Midwest Studies in Philosophy
Volume XII

MIDWEST STUDIES IN PHILOSOPHY

EDITED BY PETER A. FRENCH, THEODORE E. UEHLING, JR., HOWARD K. WETTSTEIN

Many papers in MIDWEST STUDIES IN PHILOSOPHY are invited and all are previously unpublished. The editors will consider unsolicited manuscripts that are received by January of the year preceding the appearance of a volume. All manuscripts must be pertinent to the topic area of the volume for which they are submitted. Address manuscripts to MIDWEST STUDIES IN PHILOSOPHY, University of Notre Dame, P.O. Box 601, Notre Dame, IN 46566.

The articles in MIDWEST STUDIES IN PHILOSOPHY are indexed in THE PHILOSOPHER'S INDEX.

Forthcoming Volumes

Previously Published Volumes (All, but Volume I, are available.)

Midwest Studies
in
Philosophy
Volume
XII
Realism and Antirealism

Editors

PETER A. FRENCH
Trinity University
THEODORE E. UEHLING, JR.
University of Minnesota, Morris
HOWARD K. WETTSTEIN
University of Notre Dame

University of Minnesota Press • Minneapolis

Copyright © 1988 by the University of Minnesota.
All rights reserved. No part of this publication may be reproduced,
stored in a retrieval system, or transmitted, in any form or by any
means, electronic, mechanical, photocopying, recording, or otherwise,
without the prior written permission of the publisher.

Published by the University of Minnesota Press,
2037 University Avenue Southeast, Minneapolis, MN 55414.
Published simultaneously in Canada
by Fitzhenry & Whiteside Limited, Markham.
Printed in the United States of America.

Library of Congress Cataloging-in-Publication Data

Realism and antirealism

  (Midwest studies in philosophy; v. 12)
  Includes bibliographies.
  1. Realism. I. French, Peter A. II. Uehling,
Theodore Edward. III. Wettstein, Howard K. IV. Series.
B835.R32 1988   149'.2   87-16229
ISBN 0-8166-1620-5
ISBN 0-8166-1621-3 (pbk.)

Chapter 4. "Pragmatism, Phenomenalism, and Truth Talk," copyright
© 1987 by Robert Brandom.

The University of Minnesota
is an equal-opportunity
educator and employer.

Midwest Studies in Philosophy
Volume XII
Realism and Antirealism

Midwest Studies in Philosophy
Volume XII

Strange Thoughts of the Third Kind

ELI HIRSCH

I

A thought may be strange for the simple reason that it seems wildly false or incredible. The strange thoughts that trouble me, however, are of a quite different sort. These thoughts are true, indeed obviously true, yet they seem strange and baffling.

A familiar example is "This is grue." Since "grue" applies (let us suppose) to anything that is either green and examined before the year 2000 or blue and not so examined, if someone now says, "This is grue," in reference to an obviously green object, he has said something obviously true. All the same, there is something remarkably strange about "This is grue."

We might in fact distinguish between three kinds of strange thoughts. The first consists simply of thoughts that are wildly false or incredible. A second kind of strangeness is exemplified by those English statements that are logically equivalent to the Grue statements, such as "It's either green and examined before the year 2000 or blue and not so examined" (whether this statement is *synonymous* with the Grue statement will be discussed shortly). The second category of strangeness might be said to encompass roughly any statement in ordinary term that seems to involve an absurd excess of logical complexity. Another example would be "Either it's green or it's green." Strange thoughts of the second kind may strike us as philosophically rather trivial, though I do not doubt that there may be some interesting questions to raise even here.

My concern in the present paper is with strange thoughts of the third kind. These are thoughts that are expressed by sentences logically equivalent to ordinary sentences but containing extraordinary terms like "grue." Only in this third kind of case are we confronted with strange (fragments of) *languages* and what we would, at least in one important sense, be tempted to regard as strange *concepts*. By calling such languages or concepts "strange," I mean only to imply that they are likely to strike us that way, as strange, bizarre, unnatural (of course, this may be a matter of degree). The philosophical question prompted by such strange thoughts is whether they are in fact worse than ordinary thoughts, and if so, why.

II

Let me first distinguish between two important cases of the third kind of strange thought. I will then delineate some likely philosophical responses to these cases.

The Grue language presents us with a case of *classificatory strangeness*. Another example, in many ways less problematical, would be a language containing a term, say "gricular," that applies to anything that is either green or circular. That strikes us as a strange classification.

Classificatory strangeness can be distinguished from *individuative strangeness*. I will use two illustrations to introduce the second idea. Sydney Shoemaker discusses a language containing the word "klable," which functions in the following way: "If a household has exactly one table in the kitchen and exactly one in the living room, let us say that there exists a 'klable' having as its history the series of stages consisting of the stages of the kitchen table from midnight to noon and those of the living room table from noon to midnight."[1]

As a second illustration, let me allude to a strange language I have discussed elsewhere.[2] This language contains the word "cperson," which functions in the following way: If two people *A* and *B* are in physical contact exclusively with each other during an interval of time, then there exist two "cpersons," one "cperson" having as its history the stages of *A* before the interval of contact followed by the stages of *B* during the interval followed by the stages of *A* after the interval, and the other "cperson" having as its history the stages of *B* before the interval followed by the stages of *A* during the interval followed by the stages of *B* after the interval. In other words, it is a rule of "cpersonal identity" that during an interval when two "cpersons" come into contact exclusively with each other, they temporarily exchange all their physical and mental characteristics. We can imagine that in this language various "cpersonal pronouns" function in the intuitively obvious way; for example, it would be correct to say, "Any cperson uses 'I' to refer to that cperson."

It is clear that classificatory strangeness need not imply individuative strangeness. The Grue language may acknowledge precisely the same entities acknowledged in ordinary language. Although the following point is considerably less obvious, I would say that in the most important sense, individuative strangeness need not imply classificatory strangeness. Given that a language acknowledges individual klables or individual cpersons, it seems not strange at all, but quite inevitable, that the language would classify these individuals under such terms as "klable" and "cperson" (things that are otherwise like tables, but that instantaneously exchange their properties twice a day, might naturally be classified together, and the same is true for cpersons). This suggests that the crux of the strangeness has to do with principles of individuation rather than with principles of classification.

Besides the cases of classificatory and individuative strangeness, one could probably distinguish several other cases. For example, *strangeness of logical constants* might encompass strange connectives (such as the stroke function) and perhaps strange devices for binding predicates together (such as Quine's language without variables).[3] Sundry other examples of conceptual oddity might no doubt be imagined. However, I shall concentrate exclusively on the classificatory and individuative cases, which have perhaps some claim to being philosophically most central.

III

Let us consider some likely philosophical responses to these strange thoughts:

1. The strange thoughts necessarily depend on their ordinary correlates (that is, the thought of grue necessarily depends on the thought of green and blue, the thought of klables necessarily depends on the thought of tables, and so on), but not vice versa.
2. The strange thoughts present a distorted picture of the structure of the facts.
3. The strange thoughts would lead to making false predictions.
4. The strange thoughts could not express correct explanations.
5. The strange thoughts do not conform to our sensory experience.
6. The strange thoughts could not serve our practical needs.

These responses are not mutually exclusive; indeed, some are very closely connected. The responses are supposed to be in some sense *critiques* of the strange ways of thinking, showing why these ways of thinking are impossible or unreasonable. A philosopher who rejects any such critique (with respect to a given case) might be called a certain kind of *relativist* (with respect to that case). Relativists might be further divided into conventionalists and *innatists*. The conventionalist holds that thinking in the ordinary way rather than in the strange way is an arbitrary convention that we could alter. A relativistic innatist, on the other hand, holds that we are, though for no good reason, innately disposed to think in the ordinary way. (Note that an innatist, of course, need not be a relativist, for an innatist might adopt one of the critiques of strangeness to explain our innate disposition toward ordinariness.)

The subsequent discussion will suggest that an antirelativist position is not easy to defend and that, to the extent that it can be defended, this might be less difficult with respect to classification than with respect to individuation. In both cases I am inclined to assume some form of innatism, though I shall touch on this issue only slightly.

IV

Let us begin by considering the first response with respect to the Grue language. I will call this response the *dependency claim*. It might be useful to reformulate this as follows: It is logically (metaphysically) necessary that if someone understands a term with the specified meaning of "grue," then he understands two terms with the ordinary meanings of "green" and "blue"; whereas, the converse is not logically necessary.[4] I will often express this by saying simply that understanding "grue" necessarily depends on understanding terms meaning the same as "green" and "blue." (In what follows, "dependency" is always to be understood as a one-way relationship.)

Perhaps there are ordinary terms (for example, "bachelor") that stand to other terms (for example, "male" and "married") in the same kind of dependence relationship that, according to the dependency claim, "grue" stands to "green" and "blue." If so, this claim could not by itself serve to show that "grue" is worse off than an ordinary term like "bachelor." It might show, however, that "grue" must lack the status of basicness or primitiveness often associated with such terms as "green" and "blue."

It might seem possible to argue for the dependency claim by appealing to the fact that "grue" means the same as "either green and examined before the year 2000 or blue and not so examined." It seems that understanding the latter term necessarily depends on understanding "green" and "blue." Hence, understanding the former term necessarily depends on understanding terms meaning the same as "green" and "blue." Here we are appealing to the plausible-sounding principle that if two terms mean the same, and understanding one of them necessarily depends on understanding a third term, then understanding the second term necessarily depends on understanding a term meaning the same as the third.

What needs to be questioned, however, is the assumption that "grue" means the same as "either green. . . . " We are given that these terms are *logically equivalent*, that is, that they have the same *intensions*, that they apply to the same actual and possible things.[5] But logical equivalence cannot (at least for the purposes of the present argument) be taken to imply synonymy or sameness of meaning. Otherwise we should also have to say that "green" means the same as the logically equivalent term "either grue and examined before the year 2000 or bleen and not so examined" (where "bleen" applies to anything that is either blue and examined before the year 2000 or green and not so examined), which would then lead by the principle mentioned in the preceding paragraph to the absurd result that understanding "green" necessarily depends on understanding a term meaning the same as "grue."

There are various accounts of synonymy in the literature, but it seems that any account that implies that "grue" means the same as "either green . . . " whereas "green" does not mean the same as "either grue . . . " must already presuppose the dependency claim and hence could not be used to support it.

According to one familiar approach to synonymy, two expressions (including sentences) mean the same if it is logically necessary that anyone who understands both expressions and assents to the application (or truth) of one also assents to the application (or truth) of the other.[6] But how could this synonymy test show that "grue" means the same as "either green . . . " whereas "green" does not mean the same as "either grue . . . "? It seems plain that the test could yield this result only if it is assumed that understanding "grue" depends on understanding "green" and "blue" in a way that understanding "green" does not depend on understanding "grue" and "bleen." Hence, it seems that applying this synonymy test presupposes the dependency claim and cannot be used to substantiate that claim.

It may be useful, in the present context, to consider Carnap's view of synonymy. According to Carnap's idea of "intensional isomorphism," two expressions mean the same if they have the same syntactic structure and contain corresponding parts that are logically equivalent.[7] This synonymy test appears to imply that a syntactically complex expression can never be synonymous with a simple expression, so that "grue" would not mean the same as "either green. . . . " It has been proposed that Carnap's test be applied only at the "underlying" level of primitive or undefined expressions.[8] Expressions at the "surface" level would be synonymous if they derive from the same or synonymous underlying expressions. (As a limiting case, a surface expression is synonymous with the underlying expression from which it derives.) So, the modified Carnap test would imply that "grue" means the same as "either green . . . " if we can assume that these expressions derive from the same or synonymous underlying expressions. Now, the underlying expression from which "either green and examined before the year 2000 or blue and not so examined" derives presumably contains "green" and "blue." Hence, we can assume that "grue" and "either green . . . " derive from the same or synonymous underlying expressions only if we can assume that "grue" derives from an expression containing terms meaning the same as "green" and "blue." But to assume that this must be so seems tantamount to assuming the dependency claim. So we cannot defend that claim by appealing to the modified Carnap test.

The issue before us might be sharpened if we hereafter distinguish between two versions of the Grue language, a strong and a weak version. In the weak version, "green" and "blue" occur at the underlying level, and "grue" is merely a surface expression deriving from "either green. . . . " In the strong version, neither "green" nor "blue" occurs at the underlying level, but "grue" does. (We might also consider a third version in which all three terms occur at the underlying level, but I will ignore this possibility.) It seems immediately plausible to suppose that a native speaker of English, who was introduced to "grue" by philosophy books, employs only the weak Grue language, in which "grue" is merely a surface abbreviation. But the dependency claim implies the much more controversial point that the strong Grue language is *logically impossible*, that "grue" could not possibly appear at the underlying level.

If there could be a strong Grue language, there appears to be no reason to regard "grue" in that language as meaning the same as any English expression. If we take "sameness of thought" to be determined by "sameness of meaning," we can say that the strange thoughts expressed in the strong Grue language cannot be expressed in English. Yet there seems to be a sense in which we could *completely describe* these thoughts or meanings in English. We could do this by first describing the intension of "grue" (that is, the denotation of "grue" in all possible worlds), then adding the decisive fact that in the language under consideration, "grue" occurs at the underlying level.

The distinction I have been assuming in the last few paragraphs between the "surface" and "underlying" expressions of a language is controversial, though to some extent this controversy concerns technical issues that are not directly relevant to the present discussion. The basic idea of the distinction is that speakers of a language can understand the "surface" expressions only insofar as they understand the definitions of these expressions, definitions that they in some sense "have in mind" when they use the expressions. The "underlying" level consists of those expressions that are not definitionally derivative, but that are semantically (conceptually) primitive, and in terms of which the definitions are couched.[9] (The "definitions" in questions may be contextual; they may be in various ways rough or vague; they may include demonstratives; they may perhaps include descriptions of stereotypes or possibly even descriptions of causal chains. All these issues can, perhaps, be left open.) In order to give the dependency claim the greatest chance of being defended, I am going to assume that a suitable sense of the surface-underlying distinction can be sustained (this assumption will be relevant but less critical for some of the other antirelativist arguments as well). I think it is fairly clear that someone who thoroughly rejects this distinction will not be attracted to the dependency claim. Only if we believe that ordinary language contains a structure of definitional dependencies can we be tempted to claim that there are some logically necessary constraints on any such definitional structure, constraints that are not satisfied by strong versions of the strange languages. The question now is what these constraints might be.

V

An argument for the logical impossibility of the strong Grue language might issue from the second response to strangeness listed earlier, that is, the response that the strange language presents a distorted picture of the structure of the facts. It may strike us that "grue" signifies a highly complex property containing as simple constituents the properties signified by "green" and "blue." (Here I casually follow C. I. Lewis's "modes of meaning," in which a general term is said to *signify* a property and to *denote* the things having the property.)[10] The reason understanding "grue" necessarily depends on understanding terms meaning the same as "green" and "blue," so that "grue" cannot possibly occur at the underlying level, it might be argued, is that the thought of a complex property necessarily depends on the thought of its simple constituents.

Let me say that a general term is *basic* if it is syntactically simple and occurs at the underlying level. The preceeding argument might then be formulated in terms of the following *property picturing principle*: a basic term necessarily signifies a simple property. This deserves to be called a picturing principle because it requires general terms (at the underlying level) that are not compounded of other terms to signify properties that are not compounded of other properties.

Actually, various qualified versions of this principle might suffice to exclude "grue" as a basic term. The property grue strikes us as being not merely complex but complex in especially invidious ways. First, grue appears to be a *disjunctive* property. At least conjunctive properties (for example, "red and round") might be said to define "similarity classes," that is, roughly, classes of (actual and possible) things that are more similar to each other than to other things; this cannot in general be said of disjunctive properties (nor of negative properties).[11] Furthermore, "grue" seems "positional," that is, its application to an object depends on the object's temporal position (or, rather, the temporal position of the act of first examining the object). Hence, to exclude "grue" as a basic term, it would suffice to appeal to some principle that merely requires basic terms to signify properties that are not disjunctive or properties that are not positional. (Perhaps the principle could simply require basic terms to denote similarity classes.) Some such qualified principle could also serve to exclude a term like "gricular" as basic.

A qualified version of the principle may indeed answer to many of our intuitions about which terms of a language might be basic. On the other hand, it is the unqualified principle stated above that appeals most directly to the picturing metaphor, and it seems to be this principle, based on this metaphor, that has attracted many traditional philosophers, including the early Wittgenstein. I will leave open the question whether (and how) the principle ought to be qualified.[12]

Principles like this might be attacked on the grounds that there is no objective distinction, independent of language, between simple and complex properties. Another line of attack is to question the picturing metaphor. Assume for the moment that there *is* an objective distinction between simple and complex properties. Why should it be impossible at the underlying level to use simple terms to signify (even disjunctively or positionally) complex properties? In fact, the property-picturing principle seems to clash with another highly intuitive idea, that of *the arbitrariness of the sign*. This idea implies that, in principle, any sign can represent any thing, so that just as we are not required to employ red thoughts or expressions to signify the property red, we ought not to be required to employ complex thoughts or expressions to signify complex properties.

We can, in a way, reconcile the property-picturing principle with the arbitrariness of the sign by repudiating the objectivity of the simple-complex distinction. The property-picturing principle would then, in effect, define a simple-complex distinction relative to the basic terms assumed as given. So construed the principle would, of course, not rule out "grue" as a basic term.

There is, then, a rather complicated interplay between the following three ideas: (1) the idea of an objective distinction between simple and complex properties, (2) the idea that basic terms cannot signify complex properties (or at least that they cannot signify disjunctive properties or positional properties), and (3) the idea of the arbitrariness of the sign. It seems that we can retain any two of these ideas only by sacrificing (or compromising) the third.

My own ambivalent intuition favors the first two ideas. I find myself unable to doubt that there is an objective sense in which a property such as grue is complex (and indeed disjunctive and positional). And it also seems to me that basic terms could not possibly signify such properties. According to this view, strong versions of the strange classificatory languages are ruled out as logically impossible because the facts represented by language have an objective structure that must be somehow mirrored by the (underlying) structure of language (this is, perhaps, a partial analysis of what it means for language to represent the facts).[13]

VI

Before going on to the other listed responses to strangeness, let me extend the foregoing discussion to the case of individuative strangeness. On a parallel with what was said for the classificatory case, we want to interpret the first two responses to individuative strangeness as, in effect, imposing a necessary constraint on the underlying structure of any language. We will see, however, that the parallel does not fully emerge.

To begin with, it is not obvious how to formulate the underlying constraint on individuation that we want to consider. For the classificatory case, the property-picturing principle prevents basic terms from signifying strange properties such as grue and gricularity. A parallel principle for individuation might prevent basic terms from denoting strange things like klables and cpersons. Such a principle is immediately problematic, however, since it may seem that a basic term like "green" would denote green klables even with respect to a language in which klable-talk occurs only at the surface level. Or should we assume, rather, that in such a language "green" is (category) ambiguous and as a basic term it does not denote green klables? For the sake of the argument, let us make this assumption.[14] There is in any case a more central difficulty to consider.

The property-picturing principle requires basic terms to signify simple properties (or, if the principle is qualified, to signify properties that are "simple" in some qualified sense). The obvious parallel for individuation would be the following *entity-picturing principle*: basic terms must denote simple entitities. The difficulty is to understand what we could mean here by a "simple entity." If we mean an entity without parts, the principle would exclude not only klables and cpersons, but also tables and persons (unless someone thinks that persons are noncomposite).

There may be another way to interpret what it means for an entity to be "simple." Philosophers often assume that associated with any entity are *principles of individuation* in virtue of which the entity's sundry parts and aspects constitute a unity. It may be that some principles of individuation can be said to be simple or unanalyzable, whereas others are complex. The entity-picturing principle might, then, be interpreted as saying that basic terms must denote entities with simple principles of individuation.

But the entity-picturing principle still seems unable to support the desired contrast between ordinary things and the strange things. The problem is that even ordinary things seem to be associated with complex principles of individuation. Principles of individuation embrace at least principles of identity through time and principles of spatial unity. In regard to familiar bodies such as tables, there is widespread agreement that identity through time is a complex phenomenon to be unraveled in terms of various spatiotemporal, causal, compositional, and qualitative continuities (under a sortal).[15] No such agreement exists with respect to personal identity, since there is an influential tradition in which personal identity is regarded as simple and unanalyzable. Many contemporary philosophers, however, subscribe to the view, which I share, that even personal identity is analyzable in terms of certain continuities. The spatial unity of a thing, though this is not a topic much discussed by philosophers, seems clearly to derive from a complexity of such factors as boundary contrast, qualitative homogeneity, and cohesiveness.[16]

It seems to follow that a consideration of principles of individuation cannot support the intended contrast between ordinary things and the strange things. Accepting the entity-picturing principle would apparently lead us to deny that even ordinary things are denoted by basic terms. (A familiar possibility along these lines is to hold that basic terms denote momentary things, though this does not address the issue of spatial unity.) If we reject the principle, we are apparently left with no reason to deny that it would be possible for even the strange things to be denoted by basic terms.

I should emphasize that the argument is not intended to deny that the principles of individuation associated with klables and cpersons seem more complex than those associated with ordinary entities. It is difficult to see, however, how this point could support the claim that only the ordinary principles can operate at the underlying level. Is there some threshold of complexity that cannot possibly be surpassed at the underlying level? This seems quite implausible. It might still be maintained that certain *kinds* of complexity are debarred from the underlying level and the strange things are disqualified because their principles of individuation are of the forbidden kinds. I doubt that this idea can be worked out successfully, though it does seem worth exploring further.[17]

Let me briefly indicate another difficulty. Continuity, as I have said, is one condition that enters into our ordinary principles of individuation for bodies. Suppose that we define a kind of thing exclusively in terms of this one condition. Let us call this a "continuity-thing." Any continuous succession of object-stages would constitute a continuity-thing. For example, if a tree sits intact and unchanging over a period of time, one continuity-thing would consist of the early stage of the whole tree together with a later stage of the tree excluding one tiny twig.[18] This continuity-thing evidently strikes as as very strange. But if a kind of thing is eligible at the underlying level to the extent that its principles of individuation are relatively simple, continuity-things ought to be at least as eligible as ordinary bodies, whose principles of individuation include continuity plus other conditions (for example, sortal-coverage). This is not what our initial intuition seems to say. In general, by paring and simplifying our ordinary principles of individuation, we arrive at things that we are initially inclined to judge to be no more eligible at the underlying level than klables or cpersons. It is not obvious how we can possibly defend these judgments by appealing to the idea that basic terms must denote "simple things." Perhaps, then, there is no way to defend these judgments.

What seems to emerge at this point of the discussion is the rather unexpected conclusion that classificatory strangeness may be a metaphysically deeper phenomenon than individuative strangeness. The property-picturing principle (or some qualification of it) presents an intuitive metaphysical basis for relegating strange classifications to a necessarily dependent or secondary status. It seems far more difficult to formulate a comparable principle with respect to individuative strangeness.[19]

VII

Some philosophers, however, would maintain that I have ignored the most obvious metaphysical argument to exclude individuative strangeness. I will call this *the existence argument*.[20] If there could be a language like Klablese, then in this language "klable" would denote certain strange entities that move and change in amazingly discontinuous ways at noon and midnight. But, of course, there *are* no such entities. So "klable" could not possibly denote such entities. The whole idea of Klablese is nonsense.[21]

One is tempted to answer that since "There are klables" is true in Klablese, "klable" in Klablese *does* denote certain entities, except that these entities are not denoted by any expression of English. But this response is incoherent since it implies that the English expression "entity not denoted by any English expression" denotes the very entities supposedly not denoted by any English expression. The simple point is that the English expression "entity" surely denotes all the entities that there are, and there cannot be any entities left over for "klable" to denote.[22]

I think that many will share my impression that the existence argument is too simple to be true. Two considerations may serve to reinforce this impression. First, it may have been noticed that when I formulated the existence argument, I did not even bother to specify that the target of the argument is only the *strong* version of Klablese (that is, the version in which klables but not tables are denoted at the underlying level). It seems on the face of it that the argument could apply even against the weak version (that is, the version in which surface talk of klables is derivative of the underlying denotation of tables). In even the weak version of Klablese it would be correct to say such things as: "Here is one klable and here is another klable. There exists a klable bigger than that klable. This klable moved from the living room to the kitchen." Surely, then, it must also be correct to say, "And 'klable' denotes those klables." But it seems that we can make no sense of "klable" denoting anything, from which it may seem to follow that even the weak version of Klablese is impossible. But that *cannot* be right since we know that we can start talking Klablese, at least in the weak version, whenever we want to.

Consider, furthermore, the following point. Supposing that there *could* be a strong version of Klablese, in that language it would be possible to formulate an argument precisely paralleling the existence argument to prove that there could not possibly be a language in which "table" functions as in English. This is dizzying. One is almost tempted to say (incomprehensibly) that relative to English, Klablese is impossible and relative to Klablese, English is impossible.

I think that the existence argument teaches us the lesson that when we philosophize about a language like Klablese, we may find it natural to adopt somewhat loose and misleading ways of talking. The English sentence "In Klablese 'klable' denotes certain entities" is strictly false. If we are inclined to assert the sentence, this is because we find it natural when philosophizing about (strong) Klablese to shift into (weak) Klablese. But if we want to stick scrupulously to ordinary English, we have to limit ourselves to saying something like this: in Klablese "klable" functions *as if* it denotes certain entities.

When we try to imagine a strange individuating scheme, we are in effect envisioning a systematic shift in the meanings of various expressions related to individuation. These would include most prominently "exists," "entity," "identity," and the whole "apparatus of quantification," as Quine would say. The meaning shift must also affect various expressions related to change, such as "moves," which is why "Something moved from the living room to the kitchen" may be true in Klablese but false in English. Finally, the shift must affect various semantic expressions such as "denotes" and "refers." This is why the sentence "In Klablese 'klable' denotes certain entities" is true in Klablese but false in English. I do not know how to give a general characterization of the kind of "systematic meaning shift" that constitutes a "change in individuation." I suspect that the best one may be able to do is to say that this is a shift that results in a language in which expressions behave *as if* they denote strange entities. And, of course, one can illustrate the kind of meaning shift in question by pointing to examples like Klablese and the Cperson language.

The existence argument says, in effect, that there could not possibly be a language whose underlying (nonlogical) expressions fail to denote (actual or possible) entities, in the *ordinary sense* of "denotes entities." This is tantamount to insisting that our ordinary concepts of existence, entityhood, identity, and reference are the indispensable touchstones of thought and language, that these concepts could not possibly be systematically replaced by other concepts. When recast in these terms, the argument must strike us as merely begging the question, for the question is precisely whether these ordinary concepts are necessarily indispensable to thought and language.

Our problem has been to explain what the relevant difference is between tables and klables (or between persons and cpersons), which renders the former but not the latter eligible as referents of basic terms. The existence argument offers this answer: "There are tables but there are no entities occupying the same places as tables that instantaneously exchange their properties twice a day (that's the difference)." But this platitude of English usage explains nothing. I suggest that a reasonable test for any argument against the possibility of strong Klablese is that the argument be expressible in weak Klablese. This test makes explicit the policy that, as noted earlier, we often naturally slip into when philosophizing about a strange language. The rationale of the test is that if an argument against strong Klablese is legitimate, it should not simply trade on the fact that, when speaking ordinary English, we cannot speak of klables. The earlier argument from the entity-picturing principle, if it could be worked out, would pass the test. Clearly, the existence argument does not.

VIII

I turn now to the third response to strangeness, that is, that the strange languages would lead to making false predictions. Insofar as this response bears on various intricacies and obscurities of inductive logic, I can at best venture a few exploratory suggestions.

Considering classificatory strangeness first, if a speaker of the Grue language treated "grue" as projectible, she would be led to make the false prediction "Emeralds first examined after the year 2000 will be grue." But why should we assume that she will treat "grue" as projectible? Perhaps because there is a presumption that a speaker will treat any basic term as projectible (that is, prior to recalcitrant predictions, high-level generalizations, and so on). The prediction argument applies, then, only to the strong Grue language, in which "grue" is a basic term. That is to be expected since the many contemporary philosophers who speak the weak Grue language are presumably not being led to make false predictions.

The prediction argument might be challenged in several ways. First, even assuming that it is part of our ordinary inductive logic to treat basic terms as projectible (other things being equal), could we not envision a deviant inductive logic that combines propitiously with deviant classifications to yield the correct (that is, our) predictions? Perhaps the deviant logic could simply contain a *list* of basic terms that are not to be treated as projectible, including the term "grue." To this it might be answered (I do not know how convincingly) that it counts anyway as an important kind of justification of our ordinary classificatory practices that they are supported by, and support, our ordinary inductive practices.

But a second question must be raised, and that is whether it is, in fact, part of our ordinary inductive logic to treat basic terms as presumptively projectible. One might wonder how else we could begin to generalize except by initially projecting basic terms, but there are other possibilities. Perhaps we start out by projecting only terms that signify simple (or at least nondisjunctive) properties or that denote similarity classes.[23] And suppose that the Grue speaker judges the property grue to be (disjunctively) complex or judges that grue things examined after the year 2000 might be wholly dissimilar to grue things examined before 2000. Then she might have a basis for treating "grue" as nonprojectible, even given our ordinary standards of inductive logic. It might be answered that if "grue" is really basic for a speaker, she would *have* to think of the property grue as being simple (or nondisjunctive) and the class of grue things as being similar to each other. But if we are now assuming that the basic terms of a language (for example, the strong Grue language) can signify (disjunctively) complex properties, why should speakers of such a language have to assume otherwise?[24]

Perhaps the general puzzle here is simply the following: How can the mere fact that someone employs a different language, containing sentences logically equivalent to our ordinary sentences, make it impossible (or irrational) for her to agree with our predictions about the future?

But suppose that, for speakers of the strange languages, there would be a presumption in favor of projecting the strange terms. Even where there is a presumption in favor of projecting a term, this presumption can be defeated by experience, most directly by observing the falsehood of many generalizations involving the term. In the case of "grue," one would have to wait until 2000 to make the relevant falsifying observations so that a presumption in favor of projecting this term could, perhaps, indeed generate a substantial number of long-range predictive errors. The situation seems rather different when we consider other stange classifications such as "gricular." Let us first reconstruct the Gricular language so that, like the Grue language, it permits the expression of statements logically equivalent to ordinary statements. We might, for example, imagine that the Gricular language contains the three terms "gricular," "grincular," and "ngricular," which apply, respectively, to things that are either green or circular, things that are either green or not circular, and things that are either not green or circular. "Green" and "circular" will be logically equivalent, respectively, to "gricular and grincular" and "gricular and ngricular." If the Gricular speaker is initially disposed to treat "gricular" as projectible, it seems she would quickly discover the ineptness of generalizing from those instances of gricular that are grincular to those that are ngricular, that is, from instances of green to instances of circular. Hence, it seems that the predictive disability that might result from "gricular" occurring as a basic term is, at worst, highly temporary.[25]

The doubts that I am raising about the adequacy of the prediction response seem even clearer when we turn to the case of individuative strangeness. If someone speaks a language like (strong) Klablese, how could this lead her to make false predictions? Are there indeed any inductive principles that even *relate* directly to individuation?

It might be suggested that a speaker of Klablese would be led to conflate what happens to a klable when it moves in the ordinary sense and what happens to a klable at noon and midnight, for these are both cases of "movement" from this speaker's point of view. Hence, the Klablese speaker would be led to the false prediction that the discontinuous twice-daily movements of a klable have the same properties observed in the ordinary continuous movements (for example, that something resting on the klable is likely to fall off). Of course, for this prediction to be even coherent, the property in question would have to be at least logically consistent with discontinuity of motion. Even so, why should we assume that the Klablese speaker would be, in effect, blind to the inductive significance of the radical distinction between the two cases of a "moving klable"? The following example from our ordinary conceptual scheme seems essentially comparable. There are two ways to move a table, either by moving it as it is or by taking it apart, moving its separate parts, then reassembling it. I doubt that there is even an initial presumption in favor of generalizing from one case to the other, though both are cases of "moving a table"; if there is such a presumption, it is evidently defeated by experience. The Klablese speaker's situation with respect to the two "movements" of klables should be no worse.

There is a general point to consider here. Insofar as the individuation of an entity, whether strange or ordinary, depends upon a complexity of factors (see the earlier discussion of principles of individuation), it seems that it would always be possible, and indeed *rational*, to gear one's inductive generalizations to those factors (such as continuity) upon which a judgment of individuation is based. This being so, it is difficult to see how there could be any rational connection between our patterns of individuation and our patterns of prediction. The general connection between individuation and inductive logic deserves further study.[26]

<h1 style="text-align:center">IX</h1>

The fourth response to strangeness, that the strange languages could not express correct explanations, will, I think, seem initially appealing to some philosophers. There may also be the inclination to combine this response with the second one about "the structure of the facts," as when it seems to be said that our explanations must be framed in terms of classificatory and individuative principles that break up the world at its "joints" or conform to the natural kinds that there are.[27]

I find it difficult to see the merit in this idea for the following reason. If p explains q, and p' and q' are logically equivalent, respectively, to p and q, then it seems that p' explains q'. (The corresponding principle for counterfactuals seems even more obvious: if the counterfactual binding p to q is true, then the counterfactual binding p' to q' must also be true.) For example, if we have a law of physics formulated in Cartesian coordinates, insofar as we are prepared to regard a second formulation in polar coordinates as logically equivalent to the first, it seems senseless to suggest that one formulation but not the other is required to give correct explanations. This same point seems to hold for ordinary statements and their strange logical equivalents.

It would not surprise me if the principle of explanatory equivalence appealed to requires some qualification and refinement (for example, the p's and q's might have to be limited to contingent statements), but it remains to be shown how the strange languages run afoul of some explanatory requirement.[28] It might, of course, be suggested that the "strange explanations," precisely because they are logically equivalent to ordinary ones, stand in some sort of satisfactory relationship to natural kinds or cosmic joints. Be that as it may, the crucial point is that the strange explanations are apparently not disqualified.[29]

X

The fifth response to strangeness was that the strange languages do not conform to sensory experience. This response, too, seems without much promise.

Certainly, it appears correct to say that we experience such qualities as green and circularity rather than grue or gricularity, and that we experience ordinary changes in ordinary things like tables and persons rather than the strange changes of strange things like klables and cpersons. But if experience is itself a kind of judgment, an experiential or perceptual judgment, these remarks imply only that our ordinary schemes of classification and individuation are present in one ordinary kind of judgment. Nothing in this suggests why there could not be people who employ the strange concepts and who have correlatively strange experiences.

There is indeed a long-standing philosophical tradition in which an allegedly nonconceptual element of experience is posited, often under the name "sensation." In Kant, "sensation" combines with "understanding" to yield experiential judgments. If it could somehow be shown that our ordinary conceptual structures are determined by these "sensations," perhaps we would have a relevant kind of critique of the strange concepts. But if these sensations really are nonconceptual, how *could* they determine our concepts? If sensation without understanding is "blind," as Kant said, or a mere "blooming buzzing confusion," as William James said, it seems quite impossible to see how sensation could effectively favor our ordinary concepts over the strange ones. (Of course, these reflections may only serve to reinforce the now familiar doubts about the traditional notion of "sensation.")

It does, however, seem straightforwardly correct to say that the general character of our sensory apparatus (for example, the sizes of our visual fields) determines in part the character of our perceptual judgments. Assuming that we can rank perceptual judgments as more or less "immediate," depending on the extent to which they are influenced by the percipient's beliefs, it would seem to follow from the nature of our sensory apparatus that the experience of grue must be less immediate than the experience of green because the former experience would apparently require (at least implicit or unconscious) knowledge of the date when something was first examined. (I think one could argue for the stronger claim that as a matter of logical necessity *any* sensory apparatus must render the experience of grue relatively nonimmediate.)[30] Could this be grounds for arguing against the possibility of "grue" as a basic term? It might be if we have a principle to the effect that basic terms must figure in perceptual judgments of a sufficiently high degree of immediacy (perhaps one principle of empiricism). Even given the principle, one would have to consider the possibility that "grue" figures in immediate perceptual judgments of the form "That thing is either grue and examined before 2000 or bleen and not so examined," which is tantamount to the perceptual judgment that the thing is green. Or, should we also have a principle excluding such (disjunctively) complex judgments as "immediate" (perhaps only when the separate constituents of the complex judgments are not themselves perceptual judgments)? Note that although these questions might also pertain to klables, or rather to the strange jumps of klables, which are time dependent, they apparently do not pertain to various other strange concepts such as "gricular" and "cperson." Apparently nothing about the general character of our sensory apparatus (let alone the logically necessary character of any sensory apparatus) prevents these kinds of concepts from entering into immediate perceptual judgments. It seems, therefore, that the general character of our sensory apparatus as such cannot account for ordinariness in either classification or individuation.[31]

The appeal to experience is apt to take a special form with respect to the concept of personal identity. Here one is tempted to say that memory ("memory experience") constrains us to use the ordinary concept rather than some strange concept like "cpersonal identity." Imagine two people who embrace (only each other) for an interval of time during which one of them feels pain. Afterward, when he is alone, he could report the memory of "that pain I felt." In the Cperson language he would have to report instead a memory of "that pain *the other cperson* felt." One is tempted to say that the latter memory is unintelligible, that memory could not possibly operate that way.

But if the argument is merely that the speaker of the Cperson language could not possibly have our ordinary concept of memory, then let him instead have the strange concept "cmemory," which fits with his strange concept of "cpersonal identity" (it now being permissible to say that one cperson can cremember another cperson's experiences).[32] The important point is that there is no argument here to show why the speaker of the Cperson language could not make confident and reliable judgments about past experience, judgments that are "immediate" rather than based on inductive inference and that are causally linked in memory-typical ways to the experience in question. Hence, there is no argument to show why the speaker of the Cperson language could not have as much knowledge of the past as we do, even if this were knowledge by "cmemory" instead of "memory."

XI

The final response to strangeness was that the strange thoughts could not serve our practical needs. Of course, if making true predictions is one of our "practical needs," this argument may revert to the previous prediction argument. But we are now seeking pragmatic considerations unrelated to making predictions.

I have found that this pragmatic response is the most difficult to put into any reasonable perspective. Certainly it has an immediate and powerful attraction, and I cannot doubt that there is *something* to it. But consider for a moment how easy it is to imagine a philosopher who, having never heard of French, when presented with the French scheme for dividing terms and articles into "masculine" and "feminine," insists that such a scheme would be impossibly "pointless," "idle," and hence "unworkable." It works fine anyway, and nobody seems to mind. In fact, the scheme is probably seen to have its own peculiar charm and elegance (and "naturalness"). We have to worry seriously that the strange concepts could have the same status. If we want to exclude these concepts on pragmatic grounds, we must be convinced that these grounds are considerably deeper than the ones that could be presented to prove that the French scheme is impossible.

According to "relativistic innatism," we are innately disposed, though for no good reason, to speak an ordinary language. (Chomsky seems to argue for such a view in several publications.) According to this view, there would presumably be unhappy consequences if we tried to teach a strange language to a child as a primary language. But let it not be suggested that *that* is the reason why the strange languages are "impractical." Here we have no argument at all against relativism. The required pragmatic argument must at least show that the strange languages could not reasonably work for any creatures with our general (that is, noncognitive) needs and capacities; the argument cannot simply appeal to our need to think as we do.

A plausible assumption might be that any creatures with our general needs and capacities would have reason to assert essentially the same facts we do, regardless of what kind of language they were speaking. Here I use the word "fact" in such a way that any pair of (contingent) logically equivalent sentences can be said to represent the same (actual or possible) fact. If we imagine replacing the sentences we ordinarily utter by the shortest logically equivalent sentences in the strange languages, the result might often be sentences considerably more prolix than the ordinary ones. It might be suggested that this violates a reasonable practical demand for brevity in thought and communication.

This whole matter of brevity seems very cloudy, however. Certainly there is no general requirement to use as few words as possible, not even in the most austere conversations, let alone in "chitchat" and the like. I do not doubt that speakers of our language are expected to exhibit certain definite forms of brevity relative to certain definite kinds of occasions. I think it highly doubtful, however, that some general requirements of practical reason can even approximately demarcate what forms of brevity are appropriate for what kinds of occasions.[33] In any case, speakers of the strange languages might be veritable fanatics of taciturnity, utterly committed to making the sparest use of their linguistic resources. In order to criticize the strange languages by reference to brevity considerations, one would require some *language*-directed, rather than speaker-directed, principle of brevity, presumably something to the effect that any language ought to provide its speakers with a sufficient number of occasions in which they can make remarks of sufficient brevity. But what is a "sufficient number of occasions" and what is "sufficient brevity"? (Of course, we can always get *more* brevity by adding some abbreviations.) And is it clear that the strange languages would have to violate this principle? I think it is difficult to avoid the impression that these brevity considerations are both shallow and indecisive, and that they cannot by themselves support an appropriately serious critique of the strange languages.[34]

There is the temptation, I think indulged excessively in the literature, to speak breezily about "the point" of this concept or the other. "What would be the *point* of a concept like klable-identity?" someone is sure to ask. Well, what is the point of the concept of *table*-identity? What indeed is the point of any of our concepts except to enable us to say the truth, which is presumably a good thing both instrumentally and intrinsically? But the strange concepts *would* enable us to say the truth, would indeed enable us to represent the same facts we ordinarily represent (in the sense of "same fact" indicated earlier). It must, therefore, not be taken as at all obvious what could be meant by the remark that the strange concepts have less of a "point" than our ordinary concepts.

Still, the feeling persists that our ordinary concepts *fit* our lives in some deep way in which the strange concepts could not. I am highly skeptical about this claim, though I find myself unable to dismiss it.

What kind of "fit" could this be between ordinary language and ordinary life? A trivially unhelpful answer would be that our ordinary aims and interests are partly constituted by our ordinary thoughts. The serious question, however, is whether speakers of the strange languages could have aims and interests constituted by strange thoughts logically equivalent to our ordinary thoughts. In this sense, their lives would be just like ours except for the difference in their concepts.

If the language-fits-life idea can be made intelligible at all, one would expect that the easiest place to understand it would be in the area of personal identity. For here, if anywhere, is a concept that seems thoroughly interwoven in all our aims and interests. Consider our concern about death, to take the most vivid example. Imagine someone who (as in Sartre's story "The Wall") believes he will die the following day and struggles with the thought "Tomorrow I will no longer exist." If we tried to translate this thought into its shortest logical equivalent in the Cperson language, we would get something like "Either I am not now exclusively in contact with another cperson and I will no longer exist tomorrow or the cperson with whom I am now exclusively in contact will no longer exist tomorrow."[35] One is tempted to say that this bizarre disjunctive judgment could not *possibly* sustain our ordinary attitudes and behavior in the face of death, at least not if we are rational.

But why couldn't it? It seems that it ought to be, if anything, the fact of dying that determines our concern, in the sense of "fact," in which whether we think in English or in the Cperson language, we are thinking of the same facts. To say instead that it is the "logical grammar" of dying that determines our concern, rather than being a tribute to our rationality, seems only to add insult to injury.

It seems, therefore, that even in the most favored case, that of personal identity, it is not at all easy to understand the idea that there is a logical or rational fit between our attitudes and the structure of our concepts.

I have considered here the language-fits-life idea as a critique of the strange languages. The idea might be used in another and more radical way, to criticize *ordinary* language, for it might suggest the possibility that by altering the structure of our concepts, especially that of self-identity, we could beneficially change our lives and attitudes.[36] Salvation by way of strange thoughts of the third kind is an enticing idea but not, alas, a very promising one. Of course, it might turn out, as a matter of pure empirical psychology, that there are, in fact, certain correlations between our attitudes and our conceptual structures, and even (though this is much more doubtful) that we could somehow exploit these correlations to our advantage. What seems lacking, however, is any logical or rational constraint determining the nature of such correlations. In this sense, the relativist seems right.

XII

Let me summarily tie together some of the points that I have made. Relativism in the sense at issue here is evidently a matter of degree, depending on the extent to which the antirelativist responses seem convincing. I take it for granted that our initial intuition is strongly antirelativist with respect to all the cases under consideration—this is why the "strange languages" strike us as so *strange*. In attempting to articulate and defend this intuition, we find, if I am right, that our major appeal must be to perennial (and perennially obscure) analytical arguments of conceptual dependence, arguments about when understanding one thing necessarily depends on understanding something else. These are, I think, the deepest arguments we have in this area. Other arguments related to the requirements of prediction and explanation, to the nature of experience, and to the practical demands of life seem ancillary. In regard to the cases of classification and individuation, the arguments from conceptual dependence seem to bear more heavily on the former, at least if one agrees with me in placing little weight on the existence argument (discussed in section VII). The other less important arguments seem to bear equally and doubtfully on both cases (though perhaps the prediction argument, too, seems more relevant to the classificatory case). By this reckoning, the antirelativist defense is stronger for classification than for individuation, and less strong for either, perhaps, than one might have expected.

Notes

1. Sydney Shoemaker, "Identity, Properties, and Causality," *Midwest Studies in Philosophy* 4 (1979): 339. I will assume that, besides the klable that jumps at noon from the kitchen to the living room, and at midnight from the living room to the kitchen, there is a second klable that does the reverse.

2. Eli Hirsch, *The Concept of Identity* (New York, 1982), chap. 10. The present formulation of the language differs slightly from that of the book by substituting the word "cperson" for the word "person."

3. See, e.g., W. V. Quine, "Variables Explained Away," in *Selected Logic Papers* (New York, 1966). Strangeness of logical constants, yielding statements logically equivalent to ordinary ones, should not be confused with "deviant logics" that yield statements incompatible with ordinary ones.

4. This formulation of the dependency claim might commit me to the controversial assumption that thought requires language. However, if it is understood that the "language" might even be a "language of thought," the assumption is somewhat less controversial. Many of the arguments that follow could easily be recast in terms of "concepts" rather than "language," but in some cases this would be difficult.

5. Strictly, "logical equivalence" can be understood either in the sense of a priori equivalence or in

the sense of metaphysically necessary equivalence. My assumption is that these two senses coincide with respect to every example I will consider in this paper.

6. This approach seems implicit in Gottlob Frege, "The Thought: A Logical Inquiry," reprinted in *Philosophical Logic* edited by P. F. Strawson (London, 1967), especially 24–26. The point that I am about to make would apply as well to the common suggestion that synonymous expressions are those that are necessarily interchangeable in belief contexts.

7. Rudolf Carnap, *Meaning and Necessity* (Chicago, 1947), 56–59.

8. See Janet Fodor, *Semantics* (Cambridge, Mass., 1980), 46–49, and David Lewis, "General Semantics," in *Philosophical Papers*, vol. 1 (New York, 1983), 200–207. Compare with George Bealer, *Quality and Concept* (New York, 1982), 186–87.

9. As Janet Fodor explains (*Semantics*, 46–49, 124), many linguists and philosophers, though disagreeing on technical issues related to "deep structure," assume some kind of basic distinction between an underlying semantic level of primitive expressions and a surface or derivative level. (Compare Saul Kripke, *Wittgenstein on Rules and Private Languages* (Cambridge, Mass., 1982), 71–72 n.) The notion of underlying definitions has, of course, been challenged in much Quinian literature, and also, from quite a different angle, in the recent writings of certain philosopher-linguists: see Janet Fodor, Jerry Fodor, and Merrill Garrett, "The Psychological Unreality of Semantic Representations," in *Readings in Philosophy of Psychology*, vol. 2, edited by Ned Block (Cambridge, Mass., 1981), 238–52, and Jerry Fodor, "The Present Status of the Innateness Controversy," in *Representations* (Cambridge, Mass., 1981), especially 283–313.

10. C. I. Lewis, *An Analysis of Knowledge and Valuation* (La Salle, Ill., 1946), 39. Although Lewis applies his notion of "signification" to singular terms as well as to general terms, I want to be understood in the present discussion (at least in the present section) to be dealing only with general terms. Possibly some of my arguments could be extended to singular terms, but this is problematical.

11. See W. V. Quine, "Natural Kinds," in *Ontological Relativity and Other Essays* (New York, 1969), 119–23.

12. Part of the question has to do with the nebulous notion of a "simple property," that is, a property that cannot be analyzed in terms of simpler ones. For example, one may wonder whether it is possible to argue for the simplicity of many ordinary shapes such as roundness on the grounds that any analysis would presuppose properties (for example, distance and position) that are, perhaps, less simple than the shapes. Regarding secondary qualities such as blue, these are evidently not simple if they are identified either with the microscopic states that cause certain sensations or with the dispositions supervenient upon such states; yet there seems to be a (phenomenal) sense of "blue" (or perhaps "looks blue") that might be said to signify a simple quality. The unqualified property-picturing principle is in effect argued against in D. M. Armstrong, *Universals and Scientific Realism*, vol. 2 (London, 1978), 33–34.

13. A related view is defended in David Lewis, "New Work for a Theory of Universals," *Australasian Journal of Philosophy* 61, no. 4 (December 1983): 344–77. Lewis maintains that there is an a priori presumption in favor of interpreting the words of a language as signifying "natural properties," this presumption being somehow constitutive of what it means to talk and think about reality (pp. 372–77). The view I have expressed differs from Lewis's in applying only to *basic* words, and in claiming that it is a matter of necessity, not merely a defeasible presumption, that these words signify simple (or natural) properties. See also Bealer, *Quality and Concept*, chap. 8, especially 183–90.

14. The assumption might be avoidable if we could rely on the notion of a *basic sortal* as a basic term somehow connected in a special way to individuation. The underlying constraint on individuation might then be interpreted as preventing basic sortals from denoting the strange things, without limiting basic terms that are not sortals.

15. This agreement is not universal, and Saul Kripke's lectures on identity might indicate an alternative view. See also Baruch Brody, *Identity and Essence* (New Jersey, 1980), especially chap. 3. On my view (see *The Concept of Identity*, chap. 4), matter might perhaps be said to have a simple principle of identity, but this cannot be said of ordinary bodies like tables.

16. See *The Concept of Identity*, 107–10.

17. If it is suggested that the underlying principles of individuation must make no reference to particular times, then this could indeed disqualify klables, but not cpersons or the indefinite number of strange things that might be modeled on cpersons. It might be suggested next that the underlying principles of individuation must not be disjunctive. However, I am not confident either that the strange principles of individuation *are* disjunctive or that ordinary principles of individuation are *not* disjunctive. (For disjunctive formulations of ordinary principles of identity, see *The Concept of Identity*, 226, 231.) It is worth emphasizing in this connection that the terms "klable" and "cperson" surely do not appear disjunctive in the manner of "grue" and "gricular," for the former terms seem indeed to denote similarity classes. This is related to my earlier observation that, once given individual klables and individual cpersons, it seems perfectly natural to classify the klables together and the cpersons together.

18. See *The Concept of Identity*, 28–31.

19. Lewis, "New Work for a Theory of Universals," 372, briefly remarks that an ordinary thing is a "highly eligible referent" insofar as it "has a boundary well demarcated by differences in highly natural properties" and is "a locus of causal chains." It is not clear how these constraints would bear upon klables, or cpersons, or continuity-things, or various other strange things that one might concoct. More important, it is not clear why things satisfying Lewis's (complex) constraints are in any sense *simple* or why our terms should be apt to denote such things. (Perhaps Lewis in effect concedes this point in his later paper "Putnam's Paradox," *Australasian Journal of Philosophy* 62, no. 3 (September 1984): 221–36, for he says there that "rabbit-stages, undetached rabbit-parts, and rabbit-fusion seem only a little, if any, less eligible [for reference] than rabbits themselves" (p. 228, n. 14)).

20. Such an argument seems to be implied in Shoemaker, "Identity, Property, and Causality," 339, and in W. R. Carter's review of *The Concept of Identity*, in *The Philosophical Review* 93, no. 3 (July 1984): 468–71.

21. Could the existence argument also work against classificatory strangeness? Such an argument would require the following two premises: (a) In order for a language like Grue to be coherent, there must exist a property signified by "grue," and (b) there is no such property as grue. But (b) requires a narrow sense of "property" that excludes (some) complex properties and, taking "property" in this narrow sense, (a) must in effect rely on the property-picturing principle. So this does not give us a substantially new argument. (See also Lewis, "New Work for a Theory of Universals," 348–50.)

22. My assumption here is that the sentence "There are entities occupying the same places as tables that instantaneously exchange their locations and their qualities every noon and midnight" as a sentence of ordinary English expresses a proposition that is trivially false (or perhaps conceptually incoherent). If this assumption is denied (if it is held that English speakers can raise a serious question of "ontological commitment" with regard to this sentence), then it is no longer clear in what sense Klablese is a "strange language," and perhaps the whole framework of this discussion would have to be altered.

23. See Quine, "Natural Kinds," 125–28.

24. Sydney Shoemaker, "On Projecting the Unprojectible," *Philosophical Review* 84, no. 2 (April 1975): 178–219, especially 186–88, argues that someone who projects "grue" would have to operate with a "gruified" notion of similarity because one could not coherently project both "grue" and "similar" in the ordinary sense. My question, then, is why (on the present assumption that "grue" *could* be a basic term) we should not be able to imagine someone for whom "grue" is basic but who does not project "grue" precisely because she operates with (and projects) the ordinary notion of similarity.

25. My argument in the last several paragraphs might be reformulated in terms of Goodman's notion of "entrenchment": first, there appears to be no reason why we need assume that "grue" ("gricular") would achieve a high degree of entrenchment in the strong Grue language (the strong Gricular language); second, with respect to "gricular," there is excellent reason to suppose that it would not achieve a high degree of entrenchment. See Nelson Goodman, *Fact, Fiction, and Forecast*, 3d ed. (New York, 1973), 94–99.

26. One question might be phrased by asking whether the Klablese speaker ought to project "klable identity" or "klable *continuity*." This might be compared to the earlier question whether the Grue speaker ought to project "grue" or "similar" (see note 24). If it seemed problematical that the Grue speaker could

have our ordinary concept of similarity, it seems rather less problematical that the Klablese speaker could have our ordinary concept of continuity.

27. For example, Jerry Fodor, *The Language of Thought* (New York, 1975), 21–22, seems to imply that correct explanations must be couched in terms of "natural kind predicates." The idea that our explanatory aims require us to adopt certain principles of individuation seems to be implied in David Wiggins, *Sameness and Substance* (Cambridge, Mass., 1980), especially chap. 5. (Wiggins comes close to explicitly addressing the issue of strange languages on p. 144, n. 18.)

28. Peter Achinstein, *The Nature of Explanation* (New York, 1983), 363–64, in effect denies the principle of explanatory equivalence with respect to certain special cases of "emphasis." The relevance of such cases to the present discussion seems doubtful but might be worth exploring. See also in this connection Fred I. Dretske, "Referring to Events" and Jaegwon Kim, "Causation, Emphasis, and Events," both in *Midwest Studies in Philosophy* 2 (1977). The principle of explanatory equivalence seems to be taken for granted in many standard discussions of the conventionality of geometry; see, e.g., Lawrence Sklar, *Space, Time, and Spacetime* (Berkeley, 1974), 96–101.

29. It might be claimed that employing a strange language would necessarily lead to erroneous judgments about the relative simplicity and credibility of theories, and hence to erroneous judgments about what the correct explanations are. (Compare Lewis, "New Work for a Theory of Universals," 367.) However, this would be only a variant (perhaps an important one) of the epistemological issue discussed in the previous section. My present point is that employing a strange language could not prevent one from *expressing* correct explanations, leaving aside epistemological questions about how one might know that these are correct explanations.

30. It appears that Nelson Goodman rejects even the weaker claim; see S. F. Barker and Peter Achinstein, "On The New Riddle of Induction" and Goodman's response in *The Philosophy of Science*, edited by R. H. Nidditch (London, 1968). An argument for the stronger claim might perhaps proceed from some premise roughly to the effect that times as such are in principle not immediately perceivable. (Of course, any such argument must presuppose that grue is objectively positional in a way that green is not.)

31. The "general character" of our sensory apparatus, in the sense intended here, must consist of facts that are completely obvious and nontechnical. I do not, of course, deny the possibility that certain technical facts about the human nervous system (or even the human eye) explain why humans are disposed to perceive things as green or as circular rather than as gricular.

32. On how to free the concept of memory from the concept of personal identity, see the notion of "quasi memory" in Sydney Shoemaker, "Persons and Their Pasts," *American Philosophical Quarterly* 7 (October 1970): 269–85.

33. H. P. Grice, "Logic and Conversation," in *The Logic of Grammar*, edited by D. Davidson and G. Harman (Encino, Calif., 1975), has "Be brief (avoid unnecessary prolixity)" as one of his "conversational maxims" (p. 67), but he does not commit himself to there being any straightforward connection between such maxims and the general requirements of rationality; see pp. 68–69. (Is Grice's maxim supposed to apply to chitchat?)

34. Contrast with Jonathan Bennett's thesis that our ordinary conceptual scheme is justified precisely by its abbreviatory power, in *Kant's Analytic* (London, 1966), 39–41.

35. This translation assumes that contact in the relevant sense breaks off between two people as soon as one ceases to exist. Without the assumption, the translation would be even more complicated, requiring two additional disjuncts.

36. Derek Parfit, "Personal Identity," *Philosophical Review* 80, no. 1 (January 1971): 3–27, especially 25, may seem to be suggesting that, by suitably altering our criteria of self-identity, we could ease the grip on us of selfishness and the fear of death. However, Parfit himself repudiates this interpretation in "On 'The Importance of Self-Identity'," *Journal of Philosophy* 68, no. 20 (October 1971): 683–90.

Realism, Antirealism, Irrealism, Quasi-Realism

Gareth Evans Memorial Lecture, Delivered in Oxford on June 2, 1987

CRISPIN WRIGHT

I

It is, as is familiar, difficult to be precise about what is involved in realism. The realist in us wants to hold to a certain sort of very general view about our place in the world, a view that, as I have put it elsewhere, mixes modesty with presumption.[1] On the one hand, it is supposed, modestly, that how matters stand in the world, what opinions about it are true, is settled independently of whatever germane beliefs are held by actual people.[2] On the other, we presume to think that we are capable of arriving at the right concepts with which to capture at least a substantial part of the truth, and that our cognitive capacities can and do very often put us in position to know the truth, or at least to believe it with ample justification. The unique attraction of realism is the nice balance of feasibility and dignity that it offers to our quest for knowledge. Greater modesty would mean doubts about the capacity of our cognitive procedures to determine what is true—or even about our capacity to conceptualize the truth—and, so, would be a slide in the direction of skepticism. Greater presumption would mean calling into question, one way or another, the autonomy of truth, and, so, would be a slide in the direction of idealism. To the extent that we are serious about the pursuit of truth, we are unlikely to be attracted by either of these tendencies. We want the mountain to be climbable, but we also want it to be a real mountain, not some sort of reification of aspects of ourselves.

It is a remarkable phenomenon that an issue of this degree of abstractness, whose proper formulation is unclear to the point where it is prima facie hazy what shape a relevant debate about it might assume, can so command intellectual curiosity. The conviction that a real issue is being presented is the conviction that metaphysics, in the most traditional sense, is possible: that there are genuine questions about the objectivity of human intellectual endeavor, and about the constitution of reality, which it falls to the traditional philosophical methods of critical reflection and analysis to resolve, if resolution is possible. This conviction may be baseless, and may yet be shown to be so by the application of just those methods. But we should work very hard before drawing that conclusion. The intellectual satisfaction associated with properly formulating and responding to these questions will be far greater than that of a repudiation of them, however well motivated.

In any case, it is evident that progress can be consequent only on some clarifications, perhaps in unexpected directions. One deservedly influential attempt at such a clarification has been Michael Dummett's.[3] I shall begin by indicating certain causes for dissatisfaction with Dummett's proposal, and will then try to consider what more generally apt analysis of realism may be appropriate if the metaphysical issues are to emerge both as reasonably definite in content and as (at least potentially) tractable. I am bound to confess to a certain pessimism about the ultimate possibility of this project. But my suggestions here must, in any case, be sketchy. And the thought is always consoling that, often in philosophy, it is more instructive to travel than to get anywhere.

II

No one has to be a realist, or not *tout court*. It is open to us to regard only some of our commitments as apt to engage with reality in the appropriate way. Realism about theoretical science, for example, need not commit one to realism about pure mathematics — and, indeed, one may wish to be only eclectically realist within science, taking an antirealist view of quantum theory, for instance. Dummett's original view was that the distinctive and proper thesis of realism about a particular genre of statements is that each of them is determinately either true or false — that the principle of bivalence holds good for them. The point of the proposal is best appreciated if we concentrate on a class of statements — say, those concerning the past beyond living memory — for whose truth-values we cannot guarantee to be able to get evidence one way or the other. Holding that bivalence is valid for such statements is holding that each is, nevertheless, guaranteed to be true or false. It would appear to follow that what confers truth or falsity on such a statement must be something separate from and independent of whatever makes for the availability of evidence for the statement's truth-value — if anything does. Hence, in particular, such a statement's being true cannot be the same thing as its meeting even our most refined criteria for its truth. The truth is, thus, independent of human opinion, which is the key realist notion.[4]

This line of thought has its problems,[5] but here I shall assume that it is in good order as far as it goes. That, however, does not seem to be far enough. One drawback of Dummett's proposal, remarked by a number of commentators, is that a Dummettian 'realist' about a given class of statements may also be a reductionist about them. Someone who held, for instance, that statements about the mental may be exhaustively analyzed in behavioral terms could also consistently hold that the analysis would be bivalence-preserving; anyway, they would have to hold, presumably, that the analysis would respect the lack of any guarantee of available evidence, one way or the other, for such statements. But, such a view would hardly involve what we think of as realism about the *mental*. Dummett, it should be emphasized, has never been under any illusions about this[6] and would be content to add, I think, that realism must be a view about what makes for the truth of statements when they are literally and nonreductively construed. But a more serious worry concerns vagueness. If the members of the germane class of statements are vague, then we precisely do not want to hold that each of them is guaranteed to be determinately either true or false. At the same time, vague statements are capable of truth and falsity, and a realist conception ought to be possible, it seems, of what makes for the state of affairs when they do possess determinate truth-values.[7]

One response would be to suggest that, when bivalence is inappropriate for this sort of reason, Dummett's proposal should reduce, in effect, to the claim that truth may be *evidence-transcendent*: The truth of a statement, vague or otherwise, need have no connection with the availability of any ground, even in principle, for believing it to be true. I believe that the appropriateness of so construing truth is the deep question that Dummett's writings on the topic raise, and that such a construal is, indeed, a cardinal feature of certain realist positions, notably the Cartesian philosophy of mind, the Platonist philosophy of mathematics, and certain forms of scientific realism. But it leaves the realist with no opinion to hold when it comes to statements for which evidence, one way or the other, can be guaranteed to be available—effectively decidable mathematical statements, for instance, or a statment concerning the observable outcome of an experiment. More important still, it represents as the distinctive realist thesis something that someone might well want to oppose, though still wishing to endorse the spirit of realism. *Antirealism*, in the sense associated with Dummett's work, is exactly the view that the notion of truth cannot intelligibly be evidentially unconstrained—or the view, at least, that once it is so unconstrained, it is no longer in terms of *truth*-conditions that the meanings of the statements in question can be interpreted. But someone who believes that has, so far, no motive to forswear all use of the notion of truth (whatever exactly that would involve), unless it is supposed that truth is always and essentially epistemically unconstrained—a supposition that falls foul of evident fact that, for a great many types of statements, we can make no sense of the idea of their being true if we have to suppose that evidence for their truth is not, at least in principle, available. Indeed, in contrast to the direction of much of Dummett's work on this topic, it is not clear that a general antirealist semantics must be other than truth-conditional, provided the truth of a statement is always taken to require the availability of evidence for its truth. The point remains that it ought to be possible to take a realist view of what makes for the truth or falsity of statements whose truth-values are not conceived as evidence-transcendent. Dummett's antirealist, who wishes to urge that truth-value should never be so conceived, seems to have no motive to reject realism in this more basic sense.

But what is the more basic sense? It would pass for a platitude, I think, that whether or not a statement, envisaged as uttered on a particular occasion, would express a truth is a function only of the content it would have on that occasion and the state of the world in relevant respects. The more basic kind of realism involves, I suggest, the assumption of a sort of *mechanical* view of this Platitude. Truth-values are, so to speak, ground out on the interface between language and reality. What thought a particular sentence would express in a particular context depends only on the semantics of the language and germane features of the context. Whether that thought is true depends only on which thought it is and germane features of the world. At neither point does human judgment or response come into the picture. To be sure, the semantics of the language depends on institution; it is we who built the machine. But, once built, it runs by itself. Thus, of any particular statement of sufficiently definite sense, it is determinate whether it expresses a truth in any particular context, irrespective of any judgment we may make about the matter. A basic realist thought is that wherever there is truth, it is, in this way, *investigation-independent*.

Since this conception builds no epistemic constraints into the factors that determine truth, it will no doubt come easily to someone who subscribes to it to suppose that truth can transcend all evidence. And since no provision seems to be made whereby reality can fail to determine truth-values, so long as the statements concerned are of sufficiently definite sense, bivalence, too, will be a natural adjunct. But the conception is completely general, available both for the class of statements whose truth we conceive as requiring the availability of evidence for their truth and for its complement. And it does nothing to alter the essential character of this conception of truth to superimpose whatever verficationist constraints we please.

The conception remains very much at the level of metaphor. But at least it is clear that realism, as characterized by it, has two quite distinct areas of obligation. The belief that a class of statements are apt to possess investigation-independent truth-values depends on regarding meaning as strongly objective: What constitutes correct use of an expression in particular circumstances has to be thought of as settled somehow independently of anyone's actual dispositions of response to those circumstances. What fits the meaning is one thing; what, if anything, we are inclined to say is another; and any correspondence between the two is merely contingent. Naturally, one feels there has to be something to this thought, that if the notion of meaning, and with it the notions of truth and error, are not to collapse, there must be space for *some* kind of contrast between proper use of an expression and that use to which people may actually incline. But it is quite another question whether only a realist conception of the objectivity of meaning can avoid such a collapse. Wittgenstein[8] assimilated the relationship between meaning and practice to that between character and behavior. The parallel is suggestive: It is quite consistent with our attaching sense to the idea of someone's action being out of character to regard what it is true to say about character — as we do — as a function of the way the subject is actually inclined to behave. But I shall not consider further what notion of the objectivity of meaning may be appropriate to the realist's purpose.[9] My point is merely that someone who inclines to the 'more basic' realism owes an account of the matter.

A philosopher who had no qualms about the objectivity of meaning as such, however, might still be dissatisfied with this kind of realism about a particular class of statements. If there are to be things that it would be correct to say, irrespective of what anyone is actually inclined to say, then – in accordance with the Platitude – a contribution is called for from 'the state of the world in relevant respects'. Historically, the various forms of antirealism, in different areas of philosophy, have been fueled mainly by doubts about the capacity of the world to make the necessary contribution. One class of such proposals is associated with more or less austere, empiricism-inspired theories of concept-formation. Hume, for instance, believed that there is no way whereby we can form a properly perspicuous notion of causation except at the cost of not including all the features that popular thought attributes to it. Hence, understood as popularly intended, statements involving the notion of causation are of insufficiently definite sense, in the Humean view, to take on determinate truth-values. Since they, nevertheless, play a relatively determinate role in our ordinary thought and language, the proper account must be that their role is not to 'correspond to the facts' – we can attain no satisfactory conception of the relevant 'facts' – but is a nondescriptive one. The instrumentalism about scientific-theoretical statements espoused by many positivists had an essentially similar rationale: A preferred theory of meaning – here, the conviction that all significant descriptive language must ultimately be analyzable into a vocabulary of sense experience – transpired not to have the resources to accommodate such statements within the sanctuary of fact-stating respectability.

This kind of proposal has its primary motivation in the theory of meaning. The reality of causation, or of certain sorts of theoretical entities, is called into question only because it is doubted that we can form any genuine concepts of what such things could be. A second kind of proposal, to similar effect, has a more basic ontological motivation. Although it is true that nondescriptive theories of moral and aesthetic valuation, for instance, can be and were stimulated by positivistic views about meaning, they have, nevertheless, retained an attraction for many who find no virtue in positivism. Such philosophers simply find it metaphysically incredible, as it were, that the world might actually contain objective values to which our moral, aesthetic, and other value judgments may be seen as some sort of cognitive response. It is thought baffling what kind of thing an objective value could be – in what the objective value of a situation could reside – and what part of our nature might justifiably be considered sensitive to such a commodity. The alternative to so murky and pretentious a view of, for example, moral language is, again, to account for what appear to be its genuine assertions in terms of their possession of some other nondescriptive role.[10]

There are, no doubt, other kinds of motives for similar tendencies. The general conception to which they give rise is that the range and variety of our declarative discourse somehow outstrips the categories of states of affairs that are genuinely exemplified by reality. We apparently talk as if there were moral, or scientific theoretical, or pure mathematical states of affairs, but in truth there are not. One response to that conviction, of course, would be to dismiss the 'language games' in question as mythology. What is common to the forms of antirealism in which we are interested here is that they eschew that response: What might be taken to be mythological descriptions are credited, instead, with some sort of different but valid role. I shall reserve the term *irrealism* as a marker for these tendencies in general, preferring 'projectivism' for a proper subclass of irrealist proposals with which we shall be concerned later. What opposes irrealism with respect to a particular class of statements is the view that the world is furnished to play the part in the determination of their truth-values, which the Platitude calls for, that there really are states of affairs of the appropriate species.[11]

III

Our concern, then, is with the philosophical topology of irrealism. What precisely are the commitments of irrealism concerning a particular class of statements? How best might it be supported? Is it ultimately coherent? For a time, during the hegemony of so-called linguistic philosophy, the irrealist tendency seemed to be channeled exclusively into various forms of *expressive* theory. Expressive theories were proposed not merely of judgments of value, but of claims about truth and about causation, professions of knowledge, descriptions of actions as voluntary, and much else.[12] The point of the notion of 'expression' here is precisely its contrast with and exclusion of assertion, properly so regarded. When one expresses something in this sense, the intention was, one makes no claim about reality,[13] even though the syntax of the utterance is superficially that of a genuine assertion, apt to agree or to fail to agree with some putative state of affairs.

The principal difficulties encountered by these theories were twofold. First, many of the positive suggestions concerning *what* was being expressed, or more generally what, in enunciating an 'expression', people were doing, were actually quite consistent with holding that the relevant kind of sentence effected an assertion. For example, those who held that to characterize an action as voluntary was to express one's willingness to hold the subject responsible for the consequences said something that no realist about the distinction between voluntary and involuntary action would have wanted to deny. Not that this has to be an objection to the expressivist's positive claim. The point is, rather, that if the positive account offered by an expressive theory nowhere goes beyond what an opponent would acknowledge as aspects of the 'pragmatics' of the relevant class of utterances, then the theoretical obligation remains to explain why it is that these pragmatic aspects actually *exhaust* the use of the relevant sentences and are not merely consequences of their possession of a genuinely assertoric role. Historically, this obligation has not, by and large, been properly met.

Second, the syntactic similarities between the sorts of 'expression' listed and what the theorists would have been content to regard as genuine assertions are actually far from superficial. Sentences, for instance, which, according to emotivism, are apt merely for the expression of evaluative attitudes, display all the syntactic possibilities enjoyed by, for example, descriptions of the weather. They allow, for instance, a full range of tenses, appraisal as "true," "false," "exaggerated," "justified," and so on; they may feature embedded in the ascription of propositional attitudes; and they admit of compounding under the full range of logical operations. In connection with the last, Peter Geach[14] argued, in an influential note, that expressive theories have no resources with which to explain the permissible occurrence of, for example, moral sentences as the antecedents of conditionals. If "Stealing is wrong" serves only to express moral disapprobation, how do we construe its role in "If stealing is wrong, encouraging people to steal is wrong also"?

Expressivism can give no answer to this question unless it is possible to construe the antecedent of such a conditional as doing something other than hypothesising its *truth*. Dummett has suggested that it is.[15] Each kind of sentence for which expressive theories have been proposed is used to mark the speaker's undertaking of a certain sort of commitment. Accordingly, rather than view the conditional just as a device for focusing attention on the range of circumstances in which its antecedent is true, we can see it, more generally, as a device for articulating the consequences of acceptance of the commitment that, if someone were to avow the antecedent on its own, they would undertake. For instance, the effect of the conditional at the conclusion of the preceding paragraph would be, roughly:

> If I were (to be brought to) to express a commitment to the wrongness of stealing, I should also (be willing to?) express a commitment to the wrongness of encouraging others to steal.[16]

Geach's point, it could be claimed, would hardly be philosophically fundamental, in any case. If moral irrealism did, indeed, have absolutely no prospect of a satisfactory construal of conditionals with moral antecedents, that could hardly be decisive. Rather, whatever case there was for moral irrealism would become potentially revisionary of our ordinary and moral linguistic practice – compare the relation between classical mathematics and the philosophical views of the intuitionists. But such radical revisionism – in effect, the proscription of all compound moral sentences – is best avoided, and Dummett's proposal, though in some respects imprecise, at least indicates a strategy for avoiding it in the present case.

The strategy has been taken further by Simon Blackburn[17] in connection with what he styles the general program of *quasi-realism*. This program comes into play by way of supplement to the irrealist (for Blackburn, 'projectivist') view of some given class of statements. Quasi-realism's goal is to show how the irrealist account of the content of these statements need not be revisionary. It proceeds by attempting to supply alternative analyses of what appear, from an irrealist point of view, to be problematic modes of construction – conditionals, embeddings within propositional attitudes, even the truth predicate itself, and so on – which are to harmonize with what the irrealist wants to say about the basic statements in the class in question. In particular, therefore, the *quasi-realist* constructions have to proceed without any assignment of truth-conditions to these basic statements.

Actually, there are a number of significant differences between Dummett and Blackburn. Dummett's proposal consisted essentially in calling attention to the potential utility of a conditional construction that—unlike the ordinary conditional—hypothesize not the truth of its antecedent, but its utterance with a particular recognized illocutionary force. What is contemplated is a range of conditionals with antecedents like "if I were to be brought to ask whether P . . . ", "if I were to be brought to assert that P . . .", "if I were to command that P . . . ," and so on. The consequents of such conditionals may, then, either describe a further such utterance or may simply say something about the circumstances that would prevail if the speech act characterized in the antecedent were to be performed. This suggests, though it is not conclusive, that Dummett was tacitly viewing expressive theories as holding 'expression' to be an illocutionary operation on a thought, just as are assertion, wish, question, and command. Undoubtedly, this is one possible view. It promises perhaps the tidiest explanation of how 'expressions' fail candidacy for truth-value—one directly modeled on the corresponding failure of, for instance, an indicative sentence used to express a command. Of course, if one attempts to view 'expression' in this way, then there has to *be* an embedded thought, just as there is in the case of the command (namely, the thought whose truth it is commanded should be brought about). So, an account will be owing of what are the genuine, truth-value-bearing thoughts that are so embedded in, for instance, moral evaluation—a possible source of difficulty if the case is an example like "Stealing is wrong," rather than "You were wrong to steal that money."

Whether or not this was Dummett's perception of the matter, Blackburn's seems different. If an apparent assertion is not a genuine assertion, that is, a claim that something is true, it may be a different mode of illocution of something apt to be true; but it may also be construed as a different kind of speech act altogether, no sort of operation on a thought. Blackburn's reaction to the problem of construing moral compounds, and especially conditionals with moral antecedents, is in keeping with this second conception. For Dummett, such conditionals emerge as genuine assertions. Blackburn, in contrast, has it that a conditional such as

If stealing is wrong, encouraging others to steal is wrong

is *itself* an evaluation; to wit, a positive evaluation of combining a negative evaluation of stealing with a negative evaluation of encouraging others to steal.

How do these proposals cope with Geach's challenge to explain the validity of such an inference as

Stealing is wrong;
If stealing is wrong, encouraging others to steal is wrong;
So: encouraging others to steal is wrong?

On Dummett's account, the conditional premise becomes something like:

> If I ever (am brought to) negatively evaluate stealing, then I also (will be willing to) negatively evaluate encouraging others to steal.

If that conditional is true, then if I so perform as to realize its antecedent — that is, I endorse the first premise — then it follows that I thereby endorse, or at least that I will be willing to endorse, the wrongness of encouraging others to steal. So, it looks as though, modulo its inexactness, Dummett's proposal may well have the means to validate Geach's example. One might wonder, though, about whether the inference, even if valid as so construed, is properly represented by Dummett's account. The gist of the second premise ought to be not a description of a performance that I will actually (be ready to) carry out in certain circumstances, but rather, something *normative*: It is that a negative evaluation of stealing *ought* to be accompanied by a negative evaluation of the practice of encouraging others to steal.

In this respect, Blackburn's strategy of construing the conditional as itself an evaluation seems superior. But what, now, does the validity of the inference consist in — when it cannot be that the truth of the premises guarantees that of the conclusion?[18] Anything worth calling the validity of an inference has to reside in the inconsistency of accepting its premises but denying its conclusion. Blackburn does indeed speak of the 'clash of attitudes' involved in endorsing the premises of the modus ponens example, construed as he construes it, but in failing to endorse the conclusion. But nothing worth regarding as *inconsistency* seems to be involved. Those who do that merely fail to have every combination of attitudes of which they themselves approve. That is a *moral* failing, not a logical one.[19]

Generally, there is no difficulty in making out a notion of inconsistency for speech-acts other than assertion, provided they represent genuine modes of illocutionary force, that is, operations on a thought. Commands, for instance, are inconsistent just in case the thoughts are inconsistent whose truth they command be brought about; questions are inconsistent just in case the thoughts of whose truth they enquire are inconsistent; and so on. Even in these cases, the notion of inconsistency need not carry the stigma associated with assertoric case. Issuing inconsistent commands is irrational — at least if one intends that they be obeyed. But asking inconsistent questions is not. And, in any case, this seems to be, as noted, the wrong model for Blackburn's purposes. Evaluation, as he seems to conceive it, is not a mode of illocutionary force.[20]

Neither account, then, seems to cope entirely happily with the modus ponens inference. Dummett's account fails to reflect the normativity of the conditional premise; Blackburn's fails to respect the powerful prejudice that the failing of one who accepted the premises but repudiated the conclusion would not be merely moral. But there is, to my mind, a deeper cause for dissatisfaction with both approaches. What they have in common is that they see the presence of a certain kind of vocabulary — that of moral or aesthetic evaluation, for instance, or that of logical necessity and modality in general — as marking the performance of a certain kind of speech act, distinct from assertion (at least when the latter is properly regarded as the purported depiction of truth). It does not matter, now, whether the speech act in question is strictly a mode of illocutionary force or whether it is something else. In neither case are the materials at hand, it seems, for an explanation of the role of *iterated* applications of the vocabulary in question.[21] So neither proposal promises any sort of satisfactory account of the kind of applications that we seem, intelligibly enough, to be able to make of notions like logical necessity and logical possibility to statements in which such modal notions are themselves the principal operators. Such applications may not be very important in ordinary inferential contexts; but they are tremendously important in modal logic, and they are, it should be stressed, apparently intelligible. If, in contrast, affirming 'necessarily P' is some kind of projection from my inability to imagine the opposite, or marks the adoption of P as some kind of linguistic rule, or expresses my resolve to count nothing as falsification of P – or whatever the preferred expressive account is – no space seems to have been left for a construal of 'necessarily: necessarily P'.

Blackburn himself is strongly committed to the progressive character of the projectivist/quasi-realist research program with respect to modal idiom,[22] but the point is not (merely) *ad hominem*. It is that modality undoubtedly raises the same kinds of problems, in this context, as does morality. There is the same kind of difficulty in seeing our judgments, modal or moral, as responses to objective features of the world. In both cases, we feel the want of a satisfactory account of the confidence that, on occasion anyway, we repose in such judgments; in both cases, philosophers have been tempted to invoke special cognitive faculties, sensitive to states of affairs of the problematic kind, as our ordinary senses are sensitive to many of the characteristics of our physical environment. In neither case has any account of this kind achieved anything but mystery. This is not to say that an irrealist account of either can be satisfactory only if it handles both equally well. But it is to suggest that the general form of an irrealist account of morals should at least be a starter in the case of modal discourse also. There may, in the end, be good reason for rejecting the irrealist account of either or both. But we can hardly suppose that we are entertaining the strongest possible version of such an account until it is fashioned in such a way that it can be adapted to any of the areas of discourse about which an irrealist (or, more specifically, projectivist) tale may seem worth telling.

The proper response to the forgoing considerations, it seems to me, is to recognize that the step in the direction of expressive, or more generally nonassertoric accounts of those areas of discourse that, for various reasons, have inspired irrealist suspicions, is a faux pas. The irrealist should seek not to explain away the assertoric appearance, but to sever the connection between assertion and the realism, which he wishes to oppose. This direction has been largely passed over, no doubt, because of the intimate connection between assertion and truth: To assert a statement is to present it as true. So if moral, or modal judgments rank as assertions, we are bound to countenance, it seems, some notion of moral, or modal truth. If this seems a fatal step from a would-be irrealist point of view, it can only be because it is being assumed that where there is truth at all, realism is correct. But that is an error. Realism, even when characterized as impressionistically as above, evidently intends a conception of truth that should be understood along the line traditionally favored by 'correspondence' theorists. What else could be the point of the play with the idea of an 'independent' reality, one that 'confers' truth-values independently of our judgments? By contrast, it has yet to be understood why the notion of truth, which essentially engages with that of assertion, may not be the thinnest possible, merely 'disquotational' notion.

To assert a statement is to present it as true, but there need be no supposition that the notion of truth is uniform across all regions of assertoric discourse. The proper focus for the dispute between realist and irrealist tendencies in moral philosophy, the philosophy of science, the philosophy of mathematics, and elsewhere is on the notion of truth appropriate to these various kinds of statements. Actually, this is the conclusion to which Blackburn's quasi-realist program must, if successful, lead. The goal of the quasi-realist is to explain how *all* the features of some problematic region of discourse that might inspire a realist construal of it can be harmonized with objectivism. But if this program succeeds, and provides inter alia — as Blackburn himself anticipates — an account of what appear to be ascriptions of truth and falsity to statements in the region, then we shall wind up — running the connection between truth and assertion in the opposite direction — with a rehabilitation of the notion that such statements rank as assertions, with truth-conditions, after all. Blackburn's quasi-realist thus confronts a rather obvious dilemma. Either his program fails — in which case he does not, after all, explain how the projectivism that inspires it can satisfactorily account for the linguistic practices in question — or it succeeds, in which case it makes good all the things the projectivist started out wanting to deny: that the discourse in question is genuinely assertoric, aimed at truth, and so on. The dilemma is fatal unless what the projectivist originally wanted to maintain is actually consistent with the admission that the statements in question are, indeed, assertions, apt to be true or false in the sense, but only in the sense, that the quasi-realist explains. But if that is right, then the route through the idea that such statements are not genuinely assertoric but are 'expressive', or, one way or another, constitute some other kind of speech-act, emerges as a detour. Working with that idea, and pursuit of the quasi-realist program on its basis, may help us to focus on the notion of truth that *is* appropriate to the statements in question. But once that focus is achieved, we have to drop the idea — and it hardly seems credible that only by this somewhat circuitous route can the requisite focus be gained.[23]

IV

Naturally, it is questionable whether the notion of truth can, indeed, be divided up in the manner that the foregoing considerations anticipate, and also, if it can, whether reasonably definite criteria can emerge for determining which notion is applicable within which areas of discourse. And correspondence accounts, should they prove to be the stuff of realism, have their familiar problems.[24] But, still, I think there is a program here, and that the beginnings of some germane distinctions can be sketched.

How 'thin' can something worth regarding as a notion of truth be? We do not have a truth predicate if we merely have a device of 'disquotation', since such a device could as well be applied to utterances that are not assertions. And, it may seem, it will hardly do to say that a predicate that functions disquotationally just for assertions is a truth predicate; that account, if it is not to be circular, will require us to separate assertions from speech acts of other kinds without appeal to the notion of truth, an unpromising project. Actually, I believe the commitment to avoid circularity of this kind would be an impossible burden in the quest for an account of truth. But, in any case, one essential aspect omitted by a bare disquotational account of truth is *normativity*: Truth is what assertions aim for. Now, if aiming at truth is to supply a substantial constraint on assertoric practice, an assertion's being true cannot be guaranteed simply by the assertor's taking it to be true. A constraint is substantial only if we can make sense of the idea of a misapprehension about whether or not it is satisfied, or of its being satisfied independently of any particular subject's opinion about the matter. The normativity of truth is respected by an assertoric practice only if a role is provided within that practice for the notions of ignorance, error, and improved assessment.

This, I think, is the least that must be asked. Nor is it very much. What is called for is only some *sort* of notion of a proper pedigree for an assertion, and correspondingly proper grounds for criticism of assertions. We do, indeed, practice these distinctions in all the areas of discourse about which philosophers have been drawn to an irrealistic point of view. Even the sort of affective judgments—concerning what is funny, or revolting, and so on—about which almost everybody's antecedent prejudice is irrealist are allowed to be capable of being better and worse made. Judgments about what is funny, for instance, may be in bad taste, or idiosyncratic, or insincere, or just plain wrong. (There is nothing funny about what happened at Chernobyl.)

There is a connection, here, with Geach's point. We should have, in general, no use for conditional or disjunctive compounds of such judgments unless it was sometimes possible to appraise the truth-values of the compounds independently of any knowledge of those of their constituents. Otherwise, knowledge of such a compound could never be of any practical inferential use, and its assertion would always violate Gricean 'co-operative' constraints. It is, thus, a condition of practically significant embedding of the kind Geach focused on that ignorance be possible concerning the status of the embedded statements. And ignorance is possible only if there is, indeed, a contrast in content between the claim that P is true and the claim that any particular subject assents to P—the contrast that, I have just suggested, is prerequisite for paying proper heed to the normativity of truth.

It appears, then—if I am permitted a somewhat swift conclusion—that truth, assertion, ignorance, error, and significant embedding constitute a package deal. We get all of them off the ground together, or none of them. And the real significance of Geach's antiexpressivist point is that they are 'off the ground' in all the familiar cases where expressivists wanted to look away from the notion of assertion and to characterize practices in other terms. The question, then, is: What can, nevertheless, be missing? What may a region of discourse lack, even when it has all this, which may inspire doubts about its factuality?

The answer, in one unhelpful word, is "objectivity." I think that a number of separable ideas jostle each other here, and I have space only to advert to three of the more important. The first has to do with what I shall call the *rational command* of truth. The second concerns the distinction between (human) responses that, respectively, are and are not properly regarded as *cognitive*. The third I shall touch on at the end of this paper.

By the 'rational command' of truth, I mean the idea that truth commands the assent of any subject who has an appropriate cognitive endowment and uses it appropriately. Associated with this is the notion that belief is not an operation of the will. We do not choose our beliefs, but come to them involuntarily—though not necessarily, of course, as a result of involuntary processes—by putting ourselves at the mercy, so to speak, of our reason, our senses, any other 'cognitive receptors' we may have, and the external world. Truth, then, according to this feature of the concept, is what is at the origin of the beliefs we form when we function as, cognitively, we ought.

In describing this as part of our 'concept' of truth, I mean only that it is a feature of the way we ordinarily think about truth. One of the oldest philosophical lessons is that there are other, potentially destructive elements within the notion—elements that traditional skeptical arguments exploit—that threaten to reduce the correspondence, if any, between what is true and the deliverances of our better cognitive natures to inscrutable contingency. Even prescinding from skepticism, realists in the sense of Dummett will want to insist that we can understand, for at least a significant number of kinds of statements, how their truth might altogether fail to connect with any disposition on our part to believe them, no matter how meticulous and extensive our investigation. And, in the other direction, everyone must acknowledge that what we are induced to believe by meticulous and extensive investigation may still not be the truth in any examples where no such finite investigation can encompass all the material, as it were, in which evidence of untruth might be found. Explicitly unrestricted, contingent generalizations, and any statement that—like many ascriptions of dispositions—implicitly contains such a generality, are the obvious instances.

One response, which would continue to allot a dominant role to the aspect of rational command, would be to move in the direction of a Peircean conception of truth: We can mean by 'truth' only that which is fated to be agreed on by all who pursue rational enquiry sufficiently far, a "final opinion . . . independent not indeed of thought in general, but of all that is arbitrary and individual in thought."[25] Such a conception dismisses the total or partial epistemological absolutism involved in skepticism and in Dummettian realism. And it relaxes the sense in which the truth of an unrestricted generalization must command the assent of a rational investigator:

A well-founded investigation may, indeed, mislead, but if such a generalization is true, all rational investigators will, sooner or later, come justifiably to believe that it is.

This has been an influential construal of the notion of truth. But, insofar as some sort of preconception about the failure of certain statements to exemplify rational command is at work in the motivation for some kinds of irrealism, it is questionable whether the Peircean construct gets it quite right. For one thing, it very much *is* a philosophers' construct, building on but going a good way past anything that might plausibly be regarded as our intuitive understanding of truth. For another, the thought that only Peircean truths are true in the substantial sense we seek may seem to hold out too many hostages to fortune. If, for instance, Quine's famous thesis of the underdetermination of scientific theory by empirical data is true (fated to be agreed by all rational investigators?), then it seems that the hypotheses of such theories cannot pass the Peircean test. That would be too swift a resolution of the debate about scientific realism. Worse, any statement whose conditions of justifiable assent are a function of what else a subject believes are at risk in the same way. If whether you ought to believe a particular statement depends on what you already believe, Peircean convergence could be expected only among rational investigators who set out with the same baggage, as it were. And it has yet to be explained why their rationality alone should tend to ensure that that is so. Yet, almost all our contingent beliefs appear to be in this situation.

A Peircean can reply. The possibility adverted to is the possibility that there may be rationally incommensurable alternative systems of belief. If that is so, we can either retain the idea that one such system might contain the truth at the expense of the others, or we can drop the idea. To retain it is to render the connection between truth and rational enquiry utterly fortuitous. To drop it is to abandon or to relativize the notion of an accurate representation of the world. In neither case is room left for the idea that the truth is what commands the assent of an appropriately cognitively endowed, rational investigator. So the Peircean development of the notion of rational command should not be faulted on the ground that it cannot accommodate the possible consequences of the underdetermination thesis or of justificational holism. The fact is that whatever notion of truth survives for statements that fall prey to those consequences simply cannot have the feature of rational command. My own opinion is that not very much of what we are pleased to regard as factual discourse will actually fall prey to those consequences. In particular, a holistic conception of confirmation poses a global threat only if, at some level, the selection of background beliefs is unconstrained. There is no reason to suppose that this must be so, but the matter raises very large issues, which I shall not attempt to broach here.

Even so, I think the intuition of rational command should be explained along other than Peircean lines. For it is an intuition that coexists with our inclination (however unfortunate) to allow that truth may be evidence-transcendent. So, the intuitive point is not that what is true ultimately commands the assent of the rational. It is, I suggest, that what it is correct to think about any statement that is apt to be, in the appropriately substantial sense, true or false is something about which rational investigators have no option at *any given stage of investigation*. It is, more specifically, determinate of any given body of evidence whether it supports such a statement, or supports its negation, or neither. Even that is too simple. Vague statements, for instance, may nevertheless be factual. But their vagueness consists precisely in the existence of a range of cases where rational subjects may permissibly and irreducibly disagree about their status in point of justification. A similar point applies to statements, vague or not, for which the evidence is probabilistic. Different subjects may, without putting their rationality in jeopardy, have different probability thresholds, so to speak. One may require a higher probability than another before being prepared to work on the expectation that a hypothesis is true. But, so far as I can see, only in these two respects is qualification necessary. If a pair of subjects disagree about the credibility of a particular statement, and if the explanation of the disagreement concerns neither of the qualifications just noted, then either they are operating on the basis of different pools of evidence—states of information—or one (perhaps both) is misrating the evidence they share. If the states of information are different, and neither is misrating the state of information, then one state must be superior to the other: Either it must contain bona fide data that the other lacks, or it must omit spurious data that the other contains. Accordingly, we may lay down the following as a criterion for the inclusion of a statement, or range of statements within the category of those apt to be true in the substantial sense—the sense which incorporates the aspects of rational command: Disagreements about the status of such statements, where not attributable to vagueness or permissibly differing probability thresholds, can be explained only if fault is found with one of the protagonist's assessment of his or her data, or with the data being assessed. The data must be in some way faulty or incomplete, or, if not, they must have suffered a prejudiced response.

It follows that reason to think that other kinds of explanation of disagreement are possible is reason to think that the statements disagreed about are not objective in the relevant sense, and so not apt to be substantially true or false. This is one of the primary motives that have fueled expressive theories. It is surely, for instance, the mainspring of the thought that judgments about what is funny are not genuinely factual: None of the envisaged explanations may be appropriate in the case of a disagreement about humor—it may be, as we say, that the subjects have different 'senses of humor'. It is for the same reason that importance is attached, in the debates about moral and aesthetic realism, to the (much exaggerated) cultural variability of moral standards and the often idiosyncratic character of standards of aesthetic excellence.

It is another question, though, how one would actually set about showing that a given region of discourse failed to pass the test. A model dispute must be constructed whose explanation falls within none of the alternatives noted: It is not, that is to say, to be owing to vagueness in the statement(s) disputed about, nor to permissibly different probability thresholds, nor to faulty data—including inferential or observational error—nor to one of the subject's possession of a relatively inferior state of information, nor to a prejudiced assessment of agreed data.[26] But the question is, of course, what, for these purposes, counts as 'a state of information' or 'data'? What will tend to happen when this construction is attempted for a particular problematic class of statements—about humor, or value, or logical necessity, for instance—is that it will be relatively easy to construct a dispute that fits the bill, provided the 'data' are restricted to statements of *other* kinds whose factuality is not at issue. It is often possible, for instance, to give reasons for or against the judgment that some situation is funny, but, as just remarked, it seems perfectly conceivable that a pair of subjects may have an irreducible disagreement about such a judgment, although neither is under any misapprehension about any pertinent facts, or knows more than the other, or is somehow prejudicially over- or under-rating the facts that they agree about. But this way of describing the matter explicitly takes it that the 'facts' exclude whether or not the situation in question is funny. A similar possibility obtains in the case of logical necessity.[27] And it does not seem unlikely that moral evaluations, for instance, are in a like situation, although I shall not pause here to consider the construction of an appropriate dispute.

In any such case, it is open to the realist to accept the proposed criterion but to insist that the germane data may not legitimately be taken to exclude facts of the very species that the problematic of statements serve to record. The comic realist,[28] for instance, may accommodate the model dispute that opponent constructs by insisting that misappraisal of the data must, indeed, be at the root of it; it is just that the data misappraised may irreducibly concern the humor, or lack of it, in the situation.

The *structure* of this maneuver is not unreasonable. Plainly, it cannot always be the case that, for any particular class of statements whose factuality is not disputed, they would pass the test even if we restricted our attention to 'data' that excluded them; not all genuinely factual disagreements have to be owing to mistakes, or ignorance, or prejudice about other matters. But the upshot is not that the proposed test is useless, but merely that it has a part to play only in the first stage of a dialectic, which must now be pressed further. The test connects failure to agree about judgments that are apt to be substantially true or false with failure of *ideal cognitive performance*. Accordingly, the realist who responds in the way described now owes something by way of explanation of what ideal cognitive performance might be with respect to the *sui generis* states of affairs to which, as such a realist now contends, our judgments of humor, or value, or modality, or whatever, are responsive. We require to be told *how* it is possible for us to be in touch with states of affairs of the relevant kind. What is it about them, and about us, that makes them—at least ideally—accessible to us? It is no answer, of course, merely to introduce a word or phrase for some putative kind of special cognitive faculty—'the sense of humor', 'conscience', 'the reason'—that is to play the appropriate part. It is true that some of our judgments must be, so to speak, *primitively* factual, from the point of view of the test. But that is not to say that we have carte blanche to regard in this way any class of judgments that would otherwise fail the test. Where there is cognition, there must be at least the possibility of a satisfactory theoretical account of how it is accomplished.

The first preconception about a substantial notion of truth was its possession of the feature of rational command. Now we have, in effect, arrived at the second: Statements are apt to be substantially true or false only if it is possible to provide a satisfactory account of the kind of cognitive powers that a mind would have to have in order to be in touch with the states of affairs that they purportedly describe.[29] But what should 'a satisfactory account' mean here? I take it that it would not be necessary to trouble ourselves with the question if it could be shown that the judgments that the realist wishes to take as expressive of special abilities could actually be satisfactorily simulated, without collusion, by a subject who had only cognitive powers that both the realist and his irrealist opponent are agreed about. Thus, if, for instance, assertibility conditions could be laid down for judgments of logical necessity that someone could recognize to obtain, whose cognitive faculties embraced only the capacity for empirical judgments and so excluded anything sensitive to logical necessity as such, it would be, on the face of it, simply a bad explanation of our handling of such judgments to view it as expressive of anything additional. *Facultates non fingendae sunt praeter necessitatem.*[30]

The irrealist, however, may not easily be able to make out such a case. This will be the situation when the ability to make acceptable, or at any rate, sincere and apparently well-understood, judgments of the kind in question will depend on the subject's capacity to be *affected* in some distinctive way: to be amused, for instance, or revolted. If possessing such affective capacities is a necessary condition of full competence with the judgments in question, the irrealist's question has to be, rather, why see such affection as cognition? And the thought is, of course, that no 'satisfactory account' either of the affective response itself or of its causes can be given that will legitimate the realist's view. Contrast the sort of story that can be told about our perceptual knowledge of our immediate environment. Our theories of the nature of matter and of the workings of our sense organs and brains are hardly complete. But we know enough to tell an elaborate story about my perception of the telephone on my desk—about the kind of object it is, and the kind of creature I am, and about why, accordingly, I am able to be aware of its being there in the way in which I am. However, we have not the slightest idea how to extend this prototype to the cases of value or humor or logical necessity. And, though that is so, it is perfectly idle to claim that, in our judgments of these various kinds, we express cognitive responses to objective states of affairs.

The likely realist reply will be to suggest that the kind of explanatory model invoked is question-begging. In insisting that the epistemology of a certain putative range of states of affairs ultimately be accounted for in terms of existing fields of natural science, the irrealist loads the dice in favor of a naturalistic ontology. The states of affairs that pass the test implicitly imposed can only be those to which natural science assigns a causal role. Accordingly, as before, it is open to the realist to claim that the suggested criterion—that a class of judgments is apt to be substantially true or false only if a satisfactory account of the (ideal) epistemology can be given — is in itself acceptable, but that it is being applied here in a tendentiously restricted way. The moral realist can urge, for instance, that just as the 'data' that figured in the statement of the first criterion should be allowed to include moral data, so a 'satisfactory account', as the notion figures in the second criterion, should be allowed to proceed by reference to a framework that includes not only natural science, but also, inter alia, moral judgment.

Does this help? Well, it might be supposed that once moral judgments themselves are allowed to be explanatorily primitive, the account of our cognition of the truth of some particular moral judgment may straightforwardly proceed by inducing the kinds of consideration that incline us to that particular judgment, namely, a moral argument based on both moral and nonmoral premises. This, though, will hardly do. Such a model explanation of moral 'knowledge' would no doubt overestimate the extent to which our convictions on particular questions are principled, and would be inapplicable, besides, to at least some of the moral premises that applications of it would be likely to involve. But what is most basically wrong is that no real analogy is constructed with the perceptual case. It is not to our *knowledge* of neurophysiology and physics, for instance, that the explanation of my capacity to perceive the telephone would appeal, but to relevant hypotheses *within* those disciplines themselves. By contrast, the kind of 'explanation' of our moral knowledge, just canvassed explicitly, does appeal, not to certain moral premises, but to our knowledge of them. So it cannot provide what was being requested: an explanation of what it is about us, and about the moral realm, that makes for the possibility of cognitive relations at all.

In general, then, though it would be, I think, a fair complaint by an evaluative realist, for instance, that the original, explicitly naturalistic version of the second test is unfairly loaded, the prospects for the position do not seem to become much brighter if we grant, for the sake of argument, that *moral* theory be permitted to figure in the *explanans*. Indeed, prescinding from the confusion just discussed, it is unclear what, for these purposes, moral 'theory' might be taken to be, and how it might be exploited by a more liberal style of explanation. Matters look hardly more promising for modal and comic realism, but I cannot attempt a more detailed appraisal here.

V

Blackburn writes:

> Suppose we say that we *project* an attitude or habit or other commitment which is not descriptive on to the world, when we speak and think as though there were a property of things which our sayings describe, which we can reason about, be wrong about, and so on. Projecting is what Hume refers to when he

talks of "gilding and staining all natural objects with the colours borrowed from internal sentiment", or of the mind "spreading itself on the world."[31]

I have spoken more often of 'irrealism' than of 'projectivism'. The latter, it seems, is best reserved for those species of irrealism that concern commitments – to borrow Blackburn's term – founded on some specific mode of 'internal sentiment' or affective phenomenology. The root projectivist notion is the Humean one that we have a tendency to seem to ourselves to find in the world qualities that, properly, are predicated of our responses to it; more specifically, that the range of our responses that we tend to talk about as though they were cognitive, apt to disclose real features of the world, is actually much broader than the range of those which really deserve to be so regarded. Projectivism is, thus, a possible and natural form for the irrealist cause to assume in the three areas – morality, modality, and humor – that this discussion has mainly had in view.[32] Irrealism about scientific theory, by contrast, is not, in any version worthy of attention, projectivist. The most powerful arguments against scientific realism concern not whether any appropriately local response we have to scientific theory is cognitive – there is no such local response – but whether theoretical statements can survive the first of the two tests adumbrated: Must disagreements about scientific theory, insofar as they are not attributable to vagueness in the concepts involved, or to rationally permissible variations in standards of evidence, invariably be explicable in terms of prejudiced assessment of agreed data, or faulty data, or ignorance? Not if the underdetermination thesis is accepted. And not, perhaps, if the received wisdom is correct that the acceptability of any report of observation is invariably theoretically conditioned. For, then, the acceptability of any pool of data comes to depend on one's background theory. And that means that the data can exhibit the feature of rational command only if the ingredients in the background theories do. How is that to be provided for, if any data by which such theories might, in turn, be assessed will be theoretically conditioned in the same sense?[33]

In Blackburn's hands, as we have seen, projectivism starts out as an 'expressive' or nonassertoric thesis. I have suggested that this element of the view should be abandoned. The real question concerns what notion of truth is applicable to the 'projections'. The projectivist/irrealist thesis should be that only the thinnest possible notion is appropriate; we have seen, by contrast, two ways in which the notion of truth applicable to a class of commitments might, on the contrary, be 'thick'. I shall conclude by noting a potential instability in the projectivist position, and a third potentially germane distinction on the thinness/thickness scale.

The instability afflicts, paradoxically, just those cases where the projectivist line is intuitively most appealing. These are the classes of commitment that, like judgments about what is funny, seem to be most intimately associated with a well-defined kind of response, which we are already inclined to regard as affective rather than detective. The problem is that any such response can be construed as potentially detective – can be 'cognitivized', as it were – if the relevant projected 'quality' will sustain construal as a *disposition*. Suppose, for instance, that some such biconditional as this holds:

> X is funny iff X is disposed to amuse many/most/normal people in many/most/normal circumstances.

There is, obviously, scope for consideration about which version of such a biconditional might be most plausible, about whether some reference to right-mindedness, or the like, might be wanted, and so on. But if *any* such biconditional construal provides the resources for a reasonably accurate descriptive account of the relevant parts of our linguistic practice, there can be no objection to the idea that judgments of humor do have the substantial truth-conditions that the biconditional describes. And the relevant response – being amused – will take on cognitive status only insofar as finding oneself so affected will constitute a defeasible ground for the assertion that the right-hand side of the biconditional is realized.

A defensible form of projectivism, then, in making good the claim that a certain class of judgments is based on a response that is better not regarded as cognitive, has to interpose sufficient distance, as it were, between the judgments and the response to prevent a dispositional construal. And this will be possible only to the extent that the original projectivist image – that we make such judgments merely by way of reading back into the world features that properly belong to our response to it – is strictly misplaced. Projectivism has, therefore, a delicate balancing act to perform. If it stays too close to the image, it is liable to be undermined by a dispositional construal; if it departs too far from it, it may become unclear in what sense the response in question provides the *basis* for the relevant class of judgments, and why an argument for an irrealist view of those judgments may properly proceed from the noncognitive character of the response. The difficulty is well illustrated, I think, by the case of moral judgments. It is prima facie very implausible to construe moral qualities as dispositions to produce moral sentiments – not least because the ascription of such a disposition does not seem to have the reason-giving force that properly belongs to a moral judgment.[34] But just for that reason, the belief that moral passion is not properly viewed as a state of cognition seems to have no very direct connection with moral irrealism.

Consider, finally, a case where such a dispositional analysis seems appropriate anyway: the case of secondary qualities.[35] To be red, for instance, consists in being disposed to induce a certain kind of visual experience in the normally sighted, under normal circumstances. (I prescind from the considerations to do with trans-galactic Doppler effect, and so on.) So, we have a biconditional comparable to those mooted for 'funny' above:

> X is red iff X would be seen as red by normally functioning observers in normal circumstances.

Now, there is a question about how 'normality' is to be understood for the purposes of the biconditional. Suppose we understand it statistically: Normally functioning observers function like most of us actually do most of the time; normal circumstances are relevantly similar to those which actually prevail most of the time. So understood, the statement on the right-hand side of the biconditional would still qualify as apt for substantial truth by both the tests earlier considered. Disagreement about such a statement might well be owing to vagueness in its constituent concepts, or to personal probability thresholds—the disputants might, for example, each have used statistical sampling techniques. But it seems impossible to understand how there could be a disagreement that could not be explained along those lines and yet owe nothing to prejudice, ignorance, or misinformation. As for the second test, the sort of direction that an account of the ideal epistemology of such a judgment should take is, prima facie at least, clear. Nevertheless, to interpret the relevant notion of normality in this way is to impose a certain kind of reading on the biconditional—at least if it is held to be true a priori. In effect, we give priority to the right-hand side. What *makes* something red is how we, most of us, respond to it in the conditions that usually obtain.

It is possible to elicit a third and stronger respect in which the notion of truth may be substantial if we contrast with this right-to-left reading of such a biconditional an interpretation that assigns priority, instead, to the left-hand side. Such an interpretation would see redness as a property of things in themselves, connecting at best contingently with any effect induced in us under statistically normal circumstances. Accordingly, to give priority to the left-hand side of the biconditional, while retaining its a priori status, would be to impose a different interpretation on the normality provisos. The essential characteristic of a normally functioning observer will now be: one suffering from no internal impediment to the proper functioning of the capacity to *detect* red. And normal circumstances will be those in which there is no external impediment to the proper functioning of this same capacity.

I owe to Mark Johnston the suggestion of the possibility of these alternative readings of such biconditionals; he characterized them as 'projective' and 'detective' respectively.[36] I would rather reserve 'projective' and 'projectivism' in the way I have indicated. The distinction, if it can be properly elucidated, is nevertheless very important and does correspond, it seems to me, to a further aspect of our intuitive preconceptions about factuality and substantial truth. An interesting suggestion, which I suspect is not quite right, is that it also corresponds to the distinction between secondary and primary qualities. Primary qualities will sustain biconditionals for which the proper reading is detective; the biconditionals appropriate to secondary qualities, by contrast, will be properly read from right to left. However that may be, there is a distinction here—roughly, between our responses *making it true* that so-and-so is the case and their merely *reflecting* that truth—that the contrast between two ways of reading an appropriate biconditional, interpreted as holding a priori, seems to capture nicely. And this, as noted, is a distinction that comes into play for judgments that pass the tests earlier considered and are accordingly apt for truth in more than the thinnest sense. Of any such class of judgments, we can ask whether an appropriate biconditional does, indeed, hold a priori and, if so, to which side belongs the priority. If the way I introduced the distinction is appropriate, this is a question to be decided by reflection on the proper interpretation of the normality provisos. But that is not the only possible way of proceeding, and it may prove not to be best. I wish merely to suggest the thought that one important class of intuitions about objectivity—those reflected, in particular, in the attempt to draw a distinction between primary and secondary qualities—have no proper place in the disputes between realism and irrealism. Rather, when the dialectic is set up in the way I have suggested it should be, they are internal to realism.[37, 38]

Notes

1. In the introduction to my *Realism, Meaning and Truth* (Oxford, 1986). This introduction elaborates many of the themes of parts I and II of this paper.

2. A qualification even of this formulation would be necessary to make space for realism about self-intimating mental states.

3. See especially essays 1, 10, 14, and 21 in his *Truth and Other Enigmas* (London, 1978); chap. 20 of his *The Interpretation of Frege's Philosophy* (London, 1981); and "What Is a Theory of Meaning (II)" in *Truth and Meaning*, edited by G. Evans and J. McDowell (Oxford, 1976), 67–137.

4. Again, a qualification is called for, to make space for realism about statements that *concern* human opinion.

5. As it stands, it involves a *non sequitur*, generated by substituting into an opaque context: 'it is guaranteed that P' and 'it is not guaranteed that Q' do not entail the falsity of the biconditional: P $ Q. See my *Realism, Meaning and Truth*, chap. 11, section 1.

6. See, for example, essays 10 and 21 in *Truth and Other Enigmas*.

7. Dummett notes the problems posed by vagueness for his original account of realism in chap. 20 of *The Interpretation of Frege's Philosophy*, 440. This chapter substantially qualifies the original account (though for somewhat different reasons). For a useful discussion of the new account, see the appendix to S. Rasmussen and J. Ravnkinde, "Realism and Logic," *Synthese* 52 (1982): 379–439.

8. *Remarks on the Foundations of Mathematics*, I, 13.

9. For more on the objectivity of meaning, see my "Rule-Following, Meaning and Constructivism," in *Meaning and Interpretation*, edited by C. Travis (Oxford, 1986), 271–97, and "On Making Up One's Mind: Wittgenstein on Intention," in *Logic, Philosophy of Science and Epistemology*, edited by P. Weingartner and G. Schurz (Vienna, 1987), 391–404.

To avoid misunderstanding, let me emphasize that I see no commitment to the objectivity of meaning issuing from acceptance of the platitude as such: It all depends on what we see as determining the contents that, with assistance from the world and in accordance with the platitude, determine truth-values. See "Rule-Following, Meaning and Constructivism," 273–74.

10. A fascinating recent example of the second sort of proposal is provided, of course, by Saul Kripke's interpretation of Wittgenstein on rule-following and meaning in his *Wittgenstein on Rules and Private Language* (Oxford, 1982).

11. However, someone who so opposes irrealism (about a particular class of statements) need not endorse the objectivity of meaning unless, contrary to my own belief, the Platitude requires it, so need not be a realist in the 'more basic' sense described in section II.

12. Thus, Austin on knowledge: "saying 'I know' is taking a new plunge. But it is *not* saying 'I have performed a specially striking feat of cognition, superior, in the same scale as believing and being sure, even to being merely quite sure': for there *is* nothing in that scale superior to being quite sure. Just as promising is not something superior, in the same scale as hoping and intending, even to merely fully intending: for there *is* nothing in that scale superior to fully intending. When I say 'I know', I *give others my word*: I *give others my authority for saying* that 'S is P' " (J. L. Austin, *Philosophical Papers*, 2d ed. [Oxford, 1970], 99).

Compare Strawson on truth: "The sentence 'What the policeman said is true' has no use *except* to confirm the policeman's story; but . . . [it] . . . does not say anything further *about* the policeman's story. . . . It is a device for confirming the story without telling it again. So, in general, in using such expressions, we are confirming, underwriting, agreeing with, what somebody has said; but . . . we are not making any assertion additional to theirs; and are *never* using 'is true' to talk *about* something which is *what they said*, or the sentences they used in saying it" (P. F. Strawson, "Truth," *Analysis* [1949]: 93).

But the classic example is Ayer on morals: "If I say to someone, 'You acted wrongly in stealing that money', I am not stating anything more than if I had simply said, 'You stole that money'. In adding that this action is wrong, I am not making any further statement about it. I am simply evincing my moral disapproval of it. It is as if I had said, 'You stole that money', in a peculiar tone of horror, or written it with the addition of some special exclamation marks." (A. J. Ayer, *Language, Truth and Logic* [London, 1962], 107).

13. More accurately: no *additional* claim beyond the clause embedded within the expressive vocabulary if—as, for instance, in each of the examples cited in note 12—there is one.

14. P. T. Geach, "Ascriptivism," *Philosophical Review* 69 (1960): 221–25.

15. In his *Frege: Philosophy of Language* (London, 1973), chap. 10.

16. Ibid., 351–54.

17. See his *Spreading the Word* (Oxford, 1984), chap. 6, and "Morals and Modals," in *Fact, Science and Morality: Essays on A. J. Ayer's Language, Truth and Logic*, edited by G. MacDonald and C. Wright (Oxford, 1986), 119–41.

18. That still is the character of the inference when the conditional is construed in Dummett's way. The result is something on the model of:

I hereby ask whether Q;
If I ask whether Q, I expect an answer;
So: I expect an answer.

19. Bob Hale, in his excellent critical study ("The Compleat Projectivist," *Philosophical Quarterly* 36 [1986]: 65–84) of *Spreading the Word*, notes that Blackburn's construal of the conditional is, in any case, inapposite for examples like

If Jones stole that money, he should be punished,

whose role cannot possibly be to evaluate a combination of evaluations since the antecedent is not evaluative. His ingenious alternative proposal is, first, to refashion the account of

If stealing is wrong, encouraging others to steal is wrong

as a *negative* evaluation of combining a negative evaluation of stealing with *the lack of* a negative evaluation of encouraging others to steal; and, second, to include not just evaluations, but beliefs (and presumably propositional attitudes in general) within the scope of such second-order evaluations. The conditional about Jones would then emerge as a negative evaluation of the combinations of believing that Jones stole the money but fail to approve of (positively evaluate) his punishment.

No question but that this improves Blackburn's account, and may well indicate the only viable direction for it to follow. But, notwithstanding some suggestive remarks by Hale ("The Compleat Projectivist," 73–74), I do not think it deflects the criticism bruited that Blackburn must misconstrue the failing of one who accepts the premises of the modus ponens example, but does not accept the conclusion. Certainly, the character of the 'inconsistency' changes: It is now a matter not of *failing* to have every combination of evaluations of which one approves, but of *actually having* a combination—a negative evaluation of stealing and the lack of a negative evaluation of encouraging others to steal—of which one *disapproves*. However, though such conduct—"doing what you boo," as Hale describes it—is naturally described as 'inconsistent', it remains that this is *moral* inconsistency: conduct that is not true to moral principle. Someone who rejects Geach's inference is being, in addition, *irrational*—and this additional failing, separate from the moral one, is just as evident if he merely rejects the conditional:

Provided that stealing is wrong, and that, if stealing is wrong, encouraging others to steal is wrong, then encouraging others to steal is wrong

without endorsing any particular evaluation of the conjuncts in its antecedent.

A related worry (acknowledged by Hale in correspondence) is whether a projectivist who follows Hale's direction can, once having construed 'mixed' conditionals as evaluations, avoid so construing *all* conditionals. Of course, expressive theories of the conditional have their supporters, too. But there is something unhappy about being pushed toward such an account quite generally, merely by the conviction that morals are of limited objectivity.

20. Actually, and independently of the illocutionary status of evaluation, there is, of course, a notion of inconsistency for evaluations quite similar to that mooted for commands: A set of evaluations, positive and negative, is inconsistent just in case no possible world realizes all the positives but avoids realizing all the negatives. But this is of no obvious help in the present case. Whether the conditional is construed as originally by Blackburn, or as proposed by Hale (see note 19), one who endorses both 'Stealing is wrong' and 'If stealing is wrong, encouraging others to steal is wrong', but denies 'Encouraging others to steal is wrong', commits himself to no such inconsistent set of evaluations. There is, I have urged, a logical inconsistency in such a performance, different from both the forms of moral inconsistency that, respectively, are disclosed by the Blackburn/Hale proposals. But neither the logical inconsistency nor those types of moral inconsistency are instances of this interevaluational species of inconsistency. The former has essentially nothing to do with the values the subject actually accepts (compare note 19). And the latter concern not the relations among his values, but those between his values and his conduct.

21. The point is made by Hale, "The Compleat Projectivist," 78–79.

22. See, for example, his "Morals and Modals," cited in note 17.

23. For pursuit of these misgivings, see my review of *Spreading the Word* in *Mind* 94 (1985): 310–19.

24. Of which the foremost is probably Frege's regress argument, given in his paper "Thoughts," Translated by P. T. Geach, in G. Frege, *Logical Investigations* (Oxford, 1977), 3–4. See Peter Carruthers's discussion, "Frege's Regress," in *Proceedings of the Aristotelian Society* 82 (1981–82): 17–32. For a very illuminating analysis of the issues between correspondence and disquotational or 'deflationary' accounts of truth, see the contributions by Hartry Field ("The Deflationary Concept of Truth") and Graeme Forbes ("Truth, Correspondence and Redundancy") in *Fact, Science and Morality*, edited by G. MacDonald and C. Wright, 55–117 and 27–54, respectively.

25. From *Charles S. Pierce: Selected Writings (Values in a World of Chance)*, edited by Philip P. Wiener (New York, 1966), 82.

26. And 'dispute' here means, of course: genuine dispute. There must be no material misunderstanding.

27. For details of how such a dispute might run, see the dialogue with the Cautious Man in chap. 3 of my *Wittgenstein on the Foundations of Mathematics* (Cambridge, Mass., 1980). Compare my "Inventing Logical Necessity," in *Language, Mind and Logic*, edited by J. Butterfield (Cambridge, 1986), 187–209.

28. Not all realists are comic, of course.

29. I try to deploy this feature of substantial truth in the context of a strategy against traditional epistemological skepticism in "Facts and Certainty," in *Proceedings of the British Academy* 71(1985):429–72.

30. Compare *Wittgenstein on the Foundations of Mathematics*, chap. 23, 456–60.

31. *Spreading the Word*, 170–71.

32. There are important internal differences. The relation between moral sentiment and moral judgment is much more complicated than that between amusement and judgment about what is funny. For one thing, though we may wish to allow that certain moral sentiments are natural in the sense that they are untrained, the capacity for *moral* sentiment arguably presupposes possession of moral concepts. An infant's distress at his older brother's punishment is not yet a moral response. By contrast, possession of the concept of humor is not a prerequisite for the capacity to be amused. For another, judging that a cer-

tain hypothetical state of affairs would be funny involves an element of prediction missing from the corresponding moral judgment, and is defeasible by subsequent apathetic responses in a way that moral judgment need not be. Third, both moral and modal judgments are disciplined by principle: Moral sentiment, and the phenomena of conviction and unintelligibility involved, for example, in the ratification of mathematical proofs, are quite often quashed by appeal to what it is independently considered correct, morally or mathematically, to think. Humor affords a parallel to this only insofar as we moralize about it, by introducing, for example, the notion of a joke in bad taste.

33. For pursuit of this line of thought, see my "Scientific Realism, Observation and the Verification Principle," in *Fact, Science and Morality*, edited by MacDonald and Wright, 247–74.

34. But perhaps only prima facie. See the remarks on the 'Moral Sense Theory' in Michael Smith's "Should We Believe in Emotivism?" in *Fact, Science and Morality*, edited by MacDonald and Wright, 289–310.

35. The distinction I wish to use the case to illustrate is actually appreciable independently of the belief that a dispositional analysis is here appropriate, so it does not matter if the reader does not share that belief.

36. In graduate classes on ethics in Princeton, spring 1986. However, the explanation of the contrast in terms of the alternative interpretations of the normality provisos demanded if the biconditional is to hold a priori is mine and may not coincide with his own preferred account. I should emphasize that I do not, at present, regard the contrast as unproblematic.

37. Johnston wanted to commend the question whether appropriate such biconditionals for moral judgments should be read right-to-left as the pivotal issue for moral realism. Certainly, we need a more detailed examination of the relations among the three criteria of the capacity for substantial truth than I have here been able to attempt. But my present belief, to stress, is that the first two criteria are prior, and that the third comes into play only for judgments that satisfy them. However, that does not entail that Johnston was in error to lay emphasis on the third criterion. For the capacity to sustain the truth of *some* such biconditional may be regarded as the litmus test of whether a type of statement is apt for substantial truth at all—so, unapt for irrealism—with the first two criteria providing tests in turn—perhaps not the only tests—of this capacity. The correctness of such a view is one among a number of very interesting questions here in prospect.

38. I would like to acknowledge the stimulus of conversations on these matters with Mark Johnston, David Lewis, and Michael Smith, and to thank Simon Blackburn, Bob Hale, Mark Johnston, and Peter Railton for extensive and very helpful comments on a previous draft, most of which the deadline has prevented me from responding to as I would have wished.

Creative Ontology and Absolute Truth

ALAN McMICHAEL

1. INTRODUCTION

Truth is absolute and not relative to system or person. This is an ancient and commonsensical doctrine that we have good reason to accept. The most important reason is that it is an integral part of the best theories of our own use of language. If truth is absolute, the significance of a declarative utterance is exhausted—or virtually exhausted—by the conditions for its truth. But if truth is relative, there must be an additional determinant of significance, namely, the system of belief to which the utterance belongs (which may or may not be the belief system of the utterer). This additional putative determinant introduces, I claim, a useless and undesirable complexity into the relativist's view of language.

To see this, consider the simple exchange:

Joe: I saw a bat in the closet.

Susan: No, you didn't!

According to the absolutist, the significance of Joe's utterance is clear, once we know that Joe is speaking English, that "I" refers to the speaker, Joe, that the description "the closet" refers, in the context, to a particular closet, and that "bat" has, in the context, one of its two possible meanings. There is no need to inquire to what system or set of beliefs the utterance belongs. According to one who is a relativist about the truth of Joe's utterance, the situation is different. Susan is disagreeing with Joe, but disagreement is obviously out of the question unless there is something in the context that forces a particular evaluation of Joe's utterance. The relativist says, however, that the utterance is evaluable as right or wrong, only with respect to a system. So, given the existence of a disagreement here, there must be something about the context that determines the system to which Joe's utterance belongs. That something about the context is the relativist's additional determinant of significance, without which, I say, we would be better off.

Of course, if truth is not absolute, the simplicity of the absolutists' view of language is illusory. But at least it can be said that, because their view underwrites a desirable simplicity in the theory of language, they have the advantage in the debate. Relativists must provide some argument to dislodge them. We shall see that the relativists are not without arguments. We shall examine, in particular, some rather ingenious ones presented by Nelson Goodman and Hilary Putnam.[1] These arguments raise several interesting, general ontological issues. The resolution of those issues will be sufficient reward for the effort of grappling with the arguments, even for one who shares my view that, on account of their conclusions, the arguments are doomed to fail.

2. THE RELATIVISM OF GOODMAN AND PUTNAM

Before turning to the arguments, let me try to explain these authors' peculiar brand of relativism. Goodman observes that apparent conflicts between plausible statements can often be resolved by relativization to frames of reference:

> Consider, to begin with, the statements 'the sun always moves' and 'the sun never moves' which, though equally true, are at odds with each other. Shall we say, then, that they describe different worlds, and indeed that there are as many different worlds as there are such mutually exclusive truths? Rather, we are inclined to regard the two strings of words not as complete statements with truth-values of their own but as elliptical for some such statement as 'Under frame of reference A, the sun always moves' and 'Under frame of reference B, the sun never moves' – statements that may both be true of the same world. (*WOW*, p. 2)

But Goodman maintains that not all such conflicts can be removed in this innocuous way. In any frame of reference we choose, there will always exist pairs of genuinely conflicting statements, and there is no way of describing the world independently of all frames of reference:

> If I ask about the world, you can offer to tell me how it is under one or more frames of reference; but if I insist that you tell me how it is apart from all frames, what can you say? We are confined to ways of describing whatever is described. Our universe, so to speak, consists of these ways rather than of a world or of worlds. (*WOW*, pp. 2–3).

These "ways of describing" are what Goodman calls *versions*:

> The alternative descriptions of motion, all of them in much the same terms and routinely transformable into one another, provide only a minor and rather pallid example of diversity in accounts of the world. Much more striking is the vast variety of versions and visions in the several sciences, in the works of

different painters and writers, and in our perceptions as informed by these, by circumstances, and by our own insights, interests, and past experiences. Even with all illusory or wrong or dubious versions dropped, the rest exhibit new dimensions of disparity. Here we have no neat set of frames of reference." (*WOW*, p. 3)

Rather than speaking of one actual world, we may, with equal propriety, speak of many actual worlds, each described by some "right" version.

Versions consisting of statements may be logically incompatible with one another. In some cases, Goodman maintains, incompatible versions may have "good and equal claims to truth." This presents a problem:

We can hardly take conflicting statements as true in the same world without admitting all statements whatsoever (since all follow from any contradiction) as true in the same world, and that world itself as impossible. Thus we must either reject one of two ostensibly conflicting versions as false, or take them as true in different worlds, or find if we can another way of reconciling them. (*WOW*, p. 110).

Goodman selects a reconciliation that leaves room both for relativity of perspective and for irresolvable conflict. The reconciliation can, I think, be captured in four basic theses.

(1) The conflicting versions, by hypothesis, meet the standards of *rightness* for the relevant discipline. These standards, however, do not entail truth in an absolute sense. (How could they? The versions are incompatible.) (*WOW*, pp. 120–25)
(2) Contradictory statements of the two versions may, of course, be said to be *true in* their respective versions. (*WOW*, p. 120)
(3) Either version may be *taken to be true* (that is, believed) by a person provided that it coheres with other versions that person accepts. (*WOW*, p. 17)
(4) No person may rightly take both to be true. The versions represent "worlds in conflict." (*WOW*, pp. 114–116)

Assuming that the standards of rightness for a discipline single out its "truths," these theses entail at least a modest relativity of truth. In the cases Goodman envisions, there are matters about which there is no absolute truth — violations of the law of the excluded middle, one might say — but about which one is permitted to take a definite stand.

Putnam's relativism is more easily documented, since he does not employ the novel "versions" terminology. The main target of Putnam's arguments is a view he calls *metaphysical realism*:

On this perspective, the world consists of some fixed totality of mind-independent objects. There is exactly one true and complete description of 'the way the world is.' Truth involves some sort of correspondence relation between words or thought-signs and external things and sets of things. (*RTH*, p. 49)

Much of Putnam's recent writing is devoted to undermining the metaphysical realists' notion of correspondence between words and things. Several sharp replies have been made to this line of thought,[2] and I shall not try to make any direct contribution to these criticisms. But there is a second, relatively neglected[3] and apparently independent way in which Putnam attacks realism, using arguments designed to show the relativity of ontology. About objects, Putnam says,

'Objects' do not exist independently of conceptual schemes. *We* cut up the world into objects when we introduce one or another scheme of description. (*RTH*, p. 52)

But different, equally good schemes can make incompatible ontological claims, so:

"If all it takes to make a theory true is abstract correspondence (never mind which), then incompatible theories can be true. To an internalist [Putnam calls his view 'internal realism'] this is not objectionable: why should there not sometimes be equally coherent but incompatible conceptual schemes which fit our experiential beliefs equally well? If truth is not (unique) correspondence then the possibility of a certain pluralism is opened up. (*RTH*, p. 73)

Never mind the notion of correspondence. Putnam, here, is giving up absolute truth. It may be true within one scheme that a certain sort of object exists, but false within another, and there may be no absolute fact of the matter as to which scheme is correct.

These, then, are the views of my opponents. In them, we can discern the outline of the main argument for their relativism, an argument based on the existence of equally good incompatible theories or versions. In what follows, I shall discuss the argument in more detail. First, I shall explain how the existence of equally good incompatible theories would indeed pose a threat to absolutism. Second, I shall examine Goodman's and Putnam's alleged examples of equally good incompatible theories. These examples fail, in interesting ways, to be convincing. Third, I shall describe an example of a sort that is most problematic for absolutists. Even for examples of this sort, however, absolutists seem to have an adequate response. Finally, two arguments are raised against this response. The first is based on Ockham's Razor; the second, on the doctrine of the relativity of structure. Neither argument is persuasive. Absolutism emerges unscathed.

3. FROM PLURALISM TO RELATIVISM

Goodman says that "to anyone but an arrant absolutist, alternative ostensibly conflicting versions often present good and equal claims to truth" (*WOW*, p. 110).

He goes on to argue that some of these conflicts are real and irresolvable. In them, he finds support for relativism. He infers that if incompatible versions, or theories, have good and equal claims to truth, then the matters about which they disagree are matters of *relative* truth only.

But this inference is far from clear. In order to evaluate it, we must know, in particular, what a "claim to truth" is and what it is for such a claim to be "good." We cannot say merely that a theory has a good claim to truth just in case it is true. The argument would then reduce to a silly one-stepper: "Incompatible theories can both be true, but this is absurd unless truth is relative." No, if the argument is to get off the ground, the notion of a claim to truth must be *epistemic*. A theory's claim to truth consists of the reasons that favor its *acceptance*. If this is correct, it is easy to say when such a claim is good. A theory has a good claim to truth when the reasons in its favor *merit* its acceptance, that is, when we would be *justified* in accepting it. (It would be idle to say, instead, that a theory has a good claim to truth when the reasons in its favor are *conclusive*. Such reasons, in the cases under consideration, are not to be had.)

Suppose that incompatible theories sometimes have good and equal claims to truth. What follows that might be disturbing to absolutists? It certainly follows, in the case of propositions about which the competing theories disagree, that we are justified in either accepting *or* denying them. That is,

> Sometimes a person may be in a position to accept a proposition justifiably or to accept its negation justifiably (but not both).

Since this principle sanctions the development, from one and the same epistemic starting point, of alternative systems of belief, I shall call it "pluralism," a usage that seems to conform with Putnam's.

Some absolutists would be willing to accept pluralism as a permissive response to cases of essential ignorance. When we cannot know whether a proposition is true, they might say, why not let people believe what they please? But notice that this is an appropriate response only if pluralist choices are optional. Goodman and Putnam will argue, on the contrary, that they are unavoidable:

> Sometimes a person may justifiably accept a proposition or may justifiably accept its negation, but may not reasonably withhold acceptance.

This, the doctrine of unavoidable pluralism, is the strongest interesting conclusion to be drawn from the existence of equally good incompatible equivalents.

It is clear, of course, that relativism makes room for pluralism. In postulating matters about which there are no absolute facts, the relativists postulate matters about which different acceptable systems might disagree. It is less clear, however, that absolutism can make no room for pluralism, less clear that absolutism must be rejected if pluralism is correct. But if Goodman's and Putnam's examples of equally good incompatible theories are to have any persuasive force, pluralism must hold *some* terrors for absolutists. What might they be?

The problem, as I see it, is that according to any of the standard conceptions of epistemic justification, it is a conceptual truism that, at one and the same time and for one and the same person, not both a proposition and its negation can merit acceptance. For example, I believe:

> If a person is justified in believing a proposition, then she must be in a position to judge that it has a high probability of being true or, at any rate, a higher probability of being true than its negation does.

This principle rules out pluralist choice, since, assuming that we are dealing with probabilities of truth in an absolute sense, it is absurd to think that a person is allowed, at one and the same time, to judge that a proposition and its negation are more probable than each other. Alternatively, suppose we adopt a reliabilist account of justification, one according to which:

> If a person is justified in believing a proposition, then, given her epistemically relevant characteristics (for example, the evidence she has and the methods she employs), the proposition has a greater probability of being true than does its negation.[4]

Once again, pluralist choice is ruled out, since it is absurd to suppose that two conditional probabilities could be greater than each other—at least, it is absurd if these are probabilities of absolute truth.

Both of the conceptions of justification just mentioned insist on probabilities, of one kind or another, greater than one-half. This is plausible when we are considering the epistemic acceptability of individual propositions, but is arguable that matters are different in the case of *whole theories*. It is arguable that a theory may be accepted even if its probability is rather low (although the practical significance of acceptability remains to be explained). This would not, however, solve the absolutists' difficulty with pluralism. Equally good incompatible theories will differ on the truth-values of individual propositions, for which an epistemic standard requiring probability greater than one-half is appropriate. And even a conception that allows a theory to be accepted when its probability is low may still require that its probability be greater than that of any "competitor," a requirement that would rule out pluralist choice among whole theories.

In summary, pluralism does indeed conflict with absolutism, given any one of several standard conceptions of epistemic justification. And I do not think there exist any attractive alternatives to those standard conceptions. Thus, the claim that there can exist equally good incompatible theories, theories between which we must make a pluralist choice, should be examined carefully, to see if there is not something wrong with it.

4. GEOMETRIC EXAMPLES

Goodman, as I have explained, wants to invoke an unavoidable pluralism in support of his relativism. He begins by pointing out that incompatible theories, or versions, can have good, perhaps even optimal, fit with our experience. He then maintains that it is not always open to us, when faced with such theories, to withhold belief in either. We can, we must, and we do make pluralist choices. But we cannot make any sense of this necessary practice unless we adopt some sort of relativism. Putnam, who offers some very similar examples of "equally good incompatible theories," appears to endorse the very same sort of reasoning.

Goodman's principal examples of equally good incompatible theories, or systems, are hypothetical. They concern not theories that actually have "good claims to truth," but rather, "equivalent" incompatible theories, theories such that if one had a good claim to truth, then so, allegedly, would the other, and vice versa. However, should we concede these hypothetical examples, should we concede that such theories have "good and equal claims to being true," we would soon be forced to concede that incompatible equivalents exist for the theories we *do* take to be true, and so would succumb to Goodman's relativism.

Goodman's principal examples are geometric:

> A world with points as elements cannot be the Whiteheadian world having points as certain classes of nesting volumes or having points as certain pairs of intersecting lines or as certain triples of intersecting planes. That the points of our everyday world can be equally well defined in any of these ways does not mean that a point can be identified in any one world with a nest of volumes and a pair of lines and a triple of planes; for all these are different from each other. (*WOW*, p. 9)

Are these theories really incompatible? What is the sense in which they are equivalent? In answering these preliminary questions, I shall concentrate on one pair of putative incompatible equivalents, the pair consisting of the geometry with points as basic individuals and the Whiteheadian geometry of points as converging classes of volumes. It is interesting to note that essentially the same example crops up also in Putnam's arguments against metaphysical realism (*R&R*, pp. 130–31).

At first glance, the incompatibility of the two theories seems obvious, since one asserts,

(1) Points are classes and have members.

And the other asserts,

(2) Points are individuals and have no members.

Underlying the claim of incompatibility, however, is the assumption that "point" has the same meaning in the two cases. This requires some argument. Perhaps it can be plausibly maintained that the two theories are competing accounts of the meaning that "point" already possessed before the consideration of the two theories. That would suffice to show a kind of *semantic incompatibility* between the two theories. But notice that to establish semantic incompatibility, one must tackle thorny issues of meaning.[5] One cannot simply appeal to the sheer obviousness of the contradiction.

There is another form of incompatibility that the two theories might be supposed to exhibit, an incompatibility that is *metaphysical* rather than semantic. The Whiteheadian geometry of volumes is the sort of geometry that might be espoused by people who deny the existence of point-individuals. So we can imagine their geometry to be conjoined with:

(3) There are no extensionless geometrical individuals.

Let us call a geometry of volumes that includes (3) a *strong* geometry of volumes, and one that does not, a *weak* geometry of volumes. A geometry of point-individuals clearly clashes with a strong geometry of volumes, for it asserts,

(4) There are points, and points are extensionless geometrical individuals.

Notice that this metaphysical conflict does not hinge on any question concerning the meaning of "point."[6]

No doubt, we can also concoct a strong geometry of points, one that includes:

(5) There are no extended geometrical individuals. (Volumes are classes.)

The geometries of volumes assert, on the contrary:

(6) There are volumes, and volumes are extended geometrical individuals.

This particular conflict is less useful for our purposes, however, since Goodman and Putnam do not exploit it, relying on the above conflicts instead.

Are the examples presented by Goodman and Putnam intended to illustrate semantic incompatibility or metaphysical incompatibility? Some of the incompatibilities mentioned by Goodman are clearly semantic (for example *WOW*, p. 114). Putnam, on the other hand, points out some incompatibilities that are definitely metaphysical (for example, *R&R*, pp. 130–31). There is no evidence that either philosopher wishes to deal exclusively in incompatibilities of one of the two sorts. Evidently, we must examine both possibilities.

We have found two ways in which the example geometries can be claimed to be incompatible. In what way are they supposed to be *equivalent*? Goodman defines equivalence in terms of *translatability*. Two theories are equivalent, in his sense, if there is a translation of sentences in one into sentences of the other that preserves the truth-values of all sentences *that we care about*[7] So, in our geometrical case, Goodman claims that talk about point-individuals can be replaced, with preservation of all truths that we care about, by talk about converging classes of volumes. The translation Goodman has in mind is straightforward. As one might expect, the truth values that are not preserved in the translation are precisely those of the sentences that are responsible for the incompatibility of the theories. Thus, the persuasiveness of Goodman's equivalence claim rests on a presumed agreement that these truth values "don't matter" in geometry. Later, I shall challenge this presumption.

It is important to note that Goodman's notion of equivalence is but a distant relative of the notion of *empirical equivalence* used in philosophy of science. If we care at all about the truth-values of theoretical claims, then empirical equivalence clearly does not imply translatability in Goodman's sense. It may be that Goodman's translatability implies empirical equivalence, although even this can be challenged. (Suppose we do not care about S because we cannot conceive of an experiment that would allow us to determine whether it is true. Suppose we later conceive of such an experiment. In such a case, two theories might change from Goodmanian equivalents into Goodmanian inequivalents. But they were always empirically inequivalent.)

5. GEOMETRY: METAPHYSICALLY INCOMPATIBLE EQUIVALENTS

The geometry of point-individuals and the strong geometry of volumes are alleged to be equivalent but metaphysically incompatible theories. The notion of equivalence used is supposed to be sufficient for the purposes of pluralism. We are to imagine a situation in which it is reasonable to adopt one of the theories, and then we are to see that, on account of the equivalence, the other theory is equally acceptable. In my discussion of these claims, I shall take Putnam to be my chief opponent, since he is more explicit in his endorsement of them.

Putnam apparently assumes that the Goodmanian translatability of the two theories entails the equality of epistemic status required to present a pluralist choice. The two theories have equal claims to acceptance because they are Goodmanian equivalents. But Goodmanian translatability is translatability *with exceptions*, so it is certainly open to question whether it preserves epistemic status.

For example, one alleged epistemic virtue of theories is *simplicity*. Other things being equal, it is alleged, we ought to prefer theories that have simpler sets of primitive notions and postulates. Goodman is certainly among those who count simplicity among the main determinants of the acceptability of systems. He has even proposed *measures* of the simplicity of sets of theoretical primitives. Suppose that he is right and that simplicity is a genuine epistemic virtue. Then, the claim that Goodman's intertranslatable theories have equal epistemic status is open to the possible objection that at least one main epistemic virtue, simplicity, is *not* preserved under Goodmanian translatability. Indeed, the two geometries under consideration provide a plausible case of this. It is arguable, more specifically, that the geometry of point-individuals is epistemically preferable to the strong geometry of volumes, on the ground that it has the simpler set of primitive notions and postulates. Of course, it is impossible to establish this with complete certainty, since we have not laid out the two geometries in complete logical detail. Nevertheless, there are some compelling considerations in its favor.

Consider the relation of betweenness among point-individuals. What relation replaces it in the geometry of volumes? Of course, there is an analogous relation among converging classes of volumes, the Whiteheadian "points." But, since it is a relation of classes of individuals rather than individuals, it belongs to a *higher logical type* than does the original betweenness relation. That itself, in the absence of an alternative replacement, would be a good ground for claiming a higher complexity for the geometry of volumes.

If we are to challenge the simplicity claim, it seems that we must find a relation of *volumes* to replace the relation of point-betweenness. Suppose we select the relation that holds among volumes X, Y, and Z, just in case *some part* of X lies between Y and Z. Call this *V-betweenness*. Although V-betweenness belongs to the same logical type as point-betweenness, and so is not any more complex in that respect, it does lack one desirable logical property of point-betweenness, the property captured in the schema:

(*) If X, Y, and Z bear relation B, and W, X, and Z bear relation B, then W, Y, and Z bear relation B.

Counterexample:

```
YYY
YYY              ZZZ
YYY   XXX        ZZZ
      XXX        ZZZ
      XXX   WWW
      XXX   WWW
      XXX   WWW
```

In the diagram, volume X is V-between volumes Y and Z, and volume W is V-between volumes X and Z, but volume W is not V-between volumes Y and Z — a violation of the principle (*). Because V-betweenness lacks the nice logical property captured in the schema, its use is bound to lead to greater complexity in the geometric axioms. Again, the attempt to make do with a surrogate for betweenness seems to add to the complexity of the geometry. In view of such failures, it is difficult to see how the volume-theorist is to deal with the problem presented by the greater apparent complexity of his system.

My main objection to Putnam's example, however, is rather different. The example theories are geometries, and this makes it difficult for one to take their ontologies, and so their ontological differences, seriously. I can, indeed, conceive of a world in which all the phenomena of nature can *usefully be thought of* as occurring within, say, a Euclidean space. But I doubt that I thereby conceive a world in which one can justifiably believe in the existence of spatial points or their surrogates. To conceive a world in which Euclidean geometry is useful in the description of spatial arrangements, indeed, even one in which it is *in principle the most useful geometry*, is not necessarily to conceive a world in which Euclidean geometry may justifiably be taken to be true. The problem is that the most reasonable view of geometry, both in this world and in the hypothetical Euclidean world, may be an *instrumentalist* view, one that does not attribute real existence to spatial points or their surrogates. Geometry, with its abundant idealizations, such as continuity and infinite divisibility, seems to beg for an instrumentalist interpretation. Consequently, Putnam's geometrical example is ill-suited for use in an attack on the absolutists' conception of reality.

This is not to say that it is absolutely impossible to conceive a world in which the real existence of spatial points becomes a live issue. What I am saying is that in concentrating on purely geometric theories, Putnam has left out of consideration everything that would be *pertinent* to the question of the real existence of points. For example, it would seem pertinent whether the best physics available is one that assigns *properties* to individual points rather than, say, only to extended volumes. Pure geometry, however, assigns no such properties and so provides no answer. Suppose, on the other hand, Putnam were to respond by admitting the relevance of such physical considerations. In that case, the equivalence of the geometries-cum-physics would come once again into question, since there is no guarantee that the physical considerations would be evenhanded. For example, if the physics assigns properties to individual points, that provides a prima facie case in favor of the geometry of point-individuals.

Finally, if we dismiss these speculations and hold fast to an instrumentalist view of geometry, the simplicity argument comes forcefully into play. If we need not take the ontologies of the two geometries seriously, there is absolutely no reason not to opt for the simpler geometry of point-individuals. Certainly, this is true if we follow Goodman and attach great importance to simplicity of theory.

6. GEOMETRY: SEMANTICALLY INCOMPATIBLE EQUIVALENTS

What of the claim, apparently made by Goodman, that the geometry of point-individuals and the geometry of volumes, even the *weak* geometry of volumes, are equivalent, *semantically* incompatible theories? This claim rests on the assumption that the two geometries present competing accounts of the "real reference" of "point." Let us assume, for the sake of argument, that this is so. Let us also assume that the theories are translatable, and so equivalent, in Goodman's sense. Then we have a pair of equivalent, semantically incompatible theories. Have we now given up the ballgame? Must we, given our assumptions, admit that it is possible for these theories to have good and equal claims to being true? Not yet.

According to our hypothesis, there is such a thing as the "real reference" of "point," and the two theories are not mere formal systems with individual interpretations, but rather, involve attempts to capture the real reference of "point." Now we can see that the Goodmanian equivalence of these theories is entirely irrelevant to their epistemic standing. That theories T and T' are equivalent in Goodman's sense shows *at most* that if one is true, then those parts of the other that we care about are true under a "similar" interpretation. The claim of semantic incompatibility, however, rests on a certain fixity in the interpretation of "point." One theory simply says false things about the real referents of "point." The fact that there exists an interpretation for which it does not is irrelevant, for that is not the intended interpretation, not the interpretation appealed to in the claim of semantic incompatibility. For example, suppose "point" really refers to point-individuals. Then, a theory that says, "Points are classes," is plainly wrong, even though there is an interpretation of "point" for which the utterance comes out true.

In this case, there is no argument from Goodmanian equivalence to equality of epistemic standing. In the absence of such an argument, we have reason to doubt that we have been given an example in which two incompatible theories have "good and equal claims to being true," let alone an example in which equal epistemic standing forces a pluralist choice.

7. PARTICLES AND FIELDS

One of the examples Putnam offers is not of the purely geometric variety:

> Sometimes incompatible theories can actually be intertranslatable. For example, if Newtonian physics were true, then every single physical event could be described in two ways: in terms of particles acting at a distance, across empty space (which is how Newton described gravitation as acting), or in terms of particles acting on fields which act on other fields (or other parts of the same field), which finally act 'locally' on other particles. For example, the Maxwell equations, which describe the behavior of the electromagnetic field, are mathematically equivalent to a theory in which there are only action-at-a-distance forces between particles, attracting or repelling according to the inverse square law, travelling not instantaneously but rather at the speed of light ('retarded potentials'). The Maxwell field theory and the retarded potential theory are incompatible from a metaphysical point of view, since either there are or there aren't causal agencies (the 'fields') which mediate the action of separated particles on each other (a realist would say). But the two theories are mathematically intertranslatable." (*RTH*, p. 73)

Assuming that the technical details can be worked out as nicely as Putnam supposes, this example is a definite improvement over the geometric ones. As we have seen, the problem with geometry is that it seems reasonable to adopt an instrumentalist view of its ontology. This stacks the deck against any geometry that absolutely denies the existence of point-individuals. If the geometry of point-individuals is a simple and convenient instrument, and if we are not inclined to take its ontology seriously or any of the alternative geometric ontologies seriously, then there is no good ground for using, instead, some geometry based on a tortuous reduction of points to classes. In the case of particles and fields, we are less likely to accept this instrumentalist dodge. We are more likely to view particles and fields as stuff out of which the universe might be made, rather than as elements of instrumental ontologies.

Putnam does not reveal the origin of the "action-at-a-distance" theory that plays such a crucial role in his example. I take him to be referring to the "Wheeler-Feynman" formulation of electromagnetic theory. The Wheeler-Feynman theory seems, anyway, to meet Putnam's requirements, for there are conditions under which it gives the "same results" as the field theory. The simplest such condition is that the universe be "opaque" (that is, act as an adiabatic enclosure).[8] It is easy to see why equivalence would be threatened if the universe were not opaque. In that case, the field theory would allow moving particles to radiate energy into infinite space, a particle-field interaction not eliminable in favor of particle-particle interactions.

But given the right conditions, the two theories are intertranslatable in Goodman's sense. The theories agree on the laws of motion for charged particles, so statements about particle positions and motions are translatable "as is." Of course, statements of the field theory concerning the values of the field at empty field points must be treated somewhat differently. The distant-action theory does not postulate field points or their properties. Nevertheless, the distant-action theory does have the resources for calculating the same mathematical values. So, corresponding to the statement that the field has a certain value at a certain point is a statement to the effect that particles are so arranged to produce the same *mathematical* value upon solution of such-and-such an equation. The distant-action theory, however, attributes no physical reality to this value or to the alleged field point.

In what respect are the field and distant-action theories incompatible? Evidently, the incompatibility is not merely a semantic disagreement about some common vocabulary. The incompatibility noted by Putnam is metaphysical. As in the geometric cases, the incompatibility consists in the denial by one of the theories of the existence of individuals postulated by the other. In particular, the field theory asserts,

(1) Spacetime is filled by point-individuals, the field points, that have a genuine causal role.

Whereas, the distant-action theory, according to Putnam, contains a contrary assertion,

(2) There are many spacetime locations that are unoccupied by individuals or, at least, unoccupied by individuals with a genuine causal role.

As in the case of the Whiteheadian geometry of volumes, we might distinguish strong and weak versions of the distant-action theory. Putnam's version, which contains (2), is the strong one. The weak version would not have (2) as a consequence and would, perhaps, be compatible with the field theory.

The field theory and the strong version of the distant-action theory do, indeed, seem to be Goodmanian, equivalent incompatible theories. And it does not seem right to construe them as mere instruments, rather than as serious candidates for truth. Do these theories, then, provide us with a genuine example of theories between which we might, hypothetically, be forced to make a pluralist choice? Imagine, the argument would go, a situation in which we would be justified in accepting the distant-action theory. In such a situation, wouldn't the demonstrably equivalent field theory be an equally good alternative?

We should not be convinced. As I pointed out in the geometric case, there is reason to doubt that epistemic standing is preserved under Goodmanian translatability. In the present case, a crucial difference between the two theories, one that is relevant to epistemic standing, is that the field theory has a *less parsimonious basic ontology*. Both theories postulate, in one way or another,[9] particles and their charges. But there is much in the field theory to which nothing in the distant-action theory corresponds, namely, continuum-many empty field points and continuum-many possible field values. If these extra, basic entities secure no advantage for the field theory, they are "ontological idlers." We have no reason to believe in them, and the distant-action theory is to be preferred. There is, in short, a prima facie case against the field theory.

Indeed, the richer ontology of the field theory leads to two problems absent from the distant-action theory. First, the field theory is compatible with a wide range of "boundary conditions." Thus, there exists the problem of justifying a particular selection. The distant-action theory, in contrast, corresponds to a field theory with very special boundary conditions. If those are the conditions actually needed, this fact would be inexplicable from the point of view of the field theory, whereas the proponent of distant action could exclaim, "No wonder $F(in) = F(out) = 0$! There is no field!" Second, the field theory must deal with the interaction of a moving charge with *its own field*. This has led to the problem of "diverging self-energy," a problem that has been removed only with the rather artificial device of "renormalization." The distant-action theory—at least in the classical version we are considering—encounters no such difficulty.[10]

To uphold his example, Putnam must maintain that the field theory has compensating, although not overwhelming, advantages of its own. In this regard, it will not do to say only that the field theory is free from the mystery of action-at-a-distance. Action-at-a-distance is mysterious because in our everyday experience we have found that objects act on distant objects by means of material intermediaries, and when such intermediaries have not been apparent to the senses, we have found their postulation fruitful. Action-at-a-distance without a material intermediary is contrary to what we have come to expect. But it is also *not* what postulation of a field secures, since the field is not a material medium! Therefore, any argument in favor of the field theory will have to be much more subtle than a mere dismissal of action-at-a-distance.

Even if Putnam succeeds in counteracting the prima facie case against the field theory and shows that the two theories are, indeed, epistemic equals, he still faces the task of showing, in the hypothetical situation in which both theories are empirically adequate, that each theory merits acceptance. One alternative to a pluralist choice in favor of one of the two theories is that of withholding belief. That is, one might accept the common part of the two theories, namely, the laws of interaction of charged particles, but remain agnostic about the existence of an intervening field. It cannot be argued against this alternative that it leaves us wholly without "a sense of how the world is," since our ignorance, according to this alternative, is only partial.

Putnam must, therefore, say more than that there is a standoff between the two theories. Perhaps he is relying on the idea that the two theories excel in different respects, the distant-action theory in respect of ontological parsimony, the field theory in some respect as yet undetermined. Thus, a choice between the two theories might depend crucially on the relative importance of the two respects, that is, it might depend crucially on *epistemic values*. Different people, the argument might go, may rationally disagree on questions of epistemic value and, so, may make different, but equally justified, choices.

But this reasoning is just an enticing dead end. Putnam is supposed to be showing you that there can exist equally good incompatible theories. It does no good to show you that a situation in which you would be inclined to accept one of his two theories is a situation in which, *if you had different epistemic values*, you would accept the other. That does nothing to establish his conclusion. Indeed, the appeal to epistemic values simply elevates the controversy to another level. The absolutist will agree that different theories may be justified according to different systems of epistemic value, but this is not to concede that different incompatible theories may be equally justified *absolutely*. Of course, Putnam may deny that justification is ever absolute, but surely he is not entitled merely to assume this when arguing against the absolutist!

In summary, Putnam's example suffers from two serious failings. First, he has not shown that, in the hypothetical situation of pluralist choice, the two theories are, indeed, epistemic equals. In particular, he has not responded to the charge that the field theory ought to be rejected on grounds of parsimony. Second, he has not shown, under the assumption of epistemic equality, that there is anything to prevent us from remaining agnostic about the existence of the electromagnetic field.

8. PARTICLE KINDS AND PARTICLE PROPERTIES

Could it be that the defense of relativism has failed because of a lack of ingenuity? No firm relativist conclusion can be drawn from Goodman's geometries, for they may plausibly be regarded as instrumental theories whose incompatibilities need not be taken seriously. Putnam's particle-field dichotomy suffers a different fate. The ontology of one, the distant-action theory, is a proper part of the ontology of the other, the field theory. Thus the distant-action theory has an incontrovertible claim to the advantage of parsimony. Consequently, one can plausibly argue that in a case in which the two theories are empirically adequate, we are at most justified in accepting the existence of particles, not the existence of a field. But, although the examples of Goodman and Putnam fail to illustrate the alleged possibility of unavoidable pluralist choices, could it be that there are examples unthought of that would? Perhaps we can cook one up.

Let us imagine two theories. One postulates just a few basic kinds of particle. For the sake of familiarity, we may suppose that the kinds are *proton, neutron, electron, muon, positron,* and *photon*. The second theory denies the existence of these particle kinds and postulates, instead, a few basic *properties* of particles: masses, charges, and spins. Each theory, we may imagine, provides an adequate classification scheme for particles. Indeed, the schemes may be imagined to be intertranslatable, with such translations as:

(1) x is a proton ↔ x has positive charge and mass M
(2) x has charge minus one ↔ x is an electron or x is muon

But, given that the kind theory denies the existence of the properties and the property theory denies the existence of the kinds, these intertranslatable theories are actually incompatible!

This example does not suffer from the defect of Putnam's particle-field example. The translation to the property theory does not involve a one-to-one mapping from the particle kinds to a proper subset of the particle properties. The reverse translation does not involve a one-to-one mapping from the properties to a proper subset of the kinds. Thus, neither theory has an indisputable claim to greater parsimony.

One drawback of the example is that not all philosophers would agree that the theories differ in *ontology*. The true view, according to those philosophers, is simply that there are no such things as kinds and properties. Choice of a theory here involves a choice of *ideology* rather than *ontology*, a choice between two systems of *predicates* rather than a choice between two sets of *entities*. For the sake of argument, however, I shall simply dismiss this objection, since even if my example is flawed, it will raise all the right issues.

9. THE RAZOR ARGUMENT

The theory of particle kinds and the theory of particle properties are metaphysically incompatible Goodmanian-equivalent theories. Neither theory cries out for an instrumental interpretation. Neither theory is obviously less parsimonious than the other. Can we imagine a situation of pluralist choice between the two theories? That is, can we imagine a situation in which we could justifiably accept either one of the two, even though they are incompatible?

We should not leap to an affirmative answer. Notice that our two theories are incompatible because each denies the existence of the entities postulated by the other. As in the case of our pair of geometric theories, there surely are weak versions of these two theories that lack the ontological denials and, so, are metaphysically compatible with one another. Using the pair of weak theories, we may make a counter-hypothesis: The envisaged situation of pluralist choice is misdescribed. We would not be justified in accepting either of the two incompatible strong theories. Each theory contains gratuitous ontological denials. Rather, we would be justified in accepting both of the weak theories and thereby justified in accepting both the existence of particle kinds and the existence of particle properties. We might call this the proposal of *ontological toleration*. Prima facie, this is surely a sensible proposal. For, by hypothesis, the kind theorist has no good argument against the existence of the particle properties, and the property theorist has no good argument against the existence of particle kinds. Both theories, after all, are equally good.

Notice that the strategy of ontological toleration is a general one. Had the examples of Goodman and Putnam survived scrutiny, I could have employed the same strategy against them: Consider the weak version of each theory, the version that does not deny the existence of the entities postulated by the other. In the alleged situation of pluralist choice, claim that neither strong theory is acceptable but that the conjunction of the weak theories is.

Against the strategy of ontological toleration, relativists may unsheath Ockham's Razor, saying, "Entities are not to be multiplied beyond necessity. The tolerant acceptance of the conjunction of weak theories presents, in violation of this rule, a classic case of redundant ontology. Particle kinds or particle properties—each is by itself sufficient to make the distinctions we need. The acceptance of both is not justified. Hence, the ontological dilemma remains. In the hypothetical situation, at least and at most one theory should be accepted. And you cannot respond by rejecting Ockham's Razor, since you yourself have spoken in favor of ontological parsimony." Let us call this the Razor Argument. Although neither Putnam nor Goodman bases his position clearly on it, it is nevertheless an important argument that naturally springs to mind, and, therefore, an argument that must be dealt with.

Before responding to the argument itself, let me answer the last remark. Yes, in favoring the distant-action theory of electromagnetism over the field theory, I did say it has the more parsimonious *basic* ontology. But what is being claimed in the Razor Argument is not that pluralist choice secures a more parsimonious *basic* ontology than does the strategy of toleration, only that it secures a more parsimonious *total* ontology. The toleration strategy leads to acceptance of an ontology that includes both particle kinds and particle properties. *Either* the set of particle kinds alone *or* the set of particle properties alone can be taken as a maximally parsimonious basis for the whole. Pluralist choice cannot secure a less inclusive *basis*; it is simply a rejection of some of the entities that a tolerationist can count as *derived*. So, there is a very great difference between my appeal to ontological parsimony and that which appears in the Razor Argument. This difference will become clearer when I discuss proper applications of the Razor.

There is a short response to the Razor Argument that is passably effective. Everyone agrees that entities should not be multiplied beyond necessity. The disagreements come when we try to say what counts as necessity. In my introduction, I mentioned certain advantages of the doctrine of absolute truth. It is at least arguable that if we must multiply entities in order to preserve that doctrine and its attendant advantages, then we ought, after all, to do so. Ontological economy is a desideratum, but not the only one. Thus, the Razor Argument is, at best, only a piece of some more inclusive argument against the strategy of ontological toleration.

But I think the Razor Argument is even worse off than the short response suggests, for I do not think it represents a proper application of Ockham's Razor, let alone a decisive one. To begin with, we ought to be suspicious of the Razor Argument reasoning. Consider an analogous case. Suppose the behavior of hydrogen atoms is totally explicable in terms of the behavior of their component electrons and protons. Suppose, as a consequence, that all our statements about hydrogen atoms can be translated into statements about protons and electrons. Would this show, by application of Ockham's Razor, that we are not entitled to accept the existence of hydrogen atoms (given our acceptance of protons and electrons)? The same reason is available as in the Razor Argument. We can make all the distinctions we need while speaking of only electrons and protons (in the strict sense of "quantifying" only over them and not over whole hydrogen atoms).

The suggested conclusion is, on the face of it, absurd. Reduction of hydrogen atoms to protons and electrons would seem, far from depriving us of our right to affirm their existence, only to give us greater knowledge of what sort of real things they are. Moreover, if we were forced, using the Razor, to withdraw our belief in this case, we would be forced, by parity of reasoning, to still more outrageous disclaimers. We would be forced to withdraw our belief in the existence of tables and chairs, since they can be reduced to pieces of wood and metal and their uses. Belief in composite things in general would be forbidden. I know that there are philosophers who do not shrink from such conclusions, philosophers who hold that only simple things exist. But surely this thesis is counterintuitive and represents a serious burden for the proponent of the Razor Argument.

Suppose the proponent is willing to shoulder the burden of rejection of absolute truth and rejection of composite things. Is there any way to make further progress against her view? There is, if we are willing to examine the Razor itself. Let us ask: Why shouldn't we multiply entities beyond necessity? There are perfectly good, informative answers to this question, answers that may provide some guide to our use of the Razor.

Trivially, ontological economy protects us from one kind of error, the error of supposing something to exist when it does not. Less trivially, it protects us from a certain kind of practical mistake, that of taking a fictitious problem or possibility as genuine. For example, suppose that there are no immaterial minds. Philosophers who do not realize this are saddled with fruitless inquiries into the nature of mind-body interaction. And suppose there is no such thing as extrasensory perception. Then a nation is wasting its resources if it investigates the feasibility of employing ESP in espionage. For another example, recall the two problems that can arise for the field theory of electromagnetism, namely, the problem of selecting from the wise variety of boundary conditions made possible by irreducible particle-field interactions, and the problem of the diverging self-energy that results from a particle's interaction with its own field.

Notice that the uses of the Razor we have been considering do not protect us from this kind of practical mistake, the reason being that in these cases the set of *possibilities* envisaged by the proponent of ontological toleration is not wider than that postulated by the ontological economist. For example, to accept the existence of hydrogen atoms in addition to the existence of protons and electrons is not necessarily to commit oneself to new possibilities. If one believes that hydrogen atoms are reducible composites, then one believes their possible states are exactly circumscribed by the possible states and arrangements of their components. No new possibilities are generated. Similarly, acceptance of both particle kinds and particle properties need not carry with it a commitment to possibilities not recognized by a partisan of just one of the two. If one recognizes the interdefinability of kinds and properties—our Goodmanian translation scheme—then one does not generate new possibilities by following the strategy of ontological toleration.

Thus, one important use of the Razor, namely, the elimination of fictitious possibilities, is not involved in the Razor Argument against ontological toleration. Is there perhaps another legitimate use of that Razor that is involved?

A second legitimate use of the Razor is its employment against *ontological idlers*. Ontological idlers are noncomposite entities, reference to which is of no use in the description of possibilities. In Putnam's particle-field case, I argued that in a situation in which the field and distant-action theories are both adequate to the phenomena, the field points and field values would be ontological idlers. However, no such argument can be constructed in the present case. Neither particle kinds nor particle properties are ontological idlers, since each set of entities plays an essential role in its own adequate system of description.

Finally, it also seems that the Razor might legitimately be used to place some nonarbitrary bound on the *ontological categories* we accept. For example, nominalists want to argue that only individuals exist. Their plan is to show that we can have adequate theories of the world without committing ourselves to the existence of nonindividuals. Then, appealing to Ockham's Razor, they want to conclude that we ought to accept only these theories and not some "equivalents" that imply the existence both of individuals and of some other things. According to them, Ockham's Razor tells us that it is better to get along with just the category of individuals, if that is feasible. Now, I am skeptical about the prospects for their success, but it seems to me that their project is, on the face of it, a reasonable one and one that might, indeed, be reasonably based on the Razor.

Once again, however, this is not the use of the Razor involved in the Razor Argument. Particle kinds and particle properties belong to the same logical type, namely, the type of attributes of individuals, and so, as we nowadays classify things, the same ontological category. Elimination of ontological categories is not at issue in the Razor Argument. (And even if it were, there is no reason to think that we would be faced with a pluralist dilemma.)

In summary, we have found three things that can be said in defense of the strategy of ontological toleration. First, it protects the doctrine of absolute truth and the attendant advantages of that doctrine. Second, it coheres neatly with the strong commonsense conviction that there are composite things. Third, although it seems at first glance to be antithetical to Ockham's Razor, deeper analysis seems to show that legitimate uses of the Razor do not rule it out. The last point is bound to be the most controversial. If I am right about the Razor, then ontological economists can take no comfort in the number of actual things. The strategy of ontological toleration countenances a very large number of alternative ontological bases and of composite entities founded on those bases. A pleasingly small number of things might be found only within individual ontological bases. (For example, consider a case in which one says, "There are just twelve kinds of particles.") But this situation seems to me entirely appropriate. Simplicity is to be found in the space of genuine possibilities and in particularly economical descriptions of that space. Of what consequence is it that the total number of *things* should be large?

10. THE ONION ARGUMENT

In Goodman's view, to accept the strategy of ontological toleration is to embark on a slippery slope. Faced with incompatible theories of particle kinds and particle properties, we choose to weaken them and believe that both weakened versions are true. But might not we later be confronted with a new alternative that is incompatible with the theories we have accepted? Perhaps we would choose, in accordance with our strategy, to weaken the new theory and accept it as well. But is there no harm in the open-ended continuation of this process? Goodman maintains that there is. Each step of the process removes some of the "arbitrariness" or "conventionality" of one's starting theories. But this process gets us no closer to a notion of how the world is independently of all the accidents of theoretical description. Instead, the ultimate result of the strategy of ontological toleration is a system of belief that says *nothing* about how the world is. When all the layers of convention are peeled off, there is nothing left. "The onion of reality is peeled down to its empty core."[11]

Interpreted in one plausible way, Goodman's claims have no force against proponents of ontological toleration. The weakened theories they accept are certainly not devoid of logical content, and obviously logical content is not lost in the process of believing many of them—a conjunction of theories has at least as much logical content as its conjuncts. So, if Goodman is saying that the ultimate result of the expansion of belief fueled by ontological toleration is some empty tautology, he is completely wrong.

But Goodman is not saying, at least not directly, that logical content is lost in the expansion process. Rather, what is lost is our sense of the structure, order, and arrangement of things. Each individual theory provides us with an account of the structure exemplified by the things in its domain. But the structure is necessarily described only *relative* to some choice of elementary objects and primitive relations.

In accepting new, equivalent theories, we make a futile attempt to escape from the arbitrariness of those choices. Ultimately, the original choices drown in the sea of other possible choices, and all notion of structure drowns with them!

It is easy to illustrate the doctrine of the relativity of structure to theory. Consider the natural numbers. We think of them as forming a sequence, bounded at one end by zero, but proceeding infinitely away from zero. And, of course, they do form such a sequence, *relative* to the relation of succession. But they also form a sequence that is unbounded at both ends, *relative* to the relation:

Rab iff a $= 1$ and b $= 0$
      or a is even and b is the successor of the successor of a,
      or b is odd and a is the successor of the successor of b.

The ordering generated by this relation is: . . . 5, 3, 1, 0, 2, 4, 6 . . . . In general, the natural numbers are ordered, relative to some relation or other, in every which way so many ($\aleph_0$) objects can be ordered. This relativity is inherited by theories. A theory in which the successor relation is primitive is one according to which the ordering of the domain is unbounded in one direction. One in which the R relation above is primitive is one that attributes an ordering that is unbounded in both directions.[12]

For another illustration of the relativity of structure, one in the spirit of Goodman's work, consider the notion of *change*. What counts as a change, it appears, depends on one's chosen scheme of classification. The sentence "All examined emeralds will be green" is an assertion of constancy, but it is logically equivalent to the sentence "All emeralds examined before 2000 AD will be grue, but thereafter examined emeralds will be bleen," which is an assertion of change. Indeed, since the sentences are logically equivalent, the example shows nicely that Goodman is concerned with something different from logical content.

Let us now recapitulate Goodman's argument: We can attribute structure to the world, or to part of the world, only relative to some selected scheme of description. The slippery-slope process of coming to accept weakened versions of many incompatible "equivalent" theories is an indiscriminate melding of descriptive schemes. The inadvisability of such melding can be seen from its ideal limit, namely, a grand theory that combines all possible schemes of description. Because it combines all possible schemes, it attributes to its domain *all conceivable structures*. But to attribute all conceivable structures to a domain is no better than to attribute no structure to the domain and, so, no better than having no theory at all.

This is a tricky argument, so we need to understand precisely what it is intended to show. Goodman contends that it is desirable to have a sense of "how the world is" and that this sense gets lost in the tolerant acceptance of a panoply of "equivalent" theories. But this is very puzzling, for Goodman himself, being a relativist about structure, denies that there is absolutely a way the world is. If so, what *good* is it to have a sense of "how the world is," a sense that, according to Goodman's view, would be entirely illusory? Certainly none of the equivalent theories performs better or worse than the others in the anticipation of experience—that follows from their equivalence. What is to be gained by the pluralist leap of deciding, quite arbitrarily, to accept one theory as our version of "how the world is"?

Of course, not all the equivalent theories are equally good from an instrumental point of view. Some might be less useful than others because they are intrinsically more complex, postulating change, for example, where one might have found constancy. Other theories evade the Charybdis of complexity only to run aground on the Scylla of unintuitive primitives. Something of this sort happens if, in a futile attempt to preserve a Euclidean view of physical space, one chooses to sever the connection between geometric lines and their physical counterparts, such as light rays and taut strings. The resulting theory forces costly and useless detours in our reasoning. In general, we prefer, quite justifiably, simple theories with intuitive primitives. Thus, it is certainly true that not all the "equivalent" theories are equally useful.

This point, however, does not impugn the strategy of toleration, for that strategy only recommends acceptance of theories as equally *true*, not as equally useful. So we can easily construct a coherent position that is antithetical to Goodman's: Our sense of how the world is, is garnered from our search for simple theories with intuitive primitives. But to take only such theories as telling us how the world is, is not to make a pluralist decision that these theories are true and other "equivalent" theories are false. For example, it is wholly consistent both to accept a theory that represents emeralds as remaining unchanged in their optical properties and to accept as true that examined emeralds will be grue before 2000 and bleen thereafter. If there is any form of pluralism lurking here, it is not one that provides support for a relativist conception of truth.

The reason Goodman's argument misses the mark is that theories, with a few philosophical exceptions, tend, through their peculiar postulates and primitives, to *show* the structures of their domains rather than to *say* what those structures are. Faithfulness of showing, if there be such a thing, however, does not engage the concept of truth. Hence, relativism about truth receives no support from relativism about structure.

For those few theories that do attempt explicitly to say what the real structure of their domains is, to distinguish, for example, real change and real constancy, our judgment of their status depends on the status of the notion of absolute structure. If all structure is merely relative, as Goodman apparently assumes, then all these theories are either false or confused. If, on the contrary, it can be maintained that there is absolute structure, then these theories are true or false depending on whether they get it right.

It is my opinion that there is absolute structure. It may be absolutely true, for example, that we inhabit a four-dimensional universe. Certainly, it seems absolutely false to say that we inhabit a one-dimensional universe, even though that is one structure the universe has in a merely relative sense. It is our search for simple theories with intuitive primitives that yields, I conjecture, some knowledge of absolute structure. The main obstacle to adopting an absolutist perspective is the relativity of intuitiveness — one and the same primitive may differ in intuitiveness for different beings. But perhaps such differences are swamped in the drive for empirically adequate and intrinsically simple theories.[13]

One need not share this vision, however, to have a satisfactory response to Goodman. The doctrine of the relativity of structure, whatever we may think of it, cannot be brought to bear against absolute truth. So Goodman's argument fails, whether or not structure is relative.

11. CONCLUSION

The pluralist idea that we may sometimes justifiably accept one of a pair of equally good incompatible theories has been found wanting. The hypothetical examples of pluralist choice presented by Goodman and Putnam are flawed in various respects. Better examples, such as the example of particle kinds and particle properties, can be constructed, but even they do not force us to pluralist conclusions, for we may adopt the strategy of ontological toleration. The only arguments we have found against that strategy, the argument from ontological economy and the argument from the relativity of structure, are unpersuasive.

Pluralism, however, is the only prop of relativism. In pluralist choice, we are supposed to witness the creation of truth — relative truth, of course, the one and only kind of truth. But we witness no such thing, and the one prop of relativism has been removed. There is nothing left to recommend it.[14]

Notes

1. The main sources are Goodman, *Ways of Worldmaking* (Indianapolis, 1978), and Putnam, *Reason, Truth, and History* (Cambridge, Mass., 1981). Also relevant are Goodman, *The Structure of Appearance* (Dordrecht, 1977), and Putnam, "Realism and Reason," in *Meaning and the Moral Sciences* (London, 1978). I shall refer to these works, respectively, as *WOW*, *RTH*, *SOA*, and *R&R*.

2. For example, David Lewis, "Putnam's Paradox," *Australasian Journal of Philosophy* 61 (1984): 221–36. Also, Alan Musgrave, "What's Wrong With the Model-Theoretic Argument Against Realism?" unpublished.

3. An exception is Mark Wilson, "The Double Standard in Ontology," *Philosophical Studies* 39 (1981): 409–27. Wilson's general line of criticism differs from my own, but some of the points I shall make are similar to his.

4. This account is adapted from Marshall Swain, *Reasons and Knowledge* (Ithaca, 1981), chap. 4.

5. I have in mind here the kind of issue that arises for philosophers who attempt to say what numbers "really are." Natural numbers might be identified with classes of classes, or properties of properties, or classes of symbol-types (platonic numerals, one might say). Each alternative yields an appropriate structure. To argue that any one actually captures the true referents of numerical symbols, however, may be a hopeless undertaking.

6. Here, too, we do not get genuine conflict unless "extensionless geometrical individual" is taken to have the same meaning in both cases. I assume that the interpretation of this phrase, unlike that of "point," is not in contention. Of course, it could be in another context. The distinction between semantic and metaphysical compatibility appears context-sensitive.

7. Goodman, *SOA*, 9. Goodman goes on to define a more specific notion of intertranslatability, namely, "extensional isomorphism".

8. This is explained in P. C. W. Davies, *Physics of Time Asymmetry* (London, 1974), 138–43.

9. A field theorist might object that she need not postulate both fields *and* particles, that instead she can construe particles as glitches in the electromagnetic field. I do not think this would affect the point about parsimony, however, for there are exactly as many glitches and glitch-types as there are particles and their charges.

10. These points are mentioned in Davies, 143. Wilson also mentions the renormalization difficulty and considers it extremely serious.

11. Goodman, *WOW*, 117–18. The same argument is echoed against the "sophisticated realist" of Putnam, *R&R*, 131–32.

12. Bertrand Russell, in *Principles of Mathematics* (1902), sec. 231, is an earlier proponent of the relativity of structure: "All sets of terms have, apart from psychological considerations, all orders of which they are capable; that is, there are serial relations, whose fields are a given set of terms, which arrange those terms in any possible order."

13. How can there be absolute structure? Some distinction must be drawn between properties and relations that are "natural" and those that are not. The absolute structure of a domain is the structure it has relative to the set of natural relations only. One eloquent plea for making a distinction between natural properties and relations and others is David Lewis's "New Work for a Theory of Universals," *Australasian Journal of Philosophy* 61 (1983): 343–77. Another is Sydney Shoemaker's "Causality and Properties," in *Identity, Cause, and Mind* (Cambridge, 1984).

14. I am grateful to James Klagge, Alan Musgrave, Joe Pitt, and Eleonore Stump for their comments and suggestions.

Pragmatism, Phenomenalism, and Truth Talk

ROBERT BRANDOM

This essay offers a rational reconstruction of the career of a certain heroic approach to truth—the approach whose leading idea is that the special linguistic roles of truth ascriptions are to be explained in terms of features of the ascri*bings* of truth, rather than of what is ascri*bed*. The explanatory emphasis placed on the *act* of calling something true, as opposed to its descriptive content, qualifies theories displaying this sort of strategic commitment as 'pragmatic' theories of truth, by contrast to 'semantic' ones. The starting point is an articulation of a central insight of the classical pragmatist theories of truth espoused in different versions by James and Dewey. Developing this insight in response to various objections yields a sequence of positions ending in contemporary anaphoric semantics: prosentential theories of 'true' and pronominal theories of 'refers'. These theories articulate an antirealist position about truth and reference, of the sort here called 'phenomenalist'. Insofar as theories of this sort offer adequate accounts of the phenomena they address, they assert relatively narrow and clearly defined limits to the explanatory ambitions of theories couched in traditional semantic vocabularies.

I

The popular conception of the theory of truth of classical pragmatism is summed up in the slogan 'The truth is what works.' According to this view, the pragmatists were trying to give a theory of truth in the sense of offering necessary and sufficient conditions for possession of that property. Their innovation is then seen to consist in taking the possession of this property by a belief to consist in a relation not simply to what is believed, but also to what is desired. Working, or being satisfactory, in-

---

volves a further argument place beyond the standard representational or correspondence notion, for it is relative to preferences, purposes, interests, needs, or some such satisfiable states. A theory of truth, according to this line of thought, is generically a pragmatic one if it treats truth as the property of conducing to the satisfaction of some state associated with the believer, paradigmatically, desire. Specific versions of this genus of explanation will be distinguished by how they understand the state, its subject, and the sort of satisfactoriness. Thus, within the pragmatic genus, truth might be identified with properties as various as evolutionary adaptiveness for a species and optimality for felt-preference maximization by a time-slice of an individual agent.

This sort of understanding of truth as a property of utility for some end, a matter of how useful, in some sense, it is to hold the belief that is a candidate for truth, may be called 'stereotypical pragmatism'. It is important to notice what sort of a theory it is. Pointing out the apparent appropriateness of questions such as 'I believe that the theory works (for instance, makes correct predictions), but how do I know it is true?' already shows that this sort of pragmatism is very implausible if it is conceived as elucidating our concept of truth.[1] As Dewey was well aware, views of this stripe can best be maintained as revisionary proposals—not as accounts of what we mean by 'true', but suggestions that we stop using that concept and get along instead with the pragmatist's notion of utility. Any assessment of the merits of such a proposal depends on an account of what the role of our present concept of truth is, what explanatory uses we currently put the property of truth to. For only in that context can it be argued that some utility notion better serves those ends or plays that role. It is from their contribution to that antecedent question, of what work is done by our truth concept, that the significance of the classical pragmatists in the present story derives. Although their account of the role of truth talk cannot, as we shall see, in the end be counted as correct, it nevertheless provides the central idea around which an adequate account can be constructed. The answer that eventually emerges regarding the role of 'true' will make it difficult to see how stereotypical pragmatism, even as revisionary proposal, can be anything other than changing the subject, sharing only a homonym with ordinary truth talk.

There is no question that the classical American pragmatists at times commit themselves to what I have called 'stereotypical pragmatism about truth'. But there is a deeper and more interesting explanatory strategy that the pragmatists pursued as well. According to this way of setting out their account, concern for what 'works' or is satisfactory is only the final move in an innovative rethinking of the nature of truth and belief. We can and should be interested in the early moves, even if the final one does not seem satisfactory. The essential point of a theory such as James's is to treat calling something true as doing something more like praising it than like describing it.[2] Five separable theses can be distinguished in the elaboration of this approach. First is the performative, antidescriptive strategy, emphasizing the *act* of calling something true rather than the descriptive content one thereby associates with what is called true. Next is an account of that act as the personal taking up of a certain sort of normative stance or attitude. Taking some claim to be true is endorsing it or committing oneself to it. Third is a particular understanding of that stance or attitude. Endorsing a claim is understood as adopting it as a guide to action, where this, in turn, is understood in terms of the role the endorsed claim plays in practical inference, both in first-person deliberation and in third-person appraisal. Fourth, and least important, is the view that an advantage of understanding the appropriateness or correctness of adopting an attitude of endorsement in terms of its role in guiding action consists in the possibility for some sort of not merely subjective measure of that appropriateness, namely, the success of the actions it leads to. This is the only strand of the argument acknowledged or embraced by stereotypical pragmatism.

Finally, and I want to argue, most significantly, the theory claims that once one has understood acts of *taking-true* according to this four-part model, one has understood all there is to understand about truth. Truth is treated, not as a property independent of our attitudes, to which they must eventually answer, but rather as a creature of taking-true and treating-as-true. The central theoretical focus is on what one is doing when one takes something to be true, that is, our *use* of 'true', the acts and practices of taking things to be true that collectively constitute the use we make of this expression. It is then denied that there is more to the phenomenon of truth than the proprieties of such takings. I call theories of this general sort 'phenomenalist', in recognition of the analogy with the paradigmatic subjective phenomenalism concerning physical objects, whose slogan was "esse est percipi." We consider these five theory-features seriatim.

The pragmatists start with the idea that in calling something true one is *doing* something, rather than, or in addition to, *saying* something. Instead of asking what property it is that we are describing a belief or claim as having when we say that it is true, they ask about the practical significance of the act we are performing in attributing that property. We accomplish many things by talking, and not all of them are happily assimilated to describing how things are. One ought not to conclude that because truth ascriptions are expressed in the same subject-predicate grammar as descriptions, they must for that reason be understood to function as descriptions. The pragmatic approach, centering on the act of calling something true rather than the content one thereby characterizes it as displaying, has much to recommend it. It has been seized upon by a number of authors who would not go on to accept the account of the act in question that the pragmatists offer. For, stripped of those further commitments, the recommendation is for a *performative* analysis of truth talk. In Fregean terms it is the suggestion that 'true' is a force-indicating, rather than a sense-expressing, locution.

Wittgenstein notoriously warned against thoughtless assimilation of sentence-use to fact-stating, and of term-use to referring. In the wake of Austin's discussions, theorists such as Strawson offered accounts of 'true' as a performative.[3] Its use was to be assimilated to other sorts of commitment-undertaking, in a way parallel to that expressed by the explicit performative 'I promise . . . '. In the same spirit, other contemporary accounts were offered of 'good' as expressing a kind of commendation, as taking up an attitude or expressing one's own relation to something, rather than as describing it by attributing some objective property. This is the sort of assimilation James had been urging in saying that truth is 'what is good in the way of belief'. Such remarks are often misinterpreted as claiming descriptive equivalence, or coextensiveness of the predicates 'true' and 'what it is good for us to believe'. On such a reading, the allegedly uncontroversial claim 'It is good for us to believe the truth', that is, the truth is among the things it is good for us to believe, is turned on its head. Necessary conditions are treated as sufficient, and truth is defined as what-*ever* it is good for us to believe. James's intent was, rather, to mark off 'true', like 'good', as a term whose use involves the taking up of a nondescriptive stance, the undertaking of a commitment that has eventual significance for action.

What motivates such a performative analysis, for the pragmatists no less than for later theorists, is the special relation that obtains between the force or practical significance of an act of taking-true (which we might, before the performative possibility has been broached, uncritically have called an act of 'describing as' true) and the force or significance of a straightforward assertion. In asserting 'It is true that p', one asserts that p, and vice versa. The force or significance of the two claims is the same. On the face of it, this redundancy or transparency of force, the fact that adding the operator 'It is true that . . . .' to what one is going to assert does not change the force or significance of that assertion, might be explained in either of two ways. One might take it that the content expressed in a truth ascription is special, and that the redundancy of force of truth claims arises out of features of the property a claim or belief is said to exhibit when it is described as true. One must then offer an account of why attributing that property has the consequences that it does for the force of one's attribution. Compare treating claims using 'good' or 'ought' as describing properties of actions, and then needing a theory to explain the special motivational role that attributions of these properties must be taken to have for the attributor. The pragmatic theories being considered adopt the more direct path of taking the transmitted force of truth claims as the central phenomenon, one that is merely obscured by the misleading grammar of property ascription. Dewey's assertibilist theory of truth develops these ideas along explicitly performative lines using the model of utterances of 'I claim (or assert) that p'.[4] The claim that the force of freestanding utterances of this type and of 'It is true that p', are equivalent is especially liable to misinterpretation as the claim that the contents expressed by these utterances are the same. As will be seen, it is easy to show that that is not so. In any case, as a revisionist, Dewey did not even claim equivalence of force, though that was the dimension along which he assessed the relationship between his views and the tradition. Accordingly, he has often been 'refuted' on the basis of misunderstandings of theories that he did not subscribe to in the first place.

To this performative, antidescriptive explanatory commitment, the pragmatists add a particular sort of account of the act of taking-true as adopting a normative stance toward the claim or belief. In treating something as true, one is praising it in a special way — endorsing it or committing oneself to it. The stance is normative in involving what the claim to which one has taken up a truth-attitude is *good* for, or *appropriately* used for. For treating something as the truth is plighting one's troth to it, not just acknowledging that it has some property. Truth undertakings are taken to be personal in that the proprieties of conduct one thereby commits oneself to depend on one's other commitments—commitments to choose (representing preference, desire, interest, need, and so on) as well as commitments to say (assert and believe). One is expressing or establishing one's own relation to a claim, in taking it to be true, rather than recognizing some independent property that claim already had. Again, the model of promising is important. This important emphasis on the normative character of cognitive undertakings was a central Kantian legacy (rejuvenated for us by Wittgenstein). Its expression is often obscured (Peirce is, as so often, an exception) by the pragmatists' further commitment to the sort of naturalism about the norms involved that gives rise to the attribution to them of stereotypical pragmatism.

Their understanding is that the commitment undertaken in taking-true is to rely on the belief or claim in question in guiding practical activity. This in turn is understood as a commitment to using the claim as a premise in practical inferences. These are inferences whose conclusions are not further claims, but actions, that is, performances under a description that is privileged by its relation to deliberation and appraisal. Relative to the truth-taking commitment, one ought to reason practically in one way rather than another. The proprieties of practical inference concerning whether to bring an umbrella are different for one who takes-true the claim that it is raining than for one who does not. The force of such proprieties is normative, in that although they may be ignored, the significance or force of the agent's commitment is to the effect that they *ought* not to be. It is these prudential 'oughts' that appraisal of actions assesses. The stance or attitude that one adopts in treating something as true is to be understood by its role in orienting action when activated by a contextualized attempt to satisfy the desires, preferences, and so on, that the agent exhibits.

II

Pragmatism in the stereotypical sense becomes relevant when one conjoins the ideas of a performative analysis of taking-true, of the relevant performance as undertaking a personal commitment, and of the commitment as specifying the appropriate role of a claim in action-orienting deliberation, with the further idea that the measure of the correctness of the stance undertaken by a truth-attributor is the success of the actions it guides. The explanatory role played by this most notorious of the pragmatists' tenets ought to be understood in the light of the larger strategy for relating the concepts of truth and belief that it subserves. From a methodological point of view, perhaps the most interesting feature of the pragmatic approach is its commitment to phenomenalism about truth. Only in the context of a phenomenalist explanatory strategy can commitments of the first three sorts be seen as illuminating the notion of truth. For what they really supply is a theory of **taking**-true. It is in the over-arching commitment to the effect that once one understands what it is to take or treat something as true, one will have understood as well the concept of truth that the phenomenalism of this strategy consists. The force-redundancy approach to truth emphasizes the practical equivalence of taking something to be true and believing it, so another way of putting it is this: Instead of starting with a metaphysical account of truth, such as that of the correspondence theorists by opposition to which the pragmatists defined themselves, and employing that in one's account of beliefs, which are then conceived as representations that could be true, that is, have the property previously defined, the pragmatists go the other way around. They offer an account of believing or taking-true, characterized by the three sorts of commitments already canvassed, that does not appeal to any notion of truth. Being true is then to be understood as being *properly* taken-true (believed).

What I find of most interest about the classical pragmatist stories is not stereo-typical pragmatism, but the dual commitment to a normative account of claiming or believing that does not lean on a supposedly explanatory antecedent notion of truth, and the suggestion that truth can then be understood phenomenalistically, in terms of features of these independently characterized takings-true. The sort of explanatory strategies here called 'phenomenalist' in a broad sense treat the subject matter about which one adopts a phenomenalistic view as **supervening** on something else. Their paradigm is classical sensationalist phenomenalism about physical objects. The slogan of this narrower class of paradigmatically phenomenalist views is that to be is to be perceived. The characteristic shift of explanatory attention enforced by these approaches is from what is represent*ed* to represent*ings* of it. The represen-teds are explained in terms of the representings, instead of the other way around. Talk ostensibly about objects and their objective properties is understood as a code for talk about representings that are interrelated in complicated but regular ways. What the naive conservatism implicit in unreflective practice understands as objects and properties independent of our perceptual takings of them now becomes radically and explicitly construed as structures of or constructions out of those takings. Attributed existence, independence, and exhibition of properties are all to be seen as features of attributings of them.

The general structure exhibited by this sort of account is that the facts about **having** physical properties are taken to supervene on the facts about **seeming** to have such properties. Or, in the vocabulary to be preferred here, the facts about what things **are** Ks, for a specified sortal K, supervene on the facts about what things are **taken** to be Ks. According to such an explanatory strategy, one must offer first an independent account of the takings—one that does not appeal in any way to what it is to be a K in order to explain what it is to take something to be one. Thus, classical phenomenalism concerning physical properties such as *red* found itself obliged to account for states of the attributing subject in which things *look-red* or *seem-red* without invoking the redness that is attributed in such takings. Once that obligation is satisfied, it can further be claimed that there are no facts about what things are red, or what it is for things to be red, over and above all the (possible) facts about what things look or seem red.

Classical subjective phenomenalism regarding physical objects and properties notoriously failed in both component explanatory tasks. Cartesian mental acts seemed ideal candidates for the takings in question. This ontological category had been given an epistemic definition in terms of the privileged access (in the sense of transparency and incorrigibility) subjects have to the class of takings that includes perceptual seemings. That something could not seem red to a subject who did not by virtue of that very taking know that it seemed red, and that something could not merely seem to seem red without really seeming red, made this class of takings appear well suited to provide the independently characterized base of a supervenience relation. Their special epistemic status seemed to guarantee for these subjective takings or attributings the possibility of a characterization independent of what they take or attribute. For one knows all about these states just by having or being in them, apart from any relation to anything but the knowing subject and the known mental state. But this is a mistake. As various authors have shown (the locus classicus is Sellars's "Empiricism and the Philosophy of Mind"),[5] 'looks'-talk does not form an autonomous stratum of language, a game one could play though one played no other. When one understands properly how the 'seems' operator functions, one sees that the incorrigibility of such claims essentially arises from their withholding of the endorsements involved in unqualified claims about how things actually are. The very incorrigibility that recommended them as a basis in terms of which everything epistemically less certain could be understood turns out to be an expression of the parasitic relation that these withholdings of endorsement have to the risky practices of endorsement from which they derive their meaning, and by contrast to which they exhibit their special status. Whatever their role may be in the order of justification, in the order of understanding *seems-red* presupposes *is-red*.

For these reasons the classical phenomenalist basis of takings as subjectively certified seemings could not be secured with the autonomy from the properties taken to be exhibited, which is requisite for the subsequent framing of phenomenalist supervenience explanations. Those explanations had troubles apart from those regarding their basis, however. Generic phenomenalism has been characterized here in terms of supervenience. The sense intended is that one vocabulary supervenes on another just in case there could not be two situations in which true claims (that is, facts) formulable in the supervening vocabulary differed, and the true claims formulable in the vocabulary supervened on do not differ. More neutrally put, once it is settled what one is committed to as expressed in the one vocabulary, then it is settled what one is committed to as expressed in the other. Classical subjective phenomenalism about physical objects and properties typically made stronger, reductionist claims that involve further commitments beyond supervenience. These regarded the equivalence of sentences, or in the most committive cases, individual terms and predicates, in physical-object talk to sentences or terms and predicates constructible in the language of takings-as-seemings. Again, the equivalence in question might vary from the extreme of definitional and translational equivalence to mere coexten-siveness. In none of these forms are phenomenalist claims of this reductionist variety plausible today (see, for instance, Quine's "Epistemology Naturalized").[6] Attempts to work out these reductive phenomenalist strategies have shown that the conditions under which there are reliable connections between how things seem perceptually and how they are can themselves be stated only in terms of how things are. The infer-ence from things seeming red to their being red depends on there being *in fact* no filters, strange lights, retina-altering drugs, and so on. That there not *seem* to be such is far from sufficient.

These explanatory failures of phenomenalism in the narrow sense ought not to be taken to impugn the prospects of phenomenalist strategies in the broad sense. For those difficulties arise from the way its general phenomenalist commitments are specialized: in applying to perceivable physical properties, in offering an account of the relevant sort of takings as incorrigible, subjective perceptual seemings, and in insisting on reduction rather than just supervenience as the relation between them. Phenomenalism, in general, is a structure that antirealist accounts of many different subject matters may exhibit. It elaborates one way of taking seriously what Dummett calls the issue of 'recognition transcendence'. To detail a specific version of this sort, one must specify three things: what it is that one is taking a phenomenalist approach to (for example, physical objects, mental activity, semantic properties, the past, and so on), how one conceives the takings or attributings on which talk of such things is taken to supervene, and how in particular the supervenience relation is conceived. Corresponding to each specific phenomenalist claim will be a class of claims that qualify as **realist** in the sense of denying the phenomenalist's "nothing but" account of the subject matter in question. For the classical pragmatist, the facts about what is true supervene on the facts about taking-true, that is, on the actual action-guiding roles of beliefs. In order to appreciate the significance of the pragmatists' phenome-nalist strategy, one must first consider the development of the basic idea that truth locutions are force-indicating, rather than content-specifying. We will reconstruct the subsequent trajectory of this idea, and then return to the issue of phenomenalism about truth.

Before we go on to see what is wrong with pragmatic phenomenalism about truth, it is worthwhile to indicate briefly what can make it attractive. Consider the account of knowledge that this sort of approach makes available. Phenomenalism about truth permits phenomenalism about knowledge as well. So the primary interest is not in knowledge itself, but in attributions of knowledge. The pragmatist must ask: What are we **doing** when we say that someone knows something? According to a phenomenalist reconstruction of the classic justified-true-belief account of knowl-edge, in taking someone to know something, one first of all *attributes a commitment*, that is, takes someone to believe. One further *attributes entitlement* to that commit-ment, that is, takes the committed subject to be justified. What is the function of the truth condition on knowledge, then? Conventionally, taking the claim that the sub-ject is committed to as true is understood as attributing some property to it, characterizing it or describing it. But as we have seen, the pragmatist's account of taking the claim to be true is *undertaking a commitment* to it. The truth condition does not qualify the entitled commitment that is attributed, but simply undertakes it on the part of the attributor. Knowledge claims have their central linguistic status because in them commitment to a claim is both attributed and undertaken. This phenomenalist distinction of social perspective, between the act of attributing and the act of undertaking a commitment, is what is *mis*taken for the attribution of a descriptive property (for which an otiose metaphysics can appear to be required). A pragmatic phenomenalist account of knowledge will accordingly investigate the social and normative significance of acts of attributing knowledge. The account of taking-true being considered is what makes possible such a way of thinking about knowledge claims.[7]

III

On the pragmatic line being considered, it is the practical significance or force of asserting that defines taking-true, and this sense of taking-true accounts for our use of 'true'. In spite of all there is to recommend such a hypothesis, this conjunctive thesis cannot be correct. A familiar point of Frege's shows the inadequacy of the basic pragmatic claim. Truth talk cannot be given a purely pragmatic rendering, because not all uses of ' . . . is true' have assertoric or judgmental force. The force-based approach can at most account for a subset of our uses of truth-locutions. Frege drew attention to the use of sentences as components of other sentences. Assertion of a sentence containing another sentence as a component is not, in general, assertion of the embedded sentence. That is, the embedded sentence does not occur with assertional force, does not express something the assertor of the containing sentence is thereby committed to. Thus, as the antecedent of a conditional, for instance, 'It is true that p' cannot have the significance of taking-true if that is understood as the expressing of assertional force. In this sense one does not take-true the claim that p in asserting 'if it is true that p, then it is true that q'.

The pragmatic approach, then, offers an account only of the freestanding uses of sentences formed with ' . . . is true', not the embedded ones. This is the same rock on which, as Geach[8] has shown, performative accounts of the use of 'good' have foundered. It is precisely because one cannot embed, say, questions and imperatives as antecedents of well-formed conditionals, in which they would occur without their characteristic force, that their significance as askings and commandings is associated with their force, and not to be understood as features of the descriptive content they express. If the essence of calling something good consisted in doing something rather than saying something, then it should not be possible to say things like 'if that is good, then one ought to do it'. That one can sensibly say things like this shows that 'good' has descriptive content that survives the stripping away by embedding of the force associated with freestanding describings. Thus, an embedding test can be treated as criterial for broadly descriptive occurrences of expressions. According to this test,

'It is true that p' has nonperformative uses that the pragmatists' approach does not account for. And it is not open to the pragmatist simply to distinguish two senses of truth claims, one freestanding and the other embedded, and proceed from ambiguity. For then one would be equivocating in inferring from the freestanding 'It is true that p' and the conditional 'If it is true that p then it is true that q', in which it occurs embedded, that it is true that q, by detachment. So the pragmatic theory must be rejected and the phenomena it points to otherwise explained.

This sort of objection surfaces in many forms. Those who incorrectly take Dewey to have offered an analysis of 'true', rather than a candidate replacement notion, must thereby treat his assertibilism as the assertion of an equivalence of content between the sentence 'It is true that p' and the explicit performative 'I (hereby) claim that p'. The most such a made-up thinker would be entitled to claim is that the *force* of the freestanding utterance of these sentences is the same. The stronger theory is refuted by noticing that 'It is true that p' and 'I claim that p' behave differently as embedded components. For instance, they are not intersubstitutable as the antecedents of conditionals, saving the inferential role of the resulting compound. Thus, an account such as is often attributed to Dewey is subject (as Putnam[9] has pointed out in different terms) to a version of Moore's naturalistic fallacy argument. Not everyone who is committed to the conditional 'If it is true that p, then it is true that p' is committed also to the conditional 'If I claim that p, then it is true that p'. If we like, we can put this point by saying that there is nothing self-contradictory about the claim 'It is possible that I claim that p and it is not true that p'. The naturalistic fallacy point is thus just another way of putting the objection from embedding.

IV

Pointing to the sentential embedded uses of ' . . . is true,' shows the inadequacy of the pragmatists' attempt to make do with a notion of taking-true as asserting. Analyzing and identifying uses of truth locutions by means of *redundancy of force*, that is, by a formal property of the pragmatic significance of acts of asserting freestanding truth claims, is not a sufficient explanatory strategy. It is not that freestanding force redundancy is not a central phenomenon of truth talk. But not all uses of truth locutions take this form. The pragmatic account cannot, for this reason, be the whole truth. Rather than simply discarding that approach, it is possible to amend it to retain the pragmatic account for the freestanding uses to which it properly applies. For there is a more general redundancy view that has the force-redundancy of freestanding truth-takings as a consequence. Embedded uses can be explained by a notion of *redundancy of content* according to which (apart from niceties having to do with type/token ambiguities) even in embedded contexts 'It is true that p' is equivalent to p. For even their embedded occurrences are equivalent as antecedents of conditionals, in the sense that anyone who is committed to 'If it is true that p then q' is thereby committed to 'If p then q', and vice versa. Furthermore, intersubstitutability of 'It is true that p' and p in *all* occurrences, embedded or not, is sufficient to yield force redundancy in freestanding uses as a consequence. If two asserted contents are the same, then the significance of asserting them in the same pragmatic context should be the same. According to such a content redundancy view, the pragmatists have simply mistaken a part for a whole.

Redundancy views such as Ramsey's accordingly provide a generalization of the pragmatist's point, one that permits an answer to the otherwise decisive refutation offered by the embedding objection. Accounts that generalize to the intersubstituta-bility of 'Snow is white' and 'It is true that snow is white' are clearly on the right track. They show what is needed to supplement the pragmatists' account, in order to deal with some embedded occurrences. But they do not yet account for all the contexts in which the taking-true locution ' . . . is true' occurs. Such simple redundancy ac-counts will not offer a correct reading of sentences like 'Goldbach's conjecture is true'. For this sentence is not interchangeable with 'Goldbach's conjecture'. For in-stance, the former, but not the latter, appears as the antecedent of well-formed and significant conditionals. So content redundancy, though relaxing the limitations con-straining the original pragmatic account, will not apply correctly in all the contexts in which truth locutions occur.

Such cases show that the content-redundancy view must, in turn, be revised to include the operation of some sort of disquotation or unnominalizing operator. In the cases to which the simple content-redundancy theory applies, the additional oper-ation will be transparent. But in the case of sentences such as 'Goldbach's conjecture is true', the claim with respect to which the truth-taking is content redundant must be determined by a two-stage process. First, a sentence nominalization is discerned. This may be a description, such as 'Goldbach's conjecture', a quote-name, such as 'Snow is white', a 'that'-clause sortal such as 'the claim that snow is white', or some other sort of nominalization. Next, a sentence is produced that is nominalized by the locution picked out in the first stage. This is a sentence expressing Goldbach's con-jecture, named by the quote name, one that says *that* snow is white, and so on. It is this sentence that is then treated by theory as intersubstitutable with the truth-attributing sentence, whether occurring embedded or freestanding.

A content redundancy account with disquotation or unnominalization is more satisfactory and deals with more cases than does a simple content-redundancy ac-count, just as content-redundancy accounts represent improvements of theories ac-knowledging only redundancy of force. But even disquotational views will not ac-count for all the uses of ' . . . is true' that might be important. They will not deal correctly, for instance, with occurrences such as 'Everything the policeman said is true', in which a *quantified* sentence nominalization is employed. For here what is nominalized is a whole *set* of sentences, and there need, in general, be no single sen-tence that is equivalent to all of them. A further refinement of content-redundancy accounts is required if they are to deal with this range of cases.

V

The most sophisticated version of the redundancy theory, one capable of handling quantificational truth idioms, is the remarkable anaphoric analysis undertaken by Grover, Camp, and Belnap in their essay "A Prosentential Theory of Truth."[10] For the original redundancy and disquotational theories, each use of ' . . . is true' is associated with some sentence on which it is redundant, or with which it shares its content. Whatever else this may mean, it at least includes a commitment that the intersubstitution of the sentence containing 'true' and its nonsemantic equivalent, in some privileged range of contexts, preserves assertional and inferential commitments. The difficulty in extending this intersubstitutional account to the quantificational case is that there the use of the sentence containing 'true' is determined not by a single sentence, but by a whole *set* of sentences, those expressing whatever the policeman has said. Of course, disquotation or unnominalization may produce sets of sentences as well, as more than one sentence may express Goldbach's conjecture. In such cases, the sentences must all share a content or be redundant on each other, that is, must be intersubstitutable with each other in the relevant contexts, whereas there is no requirement that any two sentences that express things the policeman has said be in any other way equivalent. So what is it that the sentence containing 'true' shares its content with, or is redundant upon, in the sense of intersubstitutability? What is distinctive of the anaphoric development of redundancy theories is its use of the model of *pronouns* to show how, in spite of this difficulty, the quantificational cases can be treated as *both* redundant in the same way nonquantificational cases are, *and* as deriving their content from a whole *set* of nonintersubstitutable sentences.

It has been noticed that pronouns serve two purposes.[11] In their *lazy* use, as in 'If Mary wants to arrive on time, she should leave now', they are replaceable by their antecedents, serving merely to avoid repetition. In the *quantificational* use of pronouns, as in 'Any positive integer is such that if it is even, adding it to one yields an odd number', such replacement clearly would change the sense. 'If any positive number is even, adding any positive number to one yields an odd number' is not a consequence one becomes committed to by undertaking the original claim. In such cases, the semantic role of the pronoun is determined by a *set* of admissible substituends, which is in turn fixed by the grammatical antecedent (here 'Any positive number'). In virtue of uttering the original sentence, one is committed to *each* of the results of replacing the pronoun 'it' in some occurrence by some admissible substituend, that is, some expression that refers to a positive number.

The prosentential theory of truth is what results if one decides to treat ' . . . is true' as a syncategorematic fragment of pro*sentences*, and then understands this new category by semantic analogy to other proforms, in particular to pronouns functioning as just described. So 'Snow is white is true' is read as a prosentence of laziness, having the same semantic content as its anaphoric antecedent, perhaps the token of 'Snow is white' that it contains. The prosentence differs from its antecedent in explicitly acknowledging its dependence upon an antecedent, as 'She stopped' differs from 'Mary stopped', when the pronoun has some token of the type 'Mary' as its antecedent. Otherwise, the lazy uses are purely redundant. The advance on earlier conceptions lies in the availability on this model of *quantificational* uses of prosentences containing 'true'. Thus 'Everything he said is true' is construed as containing a quantificational prosentence, which picks up from its anaphoric antecedent a set of admissible substituends (things he said). Expanding the claim in the usual way, to 'For anything one can say, if the policeman said it, then it is true', exhibits 'it is true' as the quantificationally dependent prosentence. Each quantificational instance of this quantificational claim can be understood in terms of the lazy functioning of prosentences, and the quantificational claim is related to those instances in the usual conjunctive way.

By analogy to pronouns, prosentences are defined by four conditions:[12]

(1) They occupy all grammatical positions that can be occupied by declarative sentences, whether freestanding or embedded.

(2) They are generic, in that *any* declarative sentence can be the antecedent of some prosentence.[13]

(3) They can be used anaphorically either in the lazy way or in the quantificational way.

(4) In each use, a prosentence will have an anaphoric antecedent that determines a class of admissible sentential substituends for the prosentence (in the lazy case, a singleton). This class of substituends determines the significance of the prosentence associated with it.

There are many philosophical virtues to explicating each occurrence of 'true' as marking the occurrence of a prosentence in this sense. Quite varied uses, including embedded ones, of expressions involving 'true' in English are accounted for by means of a unified model. That model is in turn explicated by appeal to the familiar, and closely analogous, pronominal anaphoric reference relation. Not only is the semantics of such uses explained, but their pragmatic features as well – acknowledgment of an antecedent and the use of truth locutions to endorse or adopt someone else's claim. Tarski's biconditionals are appropriately underwritten, so the necessary condition of adequacy for theories of truth that he establishes is satisfied. A feature dear to the hearts of the prosententialists is the metaphysical parsimony of the theory. For what in the past were explained as attributions of a special and mysterious *property*, truth, to equally mysterious bearers of truth, namely, propositions, are exhibited instead as uses of grammatical proforms anaphorically referring only to the sentence tokenings that are their antecedents. A further virtue of the prosentential account is that anaphora is a relation between linguistic expression *tokenings*. Consequently, the use of tokenings of types such as 'That is true' as a response to a tokening of 'I am hungry' is construed correctly, just as 'he' can have 'I' as its antecedent without thereby referring to whoever uttered 'he'. An incautiously stated, content redundancy theory would get these indexical cases wrong. Finally, the uses of 'true' falling under the elegant, anaphorically unified treatment include quantificational ones such as 'Everything the oracle says is true,' which are recalcitrant to more primitive redundancy and disquotational approaches.

The pragmatists' insistence that in calling something true one is not describing or characterizing it is respected. For one does not describe a cat when one refers to it pronominally by means of an 'it'. This point is further broadened to accommodate embedded uses where the account of the describing alternative as endorsing does not, as we saw, apply. 'True' functions anaphorically and not descriptively even in such cases. And anaphoric inheritance of content explains equally why freestanding or force-bearing uses of 'It is true that p' have the pragmatic significance of endorsements of the claim that p. The prosentential account shows how the pragmatists' insights can be preserved, while accounting for the uses of 'true' that cause difficulties for their original formulation. It is thus a way of working out the content-redundancy rescue strategy.

VI

The treatment of quantificational prosentences represents an advance over previous redundancy theories. As the theory is originally presented, however, the treatment of lazy prosentences in some ways retreats from the ground gained by disquotational developments of redundancy theories. The explanatory costs associated with the original theory arise because it treats *most* occurrences of 'true' as quantificational. Thus, the official version of 'The first sentence Bismarck uttered in 1865 is true' construes it as a quantified conditional of the form 'For any sentence, if it is the first sentence Bismarck uttered in 1865, then it is true', in which 'it is true' is a prosentence of quantification. Now, one of the strengths of the prosentential account is its capacity to use the logical structure of quantification to explain the use of complicated sentences such as 'Something John said is either true or has been said by George'. There should be no quarrel with the author's treatment of these sentences that "wear their quantifiers on their sleeves." And it is clear that any sentence that has the surface form of a predication of truth of some sentence nominalization can be construed as a conditional propositional quantification. But it is not clear that it is a good idea to assimilate what look like straightforward predications of truth to this quantificational model. To do so is to reject the disquotational treatment of these lazy prosentences, which has no greater ontological commitments and stays closer to the apparent form of such sentences. Otherwise, almost all sentences involving 'true' must be seen as radically misleading in terms of their underlying logical form. The account of truth talk should bear the weight of such divergence of logical from grammatical form only if no similarly adequate account can be constructed that lacks this feature. It would be preferable to follow the treatment of sentence nominalizations suggested by disquotational generalizations of redundancy theories.

In fact, there is no barrier to doing so. The original motivations and advantages of the prosentential account carry over directly to a disquotational or unnominalizing variant. According to such an account, 'The first sentence Bismarck uttered in 1865' is a sentence nominalization, a term that picks out a sentence tokening. In this case it describes the sentence, but it could be a quote-name, demonstrative, that-clause sortal, or any sort of nominalization. Its function is just to pick out the antecedent on which the whole prosentence formed using 'true' is anaphorically dependent, and from which it accordingly inherits its content. Ontological commitment is only to sentence tokens and to anaphoric dependence, which prosententialists require in any case.

A brief rehearsal of the considerations leading the authors of the prosentential theory to do things otherwise will show that their reasons ought not to discourage us from adopting a disquotational variant of the prosentential account. They say:

> This account differs radically from the standard one since on (what we have called) the subject-predicate account 'that' in 'that is true' is always treated separately as referring by itself to some bearer of truth, whether it be a sentence, proposition, or statement. On our account cross-referencing — without separate reference of 'that' — happens between the *whole* expression 'that is true' and its antecedent.[14]

Another way to put this point is that, where the classical account takes a subpart of the sentence as a referring term, and ' . . . is true' as a predicate that forms a sentence from that term by characterizing its referent, according to the prosentential theory the only expression standing in a referential relation is the whole sentence, which refers anaphorically to an antecedent. There are accordingly *two* innovations put forth concerning reference in sentences like 'That is true'. The sentence is seen as an anaphoric proform, *and* 'that' is no longer seen as a referring term. We are told:

> Reference can involve either (or both) anaphoric reference or independent reference, and since people have not seriously considered the former, the possibility that **the** relation between 'that is true' and its antecedent may be that of anaphoric reference has not occurred to them. In ignoring anaphoric reference philosophers have assumed that **the** reference involved in 'that is true' is, through 'that', like that between a pronoun (say 'she' used independently) and its referent (say Mary). Once this picture dominates, the need for bearers of truth begins to be felt, and it is then but a small step to the claim that in using 'is true' we are characterizing those entities. [emphasis added][15]

But why should we think that we have to choose between treating the whole expression 'that is true' as a prosentence anaphorically referring to a sentence tokening from which it inherits its content and treating 'that' as a referring expression, in particular a sentence nominalization, that picks out the tokening on which the whole prosentence depends? Instead of seeing ' . . . is true' as a syncategorematic fragment of a semantically atomic generic prosentence 'that is true', we can see it as a *prosentence forming operator*. It applies to a term that is a sentence nominalization or that refers to or picks out a sentence tokening. It yields a prosentence that has that tokening as its anaphoric antecedent. To understand things this way is not to fall back into a subject-predicate picture, for there is all the difference in the world between a prosentence-forming operator and the predicates that form ordinary sentences. Nor does it commit us to bearers of truth, apart from the sentential antecedents without which no anaphoric account can do.

There is a further reason to prefer the account that treats ' . . . is true' as a prosentence-forming operator as recommended here, rather than as a fragment of the single prosentence recognized, 'that is true', functioning almost always quantificationally, as the original theory has it. For conceived in the former way, the treatment of 'true' has an exact parallel in the treatment of 'refers'. Elsewhere[16] I have argued in detail that 'refers' can be understood as a pronoun-forming operator. Its basic employment is in the construction of what may be called **anaphorically indirect** definite descriptions. These are expressions such as 'the one Kissinger referred to [or described] as "almost a third-rate intellect," understood as a pronoun whose anaphoric antecedent is some utterance by Kissinger. A full-fledged pronominal or anaphoric theory of 'refers' talk is generated by first showing how other uses of 'refers' and its cognates can be paraphrased so that 'refers' appears only inside indirect descriptions, and then explaining the use of these descriptions as pronouns formed by applying the 'refers' operator to some antecedent-specifying locution. Treating 'true' as an operator that applies to a sentence nominalization and produces a prosentence anaphorically dependent on the nominalized sentence token, and 'refers' as an operator that applies to an expression picking out a term tokening and produces a pronoun anaphorically dependent on it, permits a single theory form to explain the use of all legitimate semantic talk about truth *and* reference in purely anaphoric terms.

VII

To sum up: The pragmatists' approach to truth introduces a bold phenomenalist strategy — to take as immediate explanatory target the practical proprieties of *taking-true*, and to understand the concept of truth as consisting in this use that is made of a class of expressions, rather than starting with a truth property and then seeing what it is for us to express a concept that attributes that property. Their implementation of this strategy is flawed in its exclusive attention to taking-true as a variety of **force**, as a doing, specifically an asserting of something. For 'true' is used in other contexts, for instance, embedded in the antecedent of a conditional, and what it expresses is not exhausted by freestanding assertional uses. We have seen how content-redundancy theories can incorporate the insights of these force-redundancy accounts, and in their most sophisticated, anaphoric form account for the wider variety of uses of 'true'. Indeed, starting with an analogous pronominal account of 'refers' or 'denotes', it is possible to generate Tarski-wise the truth-equivalences that jointly express the content redundancy of ' . . . is true'. The pragmatists' strategy has been vindicated at least this far: It is possible to account for truth talk without invoking a property of truth that such talk must be understood as answering to.

Anaphoric semantics gives aid and comfort to semantic phenomenalists. Although the possibility of such an account does not enforce or entail phenomenalism about truth and reference, it enables such a view. It is tempting to conclude, in line with such a phenomenalism, that there are no semantic facts. Facts are simply true claims (and the prosententialist knows how to talk noncommittally about *these*). What look like semantic claims are assertions whose function, though complex, we can now see how to specify. When that is done, we see that these utterances ought not to be assimilated to property ascriptions, and so the temptation to look for a property of truth corresponding to 'true' talk, and a relation of reference corresponding to 'refers' talk, is seen to be misbegotten—one more disreputable metaphysical urge better outgrown than indulged. This is a view one can be entitled to only by possession of an adequate account of the use of the expressions involved. Although such an account is necessary for phenomenalism, it is not sufficient.

There are two related reasons for caution in adopting phenomenalism of an anaphoric sort about truth talk. To begin with, it is not quite true that all sorts of truth talk are recoverable by such theories. Specifically, talk in which the substantive 'truth' appears in a way not easily eliminable in favor of 'true' will receive no construal by such theories. Philosophers do say things like 'Truth is one, beliefs are many' and 'Truth is a property definable in the vocabulary of some eventual physics', which are illegitimate according to the account of 'true' offered here. The phenomenalist is not permitted to say things like this, denies that ordinary people do, and so counts it no defect of the account that it fails to generate readings for this sort of fundamentally confused remark. But this is hardly decisive. At most, the phenomenalist is entitled to claim that the burden of proof has shifted to the antiphenomenalist, to show that this kind of 'truth' talk has anything other than its sound in common with the expression that is given a use by everyday linguistic practice.

This brings us to the second reason for according a limited significance to the possibility of a phenomenalistically acceptable account of ordinary truth talk, namely, that the motivation for a realistic approach to truth may not be part of a project of reconstructing ordinary usage, but rather part of a theoretical explanatory effort. Truth is not, as it were, a property confronted in everyday discourse, but rather one that must be postulated by an explanation of certain features of that discourse that are not exhausted by talk *about* truth. For instance, a phenomenalist who offers a content-redundancy account of truth talk is obviously barred from an explication of the sort of content involved that appeals to a notion of *truth conditions*. The phenomenalist may be right in claiming that it is only by misunderstanding the role of 'true' that one could have been misled into thinking that explanatory ground could be gained by such an appeal, but this is not established simply by showing that one *can* understand truth talk in a way that condemns such talk as confused. One must show that the explanatory tasks that truth properties and reference relations have been invoked to help with are better served by other explanatory primitives.

The phenomenalist's claim is always of the "nothing-but" variety; the opposing realist insists that something more is needed. It seems good Popperian methodology to adopt the most easily falsifiable of these strategies. Methodological phenomenalism about truth would not be an ontological position, but a revisable commitment adopted for its salutary effects on the course of inquiry. On those adopting such a commitment, it imposes the task of explaining in phenomenalistically acceptable terms whatever linguistic phenomena a realistic theory claims require the invocation of taking-transcendent properties and relations. One might offer an inferential account of sentential contents,[17] and a substitutional account of what it is for such a content to purport to represent a state of affairs. Providing such a substantive account is the real work of the phenomenalist program – not criticizing realists, but providing detailed nothing-but theses for realists to respond to and discover the specific inadequacies of. Semantic phenomenalists must show how to do without truth and reference in theoretical explanation, as well as in casual discourse. This cannot be accomplished by studying the grammar of 'true'. It requires a full-blown account of linguistic practices.

Such a methodological stance leaves the realist an equally important task. Antiphenomenalists about truth, those who claim that there is more to truth than its appearance in truth talk, not only must show what is left out by a phenomenalist account, how truth transcends proprieties of taking-true, that is, show the crucial explanatory work done by the notion in some substantive theory; they must also show how that theoretical concept is related to the ordinary use of 'true' that is capturable in anaphoric terms. Only so can they vindicate their use of words that already have familiar uses, to express theoretical constructs that outrun everyday talk. For it would not suffice to settle this dispute about truth or reference to show that physical properties and relations need to be invoked to account for the use of linguistic expressions such as 'red' or 'This stone has a mass of one gram'. (In any case, surely no one could deny this much.) The challenge presented by a phenomenalistic account such as the anaphoric one whose antecedents have been traced here is to connect the theoretical concepts with our ordinary takings. Phenomenalist and antiphenomenalist each owe theories of discursive practice, which either show how to do without taking-transcendent notions of truth and reference, or show how essential these are. The anaphoric account of 'true' and 'refers' confers on the latter the additional responsibility of showing how that theory in some way elaborates on ordinary practices of taking-true. To that extent, and insofar as it is acceptable to apply here a legal concept born of a practical necessity philosophers ought not admit, namely, the necessity that all deliberations conclude with a verdict, the anaphoric account shifts the burden of proof to the antiphenomenalist camp. But what is important in the end is not what 'true' means, but how language works.

Notes

1. The point here does not concern merely the senses of the contrasted expressions, but the extensions they determine. The appropriateness of this question would have to be defended by adducing cases in which a belief apparently "worked" and was not true, or vice versa. Such cases are not far to seek. This sort of argument is considered more carefully in what follows.

2. *Pragmatism* (Cambridge, Mass., 1978), bound with its sequel, *The Meaning of Truth*, which as here interpreted ought to be titled "The Meaning of Taking-True." For an important assessment on a larger scale, see R. Rorty's "Pragmatism, Davidson, and Truth," in *Philosophy of Donald Davidson: A Perspective on Inquiries into Truth and Interpretation*, edited by E. LePore (Oxford, 1986), to which this essay is a tangential response.

3. For instance, in "Truth", reprinted in *Truth*, edited by G. Pitcher, (Englewood Cliffs, N.J., 1964), 32–53. Strawson's view is often also referred to as a 'redundancy account,' in the sense of an account focusing on redundancy of *force*.

4. *Logic: The Theory of Inquiry* (New York, 1938).

5. Reprinted in Sellars, *Science, Perception, and Reality* (London and New York, 1963).

6. In Quine, *Ontological Relativity and other essays* (New York, 1969).

7. For some further prerequisites, see my "Asserting", *Nous* 17, no. 4 (November 1983): 637–50.

8. "Ascriptivism" and "Assertion," reprinted in Geach's *Logic Matters* (Berkeley, 1972), 250–53 and 254–69.

9. "Reference and Understanding," in *Meaning and the Moral Sciences* (London, 1978), 108.

10. Grover, Camp, and Belnap, "A Prosentential Theory of Truth," *Philosophical Studies* 27 (1975): 73–125.

11. See P. Geach, *Reference and Generality* (Ithaca, N.Y., 1962), 124–43. For some complications, see B. Partee, "Opacity, Coreference, and Pronouns," in *Semantics of Natural Language* edited by Harman and Davidson (Dordrecht, 1972), 415–41.

12. "Prosentential Theory of Truth," 87.

13. The authors of the original theory may believe that for any syntactic prosentence type (paradigmatically 'That is true') and any declarative sentence tokening, there is potentially an anaphorically dependent prosentence tokening of that type that has the declarative tokening as its antecedent. On the disquotational account of lazy prosentences offered in emendation below, that formulation would not hold.

14. "Prosentential Theory of Truth," 91.

15. "Prosentential Theory of Truth," 109.

16. "Reference Explained Away," *Journal of Philosophy* (September 1984).

17. For a general discussion and a particular example, see the author's "Varieties of Understanding," in *Reason and Rationality in Natural Science*, edited by N. Rescher (Lanham, Md., 1985) 27–51.

On Always Being Wrong

Peter van Inwagen

I believe that truth is radically nonepistemic.[1] In my view, propositions that are not *about* the beliefs (or, more generally, the mental states) of rational beings are true or false quite independently of the beliefs (or mental states) of rational beings. Moreover, whatever precisely 'about' may mean, there are, *pace* Berkeley and Hegel, many propositions that are in *no* sense "about" the mental states of rational beings. One such is the proposition that Mount Everest is 8,847.7 meters high. This proposition, as I see matters, is true and would have been true if the metric system had never been devised, if theodolites had never been invented, if Mount Everest had been named Mount Lambton, if Mount Everest had never been named at all, if there had never been such a language as English, if sapient beings had never evolved on the earth, and if life had never existed anywhere in the universe.[2] (Actually, I am not quite sure about this last statement. For all I know, the existence of life in a universe like this one is so very nearly inevitable that the closest possible worlds in which there is no life whatever are worlds in which the large-scale structure of the universe is different—in which case, all bets about the height of Mount Everest are off. This sort of consideration obviously applies not only to the existence of life, but also to the existence of beliefs and other mental states: The truth-values of various propositions that are not *about* mental states may, nevertheless, be causally connected with the existence of mental states. For example, the proposition that there have been hydrogen fusion explosions near the surface of the earth is not about mental states, but it is true, and would have been false if there had never been any mental states. One who holds that truth is radically nonepistemic, therefore, must say something like this: Although mental states may be among the *efficient* causes of the truth-value of a proposition that is not about mental states, mental states are never among the *formal* causes of the truth-value of a proposition that is not about mental states. That is to say: The existence of mental states has nothing to do with *what it is* for a proposition to be true—or not unless that proposition is about mental states.)

If life had never evolved on earth, then, or so it seems reasonable to suppose, no one would ever have thought of the proposition that Mount Everest is 8,847.7 meters high.[3] Nevertheless, this proposition would have existed and would have been true. And who can doubt that there are in actuality many propositions that no one *has* ever thought of but which are true? It is, of course, impossible to give an example of one. But we can easily think of some near misses. If I had not just decided to think of a bizarre proposition—if I had sat down to write a half hour earlier or later, with a different set of associations in my mind—no one in the whole history and future of the universe would ever have thought of the proposition that fewer than one hundred and eight Paraguayans have flown to Mercury on broomsticks made of lignum vitae. But this proposition would have existed just the same, and it would have been true. The number of such propositions—propositions I might very well have thought of just now but didn't, and which no one else will ever think of, and which are true—is, I imagine, greater than the number of elementary particles. And, of course, there are vast infinites, perhaps there is a proper class, of propositions that no one will ever think of because they are too complicated. And many of these propositions will be true. (Roughly half of them, to borrow a joke of Plantinga's.) For example, for each well-ordering relation on the real numbers, there is the proposition that that relation exists. There are 2-to-the-*c* such propositions, all of them true, and no one will ever think of any given one of them. And there are other propositions that no one could ever think of that are much "nearer misses" than these. If the mean IQ of our species had been 60 rather than 100 (and if there had been no other sapient species), no one would ever have thought of the proposition that the existence of atomic nuclei depends on the fact that the bosons that transmit the color-force themselves bear color-charges. But this proposition would nevertheless have existed and it would have been true. (At any rate, it would have been true if it *is* true.) And I find it very hard to believe that there are no propositions that must remain unknown to us because of our intellectual incapacities, but which could be known to finite but more intelligent beings.[4] If the mean IQ of our species had been 180 rather than 100, then, doubtless, all manner of really interesting propositions would be known to us that will never in fact be thought of.

Truth, I maintain, is a property of propositions, items that stand to assertion as numbers stand to counting and that stand to declarative sentences as numbers stand to numerals. In saying that this property, truth, is radically nonepistemic, I am not embracing any particular theory about what the possession of this property by a proposition consists in. Most especially, I am not saying that the truth of a proposition consists in its sharing a "structure" with a part of the world, or consists in its "mirroring" or "picturing" reality. I am not saying this because I do not know what it means. (To be precise, I do not know what the words in scare-quotes mean.) And, of course, for the same reason, I do not *deny* that the truth of a proposition consists in its sharing a structure with a part of the world or in its mirroring or picturing reality. Some philosophers seem to believe that the thesis that truth is radically nonepistemic commits its holder to the thesis that the truth of a proposition consists in some sort of "Tractarian" relation between that proposition and some segment of the world. Well, perhaps this is right. Doubtless, many of the philosophical theses I hold commit me to propositions that I do not know about because I cannot understand the available descriptions of these propositions. What I am sure of is that I *do not* understand the Tractarian account of truth; and, therefore, I decline to regard myself as committed to it by my belief that truth is radically nonepistemic or by any other thesis I hold.

The sentence 'Truth is radically nonepistemic' is one way of expressing the thesis that is nowadays called realism or metaphysical realism or external realism. Or perhaps it expresses only a part of or a consequence of "realism." I don't know. I have no very reliable sense of the boundaries of what is at issue in the realism/antirealism debate. Perhaps there is more to "realism" than the thesis that truth is radically nonepistemic.[5] Perhaps some sort of Tractarian "copy" or "picture" theory of truth is an essential part of realism. Nevertheless, my conviction that truth is radically nonepistemic (understood as I have spelled it out in the preceding paragraphs) would not be accepted by any of those philosophers who describe themselves as antirealists. At least I *think* this is true. Consider the proposition that the existence of atomic nuclei depends on the fact that the bosons that transmit the color-force themselves bear color-charges. If there is an antirealist who believes that this proposition would have existed and would have been true even if there were no minds, I hope that antirealist will write to me and tell me so.

In this paper, I wish to examine and reject a certain argument that (if I understand him rightly) Hilary Putnam has employed to show that truth cannot be radically nonepistemic. This argument is not Putnam's only argument for that conclusion, nor, I believe, is it the argument that he places the most weight on. I do not claim, therefore, to have seriously undermined Putnam's defense of antirealism or to have decisively blocked his attack on realism.

Here are the bare bones of the argument:

(1) If truth is radically nonepistemic, then it is intelligible to suppose that we are all wrong about almost everything.

(2) It is not intelligible to suppose that we are all wrong about almost everything

hence, Truth is not radically nonepistemic.

We should "all be wrong about almost everything" if we were in the position Descartes imagines himself to be in in *Meditations*, i ("I shall, therefore, suppose . . . that some evil genius, no less powerful and crafty than he is deceitful, has employed all his energies in deceiving me; I shall suppose that the heavens, the earth . . . and all other external things are only illusions. . . . "), or if we were "brains in vats." I say "almost everything" because one might maintain that even if

I am a brain in a vat, I am right in thinking that I am not now in excruciating pain, and that I *believe* I am now writing a paper for *Midwest Studies in Philosophy*, and that $1 + 1 = 2$.[6] (And, for that matter, that there are brains and vats.) But I am wrong in thinking that I have limbs or that there is such a country as Austria or that Sirhan Sirhan shot Robert Kennedy: Almost all the statements I (think I) make or (think I) hear others making are false.

I concede that Putnam does not explicitly formulate this argument, or any similar argument. But if he does not mean to be defending this argument, or some argument very much like it, in the first chapter of *Reason, Truth and History*,[7] then I do not see the point of that chapter.

Most of that part of the first chapter of *Reason, Truth and History* that I take to constitute a presentation of the argument whose "bare bones" are laid out above is (read in that way) a defense of its second premise. I cannot find anything that is clearly supposed to be a defense of the first premise or of any similar proposition. And it is the first premise that will be my concern in this paper. I shall, in fact, argue that there is no reason to accept the first premise. But my argument for this conclusion will consist mainly in an attempt to show that there is no reason why someone who believes that truth is radically nonepistemic should not accept Putnam's argument for the second premise. I will begin, therefore, by examining Putnam's attempt to show that it is unintelligible to suppose that we are all wrong about almost everything.

My first reading of Putnam's argument for this conclusion was accompanied by a strong feeling of déjà vu. The argument is very nearly identical with arguments deployed by two prominent students of Wittgenstein against the intelligibility of two of the great philosophical tales of global deception. The tales are Descartes's "evil genius" story and Russell's celebrated "hypothesis" that the world came into existence five minutes ago, "with a population that 'remembered' a wholly unreal past."[8] The prominent students of Wittgenstein are O. K. Bouwsma ("Descartes' Evil Genius")[9] and Norman Malcolm ("Memory and the Past").[10] I used to be fascinated by these arguments and to believe that they were both deep and probably correct. I am now less sure about their correctness; but never, during my many years of thinking that they were probably correct, did it occur to me that these arguments ought to make me the least bit uneasy about my allegiance to a radically nonepistemic conception of truth; and I do not now think that I was missing anything.

Putnam's version of the argument goes like this. (What follows is a free paraphrase of Putnam's argument. He should not be held responsible for the details of my exposition—all the more so in that I have not hesitated to add my own "improvements" here and there—or for the absence of various subtle qualifications. The argument that follows is intended more as a reminder to the reader of the *sort* of argument that Putnam presents than as a responsible presentation of that argument.)

Let us consider the following tale of global deception: We are all brains in vats of nutrient fluid, continually supplied with artificially produced stimuli that mimic the stimuli we should be receiving from the external world if we were (or had) "normally embodied" brains. (These stimuli are supplied by a vast computer: a world-processor.) This tale obviously has no implications as regards the intrinsic qualities of our mental states. Therefore, we are tempted to say, there is no way to tell whether or not this tale is true, and it is perfectly conceivable that we are all wrong about almost everything—for, if the tale were true, we should all be wrong about almost everything.

This temptation should, however, be resisted. Here is why. The intrinsic qualities of a mental state cannot determine what extramental events that mental state represents, or what features that state represents them as having. For example, the intrinsic qualities of a mental state can no more, by themselves, make that state a memory (even a false memory) of once having met Winston Churchill than the intrinsic qualities of a pattern of lines on paper can, by themselves, make that pattern of lines a caricature of Winston Churchill. There is more than one philosophical account of what it is besides the intrinsic qualities of a mental state that is needed in order for a mental state to represent something extramental, but all these accounts agree in this: Whatever is needed for a mental state to represent extramental objects, it is something that could not be possessed by a mental state that belonged to a brain in a vat. As a consequence, when a brain in a vat "produces" a sentence like "There's a tree before me," either he [he?] says nothing at all—or he at any rate does not refer to trees or to any others of the things philosophers call "external objects." Either he speaks no language at all, or he speaks a language that is not ours—he was not brought up in the right linguistic community or even in the right kind of environment to speak *our* language—and, therefore, he certainly could not be referring to *trees*. He could not have been referring to trees for the same reason that a Cro-Magnon man could not, when engaged in some piece of paleolithic fireside chatter, have referred to neutrinos. The causal relations that held between paleolithic utterances or mental states and those elusive particles were too remote, too nearly nonexistent, for those utterances or states to refer to or represent neutrinos; similarly, the causal relations that hold between the "utterances" or mental states of a brain in a vat and external objects are too remote for "vattish" utterances or states to represent external objects. (Remember, we are not talking about a case in which a brain in a vat is supplied with an external scanner that "reports" the physical structures of nearby objects; the stimuli that the brain in our story receives are generated by a computer running a world-processing program. If the external world does happen to contain trees as well as vats and computers, that is just an accident.)

A brain in a vat, therefore, either has no language at all or has a language that is not ours. Even if he does have a language, it does not follow that he is wrong when he "says," "There's a tree before me"—for, whatever he may be saying, he is not saying that there's a tree before him. And if he is saying anything, why shouldn't he be saying something *true*? If his words have any meanings, they have *his* meanings. Why not assume that he means by this sentence something that is verified or made true by the situation he is in? (By "the situation he is in," I do not mean simply the mental states he is experiencing at the moment. I mean his total situation, which includes the program of the world-processor. A brain in a vat can be deceived by the "immediate" aspects of his situation, just as someone who is able to move about in space and manipulate physical objects can. It may well be that his situation is such that his "utterance" of the words 'There's a tree before me' expresses a false proposition, and that he would have asserted a true proposition if he had "said," "There's a full-scale papier-mâché model of a tree before me.") And isn't that what we should assume about him? Have we any choice?

We should remember that the "hypothesis" we are considering is that we are *all* brains in vats. Presumably, therefore, if any of us speaks a language, we all do. And if that is true, then many of us speak the *same* language – the one that calls itself 'English', for example. Let us concentrate on that one. What is the source of the meanings of English words? What could it be besides regularities in the behavior of English-speakers? Don't such regularities simply establish linguistic conventions? How else could linguistic conventions get established? They might, of course, be established by explicit verbal agreement. The conventions governing, for example, 'Abelian group' were so established. But no one would suppose that all linguistic conventions could be established that way; explicit verbal agreement is possible only when language (and hence linguistic conventions) already exist. Isn't what makes it true that the extension of 'red' is a certain class of objects simply the fact that a lot of people agree – the agreement being manifested in their behavior – to apply this term to the same objects?

"But doesn't that mean that if everyone agreed that the earth was flat, it would be flat?" It means that if everyone agreed to apply the term 'flat' to the earth, then 'flat' would be a correct term to apply to the earth.[11] It does not follow that 'flat' would mean what it actually means – after all, we actually agree *not* to apply the term 'flat' to the Earth. The "agreement" I am talking about is, in any case, agreement in all possible situations, including, say, observing the Earth from ten thousand miles above its surface. If we imagine a situation in which the earth is round but in which English-speakers, observing the earth from ten thousand miles up, say, "It's flat, all right," we are imagining a situation in which 'flat' means something other than what it actually means – perhaps 'round', perhaps something more complicated.[12]

Speaking of Russell's "hypothesis" of an unreal past, Malcolm says that this hypothesis

> requires that the newly created people should make judgments about the past, all of which are false. What criterion would there be, then, for saying that they have a past tense in their language? An omniscient observer ought to conclude that they do not have one. The case would be similar to that of a people who apparently speak English but whose "color judgments" are always or usually false. An observer ought to conclude that, contrary to what had first been supposed, they are not making color judgments.[13] What originally looked like that has to be interpreted in some other way. The same holds for those sentences that at first appeared to express statements about the past.[14]

And the same holds for those statements (made by the brains in the vats) that at first appeared to express statements about trees and buildings and brains and vats and the rest of the furniture of the world. In particular, this holds for statements expressed by the words 'I am not a brain in a vat'. If someone is (and has always been) a brain in a vat, then—assuming he has a language at all—he means by 'brain' and 'vat' and 'in' something different from what these words mean in the mouths of people who are, or have, normally embodied brains. What *he* means by 'I am not a brain in a vat' is something that could be true even if it were asserted by a brain in a vat. But if that is right, then the thesis that *I* am a brain in a vat collapses. If I try to suppose that I am a brain in a vat, then I must suppose that I do not speak any language (a supposition I cannot coherently make, since one can suppose that one cannot speak only if one can speak), or else I must suppose that what I mean by 'I am not a brain in a vat' is something that could be true if I were a brain in a vat. To attempt to make either of these suppositions would involve me in a pragmatic contradiction: I can no more coherently say 'I am a brain in a vat' than I can say 'It's raining but I don't believe that it's raining'. *Someone* may be a brain in a vat, just as *someone* may not believe that it is raining when it is raining. But no one can coherently say that *he* is in either of these situations. The two cases are not perfectly parallel, however. One cannot coherently *assert* that one satisfies the description 'does not believe it is raining although it is', but one can without falling into incoherency *wonder* whether one satisfies that description. But one cannot, without falling into incoherency, wonder whether one is a brain in a vat. One can coherently raise the question whether a proposition one does not assent to is in fact true, but (if the argument I am presenting is correct) one cannot even coherently raise the question whether one is a brain in a vat. If this is correct, then the question whether one is a brain in a vat is like the question whether one in fact speaks any language at all, or the question whether one is in fact capable of raising any questions. One cannot coherently raise the question whether one speaks any language, because it is a conceptual truth that a person who spoke no language could not raise the question whether he spoke any language. One cannot coherently raise the question whether one is a brain in a vat, because it is a conceptual truth that a brain in a vat could not raise the question whether he was a brain in a vat.

Most philosophers find this argument unconvincing. The easiest way to find it unconvincing is to imagine that while one is picking one's way through its intricacies, one *is* a brain in a vat and that the Vat Keeper is monitoring one's thoughts (*via* his cerebroscope) and laughing at one. ("Hey, everybody! Look! This is priceless! He's just thought of a philosophical argument that proves he isn't a brain in a vat!") Well, *if* the argument is correct, this is an impossible supposition—since it involves the impossible supposition that one is a brain in a vat.

A more profound unease, or at least one that is not open to this quick reply, can be generated if we "turn the whole thing around" and imagine ourselves in the place of the Vat Keepers. *We* examine *our* cerebroscope in *our* laboratory and discover that the brain in *our* vat thinks he is someone called 'Hilary Putnam' and that he is in a study in a (wholly fictional) place called 'Widener Library', constructing an argument proving that one cannot coherently suppose that one is a brain in a vat. We are, of course, immensely amused.

But, if Putnam's argument—the real Putnam's argument—is correct, we are misusing our cerebroscope. It is not telling us the thoughts of our captive brain; it is telling us the thoughts that *would* be "tokened" (as they say) in the normally embodied brain of an English-speaker if that normally embodied brain were in the same physical state as the brain in the vat. And that is *our* fault. *We* are the ones who calibrated (or whatever the word is) the cerebroscope. We have, evidently, in calibrating the cerebroscope, used the brains of English-speakers as our standards. But the brain in the vat is not the brain of an English-speaker, and the immensely amusing joke is on us. The brain in the vat either speaks no language at all—in which case we are certainly wrong in thinking that he is constructing a subtle philosophical argument for any conclusion whatever—or he speaks a language in which 'brain' and 'vat' and 'in' (and perhaps even 'prove' and 'coherently') have meanings different from the meanings they have in English. In the second case, the conclusion of the argument the brain is constructing, a conclusion that is perhaps not even *expressible* in English, may well be true.

Bouwsma has made a similar point. Speaking of Descartes's evil genius, he says,

> I intend to show that the evil genius is himself befuddled, and that if we exhaust some of our energies in sleuthing after the peculiarities of his diction, we need not be deceived either.[15]

Bouwsma means that a being who attempts global deceptions of the Cartesian variety (whether he stands outside Nature or merely outside a vat) succeeds only in producing a creature who, if he speaks any language at all, speaks a language that is semantically radically unlike the Global Deceiver's,[16] although it may be homophonic[17] with the Deceiver's language. This language—if it exists—is one that the Evil Genius or the Vat Keeper or the Creator of a World-That-Began-Five-Minutes-Ago cannot, for all his airs, understand. He cannot understand it because he was not brought up in a community in which it was spoken. (Nor does he belong to a community in which it could be taught to him: He and those he thinks he is deceiving have no common repertory of ostensive gestures—they, in fact, do not make what he calls 'gestures';[18] he cannot even understand what *they* mean by 'gesture' or 'over there'. If we imagine the Vat Keeper to be human and a member of our linguistic community—we have no way of imagining his two colleagues in attempted global deception, and they certainly are not members of *our* linguistic community—we can suppose that when the brain in the vat says, 'Now this is what we call a nasturtium,' a computer screen displays a picture of a man pointing at a flower. We can imagine that this picture is constructed from cerebroscopic data, eked out with information about the Master Computer's world-processing program. But a picture must be interpreted, and a picture can have more than one interpretation. If the Vat Keeper deduces from the picture he sees that the brain in the vat currently believes himself to be pointing at a flower, he is misinterpreting that picture.) If the Evil Genius or the Vat Keeper thinks he is deceiving someone about almost everything, he is deceiving only himself. Like Screwtape's unfortunate nephew Wormwood, he is an incompetent deceiver.

To complete our account of how attempted global deception looks "from the other end," we should note that the brain in *our* vat (1) cannot understand what is expressed by the *English* predicate 'is a brain in a vat', and (2) cannot coherently wonder whether he satisfies the predicate of *his* language — always assuming he has one — 'is a brain in a vat', although he knows perfectly well (and we cannot know) what is expressed by that predicate. In making this second statement, of course, I am assuming that the brain in the vat is such that, if he were caused to be normally embodied, the resulting man-shaped organism would pass the behavioral tests by which we pick out competent speakers of English — as opposed to speakers of a language in which 'is a brain in a vat' means something different from what it means in English.

This essentially completes my exposition of Putnam's argument for his second premise ('It is not intelligible to suppose that we are all wrong about almost everything'). We need only note that the "hypothesis' that we are all brains in vats is not importantly different from any other tale of global deception: If Putnam's argument shows that it is unintelligible to suppose that we are brains in vats, it could easily be modified to show, with respect to any given tale of global deception, that we cannot intelligibly suppose that tale to be true. But if we are all wrong about almost everything, then some tale of global deception must be true. Whether Putnam's argument is cogent depends on many disputed questions in the philosophy of language and the philosophy of mind. Theories of mind and language according to which this argument is certainly *not* cogent have recently been developed by several philosophers, most notably John Searle in *Intentionality*[19] and Roderick M. Chisholm in *The First Person*.[20] (Searle and Chisholm do not seem to say anything in these books that would count as a statement about the nature of truth.) It is not my purpose to try to decide who is right about the second premise of Putnam's argument. My business, as I have said, is with its first premise ('If truth is radically nonepistemic, then it is intelligible to suppose that we are all wrong about almost everything').

Why does Putnam believe this? Why does he think that a (metaphysical or external) realist should believe that it is intelligible to suppose that we are all wrong about almost everything? What premises in Putnam's argument for the incoherency of supposing that we are brains in vats must the realist reject?

In *Reason, Truth and History*, Putnam says,

Before I give the argument [the argument presented above for the conclusion that it is unintelligible to suppose that we are all brains in vats], let us consider why it seems so strange that such an argument can be given (at least to philosophers who subscribe to a 'copy' conception of truth). . . . it is compatible with physical law that there should be a world in which all sentient beings are brains in a vat. As philosophers say, there is a 'possible world' in which all sentient beings are brains in a vat. . . . The humans in that possible world have exactly the same experiences that *we* do. They think the same thoughts we do (at least, the same words, images, thought-forms, etc., go through their minds). Yet I am claiming that there is an argument we can give that shows we are not brains in a vat. How can there be? And why couldn't the people in the possible worlds who really are brains in a vat give it too? (p. 8)

What Putnam asks us to consider in this passage is the question, Why does it seem so strange to philosophers who subscribe to a copy theory of truth that there is an argument that shows that we are not brains in vats? He does not ask us to consider the question we are at present interested in: Why must philosophers who believe that truth is radically nonepistemic *reject* the thesis that there is an argument that shows that we are not brains in vats? But perhaps an answer to the former question would provide the materials out of which an answer to the latter could be constructed. The main trouble with the passage I have quoted is that it does not seem to provide us with much of an answer to the question that it asks us to consider. Insofar as it does contain an answer to this question, this answer would seem to be contained in the two rhetorical questions with which it ends. We are, presumably, to suppose that those questions are being asked by subscribers to a 'copy' conception of truth. Here is why the thesis that a certain kind of argument is possible seems strange to them: It raises (for them, if not for more enlightened philosophers) those questions.

But why? Why should it raise those questions *for them* — for them in particular? Any philosopher *might* be puzzled by the announcement of an argument that proves that we are not brains in vats; and that puzzlement might lead him to ask those questions. But why should those questions be particularly closely associated with a 'copy' theory of truth — *or* with the thesis that truth is radically nonepistemic? Why shouldn't the "copyist," when he has seen Putnam's argument for the incoherency of supposing that we are brains in vats simply say, "Oh, now I see," and continue to be a copyist? Why shouldn't the proponent of the thesis that truth is radically nonepistemic react in that way, too? This is precisely the question we have been asking. I do not know of any answer to it. I think it has no answer. (On p. 22 of *Reason, Truth and History*, Putnam says that the reason it is surprising that the brain-in-a-vat hypothesis turns out to be incoherent is that "we are inclined to think that *what goes on in our heads* must determine what we mean and what our words refer to." Well, perhaps we are inclined to think this, and perhaps it is false. But why should the inclination to think this be associated with realism? On this point, see notes 5 and 25 to the present paper.)

If Putnam is right about brains in vats, then, as we have seen, to suppose that we might all be brains in vats is to fall into pragmatic contradiction. Supposing that we might all be brains in vats could be compared with supposing that no one speaks a language, or that no one is able to suppose that some thesis is true. I expect that most philosophers, whatever theories they might hold about the nature of truth, would concede that a person who supposes that no one can speak any language has fallen into incoherency (and this despite the fact that the proposition that no one speaks any language is not self-contradictory). And this thing that all philosophers would concede does not seem to favor any given theory about truth over any other. In particular, the (metaphysical) realist can accept it with perfect equanimity. But then what prevents the realist from accepting the corresponding thesis about supposing that everyone might be a brain in a vat? To suppose that everyone might be a brain in a vat is either to fall into a pragmatic contradiction or it is not. In the latter case, Putnam's argument is unsound. In the former case—well, the realist admits that there are *some* self-consistent propositions such that a person cannot, without contradiction, suppose with respect to one of those propositions that it is true—why should a proof that any particular proposition falls into this category disturb him?

It may be instructive to substitute some other one of these propositions in the argument I have attributed to Putnam. For example:

(1a) If truth is radically nonepistemic, then it is intelligible to suppose that no one speaks any language.

(2a) It is not intelligible to suppose that no one speaks any language.

hence, Truth is not radically nonepistemic.

In this case, I dare say, almost everyone would grant the second premise. But why should anyone grant the first? And why is the first premise of Putnam's argument—that is, of the argument I have attributed to Putnam—any more plausible than (1a)? (It will not do to argue that 'We are all wrong about almost everything' has epistemic implications, and is thus particularly apt to have some sort of conceptual connection with 'truth is radically nonepistemic'. To speak a language entails being right about many, many things. For example, to speak English entails being right in believing that 'cat' does not mean the same as 'dog', that 'colored' applies to anything 'red' applies to, and so on. Therefore, the thesis that no one speaks a language has epistemic implications only slightly less profound than those of the thesis that we are all wrong about almost everything.)

In my view, there is no answer to this question, and Putnam's argument for the incoherency of the "hypothesis" that we are brains in vats has, even if it is correct, no implications whatever for the thesis that truth is radically nonepistemic. What Putnam's argument shows (assuming it to be correct) is that the *capacity to state and believe propositions* is "radically epistemic": If we were not right about most things, we could not even be *wrong* about very much. Thus, the supposition that we are all wrong about almost everything is (if Putnam's argument is correct) incoherent. But this is a far cry from saying that *truth* is radically epistemic. The only truths that depend for their status as truths on our knowing lots of things or on our almost always being right are the truths that everyone would admit had that feature, and the types of dependence involved are obvious and boring: It is because (formal cause) our beliefs are almost always right that it is true that our beliefs are almost always right; it is because (efficient cause) we are often wrong about our own motives that our judgments about other people's motives are often wrong. And so on.

The realist will distinguish in the following way between the conditions necessary for the acceptance and statement of propositions and the conditions necessary for the existence of truths. (At least many realists will. At least I will.) Suppose someone believes that Mount Everest is 8,847.7 meters high. Or suppose he says, "Mount Everest is 8,847.7 meters high." (Let us concentrate on the problems raised by the former supposition, for what we shall say about belief can be adapted easily enough to the case of assertion.) What he believes is true. The fact that what he believes is true is (as the realist sees matters) in a fairly obvious way a conjunction or combination of two facts:

> (F1) He believes (or, as I prefer to say, accepts) the proposition that Mount Everest is 8,847.7 meters high.
>
> (F2) The proposition that Mount Everest is 8,847.7 meters high is true.

Understanding the nature of the former fact is a deep problem in the philosophy of mind. (I should say that it was one of the two central problems in the philosophy of mind, the other being the problem of the nature of sensuous experience.) Some philosophers (Chisholm and Searle, for example) say that the existence or holding or obtaining of a fact of this sort is entirely a matter of what goes on in the subject's head (or in his mind or soul—the mind-body problem is not what is at issue here). Other philosophers (Putnam and Kripke, for example) say that it involves other things as well—perhaps the subject's being a member of a certain linguistic community, or his being causally related to a certain large mass of rock. If Putnam's argument for the incoherency of supposing that everyone is a brain in a vat is correct, then Chisholm and Searle must be wrong; it certainly does follow from their position that a person's "vat-Doppelgänger" accepts exactly the propositions that that person accepts. (In saying that this is a consequence of their position, I pass over the issue of propositions expressed by sentences containing indexicals.) And, if Putnam's argument is correct, then either one's vat-Doppelgänger accepts hardly any propositions at all, or else he accepts a set of propositions most of which one could not even grasp. From the realist's point of view, Putnam's argument has nothing to do with the nature of truth. It has nothing to do with the nature of the relation that must hold between a proposition and the world in order for the latter to *confer truth on* the former. It has, rather, to do with the nature of the relation that must hold between a proposition and a subject in order for the latter to *accept* the former. The realist who accepts Putnam's argument will describe its import like this: Putnam has shown that certain of the necessary conditions for accepting the proposition that everyone is a brain in a vat—or for accepting *any* proposition about brains and vats—could not be satisfied by anyone if everyone were a brain in a vat. Of course (the realist might add), if everyone were a brain in a vat, this proposition would be *true*; it is just that no one would be able to accept it or grasp it or consider it.

The nature of the second fact, (F2) – that the proposition that Mount Everest is 8,847.7 meters high is true – represents a problem of an entirely different sort. (This problem is not the problem solved by Tarski:[21] the problem of giving a mathematical characterization of the set of sentences in a formal language L – a language satisfying certain constraints – that satisfy the predicate 'expresses in L a true proposition'.[22] It has next to nothing to do with *that* problem. Nor does it have much to do with the important extensions of Tarski's work by Saul Kripke[23] and by Anil Gupta,[24] which treat formal languages that are in a certain philosophically important respect more like natural languages than is the sort of language for which Tarski solved the problem. I do not mean to depreciate the work of Tarski, Kripke, and Gupta, but merely to classify it. The classification, moreover, represents a philosophical position: When I say that Tarski's results have next to nothing to do with the problem of what it is for a proposition to be true, I do not claim to be stating an obvious fact; I am only saying where I stand.) I have little to say about this problem. I note only that, as a realist, I have the following picture: Propositions, like numbers, are necessarily existent, abstract objects; the same propositions exist in every possible world; in different possible worlds, there are different concrete objects, and even in two worlds that have the same population of concrete objects, these objects may have different intrinsic qualities and be related differently to one another; what change from world to world, therefore, are the population, qualities, and arrangement of concrete objects, and it is these features of concrete objects that are the formal causes of the truth and falsity of propositions. The problem of the nature of the fact (F2) is, in its general form, the problem of the nature of the relation that holds between a world composed of certain objects having certain intrinsic qualities, and related to one another in a certain way, on the one hand, and a proposition, on the other, in virtue of which the world is the formal cause of the truth-value of the proposition. The realist position is: This relation has nothing to do with the existence of minds, or with their contemplation of the proposition or of the arrangement of objects that causes it to be true. *Some* worlds, indeed, contain minds, and some propositions are about minds, but the relations "makes true" and "makes false" hold not only in those worlds, but also in worlds (if such there be) wholly devoid of mind.

This is the realist position on the nature of truth. Perhaps it is an obscure position. It is, after all, a position on a fundamental philosophical question, and these positions tend to be obscure. It is certainly no more obscure than the antirealist's position on the nature of truth (rather less so, if you ask me). But its obscurity or lack of it is neither here nor there. The essential point for our purposes is this: Putnam's brain-in-a-vat argument has nothing to do with this position. The brain-in-a-vat argument is relevant only to this question: What is it for a proposition to be accepted, grasped, or entertained? It is not relevant to the question: What is it for a proposition to be *true*. I do not, as I have said, understand a "copy" or Tractarian account of truth. But I see no reason why an adherent of a copy account of truth should not accept Putnam's argument. I can see no reason why he should find it "strange" that such an argument can be given.[25] Why shouldn't the "copyist" say this: "I accept the proposition that Mount Everest is 8,847.7 meters high. And this proposition is true because it and a part of the world have the same structure. My vat-Doppelgänger accepts a proposition that *he* expresses by the words 'Mount Everest is 8,847.7 meters high'. This proposition is true because it and a part of the world have the same structure"? As far as I can see, the only thing that could prevent his saying this would be certain theories in the philosophy of mind, theories that, although consistent with realism, are by no means entailed by realism, theories according to which the propositions accepted by a thinker are entirely determined by "what is in his head."

The same point can be made about the philosopher who believes that truth is radically nonepistemic. Why shouldn't he say: "I accept the proposition that Mount Everest is 8,847.7 meters high. The way the world is makes this proposition true, and this 'making true' relation is one that would hold between the way the world was and certain propositions even if there were no minds. My vat-Doppelgänger accepts a proposition that *he* expresses by the words Mount Everest is 8,847.7 meters high'. The way the world is makes this proposition true, and this 'making true' relation is one that would hold between the way the world was and certain propositions, even if there were no minds"? There is, of course, one important difference between you and me and the propositions about Mount Everest that *we* accept, on the one hand, and the propositions expressed by "Vat-English" sentences containing the words 'Mount Everest', on the other. The propositions about Mount Everest that you and I accept (the geological ones, anyway, as opposed to the historical and sociological ones) do not depend for their truth-values on the thoughts or actions of human beings. But the proposition expressed by the Vat-English sentence 'Mount Everest is 8,847.7 meters high' would have been false if the world-processing program controlling the stimuli received by the brain in the vat had been different in certain minor ways, or, *a fortiori*, if it had never been written. That proposition would have *existed* even if there had never been a physical universe (like all propositions, it is necessarily existent), but its truth-value is intimately connected with the specific actions of specific human beings. But that does not affect my point. That is only to say that the thoughts and actions of human beings are among the efficient causes of the truth of this proposition; it is not to say that the thoughts and actions of human beings have anything to do with *what it is* for that proposition to be true. (We should note, by the way, that the sentence 'The fact that Mount Everest is 8,847.7 meters high in no way depends on the thoughts or actions of human beings' expresses, in Vat-English, a true proposition.)

I conclude that defenses of antirealism, and attacks on metaphysical realism and the copy theory of truth and the thesis that truth is radically nonepistemic, must be based on something other than arguments showing that we cannot coherently suppose that we are brains in vats.

Notes

1. Compare Hilary Putnam, "Realism and Reason," in *Meaning and the Moral Sciences* (London, 1978), 125.

2. I do not, however, wish to deny that if someone were to say, "Mt. Everest is 8847.7 meters high" (that is, if someone were to pronounce those words in a context in which his pronouncing them would constitute his saying that Mt. Everest was 8847.7 meters high), then his saying this would have certain "conversational implicatures" or presuppositions that would be false if various of the states of affairs enumerated in the text failed to obtain. For example: that 'Mt. Everest' is a name for a certain mountain; that he has some way of knowing how high that mountain is; that 'meter' is a name for a unit of linear measure. But none of these propositions whose truth is presupposed by his asserting the proposition that Mt. Everest is 8847.7 meters high (in those words) is entailed by that proposition.

3. Or no one but God. I do not quite know how to deal with God—that is, with a necessarily existent and essentially omniscient being—in a discussion of the present topic. I should *like* to say that even though (because of God's necessary existence and essential omniscience) there is no proposition that no one ever thinks of, and no true proposition that is not believed by anyone, this fact is somehow irrelevant to what is at issue in the realism/antirealism debate. But I am not sure how best to articulate this inclination. Tentatively, I would say this: Although God's "mental states" are among the efficient causes of the truth-values of all contingent propositions, they are not among the efficient causes of the truth-values of necessarily true or necessarily false propositions—for the truth-values of noncontingent propositions have no efficient causes. And both of the following propositions are necessary truths: (1) the proposition that snow is white exists; (2) if snow is white, and if the proposition that snow is white exists, then that proposition is true. These two necessary truths, together with the contingent truth that snow *is* white, entail that the proposition that snow is white is true. God's "mental states" are doubtless among the efficient causes of snow's being white. They are, therefore, among the efficient causes of the truth of the proposition that snow is white. But they are not among its formal causes; they are not constituents of the fact that the proposition that snow is white is true; they need not be mentioned in a correct account of what it *is* for that proposition to be true. An account of what it is for that proposition to be true—I do not have a nontrivial one—need mention only the intrinsic or nonrelational properties of the proposition that snow is white, and the fact that snow is white (how the whiteness of snow came about would not be relevant).

The philosopher who believes that truth is radically nonepistemic, and who is also an atheist, has available to him an effective "intuition pump" (in Dennett's sense) that he can use in good conscience. He can imagine a world in which there are no minds, but (of course) lots of truths and falsehoods. I have made some use of this intuition pump in the text, but not in very good conscience, since I do not believe that there are any such worlds. My only defense is that my use of this pump is not supposed to constitute an argument for the mind-independence of truth, but only to provide the idea that truth is mind-independent with some intuitive content—and, anyway, the present paper is not a defense of the mind-independence of truth.

4. 'Known to' here refers to "knowledge by acquaintance." The proposition that the truths of arithmetic can be specified recursively is a *false* proposition that is "known" to us in this sense, and which could not have been known to us if we had been very much less intelligent than we are.

5. In "Realism and Reason" (p. 125) and elsewhere, Putnam says that metaphysical realism is the thesis that there is a "determinate relation of *reference*" between the terms of a language and pieces of "the world." (In "Realism and Reason," Putnam writes 'THE WORLD' rather than 'the world'. I think we may take the world—lowercase or capitalized—to be constituted by those objects, if such there be, whose existence and attributes are independent of the mental states of the speakers of the language in question, or whose existence and attributes "depend" on those states only in a crude, causal sense. The function of the capitals appears to be to suggest that realists treat the attribute of mind-independence as conferring a sort of quasi-religious awfulness on its possessors.) If this is what "realism" is, then I am a realist in this sense, too. Putnam tells us in "Realism and Reason" (p. 125) that the thesis that truth is radically nonepistemic is a "consequence" of the thesis that there is a determinate notion of reference. I have a certain amount of trouble with this contention in that, in my view, truth is a property of items that do not belong to any language—propositions—and, thus, I see the connection between theses about reference and theses about truth as rather problematical. Perhaps Putnam's contention is this: The thesis that there is a determinate relation of reference entails the thesis that *expressing some true proposition or other* (a

relational property of some sentences) is radically nonepistemic. I shall not discuss this contention. I should say that in accepting the position that there is a determinate relation of reference, I do not mean to commit myself to any theory about the "determinants" of this relation; in particular, I do not mean to commit myself to the thesis that the referent of, for example, 'Mt. Everest', as used by Sir Edmund Hilary, is wholly determined what goes on "in the head" of Sir Edmund. (Compare note 25.) I should also say that, because I do not understand the "copy" theory of truth, I decline to regard my belief in a determinate relation of reference as committing me to that theory.

Putnam also suggests in "Realism and Reason" (p. 125) that "realism" is the thesis that an ideal scientific theory might be false— " 'ideal' from the point of view of operational utility, inner beauty and elegance, 'plausibility', simplicity, 'conservatism', etc." I will not discuss this form of "realism," except to remark that the conceivability of a false ideal theory seems extremely plausible on scientific grounds. It seems plausible that there might be two competing and logically incompatible theories, each of which was "ideal" in this sense—and one of them, presumably, would have to be false. Two incompatible competing theories might both be "ideal" because it might be physically impossible (even demonstrably physically impossible) to perform any experiment of the sort that would be needed to choose between them. (And this physical impossibility might be a consequence of both theories.) Current physical theory suggests that this is not only a logical but an epistemic possibility. Some physicists have speculated that an experiment that could choose among competing versions of the "Grand Unified Theory" would require energies on the order of those that would be produced by a linear accelerator light-years in length and powered by the total output of several stars. It is reasonable to suppose that, given the actual distribution of available energy in the universe, the production of such energies would be not only technologically impossible, but thermodynamically impossible. And what if it could be shown that the production of such energies would be thermodynamically impossible in any comic epoch in which the average energy-density of the universe was compatible with the existence of living organisms?

6. One might maintain these things—or one might not. It is consistent with everything I shall say later to suppose that a brain in a vat is not right even about simple a priori truths or about its own pains and beliefs.

7. Cambridge, 1981.

8. See *The Analysis of Mind* (New York, 1921), 159–60.

9. *The Philosophical Review* 58 (1949): 141–51.

10. In *Knowledge and Certainty: Essays and Lectures* (Englewood Cliffs, N.J., 1963), 187–202.

11. Compare Wittgenstein, *Philosophical Investigations*, 241.

12. It might not be a shape-predicate at all—if, for example, they refused to apply it to billiard balls.

13. Here, I believe, Malcolm overstates his case. All that follows is that they are not making the color judgments we should make using the same words: Perhaps they use 'red' to mean what we mean by 'yellow', and so on. Malcolm's conclusion would require a stronger set of assumptions; it would require at least the assumption that their apparent color-judgments are not related systematically to the colors of the objects in their environment.

14. "Memory and the Past," 196.

15. "Descartes' Evil Genius," 142.

16. I imagine that Bouwsma would have smiled to read this highfalutin paraphrase of his words: " 'Semantically radically unlike—so *that's* what I meant! My, my!'"

17. Whatever, exactly, homo*phonic* may mean in this context.

18. To my mind, this is a good reason for saying that the brain in the vat does not speak any language at all.

19. Cambridge, 1983.

20. Minneapolis, 1981.

21. "The Concept of Truth in Formalized Languages," in *Logic, Semantics, Metamathematics* (Oxford, 1956), 182–278.

22. Tarski, of course, would say 'is true in L,' where I say 'expresses in L a true proposition' or (even better) 'expresses in L some true proposition or other'.

23. "Outline of a Theory of Truth," *Journal of Philosophy* 72 (1975): 690–716.

24. "Truth and Paradox," *Journal of Philosophical Logic* 11 (1982): 1–60.

25. Nor do I see any reason to suppose that an adherent of the thesis that there exists a "determinate relation of reference" should find it strange that such an argument can be given. Such a philosopher will contend that this determinate relation of reference (or, more generally, extension) holds between the English word 'vat' and certain large containers. And, if he accepts Putnam's argument, he will contend that the "Vat-English" word 'vat' bears this same determinate relation to something-we-know-not-what — provided that there *is* such a language as Vat-English. He must, of course, deny that what determines this relation to hold between the words of a given language and various objects or sets of objects is entirely "inside the heads" of the speakers of that language. Compare note 5.

Putnam, Reference, and Realism

MARK HELLER

This paper is a discussion of Hilary Putnam's argument against realism. It is also meant to shed some light on certain general aspects of the realism/antirealism debate. Since 'realism' and 'antirealism' are used in many ways, the first step in any discussion of this topic must be to explain which debate is really being discussed. I will begin, therefore, by distinguishing two broad senses of 'realism' and, correspondingly, of 'antirealism'. Even in the sense that is relevant to Putnam's argument, there are different kinds of realism. I will argue that there is a weak kind that is invulnerable to Putnam's attack. Then I will show that this weak realism can be used to show that Putnam's argument does not work even against the strong realism that is his intended target.

We can distinguish two broad senses of 'realism'. In the first, to be a realist about some particular thing or kind of thing is to believe that that thing or kind exists (or that that kind has members). In this sense, the antirealist believes that the thing or kind in question does not exist.[1] In this first sense, some philosophers are realists about tables but antirealists about electrons. Others are realists about electrons but antirealists about tables. There are some who are realists about both kinds of objects and others who are antirealists about both.

Since these realists and antirealists are debating the *existence* of particular entities or kinds of entities, we might call them 'existential realists' and 'existential antirealists'. All these philosophers are in the same broad philosophical camp. They all believe that there is a right answer to the questions of whether there are tables and whether there are electrons. All they disagree about is what that right answer is. It is their common belief in some right answer that makes them all realists about tables in my *second* sense of 'realism'.

In this second sense, to be a realist about some particular object or kind of object is to believe that there is a fact of the matter as to whether that object or kind exists. To be an antirealist, in this second sense, is to believe that there is no fact of the matter about these things. An antirealist might accept a fact of the matter relative to a conceptual scheme or to a background theory, but there is no nonrelative fact of the matter. Henceforth, I will follow Putnam in using the terms 'externalism' and 'internalism' to pick out realism and antirealism in this second sense. Where there might be confusion I will use the longer expressions 'metaphysical externalism' and 'metaphysical internalism' to distinguish these views from the epistemological theses with similar titles.

There are several kinds of arguments for metaphysical internalism. I confess that I often find many of them persuasive. The purpose of the present paper will be to offer a defense against one of these arguments. I am not defending externalism against all objections. I am not yet sure that that can be done. Nor am I defending an existential realism about any particular kind of object.[2] Putnam's argument, if properly understood, is not an argument against any existential realism. It is an argument directly against there being any nonrelative facts of the matter about certain issues.[3]

In *Reason, Truth and History* Putnam describes externalism:

[According to metaphysical realism] the world consists of some fixed totality of mind-independent objects. There is exactly one true and complete description of 'the way the world is'. Truth involves some sort of correspondence relation between words or thought-signs and external things and sets of things. I shall call this the *externalist* perspective, because its favorite point of view is a God's eye view. (*RTH*, p. 49)

This description includes a version of a correspondence theory of truth. There is supposed to be something that the world is like independent of how we conceptualize it. To express a truth, then, should be to give an accurate account of what that unconceptualized world is like. Giving such an account requires a correspondence between an utterance and the unconceptualized world. The main thrust of Putnam's argument in *Reason, Truth and History* is that there is no plausible theory of the correspondence. He attempts to show that no reasonable theory of reference will allow for the desired correspondence.

His argument can most perspicuously be broken up into two main premises, though Putnam does not actually present the argument in this way. The first premise is that externalism requires the ability to refer to objects as they are in themselves. That is, any truth must be *about* the objects that really compose the world, not merely about the objects as our theory posits them. The second premise is that we cannot have the required ability to refer; we can refer only to bits of the world as it is conceptualized by us. If both premises are accepted, externalism must be surrendered.

I will reject both of Putnam's premises. I will argue against the first premise by presenting a weak form of externalism that does not require the ability to refer to objects as they are in themselves.[4] I will then argue against Putnam's second premise by showing that if we accept weak externalism about the right sorts of questions, we can undermine Putnam's argument against our ability to refer to the world as it is in itself. For all of Putnam's ingenuity, I will conclude, there may still be a world as it is in itself, independent of any conceptual scheme; moreover, this world may be referred to and known as it is in itself.

Putnam writes in *Meaning and the Moral Sciences*:

> The most important consequence of metaphysical realism [externalism] is that *truth* is supposed to be *radically non-epistemic* — we might be 'brains in a vat' and the theory that is 'ideal' from the point of view of operational utility, inner beauty and elegance, 'plausibility', simplicity, 'conservatism', etc., *might be false*. 'Verified' (in any operational sense) does not imply 'true', on the metaphysical realist picture, even in the ideal limit.[5]

So, it is a consequence of externalism that we can have a theory T1 that is ideal with respect to all operational and theoretical constraints, and yet false. In spite of T1's being ideal, there is another theory T2 that really is true even though it is no better with respect to operational and theoretical constraints than T1. (It may even be worse; for instance, it may not be as simple or beautiful as T1).

Putnam rejects this consequence of externalism, thereby rejecting externalism itself. To show the implausibility of holding T1 false and T2 true in any nonrelative sense, Putnam points out that there are some interpretations of T1, some ways of mapping the terms of T1 onto the world, such that *relative to those interpretations*, T1 is true. (He shows this briefly in *MMS*, pp. 125–26, and in more detail in *RTH*, pp. 33–35 and in the appendix, pp. 217–18.) Furthermore, the same reasoning can be used to show that there are some interpretations relative to which T2 is false. Now compare interpretation I1, according to which T1 is true and T2 is false, and interpretation I2, according to which T2 is true and T1 is false. If it turns out that there is no fact of the matter as to which interpretation is correct, then it follows from this that there is no fact as to which theory is correct.

The externalist seems forced to hold that I2 is the correct interpretation: the terms in T2 do, in fact, refer to the pieces of the world that I2 maps them onto, not to the pieces that I1 maps them onto. If it turns out that these facts about reference are themselves true only relative to a particular theory or conceptual scheme, then, of course, we would be left with T2's truth and T1's falsity also being relative. So a term's referring to a particular piece of the world must itself be theory-independent. It seems, then, that externalism requires that we refer to pieces of the world as they are in themselves, not as they are relative to a conceptual scheme. Thus, the externalist seems committed to Putnam's first premise.

Externalism insists that, independent of our theories about the world or our way of conceptualizing the world, there is a way the world really is. This is supposed to lead to the first premise, since there can be two incompatible theories about the way the world is, each of which is true relative to some particular mapping of terms to world. The world cannot be both ways. Yet, if we deny the first premise, in effect denying that there is any theory-independent mapping, we will be unable to find anything in the world itself that makes one theory true rather than the other. To attack the first premise, I suggest that there is an assumption here that must be doubted.

Why should we be so sure that the world cannot be the way that T1 says it is and also the way that T2 says it is; why should we be so sure that the two theories are incompatible? Of course, we can simply stipulate that they are, but such a stipulation presupposes that there is a correct nonrelative interpretation for each of the theories after all. Certainly, under some interpretations of each theory they conflict. Perhaps we can even go further and say that no single interpretation can map the terms of both theories onto the world in a consistent way. But in order to conclude that there is no nonrelative way that the world is, we need a stronger kind of incompatibility. The two theories would have to be incompatible in that there is no way that each theory could be given a true interpretation. That is, it must be that the unique, nonrelative way that the world is cannot be described by both theories. And this is precisely what Putnam shows to be false.

This response to the first premise can be put less abstractly. T1, the supposedly false but otherwise ideal theory, is true under interpretation I1 and false under interpretation I2. T2, the true, though perhaps less than ideal, theory (perhaps it does not fit such theoretical constraints as "plausibility"), is true under I2 but false under I1. This suggests that there *is* a nonrelative way the world is. It is the way that T1 says it is if T1 is interpreted under I1, and it is also the way that T2 says it is if T2 is interpreted under I2. T1 under I1 and T2 under I2 are perfectly compatible. There is a unique way that the world can be such that its being that way makes T1 under I1 true and makes T2 under I2 true. In fact, if the two theories, under the appropriate interpretations, are complete theories of the world, they are in total agreement. In this case, depending on how we individuate theories, we might even say that T1 under I1 is the very same theory as T2 under I2.

The question of which *un*interpreted theory is correct is illegitimate. If theories are the kinds of things that need to be interpreted, then an uninterpreted theory has no truth value at all. This is not surprising and should not by itself be taken to undermine externalism. It is no more surprising, for instance, than the obvious truth that a sentence has no truth value except relative to a language. If Putnam's second premise is true, then no interpretation is available to us independent of a conceptual scheme. This might force us to accept that we cannot ever express or believe the true theory (except relative to a conceptual scheme), but that is consistent with there being a nonrelative way that the world is. At worst, it is the formulation of theories about the world that is somehow relative. The world is the way it is, independent of our being able to talk about it or think about it.

Consider the following quotation from Putnam:

> Sometimes incompatible theories can actually be intertranslatable. For example, if Newtonian physics were true, then every single physical event could be described in two ways: in terms of particles acting at a distance, across empty space (which is how Newton described gravitation as acting), or in

terms of particles acting on fields which act on other fields (or other parts of the same field), which finally act 'locally' on other particles. For example, the Maxwell equations, which describe the behavior of the electro-magnetic field, are mathematically equivalent to a theory in which there are only action-at-a-distance forces between particles, attracting and repelling according to the inverse square law, travelling not instantaneously but rather at the speed of light ('retarded potentials'). The Maxwell field theory and the retarded potential theory are incompatible from a metaphysical point of view, since either there are or there aren't causal agencies (the 'fields') which mediate the action of separated particles on each other (a realist would say). But the two theories are mathematically intertranslatable. So if there is a 'correspondence' to the noumenal things which makes one of them true, then one can define another correspondence which makes the other theory true. If all it takes to make a theory true is abstract correspondence (never mind which), then incompatible theories can be true. (*RTH*, p. 73)

Here we seem to have two incompatible theories about the way the world is. Yet, working under the assumption that there is nothing in the world itself that makes one interpretation right rather than another, each theory has as good a claim to truth as the other. That the theories are intertranslatable guarantees that if either theory is true relative to some particular mapping of terms to world, then there is some mapping that makes the other true. If there is some correspondence between one theory and the world, then there is also some correspondence between the other theory and the world. The world cannot be both ways, yet there can be nothing in the world itself that makes one theory true rather than the other.

The externalist response that I have been proposing is to emphasize that the apparent conflict between the two theories is a real conflict only relative to certain interpretations. If the two theories are understood as already interpreted in such a way that they really do conflict, their being intertranslatable does not count against one being true and the other false. At worst, the intertranslatability shows that the two theories will be equally confirmed or disconfirmed by any possible evidence. This may generate a standard skeptical argument for the conclusion that we cannot *know* which is true and which is false, but even if this conclusion were accepted, that would not count against there being a fact of the matter.[6]

On the other hand, if both the retarded potential theory and the field theory are to be understood as corresponding to the way the world really is, they must be mapped onto the world relative to different interpretations. In this case the two theories do not conflict. Either the world is such that in order to get the retarded potential theory to correspond to the way the world really is we must interpret it so that it is committed to the existence of fields after all, or the world is such that in order for the field theory to correspond to the way the world really is it must be interpreted in a way that does not commit it to the existence of fields. We may, at worst, never know which interpretation is the one that gets us to the way the world really is, but this does not count against there being a way that the world really is.

There is, then, a weak form of externalism that does not require a nonrelative mapping of a theory's terms onto pieces of the world. Even if we have no nonrelative way to refer to the world, there is still a nonrelative fact about what the world is like. It is our descriptions of the world that are relative to conceptual scheme, not the world itself. However, Putnam would object that this weak version of externalism is so limited as to leave externalists with little of what they really desire. For instance, it seems that although there is a nonrelative way that the world is, we can have no nonrelative access to the way the world is. Any given theory that might be put forth will have many possible interpretations. The truth value of any theory will depend on what interpretation that theory is given. Unless interpretations are themselves nonrelative, the truth value of the theory will still be relative.

One consequence of this is that I can hold no true theory, and hence have no knowledge, except relative to a conceptual scheme or a background theory or something similar. But things are worse still. It seems that I cannot even speculate about which theory is true except relative to some interpretation. When I try to choose between the field theory and the action at a distance theory, I cannot even evaluate the theories until they are given some interpretation. This is no problem if there is a definite fact of the matter as to which interpretation each of the theories should be given, but there being such a fact is exactly what Putnam raises doubts about. He thinks that no interpretation is more privileged than any other. This yields a far more extreme skepticism than even Descartes would have imagined. It is not just that I cannot know which of two observationally equivalent theories is true; I cannot even know what the world would have to be like for either of the theories to be true.

Unless there is a nonrelative fact of the matter as to which interpretation our theories should be given, those theories would not really be about the external world as it is in itself. The so-called field theory would not tell us that there are really fields out there in the world, since there are interpretations according to which field theory comes out true even if there are no fields. Of course, if my use of the term 'field' is given the same interpretation as the field theory's use of that term, it will be contradictory to say that the field theory does not tell us that there are fields. My point is that the world can be radically different ways and still be "truly" described by field theory under different interpretations. Unless one interpretation is somehow privileged, there will be no unique way that the world has to be in order for field theory to be true. In this way our theories would be divorced from the world as it is in itself, and we would be led to an extreme skepticism. If our theories do not tell us what the world is really like, they cannot be instances of knowledge.

Putnam makes this very point. In discussing an argument against externalism that is very closely related to the argument that I have been focusing on, Putnam considers and rejects something very similar to the defense that I have offered. His rejection is not based on any weakness in the defense, but rather on the weakness of the position being defended. He writes:

In the past I argued, that [alternative descriptions of the world raise] no problem for the realist—it's just like the fact that the earth can be mapped by different 'projections', I said (Mercator, Polar, etc.).

In particular, I believed, it can happen that what we picture as 'incompatible' terms can be mapped onto the same real object—though not, of course, within the same theory. Thus the real object that is labelled 'point' in one theory might be labelled 'set of convergent line segments' in another theory. And the *same* term might be mapped onto one real object in one theory and onto a different real object in another theory. It is a property of the world itself, I claimed—i.e. a property of THE WORLD itself—that it 'admits of these different mappings'.

The problem—as Nelson Goodman has been emphasizing for many, many years—is that this story may retain THE WORLD but at the price of giving up any intelligible notion of *how* THE WORLD is. Any sentence that changes truth-value upon passing from one correct theory to another correct theory—e.g. an equivalent description—will express only a *theory-relative* property of THE WORLD. And the more such properties there are, the more properties of THE WORLD will turn out to be theory relative. (*MMS*, p. 132)

Putnam is claiming that a certain unacceptable view, an extreme skepticism, is forced on anyone who takes the approach that I am advocating. There may be a way the world is, but anything we can do to say what way that is, is doomed to failure. Every property we attribute to the world will be theory relative. The properties that the world really has are inaccessible to us, because those properties are supposed to be independent of any theory.

Michael Devitt, himself an externalist, agrees that any form of externalism that leads to such an extreme skepticism is unacceptable. In the following passage, he calls the view 'weak realism', and in his criticism he quotes from Goodman:

The very weakest form of realism is completely unspecific about what exists; it requires only that *something* does. When the independence dimension is added this 'weak realism' amounts simply to the claim that something objectively exists independent of the mental. This commits realism only to an undifferentiated, uncategorized, external world, a Kantian 'thing-in-itself'. . . .

The weak realist's world is one that perhaps even Goodman would allow, a world 'without kinds or order or motion or rest or pattern'. As Goodman points out, this world 'is not worth fighting for'. What difference does believing in it make? It is a world we cannot know about or talk about. It cannot play a role in explaining any phenomenon. It is an idle addition to idealism: antirealism with a fig-leaf.[7]

Devitt is using a sense of 'antirealism' in which idealism would be a form of antirealism. But I take it that he would have the same objection to externalism as I have explained it. His criticism is based on the distastefulness and impracticality of skepticism. The reason to reject the world of the weak externalist is that we can know nothing about it, and it can do no work for us. I have my doubts about this objection. In particular, I doubt whether either the sort of externalism defended by Devitt (given his way of defending it) or the sort of internalism that Putnam or Goodman propose is any better, from a practical point of view, than the weak externalism that they all are trying to avoid. But that is a topic for future discussion. My present concern will be to deny that my defense of externalism protects only weak externalism.

If I am granted the weak externalism that I have argued for so far, I can use that to support a much stronger externalism, an externalism that is not committed to any kind of skepticism. I will use the weak externalism to undermine what I called Putnam's second premise—his claim that there can be no reference to the world as it really is. The things we refer to are real pieces of the world as they really are. The properties we attribute to the world are not mere theoretical properties. Hence, even if a strong externalism does require reference to the world as it is in itself, that will be no objection to strong externalism, since this sort of reference is possible.

It will be helpful to clearly distinguish Putnam's argument for the claim that externalism leads to skepticism from more standard arguments for this same claim. If we have two observationally equivalent theories, no amount of evidence will enable us to tell which is true. Descartes's evil-genius theory is an example of one that is observationally equivalent to our standard theory of the world, though in obvious conflict. From an internalist perspective, we might deny this conflict; we might be able to say that each theory is true relative to some particular conceptual scheme. But from an externalist perspective, we must view the two theories as truly in conflict (at least, assuming the most obvious interpretations of these theories). If no observations can favor one of the theories over another, it would seem that a belief in either theory must be unjustified.

The most promising line to take against such a skeptical argument is some form of epistemological externalism. This position should not be confused with the metaphysical externalism that we have been discussing so far. Indeed, it may be just a confusing accident that both the metaphysical and the epistemological views are called 'externalism'. We should not assume that metaphysical externalism and epistemological externalism are two forms of the same general kind of thesis. The epistemological externalist holds that justification is partly a function of certain external facts, external to the believer's evidence (in even the broadest senses of 'evidence'). A belief is justified not merely in virtue of the observations on which that belief is based but also on certain unobserved facts. These unobserved facts may be about the reliability of the belief-forming mechanism[8] or about the existence of justificatory defeaters.[9]

Since some of the relevant facts are unobserved, we can be justified in believing some B without being justified in believing that we are justified in believing B. We are justified in believing B as long as the relevant conditions are met. But since we may not be justified in believing that those conditions are met (we may have no idea one way or the other about that), we may not be justified in believing that we are justified in believing B. It may even turn out that the relevant unobserved facts are unobservable, and that we have no observation-independent way to know anything about them. If this were the case, and if second-order justification requires knowledge of the truth of these unknowable facts, it would be impossible for us to be justified in believing that we are justified in believing B. If this were the case (and it may well *not* be the case), we would be stuck with a second-order skepticism, but this would not impinge on our first-order knowledge. We would still be able to know which of the two conflicting theories of the world is true, though we could not know that we knew this. Similar considerations show that second-order knowledge does not require third-order knowledge, and so on.

The distinction between epistemic levels plays a central role in the defense against standard skeptical arguments.[10] Once we deny that knowing p entails knowing that we know p, we can accept that someone can have knowledge without knowing that the relevant conditions for knowledge are met. What we will see is that a similar distinction of levels can play a similar role against Putnam's skeptical argument. In responding to that argument we will distinguish between levels of interpretation instead of levels of justification. We will find that in order to have knowledge at any given level, what is necessary is that our beliefs must have a nonrelative interpretation, but that interpretation does not itself have to be knowable. This fact will end up undermining Putnam's argument against nonrelative interpretations.

The standard argument for skepticism, as I have stated it, focuses on the justification condition for knowledge. If knowledge is at least justified true belief, and if our beliefs cannot be justified, then we cannot have knowledge. Putnam's argument for the externalist's commitment to skepticism focuses on the truth and belief conditions. We cannot have beliefs about the world except relative to an interpretation, but, since no interpretation is privileged, any belief that is relative cannot really be true. Put another way: in order to have a true belief, we must have a belief about the world that really corresponds to the way the world is. But according to Putnam, none of our beliefs can be about the world as it really is, since any property that we can attribute to the world must be a theoretical property. Put yet another way: for *any* belief there is some interpretation relative to which that belief corresponds to the way the world really is, and for *any* belief there is some interpretation relative to which that belief fails to correspond to the way the world really is. The externalist cannot appeal to a select class of true beliefs unless there is some definite, theory-independent way that beliefs map onto the world. It is this theory-independent mapping that Putnam denies.

In arguing against there being any theory-independent interpretations, Putnam appeals to the fact that in stating the interpretation we must use sentences that themselves need interpreting. In general, any meta-theory about what the appropriate interpretation is for a given theory will itself be true only relative to certain interpretations. Presumably, this regressive relativity is independent of whether anyone ever tries to formulate the meta-theory. Since there is no absolutely true meta-theory about what interpretation should be given to a particular theory, there is no privileged interpretation except relative to a further background interpretation. And, of course, for the same reasons, there can be no absolute fact as to which of those background interpretations is privileged. Hence, Putnam is led to adopt a "verificationist semantics all the way up (or down) — in the meta-language, the meta-meta-language, etc." (*MMS*, p. 129).

My response is that Putnam's demand is too great. In order for a certain theory T to be true, for the externalist, there must be a theory-independent interpretation of T. But this does not mean that there must be a true theory T* about the interpretation of T. As long as the world is a definite way with respect to T's interpretation, it does not matter whether there is any way to talk about or refer to the way that the world is with respect to T's interpretation. We do not need to be able to state a relevant T* in any metalanguage. If we accept the weak externalism for which I have already argued, then even if there is no way to formulate a theory about the way the world is, there is still the way the world is. What I am arguing now is that that is all the strong externalist needs. As long as T has a definite interpretation, regardless of whether that interpretation is knowable, T can be both true and believed. Assuming that it can also be justified, T can be known. These same considerations apply at the next level when discussing a theory about T's interpretation.[11]

Although we know T without having a theory about T's interpretation, it might still be desirable to have one. We can now see that there is no reason to believe that we cannot have true beliefs about the meta-theory T*. Putnam's objection to our having true beliefs about T* is that we would need a meta-meta-theory T** to tell us the appropriate interpretation of T*. But again this demand is too strong. There need not be such a meta-meta-theory. All that needs to be the case is that the world be a certain definite way with respect to T*'s interpretation. Of course, similar remarks apply to our ability to know the meta-meta-theory and the meta-meta-meta-theory, and so on.

It might be objected that the weak externalism that I defended is too weak to serve my purposes. It is one thing to say that there is a definite way that the world is; it is quite another thing to say that there is a definite way that the world is with respect to interpretations or with respect to chairs or with respect to any other particular kind of thing. To say that the world is a certain way *with respect to* a certain kind of thing is already to suppose that that kind of thing is not merely theoretical, that the world really contains such things. To say that the world is a certain way with respect to chairs is to presuppose that our word 'chairs' maps onto pieces of the world in a definite way. But this is to presuppose strong externalism, and hence cannot be used as part of an argument for strong externalism. My argument for strong externalism required as a premise that there is a certain way that the world is *with respect to T's interpretation* — it may be a way that we cannot know anything about, it may even be a way that cannot be expressed in any theory, but there at least must be such a way.

But my point is not that weak externalism *entails* strong externalism or entails even that there is a definite way that the world is with respect to any particular kind of entity. Rather, the point is that weak externalism allows for the possibility of strong externalism. If there is a definite, nonrelative way that the world is, it may well be that the world is such that there is a definite interpretation for our theories. Of course, any externalist about interpretations must be prepared to accept that we could be wrong in supposing that there are such interpretations. If there are nonrelative interpretations for our theories, the claim that there are is itself a theory. And, just like any other nonrelative contingent theory, this one could be false (even if it has certain theoretical advantages over its denial). But the point is that Putnam's arguments need not persuade us of this theory's falsity. As long as there is some way that the world is in itself, it may be exactly the way that it needs to be in order for our theories to be true.

With the help of weak externalism, the levels ploy can be applied directly to Putnam's text. For instance, after arguing that any theory has several interpretations that are equally good with respect to operational and theoretical constraints, Putnam claims:

> Notice that a 'causal' theory of reference is not (would not be) of any help here: for how 'causes' can uniquely refer is as much of a puzzle as how 'cat' can, on the metaphysical realist [externalist] picture. (*MMS*, p. 126)

Putnam seems to be insisting that we have the meta-theory before we can accept the theory; we need to have a theory of reference for 'cat' before we can have true beliefs about cats. My response is that there may be a fact of the matter as to how 'cat' refers independent of there being any theory about how 'cat' refers. Furthermore, it may be that in fact there is a theory about how 'cat' refers, and that the true theory is the causal theory. For this to be the true theory, there must be a fact of the matter about how 'causes' refers. There can be such a fact of the matter independent of whether there is a theory of how 'causes' refers. Still further, it may even be that there is a true theory of how 'causes' refers, and that theory itself may be a causal theory.[12]

Nothing in this is circular. There is a certain feature of the world in itself in virtue of which 'cat' refers to the object it does. There is a similar feature in virtue of which 'mat' refers to the object it does. This general kind of feature is referred to by the word 'causes'. 'Causes' refers to that kind of feature in virtue of a certain feature of the world in itself. That feature is, in fact, of the same kind as the feature responsible for the reference of 'cat' and the feature responsible for the reference of 'mat'. Hence, what makes 'causes' refer to the kind of feature it does is itself a causal relation. To say that it is a causal relation is to say nothing more than that it is of the same relevant kind as the relations that fix the referents of our other terms. What makes a relation a member of that kind is that it has the relevant properties. There is a definite fact as to which the relevant properties are, regardless of whether we are capable of stating that fact.

Similar remarks apply to Putnam's more elaborate dismissal of Hartry Field's view of reference as a physicalistic relation that is discoverable by empirical science. Even if we accept that

(1) *x refers to y* if and only if *x bears R to y*
(where R is a relation definable in natural science vocabulary without using any semantical notions),

we are still left with the fact that (1) itself requires interpretation. "The interpretation of 'x bears R to y' will fix the interpretation of 'x refers to y'. But this will only be a relation *in each admissible model*; it will not serve to cut down the number of admissible models at all" (*RTH*, p. 46).

Putnam acknowledges Field's response, but pushes on in his criticism:

> What Field is claiming is that (a) there is a determinate unique relation between words and things or sets of things; and (b) this relation is the one to be used as the reference relation in assigning a truth value to (1) itself. But this is not necessarily expressed by just *saying* (1), as we have just seen; and it is a puzzle how we could *learn to express* what Field wants to say. (*RTH*, p. 46)

But what we should notice is that Putnam is making several unacceptable demands.

In even requiring that we come up with a theory of reference, he is assuming that our words cannot refer unless there is a theory of how they refer. We have already seen that there can be a fact of the matter without there being a theory that describes that fact of the matter. Still, it is reasonable to desire a theory of reference. But here he demands of Field's theory that it be interpreted, requiring not only that there be a unique appropriate interpretation for his theory of reference, but also that we be able to state it. Again, this requirement should be rejected. In the end, Putnam leaves us with the "puzzle of how we could learn to express what Field wants to say."

The answer should be clear. In spite of Putnam's claim to the contrary, in order to express Field's theory we need only say (1). As long as there is a unique determinate interpretation of (1), our job is done. We need not produce the interpretation. If we, for some independent reason, do want to know what the interpretation is, then we can do that with another sentence; presumably, the scientists will tell us what the right sentence is. That sentence, too, requires an interpretation, but it, too, does not require that the interpretation actually be produced.

My line of argument might seem to suppose that reference is somehow a brute metaphysical fact. Indeed, this is Putnam's final criticism of Field.

> If (1) is true, . . . what *makes* it true? Given that there are many 'correspondences' between words and things, even many that satisfy our constraints, what *singles out* one particular correspondence R? Not the empirical correctness of (1); for that is a matter of our operational and theoretical constraints. Not our intentions (rather R enters into determining what our intentions signify). It seems as if the fact that R *is* reference must be a metaphysically unexplainable fact, a kind of primitive, surd, metaphysical truth. (*RTH*, p. 46)

In answering Putnam's question of why R is reference, we must distinguish two different questions that he might really be asking, a linguistic one and a metaphysical one. The linguistic question is why 'reference' refers to R. If we have to say that there is no answer to this question, that it is just a brute fact, then we would, as Putnam claims, be stuck with "a magical theory of reference. Reference itself becomes what Locke called a 'substantial form' (an entity which *intrinsically* belongs with a certain name) on this view" (*RTH*, p. 47). Fortunately, the linguistic question does have an answer. 'Reference' refers to R because it bears the appropriate relation to R. That appropriate relation, it turns out, is R.

There is an obvious problem with this response. Given that there is some other relation R' such that 'reference' bears R' to R', why should we say that 'reference' refers to R rather than to R'? Why should we think that R is the relation that 'reference' needs to bear to a relation in order to refer to that relation? We seem forced to accept as a primitive fact that bearing R to a relation is sufficient for referring to the relation. Here, again, there is a linguistic question and a metaphysical question. And, again, the linguistic question has an easy and uninteresting answer. The relation that 'reference' must bear to R in order to refer to R is the relation that is in fact reference; that relation is R. No matter how many times we ask the question of why that relation is reference, if this question is understood as a linguistic question, it will continue to get the same answer.

It is the metaphysical question that is interesting, and it is because it is so difficult to separate the metaphysical question from the linguistic question that my answer to the linguistic question might seem unsatisfactory. In order to even understand what this metaphysical question is, we should think about why reference is so important to the externalist. There is a world in itself, regardless of whether we have any ability to say anything about it. What reference is supposed to do is to give us a way of saying things about that world as it is in itself. The metaphysical question, then, is why R's holding provides us with this ability. Why does the complex causal relation R do the job, though some other relation does not?

This is a difficult question, and I have no answer to it. Perhaps it is a question to be left to scientists, perhaps not. In any event, it is not at all implausible to suppose that this question can be answered. We do not seem forced to accept it as simply a brute fact that R does the job the externalist requires and that no other relationship would. The question can be broken into two: "What is the relevant role that a relation would have to play in order to satisfy the externalist's needs?" and "What relation, in fact, plays that role?" These questions do not seem unanswerable.

Furthermore, even if it does turn out to be a brute fact (though I think it will not) that R plays the relevant role, this need not force us into accepting a magical theory of reference. The brute fact is not that a certain word attaches to a certain object. The mere bruteness of the fact should not intimidate the externalist. It seems likely to me that the externalist is going to have to accept some brute facts anyway. It seems to be a primitive, unexplainable fact that *modus ponens* is valid. Perhaps the same should be said of the laws of nature. Why should we not hold that the fact that R is reference—the fact that R plays the relevant role—is also primitive? This does seem as fundamental for language as laws of logic are for reasoning and as laws of nature are for science.

As far as I can tell, then, there is nothing to be said against even a strong externalism. The need for a definite, nonrelative interpretation for any theory does nothing to threaten externalism, since there is no reason to believe that there is no such interpretation. In defending *weak* externalism, I showed that the world can be a definite way regardless of our ability or inability to refer to the world. Hence, it can be that there is a definite fact of the matter as to what the appropriate interpretation is, even if the only way to get at that fact is by way of a statement or mental state that will itself need an interpretation. If there is a definite fact as to how any given theory should be mapped onto the world, then there is also a fact as to which theories are true and which are false. If we are granted weak externalism, we have no reason to surrender strong externalism.[13]

Notes

1. Following W. V. O. Quine, "On What There Is," in *From a Logical Point of View* (Cambridge, 1953), this point should be put more carefully: the antirealist believes that the relevant predicate has a null extension.

2. It may seem that I have explained realism in such a way as to commit all realists to the existence of such entities as facts of the matter. However, those who do not want to be committed to such entities should be able to offer a paraphrase. For instance, instead of saying that there is a fact of the matter as to whether there are electrons, they might say that the sentence "There are electrons" is either true or false. If no paraphrase is available, this will force the realist to be an existential realist about facts of the matter, but I will not pursue this issue in the present paper.

3. Putnam stresses this point throughout his work; one glaring example is in his comments on reductionism in *Reason, Truth and History* (New York, 1981), 56–57. Henceforth I will cite this text in the body of the paper, referring to it as *RTH*.

4. Actually, the weak externalism that I will defend requires only that there be an unconceptualized world—a way things are independent of how we conceptualize them—it does not require that there be any description of the unconceptualized world. Hence, it does not satisfy Putnam's definition of externalism. For all that Putnam says against externalism, he may still accept my so-called weak externalism. In "Putnam's Paradox," *Australasian Journal of Philosophy* 62 (September 1984): 231–32, David Lewis points out that Putnam's attack, even if it were successful against the theory that Putnam calls 'externalism' or 'metaphysical realism', would leave much of "traditional realism" unscathed. In denying Putnam's first premise, I agree with Lewis.

The crucial point of my paper is that accepting weak externalism undermines Putnam's argument against the strong externalism that he intends to attack.

5. *Meaning and the Moral Sciences* (Boston, 1978), 125. Henceforth I will cite this text in the body of the paper, referring to it as *MMS*.

6. This sort of "skeptical argument" can be used in support of internalism if some kind of verificationism is accepted as a premise. But Putnam intends to be arguing for verificationism, so he cannot appeal to it in his argument.

7. *Realism and Truth* (Princeton, N.J., 1984), 15.

8. See, for instance, Alvin Goldman, *Epistemology and Cognition* (Cambridge, 1986).

9. See, for instance, Peter Klein, *Certainty, A Refutation of Skepticism* (Minneapolis, 1981).

10. See William P. Alston, "Levels-Confusions in Epistemology," *Midwest Studies in Philosophy* 5 (1980): 135–50.

11. In "Realism and the Renegade Putnam: A Critical Study of *Meaning and the Moral Sciences*," *Nous* 17 (1983): 298, Devitt writes, "What the realist needs to say is that *at any point* in our theorizing, even at the point of the ideal theory T1, we can stand back from our theory and raise epistemic and semantic questions. The answer to these questions will be further theory from which we can also stand back."

12. Ibid, 298–99, and Lewis, "Putnam's Paradox," 225–26.

13. My thanks to Harold I. Brown, Paul Hrycaj, Peter Unger, and especially Hilary Kornblith.

Metaphysical Internalism, Selves, and the Invisible Noumenon (A Frego-Kantian Reflection on Descartes's *Cogito*)

HECTOR-NERI CASTAÑEDA

1. MODEST TRANSCENDENTAL REALISM: THE *COGITO*, THE BALLOON, AND THE TRUE

The most radical forms of skepticism force us into Metaphysical Internalism. This is, very roughly, the view that all thought and talk about the world and the reality underlying it are internal to experience, whatever reality may be in itself beyond experience, indeed, even if there is no reality beyond experience.

The world we encounter might certainly be all illusory, exhausted in its own appearance. Our lives could be coherent hallucinations created by an Evil Demon. Each of us could be a brain in a cask, perversely, or happily, manipulated by a clever experimenting scientist. I might have always been just an immobile, computerlike artifact at the center of a huge spaceship the likes of which will not yet be dreamed of on earth for centuries, and my experiences and beliefs, piecemeal hallucinatory, could be caused by the interaction of cosmic rays and waves impinging on my electronic parts made of some unfathomable materials.

These are, of course, mere philosophical fantasies. Nevertheless, they are philosophically salutary—if we do not, depressed, stay with them. They can be neither proved nor disproved. Obviously, any argument offered, whether pro or con, if its premises are not inconsistent, can always be rejected by an opponent. The rejection recipe is simple: Choose one premise, claim that *at it* the argument begs the question, and demand a proof of that premise; repeat the procedure for the new argument, and for each of its successors; if, at some round of argumentation, you are tempted by the premises, complement the argument with a modus tollens, and take it as a proof that the least attractive premise is false.[1]

My purpose here is neither argumentative nor dialectical. I am not concerned with building an argument that finally, and conclusively, establishes radical skepticism. I immediately surrender to Descartes's nondemonstrative hyperbolic techniques of doubt. Thus, obversely, I desire NOT to engage in a refutation of radical skepticism to secure the metaphysical basis for our daily living. Radical skepticism is cathartic: It *can* be treated optimistically: In the final analysis, it must be swallowed whole in one gulp and then allowed to do its job in oblivion. (But I understand the manifold passions for professional skepticism.) My aim here is hermeneutical and constructive, namely, to subject the phenomenon of radical skepticism to exegesis in order to distill the deep reality-content of the world in which we find ourselves.

Most of us do not believe the skeptical arguments. But are we justified in supposing that there is a reality beyond, and underlying, experience?

The mere affirmative answer to this question is *Minimal Transcendental Realism*. It is compatible with Metaphysical Internalism. As I interpret Kant, his Copernican Revolution is his adoption of Metaphysical Internalism. Some philosophers would say "antirealism"; this expression is, however, not adequately descriptive. Kantian terminology, albeit archaic and tainted with the suggestions and images of Kant's own views, is more apt: Radical skepticisms strangle our complacency with transcendent metaphysics and thrust us into transcedental idealism. The outcome is that, with the exception of the account of what he calls the problematic noumenon, we are limited to do, as I have sometimes called it, phenomenological ontology.[2] His claim that, properly speaking, we have only a *negative* concept of the noumenon is his endorsement of Minimal Transcendental Realism.[3]

According to Metaphysical Internalism, I must not try to break my possibly nonexisting head attempting to beat the skeptical arguments: I must yield to the deepest skeptical doubts and concede that all my experiences could, in principle and in fact, be illusory. I must, then, turn to inside experience and follow Leibniz's internalist advice,[4] making my problem that of understanding the contents and the structure of the experienced world, however illusory these may be. I must understand them from *inside*, not from without, as God may see them; even the skepticism of the past, whether composed of events in the external world or of speech acts that have a semantic unit across time, should be granted, and acknowledge that the past is posited within the bounds of present experience.

Enter Minimal Realism. We fasten to a minimal transcendent-pointing framework—we may call it *transcendental*—within which we must vicariously and holistically connect our experiences to a reality beyond merely pointed to. Within the structures of that framework, we can posit a hierarchical quilted world with varying degrees of uncertainty. By fastening to those posits, we can live our autobiographies with variegated degrees of limited certainty. Happiness? It must lie somewhere in the interaction of those posits and the succession of our experiences.

Minimal Realism is indispensable if the whole of experience is not to become lost in a total circle of fiction. Clearly, a character in a fictional story may be said to engage in, say, skeptical doubts concerning the possibility of an Evil Demon who deceives him at every thought. But the character is *said* to do that, he does not *actually* do anything. This difference spans the difference between literature, or science fiction, and artificial intelligence. Thus, when I (whatever I may really be) engage in that reflection, I indeed *engage* in it. More generally, as Descartes pointed out (at the beginning of his second *Meditation*), regardless of how much the Evil Demon may deceive me, he cannot deceive me about two things: (i) that I think, and (ii) that I am having such and such thoughts. These are for real.

(D.2) But I am persuaded that there is nothing in the world. . . . But [I have supposed] there is an I don't know what that deceives, too powerful and too cunning, who uses all his skills to deceive me always. Then there is no doubt that I exist, if he deceives me, and that regardless of how much he deceives me to the full extent of his wish, he will never be able to make me nothing, as long as I *think* that I am something [whatsoever mistaken this thought may be]. This way then, after thinking attentively, having examined all these matters carefully, it is necessary to end [conclude], and to record as a constant [i.e., as an unchangeable truth] this proposition *I am, I exist*, which is necessarily true whenever I assert it, or I conceive it in my mind.

This is the end of Descartes's methodological, nondemonstrative doubt. He was making several connected points.

First, in (D.2) Descartes is remarking that we can conceive all alleged truths about the external world to form an exhaustive set or whole, which I will hereafter call *The Balloon*, and, further, that the arguments for radical skepticism put the doubter in a position of transgressing all particular experiences in which she deals with parts of the world, in order to transact with the world as a whole, thinking The Balloon, so that the situation can be depicted thus:

(1) I think that (The Balloon).

In other words, Descartes was making a wholesale application—of the sort Kant would have called "transcendental"—of Kant's general *I-think* principle: "It must be possible for the 'I think' to accompany all my representations" (Kant 1781, B131).

Second, Descartes in (D.2) observes that the Evil Demon can make me doubt The Balloon in its entirety, the whole of it, and, distributively, each part of it. But the prefix *I think that*, hereafter called (in Kantian style) the *transcendental prefix*, is beyond doubt. Therefore, its components, which we shall henceforth call the transcendental *Thinking I* and the transcendental *Think*, reach metaphysical rock bottom. Of course, it is part of that rock bottom that the *Think* has The Balloon as its total tail, whether this is wholly illusory or not, and that on particular occasions of customary thinking certain parts of The Balloon will function as partial tails of my thinking. The Balloon may be a fiction, but that I exist thinking The Balloon or parts thereof is NOT a fiction. Hence,

(mTR*) There is a minimal transcendent dimension of experience underlying what is thought through the transcendental Thinking I.

Third, a crucial point Descartes makes in (D.2) is that the certainty of *cogito* (I think-I exist) is NOT the certainty of a deduction. As he well knew and insisted all along, his search for a fundamental certainty cannot be derived from anything else. The certainty of the *cogito* is fundamental because it is the terminal certainty of his quest. He makes deductions: His skeptical arguments are deductions and generalizations; but the proceedings culminate with reflections on the role of the Evil Demon's deception or the wholesale illusion of experience for whatever causes. These reflections are doings and they conclude, that is, end up, with the doubter's *metaphysical-phenomenological grasping* of an ultimate reality — this is the metaphysical aspect of the grasping — that appears — this is the phenomenological aspect — as a thinking I confronting a whole but perhaps wholly empty world, including the I's own embodiments in that world.

Fourth, the transcendental I of the methodological doubt exists with certainty only *during* the skeptical experience. Descartes says "with necessity," but it is not clear that by 'necessary' he means, etymologically, nonceasing, that is, constant, which is another word he uses. The doubter's existence as well as his or her thinking are constant parameters during the whole skeptical proceedings. In any case, Descartes leaves it, in (D.2), quite open that the transcendental I of a particular skeptical experience may vanish when the experience ends, that if the experience is repeated, the transcendental I's involved may be entirely different.

This brings us to a *fifth* crucial point that pervades (D.2) throughout, which Descartes did not appreciate fully — at least he did not dwell upon it as fully as he should have done. The point is that the I on which the hyperbolic doubt concludes is not internal to The Balloon. That is why Kant called it *transcendental*, transcending The Balloon without being transcendent in the sense of being beyond experience, that is, the experience of the methodological hyperbolic doubt. That I is beyond the world in The Balloon, and it is all of reality as this can be grasped in that encompassing doubt. Hence, the empirical I's within The Balloon may be different from the transcendental I thinking of them as the same as itself inside The Balloon.

Descartes did not savor fully the nonworldliness of the transcendental I of his *cogito*. Having realized that the *cogito* ended with an existent, but with no content, aside from facing a whole world of experience, he hastened to ask *what am I* ? But this question involved a tremendously important, though apparently insignificant, shift of sense and referent in his new use of the little word 'I' (or 'je' and 'ego'). This question is NOT the question about the transcendental I that thinks The Balloon. This latter question would ask about the structures connecting the transcendental I without and The Balloon within or as the accusative of the transcendental Think. Descartes's question, on the other hand, is about *an I within The Balloon*.

We must ask the unasked question and then try to fill in an account of the connection between the nonworldly transcendental I and the many I's within The Balloon.[5]

Now, the *cogito* possesses a second dimension of transcendental realism. It has to do with the transcendental *thinking* of The Balloon. The thinking of The Balloon is also externally real, as real can be, indeed *thinking* as such is the internal, experienced manifestation of whatever it may be in the reality beyond, which underlies experience. Thinking *is* itself a real representing—whatever this may ultimately really be—of a perhaps empty representation of a hallucinatory world.

Moreover, in the reality beyond experience lies the source, the *transcendent source*, of the thinking of what is thought in The Balloon. The nature of that source is, of course, at the level of the radical skepticism of the Evil Demon, as unknowable as the transcendent self underlying the transcendental I. For instance, according to the Evil Demon "hypothesis," the transcendent source is the Demon's network of deceptive operations; according to the Clever Scientist "hypothesis," the Scientist's manipulations; in the case of the self-propelled isolated computer or brain, it is the electric or physicochemical activity inside the computer or brain. To be sure, wilder hypotheses come forth with their own unknown transcendent sources. In particular, the self-propelled computer shows that the transcendent self may be at the core of the transcendent source. We include both dimensions of transcendence under the heading of Minimal Transcendental Realism. Of course, none of these so-called hypotheses is a genuine hypothesis. They are nothing but suggestive analogies of how noumenal reality could be conceptualized within our experiential resources; there is absolutely nothing to elicit a preference for one over the others. This total parity concerning their validity shows (as Kant well knew) that once we recognize the force of radical skepticism, we must simply aquiesce in the ineffability of the underlying reality.

Two additional aspects of transcendence must yet be latched on to Minimal Transcendental Realism.

To begin with, The Balloon is precisely what may be wholly illusory. Yet it also has a two-directional dimension of transcendence. On one direction, it has a transcendent source. At worst, exactly the same transcendent source of my *thinking* The Balloon is also the very same source of my thinking *the contents* of The Balloon. On the other direction, there is an internal pointing to transcendent reality within the experiences inside, composing The Balloon. The fundamental *attitude* we must take toward the world is that of transcendent realism. We must live our ordinary experiences as if normally what we experience is real beyond them. Any questioning stops the natural flow of one's autobiographical living; it may, of course, start a stream of philosophizing. After all, the metaphysical possibility of error does not affect the order of experiences. We simply take—and must take—it for granted in our basic daily experiences that we are not the toys of an Evil Demon or the thinking gadgets of a clever scientist, or the accidental connivance of we do not know what that causes us to have wholly illusory experiences.

Second, experience is hierarchical. We ascertain within it different layers of *irreality*. We have within our experiences of The Balloon what we call simple illusions, misperceptions, delusions; we distinguish within experience tiers of fiction: original fiction, and fiction created within fiction, and so on, and variegated mixtures of so-called reality and fiction. These hierarchies of internal nonreality presuppose a *ground floor* of The Balloon on which we set them up.

The metaphysical doubt is, in effect, the overall doubt about the ground floor we need. This is the realm of physical objects orderly interacting in spacetime. It is this ground floor of The Balloon that we take in our naive attitude to be real in the strongest metaphysical sense. Thus, our transcendental pointings of our naive attitude are pointings to the reality beyond experience of the ground floor. The metaphysical doubt is, in effect and essence, a sweeping doubt about the physical ground floor of The Balloon. It succeeds, its polemical tone aside, in establishing that the customarily unquestioned ground floor taken for granted in daily living is not logically or mathematically secure.

Notwithstanding, still, within the morals of what Descartes taught us, each of us can affirm a transcendental experience of radical skepticism:

(Di*) Regardless of how much Evil Demon, the Mad Scientist, or the Reality Beyond may deceive me, it cannot make me doubt that I need a ground floor of believed content of experience at the basis of, and inside, The Balloon, through which I point in every act of thinking the contents of that ground floor to the transcendent reality underlying experience holistically.

Doubtless, here we still lack metaphysical certainty about transcendent reality. We merely acquire an *ontologico-epistemological* dimension of realism: Experience rests on a fundamental transcendental, taking for granted both that it has a ground floor and that, so to speak, each placing of a tile on that ground floor, through the rehearsal of a belief about physical reality, is a pointing to the reality beyond experience.

The transcendental *Thinking I* and the transcendental *Think* deliver pointings to transcendent reality. They deliver transcendent reality as target, so to speak, as blindly and merely hooked at the ends of their long harpoons. The Balloon delivers a network of pointings. For instance, each perception we take to be veridical, each belief we come to adopt considering it to be true, is a pointing in the direction of transcendent reality. The pointing is, continuing to use Kant's jargon, transcendental: It reveals that something lies beyond, but it does not reveal *what* it intrinsically is.

What the transcendental *Thinking I* harpoons and what the transcendental *Think* harpoons may, for all we can ever *really* know, BE one and the very *same* thing. That same thing is precisely what, in constructing The Balloon, we may be pointing to. Indeed, we can say very little more than this about transcendent reality. It is of the utmost importance to appreciate that as far as we can consider it, it is an INDIVISIBLE WHOLE. As Kant remarked about his negative problematic concept of the noumenon, it is so far beyond our experience that even calling *it* "it" is already too presumptuous, if we do not dissociate from this use of 'it' semantic contrasts that give it its meaning – for example, its being a singular pronoun; of course, the plural 'they' is by far much more misleading.

Frege appreciated well Kant's insight into the noumenon. He understood deeply both the holistic role of the noumenon in the total unified experience of the world at large and its iterative role in the piecemeal transcendental pointings to it in each of our believings. In each claim of truth we make we point holistically to the problematic noumenon, and for us then the only-blindly pointable transcendent reality is what underlies and undergirds the undifferentiated *The True*, which Frege postulated as the ultimate indivisible convergent referent of all true propositions. Propositions, or Thoughts, are internally to experience what they really are, and when we take them to be true, we represent to ourselves a GUISE of a small part of The True. But there is no reason to suppose that that part is a transcendent part of The True. *Frege's The True is inside experience the fundamental internal guise of the Kantian noumenon.*[6]

We have discussed three several-pronged, transcendental dimensions of the transcendental prefix. Together we shall call these *Modest Transcendental Realism*. Patently:

(MI.Mr*) Modest Transcendental Realism is compatible with Metaphysical Internalism and anchors it to transcendent reality (The True, the Whole Indivisible Problematic Noumenon).

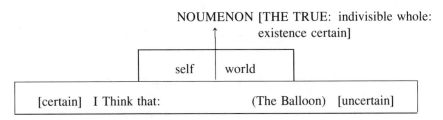

2. THE ONTOLOGICAL SEMANTIC DIMENSION OF ORDINARY WORDS

The three aspects of the noumenon, subsumed under Modest Transcendental Realism, are about all we can say concerning transcendent reality. From there on, everything we can say will have to be *internal* to the complex:

(1)   I Think (The Balloon).

In particular, the vocabulary for making reality claims — for example, first-order mechanisms like existentially meant verbal inflections and words like 'exists' and 'really', as well as second-order mechanisms like 'true' — have full-fledged metaphysical applications only as allowed by Modest Transcendental Realism. That is, these words serve their speakers to *perform* metaphysical pointings to The True, but their meaning consists of their essentially internalistic, or phenemenological use.

In the most common, internalistic, use of the word, reality is the ground floor of The Balloon, in particular, the physical world. The Balloon, of course, includes much more. As we observed, it has a hierarchical structure: reality or brute facts at the bottom, our experiences thereof, and the diverse tiers of nonfacts or nonreality above – illusions, hallucinations, dreams, conjectures, unverified hypotheses, intentions, unrealized plans, obligations, unfulfilled duties, fiction, and so on.

The ordinary vocabulary of natural languages for claims about reality has an *ontological semantic dimension*. Ordinary reality claims are about the ground floor of the world we confront in experience. Each making of a reality claim includes a pointing in the direction of transcendent reality as well as a positing of a part of the ground floor, and carries with it the suggestion that what is so posited may, in fact, be itself in, or have a counterpart in, The True beyond. To illustrate, while being deceived by the Mad Scientist, I distinguish between my veridical perceptions and my dreams, and from both my imagined situations and my creation of pieces of fiction. By claiming that my perceptions are *veri*dical, I am claiming, *internalistically*, that the acquired perceptual content belongs to the ground floor of the totality of my experienced contents, to the (internalistically) real world, namely, the ground floor of The Balloon. Underlying this internalistic claim of reality is the deeply seated *taking it for granted* that there is *beyond* a noumenon, which is somehow responsible both for my having the perceptions in question and for these possessing the content they have.

3. THE FIVEFOLD ONTOLOGICAL DIMENSIONS OF CERTAINTY

Reflection on the Evil Demon challenge, or on its alternatives, has unveiled two dimensions of *cogito* certainty:

(a) The *metaphysical* certainty of the three aspects of Modest Transcendental Realism: This is a wholly existential and contentually unspecific knowledge that there is simply a reality, to which we can point as a whole in every experience, which underwrites the metaphysical fact that there is experience of a (perhaps wholly illusory) world, and which is directly but blindly harpooned by the Thinking I (whatever and however this may in itself be).

(b) The *ontological* or *semi-internalistic* certainty that the transcendental Thinking I of the radical doubt exists confronting, even surrounding, the world, indeed The whole Balloon, with its Thinking.

A quick reminiscence suffices to remind us that The Balloon may very well contain, so to say, its local I's. There are inside The Balloon many first-person propositions (possible states of affairs, thought contents) like the following:

(B1) I am shorter than Robert Sleigh, Jr.

(B2) I feel a pain on my neck.

(B3) I read Sellars's *Science and Metaphysics* many years ago.

The Evil Demon may definitely sweep away (B1)-(B3) with its tornado of doubt. My height and my eyes, Sleigh and Sellars, my neck and Sellars's book, all might be mere figments of my imaginings forced by the Evil Demon. Can He make me believe that I have a pain that does not exist? Here I want to set this question aside. Here is something of much greater importance. This is I. Can the Evil Demon mislead me about me, that is, I as I appear in (B1)-(B3), *inside* The Balloon? We have grasped the indubitability of the I without The Balloon, which doubts (B1)-(B3) and the rest of The Balloon. But here we have local, internal (empirical) I's. *If* these I's are the SAME in some strong sense of 'sameness' as the Thinking I of the transcendental prefix of (1), then the certainty of the Thinking I spills over into The Balloon over the local I's. Hence, if so, two further dimensions of certainty surface:

(c) The *metaphysico-ontological* or *trans-internalistic* certainty that the local I's in The Balloon are also anchored to transcendent reality.

(d) The *phenomenological* or *internalistic* certainty that within the domain of the appearances constitutive of The Balloon, the local I's in The Balloon are on the ontological ground floor of The Balloon: The ultimacy of the reality of the transcendental I supports The Balloon, and this support also spills over the local I's and disperses throughout them. The force of this internalistic certainty is epitomized in the following implication (signaled by the double-stemmed arrow):

(C*.Ex) *Internal Cogito Axiom:*

S(I) $\implies$ I exist

where 'S(I)' is any sentence in direct speech, containing uses of the indexical first-person pronoun signaled by 'I'.[7]

This ground floor, dispersed existential certainty of the transcendental I, requires the certainty of the embodiment of those local I's, that is:

(e) The *phenomenological* or *internalistic* certainty that every local I in The Balloon must be tied down to, that is, must be the *same* as, a ground floor resident of the world, that is, a resident so chained by the structure of the world that it cannot leave The Balloon. Such a native resident of the world is, of course, a natural victim of the radical skepticism of the Evil Demon. Thus, here again, we find the certainty of the phenomenological necessity of *there being* something in the ground floor, but not the certainty or necessity of anything in the ground floor that realizes or embodies any local I.

4. SELVES, I-GUISES, AND THE MULTIFARIOUS SEMIOTICS OF FIRST-PERSON REFERENCE

According to (c) the I's in The Balloon have a full-fledged transcendent existence, (but, to be sure, unspecifiable in transcendent content) — provided that, and to the extent that, they are the *same* as the Thinking I of the transcendental prefix. This proviso needs attentive examination. Undoubtedly, from the mere linguistic fact that we have the same mark 'I' in (B1)-(B3), it follows neither that the three occurrences of 'I' are used to think the very same entity, nor that what they denote is exactly the same as what the word 'I' denotes in the transcendental prefix of (1). The issue is *not* that different persons may be uttering (B1)-(B3). We are assuming that there is a personal unity of reflection, experience, and world throughout this meditation. In a general sense all the uses of 'I' that we are considering are uses of the first-person pronoun by the same ordinary person. In that sense, we assume that they all are uses by that speaker to refer to the same entity. But obviously, there is more to the thinking reference of the speaker than that general sameness. The meditation occurs in the first person, for the first person, and all the samenesses that the thinker-speaker does not know are unavailable to her. Yet her thoughts have a definite content. Thus, by using the first-person pronoun, the speaker is somehow referring to an entity — which in *some* sense, loudly crying out for analysis, is, of course, the *same* as the speaker. Besides all that, which may be inaccessible to her, she is thinking of an entity *as* a thinker of such thoughts in such and such circumstances. And this makes an enormous difference. For instance, the thinker engaged in the transcendental meditation responds to the brain-in-the-cask "hypothesis" without any assumption of her being embodied; the thinker that thinks (B1) to be probably true must perforce be embodied; the thinker thinking (B3) must think of himself as having a history. This raises a serious question about the sense of diachronic identity between I's.

Let us say that an entity conceived *as* in some way or other is a *gross individual guise*. We may say that a gross individual guise is an ordered pair (x, G), where x is conceived as, *qua*, the G. Applying this idea to the I's, we have been considering, let us introduce some terminological order. We call each I thought of in a given unitary propositional text pertaining to the ground floor of The Balloon an *empirical gross I-guise*. Temporarily, let us conceive the unitary manifolds of such gross I-guises as somehow constituting entities to be called *empirical selves*.

The metaphysical certainty of one's own existence is the assurance that there *exists* something problematic, unspecifiable, beyond experience, which underlies one's own uses of the first-person pronoun. These uses are semiotically complex. The uses of 'I' in the transcendental prefix *I Think* in (1) have at least the five crucial roles we pass on to discuss.

First, 'I' in (1) represents a successful gesture of *pointing to* the transcendent self.

Second, 'I' *depicts* in the context of sentence (1) the semi-internalistic role of the Thinking I vis-à-vis The Balloon. To think proposition (1) is to think of oneself as without The Balloon; yet this *without* is not a transcendent 'without'. The I-Thinking-that in (1) is apprehended in (1) as at the boundary of The Balloon, and it is *internalizable* by its being thought of within a larger Balloon:

(2) I Think that {I think that (The Balloon)}).

In proposition (2), we have the Extended Balloon: { *I think that (The Balloon)* }. This process is iterative with no end. This iterativity makes it clear that the Thinking I is already in (1) a Thought-of I. In a sense, then, the true Thinking I is the *unthought of* I, which thinks (1), or (2), or any other more emcompassing proposition of this sort. The iterative embedding of (1) or its successors in a more emcompassing Extended Balloon merely introduces *another* thought-of I, thus, revealing by adumbration a semi-internalistic, inexhaustible reservoir of Thinking I's from which Thinking-Thought-of I's can be extracted. Let us call that inexhaustible reservoir the *transcendental I.*

This brings in a *third* role of the first-person pronoun 'I' in (1) and (2): Also semi-internalistically, each use of 'I' points to the internalizability of the transcendental I, or rather, to its sliceability in Thinking-Thought-of slices (hereafter called *transcendental gross I-guises*) that can be internalized in Extended Balloons.

A *fourth* role of depiction by the first-person pronoun in (1) is this: The internal inexhaustibility of the transcendent I is an internal representation within (extended) experience of the inaccessibility of the transcendent self.

Fifth, as already noted, the 'I' in the transcendental prefix of (1) anchors the uses of 'I' to denote an empirical self within The Balloon.

The structure of the internalistic certainty of the empirical I's includes the substructures of indexical reference in general. Referring to oneself *qua* oneself as in the midst of the world is to refer as such to a thinker as *presently* involved in the very experience of making the referring in question.

The nonworldliness of the transcendental I infects the empirical I's. But we cannot go into this here. Furthermore, first-person reference is just one case of demonstrative or indexical reference to items that are presented or present in an experience, which is lived through the very structure of the references in question. Therefore, to understand fully the structure of the internalistic certainty of one's existence, it is necessary to place the psycholinguistic phenomenon of first-person reference within the context of its general type of *indexical reference.* Additional aspects of the semantics of the first-person pronoun become crucial. And the nonworldliness of the I's turn out to be hand in hand with the nonworldliness of the strict denotata of all other indexical references.[8]

5. THE I-MANIFOLD; STRICT SEMANTIC DENOTATION VERSUS DOXASTIC DENOTATION

We have encountered a somewhat bewildering multiplicity of entities at the end of the semantics of the first-person pronoun. We have also felt pressure for some sort of identification among them. Here we cannot tackle the problem in full. If we yield to the pressure for indentification, we find a long, impressive array of equations. We deliberately formulate them by means of the problematic word 'same', intending to pose a problem at it. To begin with, we have, where for convenience the adjective 'gross' is left tacit:

Ontological Unity of the World of a Given Subject:

(TI.TI*)   Each transcendental I-guise, that is, each Thinking-Thought-of I, is *the same as* its corresponding transcendental I.

(TI.TI*.1) I [Thinking an Extended Balloon] am *the same as* my (semi-internalistically) underlying transcendental I.

Metaphysical Anchoring of Experience:

(MA*) The transcendental I is *the same as* its transcendent self [which underlies from beyond experience its thinking a Balloon].

By equation (TI.TI*) all the members of the iterative infinite sequence of Extended Balloons have the unity of one and the same underlying unthought-of transcendental self. Since each Extended Balloon thought of is explicitly encompassed by a transcendental I-guise, (TI.TI*) derivatively unifies both the Balloons and the possible experiences of a given subject. Equation (MA*) is, by contrast, a *metaphysical*, trans-semi-internalistic principle tying the knowable world of experience to the (problematic, indivisible) noumenon.

Moving into The Balloon we find the *empirical I-guises*. Here, again, positing a unity of reference is the simplest and most straightforward justification of the use of the first-person pronoun. We postulate:

Internalistically, within The Balloon:

(Ei.ES*) Each empirical I-guise is *the same as* the empirical self.

Semi-internalistically, a Bridge between the Prefix and The Balloon:

(Ti.Ei*) Each transcendental I-guise [of the prefix], is *the same as* each of the empirical I-guises [in its corresponding Balloon].

(TI.ES*) Each transcendental I *is the same as* the empirical self it encompasses.

Some of these equations can be derived from others by the transitivity of sameness, but this is part of the problem. Also by transitivity, (Ei.ES*) identifies all the empirical I-guises. This requires investigation concerning the unity and identity of empirical selves across time. Equations (Ei.ES*) and (TI.ES*) raise, and are contributions to, the fundamental problem of the synchronic unity of an I.

By the above equations, all the uses of the first-person pronoun captured in (1), (2), and (B1)-(B3), from the perspective of one person, denote the same everywhere. This cries out for elucidation.

As we have pointed out, we are considering entities as they are thought of and referred to by a thinker putting her world together after the skeptical devastation brought about by the Mad Scientist, or the Evil Demon. Thus, we found the thinker thinkingly referring to individual guises. If that thinker's thinking is deployed or embodied in language, then there is a *fundamental semantic dimension* in which the *strict semantico-pragmatic denotations* of the thinker's terms are precisely what the thinker refers to, namely, individual guises. Otherwise, the terms are not capable of carrying the thinker's thoughts. If the terms in question gain their denotation in the pragmatic context of use, then these, as they exist in the thinker's psycholinguistic speech habits, do not have a denotation. Their general meaning is, then, a schema to be filled in by the pragmatics of the context of use. (In more fashionable jargon: The general meaning of a term is only a function that assigns a function of the context that assigns a denotation to the term.)

We must, therefore, distinguish different ways in which a proffered singular term, or the corresponding mental content it overtly represents, can be said to refer to, or aim at, its denotata. Here we are concerned with the referential uses of the first-person pronoun. Clearly, then, each token of 'I' *strictly (semantico-pragmatically) denotes* an I-guise being thought of; it *mediately denotes doxastically* the transcendental I, by virtue of being part of an expression of thought that *occurs* within a network of beliefs, which includes the assumption of a unity of the thinker's experience; and it *points to*, or *most mediately denotes doxastically*, the transcendent self—which in the naive attitude of daily living is not even conceived, but underwrites the naive realism of daily attitude.

6. THE VARIEGATED SAMENESS IN THE I-NETWORK

The above principles establish, but only programmatically, subject to an acoming theory, the unity across the I-manifold. That theory has to deal with the problems mentioned, as well as with others. For instance, by the transitivity of sameness, the preceding equations also imply:

(TS.Ei)   The transcendent self [BEYOND the inexhaustive transcendental prefix] is *the same as* any empirical I-guise [IN The Balloon].

This contains an important grain of truth, namely, the one that underlies the dimension of certainty (c) described earlier. But (TS.Ti) must not be understood as transferring the properties of an empirical I-guise to the transcendent self—the noumenon. This is precisely Descartes's error in his *Second Meditation* when he derives from the certainty of the *cogito* that he is a transcendent mental substance. Pointing out this error is the main task of Kant's "Paralogisms."

We must, consequently, interpret (TS.Ei) in such a way that the sameness it proclaims is *not* strict identity. Since (TS.Ei) is a consequence of the previous equations, there is at least one sameness in the latter that is not strict identity.

Having differentiated sameness from strict identity, we need a general account of identity, sameness, predication, and guises. *One* such account, built on the distinctions drawn between strict semantico-pragmatic reference and doxastic reference and pointings-to, can be found in Guise Theory.[9] Since we are now dealing with the structures inside The Balloon, we may stop this round of investigation. Perhaps one small appendix may not be amiss to round out our discussion.

7. THE TRANSCENDENTAL PREFIX AND EXPERIENCE

Our reaction to the Evil Demon hypothesis followed Descartes in considering the whole world and experience, The Balloon, encompassed by Kant's transcendental prefix *I think*. This is, however, a serious error, for as Descartes himself had casually shown, the Kantian prefix is only a fragment of the relevant prefix, to wit: *I think now*. This is, to be sure, at the heart of Descartes's claim that thinking and extension are two distinct attributes characteristic, respectively, of the mental and material substances. A comprehensive study of indexical reference suggests that the true transcendental prefix is, therefore, the extended one: *I think here now*. By the same Cartesian considerations that led Descartes to the indubitability of the doubting I, we reach the indubitability of both the *now* and the *here* of the doubting. Those considerations are simply that all doubts, regardless of how radical they may be, can always be imprisoned in the subordinated Balloon, and in so doing, a new transcendental prefix *I think here now* springs forth at every turn:

I think here now that (I think here now that [. . . The Balloon] . . .).

We may speak here of the extended *cogito* and of the indubitability of the transcendetal *I-Here-Now*'s.

This extended *cogito* is Cartesian only in structure. Its contents are anti-Cartesian. For one thing, it provides only an I that exists in time and in space. For another, there is the problem of transferring the transcendental *I-Here-Now*'s into The Balloon and determining the sense, scope, and laws of the different sameness relations connecting the transcendental times and places with their empirical counterparts, and those between the empirical counterparts themselves. Patently, we need the Guise Theory of times and places to go hand in hand with that of the I-guises and selves, and of physical objects.

Kant would have insisted against Descartes that extended transcendental prefix delivers only an *I*, and that we must add a *here* and a *now* from inside experience. The question arises in relation to Kant: Does the fact that a transcendent reality underwrites the transcendental I-Now guises also extend, first, to there being in the noumenon something like time (duration, or becoming, as Bergson suggested)? If so, is there in the noumenon something like space that underlies the Here-component of the extended transcendental I-Here-Now guises? Of course, Kant might have, on the one hand, resisted recognition of the extended transcendental I-Here-Now guises. On the other hand, he would have insisted that, although his official theory about the limits of knowledge precluded knowledge claims about the noumenon beyond its negative concept, his official epistemology and philosophy of mind made ample room for *metaphysical faith* — just as they did for theologico-religious faith. Thus, *unofficially*, one can believe — without knowledge — that the noumenon is this or that, indeed, that it is exactly as science and intersubjective experience tell us the phenomenal world is.

Notes

1. For details see Castaneda 1984.

2. In the context of developing a material and experiential semantics for ordinary language, I contrasted transcendent metaphysics with phenomenological ontology in Castaneda 1974. The proposed phenomenological ontology-semantics was later on called Guise Theory.

3. See Kant 1963, Preface to the Second Edition, A286ff, B287ff.

4. Leibniz 1690. He formulated his Internalism as follows: "Indeed, even if this whole life were said to be only a dream, and the visible world only a phantasm, I should call this dream or this phantasm real enough if we were never [internally] deceived by it when we make good use of reason." (Loemker 1976, p. 364.)

5. Descartes should have moved the rest of *Meditation* II beginning with its fourth paragraph to *Meditation* IIbis. What follows above in the main body of the essay is one (anachronistic) way of furnishing the "missing' part of what "should" have been *Meditation* II.

6. See Frege 1892.

7. Descartes is not denying (C*.Ex) when he replies to Gassendi:

For when you say that I could have indifferently concluded the same thing [that I exist] from each one of my other actions, you seriously misinterpret me, for there is nothing in them of which I can be entirely certain, that is the metaphysical certainty which is the only one at issue here, except thinking. For, for example, THIS INFERENCE WOULD NOT BE SOUND: *I walk, therefore, I exist*, if only the interior knowledge that I have is of a thinking episode, from which alone the conclusion follows. (at the end of section I of the third response to the Fifth Objections to the *Meditations* capitals are mine.)

Descartes is merely pointing out that at the transcendental level of the methodological hyperbolic doubt, the premise of the quoted inference is false, hence, an unsound transcendental argument. The inference is, of course, valid, and internalistically sound if the premise is true.

8. For a preliminary treatment of these matters see Castaneda 1981. For a sustained discussion of the self see Castaneda 1987, and for a most comprehensive of indexical reference see Castaneda 1982, 1988. See also the studies by Robert M. Adams, John Perry, and the replies to them in Tomberlin 1983, and the studies by Esa Saarinen and by David W. Smith in Tomberlin 1986.

9. For an account of Guise Theory, criticisms of it, and responses, see the essays by Alvin Plantinga, Romane Clark, and replies to them in Tomberlin 1983; the studies by Jay Rosenberg, David W. Smith, Jefrey Sicha, and replies to them in Tomberlin 1986; see also Tomberlin 1984 and subsequent reply.

References

Castañeda, Hector-Neri. 1974. "Thinking and the Structure of the World." *Philosophia* 4 (1974): 4–40. Also in *Critica* 6–18 (1972): 43–81.

Castañeda, Hector-Neri. 1981. "The Semiotic Profile of Indexical (Experiential) Reference." *Synthese* 49 (1981): 275–316.

Castañeda, Hector-Neri. 1982. *Sprache und Erfahrung: Texte zu einer neuen Ontologie*, translated by Helmut Pape. Frankfurt.

Castañeda, Hector-Neri. 1984. "Philosophical Refutations." In Fetzer 1984.

Castañeda, Hector-Neri. 1987. "The Self and the I-Guises, Empirical and Transcendental." In *Theorie der Subjektivität*, edited by Konrad Cramer, Hans Friedrich Fulda, Rolf-Peter Horstmann, and Ulrich Pothast. Frankfurt.

Castañeda, Hector-Neri. 1988. *Thinking, Language and Experience*. Minneapolis.

Descartes, Rene. 1641. *Meditations*.

Fetzer, James, ed. 1984. *Principles of Philosophical Reasoning*. New Jersey.

Frege, Gottlob. 1892. "Sense and Reference." E.g., in Geach and Black 1980.

144   HECTOR-NERI CASTAÑEDA

Geach, Peter, and Max Black, eds. and transls. 1980. *Translations from the Philosophical Writings of Gottlob Frege*. Oxford.

Kant, Immanuel. 1781. *Critique of Pure Reason*. 1st ed. (2d ed. 1787). Translated by Norman Kemp Smith. London and New York (1969).

Leibniz, Gottfried Wilhelm. 1690. "On the Method of Distinguishing Real from Imaginary Phenomena." in Loemker 1976.

Loemker, Leroy E., ed. and transl. 1976. *Leibniz's Philosophical Papers and Letters*. Dordrecht.

Tomberlin, James E., ed. 1983. *Agent, Language, and the Structure of World*. Indianapolis.

Tomberlin, James E. 1984. "Identity, Intensionality, and Intentionality." *Synthese* 61 (1984): 111–31.

Tomberlin, James E., ed. 1986. *Hector-Neri Castaneda*. Dordrecht.

Internal Realism: Transcendental Idealism?

CURTIS BROWN

I dealism is an ontological view, a view about what sorts of things there are in the universe. Idealism holds that what there is depends on our own mental structure and activity. Berkeley of course held that everything *was* mental; Kant held the more complex view that there was an important distinction between the mental and the physical, but that the structure of the empirical world depended on the activities of minds. Despite radical differences, idealists like Berkeley and Kant share what Ralph Barton Perry called "the cardinal principle of idealism," namely, the principle that "being is dependent on the knowing of it."[1] I believe that Hilary Putnam intends his "internal realism" to be a version of idealism in this broad sense; though many of his arguments concern semantic notions like truth and reference, he takes these arguments to have ontological consequences. This is strongly suggested, for instance, by his claim that " 'objects' themselves are as much made as discovered, as much products of our conceptual invention as of the 'objective' factor in experience."[2] Or again there is this rather Kantian metaphor: "the mind and the world jointly make up the mind and the world."[3] But just what *is* Putnam's ontology?

Putnam has been defending a version of antirealism in his writings of the last several years. He describes his view as "internal realism," where the term "internal" is intended to indicate his rejection of the view he calls "metaphysical realism." Putnam combines internal realism and metaphysical antirealism in something like the way Kant combined empirical realism and transcendental idealism. I would like to investigate here *one* of the numerous lines of thought by means of which Putnam has defended internal realism. The argument I shall focus on is what might be called the "argument from reference." Putnam also has arguments from vagueness, from the nature of truth, and others; I will not discuss these.

It would be interesting to undertake a full-scale investigation of the relations between Kant's transcendental idealism and Putnam's internal realism. Putnam himself invites this comparison by his frequent use of Kantian terminology and his allusions to Kant's work, and indeed the parallels are numerous. Both consider, somewhat uncomfortably, the view that there is an unknowable noumenal world behind the phenomena. Both are motivated in part by the threat of skepticism: Kant by skepticism about our ability to *know* the external world, Putnam by skepticism about our ability to *refer* to it. Both Kant and Putnam hold that the world we know and talk about is empirically real, but both hold also that it is mind-dependent. Putnam at least flirts with the Kantian idea that there are a priori truths about the world.[4] Putnam, like Kant, stresses the pervasive importance of causation, and argues that causation is partly our own imposition on the world.[5] Putnam argues that science presupposes values, in a way reminiscent of Kant's claim that science requires the regulative use of the Ideas of Reason. Like Kant, Putnam argues that the relation between morality and rationality is much closer than empiricists (from Hume to Bentham to the positivists) typically can allow.[6]

I shall not attempt such a full-scale investigation here. My purpose is to discuss one particular issue: Putnam's Kantian response to a kind of skepticism, namely that about the possibility of reference. The paper is in three parts. In section I, I discuss the view that in classifying or organizing the world into objects, we create objects. I explain what I take to be a plausible realist alternative to this view. The remainder of the paper discusses Putnam's reason for rejecting this realist account, namely, his argument that reference to mind-independent objects is impossible. I propose to accept the argument and see what follows from it. If determinate reference to mind-independent objects is impossible, this seems to leave open two possible responses. One might hold that we refer *indeterminately* to mind-independent objects, or that we refer determinately to mind-*dependent* objects. The first view retains a realist ontology at the expense of determinate reference; the second retains determinate reference by adopting an idealist ontology. In section II, I discuss the former possibility, a response Putnam rejects. Putnam claims that this view introduces the problems of Kant's notion of the thing-in-itself; I question this. In section III, I discuss the second response, that we refer determinately to mind-dependent objects. I suggest that this view is actually at least as Kantian in spirit as the one Putnam rejects. I also suggest that it is not clear that this response really succeeds in meeting Putnam's skeptical problem about reference.

I

Let us begin with what we might call "the argument from organization." According to this argument, because our language organizes, selects, categorizes, and classifies things, the things we talk about are not part of the world as it is in itself, but rather are created by us. To be sure, we do not create the raw material out of which we produce objects, but the objects themselves, as opposed to the neutral stuff of the world in itself, are our own creations. If this is correct, then the world we talk about is mind-dependent, and idealism in the broad sense I am concerned with is true.

I do not mean to suggest that Putnam is committed to this argument, at least in the unsophisticated form in which I have just phrased it. But he does say things that suggest it. He writes, for instance, that: " 'Objects' do not exist independently of conceptual schemes. We cut up the world into objects when we introduce one or another scheme of description. Since the objects *and* the signs alike are *internal* to the scheme of description, it is possible to say what matches what."[7] This suggests that if we did not "cut up the world into objects" there would *be* no objects, so that we bring objects into being by organizing the world. Again, Putnam criticizes the view that there are "Self-Identifying Objects," explaining that "this is just what it means to say that the *world*, and not thinkers, sorts things into kinds," and he opposes to this idea the view that " 'objects' are as much made as discovered,"[8] suggesting again that the fact that we organize the world shows that we create objects. To take a final example, Putnam speaks approvingly of the idea "that objects and reference arise out of discourse rather than being prior to discourse."[9]

As Putnam is well aware, similar arguments are common in contemporary thought; one particularly explicit and unapologetic defense of the view may be found in Leszek Kolakowski's "Karl Marx and the Classical Definition of Truth."[10] Kolakowski, as his title suggests, attributes the view to Marx. Just as Putnam criticizes the view that objects are "self-identifying," Kolakowski criticizes "Aristotelian realism, which posits that the species and genera into which the sciences divide reality are merely copies of the genera and species of this reality reflected more or less exactly, but ever more exactly, in the mirror of consciousness."[11] As Putnam says that objects are "as much made as discovered," Kolakowski says things like this: "Nature as composed of separate parts and species is an 'artificial' creation";[12] or again: "In this world the sun and stars come into being because man is able to make them *his* objects";[13] or again: "If, for Marx, man replaces God-the-Creator, still He is not the God of Augustine or Thomas Aquinas, a God who gives birth to the world out of nothingness; rather, He reminds us of the God of the Averroists, who organizes the world out of previously existing material."[14]

In Kolakowski especially, one gets the idea that there are only two possible views. On the one hand there is "Aristotelian realism," which holds that the universe divides itself into a single set of kinds, and that the proper role of language is to copy the world's own single set of divisions, to classify the world in its own way. This seems to be the same view Putnam criticizes in denying that the world contains Self-Identifying Objects. On the other hand, there is Kolakowski's preferred view, which seems also to be Putnam's: that the world "in itself" is *undifferentiated* (he speaks of a "pre-existing 'chaos' "[15]), and that we create objects by inventing classifications. Kolakowski's strategy seems to be to argue that since Aristotelian realism is false, his own version of antirealism must be correct.

Now if this were the antirealist's only argument that the world is mind-dependent (as in fact it seems to be Kolakowski's only argument), the realist could quite plausibly assert that it simply is not good enough. One can grant that it is false that the world has one true classification or division into objects and kinds of objects without granting that it has *no* organization of its own. A *modest* realist might well say that the world has infinitely many classifications, that it contains infinitely many different kinds of objects. Such a moderate realist could say that when we develop a language we are not imposing an organization on the world, but selecting one of the world's organizations for our own use. On this view the world "in itself" has *more* objects than we usually talk about, not fewer.

Modest realism shares with Putnam and Kolakowski an emphasis on the importance of human activity in determining what sorts of things we will be most concerned with, but, if accepted, makes unnecessary the idealistic view that in dividing up the world we are somehow populating our world with objects that were not there before.

But this is not the end of the matter. Kolakowski, as far as I can tell, simply does not consider modest realism. Or it may even be that he *accepts* modest realism, and that his talk of "creating" objects carries no really antirealist implications but is only a metaphorical way of expressing a modestly realistic view. But Putnam carries the matter further than this. He argues that determinate reference to mind-independent objects is impossible; we may take this as an argument that if the goal of language is to select from among the world's many organizations, it can never succeed in choosing just one. To this argument I now turn.

II

Putnam places a good deal of weight on an argument that determinate reference to mind-independent objects is impossible. He has discussed the argument in a number of places, most notably in "Models and Reality"[16] and in Chapter 2 of *Reason, Truth and History*. The general idea is that no amount of holding-true of sentences, including sentences that use the term 'reference', will suffice to uniquely determine referents for our terms. No matter how elaborate our theories, including our theories of reference, if they are consistent they can be made true by endless different assignments of referents to their singular terms. Indeed, Putnam argues in *Reason, Truth and History* that endless assignments of referents can even leave the truth *conditions* of all the sentences of any consistent theory the same. So no matter how we try to constrain reference from the "inside," so to speak, it will remain indeterminate.

The conclusion is strikingly similar to Quine's thesis of the inscrutability of reference,[17] and indeed Putnam speaks of himself as extending Quine's result.[18] The discussions of Putnam's recent work that I am aware of assume that the argument is successful; disagreement comes over what to conclude from it. Most of Putnam's critics have urged that, since the argument shows that "internal" constraints on reference do not suffice to pick out a single correspondence relation between words and the world, there must be some "external" constraint that does this. Two sorts of external constraints have been suggested. According to David Lewis what is needed is an "inegalitarianism" of classifications of the world, the view that the world really does in a sense come pre-divided into objects. What is needed, Lewis says, is "the traditional realism that recognises objective sameness and difference, joints in the world, discriminatory classifications not of our own making."[19] It then becomes a constraint on interpretations that they maximize the assignment of "elite classes" as referents. Not that this constraint operates because we *intend* to refer to elite classes: perhaps we do, but that intention, like all others, is susceptible to countless interpretations, including many in which "elite class" refers to classes that are *not* objectively elite. Rather, it is just in the nature of things that some classes are more gerrymandered than others, and the correct assignment of referents will maximize the assignment of the least gerrymandered classes, so far as this is compatible with meeting the other constraints on reference.

The second sort of constraint that has been proposed is causal. The idea here is that the referent of a term might be the object suitably causally connected to people's use of the term. There is a kind of standoff about this constraint. Putnam points out that we cannot from the inside determine the referent of 'cause' any more than we can other referents, so adding some such sentence as "Cats cause the use of the term 'cat' " to our total theory will not help to fix the interpretation of that theory. The total theory could be interpreted by taking 'cat' to refer to some bizarre class of objects and 'cause' to refer to some bizarre relation that relates these bizarre objects to our use of the term 'cat'.[20] Does it follow that we cannot single out a relation, causation, that narrows down the acceptable interpretations? No, as causal theorists reply. Our use of the term 'cause' is *caused* by the relation of causation, so that if the causal constraint on reference is correct it determines the interpretation of 'cause' "from the outside."[21]

Thus the standoff. If Putnam is correct that the only constraints on reference must be internal, then the causal theory of reference does not help to narrow down interpretations, since it cannot succeed in picking out a single relation, causation. On the other hand, if there can be external constraints on reference, then the interpretation of the causal theory may itself be determined by the external relation of causation, so that it can then succeed in narrowing down the possible interpretations of the rest of our theory. Nevertheless it seems to me that in one sense Putnam is in the stronger position here (and not just for the interesting dialectical reason noted by Lewis[22]). There are countless relations that the causal theorist *could*—for all internal constraints can determine—be referring to when he or she uses the term 'cause'. Granted, causality is causally related to 'cause', but then the weird relation shmausality is shmausally related to the word 'cause'. What makes causality rather than shmausality the important relation here?[23] It cannot be anything about us, so it must be something about the world. Putnam suggests that the best the causal theorist can do is "claim that a relation can at one and the same time be a physical relation and have the dignity (the built-in intentionality, in other words) of choosing its own name."[24] This seems unjust to me. But what the causal theorist *must* do is to advocate the inegalitarianism Lewis discusses. The causal theorist must hold that some relations are less gerrymandered and bizarre than others, and that what singles out *causation* as the referent of 'cause' is that, of the relations that are otherwise possible referents, causation is the most natural. If this is correct, it is misleading to think that there is a choice between causality and objective similarity as the right external constraint. Objective similarity must be appealed to whether there is a further appeal to causation or not.

For my purposes the interest of this discussion of external constraints is that it looks as though any external constraint will require what Kolakowski calls "Aristotelian realism." In section I, I suggested three possible metaphysical views: Aristotelian realism, which holds that the world has an organization of its own; modest realism, which holds that the world has countless organizations of its own; and antirealism, which holds that the world has no organization of its own. Kolakowski defends a kind of antirealism by attacking Aristotelian realism, thus ignoring the attractions of modest realism. But now it appears as though the modest realist will have to hold that reference is indeterminate, that we never manage to select a single organization of the world for our own purposes.

Let us now leave Aristotelian realism behind. I do not see that Putnam has managed to show that it is untenable, but I also do not see how to advance its discussion further. Let us consider modest realism and Putnam's internal realism (i.e., antirealism, or "idealism" in the broad sense I have been employing). Putnam's argument appears perfectly compatible with modest realism; the straightforward reading of the moral of the argument would be only that there is a surprising and disturbing indeterminacy in our reference to the real, mind-independent world. It is not the argument about reference alone, but that argument together with his rejection of indeterminacy that leads Putnam to his idealistic ontology. But why exactly does Putnam reject indeterminacy?

In *Reason, Truth and History*, the earliest of the publications I am considering here, Putnam explains that he will be exploring an alternative to Quine's view that "it is just an illusion . . . that the terms in our language have determinate well-defined counterparts."[25] But in this book he does not, so far as I can tell, offer any reason for rejecting indeterminacy. He does note that indeterminacy is disturbing because "no such 'indeterminacy' rises in the 'notional world' of the speaker,"[26] but he does not take this to be a reason to reject indeterminacy, for as he nicely observes, "the fact that in our belief system or 'notional world' no cat is a cherry means that in each admissible interpretation of that belief system . . . the referents of 'cat' and the referents of 'cherry' must be disjoint sets. But the disjointness of these sets is compatible with the (remarkable) fact that what is the set of 'cats' in *one* admissible interpretation may be the set of 'cherries' in a *different* (but equally admissible) interpretation."[27]

In *Realism and Reason*, Putnam does offer a criticism of indeterminacy. He writes of the view that reference is indeterminate: "I cannot accept it for my own language, because to do so would turn the notion of an object into a totally metaphysical notion. I know what tables are and what cats are and what black holes are. But what am I to make of the notion of an X which is a table *or* a cat *or* a black hole (or the number three *or* . . .)?"[28] Let us pause here for a moment before returning to the quotation. Isn't this description of the view unfair? First, the advocate of indeterminacy does not hold that there is some *object* that is not determinately a cat or a table or whatever. It is not the objects themselves that are indeterminate, but rather *which* objects we are referring to. Perhaps Putnam should ask rather what to make of the notion of a *word* that refers to tables *or* cats *or* black holes, etc. But this also would be unfair. For *no* intepretation of English makes it true that there is a word that refers to tables *or* cats *or* black holes. The most we can say is that some interpretations assign to 'cat' the same referents that other interpretations assign to 'table'. And even in saying this we need to keep in mind that this is only possible as part of wide-ranging differences in the interpretation of other singular terms and predicates.

Let us now return to Putnam's criticism of indeterminacy. Immediately after the last-quoted sentence, Putnam writes: "An object which has *no* properties at all in itself and any property you like 'in a model' is an inconceivable *Ding an sich*. The doctrine of ontological relativity avoids the problems of medieval philosophy (the problems of classical realism) but it takes on the problems of Kantian metaphysics in their place." But again, the interpretation of the indeterminist position seems incorrect. The indeterminist does not deny that objects have properties in themselves. The indeterminacy is in our reference to objects and properties, not in the objects or properties themselves. We can, to be sure, say that the referent of 'table' on one interpretation is hard and wooden while on another interpretation it is soft and furry; but that is not to say that there is an object which in itself is neither hard and wooden nor soft and furry, only that it is indeterminate *which* object 'table' refers to. Moreover, even the point that the referent of 'table' has different properties on different interpretations misleadingly suggests more looseness than is actually present, since on any interpretation the referent of 'table' has the property expressed by 'hard and wooden', and on no interpretation does the referent of 'table' have the property expressed by 'soft and furry'.

The problems with Kant's metaphysics come from the problematic relation between the two worlds he talks about: the phenomenal, empirical world and the noumenal world of things in themselves. The view that reference is indeterminate does incorporate the Kantian view that there are things in themselves, that there are mind-independent objects in the world. But this is just to say that it incorporates realism. It also holds that reference is to things in themselves and that knowledge is of things in themselves, though it admits that reference is less determinate than we would like. It thus avoids Kant's interposition of a made-up world between our experiences and the really real world. It thus also avoids, I would suggest, the problems of Kantian metaphysics. In the next section, I will suggest that Putnam's own view is actually more Kantian than the one he here rejects.

The paragraph of Putnam's I have just quoted and criticized is, so far as I know, the only place where he justifies his rejection of the view that reference is simply indeterminate—with the exception of one sentence in "Is the Causal Structure of the Physical Itself Something Physical?" In that paper he describes the view as "incoherent," explaining that it "requires us to believe in a world of things in themselves that have no determinate relations to our language."²⁹ This certainly describes the view fairly. But why is it incoherent? It seems to me perfectly coherent, though admittedly rather unsettling.

I have now discussed two realist responses to Putnam's argument about reference. Aristotelian realism agrees that nothing internal can fix reference, but holds that the world itself is organized into kinds and thus that there can be external constraints on reference. It thereby defends the possibility of determinate reference to mind-independent objects. Modest realism denies that any of the possible classifications of the world are inherently preferable to others, and so holds that we refer indeterminately to mind-independent objects. I turn now to Putnam's own preferred view.

III

Putnam's own view about reference, I take it, is that we refer determinately to mind-dependent objects. In *Reason, Truth and History*, after mentioning the view that reference is simply indeterminate, Putnam says that he "will explore the alternative . . . of giving up the idea . . . that words stand in some sort of one-one relation to (discourse-independent) things and sets of things."³⁰ This is puzzling at first, since it is precisely what the view that reference is indeterminate does as well. Although indeterminism gives up the one-one relation, Putnam's internal realism gives up the discourse-independence: "a sign that is actually employed in a particular way by a particular community of users can correspond to particular objects *within the conceptual scheme of those users*. 'Objects' do not exist independently of conceptual schemes. . . . Since the objects *and* the signs are alike *internal* to the scheme of description, it is possible to say what matches what."³¹

I am not at all sure I understand this. I am not sure what it is for an *object*, as opposed to a description, to be within a conceptual scheme. But I take it that internal realism is not supposed to do damage to the truths of common sense: it does not deny that there are objects that are separate from us and that we interact with causally. It is just that to some extent the character of the objects and relations is mind-dependent. Now it is tempting to ask how mind-dependence can help with the puzzle about reference. It is not at all clear that the argument that reference is indeterminate rests on any assumptions about the mind-independence of objects. Suppose that tables and cats and the rest are somehow mind-dependent. Isn't it still the case that talk using the word 'table' can be interpreted consistently either as talk about tables or as talk about cats? How does the mind-dependence of tables and cats help fix which one 'table' refers to?

On Putnam's view we ordinarily use terms to refer to objects that are mind-dependent. But Putnam's argument about reference does not appear to violate ordinary usage; it seems to use words in the same familiar way, though it manages in doing so to arrive at startling conclusions. But if we ordinarily use words to refer to mind-dependent objects, and Putnam's argument uses words in the ordinary way, it seems that the argument shows that reference to mind-dependent objects is indeterminate.

Perhaps it misrepresents Putnam's position to say that he holds that our terms correspond determinately to mind-dependent objects. He suggests that the whole notion of correspondence needs to be overthrown. When he offers a positive account of reference, he advocates a kind of disquotational theory of reference according to which "we understand 'refers to' *not* by associating the phrase 'refers to' with a 'correspondence', but by learning such assertability conditions as the following: . . . 'Cat' refers to an object X if and only if X is a cat."[32] He goes on to explain that "reference . . . is not something prior to truth; rather, knowing the conditions under which sentences about, say, tables, are true is knowing what 'table' refers to."[33]

It is not altogether straightforward to locate the difference between Putnam and the defender of indeterminacy here. The defender of indeterminacy will also say that knowing the truth conditions of sentences containing 'table' is all there is to know about reference. For the indeterminist, there are no facts about reference beyond those fixed by our use of the language; this is what distinguishes the indeterminist from the Aristoltelian realist. But, the indeterminist will point out, precisely what the argument about reference shows is that truth conditions of sentences containing 'table' are not enough to fix a unique referent for 'table'. Many different referents for 'table' will make the same sentences true, including the sentence" 'table' refers to tables." It is precisely *because* knowing truth conditions is knowing all there is to know about reference that reference is indeterminate.

I have two suggestions about what distinguishes Putnam from the indeterminist realist, neither of them very satisfactory. The first is that Putnam really wants to deny that there is any such relation as reference between words and things. 'Refers' is merely a device of semantic descent, so that ultimately it only relates words to other words: words with quotation marks around them to words without quotation marks. The relation between 'table' and the world cannot be indeterminate because there is no such relation. This view would have the consequence that, at least at the level of individual terms, language is not about the world at all. But if this were Putnam's view, he ought not to talk about the mind-dependence of objects; he ought instead to insist that talk about objects simply makes no sense.

This brings us to the second suggestion about what distinguishes Putnam from the indeterminist. Perhaps Putnam means to simply make it true by definition that reference is determinate. Perhaps he simply intends to use the word 'object' in such a way that knowing the truth conditions of sentences *does* suffice to determine what objects those sentences are about. (But wouldn't this establish the determinacy of reference in the same way that defining 'God' as 'omnipotent omniscient omnibenevolent *existing* person' establishes the existence of God?) An "object" in this sense would perhaps be whatever is common to the uses of 'table' on any intepretation that meets the available constraints: the word 'table' itself and perhaps associated descriptions and experiences. Talk about objects would then really be talk about words and descriptions and experiences. Or rather, since we surely need to preserve some sort of distinction between purely linguistic and mental phenomena on the one hand, and objects on the other, we would perhaps make up a kind of imaginary world, a notional or phenomenal world, and treat reference as reference to this phenomenal world. On this account objects would be mind-dependent in a very strong sense. But also on this account the determinacy of reference would be a kind of pretense, either pretended determinate reference to real things or really determinate reference to pretend things. There would still be real, mind-independent objects in the world, and it would still be troubling that we could not determinately refer to them.

The unsatisfactoriness of both suggestions is evidence that neither is what Putnam has in mind. I wish I had a better suggestion to offer. My guess is that the second suggestion comes closer than the first. But if anything resembling the second suggestion is correct, then Putnam's internal realism is very similar indeed to Kant's transcendental idealism. For it introduces precisely the Kantian contrast between the phenomenal world we can know (refer to) precisely because we largely make it up ourselves, and the mind-independent noumenal world to which we have no (determinate) access.

Making up a phenomenal world can hardly make the things themselves go away. Putnam himself occasionally verges on acknowledging that there must be mind-independent objects behind the phenomenal ones: "I am not inclined to scoff at the idea of a noumenal ground behind the dualities of experience, even if all attempts to talk about it lead to antinomies,"[34] and again: "Today the notion of a noumenal world is perceived to be an unnecessary metaphysical element in Kant's thought. (But perhaps Kant is right: perhaps we can't help thinking that there is *somehow* a mind-independent 'ground' for our experience even if attempts to talk about it lead at once to nonsense.)"[35] So Putnam himself is enmeshed in the Kantian distinction between appearances and things in themselves. We have seen Putnam object to indeterminacy that "it takes on the problems of Kantian metaphysics." But it now appears that this criticism may be applied with at least equal justice to internal realism itself.[36]

Notes

1. Ralph Barton Perry, *Present Philosophical Tendencies* (New York, 1912; Third Impression, Revised, 1916), 114. Perry meant this characterization to cover Berkeley, Kant, and Hegel, among others; I take it that his attempt to state what they have in common would meet with wide agreement. More recently, Thomas Nagel has suggested that the "common element" in a variety of versions of idealism, including both historical versions and the views of such contemporaries as Davidson, Strawson, and Wittgenstein, is "a broadly epistemological test of reality." Nagel, *The View From Nowhere* (New York, 1986), 91.

2. Hilary Putnam, *Reason, Truth and History* (Cambridge, 1981), 54.

3. Ibid., xi.

4. Hilary Putnam, *Realism and Reason, Philosophical Papers Volume 3* (Cambridge, 1983), papers 6 and 7.

5. Ibid., papers 12 and 16; "Is the Causal Structure of the Physical Itself Something Physical?" *Midwest Studies in Philosophy* 9 (1984): 3–16.

6. Putnam, *Reason, Truth and History*, especially chaps. 6, 7, and 9.

7. Ibid., 52.

8. Ibid., 53–54.

9. Putnam, *Realism and Reason*, p. xvi.

10. Leszek Kolakowski, "Karl Marx and the Classical Definition of Truth," in Kolakowski, *Toward a Marxist Humanism*, translated from the Polish by Jane Zielonko Peel (New York, 1968).

11. Ibid., 67.

12. Ibid., 73.

13. Ibid., 68.

14. Ibid., 78.

15. Ibid., 76.

16. Putnam, "Models and Reality," in *Realism and Reason*.

17. See especially Quine's "Ontological Relativity," in Quine, *Ontological Relativity and Other Essays* (New York, 1969), 26–68.

18. Putnam, *Reason, Truth and History*, 33.

19. David Lewis, "Putnam's Paradox," *Australasian Journal of Philosophy* 62 (1984): 221–36, at 228. Lewis credits the suggestion to G. H. Merrill, "The Model-Theoretic Argument Against Realism," *Philosophy of Science* 47 (1980): 69–81.

20. Compare Putnam, *Realism and Reason*, xi.

21. See, e.g., Michael Devitt, "Realism and the Renegade Putnam: A Critical Study of *Meaning and the Moral Sciences,*" *Nous* 17 (1983): 291–301, at 298–99; Devitt, *Realism and Truth* (Oxford, 1984), 188–91.

22. Lewis, 225–26.

23. Compare Putnam, *Realism and Reason*, 296; and "Is the Causal Structure of the Physical Itself Something Physical?" 6–7.

24. Putnam, "Is the Causal Structure of the Physical Itself Something Physical?" 7.

25. Putnam, *Reason, Truth and History*, 41.

26. Ibid., 44.

27. Ibid.

28. Putnam, *Realism and Reason*, xiii.

29. Putnam, "Is the Causal Structure of the Physical Itself Something Physical?" 6.

30. Putnam, *Reason, Truth and History*, 41.

31. Ibid., 52.

32. Putnam, *Realism and Reason*, xv.

33. Ibid., xvi; compare *Reason, Truth and History*, 52.

34. Putnam, *Realism and Reason*, 226.

35. Putnam, *Reason, Truth and History*, pp. 61–62.

36. Work on this paper was supported in part by a National Endowment for the Humanities grant to the Trinity University Philosophy Department for a curriculum development project in the history of philosophy.

Rorty's Mirrorless World

MICHAEL DEVITT

1. INTRODUCTION

In his famous work, *Philosophy and the Mirror of Nature*, Richard Rorty (1979) rejects the view that our thoughts or our sentences "mirror," or in any other way "correspond to," nature. Why? The main reason is clear. The view is part of the skeptical problematic that has dominated modern philosophy, and which Rorty thinks should be set aside.

That problematic starts from the assumption that we have mental representations (thoughts), or linguistic representations (sentences), of reality. The skeptic doubts the accuracy of these representations. The nonskeptic affirms their accuracy: They correspond to reality and so are *true*. Rorty wants no part of this. He urges a pragmatic view of truth. There is no (nontrivial) question of representations corresponding or failing to correspond to reality, and hence the problem of skepticism dissolves. Philosophy cannot "underwrite or debunk claims to knowledge" (1979, p. 3). A priori foundationalism—indeed, epistemology as a whole—is dead. The philosopher should "give up the desire for confrontation and constraint," replacing this role of "cultural overseer" with that of the "informed dilettante." We should take up hermeneutics; we should engage in "conversation" (pp. 315–18), be "edifying without being constructive" (p. 360).

In brief, Rorty thinks that philosophers are obsessed with skepticism. His message to us is: Stop it or you will go blind.

There is no doubt that the correspondence theory of truth has been part of the skeptical problematic. And "naturalistic" philosophers would agree with Rorty that we should free ourselves from that problematic and the a priori view of philosophy. Philosophy is, indeed, not an "all-encompassing discipline which legitimizes or grounds the others" (p. 6). These naturalistic philosophers are likely to welcome Rorty's fascinating historical discussion in support of this view. However, they are also likely to have two objections to Rorty's position and one worry about it.

First objection: Rorty clearly thinks that we *need* to reject the correspondence theory in order to free ourselves from the skeptical problematic. Yet, surely there is no such necessary connection between semantics and epistemology. We can abandon the skeptical problematic because we see "the quest for certainty" as essentially hopeless, and because we think that there is no place in a scientific world view for the a priori epistemology implicit in such a search. Furthermore, once we are free of the problematic, it as an open empirical question whether a correspondence theory of truth has a place in the total world view. Many naturalistic philosophers think that it has.

Second objection: Why should the rejection of skepticism and a priori philosophy lead us into hermeneutics? Naturalistic philosophers see a systematic and constructive role for philosophy in conjunction with science.

The worry: There is an aura of antirealism about Rorty's discussion. Rorty is aware of this worry and tries to allay it. A central part of his metaphilosophy is that we should move, as he puts it in the title of a very recent paper, "Beyond Realism and Anti-Realism" (in press), for that issue is at the center of the discredited problematic (1979, pp. 139–40). The naturalistic philosopher will sympathize. However, that philosopher is likely to want the issue settled firmly in the realist way before leaving it behind. It is not obvious that Rorty has so settled it. Indeed, Rorty is usually regarded as an antirealist.

My concern in this paper is to explore Rorty's relationship to naturalistic philosophy. I shall start by removing the worry about realism. I shall go on to sustain the two objections.

2. REALISM AND THE CORRESPONDENCE THEORY

The aura of antirealism in Rorty arises mainly from his rejection of the correspondence theory of truth and from his enthusiasm for Kuhn. I shall argue that Rorty is, nevertheless, a realist.

Just as Rorty thinks that the correspondence theory played an important role in the skeptical problematic, so also does he think that it played an important role in the development of the realism issue. And, of course, he is right. Nevertheless, realism should not be confused with the correspondence theory of truth. Realism is not a theory of representation, but a metaphysical and epistemological doctrine. I have argued this at some length in *Realism and Truth* (1984). I summarize in what follows.

Realism has two dimensions, an existence dimension and an independence dimension. The existence dimension commits the realist to the existence of such commonsense entities as stones, trees, and cats, and such scientific entities as electrons, muons, and curved space-time; we are more or less right in our physical posits. Typically, idealists, the traditional opponents of realists, have not denied this dimension (Hume was one exception); or, at least, have not straightforwardly denied it. This was wise, for it is so plausible on the face of it.

What idealists have typically denied is the independence dimension. According to some idealists, the entities mentioned by the first dimension are made up of mental items, "ideas" or "sense data." According to others, the entities are not in a certain respect "objective": They depend for their existence and nature on what we believe or can discover. Realists reject all such mind dependencies. Relations between minds and the world of those entities are limited to familiar causal interactions long noted by folk theory.

In insisting on the objectivity of the world, realists are not saying that it is unknowable. They are saying that it is independent of the cognitive activities of the mind. The world is not constituted by our knowledge, by the synthesizing power of the mind, nor by our imposition of concepts or theories. Kant's phenomenal world, Dummett's verifiable world, and Kuhn's world of theoretical ontologies do not have objective existence in this sense; nor does a world, believed in, perhaps, in some eastern religions, created and sustained in existence by our thoughts.

We might sum up realism briefly as follows: Physical entities objectively exist independently of the mental. This is the sort of doctrine that naturalistic philosophers take for granted (except for a few whose science makes them dubious of the commonsense entities).

My definition of realism is unfashionable. For, it is entirely unsemantic, making no mention of representations or truth.

A striking aspect of the current "realism" debate is that it contains almost as many doctrines under the name 'realism' as it contains participants. However, some common features can be discerned in this chaos. First, nearly all the doctrines are, or seem to be, partly semantic. The debate is full of talk of truth, reference, and convergence. Second, among all this semantic talk, it is usually possible to discern a metaphysical doctrine. Indeed, it would be very surprising if this were not so: Anything that is to bear on the traditional dispute between realists and idealists must be metaphysical.[1] Thus, 'realism' is now usually taken to refer to some combination of a metaphysical doctrine like the one above with a doctrine about truth, particularly with a correspondence doctrine.[2]

In response to this fashion, I begin by emphasizing that correspondence truth is in no way constitutive of realism as I have defined it, nor of any other doctrine along similarly metaphysical lines. On the one hand, such doctrines do not entail the correspondence theory nor any other theory of truth. One can be a realist and yet be eliminativist about the semantic properties of thoughts and language. This has been nicely demonstrated by Stephen Leeds (1978) drawing on the views of Quine. Indeed, many philosophers interested in cognitive science, and not in any way tainted by antirealism, are dubious of the need for a correspondence notion of truth.[3]

On the other hand, the correspondence theory does not entail realism. It is the theory that truth consists in some way in correspondence to a reality that is usually taken to be objective. Beyond that, the correspondence theory says nothing about the nature of that reality. The theory leaves open what entities make representations true.

Realism is a doctrine about the nature of reality in general; it is about the largely inanimate, impersonal world. If correspondence truth has a place, it is in our theory of only a small part of that reality – it is in our theory of people and their language.

Verbal disputes are boring. If people want to use 'realism' to cover something that is a part-metaphysical and part-semantical doctrine, who is to say they should not? Nevertheless, I think there are reasons for resisting this usage.

First, since the metaphysical doctrine of realism and the doctrine of correspondence truth *are* distinct, and require different arguments, they should be kept distinct in the interests of clarity. This is particularly so since many current doubts about truth, particularly those in cognitive science, do not arise out of any of the traditional concerns of the realism dispute. I shall return to this point in the next section.

Second, if the fashionable usage of 'realism' is followed, what are we to call the metaphysical part of its referent? We are forced, quite unnecessarily, to coin another term.[4]

Third, I think that there is little historical basis for this usage. This is not the place to argue for this claim. However, support for it can be found in the account of realism in *The Encyclopedia of Philosophy* (Hirst 1967) and in John Passmore's *A Hundred Years of Philosophy* (1966). Historically, realism has been about the nature of the world, not about the nature of language or thought.

If this is so, why has correspondence truth become so confused with realism? I shall conclude my response to the fashion by considering this question in some detail.[5]

My claim is that the correspondence theory of truth is not in any way essential to realism. This is not to say that theories of truth are irrelevant to the realism issue. Typically, they have played a very significant role in *the way the issue is argued* and the degree to which it seems interesting and controversial. But arguments are one thing, their conclusions another. The point is that correspondence truth is not constitutive of a realist conclusion.

Arguments against realism within the skeptical problematic have usually run as follows:

(1) If the realist's independent reality exists, then our thoughts/theories must mirror, picture, or represent, that reality.

(2) Our thoughts/theories cannot mirror, picture, or represent the realist's independent reality.

(3) So, the realist's independent reality does not exist.

The center of the debate about this argument has been on (2); that is to say, the center has been about the correspondence of our ideas or language to independent reality. Traditionally, the problem has come up in epistemology: "How could we know about such a reality?" More recently, the problem has come up in the theory of reference or intentionality: "How could our language or thought refer to such a reality?"

These questions have seemed metaphysically important only because (1) has been assumed, mostly without argument. Indeed (1) has seemed so irresistible that to deny a correspondence theory has often been seen as tantamount to denying realism. The Leeds-Quine view that ontology is one thing, the representational properties of our thoughts another, strikes people as paradoxical. Consider, for example, this recent statement by Hilary Putnam:

> Whatever authority [ontology and epistemology] had depended entirely on our conceiving of reality and sensations as, respectively, the makers-true and the makers-justified of the sentences we produce – not the makers-true and the makers-justified from within the story, but the things outside the story that hook language onto something outside itself. (1985, p. 78)[6]

Irresistible or not, (1) is false.

One historically important account of realism did involve correspondence truth and, hence, may bear some distant responsibility for the contemporary confusion. Descartes and the British Empiricists assume that what we immediately perceive are ideas in the mind. For them realism is the view that there are objects outside the mind that cause and *resemble* these ideas. So the only account of the objects realism is committed to is in terms of their correspondence to ideas; commitment to cats comes from commitment to things resembling cat ideas. From this perspective, of course, realism seems very dubious; Descartes's case for it required the help of a Very Powerful Friend; Berkeley demonstrated the desparate thinness of Locke's case. However, what needs emphasizing is that this way of identifying the realist world is not necessary: You can commit yourself to cats by committing yourself to cats. And the crude notion of resemblance (or mirroring) has no place in contemporary correspondence theories, as we shall see (section 5).[7]

The view that we need to appeal to ideas to identify the realist world did not survive the impact of Kant on the debate. However, a shadow of it is to be found in the contemporary insistence on the importance of interpretation. A person's realism about certain entities cannot be simply exemplified in a belief or claim that those entities exist, we are told, for we must know how such a belief or claim is to be interpreted; commitment to cats must come from commitment to a certain view of the reference of 'cat'.[8] I have argued against this at length elsewhere.[9] Briefly, we do not need to move into a metalanguage discussion of our object language claims to establish ontological commitment. Indeed, if commitment could never be established at the level of the object language, it could never be established at all. The idea that talk about the world is unclear and in need of interpretation, yet talk about language and its relation to the world is straightforward on the face of it, reflects the damage of years of living under the Linguistic Turn.

3. RORTY ON REALISM

It follows from this discussion that Rorty's rejection of the correspondence theory alone does not show him to be opposed to a metaphysical doctrine of realism like mine. Where, then, does Rorty stand on such a doctrine? He has been quite explicit. He refers to it as a "banal anti-idealist thesis," and "as no more than out-dated rhetoric" (1985, p. 354).[10] What are we to make of this dismissal?

Rorty clearly regards the existence dimension of the above doctrine as too obvious to be worth stating (see for example, 1982, p. 14). The interpretative problem is over the independence dimension. I detect three strands in Rorty's thought about independence and, hence, about realism. Strand 1 is that the independence dimension is true but boring. Strand 2 is that, insofar as the dimension is clear, it is trivial. Strand 3 is related to this. It is that the controversy was not really over this clear but trivial doctrine, but over an unclear and misguided doctrine about other sorts of entities altogether.

Strand 1 arises simply out of the abandonment of the skeptical problematic and so is congenial to the naturalistic philosopher. Once skepticism has been set aside, suggestions that the familiar and scientific physical world is in some way dependent on us have no plausibility. Antirealism can seem interesting only if we start in the wrong place, worrying about how we can know about, or refer to, the world. This procedure, characteristic of the skeptical problematic, puts the cart before the horse. We should be clear about what there is before indulging in any speculations about knowledge or language.

These remarks add to the case for keeping the metaphysical issue of realism distinct from the problem of truth. If one tackles truth before, or at the same time as, realism, truth is likely to seem particularly baffling. Worries obtrude about what there is in the world to be corresponded to, and about how we could know about such entities. But realism, not truth, is the proper home for these sorts of worries. One's best chance of freeing oneself from doubts about the external world, and from the skeptical problematic in general, is to confront those doubts directly, without the distraction of an irrelevancy like truth. Once free of skepticism, the problem of truth takes on a different light: It is an empirical problem in cognitive science and the theory of language. And until one is free of skepticism, truth should be among the least of one's problems.

I think that the naturalistic philosopher should resist the suggestion that the realism issue is *completely* boring. It *ought* to be boring, but while antirealism is alive, well, and living in Britain, France, America, the East, and even in some areas of Australia, the issue retains some interest. Realism is like atheism.[11]

The rejection of the skeptical problematic is, of course, central to Rorty's philosophy and so it is not hard to see signs of strand 1 in his work. Signs are also to be found, interestingly enough, in his discussion of Kuhn.

Rorty is enthusiastic about Kuhn, but his enthusiasm is qualified. What he really likes is Kuhn's epistemology: the rejection of the "given" and the emphasis on theory ladenness. He does not accept the two elements of Kuhn's philosophy that suggest antirealism.

First, Rorty distances himself from Kuhn's " 'idealistic'-sounding" view that the proponents of different theories " 'see different things' or 'live in different worlds' " (1979, p. 324).[12] Indeed, he thinks it absurd to say "that we make objects by using words" (p. 276).[13]

Second, he does not subscribe to the incommensurability thesis that pushes Kuhn into his idealistic metaphysics. Kuhn's incommensurability thesis is fundamentally semantic: The languages of different paradigms do not share meanings; so the theories of different paradigms cannot stand in the logical relations required for theory comparison. Rorty has an incommensurability thesis, but it is epistemic.

> By "commensurable" I mean able to be brought under a set of rules which will tell us how rational agreement can be reached on what would settle the issue on every point where statements seem to conflict. (p. 316)

He distinguishes this sense of "commensurable" from the semantic one (p. 316n). His incommensurability thesis is: There is no "algorithm for theory choice" (p. 324). This thesis is quite congenial to a naturalistic realism.

The signs of strand 1 in Rorty are not clear, because his discussion of realism is as much influenced by his Davidsonian view of the mind and language as by his rejection of the skeptical problematic. Indeed he writes—quite falsely, I shall argue (section 5)—as if the Davidsonian view is part and parcel of that rejection.

Strand 2 arises out of that Davidsonian view. More generally, it arises out of Rorty's opposition to the correspondence theory. He does not think that there is "a clear and nontrivial sense to be given" to the notion of " 'facts' and 'objective relations' independent of the mind" (1976, p. 327). For him the independence in question is to be made clear by giving a Davidsonian construal of the view that "it is the *world* that determines the truth" (1982, p. 12) of beliefs and utterances. And this construal makes the view trivial.[14]

The triviality comes from the Principle of Charity: "most of our beliefs . . . simply *must* be true." For, "what could count as evidence that the vast majority of them were not" (p. 12)? As a result, "we shall automatically be 'in touch with the world' " (p. 13); "truth as correspondence" becomes an "uncontroversial triviality" (p. 15).

Since the independence of the known world of common sense and science is trivial, Rorty thinks that the realist must be insisting on the independence of some other world. This introduces strand 3. What the realist wants is the notion of a world *so* "independent of our knowledge" that it might, for all we know, prove to contain none of the things we have always thought we were talking about . . . .[This] must be the notion of something *completely* unspecified and unspecifiable—the thing-in-itself, in fact. (p. 14)

The controversy has been over a world "which could vary independently of the antics of the familiar objects; . . . something rather like the thing-in-itself" (1985, p. 354n); "the purely vacuous notion of the ineffable cause of sense and goal of intellect" (1982, p. 15).

According to strand 3, therefore, the traditional disagreement between realists and idealists has *never* been over the familiar world mentioned in the doctrine I have defined. It is not just that that doctrine loses its interest once the skeptical problematic is set aside, as in strand 1; the doctrine is trivial, hence banal, even within that problematic.

Rorty's attitude to the mysterious thing-in-itself is brought out nicely in the title of a paper I have quoted frequently, "The World Well Lost" (1982, pp. 3–18). The claim that there is such an independent world is certainly not trivial, but it is unclear and uncalled for.

Strands 2 and 3 come from Rorty's Davidsonian semantics. In the next section, I shall consider the bearing of this semantics on realism. But first I shall briefly assess strand 3.

We can certainly do without the world that Rorty wants to lose, a Kantian thing-in-itself forever beyond our ken.[15] And there is no doubt that disputes about it have played a part in the realism issue. Nevertheless, I shall be so bold as to disagree with Rorty about the history. I think that the central issue in the realism dispute has been over the existence and independent nature of the *known* world; it has been over the doctrine I have formulated here.

Consider one of the greatest antirealists, Kant. His view of the noumenal world of things-in-themselves has been important. However, his view of the phenomenal world of appearances has surely been more so. This world is the known one of stones, trees, cats, and the objects of science. Kant's idea that this world is partly our construction—for how else could it be known?—has dominated through two centuries of antirealism.

Passmore says this about the last century:

The main tendency of nineteenth-century thought was towards the conclusion that both "things" and facts about things are dependent for their existence and their nature upon the operations of a mind. (1966, p. 174)

It is clear that the things in question are the known ones, not the ineffable ones. The popularity of the Kantian idea has not diminished in this century. It is to be found, for example, in Kuhn, Putnam, Whorf, and the structuralists. It has some claim to being the most influential bad idea in philosophy.

4. DAVIDSONIAN SEMANTICS AND REALISM

According to Rorty's strand 2, we need Davidsonian semantics to make any sense of the independence talked of in our doctrine of realism. And then, he thinks, the doctrine becomes trivial.

I think realism is clear enough without Davidsonian semantics. This is not to say that the mind-dependency claims made by *anti*realists are clear. Most of the claims are so bizarre as to require much more explanation than they are given. Is it really claimed, for example, that there could not have been dinosaurs if there had not been people? If this is not claimed, in what way could dinosaurs be dependent on us? However, the problem of clarifying such dependencies is one for antirealists. Realists reject all dependencies, whether clear or not. For they believe that the only relations between the mind and the external world are the familiar causal ones. What could be clearer than that?

Rorty's distaste for traditional epistemological and metaphysical issues like realism is so great that he hankers after a language in which they cannot be formulated (1985, p. 351). And in his latest paper on realism (in press) he writes as if he has already found such a language. I can see no justification for this rather romantic attempt to break with the past.

Before considering whether Davidsonian semantics makes realism trivial, I want to raise a more disturbing question. Does that semantics make realism *false*?

The reason for thinking that it does make it false is to be found in a passage from Rorty already quoted. Realism's independence dimension seems to require that we could be completely wrong about the world. Davidson's Principle of Charity denies that we could. As Rorty puts it,

we now know perfectly well what the world is like and could not possibly be wrong about it. (1982, p. 14)

(It was the realist's insistence on a level of independence unobtainable from the Davidsonian perspective that encouraged Rorty's strand 3 identification of the realist's world with a thing-in-itself.) So, Rorty thinks that, for the most part, if we believe that *p* then *p*. It is tempting to think that Rorty's commitment to this amounts to antirealism.[16]

However, before we give in to this temptation, we need to examine the direction of dependency. Realism is threatened only if the world is dependent on the believer. This is not the Davidsonian view. The view is, rather, that beliefs are somehow dependent on the world. Given that the world is a certain way, Davidson claims, we cannot interpret any believer-desirer as believing that it is any other way. In my view (section 7), this claim is false, but nevertheless it is not antirealist.

There is a moral in this. Semantic theories may lead a person into an antirealist metaphysics, as we saw in section 2, but such theories do not, on their own, amount to antirealism. This is as true of the Davidsonian theory of interpretation as it is of the rejection of correspondence truth.

Rorty's comforting view that we cannot be wrong about the world reflects not antirealism, but a false theory of people and their language.

Davidsonian semantics does not undermine the truth of realism, but does it make realism trivial? The semantics does trivialize the view that "it is the *world* that determines the truth." However, this view is not essential to realism. Furthermore, as we have seen, antirealists think of the world as dependent on us in various ways. It is not trivial to reject these dependencies. Davidsonian semantics alone will certainly not suffice for that rejection.

In sum, strand 1 of Rorty's thought about realism is near enough correct: Realism is true and ought to be boring. Strand 2 is mistaken: We do not need Davidsonian semantics to make realism clear; and that semantics does not make realism trivial. Strand 3 is wrong in claiming that the traditional dispute was over things-in-themselves, but right in wanting to have nothing to do with such dim entities.

Having put to rest the worry about realism, I shall move on to the first objection and the issue of correspondence truth.

5. THE CORRESPONDENCE THEORY AND THE SKEPTICAL PROBLEMATIC

Rorty's rejection of any correspondence theory of truth (other than the trivial Davidsonian one) is total. We must discard "the notion of the mind as Mirror of Nature" (1979, p. 170).

> We have to drop the notion of correspondence for sentences as well as for thoughts, and see sentences as connected with other sentences rather than with the world. (pp. 371–72)

'Truth' does "not name a relation between utterances on the one hand and 'the world' on the other" (1976, p. 322). What mainly distinguishes contemporary correspondence theories from the pragmatic view he takes from Davidson is their commitment to "word-world relationships for individual statements". There are no such relationships (1976, p. 322). Rather, the language as a whole relates to reality. "Nothing will explicate 'theory-independent truth' " (1979, p. 281). In particular, reference does not do so. We have no need of a theory of reference.

What has Rorty got against the correspondence theory? Three things: (i) The theory is guilty by association with the skeptical problematic. (ii) It requires what cannot be had: a philosophically significant theory of reference. (iii) There are a cluster of considerations that Rorty takes from Davidson. I shall have something to say about (iii), but the focus of my discussion will be on (i) and (ii), both of which are relatively independent of Davidsonian semantics. The rest of this section is concerned with (i).

Rorty sees the skeptical problematic under every correspondence theorist's bed. On the one hand, an interest in a notion of reference that makes "language safe for "truth-as-correspondence-with-reality" is taken to be an epistemological interest (1976, p. 331). On the other hand, rejection of Rorty's Davidsonian view of truth is taken to involve the belief

that we have, deep down inside us, a criterion for telling whether we are in touch with reality or not, when we are in the Truth. (1982, p. xxxviii)

Both elements are to be found in Rorty's distinction between "pure" and "impure" philosophy of language. The impure is "explicitly epistemological" (1979, p. 257) and is "roughly coextensive with" the theory of reference (p. 270). The impure is "burdened with the task of blocking skepticism" (p. 288). The "de-epistemologized" (p. 259) pure philosophy of language is near enough identified with Davidsonian semantics (p. 299). The pure is not concerned "to explain the relationship between words and the world" (p. 262) nor with " 'how language hooks onto the world' " (p. 265).

In brief, Rorty thinks that to resist Davidson is to hanker after an answer to the skeptic. It seems as if Davidsonian semantics is not to be judged simply on its merits as a theory of language. Rather, borrowing the words of one of Rorty's heroes, that semantics is needed "to shew the fly the way out of the fly bottle" (Wittgenstein 1953, §309).

Doubtless, the interest of some philosophers in non-Davidsonian semantics has been epistemological. It is plausible to suppose this of verificationists like Michael Dummett, for example. However, there is no basis for supposing it of many others, particularly those associated with the causal theory of reference.[17] There is no necessary connection between purity and Davidson.

The correspondence theory of truth and the theory of reference are parts of a theory of language, not attempts to justify knowledge. In my view, briefly, sentence meaning is to be explained largely in terms of truth conditions; those conditions are to be explained in terms of syntactic structure and the reference of words;[18] reference must then be explained, part causally, part descriptively. The notion of truth that is featured in this theory has sufficient of the properties of the traditional correspondence notion—without the obscure mirroring metaphor—to be called a correspondence notion. Skepticism has nothing to do with the theory, and is set aside anyway.[19]

Consider an example, 'Amanda is a cuscus'. This sentence has a simple structure in virtue of which its truth value depends on reference in the following way: It is true if and only if there is an object designated by 'Amanda' and that object is among the ones that 'cuscus' applies to. Structure, reference, and reality are the way they are independently of our opinions. Thus, if the sentence is true, it objectively corresponds to objective reality. This does absolutely nothing to show that it *is* true. The question of justification is left untouched by the theory.[20]

The choice between such contemporary correspondence theories and Davidsonian semantics is empirical. The choice should not be influenced by the fact that the ancestors of correspondence theories kept company with bad epistemology.

Rorty has a response to this line of thought. He raises a very good question: "What data [must] the philosophy of language explain" (1982, p. xxiv)? In particular, what do correspondence notions of truth and reference explain? He dismisses the answer, the success of science (pp. xxiv-v), quite rightly in my view (1984, pp. 106–10; in press).[21] In the next section we shall consider his dismissal of another answer. Since he can find no satisfactory answer, he suspects the worst. In denying a concern for skepticism, correspondence theorists are trying to conceal something; they are closet foundationalists:

> Semantics has *not* become completely disjoined from epistemology, despite advertisements to that effect. Most philosophers of language want . . . an account of our representations of the world which guarantees that we have not lost touch with it, an answer to the skeptic which flows from a general account of the nature of representation. (1982, p. 128)

I see no basis for Rorty's worst fears. Nevertheless, he has hit on the weakest point of the correspondence theory: the lack of a convincing, and agreed, account of why we need such a theory in the first place. It is certainly very difficult to say why we do need it. Many in cognitive science struggle with this problem.[22]

In my view, the solution has been sought in the wrong place: Truth has been thought to explain something about behavior, particularly linguistic behavior. Thus, the attempt has been to find a place for truth in psychology. I think that the theory of language is a social theory, not part of psychology. This is not the place to argue the matter, but a few (un-Davidsonian) words may help.[23]

What prompts our task in the theory of language is the striking role that certain noises, inscriptions, and so on—linguistic symbols—play in our lives, particularly in communication. The task is to explain the properties these symbols have that makes them worth producing and responding to. Linguistic symbols should not be confused with linguistic behavior. A piece of linguistic behavior is a series of bodily movements, usually of vocal chords or hands. The symbol is a datable placeable part of the physical world *produced by* the behavior with the help of the environment. An explanation of the behavior will seek a psychological description of its *cause*. An explanation of the symbol will seek a description of its *nature*. It is in the latter explanation that we have a need for truth and reference.

Some objects have economic properties—for example, having a price or having a value—in virtue of which those objects play a certain economic role in our lives. Some objects have socio-legal properties—for example, being a contract or a vote—in virtue of which those objects play a certain socio-legal role in our lives. Similarly some objects have linguistic properties. It is the task of the theory of language to study those properties just as it is the task of economics to study the economic ones. These social sciences are not irrelevant to the explanation of behavior, nor are they independent of psychological facts. Nevertheless, they are not psychology.

Perhaps this solution to the problem is wrong and another one right. Perhaps there is no solution and correspondence truth should be abandoned. Whatever the truth of the matter, skeptical concerns play no role in the debate. In insisting that those concerns are central to correspondence truth, Rorty shows all the zeal of a convert: Having rejected sin, he sees it everywhere.

Finally, Rorty's view is a little paradoxical. *Prima facie*, it is Davidsonian semantics, not the theory of reference, that attempts to answer the skeptic. Davidson claims to establish the earlier-mentioned Principle of Charity, according to which most of our beliefs must be true. What could be a more complete answer to the skeptic? Davidson himself thinks that he has answered the skeptic (1983, p. 426). Rorty deals with this embarrassment ingeniously, and at some length, arguing that what Davidson really does is not answer the skeptic, but repudiate his question (1985, pp. 342–44). I am not convinced.

I shall now move on to the second thing that Rorty has against the correspondence theory: (ii) it requires a philosophically significant theory of reference which cannot be had.

6. RORTY AGAINST REFERENCE

Rorty contemplates one task for a theory of reference, and hence for a correspondence theory, that is free of epistemology. It is the task of helping with the problem of "ancestral error" (1976, p. 324); we would like an account of our superiority to our ancestors that sees the history of theories as being one of gradual progress (p. 321). The theory of reference—in particular the causal theory—is thought to help, because it implies that our ancestors were mostly referring despite their many false beliefs. Progress can then be seen as a steady increase in the number of true beliefs that we have about the referents. We are always in touch with reality and gradually finding out more and more about it. (The New Zealand-based verisimilitude industry has shown that this idea is much more difficult to work out than one might have supposed.)

Rorty's response to this idea is dismissive. It is also extremely complicated (pp. 324–31; 1979, pp. 288–93). He draws a distinction between three notions of reference: the ordinary notion of "talking about," which is opaque and hence allows "reference to the nonexistent"; the philosophical notion featured in the causal theory, which is transparent and concerned with word-world connections; and a bridging notion between the two. He alleges that the argument for the causal theory has come from confusing these notions in considering our intuitions. These intuitions mostly concern the ordinary notion of talking about, and partly concern the bridging notion. They show that a description theory of the "cluster" sort proposed by Strawson and Searle applies to the ordinary notion except in a few "special cases" (1976, p. 327). The philosophical notion "is just not something that anybody has intuitions about" (p. 329) and should be dispensed with.

The above task for the theory of reference remains, but fulfilling it "is too slight to merit the title of 'theory' " (1979, p. 288); it simply requires

> a decision-procedure for solving difficult cases in historiography, anthropological description and the like — cases where nothing save tact and imagination will serve . . . [it] is a question about the best procedure for comparing large coherent sets of false beliefs (other epochs, cultures, etc.) with ours. (p. 293)

The procedure is constrained only by our interest in finding a description of the situation which "avoids paradox and maximizes coherence" (p. 291).

I have three comments. First, helping with ancestral error is certainly something that we should hope for from a theory of reference, but it is not the main task for the theory. That task is helping to explain language, as I have indicated (section 5).

Second, if my view of the task for reference is correct, the case for causal theories goes beyond appeals to intuitions. Description theories cannot account for the reference of all words. Description theories explain the reference of some words in terms of the reference of others; they pass the referential buck. So if the reference of any word is to be fully explained, and hence the correspondence theory justified, the reference of some words must be explained without appeal to that of others. Causal theories offer the only prospect of such an ultimate explanation, the only prospect of stopping the buck.

Third, with the help of his three notions of reference, Rorty does seem able to explain away the difficulties for his view raised by causal theorists. However, if the complexities he introduces into the account of reference are not to be ad hoc, they need a justification that is independent of these difficulties. In particular, why suppose that there are the three notions of reference? Rorty thinks that the transparent/opaque distinction supplies a justification. I disagree.

It is plausible to claim that, in its ordinary use, sentences of the form 'x refers to y' are often opaque. If they are, then 'refers' is like many other verbs in English. Examples that Quine uses in his classic discussion, "Opacity in Certain Verbs" (1960, pp. 151–56), include 'looking for', 'hunt', and 'want'. The problem for Rorty is that, if 'refers' is indeed one of these verbs, it will *also* be the case that some sentences of the above form will be transparent. Sentences containing such intentional verbs can be construed either transparently or opaquely, as Quine points out. This is not to say that the *verbs* are ambiguous. The ambiguity lies in the *constructions*; the sentences are syntactically ambiguous.[24]

It follows from this that a philosophical notion of reference cannot be distinguished from the ordinary one on the ground that the former is transparent whereas the latter is opaque. Furthermore, the ordinary notion *is* concerned with word-world connections, most strikingly so in transparent constructions. This is not to say that philosophical notions of reference do not differ from the ordinary one. The ordinary notion is very vague. Philosophers tend to make it more precise in various ways and to use it only in transparent constructions.

Since the sharp distinction Rorty draws between the ordinary and the philosophical notion of reference is spurious, the motivation for supposing that there is a bridging notion disappears.

The collapse of Rorty's sharp distinction prevents the isolation of the philosophical notion of reference, concerned with word-world connections, from the intuitions that Kripke and others relied on in arguing for the causal theory. Our intuitions must involve the ordinary notion, but if that notion is simply a vaguer version of a philosophical one, then those intuitions are directly relevant to any theory containing the philosophical one. What Kripke and others did was compare our intuitions about the truth value of ordinary transparent sentences using 'refer' with philosophical theories of reference. They claimed that the intuitions decisively favored the causal theory for names and natural kind terms. (Of course, comparison with such intuitions should not settle the fate of a theory. The intuitions simply reflect folk wisdom, and the folk may not be wise, as Rorty would be among the first to insist [1982, pp. xxix-x]. However, it is an undoubted plus for a theory to be in accord with the folk.)

The failure of Rorty's attempt to isolate the philosophical notion means that the full weight of his case against the causal theory's account of word-world connections must be born by his response to the causal theory of the ordinary notion.

We accommodate his mistaken view that the ordinary notion is opaque by considering the notion only in opaque sentences. We then have sentences about which Rorty has intuitions. He claims that, normally, you opaquely refer to whatever you *think* you are referring to (1976, p. 324); you are "the sole judge" (p. 325); you refer to the object most of your associated beliefs are true of; that object is the "intentional object" of your thought (1979, p. 289; 1985, pp. 340-41). In brief, Rorty rejects the claims of causal theorists and assumes a description theory for the ordinary notion of reference and for determining intentional objects. If he is right, this will count against the causal theory's account of the philosophical notion of reference (though, of course, Rorty does not think so because he mistakenly thinks that he has isolated that notion).

How does Rorty deal with all the Kripkean cases that seem to show that the description theory is wrong? He treats them as special cases. They are special in that "we know something [the subjects] don't" (1979, p. 289); they are what I call cases of "ignorance and error" (1981, p. 23). In such cases, he agrees, the causal theory applies, but in general the description theory is correct. This maneuver is as ad hoc as one could get. Any theory can be saved by excluding all counterexamples from its domain. Causal theorists claim to have a theory that applies to all cases. According to this theory, people are never the sole judge of the referent of the names and natural kind terms they use. A person may have the knowledge required by the description theory, but that knowledge is irrelevant to reference. If the causal theory works generally, it is clearly to be preferred to Rorty's ad hoc modification of the description theory.

What reasons does Rorty have for thinking that the causal theory does not work generally? One reason is implicit. He thinks that the causal theory cannot handle "reference to the nonexistent," which is allowed by the ordinary notion. This sort of reference is undoubtedly a problem for the causal theory. I think that it can be handled (1981, chap. 6), but shall not attempt to do so here. So far as reference to existents is concerned, Rorty assumes, in what seems a blatantly question-begging way, that a description theory normally applies. He does not respond to the evidence that the causal theory always applies.[25]

7. DAVIDSONIAN SEMANTICS

In the last two sections I have rejected two of the things that Rorty has against the correspondence theory. These are both relatively independent of Davidsonian semantics. The rest of his case against the theory, (iii), comes straight from that semantics.

I have already written at length on Davidsonian semantics.[26] Aside from that, this is not the place to tackle such a difficult subject. I shall restrict myself to a few brief comments on parts of that semantics that are emphasized by Rorty.

(1) The central tenet of Davidsonian semantics has already been aired: the Principle of Charity. In my view, this amazingly popular Principle is implausible and quite false. Rorty asks, rhetorically, what could count as evidence that the vast majority of someone's beliefs were false. The answer is a wide range of evidence about the person's behavior, learning mechanisms, history, and natural and social environment. This evidence might be such that inference to the best explanation should make us conclude that the person's beliefs are mostly false. Of course, it is most unlikely that evidence *would* make us conclude this. However, this epistemic point is irrelevant to the Principle. The Principle wrongly claims that it is constitutive of having beliefs that they are not mostly false.[27]

(2) Aside from this, Davidson's argument for the Principle is verificationist, as Rorty acknowledges (1982, pp. 5–6). I think that it should therefore be rejected. Rorty makes a valiant attempt to save the argument from the charge of verificationism by claiming that the charge depends on taking the notion of truth in question as the correspondence one, whereas it is no more than the "homely and shopworn" notion (1979, pp. 306–11). I do not think that it does so depend.

(3) Rorty attributes to Davidson the view that the only philosophy of language that we need is that of the "field linguist" (1985, p. 339). We need only what is required for that "linguist's translation-manual-cum-ethnographic-report" (p. 341). This is alleged to show that we do not need the correspondence notion of truth (p. 342).

The only argument that Rorty detects in Davidson for this limited view of the philosophy of language is that the "various 'confrontationalist' metaphors [that Rorty associates with correspondence] are more trouble than they are worth" (p. 345). This argument is surely inadequate. Why is Davidson's view any more plausible than the following: The only monetary economics we need is that of the "field economist" interested in preparing an exchange-manual? The philosopher's interest in language, like the economist's in money, is in *explaining* a social phenomenon. Restriction to the impoverished theoretical machinery of the field-worker seems completely inappropriate in both cases.

I do not suppose that field linguists need a worked-out correspondence theory of language, including a theory of reference. However, it seems likely that they *do* need correspondence notions of truth and reference in preparing their manuals; good translation will require that they have caught on to these notions even though they are unlikely to have a theory of them.

(4) Rorty describes Davidson as a "non-reductive physicalist" (p. 345). Yet Davidson's view that truth needs no definition or explanation suggests rather that Davidson is an antiphysicalist, that he exemplifies what Hartry Field calls "semanticalism" (1972, p. 92). Rorty resists this criticism by claiming that the notion of truth used by Davidson is not itself explanatory but merely "disquotational," and so is not in need of explanation (pp. 345–48). If this claim is correct, then it does avoid the criticism. And I think that it is the only way to avoid the criticism. However, despite Rorty's efforts, I find it hard to understand how the central notion in a theory of meaning cannot be explanatory.

(5) Finally, apparently under the influence of Davidson, Rorty seems to think that the correspondence theory seeks the impossible: The attempt to "see language-as-a-whole in relation to something else to which it applies" (1982, p. xix) demands

> some transcendental standpoint outside our present set of representations from which we can inspect the relations between those representations and their object. (1979, p. 293)

"It is the impossible attempt to step out of our skins" (1982, p. xix). This is reminiscent of Putnam's view that realism requires a "God's Eye View," as Rorty himself notes (1985, p. 345). And it is no more appropriate than Putnam's view. The relationship between language and the world is a natural phenomenon as open to empirical investigation as any other. There is, of course, a problem of self-reference, since a theory of language must, like any other theory, be in a language. But it is absurd to think that we have to step out of our skins to solve this (not very interesting) technical problem. There is no other reason for thinking that we have to, either.[28]

8. NO EXCUSE FOR HERMENEUTICS

This paper began by putting to rest the worry about realism occasioned by Rorty. I have now finished my discussion of the first objection to Rorty. The rejection of the skeptical problematic does not require the rejection of correspondence truth.

Furthermore, I have given some indication of the case for correspondence truth. I finish by considering the second objection.

Rorty not only rejects our past, with its interest in skepticism and correspondence; he also offers a vision of the future. Philosophers should emulate "the three most important philosophers of our century—Wittgenstein, Heidegger, and Dewey." What Rorty likes about these philosophers is that

> their later work is therapeutic rather than constructive, edifying rather than systematic, designed to make the reader question his own motives for philosophizing rather than to supply him with a new philosophical program. (1979, pp. 5–6)

He calls what we should practice "hermeneutics," though distancing himself from some of the views, particularly idealist ones, that have been associated with that term.

The basis that Rorty gives for this prescription is inadequate. I agree that we should set the skeptical problematic aside. However, we should move not into hermeneutics, but into systematic and constructive naturalistic philosophy.

One example of this philosophy is the dispute that has occupied the last few sections of this paper. Do we need a correspondence notion of truth to explain language? Rorty does not—certainly, should not—suppose that his Davidsonian view that we do not need it can be established a priori. The question is a crucial empirical one for a systematic and constructive theory of language. Of course, the question is not a *low-level* empirical one, but neither are many empirical questions in, say, physics. That we try to answer the question from an armchair does not prevent it from being empirical; we bring with us to the chair memories and books recording the relevant evidence.

Occasionally, Rorty writes as if a philosophy that has gone naturalistic is no longer philosophy (1979, pp. 188, 384–85). This seems like a boring question about what to call "philosophy." What matters is that some empirical sciences like the study of language have high-level conceptual problems, including some about the relation of those sciences to others, which philosophers are, by training, particularly suited to tackle.

Just as there is a place for a naturalistic philosophy of language, there is one for a naturalistic epistemology. Rorty rejects the possibility of such an epistemology because, following Quine, he assumes that it will simply be psychology: It will describe our ways of learning about the world but will not say how we ought to learn about the world (pp. 221–30). Rorty thinks that such a study does not merit the title "Epistemology." Perhaps not, but it is not all there is to naturalized epistemology. That epistemology does tackle the normative question. Using the evidence of our epistemic successes and failures in science and ordinary life, we theorize about how best to learn about the world. Learning about learning is an empirical activity, just like learning about anything else.[29]

The study of language and knowledge comes within cognitive science. That science generates many problems to which philosophy can make a systematic and constructive contribution. So also does physics, mathematics, and biology. And what about moral, aesthetic, political, and social theories?

In conclusion, philosophy can abandon the skeptical problematic without abandoning correspondence truth and without limiting itself to the edifying practices of the informed dilettante. Rorty has not shown us that it should abandon that truth and limit itself to those practices. The aura of antirealism in Rorty's discussion is misleading: Rorty is a realist.[30]

Notes

1. However, the metaphysics is often well-hidden. In an introduction to a collection of papers, Jarrett Leplin lists ten "characteristic realist claims" (1984, p. 1). These concern truth, reference, success, convergence, theories, and the aims of science. Not one is straightforwardly metaphysical.

2. Two examples that interest Rorty are Hilary Putnam's "metaphysical realism" (1978, pp. 123–25), and the account of realism by Arthur Fine (1984a, p. 86; 1984b, pp. 51–52).

3. See, for example, Field 1978, Churchland 1979, Stich 1983.

4. Thus, Fine introduces 'the Natural Ontogical Attitude' (1984a) for something very similar to what I call 'realism'.

5. In so doing, I go a little beyond the discussion in Devitt 1984.

6. A similar view may lie behind Kim 1980, pp. 596–97.

7. The structuralists' rejection of reference seems to come from their mistaken assumption that the only possible theory of reference is a resemblance theory (Devitt and Sterelny 1987, sec. 13.3).

8. For recent examples, see Blackburn 1980, p. 354, and Fine 1984b, pp. 53–54.

9. 1983b, section 1 (a crticism of Blackburn 1980), and 1984, sections 4.3 to 4.5.

10. These comments are on my statement of realism in a critique of Dummett; 1983a, p. 76.

11. So, Rorty's claim that I think realism "an interesting and controversial thesis" (1985, p. 354) is a bit misleading.

12. See also 1982, pp. xlvi*n*, where he distances himself from Berkeley, and xlvii*n*, where he distances himself from Goodman.

13. Rorty's reaction to such talk in Kuhn and Goodman is nevertheless sympathetic. He construes it metaphorically. I think that it is intended to be taken literally; 1984, pp. 136–40, 192.

14. The views of Davidson that have most influenced Rorty were first published in Davidson's 1973 paper, "On the Very Idea of a Conceptual Scheme," to be found in Davidson 1984. Rorty was also influenced by Stroud 1969.

15. Commitment to it is a variety of what I call "Weak, or Fig-Leaf, Realism"; 1984, p. 22.

16. I gave in to the temptation of seeing Davidson himself as an antirealist on this ground; 1984, p. 180.

17. In their criticisms of Rorty, Chris Murphy (1981, pp. 342–43) and Michael Losonsky (1985) also argue that the theory of reference is not linked to the skeptical problematic.

18. This does *not* entail that word meanings are either *learned* before (compare Rorty 1979, pp. 303–4), or are the *evidence* for Rorty 1985, p. 343), sentence meanings. Word meanings are prior in the order of explanation, not necessarily in the orders of understanding and evidence.

19. On the theory of language, see my 1981 and Devitt and Sterelny 1986. On this notion of truth as a correspondence one, see my 1984, chap. 3. On the setting aside of skepticism, see chap. 5.

20. Compare Rorty's claim that my correspondence theory succumbs to "the pre-Wittgensteinian urge" "to coalesce the justificatory story and the causal story" (1985, pp. 353–54).

21. See also Levin 1984.

22. See, for example, Field 1978, Churchland 1979, Stich 1983.

23. For a lot more, but still not enough, see Devitt and Sterelny 1987, particulary chap. 9 and sec. 8.2.

24. I have used the causal theory to explain the semantics of such constructions in 1981, pp. 263–67.

25. I think that there are reasons, arising out of Donnellan's discussion of definite descriptions (1966), for restricting the generality of the causal theory (1981, pp. 40–41), but these are beside the present point.

26. 1981, chap. 4; 1984, chap. 10; Devitt and Sterelny 1987, chap. 15.

27. Sometimes the Principle is presented as if it simply requires that our disagreements with aliens "be explicable" (1985, p. 351). This makes the Principle an innocuous methodological one: *Of course*, our disagreements should be explicable; and so should our agreements.

28. I have argued against Putnam's view elsewhere (1984, pp. 188–95).

29. On this see Chris Murphy's excellent critical notice of Rorty 1979 (1981, pp. 343–45); also, Devitt 1984, pp. 65 ff., and Kornblith 1985.

30. An earlier version of this paper was delivered at the University of Queensland in July 1986. I am indebted to Rae Langton and Michael Levin for comments on that version that led to changes. The final version of the paper was delivered at the University of Colorado in January 1987.

References

Blackburn, Simon. 1980. "Truth, Realism, and the Regulation of Theory." *Midwest Studies in Philosophy* 5: 353–71.

Churchland, Paul M. 1979. *Scientific Realism and the Plasticity of Mind.* Cambridge.

Davidson, Donald. 1983. "A Coherence Theory of Truth and Knowledge." In *Kant oder Hegel?*, edited by Dieter Henrich. Stuttgart.

Davidson, Donald. 1984. *Inquiries into Truth and Interpretation.* Oxford.

Devitt, Michael. 1981. *Designation.* New York.

Devitt, Michael. 1983a. "Dummett's Anti-Realism." *Journal of Philosophy* 80: 73–99.

Devitt, Michael. 1983b. "Realism and Semantics." Part 2 of a critical study of French, Uehling, and Wettstein 1980. *Nous* 17: 669–81.

Devitt, Michael. 1984. *Realism and Truth.* Princeton.

Devitt, Michael. In press. "Does Realism Explain Success?" *Revue Internationale de Philosophie.*

Devitt, Michael, and Kim Sterelny. 1987. *Language and Reality: An Introduction to the Philosophy of Language.* Cambridge, Mass.

Donnellan, Keith S. 1966. "Reference and Definite Descriptions." *Philosophical Review* 75: 281–304.

Field, Hartry. 1972. "Tarski's Theory of Truth." *Journal of Philosophy* 69: 347–75.

Field, Hartry. 1978. "Mental Representation." *Erkenntnis* 13: 9–61.

Fine, Arthur. 1984a. "The Natural Ontological Attitude." In Leplin 1984, 83–107.

Fine, Arthur. 1984b. "And not Anti-Realism Either." *Nous* 18: 51–65.

French, Peter A., Theodore E. Uehling, Jr., and Howard K. Wettstein, eds. 1980. *Studies in Epistemology.* Midwest Studies in Philosophy. Vol. 5. Minneapolis.

Hirst, R. J. 1967. "Realism." In *Encyclopedia of Philosophy*, vol. 7, edited by Paul Edwards, 77–83. New York.

Kim, Jaegwon. 1980. "Rorty on the Possibility of Philosophy." *Journal of Philosophy* 77: 588–97.

Kornblith, Hilary. 1985. "Introduction: What is Naturalistic Epistemology?" In *Naturalizing Epistemology*, edited by Hilary Kornblith, 1–13. Cambridge, Mass.

Leeds, Stephen. 1978. "Theories of Reference and Truth." *Erkenntnis* 13: 111–29.

Leplin, Jarrett, ed. 1984. *Scientific Realism.* Berkeley.

Levin, Michael, 1984. "What Kind of Explanation is Truth?" In Leplin 1984, 124–39.

Losonsky, Michael. 1985. "Reference and Rorty's Veil." *Philosophical Studies* 47: 291–94.

Murphy, Chris. 1981. Critical Notice of Rorty 1979. *Australasian Journal of Philosophy* 59: 338–45.

Passmore, John. 1966. *A Hundred Years of Philosophy*, 2d ed. London. 1st. ed., 1957.

Putnam, Hilary. 1978. *Meaning and the Moral Sciences.* London.

Putnam, Hilary. 1985. "A Comparison of Something with Something Else." *New Literary History* 17: 61–79.

Quine, W. V. 1960. *Word and Object*. Cambridge, Mass.

Rorty, Richard. 1976. "Realism and Reference." *Monist* 59: 321–40.

Rorty, Richard. 1979. *Philosophy and the Mirror of Nature*. Princeton.

Rorty, Richard. 1982. *Consequences of Pragmaticism (Essays: 1972–1980)*. Minneapolis.

Rorty, Richard. 1985. "Pragmatism, Davidson and Truth." In *Truth and Interpretation: Perspectives on the Philosophy of Donald Davidson*, edited by Ernest LePore, 333–55. Oxford.

Rorty, Richard. 1986. "Beyond Realism and Anti-Realism." In *Weiner Riehe: Themen der Philosophie, Volume I: Wo Steht die Sprachanalytische Philosophie Heute?* edited by Herta Nagl-Dockerl, Richard Heinrich, Ludwig Nagl, and Helmet Vetter, 103–15. Vienna.

Stich, Stephen P. 1983. *From Folk Psychology to Cognitive Science*. Cambridge, Mass.

Stroud, Barry. 1969. "Conventionalism and the Indeterminacy of Translation." In *Words and Objections: Essays in Honor of W. V. Quine*, edited by D. Davidson and J. Hintikka. Dordrecht.

Wittgenstein, Ludwig. 1953. *Philosophical Investigations*, translated by G. E. M. Anscombe. Oxford.

The Elusiveness of Reference
THOMAS BLACKBURN

Some fifteen years after it became a focus of discussion in philosophy of language the notion of a causal or historical theory of reference continues to figure in debates over "realism" in its various forms. It does so in a number of distinct ways, the range of which I can only roughly indicate here.

First, there are still those for whom such a theory represents the best hope for a reply to the threat of idealism, skepticism, or (as Rorty puts it) "something unwholesomely relativistic."[1] Linguistic reference (as determined by causal or historical chains) is invoked as that by which our words may "hook onto" the world, independently of the accuracy of our current beliefs, statements, or theories.[2] Second, there are those who see naturalistic accounts of linguistic reference not as aimed at epistemologically underwriting the course of inquiry, but as completing science's own (realistic) explanation of its successes.[3] Finally, the promise of such theories of reference is viewed with interest by others whose main concern is with the status of semantic notions themselves. In opposition to those who would view "truth" and "reference" as having but instrumental or congratulatory value in our theories of speakers and languages, these semantic realists see our progress toward informative accounts of linguistic and nonlinguistic representation as vindicating the view that these are real relations obtaining between words and the world.[4]

The question of how much genuine progress we *have* made, however, must be confronted by one who invokes naturalistic accounts of reference in any of these contexts. The early debates on the topic were directed at the plausibility of this new *approach*, and at the philosophical implications such accounts might have were they to be worked out in detail. But it is remarkable that the "new approach" is still so much discussed and cited, when so little has been done to redeem those enthusiastically penned promissory notes which marked its inception. What had been hoped for was a revelation of the fundamental "mechanisms" of linguistic representation, locating these within that natural world to which they give us access. What we have,

I submit, is still but an intriguing approach or "picture,"[5] one whose legitimacy must be called into question (if not on other grounds) by the absence of any recognizable progress toward making good its promises.

In this essay, I propose to explore the question of why an enlightening and satisfactory account of reference has not issued from the work of the "new theorists." It is not clear to me that there are satisfactory arguments that establish a priori the impossibility of giving an adequate account of their supposed mechanism. However this may be, my more modest aim of providing a reminder of the specific difficulties facing any attempt to fill in such an account may prove useful, if only to evoke caution in those who still write as if that mechanism has already (in essence) been uncovered. In the final section of this paper I go much further, suggesting that these difficulties indicate something important about the nature of reference ascription, and therein, why there is good reason to deny the existence of any (intentional *or* nonintentional) mechanism of representation.

The quest for a theory of reference may be conducted in the hope of answering to general epistemological concerns, as a means of viewing linguistic representation as a coherent feature of the world as we know it, or as a purely semantic inquiry into the general rules in accordance with which we understand and evaluate the utterances of our fellows. My argument, in brief, is that in any of these forms, the inquiry appears to founder upon a certain predicament. Every proposed account is either mistaken (that is, it presents us with a mechanism or rule that is manifestly not that which establishes *reference*), or covertly vacuous (and, hence, not indicative of anything like a mechanism or rule at all). In the closing section, I attempt to make a start at seeing why this is so.

I

From among the various developments that have been put forth and debated among theorists of reference, I will focus only on the attempt to formulate those conditions that serve to fix or determine the reference of a proper name as it is used by an individual speaker.[6] If anything suggests progress toward uncovering a mechanism of reference, it is to be found here (rather than in theses regarding, say, the "rigidity" of proper names in modal contexts). It is, then, to suggestions that singular reference attaches to names by virtue of causal, historical, or social connections that we now turn.

The excitement over causal or historical accounts was stirred by convincing arguments to the effect that traditional theories had failed to capture the conditions for name reference by an individual. Those theories, with their reliance upon the beliefs or descriptions associated with names by their users, simply left no room for a speaker's ignorance or error regarding the referent of any name he or she used. Kripke, Putnam, Donnellan, and others forcefully pointed out the commonplace — that we are all incapable, with regard to many of the terms we use, of accurately and uniquely specifying that whereof we speak. Having come to designate a particular thing, a name retains its reference even as it is used and misused by speakers in the relevant linguistic community. The reference of the name *itself* (its "semantic reference") seems to stand independent of the representational capacities of its users, and to be determined, instead, by the causal or historical background of its use.

The task facing the new theorists is that of spelling out in detail the story of these semantically relevant connections. As is well known, that enterprise comprises two distinct undertakings, corresponding to two sorts of referential links. The envisioned account, put in terms of a chain of usage, must include the specification of that by which a name acquires its reference, and a treatment of that connection between speakers whereby they come to share in the established use of the name, "coreferring" semantically despite disagreements, mistakes, or ignorance regarding its referent. Here we will follow out only the latter attempt, in the hope that we can learn from it lessons whose applications will extend to the whole project of uncovering the mechanisms of reference.

What we are after, in effect, is an account of community membership, of the sort that is supposed to ensure coreference in the use of a particular name. Of course, it would suffice for the existence of such a community, consisting of speakers A and B, that they *each* (independently) use 'Feynman', say, to refer to Feynman.[7] But the causal theorists' critique of traditional accounts of naming reveals that this cannot be necessary for coreference. There is also, evidently, coreference that is not mere coincidence of reference—cases in which the reference of 'Feynman', as used by B, derives from and is determined by its reference for A. Our present concern is with what it is that secures such dependent, borrowed reference in the use of a name.[8]

The first response, included in every preliminary sketch of a causal or historical theory, is that if the use of the name has been "transmitted" from A to B, their coreference in its use is assured. Admission to the relevant linguistic fellowship is but a matter of having acquired the name itself from a member in good standing. Here, indeed, we find an account that delivers us a mechanism of coreference: The semantic relevance of A's usage lies in its being causally responsible for B's using the name. Here, however, we find what can be only a first approximation to the account we seek. For, if the traditional views of naming have demanded too much of individual speakers, this straightforwardly causal picture of coreference surely demands too little. It is a familiar-enough fact, documented in the literature by a wealth of "my cat Caesar" stories, that mere causal connection to some antecedent tradition of name use does not suffice for the preservation of reference. As the causal theorists have readily acknowledged, we need an account that distinguishes those cases in which prior usage is *referentially* relevant from those in which it is merely *causally* relevant to the current use of the name.[9]

We must, however, take care not to move too quickly here, for the causal theorist actually has several options at this point:

(1) Preserve the insistence upon the sufficiency of the causal connection, by denying that (genuine) shifts of reference occur.

(2) Preserve the sufficiency claim, by allowing that coreference is secured only when the causal connection between speakers is "of the appropriate sort."

(3) Preserve the sufficiency claim, by insisting that causal connection does assure coreference, in the absence of new "dubbings."

(4) Allow that the causal connection itself is *not* sufficient to assure coreference, that sufficient conditions may be obtained only by somehow augmenting the story of *B*'s relation to *A*.

In fact, it is only option (4) that we will pursue seriously, in that this is the route commonly taken both by the causal theorists themselves, and by those who seek to incorporate into a more traditional account the insights of the causal theorists. Their move is to bring in some further condition, satisfaction of which will complete the picture of successful transmission. We will examine such attempts shortly. But the appeal of this fourth option is not independent of the failings of the other three, and there is something to be gained by first noting these failings.

Let us begin with the most attractive of these, the third option. Its plausibility derives from the fact that, in the sort of "reference shifts" that come most readily to mind, there is the conscious adoption of a new referring practice—a new "dubbing." I *decide* to bestow the name 'Feynman' upon my goldfish, and the occurrence of this dubbing seems to override the semantic relevance of the causal chain of usage that leads back to a certain physicist. Indeed, were all shifts in a name's reference brought about in this way, perhaps there would be no problem. But there are problems, the most salient of which results from the fact that reference may shift unwittingly, as the product of error and misunderstanding. (Evans's 'Madagascar' case is a renowned example of this sort of shift.)[10] Once we allow, then, that a new "dubbing" (and a resulting shift in reference) may take place without the occurrence of any overt or intended bestowal of the name upon its new referent, this third proposal has become empty. It amounts only to the claim that causal connections secure coreference, so long as no referential shift has taken place along the way.

I submit, then, that reflection upon option (3) reveals it to fail in just the way that option (2) more obviously does. The latter *does* provide sufficient conditions for coreference, and also allows for reference shifts—but only by virtue of smuggling into the "account" precisely that of which an account was sought. So long as we must describe our 'Feynman'-user's reference as being the product of his being causally connected "in the right way" to another user of the name, we will have made no advance in our understanding of borrowed reference. For this "in the right way" can, it seems, be read only as "in the reference-preserving way"; and the "appropriate sort" of causal connections can be said only to be those which *do* secure coreference. To determine whether *B* does corefer with *A*, then, we should have to see whether the causal connection between their uses of 'Feynman' is of the right sort, the determination of which in turn demands that we (independently) ascertain whether *B* does use 'Feynman' to refer to Feynman. The conditions supposed to secure coreference covertly include the very fact of that coreference itself.

Options (2) and (3), then, are of interest not because they represent serious candidates for a theory of borrowed reference, but because they serve to warn us of a sort of smuggling whose attempt need not be so obvious, and against which we must be on guard.[11] Option (1), on the other hand, presents us with a more interesting challenge, despite its appearance as the most counterintuitive line of response to the problem of reference shifts. Why, after all, should the causal theorists not simply dig in their heels at this point, insisting that causal connection between uses of a name *does* assure their coreference? Why not take the line that these apparent shifts in the reference of a name are merely apparent—that, if the "new usage" involves a divergence from the referring practice that underlies it, this constitutes but a mistaken use of the name? The name *itself*, according to this line, retains its original (semantic) reference, despite its (even habitual) misuse by speakers to whom it has been transmitted.

It is important to see that our initial, most natural response to such a proposal is not sufficient to defeat it. Appeals to the case of 'Madagascar', or to more homely examples in which we might insist that an old name has been put to a new use, are of no immediate force here. These die-hard causal theorists can allow that something indeed has shifted—namely, the "speaker's reference" of the name, as reflected in the claims endorsed by its new users. But we are seeking, remember, an account of *semantic* reference and coreference, a theory of the denotation of the names themselves; the causal theory, as we have represented it, arises precisely from the recognition that the "content" we associate with a name may not pick out its actual referent. Adopting option (1), then, amounts only to the extension of this insight, so as to deny the reality of these alleged shifts of reference. To be sure, there may be changes in the "content" attached to a name, and we may come to take it to be (and use it as if it were) the name of something other than its semantic referent. But, if our use of it is causally linked to some earlier usage, the reference of the *name* has been preserved, and we (semantically) corefer with those earlier users.

There is, I believe, no direct way in which such a thesis can be shown to be wrong. The most we can say, by way of attempting to repudiate it, is that the causal theorists who take this valiant line have so cut themselves off from our ordinary intuitions and practices of reference-ascription that it is wholly unclear how we might establish that their thesis is *right*. Even more to the point, however, is the question of why (assuming that it *is* right) these notions of "reference" and "coreference" should be of any interest to us. Given this purely causal rendering, the reference of a name has become irrelevant to our actual use of it, and (as a result) the closely related notion of *literal* truth and falsity has taken on a sense that makes it incidental to our activity as critics and inquirers. The causal theorists who persevere by embracing option (1) may not be demonstrably wrong in doing so, but they have failed to give us a theory of anything about which we should care. And, in precisely this sense, they *are* wrong: They have failed to produce a satisfactory theory of *reference*.

The examination of options (1) through (3), then, reveals a simple causal theory to be either vacuous or mistaken as an account of reference-borrowing. This brings us to a position from which it appears that only some version of option (4) lies open, if we are to arrive at an account of coreference that is both informative and intuitively satisfying. What we require is the recognition that prior (or communal) usage *may* determine current reference, along with the allowance that this need not always be so, even where there *is* a causal connection to earlier uses of the name. The new theorist must find a way to distinguish (in principle) these two sorts of cases, and thereby to uncover that which does secure dependent or borrowed reference when it does occur.

As noted earlier, the common response in the literature involves the invocation of some further condition, whose satisfaction will distinguish referential linkage from merely causal linkage. This attempt has taken a number of specific forms, but these share the general feature of putting a certain degree of authority back in the hands of individual users of a name. Their central point is that antecedent or communal usage is relevant to the current user's reference with a name, insofar as he somehow recognizes or acknowledges that relevance. He may, indeed, misuse the name on occasion; he may even do so habitually, by virtue of associating with it "content" that fails to pick out its referent accurately and uniquely. In this sense the *proper* use of the name, that prescribed by its semantic reference, may not be reflected in his actual use of it, and may instead be determined by how other speakers have used that name. But these are his authorities (and this is *his* semantic reference) in that he somehow has delegated this authority to those others, thereby establishing his (semantic) coreference with them. That "chain" of borrowed reference, then, is not so much a causal chain as a chain of linguistic authority, with its links being secured by individuals' recognition of the relevance of past usage to their own.[12]

The proposed account, still put quite generally, amounts to this: *B* corefers with *A* in his uses of 'Feynman' if *B* recognizes *A* as an authority regarding its reference, if he takes *A*'s use of the name to set the standard for his own proper use of it.[13] The proposal is, of course, intolerably vague in a number of respects, and it remains to be seen whether (when it has been more fully articulated) it can provide anything resembling a satisfactory account. It should be noted from the outset, however, that this is anything but an ad hoc move on the part of the theorist of reference. It may appear so, as when Kripke suddenly introduces "intentions to use the name as it has been used" to save what was to have been a causal picture from refutation by obvious counterexample.[14] It is, however, a plausible and well-motivated emendation of the conditions for semantic coreference. We are offered here the means of accommodating both *mistaken* use of a name (in which its reference is nonetheless preserved by the social context of its use), and also the emergence of *novel* and *independent* referring practices (in which the new participants are exempted from criticism directed at their divergence from prior usage). This represents, then, the attempt to retain the causal theorists' fundamental insight, while still satisfying our demand that the semantic reference of the name be in some obvious way *relevant* to its actual use in the making and criticizing of claims.

It is worth noting, moreover, that some move of this sort may be found in the writings of virtually all recent theorists of reference who have addressed this problem, whether we look to the new theorists or to their critics. Kripke's appeal to speaker intentions, when he suggests how we might advance from a causal "picture" to a genuine "theory," has already been mentioned. Putnam, too, when he introduces that "division of linguistic labor" implicit in the social or historical approach, portrays individual speakers as linked (coreferentially) to the experts by their attitude of "cooperation" and "consent."[15] From the side of the critics, we see Dummett acknowledging this phenomenon of borrowed reference, invoking the speaker's willingness to defer to established usage as being that which effects the borrowing.[16] Others, more explicitly attempting to salvage an individualistic traditional view, make appeal to a speaker's "fall-back descriptions," whereby one may cite other users of a name to fix the reference of one's own usage.[17]

All these maneuvers, I take it, are but versions of this same general approach to the problem confronting us. Whether the resulting accounts had best be viewed as modified causal theories, or as modified versions of the traditional view, is not (at present) a matter of great concern. It is, however, significant that representatives of both camps find in such an account their best hope of treating the relevant semantic phenomena. This suggests that we may be on the verge of arriving at a workable synthesis of the insights present in each of these rival approaches. And it suggests, as well, that if this sort of ploy can be shown not to do the work demanded of it, the ramifications of this failure may extend far beyond the bounds of our hopes for a successful *causal* or *historical* theory of reference. What is at issue is whether we have advanced at all in our search for a mechanism of shared semantic reference.

For the purpose of indicating that we have not, it is not necessary that we settle on any particular formulation of this "further condition." However it is put, it involves some recognition of the linguistic authority of some other speaker or speakers, with regard to the reference (and, hence, the proper employment) of the name in question. If *B* defers to *A*, in some such sense, then *A* is the authority whose use of 'Feynman' fixes its reference for *B*. (We must allow that *A* may be someone quite far-removed from *B* and *B*'s contemporaries. *A* may, indeed, be the one who initially introduced the name into currency, and to whom *B* is linked by an extended chain of transmission and deference. This, however, is of no consequence to our present concern.) What *is* of consequence is this: If a speaker may be ignorant or in error regarding the reference of some name he employs, why might he not err as well in recognizing the relevant authority (or in recognizing the relevant chain of authority)? Indeed, precisely *in* that one may know so little about the name's referent, mistakes in picking out or cooperating with the proper authorities seem all the more likely to occur.[18] Moreover, it seems plausible to suppose that deference may be exhibited or withheld owing to factors that are clearly irrelevant to semantic evaluation. Coercion, on the one hand, and simple stubbornness, on the other, might result in deference or refusal to defer that should not be deemed matters of semantic interest.

To make clearer the difficulty here, we must consider (still in a general way) how the "deference" of one speaker toward another might be characterized. Whether it is a matter of citing, of consulting, or simply of being sensitive to certain sorts of criticism, this deference could be construed as something that a speaker *does* or *would do* in relation to others. That is, we can suppose either that on each uttering of the name our borrowing speaker *defers*; or, more plausibly, that he *would* defer if the legitimacy of his usage were challenged.[19]

Suppose we take the first option and insist that a speaker corefers with another if he *does* defer (on the occasion of each tokening of the name) to that other speaker. Even putting aside the obvious psychological implausibility of the view, we are faced with consequences that are semantically unacceptable. If we take this to be a sufficient condition of reference-borrowing, there simply can be no such thing as mistaken deference. If we take it to be necessary for such borrowing, we must conclude that if no deference is at present being exhibited, the individual is his own ultimate authority. In short, we arrive at a position analogous to (and no less objectionable than) that of the most naive sort of descriptional theorist, who leaves no room for the errant or ignorant use of a name.

If, on the other hand, we take it that a speaker corefers with those to whom he *would* defer regarding the name, we arrive at a position that is superficially much more plausible. But we also arrive at a position from which it appears that only the most stubborn of us *ever* use a name to refer uniquely and determinately. For it is psychologically indisputable that any of us would defer, in readily imaginable circumstances, to virtually anyone. To take a particularly exotic example, were I transported unwittingly to Putnam's Twin Earth, I presumably would exhibit deference to speakers in *that* world, for whom the name 'Feynman' has a reference divergent from that which it has in this world. What is of importance, however, is not the question of to whom I should *then* be referring, but that of my *present* reference in using the name. Even now, it is true of me that I *would* defer both to Earthian and Twin Earthian speakers, under different circumstances (however unlikely) that might present themselves. There are, indeed, any number of distinct (actual or possible) referring practices for the use of a particular name, to whose participants I *would* defer on a given occasion. Are we to say, then, that as I now use the name, it has indeterminate or ambiguous reference? The proposal, as it stands, appears to demand such a verdict. Only one so constituted that he or she would never defer, or would defer (under any circumstances) only to *this* or *these* speakers (participants in a single semantic practice), could ever utter a name in a way that rendered it semantically univocal and unambiguous.

Neither an occurrent nor a dispositional rendering of this notion of "deference," then, issues in a satisfactory account. What a speaker *does* or *would do*, by way of deferring to another, cannot in itself be sufficient to decide the question of whether or not the two corefer. A speaker might, for any number of reasons, defer to one who is not the relevant authority (or who is not a member of the relevant chain of authority), and fail to defer to one who is. Returning to the case of our 'Feynman'-users, the mere fact that B defers (or would defer) to A cannot be that which secures their semantic coreference in uttering the name.

What we need, it seems, is some means of distinguishing those dispositions to defer which are referentially relevant from those which are not—a situation reminiscent of that confronted by the causal theory earlier. And, intuitively, what we should like to say here is that deference to another suffices for coreference if it is displayed "in light of all the relevant information," or if it is exhibited "under ideal conditions." A *relevant* authority, we should say, is one to whom our speaker would defer, were the borrower ideally rational and well informed. Only with this sort of qualification can we discount, as it seems we must, that misplaced deference whose occurrence is psychologically possible but semantically irrelevant.

The crucial and obvious question, however, is how we are to understand this talk of "the relevant information," or of those "optimal conditions" under which B's deference to A would count as securing their coreference. What must be included in these conditions, in order that their satisfaction guarantee that B's deference to A is not misplaced? That A attaches the same "content" to the name 'Feynman'? That A indeed be the one from whom B acquired the name? It is clear that these attempts will not work, and it is clear why they will not. Neither condition, we have seen, suffices to ensure that A and B do corefer; nor, thus, that A is the rightful object of B's deference. Indeed, it was precisely the inadequacy of these (descriptional and causal) treatments of coreference that led to our bringing onto the scene the further condition of "deference."

In a quest such as this, there may well be no such thing as reaching the end of the road. But when the scenery begins to look strikingly familiar, as it does at this point, we should realize that the road simply is not getting us anywhere. What we need, by way of assurance that B's deference is well placed (and thus that it is deference of the sort that establishes coreference), is nothing less than the very fact that A and B *do* corefer in their uses of 'Feynman'. And it is obvious that, if *this* is to be invoked in our account of their coreference, we shall have the "very fact" to be accounted for figuring prominently in its own explanation. B now is seen to corefer with A in that he ideally would (or should) defer to A—a "should" whose obtaining can be explained only in terms of the fact that B does corefer with A.[20] We have, to be sure, arrived at an indisputably sufficient condition for coreference, but our journey has taken us nowhere.

What emerges is that the attempt to devise a "modified" causal theory, a synthesis of the old and the new, faces that same predicament we noted in connection with the straightforward causal account. Either the conditions for reference-borrowing are stated in such a way as to be informative but wrong ("Deference just *is* sufficient."), or in such a way as to be correct but wholly unenlightening ("*Well-placed* deference is sufficient."). In neither case have we discovered a way of picking out, in terms that do not presuppose the fact, that which secures the coreference of B with A.

II

We have been following out a very narrow and specific line of inquiry, and it is time to try to derive the lessons of it. Our attention has been restricted to questions of reference-fixing in the case of proper names, and (within that sphere) to those cases where it appears that social or historical relations between speakers are semantically relevant. But this has been intended to represent and shed light on the general nature of reference-ascription, and upon the upshot of attempts to locate general rules governing such ascriptions. As a first step, it is important to characterize more generally what has been the object of our search, and how that search has been frustrated.

We may first note that this work toward a theory of borrowed reference did *not* meet with failure because it attempted, in any obvious way, to "step outside" our discourse or our practices for assessing one another's utterances. The charge has often been made that this incoherent undertaking is implicit in philosophical theorizing about reference and truth, and that there is no sense to be made of this project of "uncovering the mechanisms of linguistic representation."[21] To be sure, the inquiry here *was* directed at uncovering such a mechanism, but it also was guided at every step by our practices of ascribing reference to terms, and might best be seen as the attempt to formulate the rules that implicitly govern such ascriptions.

Only in this light, I submit, can we understand the causal theorists' objections to traditional theories of name reference. Their charge was that these latter accounts failed to do justice to the ways in which we understand and evaluate one another's utterances in everyday discourse. It was taken as manifest that 'Feynman' may refer to Feynman, even where the speaker using the name holds mistaken beliefs or is incapable of identifying its referent. The cases brought forth are, thus, ones in which we agree (it is hoped) on the semantic facts—that 'Feynman' refers to Feynman, that 'a physicist' applies to Feynman but not to him alone. Such cases obviously could not be presented by one responding to worries over whether we are semantically "in touch with" the world; nor could the superiority of the causal or historical theory be argued from any illusory standpoint "outside" our discourse.

The only real and objectionable sense of "standing outside" that we have encountered lies in the proposal of a rule for assigning reference that does not accord with our commonplace intuitions and judgments. If what we are after is a theory of *reference* in the use of terms, then we cannot but test any such proposal against the interpretive practices it seeks to codify. One who suggests a mechanism that would result in reference assignments badly out of line with our actual assessment of one another must make out in what sense this can be a theory of reference at all.

Herein we see both what our inquiry actually aimed at and wherein it actually failed. There was nothing incoherent in that aim itself, which was that of revealing those factors which make for reference and coreference in the use of a name, by un-covering our rules for assigning reference to terms. But this inquiry did, as I see it, fail to uncover any such rules, and hence, any factor that "makes for" reference or coreference in the use of a name.

What we have seen, I suggest, is that in *no* single case of name reference can we rightly and informatively say "*This* is what secures reference here." If the argu-ments cited and presented so far are sound, their upshot is not merely that there are still certain cases of successful name reference in which we have not yet located the mechanism by which that reference (or coreference) is established. Rather, their consequence is that we cannot claim to have located such a "mechanism" — in the sense of informative sufficient conditions — for *any* case of name reference. It is not that we have only theories that are incomplete, explaining only "most" or "certain" instances of denotation by proper names. We do not have any theory that explains, in the desired sense, even the most obvious and uncontroversial cases.

These are bold claims, and it may be far from clear how one might reasonably derive such pessimism from the considerations presented in section I. We were, after all, seeking only an account of "borrowed reference"; and this was to be but a part of a more general theory of coreference (since not all coreference is the product of "borrowing"); and this, in turn, was to be but a part of a theory of name reference in general. How, from our want of a satisfactory account of borrowed reference, might we conclude that in *no* case can we say what secures the relation of reference between name and bearer? What of those cases in which coreference does not in-volve borrowing, let alone those in which *co*reference is not even at issue? Indeed, what of those cases in which there *is* deference to the proper authorities, in which a speaker does (or would) rely on the community and its experts in a manner that involves no mistakes or coercion? Can we not at least say that *commonly*, in such borrowings, it is the speaker's deference to authority that establishes the reference of the name he employs?

These questions are entirely legitimate, and certainly give evidence of the many steps that lie between the argument of the foregoing section and any general consequences of the sort I have suggested. We can make a start at filling in these steps, however, by correcting the misapprehension implicit in the last of these ques-tions. What it represents, I believe, is a failure to appreciate the general thrust of my worries concerning the theoretical treatment of the phenomenon of borrowed reference. Setting this straight is crucial to my attempt to support my more general negative thesis.

A central move in my argument against the "deference theory" lay in calling attention to the fact that we might envision deference being exhibited in one's use of a name, where this deference would not be deemed semantically relevant, or would not have been directed at the "proper" authorities. We can imagine cases, that is, in which, though B would defer to A in the use of 'Feynman', this fact would *not* secure their coreference. If this is so, however, its lesson is certainly not just that deference does not suffice in *this* case — of course it does not, since in the imagined circumstances the two do not corefer in the use of the name. The point, rather, is that deference does not suffice in *any* case. There simply is no sense in saying, in light of this, that deference is only *commonly* responsible for securing coreference. Deference, in itself, is never the whole story. It must, to be sufficient, be deference "of the right sort," or deference "which is well placed." The problem is that there seems to be no way to explicate these quoted phrases without invoking the very semantic facts at issue.

Similarly, our original appeal to "deference" was motivated not by the need to handle only those cases of reference-borrowing that could not be treated in terms of causal connections alone. The worry, again, was that causal connections in themselves *never* can be the whole story in any case of reference-borrowing, as demonstrated by the fact that such connections may obtain without the obtaining of coreference. Until the causal theorists (or any other, for that matter) can specify conditions the obtaining of which would in every case secure coreference, they cannot claim to have explained or accounted for coreference in any case. (Of course, as we have seen, it is easy enough to meet our demand through appeal, say, to causal connections "of the appropriate type." It should by now be obvious that the "smuggling" we noticed in this move is of the same sort as that concealed in the later appeal to "well-placed deference.")[22]

In general, what we must guard against is the illusion that, as we proceed down the path from descriptional theory to causal theory to deference theories, we are at each step accounting for more and more cases of name reference—uncovering, along the way, those conditions which (in various circumstances) link the name to its bearer. Seen in this light, the point of section I appears only to be that there may still be certain cases to be accounted for, still further rules (or refinements in their formulations) to be uncovered. But this dialectical path is not one of ever-mounting success, of our progressing toward a more complete grasp of what it is that secures reference and coreference. If the arguments against the traditional accounts are on the mark, if representational "fit" is not sufficient to assure semantic reference, then in *no* case can we say that reference is a matter of such "fit." If there are cases in which mere causal connection does not secure reference (or coreference), then there is no case in which it *does*. Finally, in that deference may be (or would be, in certain circumstances) directed at speakers with whom one does not semantically corefer, deference can in *no* instance be seen as establishing coreference. To genuinely and informatively explain or account for even the most clear-cut cases of reference and coreference, we must add to these accounts some further condition. I take our inquiry above to indicate that this further condition is to be found nowhere but in the obtaining of those very semantic facts that were to be explained or accounted for.

III

There is a pattern of failure here, recognition of which should dissuade us from hoping any longer that there *is* a rule of reference-assignment, or a mechanism that is singled out by our practices as *the* link between name and bearer. We must try now to discern why this is so, why this phenomenon of shared reference is so resistant to theoretical treatment, and our general standards of reference-assignment so resistant to codification.

Clues emerge from certain points made in passing during the course of our inquiry. The fundamental insight of the new theorists, in their attacks upon the traditional views, was that the reference of a name is not simply to be "read off" from the ideas, beliefs, or claims of its users. Speakers make *mistakes* in talking about things, which could only be so if the reference of the terms they use were not regarded as being dependent solely on the content of their utterances. What they say and believe of their referent may be drastically out of line with what they *should* say and believe of it, even to the point where their ("speakers") reference in using the name may differ from the reference of the name itself. In brief, the notion of the "semantic reference" of a name is introduced to play a normative role in the characterization of an utterance. The semantic referent of a name (however this is determined) is that thing for which the name is *properly* used, where that usage involves a prescription of which statements one *ought* (or is *allowed*) to make in using the name.

A first and crucial point, then, is this: To say that a name (in some speaker's employ) *really* (or *semantically*) refers to Feynman is implicitly to set a standard for its proper use by that speaker. We cannot, in general, rely on the speaker's behavior to show us what this standard is, precisely in that he or she may violate it by holding beliefs (and uttering sentences) that are badly mistaken, or that are inadequate in identifying the name's referent. Whether or not this is so, in a given case, can be decided only on the basis of an independent assignment of reference to the name. We must, that is, already have decided on the standard applicable to the speaker's utterances, before we can evaluate their truth or falsity.

On the other hand, given the multiplicity of actual and possible semantic references for any name-type, we need some way of underwriting the judgment that our assignment of semantic reference (to a name as used by an individual) indeed captures the standard by which *that* speaker's utterances should be evaluated. The failure of the simple causal theory illustrated our practice of recognizing the emergence of competing traditions of name usage, and our sense that the evaluation of a speaker's utterances must be senstitive to what that speaker deems relevant to their evaluation. The semantic reference of a name, as I use or misuse it, must bear some relation to what I do or would recognize (if only ideally) as relevant to its proper usage. Where this condition is not satisfied, we lose our grip on the sense of saying that the name "really" has this reference for me.

We can see now in a new light why those notions of "deference" and "authority" naturally worked their way into our attempted account of borrowed reference, as a means of doing justice to this sense that the reference of a name should be relevant to the speech-behavior of those for whom it has that reference. But we now can see, also, why the questions arose of specifying the "right" authorities, those to whom the speaker *should* defer. Here, again, we hit upon the fact that what counts as correct or rightly placed deference (no less than what counts as correct claim-making) can be judged only *after* we have settled the question of what the name semantically refers to for the speaker in question.

The predicament facing a theorist of reference, then, may be put as follows: We are seeking a method of assigning semantic reference to a name as employed by a particular speaker, where this amounts to deciding what rule he should follow in using it. If that proposed method involves looking solely to him—his utterances, beliefs, or deference to others—then we lose our sense of its being a *rule* for him, which he may not always follow and which his behavior may not reflect. By contrast, if we specify a method of assignment that involves some "mechanism" that is irrelevant to how he does or would use the name, we lose our sense of its being a rule *for him*. This predicament, which underlies the general difficulty noted in section II, appears to reflect a certain tension in our practices of linguistic interpretation, a tension that cannot be glossed over and that frustrates any reduction of those practices to a (metalinguistic) rule.

And yet we do (in our ordinary understanding of one another) assign reference to names, taking into account as we do so a number of factors that have emerged in our discussion. Mere use of a particular name, the beliefs or claims associated with it, the social context in which it is uttered—all provide grounds on which we make judgments of reference, judgments on which, in turn, rest our evaluations of the truth or falsity of sentences uttered by individuals.

To deny, then, that there are *facts* of reference and coreference would be, indeed, to "step outside" our ordinary discourse and practices. But the considerations presented here should not be seen as leading us into an "antirealism" regarding reference or other semantic notions. They serve to display these facts as emergent from our practices of *interpreting* speakers and their utterances, where this is an enterprise that cannot be separated from the *evaluation* of sentences and those who utter them. The hope (especially on the part of epistemologically motivated "realists") was for an account of reference assignment that displayed independent, general rules for such interpretation, so that we might rightly interpret and evaluate utterances in problematic or philosophically interesting contexts. The absence of such rules, though it renders impotent any attempt to found a realism *upon* a theory of reference, also makes evident in just what (benign) sense we *can* be realists regarding semantic phenomena themselves.

It should be noted that the normativity of the notion of "semantic reference" does not itself preclude there being a "mechanism" or a precise rule for its ascription. Our interpretive practices might have been such that we *did* take the causal heritage of a name to determine its semantic reference, just as we might have taken the truth of a claim to be determined by whether it pleases the king, or the goodness of an action to be decided by whether it accords with the prescriptions and prohibitions of a certain holy text. Within such practices as these, then, there would be a rule for the ascription of coreference or of goodness. There would, indeed, be a "nature" or "essence" of reference for the theorists to uncover. But there is not. *Our* use of 'refers' may be justified and debated through appeal to a variety of considerations, but it is not governed by any general rules that the theorist can hope to reveal.[23] The turn to social context as relevant to the determination of reference was an important insight of the new theorists. Properly appreciated, however, it is not a revelation of the real mechanism of reference; instead, it is a step toward the realization that there is no such mechanism to be found.[24]

NOTES

1. R. Rorty, "Realism and Reference," *Monist* 59 (1976): 323.

2. See, for instance, M. Devitt's *Designation* (New York, 1981), xii. "Causal theories of reference," Devitt tells us, "promise an answer to age-old questions about how language 'hooks onto' the world."

3. See, for instance, R. Boyd's "The Current Status of Scientific Realism," in *Scientific Realism*, edited by J. Leplin (Berkeley, 1984), 41–82, and M. Levin's "What Kind of Explanation is Truth?," 124–39 in the Leplin volume.

4. See H. Field, "Conventionalism and Instrumentalism in Semantics," *Nous* 9 (1975): 375–405, and M. Devitt, *Designation*, chap. 4.

5. For Kripke's distinction between a "picture"and a "theory" of name reference see *Naming and Necessity* (Cambridge, Mass., 1980), 94–97.

6. The seminal works here include K. Donnellan, "Proper Names and Identifying Description," in *Semantics of Natural Language,* edited by D. Davidson and G. Harman (Dordrecht, 1972), 356–79; S. Kripke, *Naming and Necessity* (Cambridge, Mass., 1980), first published in the Davidson and Harman volume, 253–355 and 763–69; H. Putnam, "Explanation and Reality," "The Meaning of 'Meaning'," and "Language and Reality," all reprinted in *Mind, Language, and Reality: Philosophical Papers II* (Cambridge, 1975).

7. It is to be noted here that we are concerned with the semantic reference of a name as it is used by an individual speaker. This is not, then, then to be identified with the *communal* reference of the name, though it may be that this *is* what fixes its semantic reference for individual speakers. But the notion with which we are concerned at present is that of what the name itself refers to in the individual's utterances, not with its (possibly divergent) "speaker's reference." This terminology derives from S. Kripke, "Speaker's Reference and Semantic Reference," in *Contemporary Perspectives in the Philosphy of Language,* edited by French, Uehling, and Wettstein (Minneapolis, 1979), 6–27.

8. For this limited purpose, we may take for granted *A*'s reference in using 'Feynman', and also take as unproblematic *this* occurrence of 'refers' in our account. Our story of borrowed reference will be damagingly circular only if, in specifying the conditions for *B*'s coreferring with *A*, we have to invoke *B*'s *own* reference in using the name. It is to be by virtue of his coreference with *A* that *B* refers to Feynman, not the other way around.

9. See, on this score, Kripke's remarks in *Naming and Necessity,* 93, 96–7, 163.

10. G. Evans, "The Causal Theory of Names," *Aristotelian Society Supplementary Volume* 47 (1973): 196.

11. In general, of course, the appeal to connections "of the appropriate sort" is not intended to represent part of a finished theory of reference and coreference. It is meant, rather, to mark out that which further research must uncover. Why I take there to be no hope that this "appropriate sort" might prove to be a *natural kind* of causal connection will become apparent in what follows.

12. Such an account is most explicitly proposed in A. Goldman, "Reference and Linguistic Authority," *Southern Journal of Philosophy* 17 (1979): 305–21. My own Ph.D. dissertation, "Proper Names and Linguistic Authority," (Pittsburgh, 1982) contains a lengthy discussion of its merits and failings, and is the basis for this section of the present paper.

13. Not that *A* herself need be in any better position to properly "pick out" the referent of the name.

As will be pointed out later, I am idealizing here in a manner that ignores the fact that all of *B*'s contemporaries may defer to earlier users of the name as being those whose use of it reflected its genuine, semantic reference.

14. *Naming and Necessity*, 96-7.

15. See, for instance, his "Language and Reality," 274.

16. M. Dummett, "The Social Character of Meaning," in his *Truth and Other Enigmas* (Cambridge, Mass., 1978), especially 425. See also his *Frege: Philosophy of Language* (New York, 1973), 138-40.

17. See B. Loar, "The Semantics of Singular Terms," *Philosophical Studies* 30 (1976): pp. 353-77; W. Ingber, "The Descriptive View of Referring," *The Journal of Philosophy* 76 (1979): 725-38; and M. McKinsey, "Causality and the Paradox of Names," *Midwest Studies in Philosophy* 9 (1984): 491-515.

18. This difficulty is noted by Kripke in his criticisms of Strawson (*Naming and Necessity*, 92-93). For the proposal he makes in answering to it, see note 19 below.

19. A third option should be mentioned here. In certain treatments of this problem, what the speaker *has* done is invoked as securing his coreference with another. (Kripke hints at this, with his suggestion that it is the speaker's intention at the time of his acquisition of the name that may secure the continuity of semantic reference. See *Naming and Necessity*, 96-7. Such an account founders, however, on the fact that I may have links to several distinct semantic traditions involving the use of the same name-type. For my current utterance to have determinate semantic reference, it appears that there must be something about my current state or dispositions by virtue of which this tokening of the name has determinate, univocal semantic reference. (There is, moreover, the problem that shifts of the 'Madagascar'-type may occur despite one's best intentions at the time of acquiring the name.)

20. It is important to note, in particular, that this "should" cannot be underwritten by the community's *taking* certain speakers to be the relevant authorities. Our question is precisely that of *which* community (if any) is relevant to *B*'s reference in using 'Feynman'. To say that *B* should defer to the (communally recognized) authorities is, indeed, to say something about what it is to belong to such a community; but it does not tell us by virtue of what one's membership is secured.

21. See, for instance, R. Rorty, *Consequences of Pragmatism* (Minneapolis, 1982), especially xxi-xxvi of his introduction, and Essay 7: "Is There a Problem about Fictional Discourse?"

22. From what has been said, moreover, it must be clear (at least in outline) what my concern would be regarding the other chapter of the "new theorists' " story—that of the "grounding" or initial "fixing" of reference for a name. The theorist must, if he is to fill out his account, specify conditions which would serve to make *this* thing the object of the "dubbing." But this must provide sufficient conditions to assure reference, and do so in terms which do not render the account vacuous by implicitly stipulating that the reference is that thing to which the name has been affixed. I have not explicitly argued that this demand cannot be met, but I believe the difficulties of meeting it to be even clearer in these cases.

23. This point is not meant to deny that there may, indeed, be rules governing the assignment of reference to specific sorts of terms (such as certain indexical expressions), nor that there may be local rules for determining the reference of pronouns in contexts of anaphoric linkage. (On the latter, see R. Brandom, "Reference Explained Away," *The Journal of Philosophy* 81 (1984): 469-92.) What I do deny is that any of these provide the basis for a general theory of reference, one that suggests a set of rules extending to proper names and other referring expressions.

24. A version of this paper was presented at a colloquium at Harvard University in 1984. My thanks to Hilary Putnam and the other participants for their comments and suggestions. I am also indebted to Robert Brandom, Bruce Brower, Joseph Camp, Thomas Carlson, Burton Dreben, Thomas Ricketts, Lawrence Simon, and Howard Wettstein for their encouragement and advice at various stages in the development of this work.

Types, Rigidity, and A Posteriori Necessity

ARTHUR W. COLLINS

INTRODUCTION AND SUMMARY

I make three points here on questions concerning reference and necessity that have been much discussed since the appearance of Saul Kripke's *Naming and Necessity*.[1] First, Kripke's arguments about the identity of types, phenomena, and natural kinds rely on the pattern developed in the context of individuals and the identity of individuals. But serious difficulties confront the effort to carry over essential features from the context of individuals to that of types. The difficulties, which appear unresolvable, jeopardize Kripke's claims about type identity. Second, referring expressions in natural language such as 'lightning' and 'electrical discharge', which are presumed rigid in Kripke's discussion of rigidity, are not, one might say, as rigid as all that. It seems to me that we will not find more rigid referring expressions and that the concept of rigid designation has to be regarded as an idealization from which natural language always deviates more or less. Even if we suppose that names of individuals are true rigid designators, I do not think we can say the same of names of types, phenomena, or species. Third, Kripke's claim that his view reveals *a posteriori* necessity and that this is an aspect of *de re* necessity is not actually sustained by his arguments, at least in the context of natural kinds. Within the setting of Kripke's own explanation of the "discovery of necessary identities," we are justified in saying that it is only contingent truths that are discovered, and are, thus, a posteriori.

1. KRIPKEAN BACKGROUND

Kripke introduces us to the main themes of *Naming and Necessity* in his discussion of identity of individuals. Names like 'Hesperus' and 'Cicero' are rigid designators, that is, they refer to the same individual in every possible world in which they refer to anything at all. Names of individuals are the first examples of rigid designators we encounter in Kripke's book. Because both names are rigid designators, identities that are name-equations are necessary, if they are true. In cases like "Hesperus is Phosphorus" and "Cicero is Tully," the necessity of the identities is obscured by the fact that, sometimes, we have to discover that such statements are true in the course of empirical investigations, and we are accustomed to the philosophical idea that empirical discovery is relevant only to statements that are contingent. In possible-world jargon, it seems that there is no need to investigate which possible world is actual in the context of propositions that are true in all possible worlds. The idea that, contrary to widely held philosophical opinion, there are necessary a posteriori truths is one of the radical results that has gained currency through Kripke's work.

It is in the context of name-equations that Kripke first introduces his account of a posteriori necessity. According to Kripke, "Hesperus is Phosphorus" and "Hesperus is Hesperus" are merely two ways of expressing one and the same necessary truth.[2] We are able to find out that Hesperus is Phosphorus, although it seems plain that we cannot *find out* that Hesperus is Hesperus. It seems as though Hesperus might not have been Phosophorus, but certainly not that Hesperus might not have been Hesperus. Since, for Kripke, the two formulas state the same necessary truth, the feeling that Hesperus might not have been Phosphorus is an illusion that must be explained away. Kripke says that, in *Naming and Necessity*, he has "presupposed a sharp contrast between epistemic and metaphysical possibility."[3] This contrast is meant to cover the situation where we do not know, and may come to know, the truth of an identity statement.

In the context of natural kinds, I mean to devote considerable attention to the pattern of thinking that Kripke envisions, in which we get to know that a necessary identity is true. Because I will focus on the analogy of thought about natural kinds and thought about individuals, I want to be as clear as possible about the idea of the discovery of the identity of individuals such as Hesperus and Cicero and about the related concept of epistemic possibility. When Kripke distinguishes "epistemic possibility" and "metaphysical possibility," I think it is fair to say that he does not mean that some proposition such as "Hesperus is Phosphorus" is contingent and not a necessary truth at all when it is considered from the perspective of epistemology. He does not mean that the same proposition is epistemologically contingent, although it is a necessary truth in a contrasting metaphysical sense. He means, rather, that although "Hesperus is Phosphorus" is a necessary truth (assuming that it is true) from any perspective whatever, when we consider things from the point of view of human knowledge, we may not know that Hesperus is Phosphorus and may mistakenly believe that Hesperus is not Phosphorus, and we may conjecture that Hesperus may not be Phosphorus. There is no full-blooded epistemological modality introduced here, as there would be if Kripke were to propose that, given that it is true, the answer to the question, Is "Hesperus is Phosphorus" a necessary truth? depends on whether we are speaking metaphysically or epistemologically. Therefore, we must ask ourselves how it is that we can be in doubt about the truth of a necessary identity of individuals and how it is that such doubts can be resolved.

In *Naming and Necessity*, this issue is faced much more fully in the context of kinds and phenomena than it is in the context of individuals. A variety of ideas comes to mind when we try to imagine how one might come to know a posteriori that Hesperus is Phosphorus. In the most common case, I should imagine, one learns this truth from someone else who already knows it. Finding out, in such cases, amounts to no more than asking "Are Hesperus and Phosphorus the same heavenly body?" or "Are Cicero and Tully two different Roman statesmen and writers?" and then being given the information by someone who has it and who, in turn, got it from someone else. Perhaps this pattern is suggestive of Kripke's conception of the reference of names as itself something that is passed along by a historical chain.[4] The historical chain of transmission of the knowledge of identity, however, cannot be entirely parallel with the historical chain of transmission of the reference. The historical chain by which reference is passed along begins, let us say, with a baptismal ceremony in virtue of which the referent gets the name in the first place. But we have to imagine that 'Hesperus' and 'Phosphorus' can be names in circulation for some time before *anyone* knows that they refer to one and the same individual. Therefore, not everyone who knows that Hesperus is Phospohorus can have obtained this information from someone else who already knew. In the context of the identity of individuals, the historical chain merely defers the conceptual problem: "How do we find out what is necessarily true?"

One pattern for learning the truth of necessary identities of individuals is suggested early in Kripke's discussion of reference. Although he rejects the Fregean conception of senses for names as sufficient determinants of reference, and though he also rejects cluster-theories that propose a less-than-definitional reference-determining role for senses,[5] Kripke does allow that a name can be introduced with the help of a contingently associated description, which serves to fix the reference of the name:

> When the mythical agent first saw Hesperus he may well have fixed his reference by saying, "I shall use 'Hesperus' as a name for the heavenly body appearing in yonder position in the sky."[6]

The a posteriori status of "Hesperus is Phosphorus" and the nature of the discovery of its truth can be made intelligible when we consider such nonrigid referring devices that, as Kripke says, "fix the reference" of the rigid designators. 'The heavenly body we sight in such and such positions in the morning' and 'the heavenly body we sight in so and so positions in the evening' are such contingent reference fixers for 'Phosphorus' and 'Hesperus', respectively. They enable us to make the unproblematic empirical discovery that the body sighted in the morning is, as matter of fact, the body sighted in the evening. This is not necessary at all. But it is the case. Then we can transfer the results of this discovery to the formulation "Hesperus is Phosphorus" when we reexpress the discovered truth in a terminology composed of rigid designators. The result is a necessity we have discovered to be true.

Late in *Naming and Necessity*, precisely this account of the discovery that Hesperus is Phosphorus is introduced by Kripke for the sake of comparison with the discovered identity of natural kinds.

Let R_1 and R_2 be two rigid designators which flank the identity sign. Then 'R_1 = R_2' is necessary if true. The references of 'R_1' and 'R_2', respectively, may well be fixed by nonrigid designators 'D_1' and 'D_2', in the Hesperus and Phosphorus cases these have the form 'the heavenly body in such and such position in the evening (morning)'. Then although 'R_1 = R_2' is necessary, 'D_1 = D_2' may well be contingent, and this is often what leads to the erroneous view that 'R_1 = R_2' might have turned out otherwise.[7]

I do not mind dwelling a bit on the machinery here, although it is familiar to those who are acquainted with Kripke's ideas. I will draw special attention to the structure of the situation on which Kripke bases his fundamental argument concerning the discovered necessary identity of individuals. Names are rigid designators. So, if we find that two names designate the same individual in the actual world, that is, if we find that the individual designated by N_1 is, in fact, the individual designated by N_2, we can conclude that the referents of N_1 and N_2 are the same in all possible worlds. Identity in all possible worlds is simply necessary identity in possible-worlds terminology. The point I want to emphasize, which is by no means concealed or obscured in Kripke's exposition, is that the discovery is, in the first instance, a discovery about the actual world. The thing we see in the evening is the same individual as the thing we see in the morning. We discover that truth *about the actual world* and draw the necessity of the name equation as a conclusion from the fact that it is true, and that both designators in it are rigid.

Everything hinges on the fact that we can make a certain investigation and establish a certain truth about the actual world. Necessity enters the picture when we state that discovered truth using a vocabulary confined to rigid designators.

2. THE DIS-ANALOGY OF TYPES AND INDIVIDUALS

When we turn from individuals to natural kinds such as phenomena (lightning), species (tigers), and elements (gold), that is, when we turn from individuals to types, it is difficult to see how we are to satisfy the pattern of argument just expounded. We are to understand that a statement in which we are interested, such as "Lightning is an electrical discharge," which is one of Kripke's illustrations, uses only rigid designators. Presumably, our intuitions are enough for this step, so let us assume, for the present, that both 'lightning' and 'electrical discharge' are rigid designators. Since the referring vocabulary consists only of rigid designators, we are in a position to say, according to Kripke, that "Lightning is an electrical discharge" is necessary, if it is true, which we assume it is. But this truth had to be discovered by empirical investigation of lightning. So, we need a contingently related referring term that, in fact, refers to the same thing as 'lightning'. For this second step, let us suppose that 'the phenomenon that appears as flashes in the sky' successfully *fixes the reference* of 'lightning'. We find empirically that the phenomenon that appears as flashes in the sky is an electrical discharge. This is an unproblematic empirical discovery because it might have been a nonelectrical phenomenon that appeared as flashes in the sky. Call that the third step. When we restate this finding as "Lighting is electrical discharge" and note that the referring vocabulary is all rigid, we are supposed to have discovered a necessary truth. The pattern is the same as that reviewed in connection with individuals and proper names.

There is one conspicuous problem here. "Lightning is an electrical discharge," whether true or false, necessary or contingent, is not an identity statement since, as everyone who contemplates this statement knows, there are discharges of electricity that are not bolts of lightning. So we really have something like the inclusion of one type in another, not the identity of two types. This is not an encouraging parallel for the context of names and individuals where what we discover is expressed in a strict identity, namely, the name equation. Can we argue that the assertion of the inclusion of one type in another is necessary, if true, if the referring expressions for both types are rigid? I do not think Kripke gives us any definite guidance on this question. Instead, it seems that the fact that this is not strictly an identity statement is incidental, a matter of detail to which no attention is given. After all, if the type-inclusion statement is true, then so is a related strict type-identity statement, namely, the one that identifies those electrical discharges that are bolts of lightning with lightning. Kripke may have that identity in mind. Maybe we can always reexpress an all-rigid type-inclusion as an all-rigid type-identity.

But the observation that "Lightning is an electrical discharge" is not itself an identity statement leads to another problem that may be much more troublesome for Kripke's understandings. Consider another type-inclusion statement that is true, in the actual world: "Wolves are carnivores."[8] Intuitions, of the same reliability as those we have accepted, show us that 'wolf' and 'carnivore' are rigid designators. So, we have another illustration of an assertion of class inclusion where the referring vocabulary is wholly rigid. The trouble is that, if this much is right, we ought to draw the conclusion that "Wolves are carnivores" is a necessary truth expressive of the essential character of wolves. But no one believes wolves would not be wolves if they managed to survive on a diet of berries and grass. It is just that, as a matter of fact, wolves eat meat and not vegetables.[9]

We seem to be forced to say that whether a true type-inclusion statement is necessary or not does not depend on the rigidity of the referring vocabulary used in asserting the type identity. If we say *that*, we need some foundation other than rigidity for the claim that such statements are necessary when they are true. Adopting this attitude, the analogy with the argument concerning individuals would be spoiled altogether.

This menacing problem about true all-rigid type-inclusions also appears to be a problem about true all-rigid type-identities. Let 'cardiacs' rigidly designate those creatures that have hearts, and 'renals' those that have kidneys.[10] This example is taken over from old discussions of analyticity. The fact is that "All cardiacs are renals" is true, and so is the converse. The two rigid designators pick out the very same class of individuals in the actual world. But there could be cardiacs that are not renals. It is not necessary that a creature with a heart have kidneys and vice versa.[11] It is a contingent fact that all creatures do have either both or neither. So we cannot conclude from the truth of "Cardiacs are renals" to its necessity, even though 'cardiac' and 'renal' are rigid.

One might allow this and simply reduce the argumentative burden of the concept of rigid designation saying that, when we move away from name equations, we do need a support for the claim that an identification is essential and necessary other than the fact that the vocabulary consists of rigid designators. But this would not satisfactorily reflect the aims of *Naming and Necessity*. The concept of rigid designation is supposed to enable us to understand with complete assurance that rigidly designated identities are necessary if they are true. We cannot give up this contention without substantially abandoning the perspective of the work as a whole. Instead, I am quite sure that, retaining the Kripkean spirit, we should reply that "Cardiacs are renals" and, for that matter, "Wolves are carnivores" are not appropriate expressions for type identities that are true in the actual world! From Kripke's perspective, these illustrations have not even set the stage for the application of the principle: True type-identities (or true type-inclusions) are necessary if their vocabulary is entirely rigid. We must defend this principle if we are to adhere to Kripke's understandings. Since the examples do not express necessary truths at all, we have to assume that they are not what Kripke has in mind as assertions of type identity in the actual world.

If this sounds a little daring as a response, that is, in part, owing to the way I have structured this discussion, since I wanted to bring out a kind of reasonable line of thought that makes Kripke's claims sound less than reasonable. I have done this simply by supposing that the question "Is type 1 the same as type 2 in the actual world?" means "Is the extension of the type 1 referring term the same as the extension of the type 2 referring term in the actual world?" On behalf of Kripke, let it be noted that the awkwardness created by our examples falls away if we say that he is talking about the identity of properties, not about the identity of extensions. The facts that the property of being a wolf is exhibited in the actual world only by carnivores, and that the property of having a heart is exemplified by all and only those creatures that exemplify the property of having kidneys, do not tend to show that the property of having a heart is the property of having kidneys, nor that the property of being a wolf includes that of being a carnivore. Therefore, we cannot say that the relevant assertions "Wolves are carnivores" and "Cardiacs are renals" express type-identities that are true in the actual world, and the question of the necessity of the truth of type identities is not even raised with the help of these examples.

At this point, I want to remind the reader of the nature of the difficulty that

I find here in Kripkean views. In the case of individuals, we discover that two rigid designators name the same thing in the actual world, and this discovery sets the stage for the claim about *a posteriori necessity*. The truth of the identity in actuality has to be established if we are to assert that it is a necessary truth. The focus of the difficulty that I see in Kripke's exposition comes to light in the question "How do we discover the identity of properties in the actual world?"

We have seen that identity of extensions is patently inadequate and that adoption of this standard of identity of a property in a world would force abandonment of a major Kripkean idea. What remains to us as a vehicle for what we called step three: the discovery that A is B? In one sense, the answer to this question depends on the illustration. We are going to use a nonrigid reference fixer for the natural kind in question, and the technique for discovering the nature of the referent will vary from case to case. In this sense, scientists will decide how to investigate phenomena that are the designata of a nonrigid reference fixer. Scientists have to figure out how to study those phenomena that appear as flashes in the sky so as to find out what they really are.

But, at the outset, we can make a global point. The discovery is not a conclusion about extensions, but about *possible extensions.* We could silence a claim that Property 1 is Property 2 by exhibiting an individual in the actual world that has P_1 and lacks P_2. But this is not feasible if all and only those individuals that have P_1 also have P_2. What we want to say in order to assert nonidentity of properties in the face of identity of extensions is expressed in the counterfactual statement: "There could have been individuals that have P_1 but lack P_2." And the assertion of identity of properties goes beyond mere coextensionality in a way that is captured by the modal generalization "Whatever has P_1 *must* have P_2."

I do not know whether we should suppose that Kripke's conception of identity of properties is a conception of identity of extensions in all possible worlds. The issue becomes important to his thinking at this juncture. If we accept this ontologically moderate idea about property identity, we have to conclude that the argument about the discovered identity of types does not achieve a satisfactory analogy with the argument about discovered identity of individuals. For, on this interpretation, the assertion of type identity is a claim about all possible worlds and there is really no sense to be given to the assertion of type identity, much less the discovery of type identity *in the actual world.*

In the context of names and individuals, we discover that the identity is true in the actual world and then, shifting to the all rigid vocabulary, we are able to assert a necessary truth. We do have a conception of a contingent identity of a nonrigidly designated individual, that is, we can speak of individual identity *in the actual world.* But, so far, we have not got any conception of property identity in the actual world at all.

Recall that the pattern for discovered identity requires a nonrigid designator that will bring our attention to some instances in the extension of the type in the actual world. We will study these individuals with a view to determining what makes them the phenomenon, species, or other natural kind that they are. This will involve ignoring some features as inessential, even if they are present in all the contingently referred to examples. The investigation of the essence of the type will proceed by invoking the thought that certain features need not appear in individuals of the type. This is because the idea of the type, as opposed to the idea of the extension of the type, is the thought of what is required to be of that type in any world. In this sense, the type is not itself something we can examine in any one possible world or in the actual world. What is examinable is only a local extension comprised of individuals of the type in question.

Consider the property of being a tiger. Our nonrigid reference fixer, 'Those ferocious striped fellows over there and ones like them', leads us to individuals in the extension of 'tiger' in the actual world. Then we study these individuals and, let's say, we come up with the DNA that engenders tigers. We offer having this DNA as identical to the property of being a tiger. We do not mean to say, at this stage, that the property of being a tiger has been discovered to be the property of having a certain DNA *in the actual world*. There is no function for this qualification here. We are saying from the outset that what makes these actual world creatures what they are is their DNA, which would make them tigers in any possible world – even in worlds in which they are neither striped nor ferocious. If we try to remove the reference to DNA, which is rigid, in favor of some nonrigid referring term for DNA, we will not get an expression of the discovery at all. This can be asserted without examining proposed, contingent reference fixers for the DNA in question. The contingency of the proposition, which refers to something we can find in the actual world, will guarantee that it is not an assertion of property identity. Therefore, the reexpression of an identity discovered to hold in the actual world between nonrigidly designated types using an entirely rigid referring vocabulary will not express a type identity and a necessary truth. In order to satisfy the pattern that worked for individuals, we would have to be able to assert a type identity in nonrigid referring terms, find that it is true in the actual world, and attain the level of necessary type-identity by moving to rigid vocabulary. None of this can be done, because no identity statement expressed in terms of nonrigid referring terms is an assertion of a type identity.

The difference between natural kinds and individuals reflects the fact that both contingent and rigid references to individuals refer to constituents of the actual world, but terms that refer to properties do not refer to constituents of the actual world that may be studied and checked for identity. Individuals are constituents of the actual world, so identity of individuals can meaningfully be discovered in the actual world. Properties are represented in the actual world in that individuals exemplify those properties that, thus, have a nonempty extension in all possible worlds in which they are exemplified. Therefore, if an assertion speaks only of the actual world, it cannot assert an identity of properties.

One feels like saying that property identity is a feature of the system of all possible worlds and that individual identity is a feature of each possible world. The only manifestation of property identity in a particular world is coextensionality; but this is only a necessary condition and not sufficient for property identity.

The very idea of natural kinds carries with it a measure of informal nominalism. To say that kinds are "natural" is to oppose, in a broad way, the idea that they are Platonic or divine archetypes that exist in addition to their actual and possible exemplifications. Natural kinds are not the constituents of a special realm intuitable only by God or by philosophers. Discourse about natural kinds does not presuppose any existential commitments beyond commitment to the individuals who are of these kinds. Comparisons of individuals are what give rise to the language of properties, which are *only* ways in which individuals resemble one another. Assertions about essential resemblances and counterfactual discourse (and/or possible-worlds discourse about resemblances) brings with it modal assertions about membership in resembling classes. Identity of properties does not make sense until we reach this level. At the level of reality, the actual world, we have nothing but the facts of coextensionality. It is simply not a fact about the actual world that the property of being a cardiac is not the same as the property of being a renal. This seeming fact is nothing at all if it is not the assertion that there could be cardiacs that are not renals or renals that are not cardiacs or both, although in fact, all and only cardiacs are renals. And this is a statement that goes beyond the actual world.

It may be that with a more realistic conception of properties than that which I have envisioned, Kripke's argument about individuals can be replicated as an argument about property identity in the actual world, restated as necessary identity through the use of a vocabulary of rigid designators. Although the possibilities in this direction are hard to judge in advance, the prospect is not good. For very realistic conceptions of properties are likely to offend common sense in ways that Kripke characteristically avoids, and, as I have already remarked, the notion of natural kinds itself militates against any strongly Platonistic conceptions of types. To identify a property we need, not an intuition of that property, but something much like the intension or the Fregean sense of a term referring to the property. We know that the individuals that exemplify one property can be different in different possible worlds. But this is not to be explained by trying to locate the property itself, as well as exemplifications of it in the actual world, as though investigators could disregard items in the extension and just study and identify the property.

There is a way of introducing contingent designation of properties that might make identity of properties in the actual world feasible. Suppose that at 3:00 I'm thinking about redness, and again at 4:00 I'm thinking about redness. The two contingent designators 'The property AC was thinking about at 3:00' and 'The property AC was thinking about at 4:00' actually designate one and the same property, namely, redness. Here we have a contingent identity statement true in the actual world, because AC might have been thinking of blueness at 4:00 and redness at 3:00.[12]

A noteworthy point here is that this idea does not seem to require that redness exist in the actual world. It is not as though something that exists in the actual world is referred to in two different ways, and it is discovered that the referring expressions actually designate one and the same real-world constituent. This might be so if we thought that properties exist in the actual world as well as exemplifications of them. But that obscure doctrine is not required to make sense of the contingent truth in the illustration. In order to make sense of this contingent truth, we do not need to suppose that properties exist in the actual world. There is something about the illustration that seems compelling even if we analyze "property" nominalistically. What is it that is compelling?

If we are nominalists, we might say that thinking about redness is thinking about the predicate 'red'. It seems to me, however, that AC, for one, is not thinking about a predicate when he thinks about redness. Reluctance about this formal-mode style of nominalism does not press us at once to reify properties. Properties, in the relevant sense, are not referents at all, but possibilities for exemplification. Since redness is what I am thinking about at 3:00, I am not thinking about something that can be identified in the actual world, since redness is not an existent in the actual world. I am thinking about a potentiality for exemplification in the actual world, in this case it is a potentiality of which there are actual instances, namely, red things. According to this understanding, the identity statement in its contingent form, "The property I think of at 3:00 is the property I think of at 4:00," is not an assertion to the effect that two referring expressions designate one and the same actual-world referent. It is a contingent fact that I was thinking about the same property at two different times. Although we have a contingent identity statement here, we have not realized the pattern of Kripke's argument concerning individuals in the context of properties. For we have not identified something in the actual world and then generated a necessary identity by using rigid referring terms.

If I try to introduce an actual-world referent here, I will have to turn to exemplifications and delete 'redness'. But the identity of exemplifications is not the one in which we are interested. Kripke's discussion of type identities yielded by scientific investigation promotes a commonsense picture of the accessibility of properties via exemplifications. Individuals in the actual world do have properties after all. So we can study things in the world and find out what their properties actually are. Have I been simply denying what is obviously done when I deny that scientific investigation can identify properties in the actual world?

Consider two contingent reference fixers for properties actual things happen to have: 'The color of my house at t,' and 'the color of your house at t.' If both houses are red at t, we can contingently discover that the color of my house is the same as the color of your house at t. Now we move to a rigid vocabulary. Suppose we rigidly designate the color my house has at t 'red' and we rigidly designate the color of your house at t 'the color of things that emit such and such radiation.' Now we are ready, so it seems, for a rigidly reexpressed property-identity statement

Red is the color of things that emit such and such radiation.

Is this the assertion, "The color of my house at t is the color of your house at t", rigidly reexpressed?

From any roughly nominalist viewpoint, another possible world that does not have these two houses in it does not contain the things that are found to be identical in this world, namely, the color of my house and the color of your house. Put in another way: Kripke's argument about the necessary identity of Hesperus and Phosphorus appeals to numerical identity and has its force because we can say that *this very thing* will be what it is in other worlds in which it exists. But the properties of my house do not exist in worlds in which my house does not exist. It is merely the case that other things exist in such worlds that are similar to my house in being of the same color.

From this point of view, sameness of color "in this world" is a matter of two exemplifications of a property and, of course, it is not being asserted that they are one and the same exemplification. The assertion of property identity is an assertion of qualitative identity of two individuals (with respect to a description). If these two houses did not exist, then, from the perspective of ontology, the properties of these two houses would not exist either. To deny this would be to assert that the house's color could exist without the house.

Maybe the example – identity of two houses with respect to color – is on the wrong track altogether, just because the two exemplifications are so clearly *two* and not one. Let us consider the study of one exemplification that the contingent designator "the color of my house at t" picks out. Scientists find, we may imagine, that "The color of my house at t is the color of things that emit such and such radiation" is a true contingent identity statement. Restated rigidly this yields "Red is the color of things that emit such and such radiation," and this is a necessary truth because all the vocabulary is rigid. I think this is closer to the commonsense idea of scientific discoveries about properties that Kripke's discussion encourages, but it cannot be allowed. We build our confidence that we can study a property in the actual world by using a referring expression that designates one exemplification of the property, namely, "the color of my house at t." But if this is the referent that is contingently identified, any restated rigid identity statement must make an assertion about this referent in all possible worlds in which it exists. This is not the statement made by "Red is the color of objects that emit such and such radiation," which covers red things in possible worlds in which neither my house nor the exemplifications of properties by my house exist.

Put generally, there is an intuitive point of view from which one can say that two possible worlds might differ in that nothing that exists in one also exists in the other. It would be entirely consistent with this intuitive premise to assert that some properties are exemplified in both worlds, although the worlds have no constituents in common. Given this way of speaking, which, again, can be called broadly nominalistic, it is plain that only qualitative identity at the level of properties can be established in the actual world. Numerical identity of properties requires the thought that numerically different exemplifications are exemplifications of a numerically identical property. In order to assert numerical property identity in the actual world, it would be required that properties exist in addition to their exemplifications, and it would also be required that properties exist *in the actual world* in addition to their exemplifications. Perhaps some significance could be given to this very perplexing way of thinking about properties, but it has no intuitive base comparable to our intuitive thought that individuals exist in actuality and the very same individuals exist and do not exist under various counterfactual hypotheses. Because of this intuitive disanalogy, Kripke's argument at the level of properties does not replicate the argument at the level of individuals. Instead of trying to assign a sense to the existence of properties in the actual world in addition to exemplifications of those properties, it is easier and more natural to suppose that assertions of property identity are always modal assertions and, therefore, that their force always goes beyond the actual world. Then, the analogy with individual identity fails.

Probably the strongest intuitive picture for Kripke's contentions about types is as follows. We refer contingently to tigers with the help of something like 'those ferocious striped animals over there, and others like them.' Then scientists examine these very creatures in the actual world and discover that they have certain DNA. In the actual world they discover, that is, that having this DNA is what causes creatures to be like these, that is, to have the appearance that these striped and ferocious animals actually do have. This is something about the actual world because the DNA in tigers would have different effects if other circumstances obtained. In particular, it is only under the existing circumstances that the DNA causes features that appear as stripes to observers with perceptual equipment like ours. But the property designators, 'being a tiger' and 'having such and such DNA', are both rigid. The discovered contingent truth

> The property that causes these animals to look as they do in the actual world (for example, to have stripes) is having a certain DNA

is reexpressed rigidly as

> Being a tiger is having such and such DNA.

And this is a necessary truth.

One difficulty with this is that there is no reason to expect that scientists will feel under a special obligation to explain the possession of the appearance by appeal to which we can contingently refer to tigers. Although the DNA is counted as the essential character of a living thing because it carries the inherited information that determines the features of members of the species, the claim about DNA does not depend on our succeeding in explaining the stripes and other matters of surface appearance. We do surmise that the essential nature of the species does explain the appearance of individuals under actual circumstances. That is, we think tiger DNA does explain the stripes of tigers. But it might not. The stripes might come about accidentally and might have nothing to do with the essence of the creature even under actual circumstances. This way of connecting the contingent reference fixer with the

right property is not always part of the story of scientific discovery. We have to imagine, as Kripke himself makes clear, that the creatures to which the contingent
reference fixer draws our attention may not even have the features that the contingent
reference fixer mentions. It may be that tigers merely look striped and that none of
them is actually striped. Or it could be that there is some secret society that, for its
own dark reasons, paints stripes on tigers when no one is looking. The point is not
that there is some likelihood of this, but only that if it were the case, the functioning
of the contingent reference fixer that appeals to the stripes would not be affected and
scientists would rightly accept the DNA as the essence of tigerhood although it has
nothing to do with the stripes.

What is the underlying relevance of all this? If the scientific discovery of the
essence of the species could somehow be linked to the appearances that make possible a contingent reference fixer, then we could understand that a causal, and thus
scientific, account of appearances naturally engenders a rigid designator for things
that, in fact, have such an appearance. Kripke's examples, such as "Heat is what
causes the sensation of heat in us," suggest this very picture. Scientists get to work
and discover what it is that causes the appearance of the phenomenon, that is, these
sensations. The cause of the sensations turns out to be molecular motion. Then we
express the discovery using an all-rigid referring vocabulary as "Heat is molecular
motion." The scope of the right discovery seems to be determined by the ingredients
of the contingent reference fixer. But if the explanation of the appearances mentioned
in the contingent designator is entirely expendable, we require some other understanding of the goals that the scientific investigation sets itself. It must be that we
have some intuitive feeling about what is essential for being a creature of a given
species, and when we study individuals, we use these standards in deciding that certain features are essential and others may be merely universally present. Such understandings operate in reaching the conclusion that having a particular DNA is the essence of being a tiger. But, if this is correct, the necessity of the assertion "Tigers
have such and such DNA" rests on these convictions about essence and is not simply
read off from the fact that both 'tiger' and 'having such and such DNA' are rigid designators. In the case of individuals, the necessity of the rigidly restated identity is simply read off from the fact that the referring vocabulary is rigid.

If we really thought that scientists simply studied the animals to which the contingent reference fixer drew their attention and found in all of them a certain DNA,
and if we then reflected that 'has such and such DNA' is rigid, as is 'tiger,' we could
not conclude that 'Tigers have such and such DNA' is necessary. It is, as we have
noted, only because the scientists think, apart from the concept of rigidity, that tigers
would not be tigers without the right DNA that they think of the assertion as necessary. But the rigidity of the vocabulary is not what the judgment of necessity rests
on. Once again, the dis-analogy with the context of individual identity emerges.

Property identity is only one of the conceptions that is likely to come to mind
in contemplating Kripke's arguments about types. The particular difficulties that we
have encountered in connection with properties may not reappear if we drop talk of

properties in favor of other conceptions of types in our efforts to articulate an argument in Kripke's spirit about identity at the level of types. Events, for example, have an evident advantage over properties in that it is quite in order to think that events occur in, and are studiable elements of, the actual world. The identification of properties in the actual world cannot be carried out, because properties only exist in the actual world in that individuals exemplifying those properties exist. But we do not feel that any corresponding qualification attaches to the idea that events unfold in the actual world. The question, therefore, arises whether we can produce a satisfactory analogy for Kripke's argument concerning individual identity if we exploit the concept of event identity rather than property identity.[13]

The nonrigid referring expression 'the phenomenon that appears to us as flashes in the sky' designates certain events in the actual world, let us say, and scientists study these events and discover that they are discharges of electricity. The rigid term for these very events is 'lightning', so that we are able to restate the discovery as "Lightning is an electrical discharge." But all the referring vocabulary is now rigid, so that the assertion is a necessary truth, if it is true. Is this a satisfactory replication of the essential move in Kripke's argument that goes from a discovered identity about the actual world to a restated identity about all possible worlds?

It seems to me that, if anything, it is easier to see that this exposition of the Kripkean argument is inadequate than it is to reach the same judgment concerning an exposition framed in terms of properties and property identity. If we take literally the idea that scientists investigate events that occur in the actual world and discover of those events that appear as flashes in the sky that they are discharges of electricity, we cannot possibly restate *that* discovery by asserting "Lightning is an electrical discharge." For the term 'lightning' does not designate those actual world events that scientists have identified in all possible worlds in which those very events exist. 'Lightning' designates lightning in all possible worlds, and that means in many worlds in which none of the actual world events that have been identified by scientists exists at all. This is, on reflection, obvious. Suppose a particular bolt that destroys Farmer Brown's barn at t is among those identified as an electrical discharge by scientists. We can entertain counterfactual hypotheses about this event by supposing, for instance, that Brown had installed lightning rods at t − n, as Mrs. Brown always told him he should. Then this very event, this discharge of electricity, would not have destroyed the barn. In the same way, we can readily imagine possible worlds in which this event does not occur at all. We can say, "Had this discharge of electricity not occurred, Farmer Brown's barn would still be standing." The same holds for all the other actual bolts of lightning. There are possible worlds in which none of them occur. Not all of these are possible worlds in which there is no lightning. Some are worlds in which there is lightning but each bolt of it is an event other than any event in the actual world. The mere coherence of this statement shows that 'lightning' is not a rigid designator for a set of actual world events. If 'lightning' were to designate rigidly just those bolts that have been identified, it would refer not to lightning but only to those particular events.

Even this relatively transparent argument can seem elusive and difficult. After all, it is always and inevitably the case that our scientists investigate phenomena in the actual world, apart, perhaps, from cases where they are doing thought experiments. So their conclusions will always be that these phenomena, and others essentially like them are each and every one an electrical discharge. Their conclusion, when they have understood what makes these events what they are, holds for the whole type of and not just for the actual world tokens. But I seem to be faulting the Kripkean argument on the inappropriate ground that scientists investigate only actual world events. This is, it may be urged, a fallacy. Scientists are finding out what this type of event is by investigating some examples. How could they possibly do otherwise? But this is precisely how scientists do find out what a certain phenomenon essentially is.

Quite a bit is obvious and true in this imagined, impatient rejoinder. But it is actually another way of insisting on the criticism of Kripke that I am making and not a rebuttal of that criticism. For I am arguing that we are not able to replicate a certain feature of Kripke's arguments about individuals. In the case of individuals, we can discover the identity of something that exists in the actual world, and then, by rigidly designating *that very thing*, we can reexpress the discovery as a necessary truth. We do not pretend, in the context of individuals, to be able to assert something about things that do not exist in the actual world at all on the basis of our contingent discovery. The contingent discovery presupposes the existence of the individual whose identity is discovered, and it is just the identity of this individual that is said to be necessary.

We introduced the concept of events precisely because events do exist in the actual world and they seem to offer the beginning of a parallel for type identities that properties do not offer. But if this is the appeal of events—that they provide something actual to be identified contingently—we would only be able to reexpress rigidly the discovered identity of these actual events. Such a reexpressed identity would be a necessary truth (I have no idea what an example would be), but it would not be an assertion like "Lightning is an electrical discharge," precisely because this assertion, in intention, covers all sorts of events that do not actually occur.

When we insist, with common sense on our side, that scientists' discoveries about events hold for event types and mean to include their actual and possible instances, this is just another way of saying that there is no level of scientific investigation the fruits of which are expressible as an identification of some actual-world events. Of course, we can suppose that B_1 is the first bolt studied and it is discovered to be an electrical discharge, and then B_2 is also discovered to be an electrical discharge. This much might generate the hypothesis "Lightning is an electrical discharge." But it is certainly not the case that this hypothesis is a rigidly reexpressed assertion of "B_1 and B_2 are electrical discharges." Nothing that is identified in the actual world is then redesignated rigidly in reaching the scientific hypothesis. But that is what would be required to replicate this key step in Kripke's argument concerning the identity of individuals.

We could try to consider other conceptual vehicles for recasting Kripke's arguments in the context of type identity. Perhaps this is not really necessary. When these examples are looked at attentively, I think it becomes intuitively clear that an actual-world identification is not going to be forthcoming in the context of types. We will not find anything in the investigation of types to play the role that "The thing we see in the morning is the thing we see in the evening" plays in setting up the necessity of assertions of the identity of individuals.

3. IDEALIZATIONS INVOLVED IN THE CONCEPT OF RIGID DESIGNATION AND IN ITS APPLICATION

A rigid designator is a referring expression that refers to the same thing in every possible world in which it refers to anything at all. This idea is surely clear enough. What is not so clear in some contexts is what counts as "the same" from one world to the next. Another possible world with Reagan in it has to have the very individual that is Reagan and not a Reagan look-alike. This way of talking raises the problem of identity across possible worlds, which I think is a pseudo-problem, following Kripke's lead. There are no other worlds full of people some of whom might somehow be identical to the people who are "also" here in this world. We are talking about counterfactual hypotheses. That Reagan might have lost the election makes sense only on the hypothesis that we can understand that things might have been different in such a way that Reagan would still have existed though he would not have been the president. Things could also have been different in such a way that Reagan would not have existed if, for example, his parents had never met or had died in infancy. But to say that Reagan might have lost the election is to say, as Kripke likes to emphasize, that this very man might have lost.

It is all right to pronounce the words "this very man" with pedantic emphasis to make the point here, but doing so does not provide a criterion for deciding whether someone can be said to be Reagan or not under a counterfactual hypothesis. At one point, Kripke says that possible worlds are given by "stipulation".[14] Thus, when we say, "If Reagan had been defeated in 1980," a counterfactual situation is stipulated in which the very man who is now President of the United States is defeated and does not become president in 1980. But stipulation cannot solve all the problems that will arise. We can stipulate a world in which Reagan has a different wife, but perhaps not a world in which Reagan has different parents.

In *Naming and Necessity*, Kripke suggests that originating from the union of a particular sperm and egg is necessary for the identity of an individual person. Nothing that did not come from that very pair of cells could be *that very person*. This is reasonable, but it does link the stipulations we can make about identity of people to our understanding of what will be "the very same egg and sperm cells" under counterfactual hypotheses. If a person's parents had somewhat different lives, for example, had they eaten differently, would it be right or wrong to say that the very sperm and egg pair that generates an individual might still have existed? The more radically different the lives of the parents, the less plausible it will be to speak of the same egg and sperm cells. How could one such cell count as the very same if an individual leads a totally different kind of life in a different place with a different diet and so on? For small differences or differences that *seem* to be irrelevant to the constitution of cells, sameness of cell can be *stipulated* like sameness of man. Then there will be intermediate cases where we could say one thing and we could say another about cell identity.

As a consequence of uncertainties about other identities, such as cell identities, whether a certain individual could be said to be "this very man" under a counterfactual hypothesis or not may not be an easy thing to decide, and it seems reasonable to surmise that there will be an element of arbitrariness or creativity in the decisions on which this issue will come to depend. This does not take away from the definiteness of the concept of a rigid designator, for it must still be the case for any individual under any counterfactual hypothesis that that individual either is Reagan or is not Reagan.

The difficulties we have illustrated are unsettling because they suggest that what is the same referent under counterfactual hypotheses is not independent of our free decisions. This admixture of our decisions and reasons for saying one thing rather than another can seriously diminish the force of the idea that we are dealing with *de re* necessity. When we think that Reagan is the individual he is, and think that it is just his nature that determines whether some individual in another possible world is Reagan or not, the atmosphere of metaphysical necessity *de re* flourishes. But insofar as we think of cases where the individual that is Reagan in another possible world depends on which differences we decide to take into consideration and which we are willing to overlook, the resulting application of the name acquires a *de dicto* flavor.

I imagine that we can stipulate that Reagan might have had a twin brother who originated from the same pair of cells.[15] Which of the boys is Reagan? The reply "The one that is this very man," accompanied by a gesture pointing to Reagan, does not accomplish anything. Yet Reagan has to be one twin and not the other. We could say under counterfactual stipulation that one twin grows up to be president and that is Reagan, but we could also say, under like stipulation, that Reagan is the one who does not become president. We could tell a story about the Reagan twins and fill in the life history of the two boys in maximum detail and, having described everything, we would be at liberty to decide which of the two is Reagan. Are there two possible worlds that are alike in every particular except that in W_1 Reagan is one of a set of twins and in W_2 Reagan is the other? What kind of difference between possibilities is this? If it is simply a difference in what we choose to say, the necessity of "Reagan is the very same man in counterfactual circumstances" loses its *de re* atmosphere.

More serious difficulties beset use of the concept of rigid designation in connection with names for phenomena, names for elements, for natural kinds, and for species. In *Naming and Necessity*, Kripke encourages us to suppose that the referring expressions 'heat', 'molecular motion', 'lightning', 'electrical discharge', 'tiger', 'water', and 'pain' are all rigid designators. Powerful intuitions support this contention about these referring expressions, which are not names for individuals. For the sake of discussion, let us put aside our misgivings about possible-world jargon, as Kripke himself usually does, and think of counterfactual hypotheses as descriptions of other possible worlds that a metaphysical traveler might visit. We ask him whether lightning, or heat, or tigers are exemplified in a nonactual possible world W. That these are rigid designators means that the traveler will only be justified in saying that W has X in it, if it has things *of the very sort* that we call 'X'.

We saw that, in the context of names, the rigidity of 'Reagan' does not automatically make clear whether or not Reagan exists under a given counterfactual hypothesis. In the same way, the rigidity of 'lightning', 'heat', and 'tiger' leaves doubts concerning questions like "Is there lightning in the nonactual possible world W?" Suppose our transworld traveler goes to W and finds that there are storms with darkenings and winds and rains, and in these storms bright bolts pierce the gloom, momentarily followed by violent claps and heavy rumblings. These flashing bolts split great trees and set houses in W afire. But the flashes are not an electrical phenomenon in W. I think it would be at least as reasonable for a world traveler to report "W has nonelectrical lightning" as it would be to report "W does not have lightning but has another phenomenon that is a lot like lightning but is not electrical."

This intuition is much strengthened by the thought that there might be other phenomena that are very much like electricity. Just as the decision to say that an individual is present in another possible world can lead us back to questions about the identity of egg and sperm cells in other worlds, so the question of the identity of lightning leads to questions about the identity of electrons. How much like our electrons do particles in W have to be in order to be electrons? One possibility that seems to me to be a live one is this: Our traveler might find that W has particles that are significantly different from our electrons, so different that, if those particles were found in the actual world along with electrons, they would constitute another kind of particle and not a variety of electron. But in W there are no particles just like our electrons. *Instead*, one might say that, in W, these particles similar to electrons play some or all (here we could have a range of counterfactual hypotheses) of the characteristic roles that electrons play in the actual world. They explain combining weights in W, there are flows of them constituting phenomena much like electrical currents, and they figure in laws expressed in terms of charge, resistance, conductivity, and so on. Won't a transworld traveler be inclined to say that W has electricity but it is different from ours? Won't he say this, even though we would not call those particles "electrons" and that phenomenon "electricity" if we had them *in addition to* our electrons and our electricity? I think intuition tells us that he would. But notice that, if the actual world did have exemplifications of both electrons and these similar particles found in W, then, since we would not say that these actual-world electronlike particles are electrons, we would not report that there are electrons in W as a consequence of the presence of the similar particles. In short, whether 'electron' refers to something in W or not depends on what else happens to exist in the actual world.

This leads to serious problems for the concept of rigid designation. First, whether certain realities of W are "the same" as realities in the actual world is not independent of other factual questions about the actual world. Second, consider a possible world W′ that contains particles just like our electrons and also contains particles just like the electrons found in W. We have already considered W′ when we said that, the small differences between the W particles and actual-world electrons would be enough to exclude them from the extension of "electron" if both existed. We call them electrons in W only because they are the only electron-candidate W offers, and the actual world does not have them. But this pursuit of (stipulable) counterfactual hypotheses compromises the rigidity of 'electron.' For we are saying that the very particles that are electrons in W are not electrons in W′, and this violates the defining feature of rigid designators, namely, that they refer to the same things in all possible worlds in which they refer to anything.

At this point we could "correct" our intuitions a bit in view of this outcome. We can say that no matter how much like our electrons particles in W are, and no matter how many analogies to actual-world phenomena these particles enter into, and no matter how many analogues of actual natural laws those particles in W satisfy, they are not electrons. This will preserve the rigidity of "electrons" and delete the dependence of the reference of "electron" in W on the issue of the existence of near-electrons in the actual world. But I can think of nothing in favor of this ruling except that it performs these ad hoc functions. I say that it is at least as reasonable to think that our conception of reference in other possible worlds is idealized in the concept of rigid designation. Plausible contexts for thinking about modalities show us that we are not entitled to the degree of definiteness that the theory of rigid designation presupposes.

Our reflections do show that it is hard to assert with the confidence that Kripke presupposes that terms like 'lightning' and 'electron' are rigid designators in their actual use. Instead, it seems that they are concepts that constrain use in the context of counterfactual hypotheses but not to the degree required for rigidity. Ordinary terms like these are not libertine designators forming casual unions with different referents in different worlds, like a sailor with a girl in every port. Their counterfactual designata are reasoned projections from actual world designata. But we cannot say that the concept of rigidity fits these terms and transfer the slack to criteria for "same phenomenon," because we have seen that the slack generates cases where, whatever criteria we use, we will not refer to the same things (electrons, in the example) by the same candidate "rigid" designator in all possible worlds. There will be counterfactual hypotheses within which certain particles are electrons and other hypotheses within the scope of which those very particles are not electrons.

If we find that some reasonable speakers would call phenomena that do not involve electrons "lightning," we might handle the case by saying that those speakers are not *using* 'lightning' *as a rigid designator*. Kripke himself provides a precedent for this concept of the status of *a use* of a referring term *as a rigid designator*.[16] But the attendant loosening of the notion threatens to jeopardize the whole project of rigid designation. At most, if we mean to keep a usable concept of rigidity, we might invoke the thought that, vis-à-vis rigidity, a speaker could use a term in a deviant, idiosyncratic, or metaphorical way. If this is how we try to understand all the difficult cases, one can still ask of a natural-language referring term like 'lightning', "Is this a rigid designator or not?" and one can expect a definite answer. The question cannot generally be made to be one of the intentions of the individual speaker without surrendering the significance of the concept.

Apart from appeal to use of a term *as a rigid designator*, we could *try* to take up the slack indicated by the reflections presented here without diluting the claim that 'lightning' and such terms are rigid. This would require that we abandon concepts like 'electrical' and 'electron' (and any other terms in which problems may become visible) as devices for helping to indicate just what "the very same phenomenon" in W is. We do not now have an alternative vocabulary yielding a system of criteria for sameness within which we can defend the contention that "thus and thus designated phenomena" are rigidly designated. Furthermore, there is no reason to think that any alternative vocabulary for expressing the essence of phenomena will not engender lapses of rigidity just as the referential vocabulary that now exists does.

At times it appears that discussions of these matters generate illusions because they can be conducted with rigidity and criteria for sameness presupposed in general without being illustrated in much detail. When we reflect with Kripke that lightning must *be the phenomenon that lightning is*, this seems to call into operation an absolute essence of phenomena that we might have trouble discovering but that surely exists, for, without it, things would not be what they are. It is precisely this flavor of absoluteness that seems to crumble when one considers what we would say is "the very same" phenomenon under detailed counterfactual hypotheses. If it is agreed that vocabulary like 'electrical' and 'electron' fall short of rigidity, we cannot repose much confidence in the hope that referring terms will emerge in the future that will not generate the same quandaries and ultimately fall short of absolute rigidity in the same ways.

4. CAN WE DISCOVER WHAT IS NECESSARILY TRUE?

Up to this point, we have questioned the analogy between arguments concerning the identity of named individuals and arguments concerning the identity of rigidly designated types (section 2), and we have raised doubts about the absolute rigidity of ordinary language terms for types and phenomena (section 3). I want to set aside these issues here in order to consider Kripke's striking doctrine of *a posteriori necessity*.

It is important to bear in mind that Kripke asserts only conditional propositions of the form

(i) If "Lightning is an electrical discharge" is true, then it is a necessary truth,

(ii) If "Heat is the motion of molecules" is true, then it is a necessary truth, and,

(iii) If "Tigers are mammals" is true, then it is a necessary truth.

In such cases, according to Kripke, we make use of contingent referring devices or "reference fixers," such as 'the phenomenon that appears as flashes in the sky', which contingently designates lightning; 'the phenomenon that causes sensations of heat in us', which contingently fixes the reference of 'heat,' and 'the species to which those ferocious looking striped creatures and their fellows belong', which contingently picks out tigers. The availability of a contingent reference fixer in the context of the discoveries in question is required for any such discovery to be made. An appropriate nonrigid designator makes it possible to formulate a contingent statement about the essential character of the phenomenon or species in question. The discovery of the necessity of the identification statement, when properly understood, presupposes and appeals to the discovery of the associated contingent truth. Thus, when the contingent assertion "The phenomenon that appears as flashes in the sky is an electrical discharge" is discovered to be true, the discovery extends to the truth of the proposition "Lightning is an electrical discharge," and once it is recognized as true, this statement is also understood to be necessary because the vocabulary is rigid.

The thought that propositions (i), (ii), and (iii) concern necessary truths is not easy to reconcile with the concept of investigations that issue in the discovery of their truth. The thought is that we knew, at one point, that lightning is a phenomenon of some specific character or other, but that, at that time, we did not know what that phenomenon is. We might imagine a stage of investigation in which there were two hypotheses under active consideration, which we can call two *theories* about the nature lightning:

Theory 1: Lightning is an electrical discharge, and

Theory 2: Lightning is λ (some nonelectrical phenomenon).

At this stage, observers will have said

Lightning may be an electrical discharge and it may be λ.

It was understood that the question could be resolved by scientists and that, once resolved, we would know that "Lightning is an electrical discharge" is true, or we would know that "Lightning is λ" is true. Whichever proves true, we understood, the other will be false. Both accounts were live possibilities. This situation does not seem to go beyond the thought shared by Kripke and those who mistakenly spoke of "contingent identity," namely, the thought that the nature of lightning had to be discovered via empirical investigation. Of course, it is not inevitable that there be two clear candidates before the identification. Putting matters this way helps make things clear and does not introduce any distortions since, logically speaking, the thought that lightning might be something unspecific, but other than an electrical discharge, plays the same role as the thought that a specific nonelectrical candidate may be envisioned.

Although the above description of the investigative situation seems intuitively natural, it is not clear that the description is even coherent under the hypothesis that the truth about the nature of lightning is a necessary truth. For, supposing, as we all do suppose, that lightning is an electrical discharge and not λ, then lightning is necessarily an electrical discharge and "Lightning is λ" does not indicate another possibility since it is necessarily false. Therefore, investigators were mistaken in their assertion that "Lightning is λ" may be true. There was never such a possibility to be canvassed.

We might try to retain the idea of the two theories, although we now recognize that the second theory was never a possibility at all. To take that view would be to say that the investigators thought Theory 2 was a possibility, but this is one of the things they discovered they were wrong about when Theory 1 proved correct. The discovery, when it is made, excludes not only the truth but also the possibility of alternatives. This is the situation when we investigate a mathematical proposition of which we know that the truth, whatever it is, is a theorem and a mathematical necessity but, for the time being, we can seem to contemplate alternatives. This way of putting things coheres with the idea that the discovery establishes not only the truth but also the necessity of one identification. That seems to be what is expressed in the conditional formulations (i), (ii), and (iii).

However, this way of handling the idea of the discovery of the essential nature of a rigidly designated phenomenon is not successful. We need to give a more full-blooded status to the notion of alternative identifications of lightning, for we do not now have an epistemic perspective on alternative identifications superior to that which existed before the discovery that lightning is an electrical discharge. We are not able to think of the judgment that lightning might have been nonelectrical as a now-discarded but understandable error. If this was an error, it seems that we are condemned to make it ourselves, even after the successful investigation of lightning, that is, after we have learned that lightning is necessarily an electrical discharge.

This is brought out by the fact that the necessity enunciated by Kripke must be stated in the conditional form of (i), (ii), and (iii) if we are to speak with complete rigor. Kripke himself likes to stress this. He repeatedly uses the formulation "Such and such is necessary, *if it is true*," and he glosses Putnam as having shown that it might turn out that cats are not animals at all, even though, if they are animals, as seems very likely, they are necessarily animals. In a similar context, Kripke says that the empirical status of the theory that assigns the atomic weight 79 to gold entails that the theory might be false and that gold may *in fact* have some other atomic weight, even though, if it does have the atomic weight 79, the assertion that it does is a necessary truth. But all this means that, though we repose confidence in scientific findings, from a logical point of view, we recognize the possibility that all theories that have empirical foundations could be wrong. This possibility is convertible at once into the possibility that statements contrary to these supposed necessary truths may, in fact, be true. We are left in the awkward position of saying (when we are expressing the findings of science) that "Lightning is electrical discharge" is necessary, and also saying (when we are reminded that this rests on empirical premises) that "Lightning is nonelectrical" may be true and this is a possibility that has not been eliminated by the success of the investigation. It will never be eliminated, in principle, because the investigation is empirical and further empirical results could lead us to reverse our present understandings. The case is not like that of a discovered mathematical truth, because mathematical propositions are proved, and identifications of phenomena rest on empirical evidence that is always and in principle revisable.[17]

The same difficulty can be expressed in terms of the language to which the word "lightning" belongs according to Kripke's understanding. The discovery that lightning is an electrical discharge is empirical, and this, by itself, seems to require, as Kripke notes, that things might have come out otherwise. Our naive way of expressing the alternative is captured by the thought that lightning might have turned out to be λ and not an electrical phenomenon at all. But how could this have been a possibility? The assertion that lightning is necessarily an electrical discharge is just the assertion that it could not be anything else and is not nonelectrical under any counterfactual hypothesis whatever. Therefore, we have to redescribe what was really possible.

The revised account that meets Kripke's needs will run as follows: There could have been a phenomenon that made flashes in the sky followed by loud bangs and so on, and it could have turned out, on investigation, that that phenomenon was nonelectrical. We cannot, strictly speaking, say that, under this hypothesis, lightning is nonelectrical, because it would not be lightning that flashed in the described circumstances. It would be another phenomenon that appears in that possible world to us as lightning actually appears to us.

If we apply this understanding to the context of investigation, we have to say that, had Theory 2 turned out to be the true one—which has to be considered a real possibility in order to make sense of the empirical status of the discovery that Theory 1 is correct—then 'lightning' would not have been our word for lightning. Under this hypothesis 'lightning' would have been our word for λ. The real alternative possibility is that we might have found ourselves in epistemological circumstances qualitatively indistinguishable from those in which we detect lightning (that is, flashes in the sky that precede bangs, and so on), and in those circumstances we might have said, "Let us (rigidly) designate that flashing phenomenon 'lightning'," and then we could have discovered that what we called lightning under the hypothesis is the nonelectrical phenomenon λ, and that would be a necessary truth.[18]

This way of looking at matters means that Theory 1 and Theory 2 describe two different possible worlds, which differ not only in the character of what flashes in the sky but also differ linguistically vis-à-vis the word 'lightning', which is a different word in each theory. Theory 1 is about a world in which there is a word 'lightning' that rigidly designates electrical discharges. Theory 2 is about a world in which there is a word 'lightning' that rigidly designates a nonelectrical phenomenon λ. This gives us a way of representing the real contingency that cannot be rendered as the possibility that lightning is nonelectrical. But this device, which is in the spirit of Kripke's own discussions, still leaves difficult questions unresolved. Now it becomes impossible to justify the descriptions that we gave of the two theories as alternative accounts of the nature of lightning. The two theories have different vocabularies, and the appearance of the shape 'lightning' in the statement of each of them does not indicate that these are two efforts to identify the same phenomenon. For 'lightning' refers to an electrical phenomenon in Theory 1 but not in Theory 2, where it refers to the nonelectrical phenomenon λ. More important than even this striking difference, as far as reconstruction of the idea of alternative theories is concerned, we now have to say that both of the theories are correct. ' "Lightning' in Theory 2 rigidly designates not lightning, but the nonelectrical phenomenon λ. And Theory 2 says of this nonelectrical phenomenon that it is the nonelectrical phenomenon λ. That is certainly not a claim that any investigation would want to rule out. Therefore, the two theories are not alternatives *in any sense*.

Perhaps we could accept this and construct a way of describing what is discovered and what is necessary that avoids the incompatibility of the necessity claim and the idea that before the discovery (and afterward), we contemplate alternative identifications. Even if this can be done, it will be done at a sacrifice of intuitive intelligibility. This is a significant misfortune for Kripke's viewpoint. The statement "Lightning may be an electrical phenomenon and it may be λ," seems intuitively unobjectionable, but now we are saying that it uses the word "lightning" in two different languages at the same time.[19] The seeming expression of alternatives is now construed as alluding to two different necessary truths. The intuitive appeal of "Lightning might be this or it might be that" is not explained by the thought that there might have been another word 'lightning' and a necessary truth linking it with the phenomenon it rigidly designates. Kripke himself does not disparage but, rather, exploits the use of the statement " 'Lightning is and electrical discharge' had to be discovered." Yet it is impossible to retain this usage while rejecting the idea that no alternative identifications for lightning could ever be contemplated.

There is a slipperiness here that may promote illusions about the impact of Kripke's substantial insights. If we are not allowed to say, when we speak properly, "Lightning might have been nonelectrical," then we should be not allowed to say, when we speak properly, "We had to discover what the nature of lightning is." If we must always replace the first with the correct assertion "What flashes in the sky might not have been an electrical discharge," then we must always replace the second with the correct version "We had to discover the nature of the phenomenon that we perceive as flashes in the sky." In many passages Kripke endorses these rephrasings as the perspicuous vehicle for grasping what is going on in a discovered identification of a phenomenon. For example:

> The loose and inaccurate statement that gold might have turned out to be a compound should be replaced (roughly) by the statement that it is logically possible that there should have been a compound with all the properties originally known to hold of gold. The inaccurate statement that Hesperus might

have turned out not to be Phosphorus should be replaced by the true contingency . . . : two distinct bodies might have occupied, in the morning and in the evening respectively, the very positions actually occupied by Hesperus-Phosphorus-Venus.[20]

If we are not going to be "loose and inaccurate," we will abandon the claim that the new point of view introduced by Kripke includes the idea that certain necessary truths are a posteriori. For it is only the restated identification of the flashing phenomenon for which we really contemplate alternatives, make discoveries and establish something a posteriori. We find a posteriori that the contingent proposition "The flashing phenomenon that we call 'lightning' is an electrical discharge" is true. We do not find a posteriori that the proposition "Lightning is what it is" is true. This is necessary but is no discovery. As Kripke likes to say, we cannot say that lightning might not have been an electrical discharge (assuming that it is) because this would mean that lightning might not be what lightning *is*. If this is how we are to speak, then we no more discover that lightning is an electrical discharge than we discover that it is what it is. All the discovering that is done is discovering contingent truths.[21]

The retention of the usage "The discovery that lightning is an electrical discharge," and so on, is understandable because we all feel a compelling intuition to the effect that such things are discovered. If we back that intuition to the end, we must, as I have already argued, agree that lightning might not have been electrical and, thus, drop the claim of necessity. We will also be forced to abandon either the idea that being electrical is essential to being "the same phenomenon" or the idea that 'lightning' is rigid. In the last analysis, however, the retention of the Kripkean spirit means that we must set aside the intuition that "Lightning is an electrical discharge" is really discovered at all. If this is correct, the segregation of truths into a priori truths, which are not discovered empirically, and a posteriori truths, which are, does not seem to be defeated by Kripke's analysis, although that analysis does reclassify identifications as necessary that had been thought contingent heretofore.

I think Kripke comes close to rejecting a posteriori necessity more or less expressly in at least one passage in *Naming and Necessity*. Toward the end of the book, he addresses this issue in a general discussion meant to cover identities expressed in name-equations and also propositions identifying phenomena and ascribing necessary properties such as atomic weight to elements. The idea that one of these assertions could be discovered to be true is wrapped up, as Kripke appreciates, with the thought that the investigation "could have turned out otherwise." Putting a challenge into the mouth of an imaginary critic, Kripke says,

> I gather that Hesperus might have turned out not to be Phosphorus. What then can you mean when you say that such eventualities are impossible? If Hesperus might have *turned out* not to be Phosphorus, then Hesperus might not have *been* Phosphorus. And similarly for the other cases: if the world could have *turned out* otherwise, it could have *been* otherwise. To deny this fact is to deny

the self-evident modal principle that what is entailed by a possibility must itself be possible.[22]

The imaginary critic goes on to show that we cannot assimilate the idea of things turning out otherwise to the illusion of possibility that exists when we do not yet know whether a mathematical proposition is a truth or not. In such cases we do not really envision alternative possible outcomes. In the context of a mathematical proof, unlike empirical discovery, we have to say that it was "impossible for the answer to turn out other than it did." In contrast, the critic continues,

> in your favorite cases of essence and identity between two rigid designators, it really is logically possible that gold should have turned out to be a compound, and that this table might really have turned out not to be made of wood.[23]

In the same spirit, the critic might add that lightning might *really* have turned out not to be electrical. This line opposes the understanding Kripke offers throughout *Naming and Necessity* in accordance with which things could neither have been, nor have turned out to be, other than as they are in the rigidly expressed identities and identifications with which we are concerned. Kripke goes on at once to answer the imagined critic and to give an account of just what is logically possible here that invokes essentially epistemological ideas:

> What does the intuition that the table might have turned out to be made of ice . . . amount to? I think it means simply that there might have been *a table* looking and feeling just like this one and placed in this very position in the room, which was in fact made of ice. In other words, "I . . . could have been qualitatively in the same epistemic situation that in fact obtains, I could have had the same sensory evidence that I in fact have, about *a table* which was made of ice.[24]

Kripke then notes that this explanation resembles the discourse of counterpart theorists who explain counterfactual hypotheses by appeal to truths about different individuals in different possible worlds.

> Something like counterpart theory is thus applicable to the situation, but it applies only because we are *not* interested in what might have been true of *this particular* table, but in what might have been true of *a table* given certain evidence. It is precisely because it is *not* true that this table might have been made of ice from the Thames that we must turn here to qualitative descriptions and counterparts. To apply these notions to genuine *de re* modalities is, from the present standpoint, perverse.[25]

Kripke means that the statements about counterparts do not show that Hesperus might not have been Phosphorus and it is perverse to interpret them as though they could introduce an element of contingency into these necessary truths. They show merely that something else, something that is not Hesperus, might have been sighted in the situations in which Hesperus has been sighted. When we confine our attention to *this very individual*, the explanation of apparent contingency does not confer any real contingency in any sense on the statement "Hesperus is Phosphorus." Just what would be "perverse" according to the last sentence just quoted? Surely, Kripke means that it is perverse to say that Hesperus might have been a different body when this means only that we might have been looking at a different body and calling it "Hesperus." The "genuine *de re* modality" is the thought that the particular body that we do call "Hesperus" is necessarily the body it is. We come around again to the unimpeachable security of "*This very body* could not be something that it is not." We might have discovered that some other body is the thing we call Hesperus. It would be, as Kripke says, perverse, to present discoveries about something else as if they were discoveries we might have made about Hesperus. But, then, it ought to follow that the only thing that we really discover is that the body that we observed in the morning is the body that we observed in the evening. Just as the facts about counterparts would be perversely described as introducing contingency into "Hesperus is Phosphorus," so, too, the claims about counterparts are perversely said to make room for the *a posteriori* discovery of what cannot be other than it is.

Applying this to the context of the identification of phenomena, we can say that some other phenomenon might have been called 'lightning' and we could have discovered the essential nonelectrical nature of that phenomenon. But the very perverseness Kripke warns of would attach to our effort to advert to this possibility in explication of the alleged discovery that lightning is electrical.

Is there not an ineliminable epistemological fact that we are ignoring here? At one time we do not know whether the statement "Lightning is an electrical discharge" is true, but we do know that, if it is true, it is a necessary truth. Then some scientific investigations are carried out and with their completion we do know that "Lightning is an electrical discharge" is true, and necessary. So, it seems that we found this out. As a consequence, Kripke speaks of a posteriori necessity here, and this conception is understandably regarded as one of the radical realignments in our thinking that has been wrought by *Naming and Necessity*.

We called lightning "lightning" before we knew what it was. This contingent fact contributes a lot to the atmosphere of discovery of necessity. Let us imagine introduction of the rigid designator after the discovery to try to shed light on what is at stake here. Suppose we did not introduce any rigid designator for lightning and always spoke of "the phenomenon that appears as flashes in the sky." Then imagine that we made a scientific discovery expressible in the assertion "The phenomenon that appears as flashes in the sky is an electrical discharge." At this point, with the discovery completed, suppose we agreed to use 'lightning' to designate rigidly this phenomenon that appears as flashes in the sky, that is, the phenomenon that has already been discovered to be an electrical discharge. If this is to be our use of 'lightning', why, of course, "Lightning is an electrical discharge" is a necessary truth and in no possible world can lightning be anything nonelectrical. It will be obvious that this is not also a discovery at all, and not a posteriori. Furthermore, under these circumstances, the necessity of "Lightning is an electrical discharge" is *de dicto* and not *de re*. As things actually stand, we use 'lightning' to refer to this phenomenon before we know which phenomenon it is. As a consequence, we get a kind of blank-check *de dicto* necessity, since we know that, whatever it is that appears as flashes in the sky, that is what lightning is. That we can use 'lightning' in this way before the discovery, just as we can introduce it for this purpose after the discovery, does not carry with it any special significance for the kind of necessity that attaches to the proposition "Lightning is an electrical discharge."

In discussing Putnam's ideas, Kripke introduces rather casually a distinction between necessity in an epistemological sense as opposed to necessity in a nonepistemological sense. It is, he says, "the latter sense of necessity that is advocated in these lectures."[26] Is this supposed to mean that "Hesperus is Phosphorus" and "Lightning is an electrical discharge" can be said to be epistemologically contingent, although they express metaphysical necessities? What could we mean by saying these propositions are epistemologically contingent when we have just emphasized that there is no sense in which these propositions could have turned out to be false? Since the actual discovery we might make is about another body and not about Hesperus, or about another phenomenon and not about lightning, to speak of "epistemological contingency" on the basis of these discoveries would be just the perverseness of construing truths about counterparts as possibilities for real existents to which Kripke is sensitive himself.

I think this conclusion is consonant with one powerful strand of Kripke's thinking, for ordinarily Kripke is not receptive to a proliferation of conceptions of necessity. If we emphasize this Kripkean motif, we will regard "epistemological contingency" as a mere manner of speaking in complicated contexts wherein an ordinary empirical truth (such as "The phenomenon that appears as flashes in the sky is an electrical discharge") and a straightforward nonempirical truth (such as "Lightning is whatever the phenomenon that flashes in the sky is") are combined to yield an ordinary necessary truth "Lightning is an electrical discharge."

Notes

1. A number of colleagues have helped me in thinking about these questions and in writing this paper. Michael Levin criticized a sequence of drafts and made many helpful suggestions, as well as pointed out defects. Arnold Koslow, Alex Orenstein, and David Rosenthal gave me advice and criticism. Over the long term, I have profited from many discussions of reference and of Kripke's thought, in particular, with Howard Wettstein.

2. See also Saul Kripke, "A Puzzle about Belief," 241.

3. Ibid., 243.

4. See Saul Kripke, *Naming and Necessity* (Cambridge, Mass., 1980), 59n and 91–97.

5. See, for example, Kripke, *Naming and Necessity*, 59ff.

6. Ibid., 57.

7. Ibid., 143–44.

8. Examples such as this were brought to my attention by Joseph Almog.

9. I find that there are some who think that "Wolves are carnivores" may be a necessary truth. They

reason that this necessity may be discovered. We may, that is, discover that the DNA in wolves guarantees a digestive system that could not survive on a diet of vegetables. If we suppose that possession of a specific DNA is the essence of belonging to a species, we might believe that a creature could not be a wolf unless it was a carnivore. Although this is intelligible, it seems to me a fragile defense of what appears to be the Kripkean ruling: "Wolves are carnivores" is necessary, if true, because 'wolf' and 'carnivore' are both rigid. The 'scientific' intuition about DNA and diet seems to me successfully challenged when we reflect that wolves might retain just the dietary needs they have but become vegetarians if vegetables were to exist that, unlike the vegetables we know, satisfy the needs of wolves as presently constituted. In the same way, wolves might become vegetarians if their intestines are colonized by organisms that convert plant nutrients into a form usable by wolves, in the fashion of termites who rely on such colonies to get nutrition from wood, which makes, ironically, an unsuitable diet for the termite per se.

10. This illustration and the terminology chosen for it were devised in a discussion with my colleagues Arnold Koslow and Alex Orenstein.

11. Again, some intuit a necessary status for "All cardiacs are renals" based on DNA. The considerations canvassed in note 2 seem to tell against this claim. In particular, supposing that creatures with hearts will inevitably need the use of kidneys, it is hard to see how we could rule out the possibility that a symbiotic relationship might develop between two creatures that permitted the kidneys of one to atrophy out of existence because of the availability of the kidneys belonging to the other creature.

12. This suggestion and the example were provided by Michael Levin.

13. The desirability of considering event identity and the salient differences between reconstruction in such terms and reconstruction via property identity were suggested to me in discussion by David Rosenthal.

14. See Kripke, *Naming and Necessity*, 44.

15. The idea that twins are an especially forceful example of the arbitrariness of our conception of who Reagan is under a counterfactual hypothesis was suggested to me by Margarita Levin.

16. "If 'C-fibers' is not a rigid designator, simply replace it by one which is, or suppose it is used as a rigid designator in the present context." Kripke, *Naming and Necessity*, 149.

17. This separation of questions about the identity of phenomena as unlike the case of discovered mathematical necessities coheres with the stand Kripke himself suggests on p. 41 of *Naming and Necessity*.

18. Kripke makes it clear that this is his understanding in this passage: "To clear up one thing which some people have asked me: when I say that a designator is rigid and designates the same thing in all possible worlds, I mean that, as used in *our* language, it stands for that thing, when *we* talk about counterfactual situations. I don't mean of course that there mightn't be counterfactual situations in which in other possible worlds people actually spoke a different language." *Naming and Necessity*, 77.

19. This way of putting the matter has profited from suggestions made by Michael Levin. Jawad Azzouni pointed out to me that it looks as if "lightning" will belong to one language in Theory 1 and to another in Theory 2, and it would have to belong to two languages at the same time in sentences like "Lightning is an electrical discharge or λ."

20. Kripke, *Naming and Necessity*, 143.

21. A similar point is made by Michael Levin in "Two Applications of Rigid Designators," *Philosophy of Science* 54, no. 2 (June 1987): Levin shows that Kripke's views do not alter the traditional conception of scientific truth as essentially empirical and contingent. He emphasizes that Kripke's analysis does not affect the status of any assertions relevant to the identification of a phenomenon except for assertions like "Lightning is an electrical discharge," where the rigid name introduced for some apprehended phenomenon is linked with its discovered essential character. I am stressing that the necessary status of this one assertion in the setting of such discoveries has to be understood as a consequence of the fact that we use "lightning" or analogous designators for types of phenomena rigidly, and not for some metaphysical necessity that was overlooked by previous thinkers. It is because we use "lightning" as a rigid designator for a phenomenon that is discovered to be essentially electrical that the identification "Lightning is an electrical discharge" is necessary.

22. Ibid, 141.
23. Ibid.
24. Ibid., 142.
25. Ibid.
26. Ibid., 123.

Explanatory Realism, Causal Realism, and Explanatory Exclusion

JAEGWON KIM

I

Explaining is an epistemological activity, and "having" an explanation is, like knowing, an epistemological accomplishment. To be in need of an explanation is to be in an epistemologically imperfect state, and we look for an explanation in an attempt to remove that imperfection and thereby improve our epistemic situation. If we think in terms of the traditional divide between knowledge and reality known, explanations lie on the side of knowledge—on the side of the "subjective" rather than that of the "objective," on the side of "representation" rather than that of reality represented. Our explanations are part of what we know about the world.

Knowledge implies truth: we cannot know something that is not the case. On a realist view of knowledge, every bit of knowledge has an objective counterpart, the thing that is known which is itself not part of knowledge—at least, not part of that particular bit of knowledge. But exactly what is it that we know when we have an explanation? Exactly in what does *explanatory knowledge* consist? If explanations constitute knowledge, it makes sense to ask, for each explanation that we "have," exactly what it is that we know in virtue of having that explanation. And when we gain a new explanation, precisely what change takes place in our body of knowledge? We usually think of knowledge as consisting of a set of "propositions," thought to represent "facts" of the world. These propositions are discrete items, although they form a complex network of logical and evidential connections. How are we to represent explanatory knowledge within such a picture? Where do we locate explanations in a scheme of propositions?

We can think of an explanation as a complex of propositions or statements divisible into two parts, *explanans* and *explanandum proposition*.[1] Since explanations can take a variety of linguistic forms, this division is rough; in particular, it

225

is not to be taken to imply that an explanation is an argument or inference, with the explanans as premise and the explanandum as conclusion. Let us focus on explanations of individual events. Such explanations typically explain an event (why a given event occurred) by reference to another event (or set of events). Let E be the explanandum, to the effect that a certain event e occurred. Let C be an explanans for this explanandum. C, let us assume, is the statement that event c occurred. Suppose then that we "have" this explanation—that is, C and E are related as explanans to explanandum in our body of knowledge (call this the "explanans relation"). What is the relationship between events c and e?

What I want to call *explanatory realism* takes the following position: C is an explanans for E *in virtue of* the fact that c bears to e some determinate objective relation R. Let us call R, whatever it is, an "explanatory relation." (The *explanans* relation relates propositions or statements; the *explanatory* relation relates events or facts in the world.) The explanatory relation is an objective relation among events that, as we might say, "ground" the explanans relation, and constitutes its "objective correlate." On the realist view, our explanations are "correct" or "true" if they depict these relations correctly, just as our propositions or beliefs are true if they correctly depict objective facts; and explanations could be more or less "accurate" according to how accurately they depict these relations. Thus, that c is related by explanatory relation R to e is the "content" of the explanation consisting of C and E; it is what the explanation "says."

Although the attribution of truth or correctness to explanations is essential to explanatory realism, it by itself is not sufficient; those who reject explanatory realism in our sense, too, can speak of the truth or falsity of an explanation—for example, in the sense that propositions constituting the explanans are all true. What matters to realism is that the truth of an explanation requires an *objective relationship* between the events involved. By an "objective relation," I have in mind a relation that at least meets the following condition: that it is instantiated does not entail anything about the existence or nonexistence of any intentional psychological state—in particular, an epistemological or doxastic state—except, of course, when it is instantiated by such states. I am not suggesting that the explanatory relation holding for events is all there is to explanations, or to the explanans relation. Just as knowledge requires more than truth, explanations presumably must meet further requirements ("internal" conditions—perhaps logical and epistemic ones), although exactly what these are does not concern us here.

What could such an R be in virtue of which an event is correctly cited in the explanation of another? The obvious first thought is this: R is the *causal relation*. Perhaps there are noncausal explanations of individual events; however, few will deny that the causal relation is at least one important special case of R. And there are those who hold that the causal relation is the only explanatory relation—at least the principal one.[2]

Explanatory irrealism, on the other hand, would be the view that the relation of being an explanans for, as it relates C and E within our epistemic corpus, is not, and need not be, "grounded" in any objective relation between events c and e. It is solely a matter of some "internal" relationship between items of knowledge. Perhaps, there are logical, conceptual, or epistemic relationships among propositions in virtue of which one proposition constitutes an explanans for another, and when that happens, we could speak of the events represented as being related by an explanatory relation. That is, given the explanans relation over propositions, a relation over the events they represent could be defined: c explains (is related by R to) e just in case C is an explanans for E. But an R so defined would fail to be an objective relation, as required by realism, for it would depend crucially on what goes on within our body of knowledge and belief.

In the following passage Wesley Salmon gives a clear and forceful expression to the realist view of explanation:

> We need not object to [the purely psychological conception of explanation] merely on the ground that people often invoke false beliefs and feel comfortable with the 'explanation' thus provided. . . . We can, quite consistently with this approach, insist that adequate explanations must rest upon *true* explanatory bases. Nor need we object on the ground that supernatural 'explanations' are often psychologically appealing. Again, we can insist that the explanation be grounded in *scientific* fact. Even with those restrictions, however, the view that scientific explanation consists in release from psychological uneasiness is unacceptable for two reasons. First, we must surely require that there be some sort of *objective* relationship between the explanatory facts and the fact-to-be-explained.[3]

However, merely to hold that C is an explanans for E just in case c is a cause of e is not necessarily to espouse explanatory realism. Whether that is so depends on one's conception of causation. Consider, for example, Hanson, who writes:

> The primary reason for referring to the cause of x is to explain x. There are as many causes of x as there are explanations of x.[4]

> Causes certainly are connected with effects; but this is because our theories connect them, not because the world is held together by cosmic glue. The world *may* be glued together by imponderables, but that is irrelevant for understanding causal explanation. The notions 'the cause x' and 'the effect y' are intelligible only against a pattern of theory, namely one which puts guarantees on inference from x to y.[5]

For Hanson, causal relations essentially depend on an appropriate conceptual interlocking of our descriptions as provided by the theories we accept. He makes it evident, in the quoted passages, that he views the causal relation between x and y as derivative from an inferential relation from x to y, and the inferential relation as intimately associated with explanation; it is also evident that he does not take the dependence of causation on inference and explanation to be merely epistemological. If one accepts this view of causation and causal explanation, there is nothing realist about the position that causal explanations hold just in case the causal relation holds. For causal relations, on such an approach, depend on inferential-explanatory connections which are primary and more basic.

More generally, if one wants to *analyze* causation itself in terms of explanation,[6] one would be rejecting explanatory realism—unless one could identify an objective relation other than causation as the explanatory relation. But what could such a relation be? One might wish to propose the *nomological* relation as a candidate. The idea is this: that two events, c and e, are "subsumed under," or "instantiate," an appropriate law is the objective correlate of the explanans relation for C and E. Giving an account of "subsumption under a law" without presupposing causal notions is not an easy task, but let us not press this issue.[7] The point to consider is how we understand the notion of "law." If a law is taken as "mere Humean constant conjunction," with no modal or subjunctive force intimating some tie of "necessitation," this approach would give us realism. But it is highly dubious that a conception of an explanatory relation based on such a notion of "law" could provide a basis for an adequate account of explanation; it is even more dubious that an analysis of causation based on such a conception of explanation will come close to capturing our concept of causation. On the other hand, if laws are endowed with sufficiently strong modal force, it is doubtful whether the nomological relation will be distinguishable, in any meaningful way, from the causal relation.[8] Indeed, the nomological account of causation is one of the more influential approaches to the analysis of the causal relation. An analysis of causation in terms of a conception of explanation that in turn is based on the nomological relation as the explanatory relation will essentially be just a nomological analysis, possibly with some psycho-epistemological embellishments. It would be difficult to see why one should not just go for a direct nomological analysis of causation, and use the causal relation as one's explanatory relation.

We must conclude that any attempt to analyze causation as explanation will result in a form of explanatory irrealism. For an analysis of causation to be a genuine explanatory analysis, the concept of explanation assumed as the basis of analysis must be a robustly epistemological and psychological notion whose core is constituted by such notions as understanding and intelligibility, not some pale, formal reconstruction of it. If, for example, the Hempelian deductive-nomological conception of explanation is used to explain causation, the result is not a genuine explanatory analysis of causation but rather the old standby, the nomological-subsumptive, or quasi-Humean, analysis. Thus, on a real explanatory approach to causation, causation will turn out to be a nonobjective psycho-epistemological relation and, therefore, fail to serve as an objective correlate of the explanans relation.

II

It is plausible to conclude, therefore, that explanatory realism requires the causal relation as an explanatory relation. As I said, we may leave open the question whether the causal relation is the only explanatory relation. But at least this much is certain:

in both everyday and most scientific contexts,[9] explanations of individual events are predominantly *causal explanations* in the sense that the events cited in the explanation of an event are its causes and, further, their explanatory efficacy is thought to stem from their causal status. And when each of a class of events can be given a similar causal explanation, we may have a causal explanation of a regularity. We shall in this paper focus exclusively on the causal relation as our explanatory relation; our general metaphysical points should be valid, *mutadis mutandis*, for other explanatory relations if any exist. Explanatory realism says this about causal explanations: a causal explanation of event e in terms of event c ("e occurred because c caused it") is *correct*, or *true*, just in case c did as a matter of objective fact cause e. That the causal relation holds between the two events constitutes the "factual content" of the explanation. This may sound obvious and trivial.

Perhaps it sounds obvious only because we take explanatory realism for granted. But it certainly is not trivial. It requires, for its intended realist purposes, that causality itself be an objective feature of reality. This doctrine, which we may call *causal realism*, has not gone unchallenged. Hume's celebrated critique of "necessary connection" as an objective relation characterizing events themselves was perhaps the first—clearly the most influential—expression of a systematically articulated, irrealist position on causation. He wrote, "Upon the whole, necessity is something that exists in the mind, not in objects".[10] Hume well understood the causal realist's sentiments:

> But though this be the only reasonable account we can give of necessity, the contrary notion is so riveted in the mind from the principles above-mentioned, that I doubt not but my sentiments will be treated by many as extravagant and ridiculous. What! the efficacy of causes lie in the determination of mind! As if causes did not operate entirely independent of the mind, and would not continue their operation, even though there was no mind existent to contemplate them, or reason concerning them. Thought may well depend on causes for its operation, but not causes on thought. This is to reverse the order of nature, and make that secondary, which is really primary.[11]

Hume was understanding, but in the end dismissive:

> I can only reply to all these arguments that the case here is much the same as if a blind man should pretend to find a great many absurdities in the supposition that the colour of scarlet is not the same with the sound of a trumpet, nor light the same with solidity. If we have really no idea of a power or efficacy in any object, or of any real connection betwixt causes and effects, it will be to little purpose that an efficacy is necessary in all operations.[12]

Hume regarded the other ingredients he identified in the causal relation, namely temporal precedence, spatiotemporal contiguity (or connectability), and constant conjunction, as objective and mind-independent features of causally connected events;[13] but evidently he thought that necessitation, too, was an essential element in our philosophically unenlightened (by his light) concept of causation. Most philosophers will now agree that an idea of causation devoid of some notion of necessitation is not *our* idea of causation – perhaps not an idea of causation at all. According to most conceptions of causation now current, at any rate, Hume was a causal irrealist par excellence.

Hume, our original causal irrealist, had some illustrious followers. Russell ridiculed causation as "a relic of a bygone age," recommending the "extrusion" of the word "cause" from the philosophical vocabulary;[14] Wittgenstein said, "Belief in causal nexus is superstition."[15] The positivist-inspired suspicion of modalities, counterfactuals, and the like, which characterized much of analytic philosophy during the first two-thirds of this century, is of a piece with Hume's causal irrealism in their fundamental philosophical motivation, and it seems that many prominent philosophers in the analytic tradition during this period consciously avoided serious discussion of causality, making little use of it in their philosophical work.[16] More recently, Hilary Putnam has attacked the idea of "non-Humean causation" as a physically real relation.[17] I think it is more difficult than one might at first suppose to find philosophers who have consciously advocated in an unambiguously realist conception of causality.[18]

According to causal realism, therefore, causal connections hold independently of anyone's intentional states – in particular, epistemological or doxastic states – except, of course, when the causal connections concern such states. The realist believes, as Hume observes in the quotation above, that causal relations – the same ones – would hold even if there were no conscious beings to "contemplate them, or reason concerning them." This means that according to causal realism every event has a *unique and determinate causal history* whose character is entirely independent of our representation of it. We may come to know bits and pieces of an event's causal history, but whether we do, or to what extent we do, and what conceptual apparatus is used to depict it, do not in any way affect the causal relations in which events stand to other events. This entails that the existence and character of events themselves must be an objective and determinate fact; that is, causal realism makes sense only in the context of global realism.

Earlier, we raised the question of how explanatory knowledge is represented in our body of knowledge – that is, what it is that we know when we have an explanation of an event. The explanatory realist appears to have a simple answer: To "have an explanation" of event *e* in terms of event *c* is to know, or somehow represent, that *c* caused *e*; that is, explanatory knowledge is causal knowledge, and explanations of individual events are represented by singular causal propositions. Thus, explanatory knowledge is propositional knowledge of a certain kind, and to gain an explanation of an event is to learn *a further fact about that event*.

But is there an alternative to representing explanations as additional bits of propositional knowledge? Isn't explanatory knowledge a kind of knowledge, and isn't all knowledge, in an epistemologically relevant sense, a matter of knowing *that*? Although I do not know whether anyone has held a view like this, it is possible to hold, I think, that explanations are essentially a matter of how a body of knowledge is organized or systematized—a matter of there being certain appropriate patterns of coherence among items of knowledge. That is, to "have" an explanation of why E in terms of C—that is, to "have" C as an explanans for E—is simply for the two propositions C and E to be appropriately related within our epistemic corpus; it is not a matter of there being a further proposition within it. According to this view, therefore, explanatory knowledge supervenes on nonexplanatory knowledge: if you and I know exactly the same first-order, factual propositions (roughly, propositions that can serve as explananda and elements of an explanans), we would share the same explanations. Various considerations might lead us to qualify this conclusion; for example, one might construe the notion of "having an explanation" in such a way as to require the subject's awareness that the explanans is appropriately related to the explanandum. Thus, one might want to suggest that the presence of the two propositions in our body of knowledge is not enough, even if they in fact instantiate a required explanatory pattern, and insist that we must somehow mentally "bring them together" and "see" that they do so. Caution is required, however; pursuing this line may take one back to the propositional view of explanatory knowledge. At any rate, the nonpropositional, "pattern" view of explanatory knowledge differs from the propositional view on the following point: gaining a new explanation, on the pattern view but not on the propositional view, does not necessarily involve acquiring new information about facts of the world.

It seems clear that explanatory realism leads to the propositional view of explanatory knowledge; it makes "having" an explanation a matter of knowing a certain proposition to be true. On the other hand, explanatory irrealism, although it has an affinity for the pattern view, is not committed to it; it appears consistent with the propositional view. One might hold, for example, that a certain conceptual-epistemic relation between an explanandum and its explanans is what is fundamentally constitutive of an explaining relation, there being no independent objective relation characterizing the events represented by the explanans and the explanandum that grounds it,[19] but that "having" an explanation *is* a matter of *knowing that* this relationship does in fact hold for the explanans-explanandum pair. This, however, may not be a plausible view; it is naturally construed as requiring anyone who "has" any explanation of anything at all to know what the explanans relation is, something that few philosophers would confidently claim to know. In any case, those who find the propositional view of explanatory knowledge too simplistic, or otherwise unpalatable, would have to settle for explanatory irrealism; explanatory realism is not an option for them.

What difference does the choice between explanatory realism and irrealism make? We have already seen that explanatory realism plausibly entails causal realism. Does explanatory irrealism entail causal irrealism? There evidently is no strict inconsistency in holding both explanatory irrealism and causal realism. However, the combination seems somewhat incongruous and difficult to motivate: though acknowledging causation as a genuine relation in the world, the position denies it any essential role in explanation, severing the intuitive and natural tie between causality and explanation.[20] What, then, would be the point of the causal relation? The concept of causation, of course, has many roles to play, but it seems that its explanatory role is a central one, being closely tied to its other important roles. I think that the combination of explanatory irrealism and causal realism, though logically consistent, is not a plausible position.

We have also seen that explanatory realism entails the propositional account of explanatory knowledge, whereas explanatory irrealism, again, seems consistent with each of the two alternatives, the propositional view and the nonpropositional, pattern view. I think that the issue of causal realism versus irrealism and that concerning the nature of explanatory knowledge are significant issues, both interesting in themselves and important in what they imply for other philosophical problems. Problems about what explanatory knowledge consists in—that is, what "understanding" something amounts to—have been almost entirely neglected within traditional epistemology; this is surprising in view of the centrality of explanation in philosophy of science, which, by and large, is the epistemology of scientific knowledge. The issue of causal realism is obviously important: whether causal relations are real and objective, or mere projections of the cognizing mind, is an issue that directly affects the significance of causation within both science and philosophy. If it is an objective relation characterizing physical events in the world, is it physically reducible, or physically based in some sense, as we expect of other physical properties and relations? If not, what accounts for its special status? Which of the special sciences are responsible for investigating the properties of the causal relation itself?[21]

As for the philosophical implications of the choice between causal realism and irrealism, it is an interesting question, for example, whether any of the so-called causal theories (of perception, memory, knowledge, action, event-identity, reference, time, persistence, properties, and no doubt many others) will be able to retain, under an irrealist conception of causation, what plausibility it enjoys. It is also an interesting question whether a substantive version of global realism can be combined with causal irrealism. I suspect that if all causal facts are taken away from the world, not much of interest may remain—the world would become so impoverished, a pale imitation of a world, that we may not care much whether it is real or only "ideal." (If all those "causal theories" mentioned above are true, a world devoid of causal relations would be one in which there is no perception, no knowledge, no naming or referring, no intentional action, no time, no persisting object, and none of the rest. It would also be world in which there are no killings, no breakings, no pushings or pullings, and so on.)

Some may consider it a disadvantage of explanatory realism that it comes only in a package with causal realism, whereas explanatory irrealism can in principle be purchased separately. However, others may consider that an advantage: causal realism gives more content to explanatory realism, and as a result explanatory realism can do work that its rival cannot. Moreover, there is a certain satisfying unity in the combination of explanatory and causal realism. In any case, there seems to be some incongruity, as we saw, in combining explanatory irrealism and causal realism, so that an explanatory irrealist may in effect have no real choice but to embrace causal irrealism as well. In what follows, I will explore the implications of the realist view of explanation for the issue of "explanatory exclusion" and the irrealist (or "internalist") implications of the Hempelian inferential view of explanation.

III

I have argued elsewhere[22] that proffered explanations of a single event, with mutually consistent explanantia, can exclude one another in the following sense: there can be no more than a single *complete* and *independent* explanation of any one event, and we may not accept two (or more) explanations of a single event unless we know, or have reason to believe, that they are appropriately related — that is, related in such a way that one of the explanations is either not complete in itself or dependent on the other. This constraint on explanations, which we may call *the principle of explanatory exclusion*, has two clauses: the first is about the *existence* of explanations, the second about *acceptance* of explanations. The first clause, I shall argue, can be seen as a plausible thesis if we assume explanatory realism. We shall not discuss the second clause here.

Suppose, then, that each of C_1 and C_2 is claimed to be a causal explanans for E. Let c_1, c_2, and e be the events represented by C_1, C_2, and E. According to explanatory realism, it follows that c_1 caused e and also that c_2 caused e. How are we to understand this situation? There are various possibilities:

1) It turns out that $c_1 = c_2$. A single event is picked out by nonequivalent descriptions. Here, there is in reality only one pair of events related by the explanatory relation (that is, the causal relation), and this gives sense to the claim that there is, here, one explanation, not two. The exclusion principle makes sense only if a criterion of individuation is assumed for explanations — that is, only if we can make sense of "same" and "different" as applied to explanations. Now, explanatory realism yields a natural way of individuating explanations: explanations are individuated in terms of the events related by the explanatory relation (the causal relation, for explanations of events).[23] For on realism it is the objective relationship between events that ultimately grounds explanations and constitutes their objective content. This provides us with a basis for regarding explanations that appeal to the same events standing in the same relation as giving, or stating, one explanation, not two — just as two inequivalent descriptions can represent the same fact. Thus, on explanatory realism, we can make good sense of the idea that logically inequivalent explanations can represent the same explanatory relation, and therefore state the same explanation. To the explanatory irrealist, this way of individuating explanations would be unmotivated: explanations would be more appropriately individuated in terms of descriptions or propositions and their internal logical, conceptual, and epistemic relationships. Nothing needs to prevent the explanatory realist from accepting this "internal" individuation criterion as well, as defining *another* useful sense in which

we can count explanations. The point is only that explanatory realism motivates an "objective" individuation of explanations, which is both intuitively plausible and well suited for the exclusion principle.

(2) C_1 is reducible to, or supervenient on, c_2. This sort of relationship might obtain, for example, on some accounts of the mind-body relation, which, though eschewing an outright psychophysical identification, nonetheless recognizes the reductive or supervenient dependency of the mental on the physical. In such a case, the causal relation involving the supervenient or reduced event must itself be thought of as supervenient or reducible to the causal or nomological relation involving the "base" event.[24] In this sense, the two explanations are not independent; for the one involving the reduced causal (that is, explanatory) relation is dependent on the one representing the "base" causal relation. This, again, is an example of realist thinking: dependency between explanations is understood in terms of the dependency between the objective explanatory relations that they represent.

(3) c_1 and c_2 are only partial causes, being constituents in a single sufficient set of causal conditions. Example: You push the stalled car and I pull it, and the car moves. In this case, neither explanation is complete: each gives only a partial picture of the causal conditions that made up a sufficient cause of the effect. This sense of *explanatory completeness*, understood in terms of *sufficient cause*, is again entirely natural within the realist picture. For, according to the realist view, the causal relation between events constitutes the objective correlate, or content, of the explanans relation; where a particular causal relation gives us a cause event that is only a partial cause, or one among the many constituents of a sufficient cause, the corresponding explanans, too, can be thought to be only partial and incomplete. Conversely, when the causal relation provides a sufficient cause, the explanans can also be said to be complete and sufficient. The realist scheme also yields a more global sense of "complete explanation," one in which a complete explanation of an event specifies its entire causal history in every detail (as we noted earlier, under explanatory realism each event has a unique determinate causal history). This is an idealized sense of completeness, and no explanation can be complete in that sense (the notion of an ideally complete explanation, however, may be useful in explicating the concept of explanation).[25] Obviously, in this idealized sense there is at most one complete explanation of any given event; again, though obvious and uninteresting, this is not trivial, unless causal realism is trivial.

(4) c_1 and c_2 are different links in the same causal chain leading to event e. But they are not independent: the later event is, then, causally dependent on the earlier one, and, therefore, the two explanations are not independent. This, too, reflects realist thinking: two explanations are thought to be nonindependent because the explanatory relations represented by them are not independent.

(5) c_1 is part of c_2.[26] The explanations, then, are not independent; nor can they both be complete.

(6) c_1 and c_2 are independent, each a sufficient cause of e. This, then, is a standard case of "causal overdetermination." Do we in this case have a counterexample

to the explanatory exclusion principle? Why aren't both explanations, "*e* happened because c_1 caused it" and "*e* happened because c_2 caused it," sufficient and independent explanations? This is an interesting case from the point of view of both explanatory exclusion and the question of explanatory realism versus irrealism, and we shall discuss this in some detail.

Hempel has called cases like this "explanatory overdetermination:[27] suppose that a copper rod is heated while simultaneously being subjected to longitudinal stress. As a result, its length increases. Two deductive-nomological (hereafter "DN") arguments can be formulated: the first would invoke the lawlike premise that copper rods lengthen when they are heated, and the "initial condition" that this particular copper rod was heated on this occasion; the second would appeal to the law stating that copper rods increase in length when subjected to longitudinal stress, and the initial condition that this copper rod was subjected to that kind of stress. The two arguments share the same conclusion, the statement that the rod's length increased on this occasion. According to the standard DN account of explanation, therefore, each argument counts as an explanation.

It is not surprising that Hempel rejects the view that these DN arguments are not "complete" as explanations. He writes:

> It might be objected that—even granting the truth of all the premises—both accounts are unacceptable since they are "incomplete": each neglects one of the two factors that contributed to the lengthening. In appraising the force of this objection it is again important to be clear about just what is to be explained. If as in our example, this is simply the fact that *Lr*, i.e., that *r* lengthened, or that there was *some* increase in the length of *r*, then, I think, either of the two arguments conclusively does *that*, and the charge of incompleteness is groundless.[28]

Here he seems simply to affirm that, as an explanation of why the rod lengthened, "each of the two arguments conclusively does *that*." But why does he say this? The use of the term "conclusively" suggests that he was moved by the consideration that each DN argument provides a premise-set that is *deductively conclusive* for the truth of the explanandum statement. This is not surprising. For, fundamental to the DN conception of explanation is the idea that explanations are *inferences* or *arguments* of a certain form. Given this assumption, a natural sense of "completeness" or "sufficiency" emerges for explanations: when an argument has the correct DN form, it is *complete* and *sufficient*. Hempel writes:

> I think it is important and illuminating to distinguish such partial explanations . . . from what might be called *deductively complete explanations*, i.e., those in which the explanandum as stated is logically implied by the explanans; for the latter do, whereas the former do not, account for the explanandum phenomenon in the specificity with which the explanandum sentence describes it. An explanation that conforms to the D-N model is, therefore, au-

tomatically complete in this sense; and a partial explanation as we have characterized it always falls short of being a D-N explanation.[29]

As explanation is conceived under the DN model, there is nothing one can do to a
DN argument to improve it in regard to its "completeness" as an explanation. One
may be able to make it deeper, more perspicuous, more systematic, and so on; but
what could one possibly do to make it "more complete"? The DN conception of explanation does not seem to leave room for any other sense of explanatory completeness than deductive conclusiveness.

These considerations suggest that a preoccupation with the deductive or inferential character of explanation leads to a form of explanatory irrealism ("explanatory internalism," perhaps, is more appropriate), and this is certainly what we see
in Hempel. This internalist tendency is evident also in Hempel's well-known emphasis on the predictive character of explanation, and in one of his two conditions of
adequacy on explanations, that is, the requirement of "explanatory relevance" to the
effect that "explanatory information adduced affords good grounds for believing that
the phenomenon to be explained did, or does, indeed occur."[30] Hempel's idea that
explanations are arguments, his condition of "explanatory relevance," and his emphasis on the predictive aspect of explanations go hand in hand: they all point to explanatory irrealism—at least, point away from explanatory realism with the causal
relation serving as objective correlate of the explanatory relation.

Hempel's primary focus in analyzing the structure of explanation is on the logical and conceptual characteristics of statements making up an explanation (the "internal" properties, as I have called them), not on the events or other entities these statements describe and their interrelations. In fact, we get from Hempel a precise and
elaborately constructed definition of what an explanation is, but only a very intuitive
and unanalyzed idea of what it is that a given explanation is an explanation of.[31]
Hempel's treatment of causal explanation and causation is also symptomatic of this
attitude:[32] the idea of a DN argument, an essentially internal notion, is primary in
the characterization of explanations, and the idea of causal explanation falls out of
this characterization as a not-so-clearly-defined special case. Hempel evidently does
not regard the concept of causal explanation, or that of causation, as at all crucial
to a theory of explanation; his discussion of causal explanation often comes across
as a concession to the popular practice of referring to causes and causal explanations,
not something that he sees as essential to the development of his theory. From such
an internalist perspective, it is entirely natural that each of the two DN arguments
about the expanding copper is regarded as complete and sufficient in itself as an explanation.

What does explanatory realism say about the expanding copper rod? If the
heating and the stress are each an independent sufficient cause of the rod's lengthening, we have a standard case of causal overdetermination. Moreover, if, as explanatory realism seems to suggest, explanatory completeness is to be understood in terms
of sufficient cause, it follows that in the present case we have two independent and

complete explanations. Thus, explanatory realism seems to yield the same result as Hempel's irrealism: both seem to contradict the explanatory exclusion principle.

The explanatory realist who wants to save explanatory exclusion might deny that the rising temperature and the stress were each a sufficient cause of the event to be explained, and deny, more generally, that genuine instances of causal over-determination exist. Peter Unger has claimed that each event has a single unique cause (at most),[33] and if this is right, then not both the heating and the stress can be a cause of the lengthening. Therefore, there could be at most one causal explana-tion here. But Unger's thesis is a radical one, too strong to be plausible: he construes it to entail the denial of transitivity of causation, and hence the impossibility of causal chains with more than two links. And, his arguments rely exlusively on a certain kind of linguistic evidence whose point I find difficult to evaluate.

Martin Bunzl, too, has argued that there are no genuine cases of causal over-determination.[34] His basic point is that the usual examples, when closely scrutinized, turn out to be either cases of causal preemption or of joint cause. That is, one of the two alleged overdetermining causes preempts the other (by "getting there first") so that the second, in fact, is not a cause of the effect in question, or else the two causes together make up a single sufficient cause, neither of them alone being sufficient. I think Bunzl's arguments, on the whole, are plausible, though not conclusive.[35] Thus, when applied to the case of the copper rod, his analysis would probably give this diagnosis: the particular lengthening that took place was caused by the single joint cause made up of the heating and the stress. Neither of the two events was, in itself, a sufficient cause of it. Thus, a complete explanation of the lengthening must refer to both the heating and the stress as a single sufficient cause.

We must set aside the question whether genuine instances of causal overdeter-mination exist. What is of interest to us here is that under explanatory realism, the causal relation can be made to do some real work, in characterizing and constraining explanations. As we saw, the association between causation and explanation, under-written by explanatory realism, yields a principle of individuation for explanations and a notion of "complete explanation," both essential to interpreting the principle of explanatory exclusion. We also saw that if causal overdetermination is not possi-ble, that takes away one potential case of explanatory overdetermination. It seems to me that we are inclined to take these considerations involving causation as both natural and relevant in discussing the nature of explanation. What accounts for this inclination, I think, is our tacit acceptance of explanatory realism: for a causal expla-nation to hold, the explaining event must be a cause of the event explained. Given this connection between causal explanations and causal relations, we are able to use facts about the latter to say something about the former.

To return briefly to the matter of explanatory exclusion: if our considerations are generally right (especially in the treatment of the six cases in which two causal explanations are offered for one event), explanatory realism is seen to provide a sense, as well as support, for the explanatory exclusion principle—except, perhaps, in the case of causal overdetermination, which we set aside without a clear-cut resolution.[36] I believe it is more difficult, though not impossible, to interpret and argue for explanatory exclusion if by embracing explanatory irrealism we lose the causal handle on explanation.[37]

Notes

1. I shall sometimes use "explanandum" as short for "explanandum proposition (or statement)." This should cause no confusion.

2. E.g., Wesley C. Salmon, *Scientific Explanation and the Causal Structure of the World* (Princeton, N.J., 1984); David Lewis, "Causal Explanation," in *Philosophical Papers*, vol. 2 (Oxford, 1986). However, there are relations other than causation one might want to consider: e.g., the relation of supervenience, the micro-reductive relation. Whether or not these possible explanatory relations require the same explanandum as the causal relation is another question; see Robert Cummins's distinction between "explanation by subsumption" and "explanation by analysis" in his *The Nature of Psychological Explanation* (Cambridge, Mass., 1983), chap. 1. See also Peter Achinstein, "A Type of Non-Causal Explanation," *Midwest Studies in Philosophy* 9 (1984): 221–43.

3. *Scientific Explanation and the Causal Structure of the World*, 13 (emphasis in the original). Explanatory realism, as I have characterized it, appears closely related to what Salmon calls "the ontic model" of scientific explanation.

4. Norwood Russell Hanson, *Patterns of Discovery* (Cambridge, 1958), 54.

5. Ibid., 64. See, for a view similar to Hanson's but worked out in greater detail, William Ruddick, "Causal Connection," *Synthese* 18 (1968): 46–67.

6. See, for example, Michael Scriven, "Causation as Explanation," *Nous* 9 (1975): 3–16. I discuss Scriven's account in "Causes as Explanations: A Critique," *Theory and Decision* 13 (1981): 293–309. Some of the present material has been drawn from this paper.

7. For some general difficulties in explaining "subsumption under a law," see Donald Davidson, "Causal Relations," *Journal of Philosophy* 64 (1967): 691–703, and my "Causation, Nomic Subsumption, and the Concept of Event," *Journal of Philosophy* 70 (1973): 217–36.

8. Where the nomological and the causal relation do not match up, the former also fails to yield the explanatory relation.

9. By the qualification "most," I intend to leave out consideration of what some tell us goes on at the deepest and most abstract levels of theoretical physics.

10. *A Treatise of Human Nature*, edited by L. A. Selby-Bigge (Oxford, 1888), 165.

11. Ibid., 167.

12. Ibid., 168.

13. For discussions of this and other matters concerning Hume on causation and necessity, see Barry Stroud, *Hume* (London, 1977), chaps. 3, 4, and Tom L. Beauchamp and Alexander Rosenberg, *Hume and the Problem of Causation* (New York and Oxford, 1981), especially chap. 1.

14. Bertrand Russell, "On the Notion of Cause," *Proceedings of the Aristotelian Society* 13 (1913): 1–26.

15. Ludwig Wittgenstein, *Tractatus Logico-Philosophicus* (London, 1922), 5.1361. However, Wittgenstein may have had in mind by "causal nexus" something much stronger than what we would now understand by "causal necessity."

16. C. J. Ducasse and Hans Reichenbach were among the exceptions.

17. "Is the Causal Structure of the Physical Itself Something Physical?," *Midwest Studies in Philosophy* 9 (1984): 3–16.

18. Some possibilities among recent writers: Salmon, *Scientific Explanation and the Causal Structure of the World*; J. L. Mackie, *The Cement of the Universe* (Oxford, 1974), especially chap. 8. Quine seems to have studiously avoided discussing causation or making use of it in his philosophical work. The uses to which Donald Davidson has put the concept of causation indicate a realist attitude; consider, for example, his commitment to an event ontology and his causal criterion of event individuation in his *Essays*

on *Actions and Events* (Oxford, 1980). But he may reject the terms in which I have formulated the positions.

19. Recall our earlier discussion of Hanson; he seems to have held a view like this.

20. Peter Achinstein's views in *The Nature of Explanation* (New York and Oxford, 1983), chap. 7, seem to approximate this position.

21. See Putnam, "Is the Causal Structure of the Physical Itself Something Physical."

22. "Mechanism, Purpose, and Explanatory Exclusion" (forthcoming in *Philosophical Perspectives*, 1989).

23. If relations other than the causal relation can serve as explanatory relation, they can also be considered as a basis for individuation; however, that probably would be redundant. It is unlikely that when the explanatory relation is different, exactly the same events would be involved.

24. For further discussion see my "Epiphenomenal and Supervenient Causation," *Midwest Studies in Philosophy* 9 (1984): 257–70. I believe that the case in which c_1 "generates" c_2 in Alvin Goldman's sense (see his *A Theory of Human Action* [Englewood Cliffs, N.J., 1970]) can be handled in a similar way, although the details may have to be somewhat different.

25. Compare Peter Railton's notions of "ideal explanatory text" and "ideal causal D-N text" in his "Probability, Explanation, and Information," *Synthese* 45 (1981): 233–56; see also David Lewis, "Causal Explanation," *Philosophical Papers*, vol. 2.

26. Karl Pfeifer brought this case to my attention.

27. Carl G. Hempel, *Aspects of Scientific Explanation* (New York, 1965), 418–20.

28. Ibid., 418–20.

29. Ibid., 416–17.

30. *Philosophy of Natural Science* (Englewood Cliffs, N.J., 1966), 47–49. See also his *Aspects of Scientific Explanation*, 367–68. The other adequacy condition is the unexceptionable requirement of "testability," to the effect that the explanatory premises must be capable of empirical test in a broad sense.

31. For further elaboration of this point and some suggestions, see my "Events and Their Descriptions: Some Considerations," in *Essays in Honor of Carl G. Hempel* edited by Nicholas Rescher et al. (Dordrecht, 1969).

32. Hempel, Aspects of Scientific Explanation, 347–54.

33. "The Uniqueness in Causation," *American Philosophical Quarterly* 14 (1977): 177–88.

34. "Causal Overdetermination", *Journal of Philosophy* 76 (1979): 134–50.

35. Bunzl, however, says that his considerations depend essentially on a certain view of the nature and individuation of events associated with Donald Davidson, and that they are ineffective if we assume the sort of view of events that I myself have advocated, namely, one that takes events as property-exemplifications. See Bunzl, "Causal Overdetermination," 150. However, I am not convinced of this; I think Bunzl may have been misled by just the kind of consideration that lead Hempel to believe in explanatory overdetermination. It is interesting to note that Bunzl accepts explanatory overdetermination in Hempel's sense (p. 145). On causal overdetermination, see also Louis E. Loeb, "Causal Theories and Causal Overdetermination," *Journal of Philosophy* 71 (1974): 525–44.

36. From the point of view of explanatory exclusion, causal overdetermination is not crucial; the exclusion principle has content of sufficient interest even if causal overdetermination is simply exempted.

37. I think explanatory exclusion can hold under explanatory irrealism as well; however, unlike explanatory realism, irrealism does not, I think, provide a positive basis for explanatory exclusion. For some considerations favoring explanatory exclusion that are not based on explanatory realism, see my "Mechanism, Purpose, and Explanatory Exclusion."

I am indebted to David Benfield, Paul Boghossian, Brian McLaughlin, Joseph Mendola, and Michael Resnik for discussions of some of the issues taken up in this paper.

Causal, Experimental, and Structural Realisms

PAUL HUMPHREYS

1. DISCOVERY AND SCIENTIFIC EMPIRICISM

Our topic is scientific realism. It has been said that the opposition between realism and empiricism is old[1] and that is presumably why, if the pull of empiricism is sufficiently strong, realism may be hard to hold. This is a plausible claim in such areas as mathematical realism and moral realism. But the opposition is not a natural one, as is the opposition between empiricism and rationalism, and what is striking is that with all the talk of scientific realism, there is no corresponding talk of *scientific* empiricism. The principal thesis of this paper is that with the correct characterization of scientific empiricism, a minimalist scientific realism is supported by, rather than opposed to, scientific empiricism, and that the empiricism which is supposed to be at odds with scientific realism is an inappropriate kind of empiricism for science.

We must mark our place in the ever more complex network of realisms, antirealisms, and naturalistic denials of both. Much of the dispute over scientific realism has concerned, in one way or another, linguistic issues. The referential status of theoretical terms, the truth value of theoretical statements, the underdetermination of limit science, the correct demarcation between theoretical and observational terms, explanatory realism (when explanation is construed as a relation between sentences)—all these take the key feature of science to be its theorizing. Within this arena, the debate favors the antirealist. Yet science is more than evaluation of theoretical hypotheses. It is also, and this is prejudicial, a method of discovery, a means of discovering things about which, and of which, we should know nothing were it not for science.

One of the key features of discovery in any field is that it cannot be done in a passive way. Discoveries of new lands, of mathematical theorems, and of new elementary particles are not simply presented to us. Yet the traditional point of departure between realists and empiricist antirealists, which is at the border of the observable, carries with it connotations of phenomena merely impinging on our sensory receptors. Let us call this observable-oriented tradition of empiricism *passive empiricism*. From Hume's sensory impressions through the logical positivists' sense data to more recent observation vocabularies, humans are taken to be merely important kinds of receiving devices. Here then is a definition of passive empiricism's antiscientific-realism: *Among the entities that constitute the focus of scientific investigation, only the observables can justifiably be claimed to exist.*

Quite banal, seemingly innocuous, and it allows passive empiricists to prescribe what is for them the legitimate ontology of specific objects and, construed purely empirically, laws of nature. Yet it is, I think, an exceptionally limited characterization of scientific empiricism, for the methods of scientific investigation are not limited to observation of the world.[2] It is the availability of other methods of discovery which enables us to concede to the passive empiricist that the burden of proof is on us, as realists, to establish that unobservables exist, yet to demonstrate that his terms are not exhaustive. This will involve a defense of some version of direct realism, direct in the sense that linguistic intermediaries are not essentially involved in the argument to realism, but not, I hope, a version of naive realism. An aside on scientific discovery is needed here.

Scientific discovery was given a philosophical bad name when placed in a context opposed to the context of justification, and condemned as being of merely psychological interest.[3] The discovery process is thus regarded as a mere preliminary to the central task of the justification, acceptance, rejection, and so forth of statements. Not only is this terminology a peculiar one given the linguistic mode within which it is usually presented, for one invents hypotheses or has ideas, one does not discover them, but its emphasis on theories is an example of why it is dangerous to identify the discovery issue with truth or assertability conditions. For discoveries are not made exclusively by means of true hypotheses. Interesting cases of falsification occur when experiments and observations made on the assumption of the truth of a hypothesis produce phenomena which were not expected on the basis of that hypothesis, by means of apparatus and data collection methods constructed on the assumption that the false hypothesis is true. If interesting cases of falsification occur, it follows that genuine discoveries can be made without the availability of true theories describing them, in that the apparatus and methods are robust enough to be used independently of the truth of the tested hypothesis. Because the novel falsifiers will generally be observable, this point should be acceptable to empiricists as well as realists. What we need to show is that discoveries often involve phenomena that take us beyond the observable.

When Humphry Davy discovered potassium and sodium by means of electrolysis, the contemporary theories of electricity and of potash and soda (the alkalies from which the metals were separated) were radically wrong.[4] Moreover, since the observed samples of the metals liberated by electrolysis were formed by continuous accretions of metallic particles smaller than the limit of observability, and had properties quite different from the materials used to produce them, we have here an example of substances literally moving across the famous gap between the unobservable and the observable. Of course, once they are out in the open, as it were, the substances uncontroversially exist for both realists and antirealists, but we can discover regularities and causes as well as objects by means of experiments. Indeed, we can, without too much distortion in the empiricist tradition, view regularities as involved in all cases of experimental discovery, in part because of the repeatability condition required of all sound experiments, in part because to say that an object is observable implies that some potential or actual regularity is associated with it.[5] Thus we can construe many, perhaps all, scientific discoveries as involving the observation of a regularity that was not previously present in circumstances other than those in which the discovery is made. We then ask the question "If these regularities are real (and the empiricist does allow that, for they are observed), why do we require experimental methods to observe them?" An empiricist can, of course, refuse the request for an explanation. Such a refusal would seem to me profoundly unphilosophical, but it can always be made. If so, I cannot proceed. But as long as a need for an explanation is seen, a realist explanation can be given that is simple, in keeping with scientific practice, and methodologically fruitful. Those are virtues which instrumentally inclined empiricists should appreciate, but the explanation involves essential recourse to unobservables.

2. ANTI-HUME[6]

What is the picture that Hume leaves us with after his devastating attack on the existence of necessary connections in nature? It is one of a world of discrete events presented to us as passive observers, assessed for properties such as spatial and temporal contiguity and regular temporal succession.[7] Taken literally, this is a very restrictive account of causation. If one takes the world as it comes, there are very few regularities of this kind—the world as it presents itself to us simply is not regular in the required way. Events rarely come to us in such a pristine fashion that we can just read off the causal relationships, even by habit. So a passive Humean empiricist is faced with a real problem. He can either say that because such regular sequences are a necessary condition for the existence of a causal law, there are in fact very few such causal laws in the world (and hence few causes and causally produced phenomena), or he will have to account for why, although the laws are present, the observed sequences are not manifest.

Those who hold that subsumption under regularities (even where not causal) is a prerequisite for scientific explanation will also have serious problems with this absence of regularities. For most phenomena that occur naturally, there will be no explanation. This difficulty can be dissolved in a number of ways, but I want to suggest that adopting a realist attitude toward causal laws and causal influences allows a unified account of how certain kinds of scientific discoveries are represented and employed.

In his book *A Realist Theory of Science*,[8] Roy Bhaskar notes this scarcity of regularities in open systems, and contrasts this with the fact that such regularities are common in experimental contexts. An activist Humean can thus provide himself with a number of causal laws, and explain phenomena in closed systems. But if causal laws are a subset of the class of regularities between observed events, why do the laws appear in closed systems but not in most open systems? It surely cannot be that the experimenter created the law by creating the experimental context, and destroyed the law in opening up the closed system. A simple nonscientific example adapted from Mill will illustrate this. Consider two tug-of-war teams—realists and antirealists—pulling on opposite ends of an inelastic rope. Equally balanced, the teams produce no observable movement. I now go to the rope and cut it with a razor. Observable effects occur. Question 1: Did the razor cut produce the law that covered the subsequent accelerations of the teams? Question 2: Was my razor cut the sole cause of the acceleration? Answers: no and no. (One may agree that the cut triggered the acceleration, but it cannot have produced the acceleration by itself. Ask the team sweating on the other end of the rope.) Hence the law and the other causes must have existed before the acceleration was produced, even though the other causes produced no observed changes before the cut.

Another reason why this response is unappealing is that it creates an extreme anthropomorphism. Most laws would be dependent for their existence on the existence of human experimenters to create the regularities. No humans, few laws. In consequence, our own existence would have evolved in a world almost free of biological (and other) laws, making it a good deal more surprising than it already is. This position is possible to maintain, but unattractive.

A second option open to an empiricist is to claim that the regularity was indeed already there in the nonexperimental context, but was obscured by the presence of other factors. The regularity was, in effect, embedded in statistical noise much as Michelangelo's sculptures were already present in the Carrara marble, waiting only to be freed by his chisel. We do, on this picture, literally discover causal laws. To discover is to bare, to uncover or expose to view, a meaning largely usurped in the epistemological realm by the wider notion of obtaining knowledge of something previously unknown.

This approach is a common one, especially in scientific and philosophical methodologies that use mathematical and statistical surrogates for actual experimental methods. The essence of this approach consists in partitioning existing data so that a subset of the data reveals a regularity that is not immediately evident in the whole set. Such methods are the essence of induction by simple enumeration, gambling systems (including stock-market forecasting by trend analysis), and correlation methods (including statistical relevance methods and regression techniques). The reverse of this method, leaving a data set with no regularities, forms the basis of many relative-frequency interpretations of probability. It is a quintessentially passive empiricist device, and its deficiencies are well chronicled. Without restrictions on the partitioning methods, or on what counts as a regularity, it is trivial to find some regularity in the data.[9] More important from our perspective is the fact that this approach cannot, by itself, provide any explanation of the presence of a regularity in one context, and its absence in another. The standard devices of restricting the scope of a regularity, or of imposing ceteris paribus conditions are merely descriptive acknowledgments of this fact.

The realist answer to this problem was, curiously, provided by J. S. Mill. In *A System of Logic*, Mill argued that the distinguishing characteristic of a causal regularity was its unconditionalness, this characteristic being exactly what is meant by a cause necessitating its effect: "That which is necessary, that which must be, means that which will be, whatever supposition we may make in regard to all other things."[10] Although Mill does not give an explicit argument for the unconditionalness requirement, the argument would seem to be the following. Suppose A is asserted to be a sufficient cause of B, yet there are circumstances X within which A is not followed by B. Then in those circumstances in which A is sufficient for B, it is not A *simpliciter* that is sufficient for (causes) B but A together with the absence of X or the absence of certain elements of X. Hence the original assertion regarding the causal generalization that A is a sufficient cause of B was incorrect. Note that this is not just an argument about how we speak of causal factors, but a condition on the very way in which such factors cause their effects. This doctrine of the unconditionalness of causal influences led Mill into serious difficulties when trying to reconcile empiricism with the unconditionalness requirement. Indeed, we shall see that the unconditionalness of causation is indispensable, and forces us to adopt a realist position with regard to causes.

Although Mill was a determinist, the unconditionalness requirement can be applied to causal analyses which do not require that a cause be sufficient for its effect, as long as those analyses have causal generalizations as their focus.[11] For if a causal factor must be necessary (not merely in the circumstances, but generally) for its effect, then because its absence is sufficient for the absence of the effect, a parallel argument to the above can be given. For probabilistic causation, the situation is more complex, for it requires us to adopt a realist attitude toward propensities, which would be begging the question here. However, a similar stricture of unconditionalness has to be imposed if one holds that probabilistic contributing causes are those which raise the propensity of an effect.

A number of writers, including Mill himself, realized that although the regularity requirement could be satisfied by creating experimental contexts, the lack of regularities in the natural world makes the unconditionalness requirement extremely difficult to satisfy. In particular, causal connections can be operating in the everyday world, but observable regular sequences are not identical with them. The natural inference to draw is that the causal sequences are associated with something unobservable, that there are causal influences "beneath" the observable phenomena.[12]

It is not enough to say this is the natural move to make. We need an argument. Here is one. Consider an experimental situation S in which a regularity R has been isolated, that is, one in which a single observed factor A is uniformly associated with a second observed factor E, that is, E regularly appears whenever A is present.[13] Then introduce into S a third factor B which, in S, in the absence of A, is uniformly associated with a fourth factor F. Now suppose that instead of insisting on the unconditionalness requirement, we claimed that a straightforward Humean regularity was sufficient, in the simple situation we have described (together with certain additional features such as temporal succession—what these are does not matter here), to identify A as a cause of E and B as a cause of F. Suppose further that neither E nor F is observed when both A and B are present, and that the situation is completely deterministic. Now ask what has happened to E. Why is it not present when B appears together with A? Now, as I mentioned earlier, it is possible for someone to deny that an explanation of this fact is called for. For him, there are three brute facts: situations with only A also have E present; situations with only B have F present; and situations with both A and B have neither E nor F. I assume in contrast that the burden of proof is always on those who deny that an explanation exists for a given fact. And the case we have in mind should be taken to be the most routine, everyday kind of situation, with no exotic quantum effects. The rope example without the razor will do.

If E was initially present, but disappeared when B was introduced into S, something must have been responsible. Let us call this "the feature that prevents A from causing E in S." We must establish that this feature, although existent, goes beyond what an empiricist would allow as real. What is this a feature of? If the feature that prevents A from causing E in S is a permanent feature[14] of B, then B would, when alone in S, simultaneously possess both the feature of causing F in S and the feature of preventing A from causing E in S. This second feature, given that it is permanent, cannot be (observably) instantiated, because it is false to claim that something has the (observably) instantiated feature of preventing A from causing E in S if A, by virtue of being absent from S at that time, does not have the feature of causing E in S. This permanent, but not always observably instantiated feature gives us the required realist entity. If, on the other hand, the feature of preventing A from causing E in S is a transient feature of B, then consider the possible cases when both A and B are present. Either A permanently possesses the feature of causing E in S, or it transiently does. If it permanently possesses it, we again have a realist feature, for it is not observably instantiated when B is present in S. It cannot transiently possess it when B transiently possesses the feature of preventing A from causing E, because in that situation A's feature is not observably instantiated and would hence be permanent, because A possesses it when alone in S and when accompanied by B. If A transiently possesses its feature when B's transient feature of preventing A from causing E is absent, then we have no explanation of why A's feature does not result in E. It is impossible for A transiently to lack its feature and for B transiently to possess its feature, for B cannot possess the feature of preventing A from causing E when A does not have the feature of causing E, any more than I can prevent a demagnetized tape from recording a message. Finally, if both A and B transiently lack their properties, then we again have no explanation for why A causes E when B is absent, but does not cause it when B is present, because the fact that A lacks the property of causing E is the fact that needs to be explained, and there is nothing in B or S to explain that fact.

Thus, even without presupposing the unconditionalness requirement, we must either allow the existence of permanent features that are sometimes not observably instantiated, or claim that there is no explanation for why the factor E is present in closed experimental systems and disappears when the system is opened, even minimally. The first option is, to my mind, preferable to the second.

I want to emphasize that this kind of argument is not antiempiricist in nature. It simply maintains that empiricism is not to be identified with the passive observation of events as they present themselves to us. We must explain what happens when the activist intervention in the natural course of events that experimentation allows produces a regularity that otherwise would not have occurred, and what happens to those regularities when other causal influences are added. The argument is applicable only in those cases in which the other causal factors do not permanently alter the causal properties of the original cause. For example, by grounding an electrically charged sphere, I remove the causal disposition to move the leaves of a gold-leaf electroscope apart. But we can identify which situations are of this kind by isolating the causal factor before and after its interaction with the other factors. If the same regularity reappears, we have a case to which the argument applies. The difference between the two types of situations is commonly acknowledged in ordinary discourse, as when the physician is enjoined to treat the disease rather than the symptoms. In the case where the original cause retains its dispositional properties, it is its effect or symptoms that are counteracted; in the case where the disposition is destroyed, it is the cause itself, or the disease, that is counteracted.

3. CONSEQUENCES

This account of scientific realism and scientific empiricism in terms of the discovery of causal factors via experimental isolation requires us to say something about how it affects other philosophical issues that involve realism and causation.

At the end of the last section, we established the existence of unobserved causal features. What the argument establishes is a general claim: that there must be causal influences operating in the world that are not to be identified with empirical regularities. It does not specify what they are, or even claim that our current theories correctly describe them. The issue remains of how much further we ought to go along the realist road. That, of course, depends upon the nature of the causal features, but the arguments given in this paper do not commit us to more than a minimalist realism.

Is it a defect that this approach enables us initially to say nothing about the properties of the causal features other than that they must exist unobserved in certain circumstances? I do not think so, because much of scientific progress consists of filling in detailed causal pictures about entities of which we initially know nothing except that they are responsible for certain observed effects. This construction of causal detail can be seen in a number of areas of scientific activity. It is seen in model building. Models being a simplification of reality, they frequently concern themselves initially with only a single causal component of a system, such as the models of a hydrogen atom. Perturbation theory then successively adds causal contributions to the previous stage of modeling. Even when interaction terms are required, the causal contributions of the existing components are generally left in place. If a causal component is removed, then that is simply an acknowledgment that the previous model was incorrect. The information about successive causal contributions may be acquired either experimentally or theoretically. The former is preferable, for one of the principal purposes of experimentation is to isolate the effects of single causal factors. However, in contexts where experimentation is impossible or impractical, resort to conceptual modeling may be required. We must, however, regard models in a Campbellian sense, within which causal influences are real, not representations. Semantic accounts of scientific theories are no better at representing causal realism than are syntactic approaches. Model theoretic structures are suitable for mathematical physics (and other sciences), not for experimental physics.[15]

Accounts of scientific explanation that closely associate prediction and explanation, that require true law statements under which the explanandum sentence falls, and that use a humean regularity account of causation have serious problems in explaining phenomena that are the result of multiple causal influences. This is primarily due to their inability to separate true explanations from complete explanations, because the lack of a comprehensive regularity covering the joint set of causes results in no explanation at all being available. Science, however, almost always proceeds in explaining phenomena by specifying a partial list of causes that contribute to and counteract the observed phenomena. Two previous papers detailed how this kind of explanation works in probabilistic cases.[16] For present purposes, the important fact is that in order to provide such explanations, we do not need a complete law under which the explanandum (not the explanandum sentence) falls; we require instead a set of a true laws covering the separate causal influences on the explanandum, and it is these which experimentation will give us.

This cumulative causal picture requires us to adopt a causal atomism rather than a logical atomism. I have deliberately refrained from construing the issue of scientific realism in terms of the truth of theories or the successful reference of theoretical terms. This semantic descent must be accompanied by a willingness to allow that the extension of the term 'observable' (I prefer 'detectable') is not fixed a priori, but is a temporally dependent function of scientific and technological advances. The problem with Russell's famous dictum "Wherever possible logical constructions are to be substituted for inferred entities," which underlies such enterprises as Ramsey's second-order eliminative approach, the first-order commitment criterion of Quine, and Craig's reaxiomatization method, is that it has become too tied to passive empiricism. (The insistence by Putnam that causation must be treated linguistically[17] seems to me to be a residue of this kind of approach.) We may, in initial phases of investigation, use a referential apparatus that employs a causal descriptive operator applied to a Ramseyfied sentence without the existential quantifier, so that we are talking of "the thing which is responsible for observed phenomenon O," but the moving boundary of the observable will frequently produce a much more direct presentation of the phenomena. Many advances in observation techniques involve procedures very similar to experimental techniques—the removal of causal factors that disturb the pure display of a cause. But we have to do the removing, and that is why I prefer another of Russell's aphorisms, to the effect that if you want to find out what exists, you must *go to the zoo*. To deny that this stripping away of confounding influences results in something observed is to deny the reality of entities such as viruses, atoms, synapses, neutrinos, status structures, and the cancer cells that caused the unfortunate death of David Hume.

The isolation of causal factors by means of experiment does not require us to adopt a manipulability account of causation, because as we have seen, we can treat the resulting causal display in the closed system purely in regularity terms. We do, however, require that the other potential causal influences be controllable, in that they can be held constant or removed entirely. If one does wish to view causation in manipulability terms, the argument sheds light on how we ought to view the proper role of such accounts. In order to impose experimental controls, we must already have a certain amount of causal knowledge. It is often claimed that manipulability accounts of causation are circular, because definitions of the causal relation in terms of manipulations require reference to causal properties in the definiens as well as the definiendum. That charge is correct if we are concerned to give an explicit definition of the general term 'causes'. For the present purposes of realism, however, that is not what is wanted—indeed, such an approach runs the risk of elevating causation to the status of a universal, with the consequent risk of having to account for what kind of thing a general causal necessity is. It is easy to make this error when employing a formal calculus of a causal necessity operator. The operator for logical necessity is usually treated as being the same for all propositions. But in the case of natural necessities, there is, if any such things exist, no reason to suppose that there is one monolithic necessity that brings about things; instead there is a variegated set of causal influences of very particular sorts. For the realist, why should there be something that pervades all actual causal connections between objects of radically different types? We already have names for these different kinds of influence: electromagnetic force, sexual attraction, economic demand, status expectations, and so forth. These may or may not be reducible to a single kind of causal factor, but that is a matter for science to discover, and if it were true, the basic influence would not be the second-level influence that natural-necessity advocates wish to establish.

In a similar vein, one should be wary of too quick an inference to the existence of 'causal powers'. If one holds that every disposition has a permanent or semipermanent basis, and that the causal features in the situations I discussed are dispositions or tendencies, then we may infer the existence of unobserved structures in such cases of multiple causal influences. The permanency of the structural underpinnings to the manifest regularities, together with the fact that such structures interact in different ways with different external variables, is enough to account for the dispositional properties possessed by such structures. Nothing in the realist positions requires that there exist an infinite regress of explanations in terms of finer-grained levels of reality, and which could only be stopped by reference to mysterious causal powers. There can be fundamental structures and processes that are *sui generis*, which are not caused by anything, which have no further explanation, and which operate unobserved in conjunction with other basic processes and structures to produce observed regularities. To that extent, the empiricist is correct in denying causal powers along with modal realism, but taking unobserved structures seriously is something which is enormously helpful even if one is primarily interested only in prediction of observed phenomena. This is because empiricist theories based only on observed phenomena will generally lose their predictive power if the internal structure of the system changes. Armed with a true account of that structure, a realist will be able to predict what effects those changes will have on the observed regularities.[18]

Finally, by not putting the issue in terms of theories, we avoid being placed in a position where the 'scientific' in 'scientific realism' requires us to provide a demarcation criterion between scientific theories and other kinds of theories. Given the difficulty of disposing of theoretical holism, and the endless debates about scientific rationality that surround the demarcation criterion, that is welcome. Nor need any mention be made of the aims or goals of science, or of limit science. It is often objected, for example, that arguments for scientific realism that are based on scientific explanation are unconvincing to many antirealists because they simply deny that explanation is a goal of science. It is true that one's methods are usually determined by one's goals. However, I take experimentation to be a given fact of the scientific enterprise. It is not that we philosophers suggest to scientists that they ought to experiment (as, for example, we might suggest they do some explaining instead of just predicting), it is a given feature of at least many of the natural sciences, and surrogates for it have been painstakingly constructed in many of the social sciences. Furthermore, although limit science is a proper concern of those interested in theoretical truth, and of those who are bothered by underdetermination issues, limit science is also an exhausted science, and of no interest to those for whom discoveries constitute the evidence for realism. The minimal realism advocated here does not *require* that we say anything true of the unobserved entities, except that they exist. But if we do liberalize the notion of observability, we are in a position successively to say much that is true of discoveries, and that at least allows us to be practicing realists.[19]

4. CONCLUSION

The preceding arguments have established a minimal kind of scientific realism. They do not, to be sure, give us the kind of conclusions that arguments based on scientific theories aimed to provide. But they do, I think, provide us with a specifically scientific ontology, a class of entities of which we should not know were it not for science. And I am not convinced that realism requires much knowledge. When Leif Eriksson discovered North America, he knew virtually nothing of it upon leaving, a fact that is all too evident from *The Vinland Sagas*. But its existence had been established, and the course of scientific discovery is not entirely dissimilar, I think, to geographical discovery.[20]

Notes

1. B. van Fraassen, *The Scientific Image* (Oxford, 1980), 1.

2. An obvious but necessary point: it may well be that at the most fundamental epistemological level, observation is all we ever have. But philosophy of science is not fundamental in that sense—it has to take for granted the existence of at least some objects of scientific knowledge, the peculiarity of scientific method, and the addition of special techniques to supplement observation, in order to distinguish science from other kinds of investigation. These techniques, and those methods, may ultimately be telling us something very different from what scientists think they are telling us, but that there exists a scientific enterprise engaging in more than observation has to be an uncontroversial claim.

3. As in H. Reichenbach, *Experience and Prediction* (Chicago, 1938), 5–7; K. Popper, *The Logic of Scientific Discovery* (London, 1959), 31.

4. The article on Davy in *The Dictionary of Scientific Biography*, edited by C. C. Gillespie, claims that Michael Faraday listed a dozen incompatible theories of electrolysis, all of which he claimed could be derived from Davy's views. For Davy's work, see H. Hartley, *Studies in the History of Chemistry* (Oxford, 1971), Chapter 4. Further examples showing that discoveries can be made without access to true theories are given in Part B of Ian Hacking's *Representing and Intervening* (Cambridge, 1983). One curious feature of this piquant book is its fascination with traditional issues involving observations.

5. In everything that follows, "experiment" is to be taken in the sense of controlled laboratory experimentation, in which all but one of the factors are removed or held constant. The use of randomized experiments, statistical surrogates for experimental controls, and quasi-experimentation all introduce additional complexities into the interpretation of causal laws, even though certain kinds of regularities may be discovered by means of them.

6. The arguments in this section have drawn heavily on ideas and arguments contained in Roy Bhaskar's *A Realist Theory of Science* (Atlantic Highlands, 1975). It was Bhaskar's book which convinced me that the correct way to argue for scientific realism must be by assessing the role played by experiment in causal discoveries. Although I depart from his views about the social basis of experimentation and the nature of tendencies, I believe that his book remains the best written on this topic.

7. Hume does use the term "experiment" in Book II, Part II, section II of the *Treatise*, and also in scattered places in Book I, Part III (especially section VIII). In all these references, however, he seems to take the term to be synonymous with "observation."

8. See note 6.

9. The trivialization was highlighted by Russell in his discussion of functional determinism in "On the Notion of Cause," reprinted in his *Mysticism and Logic* (London, 1917).

10. J. S. Mill, *A System of Logic*, 8th edition (London, 1881) III, v, 1–3, 6.

11. These arguments are inapplicable to singular causal claims that are not derived from causal regularities. By building "A caused B, in the circumstances" into the claim, or by relativizing the claim to a background field, the conditionality of the causal claim is thereby introduced. Excluding such cases

will not affect our argument for realism, in part because it is a requirement on experiments that they be freely repeatable.

12. Mill was caught in a dilemma between remaining faithful to an empiricist regularity account of causation and adopting a position involving tendencies to produce effects. See Mill, *A System of Logic*, III, v, 1–3, 6, for the first view; III, x, 5, and III, v, 5, for the second view. This last section is not in the first edition, and contains Mill's somewhat obscure views on dispositions: He says that 'capacities' are not real, but are merely names for inferential habits. Whether this humean line applies to tendencies, which are active capacities, is not stated. Mill's dilemma is discussed by Geach in *Three Philosophers*, by G. E. M. Anscombe and P. Geach (Ithaca, 1961), 101–4; chapter 4 of Alan Ryan's *John Stuart Mill* (New York, 1970); Roy Bhaskar, *A Realist Theory*; and Essay 3 of Nancy Cartwright's *How the Laws of Physics Lie* (Oxford, 1983).

13. Take 'factor' to represent whatever you consider the causal relata to be: event types or tokens, changes in variables, states, conditions, etc.

14. The term 'feature' is used rather than 'property' to avoid unnecessary worries about the status of properties. Even if one does not want to allow properties as real, there are many features of the world that uncontroversially exist for empiricists.

15. In his "Galilean Idealization" paper (*Studies in the History and Philosophy of Science* 16 [1985]: 247–73), Ernan McMullin has traced the development of such modeling methods. In his "Structural Explanations (*American Philosophical Quarterly* 15 [1978]: 139–47) and "A Case for Scientific Realism" (in *Scientific Realism*, edited by J. Leplin [Berkeley, 1984], 8–40), he had already argued on philosophico-historical grounds for adopting a position on scientific realism of the kind I adopt in the present paper. I hope the arguments here complement those in his papers. Further examples of the relation between causal modeling and experiment can be found in the papers by Blalock, Duncan, Glymour and Scheines, and by Cook and Campbell in *Synthese* 68 (1986): 1–188; and from a different perspective, in P. Humphreys and J. Berger, "Theoretical Consequences of the Status Characteristics Formulation," *American Journal of Sociology* 86 (1981): 953–83.

16. See my "Aleatory Explanations," *Synthese* 48 (1981): 225–32, and "Aleatory Explanations Expanded," in *PSA 1982*, Vol. 2, edited by P. Asquith and T. Nickles (East Lansing, 1983), 208–223.

17. "Why There Isn't A Ready-Made World" and "Introduction," both in H. Putnam, *Realism and Reason, Philosophical Papers*, Vol. 3 (Cambridge, 1983); "Is the Causal Structure of the Physical Itself Something Physical?" *Midwest Studies in Philosophy* 9 (1984): 3–16.

18. A detailed argument for this claim, with illustrative examples, is given in P. Humphreys, "Quantitative Probabilistic Causality and Structural Scientific Realism" in *PSA 1984*, Vol. 2, edited by P. Asquith and P. Kitcher (East Lansing, 1986).

19. A quite different set of arguments for minimal realism has been offered by Robert Almeder in his "Blind Realism," *Erkenntnis* (Dec. 1986): 1–45. There he concludes that although some of our warranted beliefs about unobservable entities must be true, we cannot pick out which, among our current set of beliefs, those are. His discussion of Pierce's experimental demonstration that laws of nature are mind-independent brings out very clearly a key aspect of experimental, as opposed to theoretical, realism—that there are features of the world over which we have no mental control.

20. A very preliminary version of this paper was read at the University of Pittsburgh in May 1985. I thank Ernan McMullin for his supportive criticisms at that time; also Nicholas Rescher and Robert Almeder for many lengthy discussions on this issue. The work on which this paper is based was supported by NSF grant SES 8410898.

How to Be a Metaphysical Realist

EVAN FALES

1. INTERNAL REALISM AND COHERENCE EPISTEMOLOGIES

All of us have—and tend to cling confidently to—many empirical beliefs that are much more specific than the general belief that there is a spatiotemporal world containing causally connected events. We believe in the existence of any number of specific material objects and physical events, and of determinate causal relations between them. We believe we know, in many cases, what properties some physical object has, and what properties it does not have. In a more sophisticated mode, we hold a number of scientific theories, more or less elaborate, that we regard as true, or approximately true, or at least as representing progressive steps along the path to knowledge of a correct theory—a path whose terminus is a least "in principle" within reach.

The philosophical defense of some or all of these theses is a task assumed by those who call themselves scientific realists. However, scientific realism can be understood in a variety of (connected) ways, and a discussion of the topic requires some anterior reflection on the nature of the claims being defended. Thus, we can distinguish the following claims that are associated with scientific realism:

(i) a thesis about the *meaning* of statements concerning some empirical domain—namely, that their meaning is dependent on their truth-conditions or on the denotation of their terms (as opposed to conditions of confirmation, or of warranted assertibility, or the like);

(ii) a theory of truth and/or reference for a domain—specifically, the correspondence theory of truth and/or a theory of reference that posits a real relation (for example, causal) between words and the world;

(iii) a thesis concerning the existence of objects in some empirical domain (for example, "theoretical entities");
(iv) a thesis to the effect that *if* objects in a given domain exist, then we can know (or justifiably believe) that this is the case;
(v) a thesis to the effect that one can coherently entertain the thought that there exist objects whose existence we could not, in principle, ever come to know.

There are some connections between these claims. (ii) specifies the sense in which the truth-conditions mentioned in (i) are to be understood: If truth were a matter of coherence or warranted assertibility, then (i) would lack its intended realist interpretation. For any putative domain of objects, (iv) is, obviously, a necessary condition for the (justified) assertibility of (iii). (iii) is stronger than (i), for it asserts not merely that we can understand assertions as being (if true) about the world independently of our epistemic condition, but that some such assertions *are* true. (v) appears to be entailed by (i): If we can distinguish between truth-conditions and confirmation-conditions, it is an open possibility that there are hypotheses that are true but non-confirmable. Indeed, as philosophers, we seem to have encountered two such hypotheses: the evil-demon hypothesis of Descartes and the idealistic hypothesis of Berkeley, interpreted as denying the existence of independent material objects. These hypotheses, or rather minor variants of them, remain eligible (for the realist) even if he succeeds in establishing the existence of space, time, and extraphenomenal causal relations. A spirit or demon—or a sufficiently expert mad scientist—could manipulate one's experiences so that, even if one is justified in inferring the existence of space and of external influences upon one's sensory field, one may be radically misled about the nature of one's spatial environment, and the nature of the influences upon one.

Hilary Putnam (1981), in a recent examination of realism, uses (v) to characterize the distinction between what he calls metaphysical realism, and what he calls internal realism. The internal realist, as depicted by Putnam, can make use of all the semantic devices associated with realism—for example, those mentioned in (ii); only these devices are now to be understood only in relation to some background *theory* that we have about the world, and not de novo. Putnam's version of realism—a realism "internal" to some theory or other—is antifoundationalist, and represents a rejection of the correspondence theory of truth and of the causal theory of reference if these are construed as giving us linguistic access to a reality independent of our conceptual apparatus. Putnam, in fact, considers an analogue to the skeptical hypothesis I have mentioned. He asks whether we might be brains in vats; and he wishes to show, by means of a transcendental argument, that this must be false. That argument is supposed to show not only that if it were true we could never know it, but furthermore, that we could never assert or entertain it. What the metaphysical realist erroneously supposes is both that we *can* entertain this hypothesis, and that it might be *true*. He thereby makes a fatal concession to the skeptic. As I examine Putnam's argument, it will be important to recognize, however, that (v) can be divided into two theses: (v1) that it is intelligible to entertain the possibility of the existence of objects independent of ourselves, and (v2) that such objects might, in principle, lie outside the domain of the knowable.

I intend to defend "metaphysical realism," though in an important respect I shall differ with Putnam over how this position ought to be characterized. Of course, I shall not attempt a full-fledged defense of metaphysical or of scientific realism. What follows is, rather, a series of reflections prompted by issues raised in the writings of Richard Boyd, Putnam, Hartry Field, and some others. What I hope will emerge from these reflections is a programmatic sketch of the kind of strategy the realist ought to follow in his dialogue with idealism (or with relativism, or with "internal realism"). That strategy can be partly expressed by the advice: To be a realist, be a foundationalist. Given the usual partnership between foundationalism and idealism, this advice, and my defense of it, will perhaps add an interesting twist to the debate. In pursuing these reflections, I shall be making (at least) three major unargued assumptions; the third reflects the foundationalist stance just mentioned. The first is that the problem of justifying memory can be solved. The second, that a single individual can in principle pick out elements within his immediate experience, recognize and compare them, and invent and use words to denote them and their types, prior to any learning of a "public" language. Thus, I shall regard Wittgenstein's skepticism with regard to the possibility of a private language, as sometimes interpreted, to be mistaken. The third premise is that we are directly acquainted in some instances with causal relations (that is, at the level of immediate experience), and that these relations involve a species of natural necessity. The relevant experiences are those of pushes and pulls. Further, I shall adopt the view of Armstrong (1978), Tooley (1977), and Dretske (1977) that causal relations are relations between physical properties, understood as universals — except that unlike them, I hold this relation to be a noncontingent one. I argue in detail for this third premise elsewhere.[1] My present argument must be taken as an exercise in exploring the consequences of these assumptions for realism; it will also suggest grounds for doubting that metaphysical realism can be defended if any of these rather strong claims is rejected.

Before I return to metaphysical realism and brains in vats, I shall briefly discuss one argument for scientific realism that fails, and then, in a highly sketchy fashion, consider the question of how we are able to identify, think about, and refer to objects in the physical world.

Thesis (iv) is the realist doctrine most directly challenged by traditional skepticism. With respect to knowledge of the physical world, the skeptic's strategy is to argue that no amount of empirical data will select a single theory as the most favorable one. For any set of data and any proposed theory, the skeptic can always fashion a conflicting theory that explains the same data equally well. Richard Boyd (1973) has argued that the realist can block this strategy.

In order to apply a proposed theory T to produce confirmable predictions, the use of auxiliary background hypotheses—call their conjunction B—is required. Similarly, auxiliary hypotheses B^* must be employed in conjunction with any competing theory T^*. If 'T & B' predicts the same experimental results as 'T^* & B^*', how are we to justify a choice among them? Boyd's response is that the evidence can make one theory—say T—more plausible than the other, on the grounds that T is a more natural extension of theories and causal principles we already accept (on the basis of evidence). But what can justify our acceptance of these theories? The answer is that the (frequent and/or approximate) truth of these theories is the only thing that will explain the success of the following methodological principle:

> (P) A proposed theory T must be experimentally tested under situations representative of those in which, in the light of collateral information, it is most likely that T will fail, if it is going to fail at all.

Boyd's claim is that the only explanation of the reliability of (P) as a guide to when a new theory is likely to fail requires the assumption that our collateral or background information is (approximately) *true*. For if that information were incorrect, it would be a matter of extraordinary luck that (P) should be effective as a principle for eliminating theories.

This argument is unfortunately defective. It assumes that (P) *is* a successful methodological principle, and it claims that only realism can provide an explanation of this fact. But is (P) reliable? The mere fact that (P) is an accepted principle of scientific research cannot decide this question. If the success of a theory is not understood in instrumental terms, then it appears that the only way one could evaluate (P) is by comparing the number of proposed theories that are, in *fact*, false with the number that the use of (P) succeeds in eliminating. But how—independently of realistic presuppositions—could we come to know the former of these statistics? If, indeed, there *were* some way of obtaining information as to what theories are false, independently of the use of (P), then the use of (P) would be rendered gratuitous. But if—as Boyd would have it[2]—success is instrumentally construed, what is to prevent a thoroughgoing antirealist from also construing instrumentally the (realist's) theory that explains that success by making appeal to such (theoretical) notions as correspondence truth? That move gives us Putnam's internal realist; and it would seem to stalemate the contest.

In any case, it is false that only realism can explain the success of (P), assuming that (P) is successful. For suppose the evil-demon hypothesis were true. It is noteworthy that a skeptical opponent is free to postulate essentially any sorts of causal processes he likes, to explain how the demon produces in us the sensations we experience. He can cheerfully accept (though in strictness he need not) a principle of sufficient reason that requires him to oppose our favored explanations of our sensations with alternative causal explanations, rather than simply propose that they may have no explanation at all. It seems obvious that a clever demon could deceive us about the reliability of (P), by arranging it so that our theories "fail" more often when tested in putatively falsifying circumstances than when not so tested, and that a small number of such theories "survive" repeated tests. Moreover, the *apparent* reliability of (P) can be explained *equally well* on the demon hypothesis as on the realist view that the theories we *do* accept are approximately true. For it accounts for all the facts, and it is elegant: singularly elegant, as cosmologies go. This argument fails to refute skepticism. Any attempt to rule out the evil-demon hypothesis as implausible in the light of current theory is bound to be question-begging. Once we have conceded the eligibility of the skeptic's hypothesis, we will find that the only way to defeat him is to argue that we can obtain evidence that, if obtained, would independently defeat that hypothesis.[3]

Boyd, to be sure, explicitly disavows the project of defending realism against radical skepticism.[4] The limited objective of Boyd's defense of scientific realism is perhaps justified by the fact that his opponents concede realism with respect to a certain class of statements, namely, those they are prepared to classify as observational. But the reasonableness of framing the issue in this limited way should not conceal the powerful dialectical role that skepticism plays in the debate. Realists – and Boyd is no exception – try to defeat antirealism by exposing its inherent instability. Since the physicalist observation statements of contemporary antirealists are themselves already "theory-laden," there is nothing, in principle, that should bar their acceptance of full-fledged realism. When they reject that invitation, the realist suggests that their caution, consistently applied, cripples empiricism by driving them into the waiting arms of the skeptic.

Antirealists, on the other hand, are prone to argue that the very same antifoundationalism that characterizes realist epistemology (certainly Boyd's), as well as their own, cannot be sustained except by conceding some form of coherentism and thereby abandoning the fundamental commitments of realism. But this stalemate shows that skepticism (and antifoundationalism's attempt to execute an end run around the skeptic) is the specter that haunts realist and antirealist alike. A consequence of this dialectic, as I see it, is that the only hope for defending realism requires a return to a foundationalist theory of knowledge. Thus, it will not be amiss to frame the problem in such stark and uncompromising terms. In my concluding remarks I shall make some further observations about antifoundationalism itself.

2. REFERENCE

Suppose we were controlled by an evil demon. Could we, in that case, ever be in a position to think about, or refer to, the evil demon in question? Or – what is quite different – could we be in a position to entertain the evil-demon hypothesis? That the latter question is different from the former is due to the fact that the evil-demon hypothesis can be construed as a general hypothesis; it need not involve making singular reference to any *particular* evil demon. All that would be required is the possibility of specifying a sufficient number of the characteristics of such a demon to make the hypothesis an intelligible and explanatory one. The following section addresses these questions.

However, I shall begin this section not with the exotic problem of how we can speak of demons, but of how to achieve singular reference to physical particulars. How does such reference occur? Here, I shall adopt the perspective of the causal, or historical, theory of reference, various versions of which have been proposed by Putnam, Kripke, Donellan, and Devitt, among others. Such a theory fits rather naturally with a causal theory of perception. In that context it does, however, render problematical the notion of direct acquaintance, at least insofar as physical objects are taken to be objects of direct acquaintance. On the causal theory, one's use of a name must be linked by a suitable (but possibly unknown) causal history to the use of that name to name physical object O, and similarly the initial use of the name must be linked by means of a suitable (possibly unknown) causal chain to O itself. One consequence of this is that, in an epistemologically fundamental sense, it is extremely difficult — perhaps impossible — to articulate in a philosophically interesting way what it is for someone to know who or what it is that he refers to, in a manner that distinguishes identification of physical objects actually perceived by an observer from identification of those he knows merely "by description." For, in both cases, knowledge is mediated by causal processes. In any case, I shall restrict the notion of direct acquaintance so that it has application only to sense-data.

Among the many difficulties that beset the causal theory of reference, one requires attention here, for it sheds special light on the realist's program. It concerns the use of definite descriptions to fix the reference of a term, and the role of associated beliefs in determining whether the term has a referent. As we shall see, the causal theorist ought to allow that the main opposing theory of reference — what Kripke calls the Frege-Russell view — *does* contain a genuine insight which needs to be preserved.

The difficulty is this: Kripke and Putnam have given powerful arguments to show that one can succeed in using a name to refer even when one has many false beliefs about the referent, no true uniquely identifying description, and little or no knowledge of the causal history that connects the referent to one's use of the name. But does this lack of constraint on descriptive knowledge go so far that nothing whatever must be known about a putative referent in order for reference to succeed? I think a consideration of actual and hypothetical cases shows that it does not. At the same time, because reference is a human activity tailored to the needs of linguistic communication, it is highly unlikely that there are formal rules that can be universally applied to determine when reference has been achieved and when not. Our judgments about this are conditioned by considerations of interpretive charity and congruence with the needs of efficient information transfer that are too variable and context dependent for that. Nevertheless, it seems that such considerations generally militate against counting the use of a name successful if misapprehension about the nature of anything that could be taken as the referent is sufficiently drastic. If all a person believed about the referent of 'Bourbaki' was that it was a topologically complex space, when, in fact, the use of this name as a pseudonym by a group of mathematicians was causally responsible for the acquisition of the name, then in most imaginable circumstances, we would count that person as unable to refer when using this name. And consideration of historical cases within science, such as the Epicureans' use of 'atom', and the more recent use of 'phlogiston' and 'electric fluid', can serve to display the range of considerations (and perplexities) that surrounds our willingness to accord or deny referential success in the face of false beliefs — even when the users of those terms had *some* correct, "reference-fixing" definite descriptions available to them.

What has been said obviously applies to reference to natural kinds as well as to reference to physical particulars. Indeed, the examples I used make this clear. What these considerations are intended to show is that however the causal theorist may wish to characterize reference-establishing causal links, the existence of such a link is not, *in general*, sufficient to guarantee reference. Some kind of (correct) descriptive backing is also required — although such descriptions may be far from uniquely identifying.[5]

This is true, I want to suggest, even for reference to ordinary, "observable" physical objects with respect to which we are placed in favorable perceptual circumstances. On the one hand, one need not have any perceptually based, uniquely identifying description of an object in order to be said to be thinking about it, attending to it, or referring to it. One need not know where the object is, for example, even in relation to oneself and other objects in one's sensory field; nor need one have any unique description of it. On the other hand, sufficiently erroneous perceptual beliefs can undermine even ostensive reference. The most plausible cases of this are provided by deceptive optical illusions (for example, the "oasis" in the desert) and hallucinations. Of course, something is the cause here of our perceptual experiences and consequent beliefs; but nothing in the causal account sufficiently satisfies those beliefs to qualify as a referent. It might be argued that the reason for reference failure here is that the causal chain is deviant. But — particularly in the case of illusions — it is difficult to see why the causal chain should count as deviant.

If this is so, if some descriptive beliefs typically play a role in the achievement of reference to particulars and natural kinds, then the problem of reference is, in part, pushed back onto the problem of how predicates pick out properties. Unless this can be accounted for, the usefulness of descriptive backing cannot be explained. For a thing to satisfy a description is for it to actually have properties properly denoted by the descriptive predicates. Moreover, we cannot always explain reference to properties in terms of *further* backing descriptions, on pain of infinite regress. Some predicates can be handled by means of definition in terms of other predicates. But there will be a class of predicates whose semantics cannot be further specified through language, on pain of eventual circularity. How is the reference of these accomplished?

How is it, for example, that 'white' picks out the property white? It is the physical property that concerns us here, the property that some physical things have, independently of any observers, but that causes those objects to look white under suitable conditions. This look, whose content is subjective white ('white$_s$', I shall call it) can be picked out, referred to, without further ado. Referential success here depends on neither backing descriptions nor problematic causal chains. The first attempt a causal theorist might make to give semantic content to a predicate intended to denote physical or objective white (let this predicate be 'white$_o$') would be to fix its reference by means of the definite description 'that property of spatial objects which causes, under normal conditions, perceptual experiences of white$_s$'. The predicates 'spatial', 'causes', 'perceptual experiences', and 'white$_s$' can all be directly given semantic content. The problem is with 'normal conditions', and phenomenally based attempts to spell this out have not been blessed with success. A quite different strategy is called for. This strategy is suggested by the observation that white$_o$ things sometimes do not look white$_s$, and nonwhite$_o$ things sometimes do. Now, abandoning all talk of normal conditions,[6] I suggest that what we do in assigning 'white$_o$' a denotation is to first notice that the ways in which our color-experiences vary are sufficiently regular (albeit very complex) to make reasonable the hypothesis that a single property causally contributes in some salient way to a certain range of experiences (not only of white$_s$ but also of other subjective colors: for example, of pink$_s$ when objects are experienced as being illuminated$_s$ by red$_s$ illumination.) Our denotative strategy is to take 'white$_o$' to pick out that unique property whose instances play a causal role (possibly further specified in terms, for example, of spatiotemporal coordinates) in each of the experiences of some suitably diverse set of color-experiences. (This means that someone will not have mastered the use of the term 'white$_o$' until he or she is prepared to say that things that look pink under red$_s$ light, and also look blue under blue$_s$ light, green under green$_s$ light, and so forth are objects that are (probably) 'white$_o$'.) The hope is that just one property will be such that its instances play this causal role in the production of each of these experiences. But it might turn out that no single property has instances common to all these causal sequences; alternatively, that more than one does. The sorts of cases that can crop up are rather analogous to ones discussed by Kripke and others in connection with reference to natural kinds. A reference-fixing sample — for instance, a sample consisting of several pieces of metal — may serve to determine the denotation of the natural-kind term 'gold'. But the presupposition that underlies this reference-fixing strategy might, of course, turn out to have been frustrated: Some members of the sample might be of a metallic element with an atomic number of 79; others might be brass or iron pyrite. Such eventualities can jeopardize reference; so, too, in the case of 'white$_o$'. If no single property is such that its instances play a (sufficiently similar) causal role in producing the reference-establishing class of perceptual experiences, or if more than one property does, then reference is jeopardized.[7] So reference to physical properties is necessarily tentative — at least when scientific understanding is at stake. It does not follow, however, that we cannot hope to improve matters; nor that revisions of referential practice in the light of further experience cannot be regarded as increasing the likelihood of success. Our worries are (1) that more than one candidate property is present in all of the causal chains associated with the reference-class, or (2) that no property is common to all these causal chains that is not also common to many reference-fixing causal chains for other properties. Problem (1) can arise in two ways. Instances of two properties P and Q may be present in all the causal chains that are intended to fix the reference of a single property-term (say, 'P'). This may occur by accident, or because the presence of P entails the presence of Q. If P entails Q (as, for example, *being red* entails *being colored*), Q can be eliminated by stipulating that P *not* be a property common to all the causal chains of some other reference-class(es). This strategy will also help in the former case, where it is accidental that P and Q occur together in the original reference-class, as will enlarging the class. On the other hand, suppose that P and Q are nomologically equivalent. That is to say, suppose their instances occur together in space and time, as a matter of nomological necessity. Then, no reference-class can include one and exclude the other. But also, in that case, P and Q will be causally indistinguishable, no matter what experimental situation we envisage. They will play a single ("joint") causal role in the causal structure of the world. And in that case, as I have argued elsewhere,[8] "they" must be regarded to be a single property. We can imagine such a case of two distinct properties only because we ignore the identity-conditions that govern what it is to be a physical property.

This last observation bears on problem (2). With respect to any finite reference-class, it is possible that the perceptual effects of two different properties may be indistinguishable. Two properties may largely mimic one another in their observed effects, so that our reference-class contains some causal chains that instantiate only the one, and some that instantiate only the other. Just as a reference-class for 'gold' may contain samples of gold and others of fool's gold, so a reference-class for 'red_o' may contain chains which instantiate red_o, and others which instantiate *fool's-red$_o$*. The only way to overcome this difficulty is to subject putatively red things to as many causal environments as possible: if red_o and *fool's-red$_o$* are distinct properties, then there will be some situation, in principle discoverable, in which their instances behave differently. This is, to be sure, a "holistic" enterprise: Identifying distinct causal environments forces us to rely on our identification of instances of *other* physical properties. What we can say, however, is that our picture of the physical world (that is, what properties it has) is not "in principle" underdetermined by the data—in the ideal limit in which all relevant data are available. I shall return to this point in my concluding remarks.

3. EVIL DEMONS AND BRAINS IN VATS

We are now in a position to see why internal realism, in Putnam's sense, does not offer a defense against skepticism. To see that this defense fails is to reaffirm a transcendent, or correspondence, conception of truth. We are also in a position, I think, to see how the metaphysical realist's defense against skepticism can be fashioned. First, let us return to Putnam's transcendental deduction of the falsity of 'We are brains in vats'. Putnam's crucial claim is that if we *were* brains in vats, we could not speculate about the question, for we would not be able to *refer* to our brains (or to the vats). This is because the brains and vats would be implicated in every causal chain eventuating in perceptual experience, and not differentially in such a way that causal chains could be used to pick out these items. We could not say: Let the reference of 'vat' be fixed by 'whatever is the cause of such-and-such experiences'—for no such reference-fixing device could single out the vat. *That* would have a causal role in *all* our experiences. Moreover, merely having an "intention to refer" and a mental image—even a vatlike image—is not sufficient for referring to a vat, for such an image is not a representation *of* a vat unless it itself stands in some suitable (that is, reference-fixing) relation to a vat. Furthermore, we cannot specify the reference-fixing relation (putatively involving causation) itself without the question-begging supposition that we have a way of referring to *it*; that is, that 'reference', as used by us, picks out some determinate relation, or, if defined in terms of causation, that 'causation' does so.

It is here that I shall invoke the third of my initial assumptions, namely, that the causal relation is an object of *direct acquaintance*. Thus, if the notion of private reference is coherent (second assumption), there is no danger of begging the question at this stage. This is of considerable importance. It gives reason to expect—making allowances for the fact that an adequate causal theory of reference has yet to be articulated—that content can be given to a notion of reference that is not theory dependent or "internal" to some "circle of ideas."

But this reply to Putnam might not seem convincing, *even* if it were conceded that a causal relation is "given" to us in experience. For it could be said that all realities—even those which are "given"—must be conceptualized in the process of forming any judgments concerning them. If conceptualization is a necessary feature of every cognitive utilization of experience, then in what way has Putnam's difficulty been overcome? All judgments are mediated by concepts, and concepts are "in the mind." Hence, their relation to the reality we can hope to grasp only through them is inescapably problematic.

This objection can and must be resisted. We should admit that all making of judgments presupposes some conceptualization of that which the judgments concern. But this does not mean that concepts must "get in the way of" or distort that which our judgments are about. Perhaps our concepts of external realities are problematic in that way. But it must be demonstrated that, even in the case of the "given," we can have no assurance that our concepts are adequate to their objects. Indeed, the very opposite of this can be shown. For conceptualization itself presupposes the act of recognition. We cannot form an idea of that which we cannot identify and, in principle, reidentify. The given is precisely that which, most primitively, we recognize. It is the soil from which conceptual activity grows; this soil must contain already the element of recognizability.

Whatever conceptual distinctions we later impose as we theorize in order to assemble our experiences into a coherent or unified picture, we must begin here, with the experiences themselves, and with conceptualizations that can be brought into agreement with them. It is on this plane that I claim we anchor the notion of causal relation. And, of course, such relations are recognized, indeed utilized in our conceptual grasping of much else long before we learn to *speak* of causation, or, at a much more advanced stage, to theorize or reflect philosophically on its nature. As Plato saw, there is a large difference between being able to recognize something — justice, for example — and being able to say what it is.

What, then, about truth? If it makes sense to say that we are brains in vats, or are controlled by an evil demon, then the notion of truth must be similarly independent of the theories in terms of which we comprehend the world. Let us pursue this question also within the context of the vat-brain hypothesis.

It is important to distinguish between the hypothesis that I am (or that my body is) a certain particular brain in a particular vat, and the *general* hypothesis that I am some brain, or mass of tissue, in some vat.[9] The former requires singular reference to particular material objects; and aside from the fact that any putative reference will fail in the event that the alleged item does not exist, such a reference is an affair that is considerably more complex than being able to speak of vats, brains, or demons in general. For, to deploy the general hypothesis, it is sufficient to be able to describe things of these sorts — and that requires only giving semantic content to certain predicates. Even if demons form a natural kind, and even if reference to natural kinds requires reference to some actual *members* of that kind, we will not, given a suitable repertoire of predicates, be blocked from formulating a hypothesis that could be satisfied by beings of *some* natural kind with demonesque properties. There is no need to single out any particular natural kind of this sort. The intelligibility of such a general hypothesis (indeed of *any* general hypothesis) of the brain-in-the-vat type will serve to arm the skeptic against Putnam's refutation — and as well, to reinstate the traditional conception of truth.

An advocate of a causal theory of reference might be tempted to give semantic content to a singular referring expression — here I choose 'that demon' — as follows: "Let the reference of 'that demon' be fixed as the satisfier of the description 'whatever thing (or things) is (are) causing my current sensations'." Then, by Kripke's lights (and mine), the sentence 'That demon caused my current sensations', uttered by the causal theorist, will express a proposition that he knows a priori to be true, and yet which is contingent. At the same time, knowledge of such a proposition represents a singular lack of progress from an epistemological point of view. It is not an empty or vacuous proposition in the way tautologies are sometimes said to be empty, for its truth depends at least on there being sensations of his at the time in question, and a cause of these. At the same time, it is clear that it achieves no gain in empirical knowledge: It goes beyond the data only in *assuming* a cause for whatever sensations are being appealed to.

Intuitively, given what we take ordinary perceptual claims to mean, such reports are *false* if it turns out that the cause of the relevant perceptual experiences is a demon. If a man says, "I see a desk," he is wrong, whether or not he is facing a desk, if a demon, not the desk, is responsible for his desklike experiences. Again, if a man says, "A demon is causing this desklike experience," we shall want our semantics to reflect the fact that what he says is wrong if the cause is not a demon but a desk. An adequate semantics must allow us to express the fact that a person whose beliefs are naively derived from experience may be always mistaken. In particular, such a semantics must make intelligible the possibility that the demon hypothesis is true. How can this be done, while giving the hypothesis a substantive content that distinguishes it from the a priori proposition considered here? Only if we can do this can we say that 'A demon is not causing these experiences' is a thesis with substantive cognitive content.

Neither 'demon' nor 'desk' is a term whose semantic behavior conforms to that of pure, proper-namelike rigid designators. Each term has enough connotative content associated with it that there are a priori limits to what *could* turn out to be a demon or a desk. Neither an atom nor a star could be a desk. Nor could either be a demon. These claims do not turn on whether demons or desks are natural kinds. It is evident that, for similar reasons, dogs could not turn out to be kidneys, or puddles of water, or cosmic dust-clouds. This is not because we could not be *that* mistaken when we see dogs; it is because we have a certain conception of doghood, which is too far transgressed by kidneys, even if it need not be too far transgressed by robot dogs. If we *were* that mistaken—if what we identified as dogs proved actually to be kidneys, then we should retract the claim that there are dogs. Such a discovery would show that there were no dogs, not that dogs were really kidneys, just as the discovery of oxygen showed (indirectly) that there was no phlogiston.

What I need to show is that the notion of a demon, or of a brain in a vat, can be given *enough* conceptual content to serve the skeptic's purpose: enough content so that the hypotheses that our experiences are controlled by a demon, or that we are brains in vats, are substantive suppositions with truth-values; enough content so that if either supposition is true, then most of our ordinary empirical beliefs are false.

The conceptual limits we place on the notions we have of dogs and demons are not to be understood solely in terms of the meanings of associated reference-fixing, definite descriptions of the sort 'the cause of such-and-such experiences'. For they involve tighter constraints than this. If kidneys proved to be the systematic cause of our doggish experiences, they would not thereby have been successfully referred to by our use of the term 'dog'. On the other hand, there is no question here of resurrecting the Frege/Russell theory of reference. No uniquely identifying description is required for reference to succeed, nor even some looser stereotypical characterization of what it is to be a dog or a demon.

This much Kripke's arguments can teach us. But since those arguments do not show that a suitable causal chain is the only necessary condition for successful reference, they do not entail the claim that a backing description of some kind is never required if an attempted reference is to count as succeeding. The considerations just mentioned show that (at least sometimes) *some*thing true must be known about the nonrelational properties of the referent. So a "pure" causal theory of reference gives too simple a picture.

What does the need for descriptions imply? It means that the predicates in terms of which the description would be expressed must denote genuine properties. Giving these *predicates* their semantic content is something that *may*, in turn, be achieved solely by means of the reference-fixing strategy that makes use of causal chains, without further descriptive constraints; that is, a predicate may be taken to denote whatever is the (common) causal property in the causal chains generating a certain specified range of experiences. However, not even this is always required: It is not required for secondary properties and for certain primary properties such as the causal relation itself and spatial and temporal properties. For we can fix the reference of the predicates we use to refer to such properties directly, through acquaintance.

It is significant that that part of the evil-demon hypothesis required to give it its skeptical implications can be articulated entirely in terms of predicates that can be given *direct* reference. With the term 'demon', we can associate the description 'a being, distinct from ourselves, who is nonspatial and who thinks'; our hypothesis is that such a being alone causes all our perceptual experiences. The brain-in-the-vat hypothesis is more complex and less elegant. But one can do the job in this case also with the resources at our command. Let us associate with 'material object' the conceptual content 'spatial and temporal being with causal powers'. Instead of fixing the reference of 'my brain' via some causal chain, I shall require only that my brain satisfy the description 'a material object that sustains certain activities that are causally necessary and sufficient for my thoughts to occur'. Let vats be understood to be (at least) material objects capable of supplying causally sufficient conditions for the operation of brains. One could easily imagine a vat as having a certain shape; but obviously this is unnecessary. Nor is it required for the skeptic's purpose that a detailed account be given of the causal interactions between vat and brain. However, something more must be involved in the brain-in-vat hypothesis, to avoid trivialization. As it stands, a "vat" could turn out to be a normal living human body (minus its brain). What is demanded is the supposition that the causal structure of the vat be such that our visual impressions are not produced by objects of the proper shapes and sizes in the proper positions in our environment, and that similar correlations are lacking for our other sensory modalities between what exists around us and what, on the basis of experience, we take to exist. But, to explain the brain-in-vat hypothesis in sufficient detail to give it skeptical content, it is once again sufficient to make use only of properties to which direct reference is possible. I conclude that if we are the dupes of demons, or are brains in vats, these are hypotheses we can intelligibly entertain. They are hypotheses that are not trivial, hypotheses concerning whose truth value one might care a great deal. But having entertained them, how can we ever hope to show that they are true or false?

Skeptical hypotheses rely on the fact that more than one set of conditions can be causally sufficient for the production of a certain type of effect (in this case, a sensation). The strongest reply to skepticism that I believe it is possible to construct makes use of the fact that distinct properties are, "in principle," distinguishable by virtue of there being *some* differential condition(s) under which an outcome will depend on whether it is the one property or the other that is instantiated.[10] This means that someone who was in a position of having "total evidence" with respect to the outcomes of the indefinitely many possible collocations of conditions that the physical universe might generate would, *in principle*, be able to sort out the structure of the world. The 'in principle' in the preceding sentence carries a highly theoretical sense. Clearly, the obtaining of total evidence is not a goal that any human being — or even the species as a whole — can expect to achieve. Certainly, we can continue to collect more and more evidence. But it is extremely unlikely that the degree of verisimilitude of our world picture will be a smoothly increasing function of the amount of evidence we have. Is it possible, falling short of total evidence, to make significant progress toward a correct picture of the world — enough, for example, to eliminate the demon hypothesis? This is a question I shall not attempt to answer. Indeed, I do not know the answer. Intuitively, everyone feels that substantial progress of this sort is entirely within reach. A full defense of epistemological realism would, I think, have to justify this feeling. To do this would require showing that the scientific enterprise was not so radically holistic as to demand, in effect, that we must know everything before we can know anything. It would require showing that it is unnecessary to amass data on the result of every possible combination of physical circumstances (or, more precisely, perceptual circumstances), before any part of the system could, with some assurance, be constructed. For science does not, in fact, work that way, nor could it. Work by Glymour (1980) suggests, however, that confirmation is indeed a piecemeal process rather than a radically holistic one. It is along these lines that the best promise for a rational reconstruction of scientific knowledge seems to lie.

4. TRUTH AND WARRANTED ASSERTIBILITY

Although I cannot further explore here the large question just raised, the argument I have given does have implications for the relationship between truth and warranted assertibility. More specifically, it has implications for the relation between truth and warranted assertibility in the Peircean limit of ideal and total evidence about the world.

According to Putnam's internal realist, the latter two notions are identical. There *is* no intelligible conception of truth which places it outside the bounds of what is rationally assertible in the Peircean limit. But internal realism involves more than this identification. It understands truth *in terms* of rational assertibility. The latter is the fundamental notion, the notion on which we can get an independent grip.

According to the realism I have argued for, it is likewise the case that a proposition will be true if and only if, in the Peircean limit, it is rationally warranted. For the metaphysical realist, however, the notion of truth is the more fundamental. Our conception of (theoretical, as opposed to practical) rationality is dependent on it.

This can initially be brought out by considering a concept that plays a central role in our chief paradigm of reasoning, the notion of deductive validity. For deductive validity is understood in terms of truth-preservation; that is why the conclusion of a deductive argument known to be valid is at least as warranted as the conjunction of its premises. Nor does there seem to be any way to understand truth in terms of deductive validity: Validity cannot play the role of truth. Can truth be dispensed with in favor of coherence or warranted assertibility? Warranted assertibility involves minimally the requirement of coherence with some body of background beliefs, which brings us back to coherence; but coherence involves minimally the requirement of logical consistency, which brings us back to truth.

Of course, deductive reasoning does not exhaust scientific rationality. Can we articulate a conception of nondeductive reasoning that does not presuppose the correspondence notion of truth? The traditional conception of nondeductive modes of reasoning has been that their *telos* is truth; a method of inference is reasonable just in case, and only insofar as, it conduces to true belief, in the correspondence sense. But perhaps such a conception of rationality collapses; perhaps it must be replaced with a conception formulated in terms of such criteria as coherence, simplicity, past success at predicting future experience, and the like.

Although various attempts at such replacement have been made, they cannot serve the functions that the notion of truth serves. If coherence means mere logical consistency, then we must agree that this is a necessary contraint on any set of rational beliefs. But it is a constraint that can be passed by all but the most extreme fantasies. If coherence means more than consistency, then this additional content must be made clear. Simplicity is a criterion that also has not been given any articulation sufficiently general in application, or sufficiently precise, to offer an adequate criterion of choice between competing theories. In any case, short of stipulation, there can be two reasons for adopting such a criterion. One reason rests on the belief that, other things being equal, the simpler of two theories is more likely to be the true one. This imports the notion of truth. The other reason is that a simpler theory is easier to work with, learn, and so on. But that is a practical matter; and to speak of rationality here is to speak of criteria relevant only to practical reason.[11] The past history of success of a theory in making predictions can hardly constitute grounds for our now believing the theory, unless we have grounds for believing that past success portends future success. But that is the problem of induction.

There is an argument that demonstrates more forcefully the discrepancy between such conceptions of rationality and a conception that uses correspondence truth as the controlling notion. There is no reason inherent in internal realism to suppose that, in the Peircean limit, there will not be two or more competing theories that meet equally well the desiderata of coherence, simplicity, and instrumental success. Unless the internal realist can show that this is not so, it is clear that he cannot understand truth as warranted belief in the Peircean limit. For in that case, equally warranted, mutually contradictory beliefs will have to be regarded as true. Michael Dummett (1978) has explored the possibility of suspending the principle of bivalence in such cases. But this means that truth, understood as warranted acceptability, can be applied only in cases where such a situation does not arise. When undecidable global theories can oppose each other, it appears that *all* our empirical beliefs concerning the physical world may be such that the notion of truth (understood as warranted acceptability) is not applicable to them.

5. CORRESPONDENCE AND REFERENCE

The concept of truth has been a difficult one to give an empiricist account of because, like other highly abstract notions, it is hard to understand the role it plays in terms accessible to empirical analysis. The notion of correspondence is problematic not merely because it is difficult to define a suitable mapping from words to world, but because, more deeply, such a mapping introduces the suspect notion of a world given to us independently of what is on the side of the mind. Since the verification conditions for " '*P*' is true" are indistinguishable from those for '*P*' itself, it is tempting to conclude that, semantically, the predicate 'is true' is otiose, though its use may serve some pragmatic purpose such as emphasis. Under these circumstances a theory of truth such as Tarski's is welcome.

But Hartry Field (1972) has argued that Tarski's explication of the notion of truth is fundamentally inadequate. Tarski requires that the predicate 'is true' in a metalanguage satisfy the criterion (Criterion T) that

'*P*' is true if *P*

be a theorem of the metalanguage for every object-language statement '*P*'. Field insists that, although this is a necessary condition on truth, it cannot serve as an *explanation* of that notion. No one who did not already understand the object language in question—hence, understand what it is for '*P*' to be true—could understand Tarski's criterion. To be sure, any philosophical explanation of the concept of truth must be expressed in a language; so, to understand such an explanation, one must already have the concept of truth. But the job that we want such an explanation to perform is to tie the notion of truth to general considerations in epistemology and ontology, in such a way as to advance our understanding of what it is to have a language. As Putnam has pointed out, Tarski's theory is neutral between philosophically distinct substantive conceptions of truth—for instance, the correspondence theory, the coherence theory, and pragmatic theories.

A philosophically adequate explanation of the notion of truth ought as well to figure in theories of language-learning. It ought, in particular, to figure in such a way as to satisfy what was, after all, one of the chief motivations for verificationism: It ought to figure in such a way as to make it possible to explain how the concept of truth can itself be acquired.

Kripke has similarly criticized theories of reference whose defect parallels that of Tarski's Criterion T vis-à-vis truth. A particularly crude version of such a theory, which can be found in Kneale (1962), is that 'Socrates' means 'the man who was called "Socrates" '; more generally,

'N' means 'the object called "N" '.

Kripke's objection is that this, as an explanation of reference, is circular. It does not enable anyone to pick out the referent of 'N' who does not already know what that referent is.

Putnam's own earlier development of a causal theory of reference was closely linked to his advocacy of realism—metaphysical realism, as he now calls it. His subsequent apostasy and challenge to metaphysical realism (1981) is not only striking, but also dialectically useful because Putnam has seen so clearly and deeply into the heart of the problem. I take the crucial insight that precipitated his apostasy to be this: The causal theory of reference *does* provide (setting aside "technical difficulties") a realist way of linking words to the world (just as a causal theory of perception provides a way of linking experience to the world—that is, a way of articulating the notion that physical objects are sometimes objects of perceptual acts). *But* this linkage can be given realist credentials only if the notion of causation itself can be fixed in a language- and theory-independent way. For if reference to that notion is itself controlled by, say, global theorizing about the world, then there will be no noncircular way of anchoring our talk about the world to the world; and, moreover, no noncircular way of introducing the crucial metalinguistic notions of reference and truth that we need to express the idea that we have such anchoring.

Now, Hume's analysis of causation, stripped of its psychological components, is free of circularity-inducing dependence on physical theory. But, of course, Hume's causal relation is too weak to establish the kind of correspondence the realist needs on behalf of reference. It might accidentally be true that there exists a constant conjunction between the tokening of a word by the users of a language, and some external state of affairs. But it could not be independently ascertained by those speakers what that state of affairs is. If one does not strengthen Hume's notion, one will be confined to think about reference at best in terms of some internally coherent global theory that situates human beings in a world and is consistent with experience. A realist answer to Putnam therefore must (1) strengthen Hume's conception of the causal relation, and (2) demonstrate that we have theory-independent access to a relation of that sort. For the present purposes, I am assuming that this has been achieved. Let me summarize in the briefest way how these achievements would bear on constructing a realist theory of language.

The fundamental elements of such a theory are a causal theory of perception and a causal theory of reference. Physical properties are identified perceptually by discriminating between them on the basis of their differential causal relations. Predicate terms denoting physical properties that are not given in experience are to be understood as rigid designators whose reference is fixed via direct reference to experience; that is, as 'the causally unique feature in the production of such-and-such experiences.' Talk of individuals can proceed by way of description, by the use of reference-fixing causal chains or, more commonly, by some hybrid of these strategies, as I have previously suggested.

The tools used by someone who employs such a strategy are not colored by any theory, nor are they internal to any conceptual scheme. They are linguistic intentions (a subject I have not discussed), deductive and inductive logic, and direct, naive experience, in particular the direct experience of causal, spatial, and temporal relations. These form the basis on which we construct our conception of a world that exists independently of our own experiences, and to which we have indirect access through experience. Reference to the particulars and properties of that physical world is always problematic, or theoretical. If, however, the identity of physical properties is tied to their causal relations, then the causal structure of the world is, in principle, accessible.

Such a conception gives us an independent way of formulating what it is to have reached the ideal, or Peircean limit of investigation. This limit will have been reached when the causal powers of each thing are known as a function of the complex of properties that it possesses. In a reductively ordered hierarchy of theories, this means that the causal powers of the most elementary physical particles (if such there be) are known; the rest can, in principle, be calculated.

Is there any way in which, if one were to reach the Peircean limit, one could know that it had been reached? Perhaps not. However, one necessary condition of one's having reached this limit would be that one's theory of the world would not be underdetermined by the data. To see why this is so, it is necessary to return for a moment to the identity conditions for physical properties. When realism is combined with the view that causation is a relation between universals that orders those universals into a uniquely determined system, the identifiability of the components of the system is assured. If the system of causal relations in which a universal stands are essential to it and unique, so that different universals necessarily stand in different relations, and if our perceptual access to the world is itself causal, then it must, in principle, be possible to acquire information that will distinguish all distinct universals and, in so doing, to organize them vis-à-vis their causal relations. But to have achieved this is to have achieved an ultimate theoretical understanding of the physical world. The data (in the ideal limit) can warrant only one theory, for to say that two eligible theories remain, is to say that two ways of reconstructing the system of universals are experimentally—that is, causally—indistinguishable. But this would violate the ontological (not verificationist) precept that a difference that makes no (causal) difference is no difference at all. This feature of metaphysical realism is one that the internal realist and the instrumentalist have not shown that they can match, even in the Peircean limit.

In that limit, moreover, rational belief and truth become one. This, however, is not because truth collapses into warranted belief. It is because, in that limit, only the truth can be warrantedly believed.

How does the form of realism developed here stack up against the five realist claims presented at the beginning of this chapter? Let us summarize our results by means of a quick comparison. I shall refer to my version of realism as 'R' for convenience.

(i) *R* not commit one to any detailed theory of meaning. It is compatible with the thought that "meaning" covers a variety of distinct features of language. But it does allow at least some component of meaning to be divorced from conditions of confirmation, for terms used to describe the physical world. And it insists on giving a central semantic role to truth-conditions and reference.

(ii) *R* affirms a correspondence theory of truth, and a causal theory of reference.

(iii) *R* is not as such committed to the existence of material objects of any particular sort. It is not even committed as such to the existence of any material objects. But when *R* is combined with the experiences we do have, it can reasonably be hoped to yield the conclusion that there are such objects.

(iv) *R* further asserts that scientific investigation (and even the ordinary use of "common sense") can tell us about these material objects, in the sense of being able, in principle, to justify beliefs about them. (However, it must be admitted that *R* has not been spelled out in sufficient detail to address all the skeptical objections to this claim and the previous one. So these assertions are only programmatic.)

(v) This thesis, used by Putnam to characterize metaphysical realism, is one that *R* rejects. For *R* yields the conclusion that the world is, "in principle," fully accessible to empirical investigation. As such, *R* does not postulate any impenetrable reality. It asserts that the evil demon, if he exists, would come to light under the onslaught of sufficiently persistent scientific scrutiny.[12] Thus, *R* rejects the doctrine I earlier called v2. Yet *R* accepts v1, for it also asserts that we can coherently entertain the hypothesis of an evil demon long before we have any evidence that could be decisive in deciding whether the external world confirms Cartesian demonology, or whether it confirms the common-sense picture we all know and love.

We come to philosophical reflection with the aboriginal conviction that sensation is reliable. If the picture I have drawn here is correct, the information with which sense experience affords us is bound to be always partial and often seriously defective. Nevertheless, the way in which experience and environment are connected cannot be arbitrary or capricious. It is not enough, of course, for sensory processes to be reliable, if partial. We must know that they are so.[13] Reliabilists often seem to deny this. They maintain that if a belief is obtained by reliable means, and is true, then it is known to be true. But if we do not know that the means are reliable, then reflective doubts about these beliefs are not merely hyperbolic. So, reflection puts us in a position in which we find that we are no longer sure that we know what we formerly believed. Perhaps we do still know what we now find subject to doubt; but we do not know that we have this knowledge. We are in the paradoxical situation of being epistemically alienated from our own knowledge. It is this situation that a foundationalist finds unintelligible. A reliabilist who understands knowledge as reliably acquired true belief must either absolve us of the responsibility of knowing that we know, or face the further task of certifying the means.

But reliabilism can take two forms. An external reliabilist holds that the processes that underwrite reliable belief-acquisition include ones like the physical operation of bodily sense-receptors, whose operation we understand, if at all, only at the end of a chain of scientific inferences. An externalist recognizes that our epistemic relation to such processes is on a par with our epistemic relation to the external world generally. An internal reliabilist, on the other hand, would seek to characterize the epistemic states and processes that underwrite knowledge as ones of whose reliability we are immediately aware.

Nevertheless, a consistent externalist could hold that we *do* know that our sense organs are reliable.[14] He could defend this by maintaining that we correctly believe these processes to be reliable, and that this belief is itself acquired by reliable means.[15] But surely this move is more clever than convincing. It does not differ in kind from a familiar proof of Biblical infallibility. That proof uses the Pauline passages which say that God cannot lie (Titus 1:2) and that all scripture is inspired (2 Timothy 3:16) to draw the desired conclusion. If the problem of skepticism has any bite at all, if it can get an initial foothold, then such a maneuver can only be seen to be question-begging. And it is skepticism, after all, that drove us to philosophy — or, anyway, to epistemology.

We must somewhere stop the regresses that such theories of knowledge invite. I have argued that an initial and crucial step in the reconstruction of the process through which we gain the world is one that requires that we focus attention once more on the natural starting point: experience itself.

Notes

1. See Fales forthcoming.

2. See Boyd 1985, p. 4.

3. For other doubts about abductive defenses of realism, see Fine 1986; see also Fine 1984 and Laudan 1984. Boyd is aware of these difficulties, but tries to outflank them by means of a holistic and naturalized epistemology (see Boyd 1984). My concluding remarks will make clear why I do not think that strategy can succeed, either.

4. See Boyd 1985, p. 4.

5. Nor are these two conditions jointly sufficient. I am, indeed, skeptical about formulating any general set of necessary and sufficient conditions, though not prepared to abandon hope for a *theory* of reference. In most cases, an additional necessary condition is an intention to *use* a term referringly.

6. That the invocation of "normal conditions" is unhelpful can be supported by the following parable. Twin-Earth is a world just like ours in all respects except that it is a planet of a star that is a red giant (suppose this is physically possible). Twin-English-speakers even use the word 'white' to describe the color of things like Twin-milk, Twin-chalk, and Twin-Taj Mahal. An Earth-Englishman transported to

Twin-Earth would also say that these objects were white; he would insist, though, that under conditions of illumation that normally prevailed on Twin Earth, these items all *looked* pink.

7. This story about how we give physical property terms denotation is naturally an idealization. We do not need to have some *definite* remembered set of perceptual experiences in mind to serve as our reference-fixing class, any more than some definite set of gold objects needs to be assumed to have played that role in establishing the semantics of 'gold'. Moreover, we can improve the prospects of referential success by loosening the requirement that *all* the members of the reference class be instances of the same property (natural kind). Perhaps only a "sufficient number" of them need to be. This is vague, but I do not see that it undermines the strategy.

8. In Fales forthcoming. See Shoemaker 1980 for a similar theory of property identity.

9. Similarly, it is important to distinguish between speculation about a particular evil demon and speculation about the existence of *some* evil demon.

10. See Shoemaker 1980.

11. Maintaining the separation between theoretical reason and practical reason is sufficiently central to our conception of rationality that it should not lightly be given up. I may, for example, have strong practical grounds for acting on a proposition (acting as if it were true), even when I have no grounds, or weak grounds, for believing that it is. Pragmatism attempts to reduce theoretical reason to practical reason. But utility calculations are blind unless guided by factual beliefs about the future; and, unless there is reason to suppose that those beliefs correspond to what is the case, they can hardly serve to guide the person who is rational and serious about his or her actions.

12. I have not explicitly argued that mental properties must, like physical ones, be included in a causal web. But considerations similar to those I have given suggest this must be so, at least for those properties of a demon by virtue of which he would be able to cause our experiences.

13. And we must know when to suspect error and how to correct for it.

14. I am indebted to Richard Fumerton for pointing this out to me.

15. By so arguing, he threatens to undermine the distinction between his position and that of the internalist. For he now can agree—or appear to agree—with the internalist that it is necessary to justify the reliability claim, necessary to back up a claim to know that *P* with the further claim to know that belief in *P* was acquired by reliable means. But that is not the central issue for us.

References

Armstrong, David M. 1978. *A Theory of Universals*. Vol. 2 of *Universals and Scientific Realism*. Cambridge.

Boyd, Richard. 1973. "Realism, Underdetermination, and a Causal Theory of Evidence." *Nous* 7: 1–12.

Boyd, Richard. 1984. "The Current Status of Scientific Realism." In *Scientific Realism*, edited by Jarrett Leplin. Berkley.

Boyd, Richard. 1985. "Lex Orandi est Lex Credendi." In *Images of Science: Essays in Realism and Empiricism*, edited by Paul M. Churchland and Clifford A. Hooker. Chicago.

Dretske, Fred. 1977. "Laws of Nature. *Philosophy of Science* 44: 248–68.

Dummett, Michael. 1978. *Truth and Other Enigmas*. Cambridge, Mass.

Fales, Evan M. forthcoming. *Causation and Universals*. Unpublished manuscript.

Field, Hartry. 1972. "Tarski's Theory of Truth." *The Journal of Philosophy* 69: 347–75.

Fine, Arthur, 1984. "The Natural Ontological Attitude." In *Scientific Realism*, edited by Jarrett Leplin. Berkeley.

Fine, Arthur. 1986. "Unnatural Attitudes: Realist and Instrumentalist Attachments to Science." *Mind* 95: 149–79.

Glymour, Clark. 1980. *Theory and Evidence*. Princeton, N.J.

Kneale, William. 1962. "Modality, De Dicto and De Re." In *Logic, Methodology, and the Philosophy of Science: Proceedings of the 1960 International Congress*, edited by Ernest Nagel, Patrick Suppes, and Alfred Tarski. Stanford, Calif.

Laudan, Larry. 1984. "A Confutation of Convergent Realism" In *Scientific Realism*, edited by Jarrett Leplin. Berkeley.

Putnam, Hilary. 1981. *Reason, Truth and Reference*. Cambridge.

Shoemaker, Sydney. 1980. "Properties, Causation and Projectibility." In *Applications of Inductive Logic*, edited by Jonathan Cohen and Mary Hesse. Oxford.

Tooley, Michael. 1977. "The Nature of Laws." *Canadian Journal of Philosophy* 7: 667-98.

Mathematical Realism

PENELOPE MADDY

I

To be a realist about set theory is to think that set-theoretic statements usually have unambiguous truth values and that they have these values depending on the properties of something objective. I say "usually" because even in set theory there might be occasions when the questions we are tempted to ask turn out to be vague or ill-formed, analogous to questions about whether or not a certain shade is red, or about the hairstyle of the present king of France.[1] Still, the realist holds that most garden-variety statements of set theory do have unambiguous and objective truth-values. As a litmus test for realism of this type, I suggest a belief in the truth or falsity of the Continuum Hypothesis. The realist will hold that this truth value is a matter of objective fact, despite our current ignorance, or even—heaven forbid!—the possibility that we shall never know.

The simplest and most obvious way to explain this objectivity of truth value is to suppose that set-theoretic statements are true or false depending on the properties of an objective realm of things, namely, the universe of sets. Realism of this sort is usually called "platonism" in the philosophy of mathematics, regardless of whether or not the sets themselves are taken to be "platonic" in any sense whatsoever. Platonistic realism allows us to extend our crudely Tarskian semantics—statements are true if the things their names name stand in the relations their predicates specify—to the theory of sets. Godel advocates a slightly mystical version of this position; I have suggested a more naturalistic reading called "set-theoretic realism."[2]

As is well known, two very general considerations threaten platonistic realism. First, it seems natural to suppose that we embodied creatures learn facts about things by coming into cognitive contact with those things, by seeing them, hearing them, touching them. Sets, as commonly understood, are abstract objects, and thus seem outside our epistemological range. Second, if set theory encompasses number theory, then there is the question of which sets are the numbers. How can three be this particular object when the only properties it has seem to arise simply from its coming third in the series of natural numbers? Any object can come third in some infinite progression, so any object seems to have as much claim as any other to being three.[3]

Attention to these problems, especially the second, has led several contemporary philosophers of mathematics[4] to a new position: structuralism. The leading idea is that mathematics is the study of structures, not of objects.[5] Thus there is no need to identify the numbers with particular objects, particular sets; rather, number theory is the study of the natural number structure. This move provides some hope on the epistemological front as well, because humans are capable of perceiving at least finite structures (or patterns) in the physical world around them. This structuralism, then, is promoted as an alternative to our embattled platonistic realism. If it steers clear of if-thenism, it should remain a realist theory, because the continuum hypothesis is either true or false in a full, iterative set structure.[6] Let's call this "structural realism."

II

I have something to say about the relationship between structural and platonistic realism, but let me sneak up on it by returning for a moment to the second standard objection to platonism. Numbers aren't particular sets, because any set can play the role of any number simply by occupying the appropriate position in an omega sequence. Elsewhere[7] I have argued that from the point of view of the set-theoretic realist, numbers should be viewed as universals, as properties of sets, and number theory as that part of set theory concerned with the number properties of finite sets. Furthermore, these number properties should be individuated along the lines of scientific properties like length or heat, that is, by something other than synonymy or conceptual identity. From this point of view, it is possible to affirm, for example, that

the property 'equinumerous with $\{0, \{0\}, \{0, \{0\}\}\}$'

$=$ the property 'equinumerous with $\{0, \{0\}, \{\{0\}\}\}$'

This explains why the choice between various "reductions" of number theory to set theory is only a matter of convenience.

We might try to compare structural and set-theoretic realism by asking a simple question: what is 3? The platonistic realist answers, "the property of being equinumerous with the set $\{0, \{0\}, \{0, \{0\}\}\}$" where this very property has many other descriptions. The structural realist would say that 3 is "the third position in the natural number structure," or "the third position in the pattern exemplified by the von Neumann ordinals," or even, "the position of $\{0, \{0\}, \{0, \{0\}\}\}$ in the sequence of von Neumann ordinals."

These answers sound different, but given that the question isn't a happy one for either view (since both deny that 3 is an object), and given that the level of abstraction involved is somewhat dizzying, it remains possible that they aren't different in any important way. To test this, let us shift our attention to a more down-to-earth question. Suppose we all agree that there are three apples on the table. Let's ask our two realists what makes this statement true. More comfortable this time, the platonistic realist answers that there is a set of apples on the table and that this set is equinumerous with $\{0, \{0\}, \{0, \{0\}\}\}$. Similarly relieved, the structural realist says instead that there is a physical aggregate on the table which instantiates the same pattern as the first three von Neumann ordinals under the successor relation.

In both cases, we are told that a mass of physical stuff has certain properties. In one case, the stuff is so arranged that it constitutes a set, and that set has a further property; in the other case, the stuff is so arranged as to instantiate a certain pattern, and that pattern is shared by a certain sequence of sets. In both cases, an aggregate of physical stuff is said to be organized in a certain way. According to the platonist, to be so organized is to be a set. According to the structuralist, to be so organized is to instantiate a structure. The further property of the platonist's set is being in one-to-one correspondence with $\{0, \{0\}, \{0, \{0\}\}\}$. The further property of the structuralist's structure instantiation is that $\{0, \{0\}, \{0, \{0\}\}\}$ under successor instantiates the same structure.

By now it should be obvious what I'm getting at here, namely, that the similarities between these two positions are far more striking than the differences. It seems to me quite possible that those differences are simply terminological variations between two descriptions of the same phenomenon. A comparison of the platonist's and the structuralist's attempts to meet the epistemological challenge encourages this impression. Both begin with simple perceptual knowledge, the sort of thing we gain when we look at the apples on the table. I would bet that any naturalistic theory of how we come to know that there is a three-membered set of apples there could be easily converted to a naturalistic theory of how we come to know that the apple-stuff there instantiates the same pattern as the first three von Neumann ordinals under successor.[8] And vice versa. Two such theories should qualify as "definitionally equivalent" if anything does.

III

I have suggested, then, that platonistic and structural realism don't differ in any significant way in their treatment of the natural numbers. The same should go for the real numbers, and anything else the platonistic realist sees as reducible to set theory. But what about set theory itself? Our platonistic realist might be willing to embrace structuralism with respect to other mathematical entities, and to see this as little more than reducing those entities to sets, but what about those sets themselves? Local structuralism might go hand-in-hand with set-theoretic realism, but what about a global structuralism that includes the set-theoretic hierarchy itself?

Notice first that every structure studied by the local structuralist has an instantiation within the set-theoretic hierarchy. Where the set-theoretic realist studies a certain set, the local structuralist studies the structure instantiated by that set, but methodologically, there is no real difference. Things aren't so simple for the global structuralist. Without the world of sets, there is no guarantee that even the natural number structure has an instantiation.[9] Thus, the global structuralist is faced with a choice between postulating the necessary uninstantiated structures and finding something to instantiate those structures.

In pursuit of the second option, global structuralism sometimes allies itself with another popular trend in contemporary philosophy of mathematics: modalism.[10] The study is not of actual structures, but of possible structures, where "possible" here means a form of mathematical—as opposed to physical, logical, or metaphysical—possibility. Important structures that happen to be uninstantiated in our world are instantiated in other possible worlds, as, for example, (some initial segment of) the set-theoretic hierarchy structure could be instantiated by physical objects in a possible world richer than our own.[11] This position remains a form of realism, because set theoretic truth is defined in terms of truth in possible full models of the set-theoretic axioms. Once again, it isn't important that these models be "physically possible," but they must present a real "mathematical possibility."

For purposes of comparison, we should ask the modal realist the same questions about apples earlier presented to the platonist and the structuralist. Unfortunately, presentations of modalism most often begin with talk about possible models of infinitary set theory, skipping over the more down-to-earth parts of mathematics. Perhaps when we see the applies, the modalist would say that we see a possible, indeed actual, set, or a possible, indeed actual, pattern, thus agreeing at the most basic level with our other realists. Let us assume that something of this sort is correct. After all, it was the question of uninstantiated, infinite structures that raised the issue of modalism in the first place.

Here the modal realist says that infinitary mathematics studies structures that are only possible in this world, but actual in other possible worlds. This raises several questions. First, what is the difference between this impoverished world and that other possible world with lots of mathematical structures? If that world has the same physical stuff as our world, I don't see what gives it the mathematical structures ours lacks. On the other hand, if it has different physical stuff, it's hard to see why we should be interested in the mathematical structure of that stuff rather than our homegrown variety. If mathematics depends contingently on the physical makeup of the particular possible world, it would seem that our science and our mathematics should be most interested in the structure of our world. On the epistemological side, modalism would require a naturalistic theory of how we come to know about other mathematically possible worlds. To my mind, knowledge of this world should be more accessible than knowledge of other possible worlds, so I doubt that the modal move will do any good.[12]

Instead of trying to instantiate the uninstantiated in another possible world, the global structuralist might choose the simple expedient of postulating structures that exist uninstantiated in this world.[13] Thus, the natural number structure is uninstantiated, but it exists nevertheless. Similarly for the all-inclusive iterative hierarchy structure. Here I suspect that the reasons the global structuralist might give for believing various things about the set theoretic structure—for example, that it contains an infinite set, that it contains a power set for every set, and so on—would sound very like the set-theoretic realist's defenses of the particular axioms of set theory.[14] Earlier I suggested that on the most basic perceptual level, the epistemological theories of the structural realist and the platonistic realist would be nearly indistinguishable. Now, at the more theoretical level of justifying assumptions about the infinite, I suggest they would remain so.

But surely the ontologies are quite different; where one postulates structures, universals, the other postulates objects, sets, in the iterative hierarchy. Here again, I question the profundity of this difference. Recall that set-theoretic realism agrees with structuralism locally, that is, on the status of numbers and other mathematical "objects" that are reducible to sets; these are really properties of which the set theorist studies particular instantiations. The disagreement, if there is one, is between the global structuralist and the set-theoretic realist on the status of the set-theoretic hierarchy itself. Here the global structuralist sees unstructured positions related by a single membership relation, and the set-theoretic realist sees sets related by the same relation. We could point to a real difference between these if we could locate properties of sets that are not determined simply by their membership relations; the structuralist's positions would lack these. But are there such properties? Is there anything true of the power set of the set of von Neumann ordinals that isn't true by virtue of its membership relations? Of course not. Thus, the purported ontological distinction between global structuralism and set-theoretic realism seems elusive.

I should point out that some structuralists also sense the possibility of a rapprochement with set-theoretic realism. Consider, for example, Shapiro's discussion of the relationship between mathematics and the physical world:[15]

> The claim that a structure is exemplified in physical reality amounts to a claim that there are entities of some sort that answer to the places within the structure. Many of the structures studied by mathematicians and used in science have an infinite number of places and, thus, there are not enough observable physical objects to exemplify them. The application of an infinite structure amounts to the postulation of infinitely many theoretical entities.

He concludes that

> science does proceed by discovering mathematical structures in physical reality, but the discovery is often indirect and involves the postulation of theoretical entities. The situation might best be described as scientific theories *incorporating* mathematical theories.

For example, when real number theory is applied to space-time, the physical scientist hypothesizes that there are points in physical reality answering to the positions in the real number pattern. In a footnote, Shapiro points out that this picture is easily adapted to platonistic realism:

> Instead of speaking of mathematical structures underlying physical reality, a Platonist can speak of *isomorphisms* between systems of mathematical objects and systems of physical objects.

Instead of postulating enough space-time points to instantiate the real number pattern, the physical scientist postulates enough to produce an isomorphism between the space-time points and the power set of the natural numbers under a certain ordering. Shapiro acknowledges that the difference between this reading and his own are negligible, and thus admits that a sufficiently naturalistic, platonistic realism could preserve the central insights of his structuralism.

IV

Supposing, then, that the structural and the platonistic realist are in search of very similar, if not identical, epistemological theories, let me say a few words about the direction in which this search might lead them. First, exponents of both views argue that the most basic level of knowledge must be accounted for in perceptual terms. The finite structures instantiated by physical objects and the finite sets of which physical objects are members are alike in being accessible to our senses. Determining the correct account of this accessibility is naturally a job for psychology as well as philosophy.

But mathematics rises to grander things than mere counting. In higher mathematics, for example, in axiomatic set theory, theories are posed and tested using a methodology reminiscent of the physical sciences. Holistically minded philosophers might claim that these two methodologies are one, that success in science is the ultimate justification for mathematical theories, and that the standard physical evidence for a scientific theory is the sole support for the mathematics applied there. What about the sorts of evidence the mathematicians themselves put forth: proofs and various plausibility arguments in favor of the axioms? On the strict holistic account, these are just so much talk. Only the mathematics useful to science is justified, and its justification is that usefulness.

It's not even clear that this position should count as realism. If a decision on the size of the continuum has no ramifications in science, perhaps our holist would dismiss it as meaningless.[16] Leaving this issue aside, there is the simple fact that this position flies in the face of mathematical practice. Along with proofs, mathematicians cite a wide range of facts and arguments as evidence for or against their statements.[14] Even the most cursory survey of these justifications shows that they cannot be subsumed under the canons of rationality displayed by some physical science like physics or biology. To dismiss them on that account is the most blatant parochialism.

Mathematics, then, has a methodology of its own, and it is the job of our realistic epistemologists to describe and explain it. This is not to say that the success of mathematics, particularly in science, is irrelevant. Rather, that success should be seen as supporting the mathematical edifice as a whole. Where the old-style holists see the application of mathematics as justifying our belief in its ontology, we should also see it as evidence for the overall rationality of its methods.

But if mathematics isn't subservient to physical science, what is the relationship between the two? Are there two realities, one mathematical, one physical, and if so why should the theory of the one be relevant to the theory of the other? Obviously, both structuralism and set-theoretic realism have moved away from the more familiar platonistic picture of a realm of mathematical objects completely divorced from the physical world. According to the structuralist, physical configurations often instantiate mathematical patterns. According to the set-theoretic realist, the proper study of both mathematics and physical science is the iterative hierarchy of sets erected over the physical objects as urelements. In both cases, the physical and the mathematical are closely intertwined.

In fact, I think there may be a way of seeing the connection between the two as even closer still. I mention this mainly for the benefit of the materialistically minded, those for whom any physical/mathematical dualism is a challenge to eliminate all but the physical. I want to suggest that the two might be seen as so interdependent that no separation, let alone elimination, is possible. Unfortunately, my current state of understanding allows me to do no more than point in the general direction of this position.

I propose two thought experiments. The first concerns our perceptual access to the simple mathematical facts discussed earlier in the example of the three apples. Both our realists can effectively argue that there is a perceptual difference between seeing an undifferentiated blob of physical stuff and seeing that stuff as instantiating a pattern, or constituting a set. I've given such arguments elsewhere[17] and won't rehearse them here.

Suppose, this time, that there is just one apple on the table. Is there a perceptual difference between the apple and its singleton?[18] It would seem that the answer is no. The actual difference is that the singleton has an unambiguous number property—one—whereas the physical blob that makes up the apple is one apple, many cells, more molecules, even more atoms, and so on. The fact remains, however, that a normal adult with the usual ability to perceive individuated physical objects can hardly help seeing the apple as a unit. Indeed, the very question can be formed so as to beg it: is there any perceptual difference between a single object and its unit set? Once a single physical object has been individuated, separated from its surroundings, it already has a number property. Further consideration of its unit set adds nothing, and ipso facto, nothing perceivable.

Does this mean that there is no difference between a physical blob and a set? No, because a physical blob has no unique number property and a set does. What this example does suggest is that once a physical blob has been isolated as a separate individual, there is no important distinction between it and its unit set. From this point of view, it makes good sense to identify an individual (not an unindividuated blob) with its singleton.[19] This means that an individual "physical" object is not purely physical; it is already mathematical as well. The physical world, understood as made up of physical things, already has mathematical structure, is already populated with sets.

Now let's try a second thought experiment: imagine the purely physical world. This would have to be a giant aggregate composed of all the physical stuff in the universe. There is nothing nonphysical in this, but most philosophers, even nominalists, prefer a less amorphous characterization; they begin with all physical objects, or all particles, or all space-time points. Indeed, it is typical to describe applied set theory as the theory of the impure cumulative hierarchy, the result of applying endless iterations of the operation "set of" to the range of physical objects.

What now seems obvious is that to add even this small amount of structure — the differentiation of the amorphous mass into individuals of some kind — is already to broach the mathematical. If we were to consider the mass of physical stuff divided into finite collections, everyone would agree that we have more than the physical. What our apple example shows is that the same is true when the physical stuff is simply divided into individual objects, because these are already mathematical. The only way to confine ourselves to the purely physical is to refrain from any differentiation whatsoever.

Is this possible? Could there be a physical world with absolutely no mathematical structure? Whatever our level of success or failure in this shamelessly philosophical imagining, I think it is plain that our world is not one such. Our reality is structured in many ways, into individual objects, into natural kinds, into patterns and structures of many sorts,[20] and (at least some of) this structure is mathematical. We might say, with the structural realist, that physical reality itself has mathematical structure; we might use the set-theoretic realist's idiom and say that physical reality comes divided into sets. Either way, the idea that physical reality can stand alone, that it comes first and that mathematics is separate, secondary or imposed, must be rejected.[21]

This view can be made even more materialistic by replacing the usual set-theoretic hierarchy over the physical objects (that is, singletons) with the iterative hierarchy of nonempty sets over this same basis, that is, by eliminating the pure sets[22] The theory of this radically impure hierarchy is essentially the same as that of the radically pure hierarchy that forms the official subject matter for set theory. The practice of studying pure sets can be explained and excused by its convenience; theorems are proved about the fictional pure sets, then transferred to the real world of the radically impure sets.

Philosophically, this perspective further promotes the inseparability of the mathematical and the physical. All radically impure sets have physical stuff in their transitive closures, and all physical objects are essentially mathematical. If we then ask our question about the relationship between the mathematical and the physical in Cartesian form[23] — are there two distinct substances, mathematical and physical? — I think the realist has the beginnings of a negative answer. The existence of mathematical entities is just the existence of physical stuff with certain structural properties; the existence of numerable physical objects is the existence of mathematical ones.

The picture I'm suggesting shows a single reality that is inseparably physical and mathematical. Physics and mathematics are two sciences, along with chemistry, biology, psychology, and others, that study aspects of this reality. Each science has its own subject matter, its own techniques and methods, but this does not mean that the world itself is divided into the physical, the mathematical, the chemical, the biological, the psychological, and so on. Rather, the world is a complex whole with many interlocking aspects.

But finally, no matter what the merits or demerits of this attempt at bonehead monism, this much remains clear: once we see how strange a completely nonmathematical world would be, our own world begins to reveal itself as intensely mathematical. It contains individuals — singletons — and it contains things with higher number properties — finite sets of physical objects. Given the success and the naturalness of ordinary arithmetic, such elementary set-theoretic axioms as Pairing and Union become reasonable assumptions. Higher set theory, via Infinity and Power Set, provides us with an instantiation of an important mathematical structure — the continuum — which we then postulate to be instantiated by the points of space-time.[24] The resulting physico-mathematical theory is again highly successful, from the point of view of both physical and mathematical methodologies.

V

My central point here has been that various naturalistic versions of mathematical realism are more similar than they are different. The moral is that instead of concentrating on the painstaking description of these (possibly nonexistent) shreds of disagreement, we would do better to concentrate on the much more pressing, much more serious, and much more important issues that we face together. What are those?

It has been remarked that the Continuum Problem is at least partly a philosophical one. On the one hand, we need mathematical facts about the interrelations of various new hypotheses, and their consequences and potential consequences for the size of the continuum; contemporary set theorists are providing these. On the other hand, we need a philosophical/psychological theory of how we know about sets; we need philosophical clarification of the concept of set itself; we need a philosophical/sociological study of the actual methods used by set theorists to try to resolve the disputes between the hypotheses under consideration; and we need creative suggestions, based on our study of actual methods, for how those methods might be rationally extended to produce new, more powerful hypotheses. To pull our weight in this endeavor, we realistic philosophers of mathematics should work together to provide these.[25]

Notes

1. I don't intend to give any examples of such questions; I insist only that the realist is not committed to their nonexistence. Notice that set-theoretic statements might also be ambiguous because there are distinct set-theoretic universes. I discuss this possibility in *Realism in Mathematics*, forthcoming.

2. See K. Godel, "Russell's Mathematical Logic" and "What Is Cantor's Continuum Problem?" in *Philosophy of Mathematics*, edited by P. Benacerraf and H. Putnam (Cambridge, 1983), 447–69, 470–85, and P. Maddy, "Perception and Mathematical Intuition," *Philosophical Review* 89 (1980): 163–96, and "Sets and numbers", *Nous* 15 (1981): 494–511. I discuss the differences between Godel's position and my own in *Realism in Mathematics*.

3. These two problems, both much discussed in the literature, can be traced to Benacerraf's two articles, "Mathematical Truth" and "What Numbers Could Not Be," in *Philosophy and Mathematics*, edited by Benacerraf and Putnam, 272–296, 403–20. (I attempt platonistic responses in the first articles cited in note 2.) Benacerraf's statement of the epistemological problem depends on the causal theory of knowledge, but I argue in "Mathematical Epistemology: What Is the Question?" (*Monist* 67 (1984): 46–55) that the underlying difficulty for mathematical platonism is independent of that particular theory.

4. For example, see S. Shapiro, "Mathematics and Reality," *Philosophy of Science* 50 (1983): 523–48, M. Resnik, "Mathematics as a Science of Patterns," *Nous* 15–16 (1981–82): 95–105, 529–50, and "How Nominalistic Is Hartry Field's Nominalism?," *Philosophical Studies* 47 (1985): 163–81.

5. By "object," here and elsewhere, I mean object in the sense of the preceding paragraph, in the sense that "any object can come third in some infinite progression." (In infinitely many, of course.) When structuralists refer to "objects," they mean positions in a structure "which derive their being from being positions in that structure" (Resnik, "How Nominalistic . . . ?" 177). A fullblown ontological relativity, would jeopardize this distinction, but I'll leave that issue aside for now.

6. This is the structure determined by the epsilon relation. Sets are not objects, but positions in this pattern. Shapiro steers clear of ontological issues, calling himself a "methodological realist" ("Mathematics and Reality," 536). Resnik, on the other hand, characterizes himself unblushingly as a "platonist" ("Mathematics as a Science", 529).

7. See Maddy, "Sets and Numbers."

8. This surely goes for the perceptual theory sketched in Maddy, "Perception and Mathematical Intuition." Incidentally, my goal in that paper was to make plausible the claim that a naturalistic theory of set perception could be given; the question of which such theory is the correct one is far beyond my small range of expertise.

9. Shapiro claims that the natural number structure is instantiated by "an infinite sequence of strokes /// . . . " ("Mathematics and Reality," 534), but this is obviously not true in any physical sense.

10. For example, see H. Putnam, "Mathematics without Foundations," in *Philosophy and Mathematics*, edited by Benacerraf and Putnam, 295–311. Putnam's position is developed by G. Hellman, "A modal Interpretation of Mathematics," circulated manuscript, 1986. Traces of structuralism can be found in both these writers. I apologize in advance for the brief discussion of modalism in the text. It suffers because I've never really been able to appreciate the gain purportedly won by moving from mathematical objects to possibilities. Perhaps as a matter of philosophical predisposition, I, with Quine, "prefer . . . abstract objects to modal operators anyway. Leveling modalities is in my view a major service of abstract objects." ("Review of Parsons's *Mathematics in Philosophy*," *Journal of Philosophy* 81 (1984): 783–94, especially 784.) Resnik takes a similar position in "How Nominalistic . . . ?" I should point out that sets, as I understand them, aren't "abstract" if this means they must lack spacio-temporal location. See G. Katz, *Language and Other Abstract Objects* (Totowa, N.J., 1981), 219, note 29. See also J. Mayberry, "On the Consistency Problem for Set Theory I," *British Journal for the Philosophy of Science* 28 (1977): 1–34.

11. See Putnam, "Mathematics without Foundations," 309.

12. Less picturesquely phrased, the question is: why should it be easier to explain knowledge of mathematical possibilities than to explain knowledge of mathematical objects? In "How Nominalis-

tic . . . ?" Resnik argues that an epistemology adequate for Field's version of modalism can be altered to provide an epistemology for realism. (Though Field's modalities are logical, Resnik points out that our knowledge of logical truths need not be—and in this case probably isn't—logical.)

13. Resnik is explicit on this point. See "How Nominalistic . . . ?" 177.

14. These reasons are considered in some detail in my "Believing the Axioms," forthcoming in the *Journal of Symbolic Logic.*

15. See Shapiro, "Mathematics and Reality," 539–40. P. Kitcher also leaves open the possibility of reconciliation with platonistic realism (see *The Nature of Mathematical Knowledge* [New York, 1983], 148). A. Hazen (in "Platonism and Structuralism") also argues that structuralist realism and platonistic realism are equivalent in some sense.

16. See Quine, "Review of Parsons," 788.

17. See, for example my "Perception and Mathematical Intuition" and *Realism in Mathematics.* The one-apple example below is Chihara's in "A Godelian Thesis Regarding Mathematical Objects: Do They Exist? And Can We Perceive Them?" *Philosophical Review* 91 (1982): 211–27.

18. For the structural realist, the question is: is there a perceptual difference between the apple and the configuration instantiating the same pattern as the first von Neumann ordinal under successor? To avoid clumsiness here and elsewhere, I occasionally express issues from the point of view of the set-theoretic realist without paraphrasing to the structural perspective as well.

19. Quine has recommended this identification as a formal expedient for simplifying the extensionality axiom, among other things, in set theory with individuals. See *Set Theory and Its Logic* (Harvard, 1969), 30–33. I'm suggesting that there might be other reasons as well.

20. The semantic role of the idea that reality comes with structure is discussed in my "How the Causal Theorist Follows a Rule," *Midwest Studies in Philosophy* 9 (1984): 457–77. A similar position, that natural individuals and natural kinds "carve reality at the joints," can be found in D. Lewis, "New Work for a Theory of Universals," *Australian Journal of Philosophy* 61 (1983): 343–70.

21. This is reminiscent of Putnam's position in "What Is Mathematical Truth?":

> Mathematics makes assertions that are objectively true or false, independently of the human mind, and . . . *something* answers to such mathematical notions as 'set' and 'function'. This is not to say that reality is somehow bifurcated—that there is one reality of material things, and then, over and above it, a second reality of 'mathematical' things. A set of objects, for example, depends for its existence on those objects: if they are destroyed, then there is no longer such a set.

(*Collected Papers*, vol. 1, 2d ed. (Cambridge, 1979), 60.) Notice, however, that Putnam counts material objects as nonmathematical.

22. In this connection, note that Zermelo explicitly refers to the empty set as "fictitious" in his "Investigations in the Foundations of Set Theory," in *From Frege to Godel*, edited by van Heijenoort (Harvard, 1967), 199–215, especially 202.

23. This classical way of posing the question was suggested to me by Pat Manfredi.

24. Again, some of the actual arguments used to support set-theoretic axioms are described in my "Believing the Axioms." I should also note that even so staunch a nominalist as Hartry Field admits that once some sets are admitted, various scientific and mathematical considerations would naturally lead to the rational postulation of more. (See his *Science without Numbers* (Princeton, 1980), 4–5.) Indeed, at least one of Field's positions is "realist" in the sense used here because it assigns a truth value to the Continuum Hypothesis. (See M. Resnik, "Ontology and Logic," *History and Philosophy of Logic* 6 (1985): 191–209, especially 198–99.) Finally, Shapiro also sees connections between his structuralism and Field's "nominalism." (See Shapiro, "Mathematics and Reality," § 6.)

25. This material is based on work supported by the National Science Foundation under Grant No. SES-8509026, and by the University of Illinois at Chicago. I am grateful to both institutions. My thanks also go to Stewart Shapiro and to Michael Resnik for their helpful comments on an earlier draft.

Conscious Beings in a Gradual World

PETER UNGER

There are certain rather deep-rooted beliefs we have about ourselves that, as I hope to make convincing, run counter to the objective view of the world our scientifically oriented society has achieved over the past several centuries. From my own perspective, one of the most central of these beliefs is this: To the question of whether some future entity will be *me*, there will always be a definite answer, either "yes" or else "no." A closely related belief is that this answer will be ensured by the metaphysics of the situation, not merely by some conventions of our language (for delimiting the range of application for 'me' and kindred terms). Perhaps the question of whether some future entity will be a certain present chair, or a certain bush, also will always have a definite answer, either "yes" or "no." But any belief we have to that effect is less firm, not so deep-rooted. And we believe that if the latter question always has such a definite answer, that will be owing, very largely, to linguistic conventions governing the range of the terms involved, of 'chair' or of 'bush', not to any deep facts about chairs or bushes.

Along with these deep-rooted intuitive beliefs that we have about ourselves, we have intuitive, and equally unscientific beliefs, about consciousness. To the question of whether some being is, or will be, conscious, we intuitively believe that there must always be a definite answer, either "yes" or else "no." And we believe, intuitively, that the definiteness of this answer is due to some deep fact about consciousness, to the metaphysics of being conscious, not merely to conventions governing 'conscious' and kindred terms.

These intuitive beliefs about ourselves, I feel certain, are strongly connected with the intuitive beliefs about consciousness. As we strongly believe, we are involved with the phenomenon of consciousness in such a way that it is true that we are each a conscious being. But few of us strongly believe that chairs, or even bushes, are so involved with, or connected to, consciousness; as we mainly believe, they are not conscious beings.

What is far from certain is the nature of the connection between our belief in the all-or-none character of our existence and our belief in the all-or-none character of consciousness. Perhaps one way that the beliefs are connected is via some such believed proposition as this: For any particular one of us to exist, there must be a certain capacity for consciousness; the required capacity will then be that individual's capacity for consciousness. If my capacity for consciousness really is no more, then there is no more me. We do not think such a thing about any particular chair or, for most of us, even about any particular bush. But I do not want to dwell on, or to refine, the details of the hypothesized connection. For present purposes, a methodological point will suffice: We are likely to reevaluate our intuitive beliefs about ourselves only to the extent that we also reevaluate our beliefs about consciousness.[1]

As I will argue, our intuitive beliefs about both matters should be reevaluated as seriously as possible. That is because these beliefs conflict with our well-evidenced and strongly believed scientific view of the world. The conflict is one of substance, not one of marginal detail, and is not likely to find adequate resolution. Faced with a choice, we are most rational to favor views of the self and of consciousness, however their details might be worked out, that are in harmony with our developing science and, to the extent that it is psychologically possible for us, to abandon our deep-rooted, less reflective beliefs. This is true because we are more deeply confident of the main thrust of our scientific view than we are of those deliverances of intuition.

As with any very general philosophical matter, it cannot be conclusively demonstrated that there is this conflict between these intuitive beliefs and our web of scientific belief. But I do think that it can be argued rather convincingly that there is, indeed, such a conflict. A main way to do this is to notice what we believe about certain *spectra* of cases. The spectra that are simplest, most directly relevant, and, thus, most persuasive are sequences of cases that form the core of certain sorites arguments that I first presented in another connection.[2] But some related spectra can serve as useful complements, reinforcing whatever case can be most simply and directly made.[3] In as relevant a fashion as we can manage, we will confront our intuitive beliefs about our existence and about consciousness with fine-grained sorites-style spectra of cases. It is hoped that this confrontation may cause us to reevaluate seriously these intuitive beliefs.

Reconsidering these beliefs may lead to rejecting them, at least when we are involved in articulating our more theoretical, philosophical, and scientifically endorsed thinking. This may lead us to reevaluate some related beliefs as well, which, in general, will not be such intuitively appealing ones.

Reevaluating our deep-rooted beliefs, in particular those about our own existence and identity, is not just a theoretical endeavor, however difficult or interesting. It is as well, I believe, a line of thinking that might rationally affect our *attitudes* toward ourselves. First, the appropriate consideration of the sorites spectra can help us toward the view, though, of course, cannot conclusively establish the view, that most of what rationally matters most to us in the neighborhood of our (strict) survival is not our survival itself but, rather, the obtaining of certain continuities that, in ordinary cases, do so much to ground the truth of judgments of survival. Along this first line, there may be another, and perhaps a larger, lesson that these metaphysical reflections can teach us: The pattern of our rational self-concern should reflect what we take to be the true facts of natural reality; if the latter really is a highly gradual affair, then our pattern of self-concern should be, if not quite so gradual, at least rather similarly gradual. This gradual pattern of concern will be the rational one for a person to have, of course, not only with regard to his own existence, but also with regard to anyone else he cares much about: members of his family, his friends, and so on. Now, as should be emphasized, although these two points rather naturally go together, neither one logically implies the other: So it might be, or it might turn out, that our pattern of self-concern, or of personal concern, should be relevantly gradual, whether or not matters of personal identity, or strict survival, always go together with "what most matters in survival." Still, I suspect that certain considerations of spectra may move us toward rationally accepting the natural pair of ideas that these two points together form. But to argue persuasively from considerations of spectra for either member of this pair, let alone for both, would in itself require a lengthy essay. So I postpone for another time a treatment of issues of "what matters," or of rational personal concern.[4]

There is a second main way that the reevaluation of our intuitive beliefs, about our existence being all-or-none, may affect our attitudes about ourselves. We are strongly disposed to think of ourselves as *entities*, each one of us an entity in his or her own right, and not *merely* as aspects, parts, or regions of some entity, at least of the universe as a whole. Thus, in this fundamental respect, we take ourselves to be very different from, say, noses, mountains, and the Atlantic Ocean. The entityhood or individuality of these latter seems much more vulnerable to serious questioning.

The thought that I am an entity, and am an individual, encourages me to have ideas and attitudes about myself that are positive, as well as others that are negative. On the positive side, I can feel that I am an autonomous agent, that, for being an individual, I have a certain dignity. On the negative side, I can feel that I have a certain aloneness, that I am all too isolated from the rest of the world. If I were a Cartesian soul, or a Newtonian atom, I might very clearly be an entity. Then I might enjoy those advantages, but perhaps only at the cost of such fearful isolation.

Appropriate sorites spectra can discourage in us the idea that we are each entities. They might at the same time encourage in us, at least to some extent, the thought that we are each merely regions, aspects or parts of whatever is sufficiently greater. This opposite thought has its own emotional advantages and disadvantages, ones that are quite the opposite of those associated with the idea that we are each entities in our own right. On the positive side, as a mere region, aspect, or part of the universe as a whole, I am not isolated and terribly alone, but am at one with the rest of the world. On the other side, I now seem swallowed up by, or merged into, so much else. Consequently, I seem to have so much less, perhaps nothing at all, in the way of autonomy and individual dignity. These are the attractions of, and the costs of, a conception of ourselves as not entities in our own right, as might perhaps have been advocated by Buddha and, perhaps, by Spinoza.

We are torn between these two conceptions of ourselves, each of which is at once appealing and repellent. Or, perhaps we uncomfortably bounce back and forth between the two. But, in any event, what is the truth about ourselves? As far as our best evidence indicates, are we entities or not? As I suggested before, our sorites spectra will at least seem to encourage the idea that, given the general truth of science, we are not so much as entities. But perhaps we may achieve a deeper, at least a more interesting, understanding of what idea it is that these spectra really do most strongly encourage.

On any reflection, the most plausible, even if not the most interesting, view of these matters will be one associated with a semantic approach advocated by David Lewis.[5] In my recent book, *Philosophical Relativity*, I called this view *contextualism*, and discussed it at some length.[6] On this contextualist approach, statements to the effect that we are entities, or individuals, will have their truth-values determined, in substantial measure, by the contexts in which the statements are made and understood, in general, and, in particular, by the interests we have when in those judgmental contexts.

Applying some reasoning that I presented in that recent book, we may arrive at what may be the most interesting, even if not the most plausible, hypothesis about the topic area: Perhaps our sorites spectra will encourage the idea that, given the general truth of science, there simply is *no fact of the matter* as to whether we are entities or not, no fact of the matter as to whether we are entities each in his or her own right or merely aspects, regions, or parts of an appropriately great entity. Our spectra may help show us that, given our best evidence, we may avoid, or even be forced away from, the perplexing dichotomy about ourselves. Insofar as reason has any say in these matters, we may be all but forced to relax, and not worry, about whether we are too deeply isolated and alone; so there may be no real worry for us, either, about whether we are too deeply lacking in autonomy and individuality. At least insofar as reason and our conscious thought processes have a say, this may allow us to have a more balanced attitude toward ourselves, neither lusting after nor fearing what we may mistakenly believe to be extreme real possibilities for human beings, for the human condition.

There is a long way to go before we can make credible, even to a moderate degree, the hypothesis that there is no fact of the matter as to whether we are entities. Indeed, the first part of that journey, which will occupy something like half of this essay, is far from easy going. That is the presentation of the argument that, given our best evidence, matters of our existence, and of consciousness, are metaphysically indeterminate matters. To prepare the way for this argument, I want to suggest some sources of our intuitive beliefs to the contrary.

In earlier work, I argued at some length that these unreliable sources are indeed at work with us, at least in regard to the matter of our own existence.[7] Now I will suggest that they are at work in regard to the matter of consciousness as well. Once the former suggestion is found plausible, the latter should also seem plausible. Once we find it at least plausible that some of the sources of the intuitive beliefs are unreliable, perhaps even are false views that we implicitly maintain, we will be more ready to accept arguments against these beliefs. Accordingly, I will begin by outlining conflicting views of ourselves, which, in something of an unstable competition, pull us in different directions when we think philosophically about ourselves and about our relation to consciousness.

1. THE OBJECTIVE VIEW, THE SUBJECTIVE VIEW, AND COMPROMISE VIEWS OF THE SELF

Our developing scientific view of the world includes a developing view of ourselves, of all conscious beings, as parts of the world. This means the development of what I have called the *objective view of the self*. On this view, we are each entities in objective space and objective time and, at least as the evidence has it, entities that each occupy a finite portion of that space for a finite portion of that time. Because of this, there is not much trouble in understanding how it is that, on this view, we might enter into causal relations with each other, and with other things in objective space and time. Because of that, there is not much trouble in understanding how it is that we might learn a good deal about each other, and about other spatiotemporal things.

On the objective view, a conscious being need not always be conscious. And, as the evidence has it, we go through periods when we do not have conscious thought or experience: certain periods of ordinary deep sleep, periods when we are strongly under the influence of a powerful anesthetic, periods when a few of us are in comas. But it may be that this objective view requires each of us to be related to consciousness in at least some such way as this: In *at least a very weak* sense or way, each of us must have the *capacity* for consciousness. Even if existing technology cannot bring some people out of comas before they die, there must be some as yet unavailable processes that would have this effect without, at the same time, changing who they are. Otherwise, their brains will be so unstructured as to be little more than living meat, and no other parts or aspects of them will do any more to subserve their existence.

At all events, we may view one of the main aims of science as filling in the details of some such objective view of ourselves. Only in that way, it seems plausible, can science help us to achieve a detailed understanding of ourselves.

We all deeply believe in such an objective view of ourselves and, largely for that reason, fear physical death if we are anywhere near our prime and our lives are going even reasonably well for us. But we also have deeply ingrained in our thinking a quite opposite view of ourselves, what I have called the *subjective view of the self*. On this conflicting view, none of us exists in objective space, nor even in objective time, but each has his own subjective time, the only time relevant to assessing matters of his own existence. Moreover, on the subjective view, the relationship we have to consciousness is most clear and direct: Each of us must be conscious at every moment of our existence, where these moments are those of the subjective time of the being in question.

One thing that leads us to the subjective view is our inability to make our objective view seem anything like a complete and adequate account of things. We find it hard to find a place for the way things *appear to a conscious subject* anywhere in the objective order. So we seem to find a place for them elsewhere: in the conscious experience of subjects, ourselves, who are really nowhere in the objective order at all. Another thing that can make some such view seem appealing is the ability, which we seem to have, of imagining away as mere inessentials everything but our consciousness. Descartes's discussion of this is the most famous, of course, but even I remember going through some such musings as a child. Once a view of ourselves as so apart from the world is at all appealing for intellectual reasons, however confused those may or may not be, a more emotional motivation may come into play as well. As pure subjects, we seem much less vulnerable to complete cessation: Whatever happens to any brain or body I may have, there may be more conscious experience left for me yet, even if it is only within my own subjective time. And, other things equal, I would very much like more such experience for me. It should not seem surprising, then, that, perhaps in conflict with other self-views, and so perhaps in a somewhat weak and unstable manner, we implicitly maintain such a pure subjective view of ourselves. We may continue to do this even as we increasingly come to recognize difficulties for such a view.

On the subjective view, it is very difficult, perhaps impossible, to understand how we might be involved in any causal relations with each other, or with any of the objective things in objective space and time. Because of that, it is hard to understand how, on this view, anyone might learn anything much about anything beyond the contents of his own mind, that is, beyond his own conscious thought and experience. Partly for these reasons, our belief in the objective view is stronger, in most contexts psychologically more efficacious on us, than is our belief in this conflicting subjective view.

Because both views pull on us, we are apt to form and hold compromise views as well. Such compromise views may have a certain instability, for their aspects come from radically different views of the self whose parts do not fit together well or easily. But some compromise views may have a certain influence on us, intermittently and temporarily. All of us may implicitly contrive such compromise views, but only philosophers will ever bother to articulate them. And only very able philosophers will be able to express a compromise view for the first time, or to newly express such a view in a way that is at all appealing.

Descartes's official view of the self is, I think, one such compromise view. The self does not occupy, nor perhaps even exist in, objective space. But the self does exist in, and even persists through, objective time. So, there is an objective aspect here as well as a subjective one. For Descartes, there is another feature taken from our subjective view as well: The self is conscious at every moment of existence – and its existence is continuous with respect to its relevant time. Because Descartes has the relevant time be objective time, he must posit that we all really do have conscious experience at every moment we are sleeping, we just forget a very great deal of it almost immediately. Because of this tremendous forgetting, we falsely think that we dream only intermittently, rather than the whole night through. And that is the sort of thing, for Descartes, that happens with people who go into, and then come out of, a deep coma.

Butler and Reid present a compromise view that is, on the whole, more appealing. That is because it draws more from the objective view, which we more strongly believe, and less from the conflicting subjective view, an outlook of whose truth we are less fully convinced. On their view, as I understand it, we need not have so direct a connection with consciousness as the subjective view demands. Rather than always be conscious, what we must always have is only the capacity to be conscious. As with Descartes, the "always" here refers to objective time, not to the subject's very own time, and the subject must persist through objective time continuously, or else cease completely and never again exist. As with Descartes, this subject will have no spatial structure; perhaps he will not occupy space at all; perhaps he will not even be at any point in objective space. Nor does it seem possible, on this view, for the subject to have any structure at all, as the subject must be absolutely indivisible, in every conceivable sense or way.

How it is that a subject with no structure will, even while not conscious, possess the capacity for consciousness is hard to understand. The view seems to present us with other mysteries as well. Nonetheless, it is at least a somewhat appealing compromise view. I suggest that it is something like this that most of us (weakly and intermittently) believe, insofar as we believe that we each have separate souls whose persistence beyond physical death might allow us strictly to survive such an awful but inevitable event.

On the subjective view of the self, and on such compromise views, whether a given person exists at a given time is a question that will always receive a definite answer, either "yes" or else "no." And the (definiteness of the) answer will not be owing, in any substantial way, to any conventions that we implicitly maintain. Moreover, the conception of consciousness that fits best with all these views is one on which any question regarding the presence or absence of consciousness will also receive a definite answer, an answer whose definiteness will not (importantly) depend on our conventions governing the semantics of 'conscious' and kindred terms. That is because, on these views, there is no ready way to think of consciousness as importantly depending on processes, structured entities, or relations among such things, the obtaining of which is a matter of degree.

If this is right, then our deep-rooted belief that our existence is metaphysically all-or-none, or is *metaphysically determinate*, may be motivated in very large part by our very deep, even if not extremely efficacious, adherence to the subjective view. So may be our deep-rooted belief in the metaphysically determinate character of consciousness. The subjective view may motivate these beliefs in two ways: directly and indirectly. At this point, the direct motivation needs no comment. But it may be useful now to offer this reminder about indirect motivation: Our subjective view motivates indirectly by contributing to at least somewhat appealing compromise views, like that of Butler and Reid, which in turn motivate the intuitive beliefs about metaphysical determinacy.

I have argued, previously and at some length, that we should strive to develop only our objective view of ourselves, in a way that is informed by scientific development, and place to the side as unpromising our other implicitly held views of ourselves, both the subjective view and compromise views.[8] Only in that way will we do much to increase our understanding of ourselves and how we relate to the rest of the world.

This route of development means tracing out the main implications of our scientifically informed, objective view, of that version of it as is best evidenced by scientific findings that seem fairly well established. Such a version of the objective view will include the idea that, among such processes and things as are at the middle level of the objective order, from cells to solar systems and somewhat beyond, almost all involve an enormous amount of *gradualness*. We may be able to trace out these implications of gradualness if we focus on certain sorites-style spectra of cases, certain of those that our scientific view endorses as spectra whose cases are *real possibilities*.

When we proceed to develop our objective self-view, we may draw conclusions that go against ideas motivated by our subjective view, both directly and by way of compromise views. Sometimes we will find ourselves resisting these conclusions. But if our resistance to them is mainly motivated by these other, conflicting self-views, we may do well to accept those conclusions anyhow. That may be a benefit, perhaps ultimately the greatest benefit, of articulating our implicitly held views of the self that conflict with our objective self-view. I suggest that two of these conclusions, related to each other, will be the falsity of our belief that matters of our existence are metaphysically determinate and the falsity of our belief that matters of consciousness are likewise all-or-none.

2. THE SELF, CONSCIOUSNESS, AND THE SORITES OF DECOMPOSITION

More than two thousand years ago, in ancient Greece, there was developed the paradox of the heap, of the *soros*, also called the *sorites paradox*. The original sorites was an argument to the effect that there are no heaps of things: Our attempts to think coherently about any such alleged entities are incoherent and futile. This nihilistic argument took two forms: as a direct argument and as a *reductio ad absurdum*, or indirect argument. In both forms, it is a powerful and perplexing argument, one that has received many mutually incompatible responses. As the disagreement among them serves to indicate, none of the responses is impressively adequate or sufficiently illuminating.

In its direct form, the argument can proceed like this: Consider a situation where it is clear that there is no heap of beans; for example, a tabletop with only one bean on it. Do nothing but add a single bean to the situation in a way, whatever it may be, that is most conducive toward creating a heap of beans there. Assume that the only change is the one just made by your bean placement (and whatever is logically entailed thereby). The difference of one bean, however placed, will not mean the difference between a situation with no heap of beans and a situation with at least one such heap. This is the argument's main principle, intuitively compelling. So with two beans, there is no heap of beans there, a result that is most acceptable in any case. Place another bean there, as conducively as you wish, that, then, making the only change. Owing to the principle, there will not be a heap of beans there even so, a result that seems acceptable enough. This bean-by-bean procedure is repeated however many times, say, one hundred times. By the principle, there is no heap of beans on the tabletop, even though a hundred beans are so nicely arranged. But if there are ever any heaps of anything, then there will be a heap of a hundred beans there then. So, there never are any heaps at all.

The conclusion is most disagreeable, though not in itself of any great philosophical import. Heaps, whether real or only putative, were never an important part of any philosopher's ontology or metaphysics. But the reasoning is intriguing and troublesome. We want to object, of course, that with a hundred beans well arranged there most certainly is a heap of beans. Probably that is right: Suppose an almighty God made his existence known to you, by way of amazing miracles and such, and offered you a bet. Pick one of two incompatible propositions. If the one you pick is true, you get a million dollars and nothing bad. If the one you do not pick is true, you get a hundred thousand dollars and nothing bad. The propositions are: There is at least one heap of beans on the tabletop with the well-arranged hundred beans. There is not even one heap of beans there then. All of us would pick the first of these two propositions, not the second, its negation. So, whatever we may also believe to opposite effect, our main belief is that there is that heap; that there are many heaps; that the sorites argument is unsound. But we may have no adequate idea of how or why the argument is unsound. If so, as seems almost certain, then we have no adequate idea of why or how our belief that there are heaps is true, of why or how it fares better than a nihilist's assertion that there are no heaps. So, we have here an interesting logical problem, and perhaps an interesting semantic problem. But as heaps are not metaphysically important, the interest of the problem is confined to those areas. In a certain basic sense, though the problem is logically interesting, it is not philosophically deep or encompassing.

The same remarks apply to the indirect form of the argument, to the *reductio*. The ancient considerations take us no further than this. How is the sorites argument relevant to our metaphysically more interesting thought and, in particular, to our thought about ourselves? Modern considerations can show us that it is highly relevant in several ways. What are these modern considerations? They are apparently well-evidenced views to this effect: The mental aspects of our lives depend on the biological aspects. As the latter may be placed on instructively troublesome gradients, so may the former be so placed, and in a clear, detailed, and convincing way. (Moreover, the biological aspects of our lives depend on the chemical and even the physical composition of our biological parts. As questions of such composition may be treated along such gradients, so may the biological aspects of our lives.) That is the reason why even what might intuitively seem utterly unique and discrete mental phenomena, conscious thought and conscious experience, may be treated in this instructively gradual way.

Numerous sorites arguments about ourselves take advantage of these general features of modern science. Here is one that I have invented that is mildly, not wildly, hypothetical, that is rather clear in detail and, largely for those reasons, that is well suited for jolting our minds away from a lazy or complacent treatment of these issues. I will not now, as I have done before, try to be, or pretend to be, a nihilist about the self as a result of considering this *sorites of decomposition*.[9] Rather, we will assume that the reasonable bet with the generous God is the right one and, on that assumption, try to learn as much from this argument as we can.

As a matter of fact, we all strongly believe, each of us is constituted of, or is at least causally dependent on, very many small entities suitably arranged and working together: many organs, which are dependent on many tissues, which are dependent on many cells, which are dependent on many molecules, which are dependent on many atoms, which are dependent on many smaller and simpler things. We might choose to focus on, say, atoms, but let us focus now on cells.

Just as my brain is a more important, more central part of me than is my stomach, so my nerve cells, especially those of my brain, are more important cellular parts of me than are, say, the fat cells of my legs. But no single cell, nor any very small group of cells, is terribly important to my existence, not even any neuron, or any ten neurons, of my brain. All of us strongly believe this to be so, influenced as we are by centuries of science.

Take away one cell from me. If I exist in the first place, I will still be there. As I just said, one cell is not all that important. Indeed, let us be cautious and conservative about all this. Take away a least important cell, presumably any one of many billions, in a most innocuous manner, say, gently scrape a peripheral skin cell off my leg. No such most innocuous cellular removal will mean the difference between a world with me in it and no me anymore. Any such net removal of one cell will not mean anything that momentous. Because we have this compelling principle, more compelling even than in the case of the alleged heaps, we can repeat this little procedure any number of times, billions upon billions of times. The end result will be, say, this: With only one cell left, I will still be around. But that is absurd; one cell, no matter which one, is not enough; I will not be around. We derive a contradiction. Perhaps the contradiction reflects badly on the supposition of my existence in the first place. More likely, we believe, it reflects badly on that compelling principle. But in what way does it do so?

Is the principle at fault because of some substantial fact, or to anything of much metaphysical significance? At first it might seem so. Perhaps at some point the removal of a cell killed me, I just could not take any more. I do not think that is right, but it does have some plausibility. Let us accommodate this worry that there may be a real line between life for me and death, a line due to some (instantaneous?) chain reaction, perhaps, that can be initiated by the removal of a single cell. In a manner that is mildly hypothetical, we can do this quite simply and effectively. We interpret our argument in the following way, or reformulate it to that effect.

Well before any biological danger occurs, we bring in life-support systems that will keep me going well beyond the points at which such danger might otherwise threaten. The components of these systems will be arranged so that they never become parts of me. So, at some fairly late stage, for example, I am, or consist of, a brain floating in a nutrient bath in a vat, stimulated and supplied with whatever is needed to keep me functioning optimally. The vat is not part of me, nor is the bath, nor are the computers that are sending in the stimulations and supplies. There may well be largely manufactured men, but this sort of case is not one that includes any such.

Here we have something of an assumption, but one that most of us believe, even if not with enormous confidence: Any of the processes going on in any (but the extremely minute sorts of) parts of me do not in any very *strong* way causally require those parts to be surrounded by my other parts, nor by entities very like those surrounding parts of mine. Processes going on in my liver, for example, can go on just as well, we think, under certain naturally possible conditions where that liver is not surrounded by my body, nor by an exact or near duplicate of my body, nor by any liverless organism at all. The liver may be placed in some suitable vat with a nutrient bath, and with artificial means of affecting it in exactly the ways the rest of my body ordinarily would. In *certain* of these cases, we must agree, the liver and what supports its continued functioning would form a notably organic whole, even if a whole most of whose parts were artificially produced and did not consist of protoplasm or even of organic compounds. But there are *other* such cases, we also believe, in which the liver does not combine with the rest to form anything of any such description. Even in these latter cases, the liver will not "know or care" that what provides its supporting and stimulating input is not integrated with it in such a special way. The rest of the world, by way of relevant parts thereof, can "fool" the liver into functioning just as it does now in my body. Whatever (nonrelationally described) processes my liver is going through now in me, it could go through just as well as a sufficiently supported but isolated organ. The same considerations apply as well to my brain, and to any (contiguous) part of my brain.

Like the liver, my brain, or as much of it as any relevant situation contains, can be "fooled" into undergoing any of the processes it would undergo in the most ordinary surroundings. Even when it is isolated and not part of any interesting organic, let alone personal, whole, the brain, or any relevant part thereof, can be "fooled" into reacting as if it were suitably attached to ever so many suitably arranged cells so as to form a quite normal, whole human being. We might call the somewhat weakly believed proposition that we employ when thinking about our decomposition spectrum the *assumption of complete functional indifference*. This assumption is far from obvious, and we are not terribly confident that it is true. Nonetheless, on the whole, we believe that it is true. It is worthwhile to trace out the consequences of such a believed assumption, and that is one thing that we are in the midst of doing.

In the next section, we will confront a naturally occurring sorites-style spectrum, one centered on the development of a fertilized egg into, eventually, a rational human person. Thinking about that spectrum can be a rather confident enterprise.

A century or two ago, it was widely believed that there was a sharp metaphysical difference between the living and the nonliving. Given the evidence available at the time, the belief was reasonable enough. Now this belief is not so widely held and is not reasonable. We know about viruses, about the way in which even human death is a *somewhat* gradual process; we know too much biology altogether. But suppose that one still believed in such a sharp metaphysical distinction.

In that case, one might think that there was a sharp difference between me and no me, owing to the difference between the living and the nonliving. This thought would be somewhat plausible. But the plausibility of the thought will fade in the light of our sorites of decomposition for oneself. In the spectrum of that argument, life is always present, even at the end, when there is just one living neuron. Because some people believe in such a sharp distinction even nowadays, this is one way in which our sorites is helpful in getting us to accept the idea that the matter of whether I exist is not metaphysically all-or-none, is not what we might call a *metaphysically determinate* matter.

Most of us are now well beyond having any strong belief that there is a metaphysical break between the living and the nonliving. But there is a related idea that we have not quite put behind us. This is the thought that there is a sharp metaphysical difference between the *conscious* and the *nonconscious*. It is this idea, I think, that lies behind so much of the appeal of the thought that our existence is always metaphysically determinate. Our sorites of the self helps us to deny this appealing and influential, but very probably false, idea.

In the spectrum of our sorites, there is almost certainly no consciousness at the end: A single neuron is, almost certainly, not conscious, nor does it constitute a unicellular being who is conscious. But at the beginning, there was a being who had a great capacity for consciousness, and who even was exercising that capacity, namely, me. In the process of cell-by-cell removal along with appropriate stimulation, when was there first no being with any such capacity? Owing to the continuous stimulation, whatever capacity for consciousness was present was always exercised.

The stimulatory systems that we employ to promote consciousness are relevantly in parallel, we most strongly believe, with the life-support systems that we have already considered. Without the help of such stimulatory systems, perhaps there would be a point, in a spectrum of suitable cell-by-cell decomposition, where there would be a "catastrophe" for consciousness. As far as our relevantly strong beliefs go, this would be a point where, in the vat, there is a greatest brain-part that, for want of a single cell, any one of many billions of equally good additions, supported no consciousness at all. But with one cell more, that brain-part would support consciousness. This would be a point in our spectrum where, without helpful outside stimulatory systems, the removal of any cell would be "catastrophic" for consciousness in relation to the organic entity in the vat. Many of us may not believe that there is such a point, but many others may believe that there is. Especially for these others, the natural possibility of appropriate stimulatory systems, we strongly believe, may avert any such catastrophe that might occur without their employment.

With appropriate stimulatory systems in place, there may be a smooth gradation in the way of consciousness associated with any greatest being at any point in our spectrum. Or can there be? A small but real worry remains. Perhaps the progressively diminished entity needs to have some periods of deep unconscious sleep, as we ordinary folks appear to require. Then let there be such periods of sleep, where, perhaps, the stimulatory system is not working full blast. We need only say this about the relation of these periods to our spectrum: Never is a cell removed during these periods, but we resume our cell-by-cell removal procedure once such a period is over. We now have no serious worry about the natural and gradual diminishment of consciousness in relation to our gradually diminished entity.

We asked the question: In the process of cell-by-cell removal along with appropriate stimulation, when is there first no being with a capacity for consciousness? Owing to the points just considered, we realize that, according to our strongest beliefs, any being in our spectrum with such a capacity will, at a relevant time, exercise that capacity. So, quite neatly, our question becomes this instructively baffling one: In our relevant spectrum of cases, when does there first occur no being that ever *is* conscious? Perhaps there is a definite answer to this question. But if there is, that answer must be owing largely to the meaning of our term "conscious," to conventions governing its proper application that we have implicitly established and maintained. There is no definite answer that is due simply to the metaphysics of the situation, to what there is in the nonconventional world. Nor is there a definite answer that is even mainly owing to such factual and substantial considerations. For, almost certainly, there never did occur any metaphysically dramatic break occasioned by the innocuous removal of just one (tied) least important (nerve) cell. This is an important point, so I should say something to make it as clear as possible.

Consider fifty men lined up according to height. At one end is a man who is seven feet tall; at the other is one who is five feet. No man differs in height by more than a quarter of an inch from any man standing next to him in the line. The man who is seven feet tall is, presumably, a tall man. The man at the other end is not a tall man. We go from the one to the other by decrements of no more than a quarter of an inch. When do we first come to a man who is not a tall man? Perhaps this question has a definite answer, even though we do not know the answer. But if it does, that answer must be mainly owing to our own conventions governing our own expression "tall man," not to substantial facts of the world or metaphysically sharp differences. There is no such difference between any two of the men in our line. That is clear as can be.

Before reflecting on the matters at some length, the matter of the difference between consciousness and no consciousness seems utterly different from the matter of the difference between the tall men and the others. Largely because of this, I imagine, the difference between me and no me also first seems so terribly different from any such highly conventional matter. Our sorites of decomposition about the self provides us with some lengthy reflection. This reasoning shows us that, very probably, there is not such an enormous difference between these matters after all. Just as the matter of the tall men involves no metaphysically important break, so the matter of consciousness, strange as it seems, involves none either. Nor is there any such metaphysically important difference involved in the question of survival in regard to any conscious earthly organism, myself included.

In addition to holding our developing objective self-view, we all favor other views of the self that clash with it. Our sorites argument convinces us how much more strongly we favor the first of these self-views that we maintain. It convinces us that other views, most of them more subjectively oriented, are not so strongly believed by us.

One clashing alternative view is the position that each of us has a soul that can survive the complete annihilation of all our physical parts, with no replacement by anything else that is physical. This is one instance, perhaps a particularly popular one, of what we have called a compromise view, a compromise between our objective view and our implicitly maintained subjective view. It is a view for which everyone in our culture has at least some sympathy, and for which some of us have a great deal. We would all like to believe strongly that, after our physical death, we survive by way of such a soul. There would not, then, come an absolute end for us, but just the end of our very intimate relation to a certain brain and body. Our sorites spectrum convinces us that, though we would like this to be true, we do not strongly believe that it is true. We may have a weak belief to this effect, but we have a much stronger belief in the opposite, more gloomy direction.

If I did have such a soul, then, at some point in the removal procedure, the removal of a single cell would make a dramatic difference. Presumably, this would occur when there were still many millions, if not many billions, of brain cells still left in the stimulating vat. At such a juncture, the removal of *any (tied) least important cell*, presumably any one of many millions, would make a metaphysically dramatic difference. Perhaps it would release my soul from my body, now from the remaining large part of my brain. Perhaps it would suddenly snuff out my soul altogether—souls not meant to endure such enormously gradual destructive procedures as this, being better suited to surviving the more abrupt failures of ordinary life. But, unless the soul is still hanging on with just that one neuron left at the end, which we strongly believe to be quite absurd, some such dramatic change must be occasioned by what is apparently such a very trivial removal. Whatever idle thoughts we may harbor in more wishful directions, almost all of us most strongly believe that no such metaphysically dramatic thing ever happens at any point in our considered sequence.

Our sorites of decomposition helps us to appreciate what are, in fact, our strongest and deepest beliefs about ourselves. These are not the same beliefs that were always so strong and deep for people. But people did not always have the developed, and still developing, scientific view of the world that we have now. In general outline, this view is almost certainly correct. That is what we strongly believe. A view of ourselves that fits with this, that is a part of this total scientific view, is almost certainly the only correct one. So, though we strongly wish and still weakly believe that we are enormously different from chimpanzees or mice or chickens or at least frogs, we do not strongly believe that we are all that different from them. Just as they do not have immaterial souls, so we do not; just as each of them will end with the breakdown of its body, so each of us will similarly end, completely and forever. From the broadest metaphysical perspective, facts like these are the main facts about our nature and the conditions of our existence. We wish that things were otherwise. But, as our sorites of decomposition helps to convince us, we very strongly believe that they are not.

In less emotional or less religious moods, we may allow that we are not all that different from chimpanzees or even frogs: both I and that frog each have a capacity for conscious experience. Perhaps we do not have souls, neither the frog nor I, but it may seem that each of us has a real essence. This real essence may concern only material reality, so that I will exist just in case a certain part of the material world is configured and functioning in just such a way as is required for my existence, and that frog will exist just in case some other part of material reality is configured and functioning in some other quite definite and particular way. In my case, just as in his, my real essence will set me apart from the rest of the world, so that we are each metaphysically significant objects, nothing like mere regions of the world in which consciousness sometimes occurs.

Thoughts like these represent versions of our metaphysics of essence and accident that have less to do with wishful thinking, perhaps, and that at least appear more naturalistic. These thoughts may do little to encourage the thought of life after physical death, but they would at least encourage an idea of ourselves, and of frogs, that gives us each some metaphysical dignity. Although it may be no great thing for us, we would like to think of ourselves as distinct entities, not as mere regions of a gradually variegated world, regions conventionally set off by the semantic conventions of certain conventionally demarcated entities, ourselves, that are not in a deeper and a less arbitrary way differentiated from the rest of the world. But our sorites considerations suggest to us that these ideas will find no more grounding in reality than appeals to an immaterial soul. Upon reflection, we are not very confident that we have *any* real essence, whether material or immaterial. Or, if we do have some such essence, we begin to think, it may not amount to very much; it may be no metaphysically determinate thing of any sort.

3. THE DEVELOPMENT OF THE HUMAN EMBRYO

The sorites just considered was an indirect argument, and it involved a spectrum of cases that is hypothetical, though not wildly hypothetical. As will be clarified later, that sorites of decomposition has certain advantages for us, at least certain psychological advantages, owing to its particular hypothetical character. Still, it would be good to have before us, in addition, a completely realistic, sorites-style spectrum that has almost all, if not quite all, the advantages of our mildly hypothetical spectrum. So much the better, too, if this spectrum can be seen in a situation that encourages a direct, rather than an indirect, sorites argument for the self. Fortunately, the world frequently presents us with a sorites, and a spectrum at its core, with both of these helpful features.

As the scientific evidence strongly indicates, there actually occurs a spectrum of cases involving each living human person that is of a gradual sorites sort. And this spectrum will encourage a nihilistic sorites argument that, though probably unsound, is a direct argument, no "mere" *reductio*. I refer to the development of a fertilized egg in the mother into a baby that is born and, for that matter, into a man or woman capable of rational inquiry. Let us consider this sorites argument, a form of what I have called a *sorites of accumulation*.[10]

We begin with the supposition that a fertilized egg, a single cell of a certain special sort, is not, and never was, me. In point of fact, this supposition is not necessary for the argument, as we will confirm shortly. But it makes for a simpler argument, and it is almost certainly correct.

No such cell is, or ever was me, or any person at all. True enough, under quite normal and common conditions, such cells develop into people. But that fact even entails that the individual cells, the zygotes, are not themselves people. For one thing develops not into something that it already is, but into something else. On reflection, there seems little truth in the idea that I was ever a single cell.

The claim just made may seem to have implications for a topic that is emotionally charged for very many people: abortion. Now, many people think that, although some abortions are wrong, some are not wrong. For most of these people, among the abortions that are all right are many that are performed very early in the process of embryonic development. But many other people think that this factor is of no moral significance, and that these early abortions are wrong, too. Some of these others feel constrained to think that fertilized eggs are people. But to defend their moral position, these people do not need to think any such thing, nor anything else that is so very likely false.

Just as it is (almost always) wrong to kill a person, so it may be (almost always) wrong to kill something that has the capacity, or the potential, to develop into a person (under normal and natural conditions.) Just as it would have been wrong at any point in my life to kill me, so it would also have been wrong to kill the zygote, and a bit later the very young embryo, that had the potential to develop into me, a potential that was in fact realized. Although I am inclined to think that in certain cases abortion is all right, that the life of the fetus is outweighed by other considerations, I am not sure whether any abortion is ever morally permissible; the question is difficult. But that question does not depend for its answer on the quite different question, apparently much easier, of whether a zygote, or even what it develops into after only three hours, is a person. And it is different from the related question of whether you or I, persons or not, were ever zygotes or were ever such small and barely differentiated groups of cells. All of this is, I think, about as clear as it can be.

But no matter how clear the point is, many will be resistant to it, or will confuse it with other points more or less closely related. The spectrum of cases presented by embryonic development, then, will remain emotionally charged for many. That is one reason why the sorites of decomposition of the self, considered in the previous section, presents a spectrum of cases that is more convincing for more people. A related reason is this: The single floating neuron left at the end of that previous sorites was not even something that, in any readily intelligible sense or way, had the potential or capacity to develop into me, or to become a person, or whatever. It was just a living cell, more or less close to the end of its narrow line.

Assuming that I was always much more than a single cell, we return to consider the actual spectrum of my embryonic development. So I was never a zygote. Still, as many people believe, about nine months later I emerged from my mother's body; there I was and here I am. What went on during those nine months? Not being a biologist, I do not know many of the details. But a lot did go on and, fortunately for me, it proceeded quite normally. About what then went on, one thing is clear even to those with the merest smattering of biological understanding: After the original division into two cells, my development did not take place by neatly adding one cell at a time onto an already existing group of cells. Rather, during any significant time interval, many cells more or less simultaneously grew and added their presence to those there before. Because my embryonic development proceeded in this somewhat less neat and simple manner, we cannot simply run in reverse the cell-by-cell sorites of decomposition just considered. If we could do that, we would have an actual sorites of accumulation that, in this respect, would be optimally convincing. But we can do almost as well.

We need only divide the time of the developmental process into sufficiently small finite units, each one (nearly) equal to the others. An appropriate unit of time might be a millionth of a second. If that seems too long, each might be a trillionth of a second. We can cut things as finely as we like, so long as we stick to a given unit once we have chosen it. Dramatic changes occur in nine months, and perhaps even in one month, but nothing much happens in any millionth of a second. If I am not there during a particular millionth, then not enough happens during the next millionth so that, for the first time, I exist. This is the main principle of the argument. To repeat our supposition, I am not there when only the zygote is there. So, by the principle, I am not there, either, just a millionth of a second later, nor a millionth of a second after that, nor a millionth of a second after *that*. We may apply our principle at will, and may consider it as thus applied, many billions of times. So, I am not there, either, after the nine months are up, nor even after forty years beyond that time. But if I do not exist as a man of forty years, then I never will exist. So there is never any me.

We will suppose that this direct argument is unsound. If so, then that is because its main principle is false, no matter how full of truth it may seem. It will do no good to question the supposition about the fertilized egg. For a similar sorites argument can show, just as well or as weakly, that there are no fertilized eggs anyway: If fertilization does occur, then it is a gradual process. It might take only a thousandth of a second, for all I know, but even that is a stretch of time. Consider trillionths of a second. If there is no fertilized egg during any given trillionth, but only an egg and a sperm, then there will not be one there during the next trillionth, either, for nothing so significant happens in that short a time. We repeat this analogous main principle analogously. So even after the whole thousandth of a second is through, and it looks as if there is a fertilized egg, there really is no fertilized egg in the situation. Then there never are any fertilized eggs at all. As should be clear now, a similar sorites can be advanced against the existence of individual sperm and individual eggs, as well as against the existence of my parents, and so on. So it is futile, and does nothing to further understanding, to challenge the supposition that I was never a single cell.

In regard to any of the relevant sorites arguments, it is the main principle that must be rejected. In particular, we will reject the one about me. But what is wrong with it? It is not to be faulted for overlooking any substantial matter of fact. There really *was* nothing much that happened in any particular millionth of a second. There was no metaphysically significant, emergent property that so suddenly flowered; there was no soul that suddenly found a physical home in these cells in my mother's womb; there was no metaphysically significant break that occurred anywhere in the process. Absolutely everything that was of any importance to my existence developed quite gradually. If the principle is at fault, and we are supposing that it is, that must be owing either entirely, or almost entirely, to its overlooking or violating certain conventions of our language: We maintain some conventions, whatever they may be, that allow such terms as "me" and "I" and "person" to discriminate situations much more finely than anyone would unreflectively suppose. That is what is going on.

Do our conventions mean that there will always be a determinate answer to the question of whether a given situation contains me? I do not know. At any rate, what I have just said is neutral on this point, though it may not appear to be. Reflection reveals this neutrality. So far as my statement goes, there might be borderline cases in the sequence, where it is neither false that I exist yet nor (fully) true either. But when do we first come upon such a case? Nothing of much metaphysical significance is happening, or is resulting from what happens, in any of the millionths of a second. There is nothing even remotely of that sort, it is all but certain, that should mean our passing from the clearly false to the indeterminate. There is no break in nonconventional reality to mark such a momentous shift. For even if this shift is not quite so momentous as that from false to true, nonetheless it is quite something. To make it happen, we must have conventions governing such terms as "I" and "me" that finely discriminate many situations from all the other situations, from all the situations where it is *not clearly false* that I exist. That is the point I made before, and now, with perhaps a bit more clarity, do well to make again.

It is hard for us to believe that our ordinary terms are so incredibly discriminating. It is almost like believing that vague terms are a species of absolutely precise terms. It is more difficult, however, to believe that anything of substantial, or metaphysical, moment occurs anywhere in the relevant processes. Perhaps hardest of all is for us to believe that I do not exist. But when we consider the enormously appealing negations of these three implausible propositions, it is the first that makes the weakest claim on us. Questions of our existence and identity, insofar as they are determinate matters at all, are settled primarily, if not entirely, by established conventions that we implicitly maintain.

For a while, some might be willing to give up the idea that nothing much happens metaphysically, rather than believe in the almost incredible sensitivity that must otherwise be ascribed to such terms as 'I', on pain of my otherwise never existing. They might look at such sorites as a proof that, science notwithstanding, after all, there are real essences for each of us, perhaps even immaterial souls that are our cores. But this thought will be to little avail. For similar sorites arguments can be leveled against twigs and cushions. And though almost all would want to maintain that such things do exist, few will want to ascribe souls, or any interesting real essences, to the twigs and cushions lying about. So we must maintain that such terms as 'twig' and 'cushion' are so enormously sensitive, finely discriminating at the level of atoms and beyond. Since we must do this for these terms anyway, and for so many other referring expressions of our language, there is almost no extra cost in making the same supposition for 'I' and 'me' and 'person'. Although some may find the acceptance of personal souls attractive for a while, in light of these considerations, few would maintain this way out of the dilemma concerning ourselves that our fine-grained spectra all but force on us.

Questions of our existence, identity, and survival are what we may call *metaphysically indeterminate matters*. Parfit sometimes says or implies that these matters are *indeterminate matters all things considered.*[11] That may or may not be. But the consideration of various spectra of cases, no matter how convincing it may be about deeper questions, does nothing to encourage his logically more ambitious idea. Nor is there any other consideration of which I am aware that does this for us. So, we must be more cautious in regard to the logic of the situation.

Instead of what Parfit holds, we should say this: These questions may or may not always have determinate answers. If they do not, then, they are metaphysically indeterminate matters, and that is why there is room for cases with no determinate answers at all. On the other hand, if they do, as well they might, then their always having determinate answers is not owing to metaphysical considerations. In *any* case, then, what our sorites spectra (almost certainly) show is that these matters are *metaphysically* indeterminate. In every case, whether or not they are settled in some *other* way, they are *not* settled by any language-independent facts about ourselves, by any metaphysically significant facts about us, by any facts regarding our real essence or nature. For, as we have ample reason to believe, and as reflection on these spectra fully convinces us, there are no such facts.

4. THE CONVENTIONALITY OF CONSCIOUSNESS

Let us return to our mildly hypothetical spectrum from the sorites of decomposition, and let us try to see better what understanding of consciousness this spectrum encourages us to have. This question, it seems to me, is of considerable interest in its own right, no matter what bearing it may or may not have on questions of the self and personal identity.

With enough of my brain in the vat, perhaps half or even a third, and that smallish entity being appropriately stimulated, there are processes going on that are correctly called instances of consciousness. With only two neurons sending electric charges to each other, there are, unless our science is very much mistaken, no such processes. About this we can be clear. Somewhere in between, it seems all but certain, processes are going on about which we cannot be so clear. Perhaps the semantics of our word, 'conscious', is so sensitive as to rule decisively with respect to every one of these processes: Then, for each process in the sequence, it is either (fully) true that it is an instance of, or supports, consciousness or it is (fully) true that it is not. Or perhaps, alternatively, there are processes for which our semantics provides no definite ruling. That matter is one we need not discuss much, for it is a question of language more than of metaphysics. So far as the metaphysics goes, we are confident, though not absolutely certain, that there is no decisive break anywhere in the sequence, between the processes "of consciousness" and the other "lesser" processes. This is surprising, but it seems that we must accept that it is so, on pain of not doing full justice to our accepted scientific world view.

We do not have any clear conception about the nature of the best of these lesser processes, of processes that barely fail to be (completely, correctly called) processes of consciousness. There is nothing much that I, at least, can say to describe them positively. Very unhelpfully, I might say that they are a little bit like the experiences I have just before falling asleep. Perhaps better, I might say that they are to those presleep experiences much as the latter are to the ordinary experiences of waking life. (Those humble processes are, perhaps, too far down the relevant gradients to be properly called experiences at all; on the other hand, if the phrase 'nonconscious experience' is coherent, perhaps at least some of these barely failing processes are nonconscious experiences.) What does this great difficulty of conception and description show? It shows very little, if anything, about the processes themselves;

it shows much more about our own impoverished understanding of them. But although we cannot helpfully describe these processes, we have strong indirect reason to believe that they exist, as our sorites spectra inform us.

In certain ways, the matter here is like that with phenomenal color. Spectra of color patches can convince us that, relative to our classification of colors, a standard question about what color is present must be, in a suitable sense, a matter of degree, and even a matter of convention. There may be patches of color between clear orange and clear yellow for which we have no good word or words. But those patches do exist. Because such patches exist, there is a good deal of truth to a remark like this: In large measure, the "familiar" colors are conventional phenomena; there is not much "metaphysical reality" or metaphysical significance to red, orange, yellow, and so on. If anything in the neighborhood has metaphysical significance, it is the phenomenon of color as a whole, or the modality of color (including black and white). (Perhaps there is some metaphysical significance, too, to each of the enormously many, perhaps infinitely many, absolutely specific shades of color.)

As well as there being disanalogies, there is a certain parallel with consciousness. Owing to what our sorites spectra teach us, we may be confident that consciousness must likewise be a matter of degree and, in a suitable sense, even a matter of convention. Consciousness itself has little metaphysical significance. Rather, there is some "larger" modality or phenomenon, certain stretches of which we deem to exhibit consciousness. If anything in the neighborhood has much metaphysical significance, it is a more encompassing phenomenon, perhaps present to a very small degree when there are only two or three neurons firing away at each other.

Poorly described colors, or regions of the modality of phenomenal color, are as easily experienced by us as is a paradigm patch of orange, or at least very nearly as easily. But, almost by definition, we do not experience the difference between processes that barely qualify as conscious and those that barely fail. We have no direct experience, or no conscious experience, of the latter processes (even if we may sometimes observe them externally and indirectly in other beings). That is an interesting disanalogy with color. But I suggest that the interest of this disanalogy is more epistemological than metaphysical.

In any case, there is not much of a disanalogy here between consciousness and life. For we do not have direct awareness of the difference between the living and the nonliving, nor do we directly experience processes that barely fail to qualify as instances of life.[12]

While there are other people who can do so, I cannot say anything very informative about beings or processes that are on the borderline of the living and the nonliving, or that barely fail to qualify as living. Viruses, I understand, are examples of this. But I cannot say what it is about viruses that makes them such examples. Our sorites of decomposition shows us, well enough, that we are all in the same position with respect to certain processes going on in that vat that I, but not certain biologists, am in with respect to so many processes going on in ordinary viruses. In any case, what viruses and certain other examples show is that life is a matter of degree and, in a sense, even a matter of convention. It has no great metaphysical significance. If anything in the neighborhood has such significance, it is a more encompassing phenomenon, some stretches of which we call living, or deem processes that manifest life.[13]

In line with our deep-rooted intuitive belief that consciousness is metaphysically determinate, we employ certain models of conscious experience. These models can make those beliefs more vivid, and may make them seem yet more compelling. One is a "dimmer-switch model," articulated (in his correspondence to me) by Mark Heller: Consciousness is similar to a light that is controlled by a dimmer switch. As the switch is gradually turned down, the light gradually fades. At some points it may be extremely difficult, perhaps impossible, for us to *tell* whether the light is on or off. But there is a definite fact, nonetheless, when the light actually goes off; there is a definite last moment at which the current is flowing. How does reflection on the spectra from our sorites of decomposition rationally affect our attitudes toward such a model?

Such spectra do not conclusively demonstrate that such a model is inappropriate or inaccurate; they do not conclusively demonstrate that consciousness is a matter of degree, and is not metaphysically all-or-none. But they do convince us that it is unlikely that such a model is appropriate, that it is unlikely that consciousness is all-or-none. When the dimmer switch is turned off, there is no light at all; perhaps when it is turned on, there is always some light, however little or weak the light may be. Let us allow this. But, given our belief in our scientific world view, it seems unlikely that there is any point in our sorites spectra corresponding to the turning off (or, in reverse, to the turning on) of any switch. Let us recall what happens in such a spectrum.

At each stage, a single cell is removed from the remaining whole, and what remains is supported at an optimal level for sustaining whatever in the way of consciousness is then naturally possible. Support systems will always be at work to attempt this. So, at any points near any plausible borderline for consciousness, there will always be extremely complex processes involving many millions of connected neurons in our vat. Any differences in the processes at one stage and at the next seem extremely slight, even trivial, in comparison with the similarities between the processes.

Materialists would *identify* the processes occurring at higher stages with instances of consciousness, but not the processes occurring at sufficiently lower stages in such spectra. On a materialist view, it is all but unintelligible that consciousness should metaphysically be all-or-none. Suppose that we are dualists, not materialists. Then we might hold that consciousness will, for metaphysical reasons, *supervene* on higher processes but, right after some fine borderline, it will fail to supervene. Insofar as we can understand what such supervenience might be, which is no easy matter, we can make this an intelligible proposal. But for the most part, it is not compelling. Although we might have some weak belief that some such break in supervenience will occur, we have a stronger belief that nothing so momentous will occur on the basis of such trivial differences in the underlying material processes.

If we are dualists, we might instead think that certain material processes *cause*, or *causally support*, nonmaterial consciousness, though others do not. For some, this might allow more intelligibility for the proposal that there is, even in our spectra, a metaphysical borderline between consciousness and its absence. But even if we think we understand it better, the proposal is still unconvincing. For the most part, we will believe that when certain very complex neural processes causally support consciousness, then extremely similar neural processes will support, if not consciousness itself, at least some sort of "mentality" whose difference from consciousness is not metaphysically significant. It is only conventions implicitly governing our term 'conscious', and kindred expressions, that make it true that only the former mentality is an instance of consciousness, but the latter is not.

The dimmer-switch model has a certain appeal. But our sorites spectra have swamped this appeal. They have done so in several ways. But one interesting and unobvious way may concern an intuitive belief about the epistemiology of consciousness: We have the intuitive belief that consciousness is a metaphysically all-or-none phenemonon that is utterly transparent to any subject to whom it occurs. So, a conscious subject will always be able to tell that he is conscious, and can never be in any situation in which he would judge this as being uncertain in itself or in any way indeterminate. But our spectra include subjects who, we mainly believe, are not in a position to tell confidently whether they are conscious or not—no more so, perhaps, than someone observing them from the outside. If these subjects can make nonconscious judgments about themselves, they would not be sure whether to judge themselves conscious or not. So, we become convinced that consciousness is not utterly transparent to all of its subjects. That helps to convince us that consciousness is not metaphysically all-or-none, but is a matter of degree. Then we may become convinced that the dimmer-switch model is inappropriate to consciousness after all.

We do not have much of an understanding of what consciousness is. But even without any detailed understanding, the web of belief that we actually do have strongly enocurages the thought that consciousness is only whatever our term 'consciousness' conventionally picks out of the flux of metaphysically significant phenomena, and is not in its own right a phenomenon of much metaphysical significance. Our sorites-style spectrum brings this to our attention.

As I have suggested, our intuitive belief that matters of our own existence are metaphysically determinate is motivated largely by our unreflective belief that consciousness is metaphysically all-or-none. This is not to say that the former belief is entirely motivated by or, in our psychology, entirely dependent on, the latter. On the contrary, it is not. For if there is anything in the neighborhood of consciousness that we implicitly deem essential for our existence, it is not consciousness itself but the *capacity* for consciousness. Unlike Descartes in his official philosophy, we are prepared to allow that we may, and often do, survive periods of deep sleep, and sometimes periods of anesthesia, when we have no conscious thought or experience at all. Even if that is so, that will not, as we most strongly believe, mean an end to us. Nor will it mean that we have intermittent existence. Even while there is deep sleep, we continue to exist; it is you or I who, while wholly unconscious, will be undergoing such sleep on such occasions.

Consciousness, as we believe, is not of our essence. Yet we may require, to exist, a capacity for consciousness. Suppose that this, or something very much like this, is the case. Then there seems to be an opening for the idea that our existence itself is not metaphysically determinate, not all-or-none, but is a matter of degree. This is because, at least as a general rule, whether or not a given entity has a given capacity seems to be a matter of degree, and whether or not a given capacity is instanced in a given situation seems to be a matter of degree. That is why it is hard to think that our belief in the metaphysical determinacy of our existence is entirely motivated by our belief in the metaphysical determinacy of consciousness. On the other hand, we may have this belief as well: Although it is generally the case that matters of capacity are matters of degree, this is not universally the case; one such area is the capacity for consciousness. And, we may believe as well that one reason this is so is that consciousness, unlike, say, speaking French, is metaphysically all-or-none, not a matter of degree. These may be strong beliefs even if we have better-grounded beliefs that conflict with them. If this is so, it explains how our belief that consciousness is determinate underlies, or helps to motivate, our belief that our existence is metaphysically determinate.

In any event, there is at least some connection in our psychology between these two intuitive beliefs. So, the extent to which we may convince ourselves that consciousness is not metaphysically determinate, and is not of any great metaphysical significance, will affect the degree to which we can seriously reevaluate, if not entirely abandon, our belief that our own existence is metaphysically all-or-none. This modest fact alone, I believe, would justify the continuing attention of those interested in questions of the self, in personal identity, toward a sustained criticism of the idea that consciousness is metaphysically all-or-none.

5. THE CONVENTIONALITY OF MENTALITY

In the previous section, we said that consciousness was a conventionally demarcated region of some larger, more encompassing phenomenon. At one point, we suggested that this phenomenon might be called *mentality*. Is there a comprehensive phenomenon of the mental, though, that might most believably be metaphysically distinct from all other phenomena? I do not think so.

Whatever considerations convince us that, given the general truth of our science, consciousness is not a metaphysically significant phenomenon will all the more easily convince us that nothing else in the realm of the mental is metaphysically significant. With our partially decomposed brain firing away optimally, the removal of just one cell, any one of the remaining many millions, will take us from consciousness to something other, perhaps into nonconscious mental processes. But, as we are mainly convinced by our scientific outlook, this tiny removal will not do this by taking us into a realm of processes lacking in something of much metaphysical significance. That is a possibility, it must be allowed, but it is not a very believable one for most of us. And if it is not so believable that a metaphysically significant break occurs at *this* "point" in this spectrum, it is even less believable that it occurs at any *other* "point." Certainly, we believe, it will not occur at any higher point. And almost as certainly, it will not occur at any lower point, either.

As we go further down this spectrum, we will come to a point where, for the first time, we will go from a stimulated brain that is involved in some *un*conscious, or *non*conscious, *mental* processes to an almost identical brain, just one least-important-cell less, that is involved only in processes that are not truly mental ones, neither conscious nor nonconscious. To think that it is *here* that we have first crossed some metaphysically significant barrier, and not before, when leaving consciousness behind, is very hard to believe. If there is *anywhere* in this spectrum, between a whole brain working optimally and, say, just two floating neurons occasionally firing back and forth, that will be between the last case of consciousness and the first case where it is lacking. But, as we have argued, even there, the most likely idea is that only conventions governing our terms separate the favored case from the less favored one, not some metaphysical leap into a dearth of a sufficiently exalted quality. So, throughout the entire realm of mental, and even quasi-mental, phenomena, there is no metaphysically interesting gulf, but only the separation of certain processes from other very similar processes by way of our (somewhat "surprisingly") extremely sensitive semantics.

Whatever processes or events are the mental ones, they do not all differ in a metaphysically significant way from all of the other processes and events of our relevantly gradual world. Nor do all the entities that are capable of mentality, all the mental subjects, "substances," or entities, differ in such a philosophically important way from all the other subjects, substances, and entities that there are. Although the opposite is not entirely absurd for us to think, what is overall most reasonable and compelling is this: There is nothing that we properly call 'mental' that differs so significantly from everything that is not properly so called.

There arises the question of what is this phenomenon of which mental processes constitute a conventionally demarcated region, or part, and of which conscious processes constitute a smaller such region or part. We have no single word, nor any short, convenient expression for naming the phenomenon. To pick it out, or refer to it, perhaps the best we can do is what we have already done in the first sentence of this paragraph, or else something along that line of extrapolative description. It is unclear to me what are the scope and limits of this phenomenon; nor am I absolutely certain that there are any limits to it at all or that its scope is less than all-encompassing. If *that* should be the case, then this phenomenon would be nothing less than the universe as a whole (or, at the least, the nonabstract part or aspect of the universe, if the universe has an abstract part or aspect). I raise this last "possibility" only as a tantalizing suggestion, not as an idea for which I have any good evidence or argument.

6. ENTITIES AND BOUNDARIES

Perhaps there is a sense of the term 'entity', a very liberal one, in which anything whatsoever is an entity: numbers, qualities, processes, regions, oceans, lumps of clay, the left half of the paper I now face, and me. But it seems clear enough that there may also be a much less liberal sense of the term in which, to put it roughly, only something that is separate or distinct from the rest of the world is an entity. It is the term in this latter sense that I wish to focus on, where the term 'entity' is, perhaps, somewhat more general than, but not terribly different in meaning from, the noun 'individual'. In this preferred sense, the term 'entity' is, I take it, rather similar in meaning to the noun 'being', in a certain, less than general sense of *that* term. In any more restricted sense that the term 'thing' has, however, this word might, for all I can tell, not properly apply to people, or to other conscious beings. For that reason, I will not employ 'thing' in the discussion to follow.

In the more restricted senses of these terms, even if we are not things, are we individuals, or beings, or entities? Or are we, at best, mere parts, regions, or aspects of some entity or entities? For that matter, is your *nose* an entity; or is it, at best, a mere part, region, or aspect of some entity or entities?

In the relevant sense, what do we mean by 'entity' and cognate expressions; in our language, what do these terms mean? For its more restricted sense, it may be hard to spell out any interesting definition of 'entity'. But perhaps we may spell out, even if somewhat vaguely and roughly, some reasonably interesting necessary condition for being an entity. Perhaps a candidate for entityhood will qualify, will be an entity, only if it is either the world as a whole or, if it is anything less than that, it is *clearly set off* from the *rest* of the world, where the rest of the world is, roughly, everything in the world that is neither it nor any region, aspect, or part of it.[14]

Suppose that a candidate is something that is in, or is a part of, the objective spatiotemporal order of the (actual) world. Then, to be an entity, that candidate must be clearly set off from the rest of what is in, or is part of, the objective spatiotemporal order of the world, roughly, from the rest of what is in, or is part of, actual concrete reality. How might this be? The candidate must have a real *boundary* that is well-defined, and this boundary must somehow deal with all the dimensions of concrete reality, and the causal processes of concrete reality, in which the candidate is involved. The most obvious thing that such a boundary must do, but certainly not the only thing, is to deal with the spatial dimensions for candidates that exist in, and that occupy, regions of space. For your nose to be an entity, it must have a real boundary that is well-defined, that among other things, clearly sets off your nose from everything in space that is not your nose, and that is not a part, region, or aspect of your nose.

Does your nose have such a boundary? On the whole, one would answer in the negative. Intuitively, we would also, on the whole, give a negative answer to the question "Is your nose an entity?" As vague and rough as this is, perhaps we are on the right track and getting somewhere with our discussion.

I have just used the expression "on the whole." What did I mean by that? There are some contexts, I suppose, where we would allow it as true that your nose is an entity. But these are unusual contexts for most people, and not often likely to come to mind. When each of us hears the question about the nose, he places it in what is, for him, a typical or average context. For most of us, most of the time, such a context will prompt us to give a negative answer. That is what I meant by saying that, on the whole, one would answer in the negative.

Doctors who specialize in the ear, the nose, and the throat might often be in contexts where the dominant interests would incline them to answer the question positively: Yes, your nose is an entity. In these contexts, they would, at least they should, also affirm that your nose had a real, well-defined boundary. The standards for a real, well-defined boundary will, then and there, be low: The reality of the boundary may be largely generated by implicit conventions, rather than by breaks in nature itself. Even if most of us would regard the (alleged) boundary as too fuzzy, or too broad, standards for well-definedness of the boundary may be in force that are very liberal on the matter: So, being that fuzzy or that broad does not preclude the boundary being well-defined, as far as those doctors are, then and there, concerned. Finally, and perhaps implicit in what has occurred with our first two points, the standards for what counts as a boundary may be low in the context. Those doctors may then allow that your nose has a boundary, perhaps necessarily real and well-defined, whereas ordinarily, and not under their influence, most of us usually would not allow that as true.

We all have a rather clear idea of an ideal case of a spatial boundary, one that fully encloses a regularly shaped, three-dimensional spatial solid, say, the boundary, or surface, of a (putative) Newtonian atom. In the ideal case, the boundary is absolutely fine and precise, has no holes in it anywhere at all, and is perfectly objective, that is, it is not in the least bit generated by our own conventions or mental activities. Whether we judge a candidate spatial boundary as successful may depend on the extent to which, as we believe, it approximates that understood ideal case. It may also depend on our dominant interests in the context in which we make, or in which we understand, the judgment. Implicitly, our judgment that a candidate is a boundary may be a judgment, then, to this effect: According to those interests most relevant in the context of judgment, the candidate approximates sufficiently closely the ideal case of a (spatial) boundary. By (perhaps unconsciously) thinking in this way, we may adaptively guide our behavior by suitable uses and understandings involving the term "boundary" in relation to the various situations that we different people face in everyday life in the actual world.

We may also have a rather clear idea of an ideal case of an entity that is in space, and that occupies space, of an entity that has a boundary. Perhaps the idea of a Newtonian atom is a clear enough idea of at least one such ideal case. In ordinary contexts, we do not encounter candidate entities that satisfy this ideal. But, in various contexts, we may often encounter candidates that measure up well enough for the purposes dominant in those contexts. For our specialist doctors, often it may be that even your nose would approximate well enough to the ideal case. Their interests may often generate contextually appropriate standards for approximation that are quite low. That is why, or part of the reason why, they often may properly (consciously) think that your nose is an entity in its own right.

Is a cloud an entity? The appropriate answer depends on a number of things including, as should now be clear, the context in which the question is asked. But other factors, independent of context, are also important. Some do not *in any obvious way* have much to do with questions of boundaries, though they may, after all, concern subtle questions of boundaries. An example of such a factor may be the causal coherence of the parts of the cloud, say, mainly of its water droplets. Typically, the causal coherence of the parts of a cloud is low, as compared to, say, the causal coherence of the parts of a rock, a bush, or your body. For this reason, as well as for others, we are not as ready, on the whole, to allow that a cloud is an entity as to allow, say, that a typical rock is an entity. But there are contexts where standards for causal coherence are sufficiently low that we may regard a cloud, or even a crowd of people, as an entity in its own right.

What I have been calling causal coherence may also be a factor that we implicitly think about in relation to an appropriate ideal. When the candidate for entity-hood is something that is material, and is an occupant of space, an ideal case may, again, be that of the Newtonian atom. Indeed, with a Newtonian atom, it is appropriate, in most contexts, to think of it as having no parts at all, any imagined parts having such an enormous, perhaps infinite, "affinity" for each other that they surpass, and are only an asymptotically approachable limit for, things that (mutually) causally cohere with each other.

Comparatively speaking, there are many contexts in which it is appropriate for us to regard a rock, or your body, as an entity. But there are not many where it is proper for us to think of a cloud, or a crowd, as an entity. Why is that? Part of the reason is this: There are many contexts in which, regarding the former two candidates, they approximate sufficiently closely the ideal case of causal coherence for the interests, and thus the standards, there dominant. But there are comparatively few contexts in which the latter two candidates approximate well enough that ideal case for the interests dominant in those contexts. Let us set aside, at least for a while, any further *direct discussion* of matters of causal coherence.

Clouds do comparatively poorly, too, in regard to questions of spatial boundaries. Some clouds do better than others, of course: Sometimes the weather is such that some clouds seem to stand alone in the sky, like huge, celestial cotton puffs; they do comparatively well. Sometimes the weather is different, and there are clouds that "sort of seem" to run together; they do comparatively poorly. It is easier for us, in most contexts, to think of the former candidates as entities. But on closer inspection and more protracted consideration, even the best candidate clouds may seem to do poorly in regard to having boundaries. There is a gradual fade-out, rather than a sudden drop-off, of the water droplets in question, between the cloud and the surrounding atmosphere. With respect to ever so many droplets, nothing in the objective order makes it at all clear whether the droplet is part of the cloud or merely in the surrounding air. Only implicit conventions of ours will help to decide whether the droplet is in the cloud or not. The objective order does comparatively little to provide even the best cloud with any spatial boundary; our conventions and mental activities must contribute a lot.

This was a rather quick and incomplete treatment of clouds and their boundaries. Elsewhere I have given a more thorough treatment.[15] There, too, I gave a rather thorough treatment of the ways in which, regarding spatial boundaries, rocks and human brains and bodies are more like clouds than is usually supposed. That excuses, I think, the brief treatment of all these subjects in the present work.

Regarding spatial boundaries, how is a rock, or a human organism, or one of a cloud's water droplets, much like a cloud? In brief, the atoms of each of these latter items are to any one of them as the cloud's water droplets are to the cloud. Of the many places on the surface of, say, a rock, there are atoms whose status is left unclear by the natural order of things: There is nothing in the world, apart from our conventions and mental activity, that determines whether one of these atoms is part of the rock or whether only part of, a tiny impurity in, the surrounding air. So that the rock may have a boundary, we must contribute something.

Even in regard to having a spatial boundary, let alone in regard to direct matters of causal coherence, perhaps nature does more for rocks and humans than for clouds. If so, then we must do correlatively less for the former than for the latter. Then, in having a real spatial boundary, rocks and humans are better approximations to the ideal case than are clouds. This may be a reason that, for most of us, there are more contexts in which we find it proper to think that a rock, or a human being, has a spatial boundary than there are contexts thus favorable for even the best of clouds. In turn, this may be one of the reasons that there are more contexts in which we find it proper to say, and think, that a human being, or even a rock, is an entity than there are contexts favorable for even the best clouds.

We may often find it appropriate to think that a rock, or a human organism, has a spatial boundary, but what is the truth of the matter? Some philosophers may hold that this is mere expediency on our part, or something of the like, and that, in fact, the ideal case must be satisfied for there to be, in a situation, something with spatial boundaries. These philosophers may hold, then, that rocks and human organisms do not really have spatial boundaries: Each of the ordinary concrete things of the world is so gradually distributed with respect to space, at least, that there is no way that any rock, or any human, is set off from the rest of the world. These thinkers may then hold, as well, that any rock, or any human organism, is thus not an entity, but is at most merely a part, region, or aspect of an entity, perhaps of actual concrete reality, perhaps of the universe as a whole.[16] Are these philosophers correct? What they offer is certainly a tempting suggestion, but can it possibly be *true*? Let us postpone discussion of this intriguing question, until we have more questions like it to discuss as well.

Now, among these intriguing thinkers, some may be materialists, or physicalists. They will hold that not only do our bodies and brains occupy space, but so do you and I. These materialists may then hold that, for the reasons in the preceding paragraph, none of *us* are entities either, nor are we, then, individuals or, in the preferred sense of the term, beings. Rather, all of us, even you, are only parts, regions, or aspects of the universe as a whole, which latter may, or perhaps may not, be an entity. Other of these thinkers may be dualists. Although these dualists may now agree that our bodies are not entities, and our brains are certainly not entities, they may persist with the idea that we ourselves are entities. For they may say that, though our bodies and brains are in space, and occupy space, we ourselves are not in space, let alone do we occupy any of it. Or they may say that only rather unimportant parts or aspects of us, our bodies and brains, are in space, but the central part or aspect of us is not in space. By making such remarks, these dualists may yet maintain that we are not merely parts, regions, or aspects of the universe. They may, then, still maintain that we are individuals and that, even in the preferred sense of the term, each of us is a being.

7. BOUNDARIES OF PHENOMENA

What these dualists have in mind is, at least, that there is some real, concrete *phenomenon* that is not physical. What sort of phenomenon might this be? One idea is that there might be a phenomenon of consciousness. Another is that there might be a more inclusive phenomenon of mentality. Is consciousness a real phenomenon, or is it, at most, *merely* a part, region, or aspect of some sufficiently great phenomenon? Is mentality a phenomenon, or is it, too, merely a part, region, or aspect of a sufficiently great, real phenomenon for which we have no name, nor any other very short and convenient expression? These questions might not be easy to answer with much confidence.

There may be a sense of the term "phenomenon," perhaps the only sense, in which any phenomenon must be set off from the rest of the world, at least from all other phenomena. It is in this sense of the term that we may best interpret our questions in the preceding paragraph. In this sense, there are many contexts in which we would allow that although color as a whole is a phenomenon, reddish orange is not a phenomenon, but is only a part, a region, or an aspect of the phenomenon of color. Reflecting on this, we may sometimes think that the ordinary colors, like red and orange, are not phenomena each in their own right, either, but are each merely qualitative regions, say, of the phenomenon of color, regions of color for which we happen to have such short, convenient names.

When we think that way about, say, orange, we are impressed with the extent to which orange lacks, or at least seems to lack, any real boundaries; we think that nothing really sets off orange from, among other "candidate phenomena," orangish red and orangish yellow. It is owing so largely to our conventions, we feel, and correlatively little to anything inherent to color itself, that orange is *in any way* distinguished from such other candidates. And *that* sort of distinguishing, we feel, is not enough in the way of setting something off from the rest of the world for the candidate to qualify as a phenomenon in its own right.

Suppose there were laws of the world that ensured that, of all of the possible shades of color, only good paradigms of the ordinarily recognized main colors were ever instanced or realized in any realm of that world, mental, physical, or whatever. So, everything of color would be, as a matter of some strict causal necessity, either a pure red, a pure orange, a pure yellow, a pure green, a pure blue, or a pure purple. In such a world, the very laws of nature would set off orange from any candidate phenomenon with which it might otherwise be merged, or confused. In almost any context, when we consider such a world, we think that orange would have real boundaries, and that orange would be a phenomenon in its own right.

Our world, the actual world, is not much like that world. In many contexts, it is proper for us to think that orange is not a phenomenon. Still, in some contexts, we may properly allow that orange is a phenomenon. We may discuss situations where people become fixated on having certain objects colored orange, attaching an almost mystical significance to their being "quite close to a pure paradigm" of just that color. We might then say, appropriately enough, that orange was a real phenomenon, but that blue and yellow, say, were just colors. So much for colors. What, now, of consciousness?

Our spectra of decomposition convinced us that there was no break in nature, nor any other metaphysically significant break, between consciousness and every other candidate phenomenon. Now, we may properly say, I believe, that, in regard to consciousness, nonconventional aspects of reality contribute more to its having suitable boundaries than is the case in regard to orange. But those objective aspects of reality do not contribute everything that might be wished. At least in some sense, there are possible worlds where consciousness is set off from everything else more objectively, or more realistically, than in the actual world. Perhaps a world with Cartesian souls is one such possible, but not actual, world. Because the objective order does not contribute everything, our conventions must contribute something, in order that consciousness be distinguished *in any way* from everything else in the world. Because of this, in certain contexts, we may think that consciousness is not a real phenomenon in its own right, but is only a part, region, or aspect of some sufficiently inclusive phenomenon.

What we have said about consciousness applies equally to mentality. Our considerations of spectra convinced us of the basic ideas involved here, and a discussion parallel to that of the preceding paragraphs will convince us of the rest. Whether we properly say (and consciously think) that the mental, or that consciousness, is a real phenomenon will depend on the context of our statement (or of our conscious token of thought). If the standards for the *boundary of a phenomenon* are not too high, it will be appropriate for us to say that consciousness, and that mentality, is a phenomenon; otherwise it will not. The standards will be determined by, among other things, the interests dominant in the context. So, in several ways, though not in all, what is going on here will parallel our talk and thought about (candidate) spatial boundaries and ordinary physical (candidate) entities.

Since there is a considerable parallel, there will be those philosophers who will be strict about consciousness and mentality. They will say that, though it may often be appropriate for us to say that consciousness is a phenomenon, and that mentality is a phenomenon, it is never true. In a world with Cartesian souls, that might be true. But we do not live in such a world. In the actual world, at least, there is at most an (intellectual) illusion that consciousness is a phenomenon in its own right; in point of fact, consciousness, and mentality as well, is at most just a conventionally demarcated part, region, or aspect of some sufficiently inclusive, real phenomenon. This last is, it appears, a phenomenon for which we have no name, but to which we can refer only by way of roundabout, complex description.

As before, the suggestions of these philosophers are both tempting and interesting. Now, what they say does not challenge a dualistic world view, nor is it meant to. Rather, it offers the idea that, regarding any salient, concrete realm that is not physical, we are as confused about its ontology as we are in our ordinary ontological conceptions regarding the physical realm. Intriguing though these suggestions are, we will forgo any detailed discussion of them. Instead, we turn to bring forward other considerations of boundary that are important to the conditions of our existence.

8. TEMPORAL BOUNDARIES

There are varieties of dualism. Some dualists do not care a fig for our scientific view of the world insofar as it may be supposed to reveal anything much about ourselves. These dualists may hold what I have called the subjective view of ourselves, or some hybrid between that and our objective view. At least in this essay, I have little to say to such dualists. But nowadays it is difficult to be a dualist of that sort. It is hard for us to believe that science has little to teach us about whatever is our true nature, or about what we may possibly lack in regard to having a true nature. Today, even a dualist will be likely to take seriously not only the idea that we exist in objective time, and exist for intervals of such time, but also that the main facts of our existence are most intimately bound up with certain things that take place in the objective spatiotemporal world, in particular, with certain of the processes in which our brains and bodies are involved. Along with more physicalistic thinkers, these realistic dualists must face whatever problems are involved with our gradual development, and with the realistically possible ways in which we may gradually decline. Anyone who is seriously impressed with the evidence of science must face certain, at least apparent problems regarding causality and, most certainly, regarding time.

Consider any candidate entity, less than (actual) concrete reality as a whole, that exists in the objective temporal order and that exists for more than an absolute instant. The candidate may exist forever, never having come into existence and never ceasing to exist. Newtonian atoms may have been treated by some scientists in this way. Perhaps certain esoteric things actually discovered by more recent scientists are relevantly eternal, and perhaps not. Regarding any much more ordinary candidates, however, our best evidence has it that they did not forever exist, and that they will not exist infinitely into the future. Then, for these candidates to be successful, for them to be entities each in their own right, they must have what we may call *temporal boundaries*. There must be a time before which they did not exist, but after which they did exist. And, as they exist for more than an instant, there must be another time at which, or during which, they exist. Finally, there must be a third time before which they exist, but after which they do not exist. For any of these relevant candidate entities, the first and third of these times are its temporal boundaries.[17]

What sorts of times are these; are they absolute instants or are they temporal intervals? A proper answer to the question will depend, again, on the context of the question. For any context, I suppose, an absolute instant will do well as a temporal boundary. Indeed, we may regard that as the ideal case of a temporal boundary. But in most contexts, we do not need so much as such an instant; rather, we may be satisfied with what, looked at from a rather metaphysical and absolutist perspective, is an interval, or a period, of time.

How short must such a period be for it to be a satisfactory temporal boundary of some candidate entity? And, what may or may not ultimately amount to the same thing: How precise or fine must be the temporal limits of such a period; can the boundary period itself be somewhat fuzzy, or must it be temporally bounded, on both sides, by absolute instants? Supposing the second question to be coherent, and to be quite distinct from the first, the appropriate answer to these questions will depend on, among other things, the contexts in which they are asked. In many contexts, most of us will be satisfied with temporal boundaries that, from any demanding perspective, are not terribly short and may be temporally quite fuzzy as well.

When did the Empire State Building come into existence? For that candidate entity to have a boundary, in most contexts many of us might insist on a period considerably less than ten years, but few indeed would insist on a second.

According to our best evidence, you did not always exist. For you to be an entity in your own right, you must have at least one temporal boundary, some time in the past. If we rely only on the natural order to provide this temporal boundary, and allow no contribution from our own conventions, we will be at a loss for any time when *you* first existed. A spectrum of embryonic development, along with a spectrum of fertilization, convinced us of this well enough. So our conventions, perhaps products of our collective mental and behavioral activity, must make their contribution. How much of a contribution? In the great majority of contexts, almost all of us would allow that they may make a very substantial contribution. In all those contexts, we would allow that, even with such a contribution, you have a real temporal boundary in the past; there really was a time, we allow, before which you did not exist and after which you did exist. Need this time be an absolute instant, or may it be a period? Almost always, we are prepared to allow the latter. How long, broad, or fuzzy will this period be?

In many contexts, most of us will insist on a period of several months, but few would insist on a period of five seconds. In other contexts, fewer in number, most of us would be even a bit more liberal than that, requiring only that there be a period beginning with "the time of your conception" and ending about the time when you first understood a fair amount of your native language, perhaps about a year after your birth. In still other contexts, the appropriate answer is simply to name the year of your birth, say, 1942; there, your past temporal boundary is a fairly broad, but also rather precise, interval of time.

An ideal case of a temporal boundary, perhaps the only ideal case, is an absolute instant, a time that has no temporal duration whatsoever in any acceptable sense of these terms. Perhaps an actually indivisible quantum of time might do as well. For any of the purposes of this essay, we need not decide this issue. In any event, when we think that a candidate entity began at a certain time, and find this time to be appropriate for a real beginning, we implicitly think, I suggest, in terms of some such ideal case. We think there is a time when the candidate first existed that closely enough approximates the ideal case: According to the interests dominant in the context in which we (consciously) think about that candidate entity, the approximation of its candidate past boundary to the ideal case of a temporal boundary is adequate.

Consider some mud that is continually moving around owing to local forces of nature acting on it. Sometimes the mud may bulge in a noticeable, even interesting way. In many of these cases, there may be, for a while, a mound of mud. Is that mound an entity? There are problems of spatial boundary here. But suppose that, in the context of the question, we are satisfied, not worried, concerning any such spatial matters. Then, it may make a difference to us how long it took the mound to form, how evenly gradual was its formation, how long the mound lasted, how long it took for the mound to "flatten out again," and how evenly gradual was the process of flattening. Holding contextual interests constant, and at some fairly typical "level," we are impressed by these factors to a great extent. If the formation process and the dissolution process were long in comparison to the period when the mound existed, that makes things difficult for the mound's candidacy for entityhood. If these processes were very evenly gradual, that makes things worse. If the times of these processes were short in comparison to many processes salient in and important for human life and experience, that makes things look worse still. With all these things holding at once, there are few contexts in which most of us would consider the mound to be an entity. In most contexts, we might allow that the mud swamp was an entity, but this fleeting mound was just a disturbance in the mud swamp. In the more liberal of *these* contexts, we might go on to allow that, for a brief while, the mound was a part of the swamp, a part of that entity, but the mound was not an entity in its own right. Even so, we can create contexts where even that fleeting mound of mud would be appropriately considered an entity by people in those contexts. With all these negative factors holding, it would be that much rarer a thing for us to generate, or to find ourselves in, such contexts where, in regard to temporal boundaries, we are so very undemanding.

We recall the philosophers who, considering the lack of an absolutely precise spatial boundary, denied that not only our noses and clouds, but even rocks and our bodies, were entities. Unlike Newtonian atoms, they said, these candidates must fail to be entities, and can be at best only parts, regions, or aspects of some sufficiently great entity (or entities). These thinkers will make trouble for us with matters regarding temporal boundaries as well.

Although it may often be appropriate for us to think that we are entities, they may say, it is never really true. In truth, we are no more entities than is that fleeting mound of mud. That is because, if for no other reason, we have no definite beginning in time, and, of course, we have not existed forever. These facts of our existence may not be a priori facts, but they are facts nonetheless. The weight of the evidence is strongly in favor of the thought that this is so. Now, among those things that have not existed forever, these philosophers will continue, only those with real past temporal boundaries are entities in their own right. And given what "boundary" really means, these philosophers will say, for it to be *true* that something has such a boundary, and not just appropriate for us to say so, that something must be an instance of the relevant ideal case. So, they will say, we may admit that a person who instantaneously came into existence might be an entity in his own right, having a real first temporal boundary wholly in the objective order of things. But none of us is like that. So none of us is an entity, or an individual, or a being, but we all are, we must realize, only parts, aspects, or regions of the universe in which we have our being.

Much as with what they said about questions of spatial boundary, what these philosophers are now saying is not terribly plausible. Nonetheless, it is not wholly implausible, either. We cannot deny that there seems to be something to what they are saying, enough, indeed, for their position to be tempting and philosophically intriguing. And now, where time, rather than space, is the dimension in focus, no appeal to any very credible form of dualism will be of any avail. So, now these philosophers have gotten us to think what are perhaps Spinozistic or Buddhistic thoughts, not only about our bodies, but also about ourselves.

9. CAUSAL BOUNDARIES AND REAL ESSENCES

Let us recall our spectrum of decomposition of the self by minute removals, a scientifically realistic group of many billions of related cases. In a certain case in the spectrum, I existed as a brain in a vat, suitably stimulated and supported by appropriate materials external to myself, a brain that had many fewer cells, and so was rather smaller, than the brain that I, in fact, now have. This is the case where, at the level of cells, I just barely exist. The innocuous removal from me of *any* of my remaining cells, almost certainly any one of the *several billions of cells* that even there I have, will make it no longer true that I exist. The only slightly smaller and less complex brain thus produced would not be me and would not constitute or "support" me;

rather, that slightly smaller brain would, at the level of cells, barely fail to be me, or barely fail to constitute or support me. Now, perhaps it would be false that this slightly lesser brain would at least support me, or perhaps it would be indeterminate; but, in any case, it would not be true that I would then exist. In the one case, I do exist, even if only barely so; in the next case, or any of the many equivalent options for the next case, it is not true that I exist. But, as far as our best evidence goes, what is so different about the two cases?

Apart from any conventions we implicitly maintain for separating cases adequately for coherent thought about the world, there is no interesting difference between them. As far as our best evidence goes, and that seems quite far enough indeed, nothing much happened when one cell was innocuously removed. The remaining cells did not break down or disappear. Nor did they suddenly start to interact in strange and peculiar ways. Nor did some immaterial soul at that point suddenly break off its attachment to the cells of the situation, and to whatever material systems they may serve to realize or constitute. There are possible worlds, we may agree, where one or another of those things would happen. In those worlds, the causal processes involved in the gradual decomposition of the self would, along the dimensions now considered, have a wholly objective and well-defined *causal boundary*. But the actual world, the only world where you and I are, is not any of those possible worlds; indeed, it is very strikingly different from them all.

In saying that I do not have the needed causal boundary, I was speaking in a context, generated by myself in a highly metaphysical mood, where the standards were high for an appropriate statement about whether a candidate was a genuine causal boundary. In most contexts, however, most of us would not have interests predominate that set such high standards, nor would there be any other way in which such high standards would be in force. Ordinarily, we would allow that relative to such a decomposition process, we did have a causal boundary, a boundary that was real, objective and well-defined. That is owing partly to facts about us in the world, but more largely to the importance for us, in terms of our actual interests, in having low standards.

The facts of the world are not as harsh as they might be. After all, to keep me going, we did have to bring in life-support systems, and perhaps stimulatory systems, without which even the removal of a single cell might have started some ultimately fatal chain reaction. A rock is not like that, nor is a log. But, we must admit, a mouse is like that, as is even, in all likelihood, a nonconscious but living bush. In regard to matters of causal boundary, then, bushes and people do not do terribly badly by way of the order of the actual world; at least we do better than rocks and logs.

This is one reason, I suggest, that some philosophers have been led to think that, among whatever is concrete but less than all of (actual) concrete reality, only what is organic, or living, is an entity. What might these philosophers say about a rock? They have two choices. More realistically, perhaps, they may say that, since rocks are not living, they are not entities, but are at best parts, aspects, or regions of the universe. More imaginatively, perhaps, they may say that, since rocks are entities, they must somehow really be organic or living, despite all the appearances to the contrary.

Although awfully vague and abstract, it is perhaps true enough that any real entity must have a real essence. Then, to have a real essence, a candidate from concrete reality that is involved in causal processes must, everywhere relative to those causal processes, have an objective and well-defined boundary. Now, all these terms can be placed in a context, as I have just done, where they *are to be treated* quite strictly. In such a context, it may be easy to think that only living candidates have real essences and, so, that only living candidates are real entities. (One may, then, even think that the universe as a whole, or at least actual concrete reality as a whole, must be alive, in order that it be an entity.) There is something right in these ideas, I think, but probably not all that much.[18]

As our spectrum of decomposition shows us, one thing wrong with this approach is that, going by any very high standards, living things simply do not everywhere have the requisite causal boundaries. By bringing in artificial support systems, we can get them to fade out, rather than suddenly break down or die. The actual nature of the world is kinder to clear examples of living things than it is to rocks, so far as letting them live up to high standards for causal boundary, thus for having real essences, thus for being entities. But it is not as kind as could be, so to say, and not as kind as some philosophers have supposed.

As far as the objective order goes, we do well, though not extremely well, in regard to having causal boundaries and real essences. In almost all contexts, though, we have dominant interests that take up the slack. These interests make it appropriate for us to say and (consciously) think that we each have real essences, and that each of us is an entity in his or her own right. Now, speaking in an absolutist mood, and in a context generated by my being in that mood and sharing it with you, we may appropriately say some things that are quite harsh and strict. We may say that there is a real difference between what we actually have in the way of causal boundaries and, thus, in the way of real essences and, on the other side, the ideal case of something (involved in causal processes) having (all the requisite) causal boundaries and, thus, having a real essence. But, then, we may turn around and say as well that, in almost any other context, we have quite different interests that predominate. According to such other interests, this difference is so small as to be negligible. Those interests, then, set standards for approximation to that ideal case according to which we are close enough to the ideal for those standards to be satisfied: Then, it is only appropriate to say that I have (all the causal boundaries needed for me to have) a real essence. And, at least where no other possible problems are taken very seriously, then it is only appropriate to allow that I am an entity in my own right.

It is often most appropriate for us to say such things as these. But are they true? Is it really true that you and I, each of us, has a real essence, and is an entity in his own right? We have encountered philosophers who would deny that it is true. According to them, the only candidates involved in causal processes that do have real essences, and that are entities, are those that are in the ideal case. In the actual world, perhaps certain elementary particles are in that position; perhaps there are certain candidates of cosmic proportions that have real essences. But you and I are not like that. So you and I have no real essence; it is not really true that we do. Because of this, if for no other reason, neither of us is an entity, really, any more than is a lump, or even a mound, of mud. Rather, we are, at the very best, merely parts, aspects, or regions of some sufficiently great entity, a being that either has a real essence or, perhaps, is so all-encompassing that it requires none in the first place.

These philosophers criticize the idea that we are entities in three ways that we have discussed: spatial boundary, temporal boundary, and causal boundary. But perhaps these three ways are not really distinct. For example, in our discussion of the spatial boundaries of clouds, we made passing mention of the causal coherence, or lack of much causal coherence, that we typically find with clouds. Questions of causal coherence involve questions of causal boundary. But questions of spatial boundary may, in subtle ways, involve questions of causal coherence: All the things, or parts of a thing, within a certain spatial boundary may, or may not, causally cohere well enough for that to be a real, objective spatial boundary; conversely they may, or perhaps may not, cohere too well with things outside the candidate boundary for that candidate to be a real spatial boundary. So questions of spatial boundary seem inseparable from questions of causal boundary. Perhaps, I suggest, all these boundary questions are inseparable from one another.[19]

Insofar as these questions are inseparable, the "absolutist" philosophers who question whether we are entities will be able to say more and more elaborate, and apparently relevant, things to us. The argumentation they offer will be that much more complex. But, as should be obvious, it will not differ in kind, but only in degree, from the argumentation already before us. Let us turn to examine, somewhat more closely, the suggestive and intriguing reasoning that these philosophers offer.

10. THE HYPOTHESIS OF SEMANTIC RELATIVITY: A SUMMARY SKETCH

According to our intriguing philosophers, in order to be an entity, a concrete candidate that has not existed forever must, for one thing, have a completely objective and absolutely precise past boundary. Otherwise it will not really be an entity, but be merely a part, region, or aspect of the universe. This past boundary, the time of the candidate's beginning or first existence, must be an absolute instant or, at the very least, an indivisible quantum of time. And these philosophers mean these words to have the strongest interpretation that they can possibly bear. Why do they think such strict thoughts?

A main reason is that these philosophers hold a certain view about language and meaning, about semantics, and about the relation of that to our thought (and perhaps to our behavior). For them, the term "beginning," to take just one example, has very strict satisfaction conditions. The real beginning of something cannot itself have any beginning. If I began to exist at a certain time, then there cannot possibly be any shorter time than the beginning of my existence; in particular, there cannot be a shorter time that was the time that the beginning of my existence first began. To say that there was a time *during* the time when I began to exist, which was *shorter* than the beginning of my existence, is to produce either nonsense or incoherence. On occasion, such (nonsense or such) incoherent talk might be useful, or appropriate, but it can never express the truth.

Moreover, for these philosophers, a real beginning must be wholly objective. There cannot be the beginning of any entity, process, or event whose occurrence is owing largely to our conventions of speech, such as our conventions for using the term "beginning," unless that be, trivially, say, some process that is itself our coming to have a certain convention. Whether things that at one time did not exist later began to exist is something that must be "decided" in the *order of the world*, and not by our conventions for talking about the world in one way or another. For these philosophers, the contribution of our own conventions to the *truth* of a statement that something began to exist cannot, except in trivial ways, be merely small; it must be zero.

According to this conception, the meaning of such terms as "beginning" and "the time when something first exists" is as strict as can be; candidate entities that can truly be said to have a beginning, or a time when they first exist, must be candidates that are in, or that satisfy, the ideal case. Nontemporal problems aside, a human being who, along with all of his constituent matter, instantaneously comes into existence may be truly said to have a beginning; it may be true that there is a time when he *first* exists. But a human being who develops gradually from a zygote does not satisfy the ideal case; strictly speaking, there is no time when he first exists, or when he begins to exist.

In *Philosophical Relativity*, I called philosophers who held this strict semantic view *invariantists*. According to an invariantist, the meaning of so many of our terms—"flat" is a vivid example—is in no way sensitive to context. When someone states "That tabletop is flat," whether his statement is true or not depends only on the configuration of the indicated table, not on nonspatial features of the context in which the statement is made, such as the dominant interests of those then understanding the statement. Invariantism has its attractions: Semantics is simple, and what makes our statements true, if anything ever does, is what seems to make them true. The truth of statements about what is flat depends only on spatial configuration, not on people's interests, often quite fleeting interests, in this or that piece of furniture. In like manner, these philosophers may hold, the truth of statements about what began when depends only on the occurrence of events and processes in objective time, not on the perhaps fleeting interest of this speaker, or of that hearer, in something taken to be some noteworthy happening.

Invariantism has its drawbacks as well. The most obvious is that so much of what we offer as true, and accept as true, will not be true. Although this is the most obvious and the most grating disadvantage, from a theoretical or philosophical point of view, it is not the most important. The important theoretical disadvantage in this conception of semantics is that what we say is so often *irrelevant* to any adaptive, or appropriate, thought or behavior in the situation toward which our statement is directed. According to this view, for example, when someone says that a certain meeting had no real beginning—some people just started talking, and then it grew and grew, what he said fails to distinguish that meeting from any other—even from a formal convening, where a gavel starts things going at what people *take* to be precisely two o'clock.

This disadvantage is important, but it is not insuperable. The invariantist need only postulate that we speakers and hearers, upon confronting so many statements whose content is irrelevant to our interests and needs, move to "focus on" related, more complex thoughts that are relevant to our contexts. For example, when the person said that the extremely informal meeting had no real beginning, we move to focus on some such thought as this: In regard to having a time when it began, the meeting is too far from the ideal case of something having a beginning to satisfy the standards for approximation to that ideal case in force in the context of this very statement. Correlatively, when a speaker appropriately may say of the second meeting that it did have a real beginning, he may get us, and himself, to focus on some such quite different thought as this: In regard to having a time when it began, *this* meeting is sufficiently close to the ideal case of something having a beginning to satisfy the standards for approximation to that ideal case in force in the context of *this* very statement.

In further contexts, we may accept as true a statement to the effect that even the first meeting did have a beginning. For example, *at least* two hours into that extremely informal meeting, someone may say, "Look, it's well over an hour since this meeting began, and we haven't made any headway at all on John's proposal; perhaps we had better discuss the alternative idea that Martha brought up a few minutes ago." In yet other contexts, we may *not* allow as true a statement that the second meeting had a real beginning. For example, a physicist may choose to contrast that alleged beginning with the beginning of a sequence of reactions involving subatomic particles, to highlight some point about what, on his view, is the quantum nature of time. He may then say, quite appropriately, that the first step in his microcosmic sequence was a real beginning of that sequence. But the so-called beginning of a formal meeting is just a conventionally demarcated period that, on a really fine, accurate, and objective measuring of time, is not only imposed on the natural order by our own conventions, but is even rather sloppily so imposed. So, the invariantist may point out, what we adaptively focus on will be sensitive to context, and often enough will be true. But such a philosopher may insist on distinguishing between these adaptive thoughts and any of the statements proffered. The statements actually made, he may say, will have nothing to do with context and, at the least, will almost invariably fail to be true.

The invariantist has a theory of our total behavior in which the semantic component, and so the psychological component of semantic understanding, is comparatively simple and small. He must then have what we take to be an unusually large *pragmatic* component, or psychological component of merely associated understanding. That is the way he cuts the cake, so to say, the way he distributes the complexity needed to adequately describe and explain our contextually sensitive, adaptive, and successful patterns of behavior.

As I discussed in *Philosophical Relativity*, there is another theory of our behavior that, in a certain respect, is the mirror image of the invariantist's. According to *contextualism*, semantics is actually much more complex than one might suspect. So, a statement to the effect that something is flat, or that something had a beginning, (almost always) *involves*, though it is *not about*, the context of the statement itself, even including the perhaps temporarily dominant interests of the main people of the context. Thus, the *semantics* of the statement "The meeting had a real beginning" is relevantly spelled out by: In regard to having a time when it began, the (indicated) meeting is sufficiently close to the ideal case of something having a beginning for those standards of approximation to that ideal case in force in the context of this very statement. All of that business about standards — which ones in force depending on contextual interests — is part of the conditions for truth of the simple statement about when the indicated meeting began. According to the contextualist view, the semantics of such seemingly context-free and interest-free terms is actually much more complex and much less objective than it appears. Thus, too, with that component of our psychological explanation of behavior that falls under the heading of semantic understanding. These are drawbacks of contextualism. But having paid this price, the contextualist is so often home free regarding pragmatic considerations. In understanding the meaning of, and the truth conditions of, the words used to make a statement about, say, the beginning of an extremely informal meeting, we are already focusing on the adaptive thought we need to guide successful behavior.

Overall, contextualism has a much greater psychological appeal than does invariantism. That is because, according to the contextualist view, but not to the invariantist view, what we say about the putative beginnings of so many ordinary items, about the putative flatness of so many ordinary items, and so on, will very often be *true*, just as we ordinarily believe it to be. According to invariantism, in contrast, our statements will so very often fail to be true. For this reason alone, contextualism is the more psychologically attractive, more comfortable, and even more plausible of these at least apparently opposed approaches.

According to the contextualist treatment of 'individual', 'entity', and 'being', in their preferred senses, it will almost always be true for us to say that we are individuals, entities, and beings. That is because there will hardly ever occur a context for us in which we lack those interests, conversational and otherwise, that will contribute enough so that it will be true for us to say these things. This may cause us to be somewhat cheerful about the matter of our individuality, as our concerns in the direction of securing it to the greatest extent possible for us are somewhat stronger, in all likelihood, than our concerns in the opposite Spinozistic, or Buddhistic, direction.

Few who think much about these matters will remain that cheerful for very long. For if, in general, it is only our own interests that take the last needed step for us to be individuals, or entities, then our individuality seems to be achieved by something too much, even if not very much, like cheating. What we really want, in this direction of our prereflective thoughtful concerns, is to be entities in a wholly objective and independent way, in no wise dependent on our own interests in talking and thinking about ourselves as entities each in his own right, rather than as mere aspects, parts, or regions. Accordingly, even if it provides the only correct account of the area, there is something about a contextualist treatment that is a good deal less than fully satisfying.

The most plausible treatment of these matters leaves us with a somewhat empty and floating feeling about ourselves. Most likely, this is all that we should ever expect. But this may not be the end of the story. Indeed, there is a third position, beyond contextualism and invariantism, that demands at least some serious consideration.

Although granting the great plausibility of contextualism, we may seriously question whether the view is correct, both generally and in the present application of it. We may seriously ask: Is there really any more truth in contextualism than in invariantism? Indeed, is there *any real opposition* between these two approaches toward describing and explaining our behavior? The *hypothesis of semantic relativity* is a proposal to the effect that there is no difference of substance between contextualism and invariantism; there is only a difference of how to label the complexity, within total theory, that is needed to explain our contextually relevant behavior. The contextualist places more complexity under the labels *semantics* and *understanding of semantic features*; he places much in boxes, so to say, that are labeled in that way, and correlatively less in other boxes. The invariantist places little of the mutually acknowledged complexity in those boxes. Rather, he prefers to place much of it in boxes with other labels: *pragmatics*, perhaps, or *understanding of nonsemantic features associated with a statement's context*. As Grice has shown, there must be a fair amount in these latter boxes anyway; the invariantist merely chooses to put a lot more in there than at first might be supposed feasible.[20]

According to semantic relativity, there is no more truth to the one way of labeling, or of distributing, the needed complexity than there is to the other. Relative to the contextualist way, semantics is complex, and so much of what we say and accept as true is indeed true. Relative to the invariantist approach, semantics is comparatively simple, and so much of what we say and accept as true is not true. As there is no fact of the matter regarding which approach is superior, there is no fact of the matter regarding how complex, how context-sensitive, is the semantics of the many terms in question. Most conspicuously, on the hypothesis of semantic relativity, there is *no fact of the matter* as to whether so many things that we offer and accept as true are indeed true, or are not true.

Creature of habit that I am, I do not actually believe the hypothesis of semantic relativity. Or, if I do believe it, I believe it only quite weakly and, then, having conflicting views in the area, more strongly believe in comfortable contextualism.

But semantic relativity is at least a moderately plausible view, as well as a philosophically interesting and intriguing view. As such it deserves, I believe, serious consideration by serious philosophers.

11. A FORM OF ONTOLOGICAL RELATIVITY

As I argue in my book, the hypothesis of semantic relativity, insofar as it is right, or as it concerns any real language that we have, will concern quite a few terms of philosophical importance, among them 'certain', 'know', 'free', 'power', 'cause', and 'explain'. Let us suppose that the hypothesis is right, or is as true as anything else in the neighborhood. Then it will apply to all those terms and more. Because it applies to all those terms and more, semantic relativity leads to an "object level" counterpart, which I call the *hypothesis of philosophical relativity*.

According to this hypothesis, (because there is no fact of the matter regarding what the philosophically important terms mean) there is no fact of the matter whether we are certain of many things, whether we know many things to be so, whether we are free to do many things, where we have the power to do much, whether the attributions of cause and effect we make are often true, whether the explanations we offer are often genuine, and so on. According to this hypothesis, then, there is no fact of the matter whether the skeptic about knowledge, or the antiskeptic, is right; there is no fact of the matter whether the incompatibilist about determinism and free action, or the compatibilist, maintains the correct position.

In line with the reasoning of our present essay, we may extend the hypothesis of semantic relativity to a range of expressions previously undiscussed in this connection, to 'beginning', 'boundary', 'set off from the rest of concrete reality', 'phenomenon', 'real essence', 'individual', 'being', and 'entity'. According to this hypothesis, there is no fact of the matter whether these terms apply only to such candidates that are, respectively, in the ideal cases for those terms or whether also to the many more actual candidates that approximate, perhaps sufficiently closely for contextual interests, those ideal cases.

We may use this result to extend the range of our hypothesis of philosophical relativity. We may use it to advocate, tentatively and unconfidently, a *hypothesis of ontological relativity*. We may then say that, because of the semantic relativity of all of these newly discussed terms, and because of the great gradualness of the actual world of concrete reality, there is no fact of the matter regarding many ontological questions: There is no fact of the matter whether noses or clouds, or rocks or planets, or bushes, or even you or I, have beginnings, or have boundaries, or are set off from the rest of concrete reality, or have real essences, or are individuals, or are beings, or are entities. And there is no fact of the matter whether consciousness, or mentality, is a real phenomenon. Closest to home for you, we may say that because of a certain indeterminacy in our language (and thought), and because of the well-evidenced scientific view of the world as relevantly gradual, there is no fact of the matter whether you are an entity or whether you are, at best, *merely* a part, aspect, or region of some suitably great entity, or entities. We say this cautiously and tentatively, of course, not confidently or complacently.

In *Philosophical Relativity*, I noted certain differences between the semantic indeterminacy that I postulate for our language and that hypothesized by W. V. Quine, principally in his *Word and Object*.[21] I noted that my conjecture of indeterminacy was somewhat more modest than, and is compatible with, Quine's famous hypothesis of indeterminacy. At this present juncture, I should mention Quine's thesis of ontological relativity, put forward in an essay of that name.[22] As far as I can discern, the form of ontological relativity that I am offering here is somewhat more modest than, and is compatible with, the thesis that Quine offers. It would be interesting to compare our two theses in some detail. But that is a task better reserved for some other occasion, and perhaps better undertaken by students of Quine's work, who are more deeply familiar with it than I am.

Let us suppose, as is at least somewhat plausible, that my hypothesis of ontological relativity is correct, or what amounts to much the same, that it is not determinately false or incorrect. Then, there is no fact of the matter whether you are an individual, a being, or an entity, or, alternatively, whether you are, at best, merely a part, aspect, or region of some sufficiently greater entity or entities. Concerning our thoughts and attitudes about ourselves, what may follow if this is, indeed, the situation?

Now, as I mentioned near the outset, there is a part of us that is very much concerned that we be entities in our own right, and not merely parts of some greater entity, or of the universe as a whole. It is this part that craves a very high form of autonomy, independence, and individuality. This part of us worries that we might not truly be entities in our own right. When we think this way, we have great sympathy for views that set us apart from the rest of the world, even if these views are unrealistic, or go against our best evidence. We are sympathetic with the view of Descartes, for example, and perhaps certain views of the self endorsed by certain forms of Christianity. But when we seek to satisfy this part of ourselves, this part of our psychology, perhaps by adhering to one of these apparently unrealistic views or perhaps in some other way, we will frustrate another part of ourselves.

This other part of ourselves, or other part of our psychology, craves identification with a sufficiently greater entity, perhaps an infinite being, and fears that each of us might be an entity in his or her own right. When thinking in this way, we see only a great and inevitable aloneness, something at least verging on a loneliness, in the prospect of one's being an entity. Then we are sympathetic with a view of ourselves perhaps like that of Spinoza, or of certain forms of Buddhism. Then we might also be more sympathetic with what may be a more realistic attempt to have us be only parts, regions, or aspects of some sufficiently great entity. But, insofar as we seek to satisfy this part of ourselves, we will frustrate our craving for individuality.

Because of this conflict in our attitudes about ourselves, we cannot win, no matter what the world is like and no matter what we are like. Now, short of unwanted brain surgery or other such unnatural intervention, nothing will ever, I believe, fully resolve this conflict in us. So anything that can cause us to worry over the conflict somewhat less seriously than we are apt to do may be of some consolation. If what causes us to be less serious, or less intense, in those worries is a rational and realistic approach to the matters themselves, so much the better.

Given the great indirect evidence for the general truth of our scientific objective view of the world, matters of our existence are not all-or-none, but are metaphysically indeterminate. According to our hypothesis of ontological relativity, there will then be no fact of the matter whether we are entities in our own right or merely parts, regions, or aspects of some sufficiently greater entity, or of the universe as a whole. On this hypothesis, then, there is nothing at all that can realistically satisfy our wish to be entities each in his or her own right, and there is nothing that can thus satisfy, either, our wish each to be merely some part, region, or aspect of the universe.

Insofar as we can accept the position of ontological relativity, we can feel this unresolvable conflict in our attitudes to be somewhat less poignant, and somewhat less troubling. That will be a benefit of accepting that relativistic hypothesis. It is not much of a reason, of course, for accepting such a hypothesis. For any really strong reason must be based on a rational assessment of our evidence, and on relevantly impartial and objective reasoning about what the evidence rationally indicates. To proceed otherwise is to engage in overly wishful thinking. But an appreciation of this possible benefit is, I think, a reason for taking this hypothesis seriously, for investigating further what evidence and argument counts in its favor, as well as against it.[23]

Notes

1. Perhaps an expression of a connection between these two intuitive beliefs is to be found in Colin McGinn's *The Character of Mind* (Oxford, 1982). Early in the book, McGinn addresses the nature of consciousness and the condition of having a mind: "There is, though, something instructive that we can say about the nature of consciousness — and this is that the possession of consciousness is not a matter of *degree*. Put differently, the concept of consciousness does not permit us to conceive of genuinely borderline cases of sentience, cases in which it is inherently indeterminate whether a creature is definitely conscious or it is definitely not. . . . If consciousness is an all-or-nothing matter, then it follows that the possession of a mind is also an all-or-nothing matter, since consciousness is what characterizes the mind. There may be many kinds of mind, but none of these is a case where it is inherently indeterminate whether there is a mind or not.

"The concept of mind contrasts in this respect with the concept of life, for it is not difficult to persuade oneself that the latter concept does admit of borderline cases" (pp. 13–14).

For two reasons, I use the word "perhaps" here, as a note of caution. First, McGinn may be, indirectly, making only a trivial point about the semantics of 'conscious', that, like 'has a mass of more than a gram', it admits of no borderline cases. But the weight of textual evidence is against this, indicating that he means his point to have at least some metaphysical depth. Second, when McGinn more directly discusses questions of our existence and identity, much later in the book, he does say that these matters, too, are all-or-nothing (pp. 102–5). But McGinn states as a necessary condition for having a self, or being a self, or someone's existing(?), the possession of self-consciousness, not just consciousness. Still, the possession of self-consciousness seems to require, minimally, the possession of just plain consciousness.

So I think it fair to attribute to McGinn an expression of these two connected intuitive beliefs that we all share, and an idea to the effect that they are connected.

Other authors may express these two intuitively appealing beliefs, that matters of our own existence are all-or-none and that so are matters of consciousness, in somewhat different ways, and may differently express, as well, apparent connections between them. However, whether any contemporary author gives expression to precisely the two beliefs I want to 'explore, there is no denying that they have a distinct appeal to us, an appeal I wish to challenge and, perhaps, to undermine.

2. To put forward a challenging form of nihilism, I introduced these sorites arguments in my "I Do Not Exist," in *Perception and Identity*, edited by G. F. MacDonald (London, 1979).

3. In a longer (unpublished) version of this long paper, I offered certain of these reinforcing spectra in some detail. These included a spectrum of brain impairments, largely a result of discussion with Stephen White, and, largely from discussion with Derek Parfit, a much-revised version of Parfit's (somewhat inadequate) physical spectrum, the original version occurring in his *Reasons and Persons* (Oxford, 1984) on pp. 234–36. There was also a discussion of why Parfit's combined spectrum, in the same book on pp. 236–43, could not even be revised to provide a spectrum useful in these regards, contrary to Parfit's claims there for that spectrum. The deep inadequacy of the combined spectrum, I should point out, has been noted by Geoffrey Madell in his fine short paper "Derek Parfit and Greta Garbo," *Analysis* 45 (1985).

In a shorter ancestor of the present paper, I offered a spectrum of brain bisections, which I also think useful in undermining our two connected intuitive beliefs. I hope to discuss all these spectra, and others, too, in a book on the human condition and our appropriate responses to it. (But that book may be a long time coming. The more I write on these subjects, the further away the book's completion appears to be.)

4. In an unpublished paper, "On Our Concern for Ourselves and Others", I discuss a number of aspects of "what matters." In other unpublished papers, I discuss some other aspects. My hope is that all of this material will, in a suitable form, find its way into the projected book cited in the previous note.

5. See David Lewis, "Scorekeeping in a Language Game," in his *Philosophical Papers*, vol. 1 (New York and Oxford, 1983).

6. *Philosophical Relativity* (Minneapolis and Oxford, 1984).

7. This is in my "Consciousness and Self-Identity," *Midwest Studies in Philosophy* 10 (1986).

8. See "Consciousness and Self-Identity," especially pp. 86–98.

9. I introduced this sorites, and the spectrum of cases at its core, in my nihilistic paper, "I Do Not Exist" (cited in note 2). I used this sorites in a still more radical nihilistic way in "Why There Are No People," *Midwest Studies in Philosophy* 4 (1979). As with any all-encompassing paradox, a sorites of this form eventually questions all of what passes for, and presumably is, language and thought. That it does that is not a terribly big mark against it, showing more about its all-encompassing character than about any substantial fault in the argument (sic). That what was offered goes so strongly, and so obviously, against so much of our common-sense thinking is a bigger mark against it.

10. I considered this "opposite" sort of sorites, and used this expression for it, in "I Do Not Exist."

11. Parfit, it seems to me, takes this line in his discussion of his combined spectrum in *Reasons and Persons*, pp. 236–43. Whether or not he does, it is a line of some logical interest, worth at least a brief discussion.

12. Perhaps it is conceivable that we should have *some* such awareness. For all I know, the laws of nature might allow each of your cells to be replaced by some tiny metallic, nonliving unit in such a way that, except for sleep when no replacements are made, your consciousness is never interrupted. Perhaps as you became less and less of a living creature, the character of your conscious experience would alter in a certain way. Perhaps when you were no longer alive at all, the character would be radically different from what it now is, as you might consciously remember. But if any of this is conceivable, it is very far from actual. Perhaps it is so far from being actual that, in some sense, it is, at best, only *indirectly* conceivable for us.

13. If they exist, perhaps enormously small segments, or points, of this encompassing phenomenon also have metaphysical significance, each then being a *quantum* with respect to that phenomenon.

14. Some people have the intuition that a universe that is infinite in all its dimensions and directions

is, in the restricted sense of the term, beyond being an entity, and so is not an entity. Perhaps this is right. If it is, that will not affect any of the main points of the present essay. Only certain formulations will have to be avoided, in favor of others. In the text, at many places I use only such more-cautious formulations; at many others, I use less-cautious ones.

15. See my paper "The Problem of the Many," *Midwest Studies in Philosophy* 5 (1980).

16. In his forthcoming book, *Material Beings*, Peter van Inwagen advocates such a view for rocks but not for organisms. Van Inwagen is not very much concerned with spatial boundaries; but he should be much concerned with what I call *causal boundaries*, discussed in section 9.

17. Perhaps Einstein's theory of relativity will require us to talk of space-time boundaries, rather than of temporal and spatial boundaries. If so, then, I should expect, points will be made in those terms that are parallel to the points I make here in our more ordinary terms.

18. I expect that some historical figures may be fairly saddled with such a view, but I am not nearly enough of a historian to do the job properly. In the forthcoming work cited in a previous note, van Inwagen offers a view that might be interestingly confronted with some of these ideas and questions.

19. Perhaps there is an interesting connection between the points I am making here and Einstein's theory of relativity, mentioned in note 17. But I do not know nearly enough physics to say anything worthwhile about this question.

20. Much of the material was presented in H. P. Grice's William James Lectures, and much has been circulated in unpublished form for many years, but little has been published. For highlights see his paper "Logic and Conversation," in *The Logic of Grammar*, edited by Donald Davidson and Gilbert Harman (Encino and Belmont, Calif., 1975).

21. *Word and Object* (Cambridge, Mass., 1960).

22. The paper is Quine's "Ontological Relativity," a version of his John Dewey Lectures, in his collection, *Ontological Relativity and Other Essays* (New York and London, 1969).

23. Many people have been helpful in giving me advice and criticism concerning the work for this paper. Let me thank Mark Heller, Mark Johnston, Thomas Nagel, Derek Parfit, Peter van Inwagen, and Stephen White.

Fearing for Our Mental Lives

ARON EDIDIN

If our science is inconsistent with the folk precepts that define who and what we are, then we are in for rough times. . . . Deprived of its empirical underpinnings, our age-old conception of the universe within will crumble just as certainly as the venerable conception of the external universe crumbled during the Renaissance.

—Stephen Stich[1]

On Tuesday, when it hails and snows,
The feeling on me grows and grows
That hardly anybody knows
If those are these or these are those.

—Pooh Bear[2]

A THREAT TO OUR SELF-IMAGE

Those of us who are inquirers by profession or inclination (and that may include almost everyone to some degree or another), as well as those of us who are just opinionated (and that probably catches most of the rest), tend to a considerable extent to conceive of ourselves in terms of what we think about things. It matters a lot to us which views we hold, which positions we espouse and which we eschew, which claims we accept and which we reject. We consider ourselves to be thinking things, even if not exclusively so, and we greatly value our lives of thought, our beliefs, and the processes that form them. Similarly, and perhaps to a still greater extent, what we want in life matters to us. Our aims, our goals, and in general what we desire constitute another central element of our views of ourselves.[3] It is, therefore, disconcerting to learn that philosophers who have considered the matter at length,

335

with care, clarity, and erudition, have concluded that it's quite possible that nobody really believes or desires anything at all. It is not unlikely, these philosophers argue, that future developments in the scientific explanation of human behavior will show that our naive picture of ourselves as (among other things) believers and desirers is simply the mistaken conclusion of a protoscientific folk theory whose ontology of belief and desire contains only fictions analogous to the vital forces, caloric fluids, demonic possessions, and luminiferous ethers of other discredited theories. Whether the correct theory of human behavior will refer to mental states or properties at all is uncertain, but even if it does, the mental states that it recognizes are apt to be vastly different from beliefs and desires as we commonly attribute them. The difference is likely to be great enough to yield the conclusion that all our everyday attributions of belief and desire are false. (In what follows, I shall use the term 'behavioral science' as a general term for the scientific investigation of behavior.[4])

Of course, the claim that there are no such things as beliefs and desires is not a new one. Versions of materialism and behaviorism that include this claim have been around for a long time. But more recent attacks on the notions of belief and desire are distinguished from their predecessors by their independence from any general hostility to mental states or events as such. Considerations specific to belief and desire lead such authors as Stephen Stich and Paul Churchland to doubt their existence.[5]

I think that these philosophers' arguments are fascinating, plausible, and intensely illuminating, but that they fail to show that our understanding of ourselves and others is apt to prove radically misguided. Considering their virtues and defects will force us to examine not only belief, desire, and the causes of our behavior, but also the relations of common sense to science and of semantic analysis to the understanding of ordinary discourse.

Before considering Stich's and Churchland's reasons for suspecting that there are no beliefs, it will be helpful to pay a bit more attention to the self-image that seems threatened by the possibility they describe. In particular, I want to focus on one crucial element of our view of ourselves as believers and desirers. I have said that we tend to conceive of ourselves in terms of what we believe and desire. At issue here is how we consciously think about ourselves, and thus the beliefs and desires that we consciously attribute to ourselves. If my own thought is at all representative, then our conscious discursive thought is largely – maybe even exclusively – a matter of talking to ourselves in languages that we also use for talking to others. I attribute beliefs and desires to myself in thought by saying to myself *in English* things like: "I believe that it will rain tomorrow in South Bend" and "I wish that it weren't raining now." As far as I can tell, my access in conscious thought to what I believe and desire is exhausted by such attributions. They thus provide me with my only resource for creating a conscious self-image in terms of what I believe and desire. Now, it seems clear to me that the meaning of such attributions when uttered silently to myself is no different from their meaning when uttered aloud to others. Since the content of a belief or desire that I attribute to myself in thought is given by the clause that follows "I believe that" or "I wish that"[6] in my self-attribution of the belief, it follows that it is essential to my conceiving of myself (even in part), in terms of what I believe and desire, that my beliefs and desires can have contents similar if not identical to those of (utterances of) such ordinary English sentences as "It will rain tomorrow in South Bend."

WHY THERE MIGHT BE NO BELIEFS OR DESIRES

Why, then, do Stich and Churchland suspect that there will turn out to be no beliefs and desires? Their expectations are based on a common premise concerning the nature of our notions of belief and desire combined with rather different predictions about the likely future course of behavioral science. The common premise is so widely shared by writers on belief and desire that it may aptly be called the received view of those attitudes: that belief and desire are among the posits of a proto-scientific "folk psychology" that proposes such content-laden psychical states as elements in the etiology of behavior. As posits of a causal theory, belief and desire are vulnerable to the empirical disconfirmation of the theory that posits them. If that theory is superseded by a successor that posits neither beliefs nor desires (nor any states to which the beliefs and desires of the abandoned theory can be reduced), then belief and desire will go the way of phlogiston, animal spirits, and the sundry other mistaken posits of mistaken theories.

We may, I think, take this shared premise as a semantic claim about the terms 'belief' and 'desire'. Put semantically, the claim is that at least part of the meanings of these terms is that that their referents have the appropriate roles in the causation of behavior. If nothing plays the right kind of role, nothing is a belief or a desire. Adopting this semantic claim lets us rule out the possibility of taking the collapse of folk psychology to show only that beliefs and desires (though real enough) simply do not figure in the etiology of behavior. Such a position licenses the conclusion that playing the right sort of role in the etiology of behavior is essential to belief and desire.[7]

Given this shared premise, it is not surprising that both Stich and Churchland base their skepticism about belief and desire on the suspicion that behavioral science will eventually replace folk psychological accounts of behavior with accounts that do not include the right sort of causal roles. But their reasons for that suspicion differ.[8] Churchland focuses on the explanatory shortcomings of folk psychology and the greater promise, as he takes it, of the explanations to be expected from a matured neuroscience. The prospect he presents is one in which a theory of causal factors whose interactions are modeled on relations among sentences (i.e., beliefs and desires interacting by virtue of their contents) is replaced by a theory in which the key causal interactions are described in biological (and perhaps ultimately physical) terms.

Stich, in contrast, does not foresee the replacement of cognitive psychology per se by physiologically based explanations of behavior. He has more confidence than does Churchland in explanatory factors modeled on linguistic items. But he like Churchland finds no role for *content* in the explanatory accounts of an adequate behavioral science. Stich thinks that the causal posits of cognitive psychology will remain modeled on linguistic items in that they will be structured *syntactically* and interact in ways determined by their syntax, but he holds that cognitive psychology ought not to attribute *content* to its syntactically structured posits.

Even if behavioral science eventually settles on theories that do not mention beliefs or desires, it may yet be that our talk of belief and desire could be saved by reduction to the terms of those theories. But it is by no means inevitable that this should be the case. Churchland and Stich present reasons for pessimism concerning the reducibility of belief and desire ascriptions to the terms of the neuroscience or cognitive psychology of the future. If their pessimism is vindicated and their semantic assumption is correct, we may expect from behavioral science the eventual verdict that we neither believe nor desire.[9]

WOULD A COGNITIVE PSYCHOLOGY OF BELIEFS AND DESIRES HELP?

What if Stich and Churchland are wrong about the future of behavioral science? Perhaps the cognitive theories of the future *will* continue to explain actions as outcomes of the agents' beliefs and desires. Even if that happens, our image of ourselves as believers and desirers may be in trouble. The problem comes from the sort of contents that must be invoked by such theories. The aim of behavioral science is to explain behavior in terms of the agent's character at the time of acting.[10] But the contents of beliefs and desires as we ascribe them is not exclusively a matter of the believer's or desirer's condition. As Putnam puts it, belief (and desire) "ain't in the head."[11] The content of my beliefs is determined partly by my condition and partly by my physical and social surroundings. (In this respect what I believe resembles what I assert, which is determined by the words I utter or inscribe together with various aspects of the context of my utterance or inscription.)[12] Now, if cognitive theories are to invoke what I believe and desire—the content of my beliefs and desires—to explain my actions, those contents must be understood to depend on my condition alone. And we cannot assume that the contents thus ascribed will correspond to those we ascribe even to ourselves in the usual context-dependent way. Even if cognitive science confirms the existence of beliefs and desires, it may judge radically incorrect my ascriptions of beliefs and desires to myself and others. ("You believe things alright, but not *those* things!")

In fact, matters are even worse than this suggests. If the contents of my beliefs and desires are to be determined solely by my condition, then those contents must be purely qualitative, in the sense that they cannot depend on the referents (external to myself) of the beliefs and desires in question.[13] Otherwise, the contents of my beliefs and desires would depend in part on what existed around me, and not solely on my own condition. But the contents of all or most sentences of natural languages do depend on the referents of some of their terms.[14] To the extent that this is so, the sentences with which we express our beliefs and desires even to ourselves will differ in content from those beliefs and desires. Most of our beliefs and desires will have contents not shared by any natural-language sentences. And this, as I insisted earlier, undercuts our entire practice of thinking of ourselves in terms of the beliefs and desires that we ascribe to ourselves.

All of this assumes that if cognitive psychology eventually attributes beliefs and desires, we should take those attributions as straightforward competitors of our everyday attributions. In a sense this is just what the received view of belief and desire requires. But here, as in the cases of Stich and Churchland's prognoses, we must allow the possibility that our everyday talk about beliefs and desires might reduce in some less-than-straightforward way to talk about belief and desire as conceived in psychological theory. Once again, though, there is no assurance that such reduction will be possible. So even if Stich and Churchland are wrong about the future of behavioral science, the threat to our self-image remains substantially what it would be if they were right.

SEMANTICS AND WHAT WE CARE ABOUT

Our view of ourselves as believers and desirers is surely a central part of our overall self-image. It is disturbing to think that it is subject to rejection in the face of likely developments in the scientific explanation of human behavior. Even if both Stich and Churchland are wrong in their detailed speculations about those developments, the vulnerability of our self-image would remain. Who knows what the future of psychology or neuroscience might bring?

There are several ways in which one might try to show that our view of ourselves as believers and desirers is immune to refutation by the progress of science. One might argue that the commonsense view is the product of apodictic a priori intuition and is thus immune from empirical refutation. A variant on this approach would be to claim that the commensense view has the status of a datum with respect to theories of the etiology of behavior, so that any adequate theory must be consistent with the commonsense view. Both suggestions would protect the commonsense view by placing limits on the possible future development of behavioral science. On the other hand, one might argue that the commonsense view, though essentially a view of the causation of behavior, is so flexible that any remotely plausible theory of the etiology of behavior would turn out to be compatible with it.[15]

None of these lines seems to me very plausible. Surely behavioral science should and will go its own way without being answerable to commonsense views of the causation of the phenomena it studies. The possibility must remain that the outcome of scientific investigation of the causes of behavior will be radically different from our present speculations about its causes. Similarly, it seems to me that if we are committed to a theory of the etiology of behavior, we must face the possibility that it will be superseded by a radically different theory as our investigations proceed.

A more promising way of defending at least our attributions of belief and desire might be to deny that the causal roles in question are essential to belief and desire. We might insist that our view of ourselves as believers and desirers could be correct even if our beliefs and desires play no role in the usual etiology of behavior. To take this line is to deny the semantic view of belief- and desire-attribution common to Stich, Churchland, and many others. I think this line is worth pursuing, and I will say a bit more about it later. But I am not at all sure how to establish or refute the sort of semantic or essentialist claim that is at issue here, and I think it is worth thinking about what would follow if the semantic position of Stich et al. is correct. It is not clear to me that the scientific scenarios that Stich and Churchland foresee would refute the most central elements of our commonsense self-image even if their semantic view is correct. Stich and Churchland claim that if things turn out as they suspect, that will show that there really are no beliefs or desires. But even if they are right, it does not automatically follow that our commonsense self-image will have proved radically misguided.

To see why not, we must very carefully distinguish two different kinds of question. These are:

> (q1) What is entailed by an ordinary concept or body of discourse (how is that concept or discourse to be analyzed or explicated)?

and

> (q2) What is central to the understanding embodied by our ordinary use of the concept or body of discourse?

It is important to recognize that the concept may turn out to be without application or the discourse to be literally false, without our being seriously misguided in our ordinary understanding of the areas within which the concept or discourse has its application.[16]

An example of a case in which the two questions might receive different answers is that of our ordinary concept of motion. We regularly speak of objects as in motion or at rest without further qualification. Surely the most straightforward analysis of our speech interprets 'is moving' as a one-place predicate and so commits us to there being such a thing as (unqualified, "absolute") motion. If the theory of relativity is correct, then "folk dynamics" is mistaken in one of its most fundamental assumptions. But this central error does not seem particularly relevant to most of our everyday thinking about moving things. It is not simply that we can use a theory that we know is false because we also know that it yields good enough prediction under most circumstances. Rather, it seems that although our discourse is committed to the existence of absolute motion, that commitment plays no role at all in most of our ordinary use of folk dynamics. The discovery that there is no such thing as absolute motion not only leaves most of our practices intact, it brings with it no sense that the universe of movable things is profoundly other than we have conceived it to be (though *some* change in our conception will be required if we had previously believed in absolute motion).[17] We could switch to talking about relative motion with some inconvenience but no sense of having undergone a major conceptual change.

We may find another example in the case of arithmetical discourse. This discourse seems best (or at least most simply) analyzed as entailing a commitment to the existence of numbers conceived as immaterial entities whose existence and arithmetical properties are independent of the activities (mental or otherwise) of arithmetizers. It seems, that is, that ordinary arithmetical discourse is committed to arithmetical Platonism. On the other hand, the discovery that Platonism is untenable (and most of our arithmetical discourse thus literally false) probably would not have much impact on the way most of us use arithmetic or think about numbers. That Platonism, though it may be right as an analysis of our arithmetical discourse, is not *obviously* right even as an analysis illustrates the fact that the Platonistic commitments of our ordinary arithmetical discourse are not a central part of the way in which we usually think about numbers.[18] Of course, it might turn out that the apparent virtues of our ordinary arithmetizing, for the sake of which we engage in that practice, are illusory because Platonism is false, but that possibility seems so remote that its neglect is well warranted.

These considerations are particularly relevant to the views of those who claim that common speech embodies commitments to various proto-scientific theories concerning its subjects.[19] These examples suggest that although common speech itself may often be so committed, its users need not be much interested in those commitments. It seems, that is, that the attitude of naive speakers toward at least some of the theoretical commitments of their speech (to the extent that they are even aware of them) will be akin to that of scientific instrumentalists. What we are apt to care most about in everyday speech is not the truth of the theories to which our discourse is committed, but rather the fitness of that discourse in some other respect. Such "other respects" need not be limited to the prediction and control beloved by textbook instrumentalists. They may also extend to the compendious expression of a view of the phenomena in question that in some perhaps vague and ill-understood respects differs from the theory literally entailed by their speech.[20]

It is important to note that whether in a given domain of discourse our principal concerns are those of "realists" or "instrumentalists" is independent of whether we characteristically take ourselves to be speaking truly in that domain. In particular, we may combine the realist's view that our statements in a domain are literally true with an instrumentalistic indifference to their truth. Indeed, matters are even more complicated than this, for we might *erroneously* suppose that the understanding embodied in a given body of discourse depends on its truth. For example, many speakers are doubtless unaware that their talk of moving things could be paraphrased to their satisfaction in terms of relative motion. Such speakers might well suppose that a world without absolute motion (in which their talk of moving things is therefore false) must be one of Parmenidean stasis, vastly different from the world of moving objects as they understand it. But such a view of the relationship between the truth of their discourse and the adequacy of their understanding would be mistaken. The discovery that there is no such thing as absolute motion leaves the understanding embodied in their discourse essentially unchallenged. Such speakers are instrumentalists in spite of themselves, mistakenly holding that the domain in question is one in which their commitments and those of their discourse are the same. The question "realist or instrumentalist?" may be asked with regard to our view of the truth of our discourse, with regard to our concern for the truth of our discourse, and with regard to the relationship between the commitments of the understanding embodied in our discourse and those of the discourse itself. The last example shows that the answers to the latter two questions may diverge, as either may diverge from the answer to the first. If the commitments of our understanding of a domain need not match the commitments of our discourse, neither are they necessarily what we take them to be.

In the cases of belief and desire as elsewhere, we may ask about either kind of commitment with regard to any putative element of these commonsense notions. We may ask whether our everyday attributions of belief and desire are committed to the presence of the element. Is it really essential to belief and desire as we ordinarily attribute them? But we may also (or instead) ask the separate question of whether the element in question is essential to the understanding embodied in our everyday attributions of belief and desire. Here, as in the case of independently existing numbers and absolute space, an affirmative answer to the first question need not entail an affirmative answer to the second. We should be prepared to discover that the element is indeed an essential part of the ordinary notion of a belief (so that if it is not present there is literally no belief) but is not a central part of the understanding embodied by attributions of belief (so that the discovery that it is never present need not lead to any serious dislocations in our understanding of people and how they work). In other words, the following plausible inference is *not* valid:

(1) Attributions of belief and desire embody essential elements of our understanding of ourselves and others.
(2) Our attributions of belief and desire are all literally false because there are no beliefs and desires, because nothing plays the right causal roles in the etiology of behavior. Therefore
(3) Our understanding of ourselves and others is radically flawed.

(3) follows from (1) and (2) only if the understanding embodied in belief and desire attributions depends essentially on the literal truth of those attributions. A parallel inference would be:

(1′) Numerical equations embody essential elements of our understanding of quantity.

(2′) Numerical equations are all literally false because there are no such things as numbers, therefore

(3′) Our understanding of quantity is radically flawed.

With regard to the challenge posed by Stich and Churchland, the questions may be put more precisely. The element in question is the causal potency of mental states that bear the sort of content that we ordinarily ascribe to beliefs and desires. Both Stich and Churchland suspect that the etiology of behavior will turn out to contain no element that bears such content. This leads to their doubts about the existence of belief and desire, since they contend that such causal potency is an essential element of belief and desire as commonly attributed. But if we are worried about how our view of ourselves and others must change if Stich or Churchland is right about the future of behavioral science, the more important question is the second: How important to the understanding embodied in our attributions of belief and desire is their putative role in the etiology of behavior? Note that the answer to this question will be a matter of degree. At one extreme, commitment to a causal role in the etiology of behavior might be *no part* of our commonsense view at all, or might even contradict that view. At the other extreme, such a commitment may be *absolutely central* to our understanding of ourselves and others. Between the extremes is a wide range of intermediate possibilities. Indeed, the really fundamental question in this domain is not the quantitative question of how important such a commitment is. It is rather the question of what elements of our self-image could and what elements could not survive the discovery that nothing plays the sort of causal role that we now attribute to beliefs.

Among philosophers of psychology, Dennett seems most aware of the distinction between what our discourse is committed to and what in the area of our discourse we most care about. Dennett thinks that we are or might as well be instrumentalists in our use of discourse committed to the existence of beliefs and desires. He suggests that we can without undue violence to our self-image take an instrumentalistically conceived version of folk psychology as either an analysis or a replacement of ordinary belief- and desire-talk. Whether or not such an instrumentalist approach captures the content of our belief and desire ascriptions themselves, Dennett thinks that it captures our central commitments as users of those ascriptions.[21]

I think that Dennett is absolutely right about what the important issues are here. I am less happy with his substantive suggestion; it seems to me that our attributions of belief and desire embody commitment to more than just the instrumental efficacy of folk psychodynamics. My own approach to the issues shall at least start out from a very different direction. But this important lesson from Dennett's approach should be borne in mind: whatever else may be involved, instrumentalist uses of folk psychodynamics are not vulnerable to the discovery that there really are no beliefs or desires.

THE ROLES OF BELIEF AND DESIRE

If Stich or Churchland is right, the progress of behavioral science may soon yield the discovery that there are no such things as beliefs or desires. This would entail that all our belief and desire attributions have been literally false. But we now know that it will take further investigation to determine whether this discovery would show that the understanding of ourselves and others embodied in those attributions is itself badly misguided.

An indication of the complexity of the latter question may be seen by considering the claim that the scientific community could discover that there is no such thing as belief. How are we to think of this discovery? Normally, we take discovering that φ to entail coming to the correct belief that φ. But if there is no such thing as belief, then, in particular, no scientist will come to the correct belief that this is so. Yet Stich's and Churchland's speculations about the future course of behavioral science do not seem obviously incoherent. What is going on?

The answer, I think, is something like this: Suppose that, as a matter of fact, no appropriately contentful state plays a central role in the etiology of behavior. This fact would neither remove the point nor impugn the genuine existence of such activities as the development, testing, discussion, and adoption or rejection of scientific hypotheses. This remains the case even if the ordinary notion of belief entails that it is just such a contentful, causally potent state. If Stich's or Churchland's speculations and semantic assumptions are correct, then scientists will not actually come to *believe* that there are no such things as beliefs, but they will develop, test, confirm, and adopt hypotheses to that effect. Of such a situation it seems natural to say that the scientific community would indeed have discovered that there are no beliefs.

If we add to these considerations the fact that we characteristically speak of the results of scientific investigation in terms of the belief of the scientists in question, it becomes clear that the understanding embodied in our ascriptions of belief is not limited to a set of (perhaps misguided) views about the causes of various actions. Suppose we discover that such attributions of beliefs to scientists in the context of discussions of scientific research have all been false because for Stichy reasons there are no beliefs. Suppose further that our account of the activities of developing, proposing, testing, confirming, and adopting hypotheses is otherwise correct. Here it seems that in the respects that most concerned us, the understanding embodied in those particular attributions of belief would have been substantially correct even though the attributions themselves were false. To see how widely this point might apply, we need to consider the various roles that we ascribe to the beliefs and desires that we attribute.

Belief and desire as we ordinarily understand them play at least three roles. What a person does is explained by reference to her beliefs and desires. (This is the dominant role of belief and desire in cognitive science and in postbehavioristic philosophy.) What it is rational for a person to do is determined by reference to her beliefs and desires. A person's view of the world as it is and as she would like it to be is constituted by her beliefs and desires. (This is the dominant role of belief in Descartes and the role that is most relevant to reports of scientific discovery.)

Our ordinary practices of belief- and desire-attribution cast beliefs and desires in all three roles. And it seems that we use but a single notion of belief to explain what people do, what it is rational for them to do, and what they think about things. The most popular philosophical view of belief in recent years takes the first role of belief attributions—their role in the explanation of action—to constitute the cornerstone of our notion of belief, and thus the essential nature of belief as we attribute it. For such authors as Armstrong,[22] Lewis,[23] Fodor, Stich, and Churchland, a belief is whatever plays the appropriate role in the explanation of action. Moreover, for these authors, the appropriate role is causal. If nothing contributes in the right way to the etiology of action, there are no beliefs. This is what I have called the received view of belief and desire, and it is this view that provides the basis for Stich and Churchland's suggestion that perhaps nobody really believes anything.

Suppose, then, that the suspicions of Stich and Churchland turn out to be correct. Suppose that the future of psychology or neuroscience shows that the causal antecedents of behavior include nothing that functions as beliefs are now supposed to do. We would then be faced with two questions about the beliefs that we had so confidently attributed. The first would be: Are there any such things? It is to this question that the received view would entail a negative answer. The second and perhaps more important question would be: How badly mistaken was the understanding embodied in our attributions of belief? This question is, as the first is not, one of degree. Moreover, again unlike the first question, it invites an answer that distinguishes among different areas of understanding jointly embodied in the attributions in question. Thus, to the extent that the purported causal role of beliefs as we understood it was central to our understanding of the etiology of behavior, the discovery that the etiology of behavior includes no such role would reveal the *etiological* views embodied in our belief attributions to have been badly mistaken. But this would not automatically entail a similar conclusion about the understanding of rationality embodied in those attributions. Neither would it automatically discredit the understanding of ourselves as thinking things—possessors of views of the world as it is and as we would like it to be—that is also embodied in our attributions of belief.

These considerations suggest that it would be a good idea to see what sort of doxic and orectic[24] notions are to be had if we take one of the two latter roles as primary. On one hand, this might provide us with an alternative to causal-role semantics for belief and desire attribution. On the other hand—supposing that the causal-role semantics are correct—it will help us to see how much of the view of ourselves embodied in our attributions of belief and desire could survive the discovery that there are no beliefs or desires. Rather than get involved at the outset with questions about the relation between the rationality of an action and its causal history, I shall try to develop a notion that focuses on the roles of belief and desire as constituents of worldviews.[25] I will then consider to what extent such a notion can serve the other roles of our current notion of belief. To the extent that it can serve in those roles without the causal potency we attribute to beliefs and desires, it will show that our understanding of ourselves as rational agents with views of the world does not depend on the causal potency of our doxic and orectic states in the etiology of behavior. Finally, I will briefly consider whether such a notion might actually turn out to *be* our current notion of belief and desire.

OPINING AND WISHING

People are inquirers. Some of us are professional inquirers and some are not, but the curiosity that makes us want to know even about matters of no practical importance seems to be a common human trait. We ask ourselves questions and we want to be able to answer them. Scientists and philosophers ask and try to answer abstruse questions about the natures of things, and their putative answers constitute scientific or philosophical theories. But each person has her own vast set of answered questions, and the answers that she accepts may be said to constitute her view of the world.

How are we to think of this answering of questions? First, it is natural to think of the adopting or endorsing of answers as an act, something we *do*. Indeed, it seems that we sometimes do it aloud. Vocal and written assertion and assent seem to be publicly observable species of this act. Of course, they are not the only species; there are silent analogues of assertion and assent. Here we give the assent or make the assertion to ourselves. We also talk to ourselves aloud, so assertion or assent to ourselves need not be silent. Indeed, assertion and assent prompted by fresh consideration of the claim in question ought probably to be seen as including the assertor in the audience even if it is also directed to an interlocutor. It seems that assertion or assent to ourselves, whether silent or voiced, is the primary way of incorporating elements into our worldviews.

When we assert or assent aloud, our assertion or assent can be observed by others as well as by ourselves. When we assert or assent to ourselves, it remains an essential part of the exercise that the assertion or assent can be noted by its intended audience. In this sense, it is of the nature of these acts that they be accessible to conscious awareness. (I leave open the possibility that we can assert or assent to ourselves absentmindedly, while our attention is elsewhere, and so fail to be aware of our assent or assertion.) Assertion and assent to ourselves are very much like Geach's acts of judgment[26] or, indeed, like belief itself as Descartes understood it. It is these acts of assertion and assent that build our views of the world. As a first approximation, we may say that a person's explicit worldview consists of those statements which she has asserted or to which she has assented (to herself in each case). To this we must add conditions to allow for changing one's mind, forgetting, and other ways of dropping elements of one's worldview. Following Dennett[27] we can call the elements of a person's worldview her opinions. Correlatively, we can call the asserting and assenting that creates opinions 'opining'.

The notion of opinion as I have described it allows in an entirely straightforward way for the familiar distinction between occurrent and dispositional doxic conditions. A dispositional opinion will simply be a claim to which the agent in question is disposed (in the right way) to assent (under the right conditions). The parenthetical qualifications are familiar from the standard distinction between occurrent and dispositional belief.[28]

I have introduced the notion of opinion as one suited to the role of beliefs as constituents of our views of the world. With our views of the world as it is we also have views of the world as we would like it to be, and it is not hard to find an orectic notion analogous to the doxic notion of opinion. As we opine, so too we wish, both aloud and to ourselves. Opining is associated with talking to ourselves in the declarative mode, wishing with the optative (as: 'Would that this paper were finished!'). Our view of the world as it is comprises our opinions, the objects of our opining. Our view of the world as we would like it to be comprises our wishes, the objects of our wishing. We may take opining and wishing to be species of the genus *affirming*, and our opinions and wishes to constitute our *affirmata*.

(It is important to bear in mind that I am here using the terms 'opinion' and 'wish' as terms of art for the components of our views of the world as we take it to be and as we would like it to be. Our opinions and wishes are the objects of our self-directed declarative and optative affirmations. Opinion in this sense is not to be taken as opposed to conviction or knowledge, and wishing is not to be taken as opposed to acting.)

My characterization of opinions and wishes guarantees that they will not play the roles in the causation of behavior that we normally attribute to belief and desire. I have said that I have an opinion (roughly) just in case I have done and not taken back the appropriate opining, and we can extend the suggestion in the obvious way to wishes. If my opinions and wishes are states of mine at all, they are states of my history, not of my present condition. To say that an opinion or wish of mine is causally potent would make sense only as shorthand for the claim that the act that made it my opinion was thus potent. Now, my public or private affirming will certainly have causal consequences of various sorts, but it seems vastly unlikely that they will have much of a direct role in the production of my behavior. (Does my saying to myself "Would that I were in Chicago!" play the role in getting me to the train station that my desire to go to Chicago is supposed to play?) In general, my behavior is in no direct way the causal product of my prior actions, among which are my various acts of affirmation. And to the extent that my past actions do influence those to come, they do not do so in the way normally attributed to beliefs and desires.

To what extent does this approach commit us to epiphenomenalism with respect to opinions and wishes? As in classic epiphenomenalism, affirmata are going to be additional products of the processes that cause our behavior (or of parallel processes. Does the difference matter?). Perhaps the "epiphenomena" play some role in the underlying processes (e.g., rehearsing as an aid to memory). It is not paradoxical to suppose that what we do has some effect on our underlying mental processes, though it is surely no part of the notion of affirming that it must have such effects.

It should be noted that this particular variety of epiphenomenalism may be put in a way that might be rather attractive, at least to intellectuals: our view of the world as a realm of facts and ends is a culminating result of mental activity on a par with other behavior rather than a dispensable byproduct of processes aimed at something else. (If this be epiphenomenalism, make the most of it!)

The central challenge to this approach is to distinguish sincere affirmation (to oneself or others) from the various sorts of deceitful or otherwise feigned affirmation: lying, playacting, trying out an assertion to see what it is like, and so on. A natural thing to say is that a sincere affirmation is of something really believed. With our approach, we may similarly say that a sincere affirmation matches the affirmer's true view of the matter, but we need some way of tracking down an agent's true views that is independent of individual affirmations even to herself (in order to allow for insincerity) and is not a matter of having the right internal affirmation-analogue. A natural way of working out the account of lying is a matter of asserting to others what you deny in your heart (to yourself) or are disposed to thus deny. On this account, *consistent* silent affirmation is per se sincere, though silent affirmation may fail to qualify as genuine if accompanied by an appropriate disposition to silent denial or doubting.

OPINIONS, WISHES, AND OUR SELF-IMAGE

Having introduced the notions of opinion and wish, we may now consider the two central questions concerning their status as potential successors to belief and desire should Stich or Churchland be right about the future of behavioral science. How well can opinion and wish perform the roles currently allotted to belief and desire? And might belief and desire as we have been ascribing them turn out to be opinion and wish after all?

The first question is the crucial one, since we want the consideration of opinion and wish to help us discover how bad a jolt our self-image must weather if Stich's or Churchland's speculations turn out to be correct. To the extent that attributions of opinion and wish can replace attributions of belief and desire in the latter's most important contexts, our view of the role of doxic and orectic elements in our makeup can remain substantially intact. The only deletions needed will involve attributions to those elements of causal agency in the etiology of behavior (and, if the causal-role semantics is correct, the characterization of the elements as "beliefs" and "desires") and the attribution of repressed, unconscious doxic and orectic states that are contentful in the usual way.

The third role, that of constituting our views of the world as it is and as we would like it to be, is that for which the very notions of opinion and wish were originally designed. Even if it turns out that there are causally active beliefs and desires, it might remain best to conceive of our views of the world in terms of our opinions and wishes. It might, for example, turn out that there are beliefs but their content is quite different from that of any sentences in natural languages. Such beliefs, with their unfamiliar and ineffable contents, would make poor candidates for the role of constituting our familiar views of the world, especially by comparison with opinions, whose contents are those of the sentences we use to express them.

If there is any serious problem for the functioning of opinion and wish in this role, it may well come from the narrowness of the explicit worldviews we get by limiting ourselves to the objects of agents' actual opinings and wishings and the difficulty of finding appropriate ways of expanding those explicit worldviews to include things like their elements' obvious consequences that the agent has never gotten around to considering. This may present no problem for our meditations upon our present views. In considering what I think about some topic, I can consider or reconsider items as I go along. When a putative element comes up for consideration I may affirm it or fail to affirm it, and its presence or absence in my view will be established. Indeed, as many philosophers have pointed out with respect to first-person attributions of belief, my assertion that I accept a claim may at the same time constitute my acceptance of it.

This sort of move is not available with respect to the description of another's worldview or of my own past view. And here it may look as though a limitation to claims that the attributee has explicitly considered could be quite troublesome. As Dennett might put it, it will come as no surprise to read that mosquitoes do not bake cakes. The claim that they do not probably is not one that you have ever considered, but it does not seem right, either, to say that your view of the world until now left the matter undecided. The natural move here, familiar from discussions of belief, is to invoke dispositions to opine; you may never before have opined that mosquitoes do not bake cakes, but you have for a long time been disposed so to opine, without need of conscious ratiocination, on consideration of the claim. In addition to your explicit worldview we ought perhaps to attribute to you a tacit view consisting of those claims to which you are disposed to assent on consideration without conscious ratiocination.

The value of dealing in tacit as well as explicit worldviews becomes more apparent when we notice that the former need not merely extend the latter. My explicit worldview may contain items that are in a sense obsolete. Here is a possibility: at some time I explicitly opine that φ. Later, I obtain information that disposes me to opine instead that $-\varphi$. But somehow I have not yet gotten around to reconsidering my opinion. When and if I do again consider whether of not φ, I will without any need of conscious ratiocination opine that $-\varphi$. In the meantime, though, I continue as it were to assume that φ. That I so assume may be revealed by my reasoning concerning other claims: I reason as if I thought that φ.[29] Here the best thing to say seems to be that I retain my explicit opinion that φ, but that my tacit worldview includes the claim (which I am now disposed to accept on consideration without need for conscious ratiocination) that $-\varphi$.

The notion of a tacit worldview characterized in dispositional terms seems necessary to the adequate construal of ourselves as worldviewers in terms of our opinions and wishes. But there are difficulties in giving a fully adequate account of such a notion. The characterization that I have been using may be too simple in holding that a claim is an element of my tacit worldview just in case I would be disposed to accept it on consideration without the need for conscious ratiocination. Suppose that I have no new information, but that I have come to be miswired in such a way that considering whether or not φ would cause a short circuit, which would in turn cause me to accept without conscious rationcination a large number of crazy claims, including the claim that −φ. According to my simple account, it is part of my tacit worldview that −φ. It may be that the problem can be avoided by amending the account of tacit worldviews to require that the worldviewer be disposed *in the right way* to accept the claims in question, with or without further specification of what ways are right. On the other hand, even apart from the evident problems with that approach, there is some reason to resist the amendment. In the case in question, my (explicit) opinion that φ *is* strikingly unstable in a way that closely resembles the instability of my obsolete opinions. Maybe the best thing to say about this case is that the opinion that −φ *is* part of my tacit worldview, but that the disposition that makes it so is very unlike those relevant to the other elements of my tacit view. Ascribing to me without further comment the tacit opinion that −φ might be literally correct but would nevertheless be very misleading.[30]

The notions of opinion and wish were designed for the role of constituents of worldviews, so it is not surprising that they perform well in that role. But what can they do with the other roles? Consider the first. How can attributions of opinions and wishes contribute to the explanation of behavior? They do not contribute causes: in general, things that I do (as we suppose opining and wishing to be) do not, at least in any very direct way, cause me to do other things. On the other hand, explanations in terms of wishes and opinions can serve at least two of the most important purposes of causal explanation. They can support counterfactuals, and (perhaps as a result) they can indicate effective strategies for influencing others' actions. Saying to myself "It looks like it's going to rain" did not in any direct way cause me to put on my hat before leaving the house, but if I had instead said to myself "It looks like it won't rain today," I would not have worn my hat, and you could have prevented me from wearing my hat by bringing me to the opinion that it was not going to rain. My opinions and wishes are correlated with my actions in the obvious way. What I do is usually what would best realize my wishes given the truth of my opinions. Moreover, this correlation is generally stable with respect to changes in my opinions and wishes. Change my opinions and wishes and I will probably act in the way that would best realize my new wishes given the truth of my new opinions.

The situation may be clarified by expanding upon Thomas Henry Huxley's use of the bell on an alarm clock as a metaphor for consciousness.[31] In terms of that metaphor, the situation is something like this: (a) The ringing of the bell is correlated with the subsequent behavior of the clock. (b) We know how to influence the ringing of the bell in ways that do not upset this correlation. As a result, we can influence the behavior of the clock by influencing the bell, even though the bell is not part of the causal process governing the clock's behavior. Presumably this is because we influence the bell by affecting the internal mechanism of the clock in ways we know nothing about. (c) The bell is our best source of advance warning of the behavior of the clock, and we can tell fairly immediately that we have influenced the bell, but only later whether we have influenced the behavior. Similarly, a person's opinions and wishes are correlated with her future actions and often provide our best means of predicting those actions; we can often influence others' opinions and wishes in ways that leave intact their correlation with subsequent action, and so use our influence over opinion and wish as a way of influencing action; we can, at least if our subject cooperates, tell what her relevant opinions and wishes are and whether they have changed long before we can tell directly what her actions will be. In a sense it will not be true that we influence action by influencing opinion and wish; rather, we presumably influence opinions and wishes by doing things that affect in ways that we may know nothing about the underlying causes of action.

Now, the sorts of things that characteristically affect our actual opining and wishing also affect our dispositions to opine and wish concerning matters that we may in fact never explicitly consider. Often it will be the case that (i) we know about what affects these dispositions (bringing matters to explicit consideration can enable us to test putative factors); (ii) the correlations between opinion and wish and action are mirrored in correlations between such dispositions and action; and (iii) the latter correlations are unaffected by the factors that we take to produce the dispositions in question. Under these circumstances, attributions of dispositions to opine and wish can play much the same role that attributions of actual opining and wishing play in the explanation, prediction, and influencing of behavior. This is particularly important in the case of wishing. Presumably I did not say to myself "I'd like to stay dry today" before donning my hat, but if I had for any reason considered the matter I would have said something like that; were I instead disposed to say "I'd like a good soaking today!" I might reasonably have been expected to leave my hat at home.

If an appropriate notion of sincere affirmation is in place, I think that most of the role of belief and desire in the explanation of action can be taken over by opinion and wish. Of course, to the extent that explanations in terms of beliefs and desires are intended to give the actual causes of the actions in question, opinion and wish will not duplicate the feat. Even in this respect, though, there will be available a fairly close analogue to the causal story in terms of beliefs and desires. In general, opinions and wishes themselves are not causal factors in the etiology of action, but the factors that influence our opinions and wishes are themselves such factors. A pre-Stich theorist might locate the cause of a given action in a complex of beliefs and desires that are themselves the products of a certain course of experience, but we may locate causes of the action among the experiences that also produced the agent's relevant opinions and wishes, taking the latter as the key to locating the former. (My hearing the weather forecast this morning presumably *was* part of what caused me to put on my hat before leaving the house.)

Of course, replacing explanations in terms of beliefs and desires with similar explanations in terms of opinions and wishes will succeed only in cases in which opinions and wishes corresponding to the previously ascribed beliefs and desires are available. The use of unexercised dispositions to opine and wish can expand the set of cases accessible to the strategy. But one important class of cases will remain in which explanation in terms of belief and desire cannot be mimicked in terms of opinion and wish or dispositions thereto. This is the class of cases in which the beliefs or desires in question are supposed to be unconscious and repressed in such a way that they would be disavowed by the agent in question. But it is precisely in such cases that commonsense or historical explanation most clearly follows a path blazed by psychological theorists. It is just here that we would expect the explanations we offer in everyday life and that historians offer in their professional works to be vulnerable to the rejection of the psychological theories to which they explicitly or implicitly appeal. Moreover, in such cases the beliefs and desires in question can play no role in an agent's conscious self-image.

Actually, even here matters are not quite so simple as the foregoing suggests. I am supposing that there are no real, causally potents beliefs and desires. I have been assuming that if all there are instead are opinions and wishes, then the only resources available for reconstructing our commonsense explanations of behavior are opinions and wishes and dispositions thereto. But that assumption is incorrect. Our explanations in terms of opinion and wish may be supplemented with the explanations available from folk psychology itself, instrumentalistically construed. We can think of this as a fictive extension of the framework of explanation in terms of opinion and wish: "It's (in relevant respects) *as if* she opined (wished) that φ" or, for that matter, "It's as if she *didn't* opine (wish) that φ."[32] In this way we can duplicate virtually all the explanations available to folk psychology, including those that invoke unconscious beliefs and desires. The cost of this means of reconstruction is, of course, that the explanations not only fail to identify actual causes of the behavior explained, but fail even to identify the explanatorily relevant characteristics of the individual. The explanations are given not in terms of what the agent *is* like, but rather in terms of what it is *as if* the agent *were* like. In this respect these explanations are unlike explanations in terms of the agent's opinions and wishes (and dispositions thereto). The latter do explain behavior in terms of facts about the agent, though they, too, fail to identify the causes of the behavior that they explain.[33]

Before I proceed to the third role of belief and desire as they are ordinarily attributed, I want to question one more assumption that I have been sharing with proponents of the received view. In common with them, I have been assuming that everyday explanation of actions in terms of their purposes is a matter of specifying some of the actions' causal or at least temporal *antecedents* in so doing, I have sought an account of the potential roles of opinion and wish that resembles as closely as possible the received account of the corresponding roles of belief and desire. If ordinary explanations of actions in terms of their ends is instead a matter of locating appropriate (actual or hypothetical) *results*, the role of beliefs and desires in everyday explanations of action is greatly diminished. This would have the double outcome of (first) making it less important to our self-image that the role be preserved, and (second) making it more likely that opinion and wish can duplicate the role (since it would by hypothesis not be one of providing causal antecedents for the actions, but rather something like predicting the ends for the sake of which the agent was apt to act).[34]

One role of beliefs and desires as attributed remains to be considered. In our ordinary view of ourselves, beliefs and desires are thought to play a role in explaining not only what we do but also what it is or would be rational for us to do. Indeed, the two roles are connected by proponents of the received view by way of the claim that only rational behavior can be causally explained by the beliefs and desires of the agent.

For an item of behavior even to be subject to evaluation as rational or irrational in the sense in question, it must be a genuine action. If there is no genuine purposive action, there will be no rational or irrational action. So, if opinion and wish are to play the role of belief and desire in the explanation of rational action, it must not be the case that the very notion of purposive action requires that belief or desire play a causal role in its etiology. If the ordinary understanding of the purpose of an action is not a matter of its antecedents, causal or otherwise, there is no problem here. But even if the received view is right that purposiveness is a matter of antecedents rather than (actual or hypothetical) results, opinions and wishes seem capable of functioning as the antecedents in question.

Here are two possible approaches to the causal explanation of purposive action: (1) psychodynamical analogues of opinions and wishes (i.e., beliefs and desires psychodynamically construed) interact to produce the actions, or (2) some other psychological mechanisms cause us to wish and opine and (usually) to act in ways that are (a) appropriate to our opinions and wishes and (b) responsive to the conditions that bring about informed changes in those opinions and wishes. The views of Stich, Lewis, Fodor et al. notwithstanding, it is not at all obvious that adopting approach 2 entails holding that there is really no such thing as genuinely purposive action. With the second approach we can distinguish actions performed by an agent of the opinion that the action would produce or facilitate a wished-for result. In such cases it will typically also be the case that had the agent been brought to the opinion that the action would produce or facilitate no wished-for result, she would not have performed the action. We can locate opinions and wishes such that if the opinions were true her action would have helped to realize the wishes, and such that had the agent opined or wished contrarily she would have acted otherwise than she did.[35]

The first and more popular approach does seem most straightforward and natural. Does that show (or suggest, or provide at least some evidence) that it is implicated in commonsense accounts of purposive action? Another explanation of its naturalness might be that it implicates as causal agents states that are modeled on familiar phenomena, whereas the second approach comes with no advance information at all about the causal agents in question. Even if common sense is best understood as committed to the first approach, it may of course be that this commitment is peripheral to the ordinary notion of purposive action and could be removed without radically undermining our views of ourselves.

If the occurence of purposive action does not require that the components of an action's purpose actually play causal roles in its production, we may consider how we might explain the rationality of actions on a view that replaces causally efficacious belief and desire with opinion and wish. First, we must distinguish two aspects of rationality: rationality as proper cognitive functioning[36] and rationality as acting for good reasons. According to the usual view, proper cognitive functioning is a matter of the agent's beliefs and desires interacting in the right way to produce actions. Actions thus produced must be appropriate to the agent's beliefs and desires, and the beliefs and desires that cause an action will be the agent's reason for so acting. It follows that on the usual view, actions that are the product of properly functioning cognitive equipment will of necessity be performed for good reasons, though the converse need not hold. If we take the second approach, the relationships will be more complicated. If your actions are inappropriate given your opinions and wishes, that will probably indicate a cognitive fault somewhere. But the fault need not be in the cognitive processes responsible for the action. It may instead be a fault in the processes responsible for your opinions or wishes, or in the coordination of the two sets of processes. It is, of course, still possible on this account for actions to be irrational in the sense of being the products of cognitive derangement. Whether an action is rational in this sense will not be determined by its relationship to the opinions and wishes of the agent. In this respect, opinion and wish ascriptions will not be able to play the normal role of ascriptions of belief and desire in explaining the rationality or irrationality of actions.[37] But this notion of rationality will remain available as long as the notion of cognitive derangement does not go by the boards. And rationality in the sense of being performed for good reasons will be explicable in terms of opinion and wish, just as it is in terms of belief and desire. An agent will have good reason to perform an action if it is the action that would best achieve the ends for which she wishes given the truth of her opinions.[38]

Opinion and wish seem well suited to each of the three roles that I have ascribed to beliefs and desires as ordinarily attributed. The only clear loss concerns the explanation of action: opinion and wish cannot, of course, play the causal role we seem to attribute to belief and desire, and they cannot duplicate the explanatory role of unconscious belief and desire. But these failures are isolated. They do not infect the rest of the role of explaining action, and they are irrelevant to the other roles. This sets a limit to the loss to our self-image that would result from the discovery that there are no beliefs or desires because nothing plays their supposed causal roles. We would lose an account of what causes us to act as we do, and we would lose the ability to appeal to unconscious motives noninstrumentalistically to explain actions.[39] But the claims that we are creatures with views of the world as it is and as we would like it to be; that these views can be used to predict, influence, and explain our actions (albeit not by giving their causes); and that the same views determine when we are acting for good reasons can all be retained by reconstruing those views in terms of opinions and wishes instead of beliefs and desires.

OPINION AND WISH AND BELIEF AND DESIRE

We are now in a position to address our second question about the relation of opinion and wish to belief and desire. So far, I have accepted the claim that the causal roles that we normally attribute to beliefs and desires are essential to those attitudes. But it seems that the causal roles attributed to belief and desire are isolated from their other roles, at least in the sense that the causal potency in question is not necessary to those other roles. This suggests, though it does not obviously entail, that the causal roles attributed to them do not constitute the essence of belief and desire.[40] If that is so, the discovery that nothing plays those causal roles would not automatically entail that there are no beliefs or desires. It seems instead that such a discovery ought to be taken to show that belief and desire are more like opinion and wish than like the causal posits of folk psychodynamics. Opinion and wish are so well suited to non-causal roles of belief and desire that if the causal role is lost, they might well turn out to *be* belief and desire.

What if the causal role is not lost? Even Stich and Churchland argue only that we must take seriously the *possibility* that behavioral science will ultimately exclude beliefs and desires from the etiology of behavior. Perhaps behavioral science eventually will posit elements in the etiology of behavior that function much as we normally suppose belief and desire to do, and to which belief and desire as they are ordinarily attributed may be reduced. In this case it would seem most natural to identify belief and desire as attributed in everyday discourse with these elements. Opining and wishing would be located among the *effects* of believing and desiring.

It should not be surprising that behavioral science should be a source of discoveries about the nature of belief and desire. We naturally expect these discoveries to appear as claims *about* belief and desire in the theories adopted by behavioral scientists. Such discoveries can take this form as long as the theories in question posit elements that are sufficiently belief- and desire-like. What I suggest is that the adoption of theories of behavior that posit *no* belief- or desire-like elements may itself be taken to embody the discovery that our beliefs and desires are our opinions and wishes.

One way or the other, if I am right about the resources of opinion and wish attribution to serve the principle purposes of belief and desire attribution, the scientific futures envisioned by Stich and Churchland would refute at most only a small part of the understanding embodied in the latter attributions. It should be noted that my consideration of possible successors to belief and desire is just one approach to the question of the import of those futures for our self-image. If I am wrong about opinion and wish as successors to belief and desire, the question remains open.

THE MORAL OF THE STORY

I have reached at long last the end of my argument for the claim that Stich's and Churchland's favorite futures for behavioral science would force no radical revision of our self-images. In spite of that conclusion, there is much to be learned from the very possibilities that Stich and Churchland anticipate. They remind us that intentional (content-invoking) psychology is not the only alternative to behaviorism as a direction for behavioral science. The failure of behaviorism does not entail the correctness of a psychology based on the commonsensical picture of action as driven by the contents of agents' beliefs and desires (or degrees of confidence and utility assignments) as these are normally attributed. Stich in particular makes a powerful case for the claim that this picture cannot be reconciled with the usual individualistic notion of psychological explanation, given the way that contents are actually attributed. The most natural account of the etiology of behavior is probably wrong. Even if this account is not an essential part of the self-understanding embodied in our attributions of belief and desire, this surely constitutes an important lesson about the relations among our beliefs, desires, and actions.

But the chief lesson to be learned from the assessment of Stich's and Churchland's claims concerns philosophical method. We must not assume that once we discover what it would take to make our claims about some important matter true (or false) we have thereby established the nature of our view of the matter. Our claims may not accurately reflect our commitments.

An effect of the complicated relationship between our assertions and our commitments is to complicate the issues involved in evaluating the claims of realists and antirealists. The central question in such a controversy – To what should we be committed? – remains unchanged. But evaluation of this question will almost surely require that we answer a second – To what *are* we committed? At the very least, identifying the intuitive, conservative answer to the first question requires that we answer the second. And to the extent that we are convinced that the understanding embodied in our discourse is not seriously misguided in the domain at issue, identifying our actual commitments will take us a long way toward identifying the right commitments. As Stich and Churchland point out, we should not be too complacent about the adequacy of our understanding. But the principal lesson learned from the evaluation of their arguments is that identifying our commitments cannot in general be accomplished by determining the truth conditions of our discourse. This means that we will not, in general, be able to tell whether we are realists or instrumentalists in a given domain by elucidating the semantics of our assertions in the domain.[41]

If semantic analysis cannot be relied upon to reveal the understanding embodied in our discourse, we need to locate other techniques. A look back to the earlier days of analytic philosophy reveals some promising candidates. One might be inclined to revive the tradition of ideal-language philosophy by trying to find ways to state perspicuously the content of our actual commitments. Alternatively, one might attempt to elucidate the understanding embodied in our discourse by careful description of the ways and concrete circumstances in which particular bits of discourse are used. If either approach proves successful, it might well be that the most salutary effect of Stich's and Churchland's work will be to set philosophical method back forty years.

Notes

1. *From Folk Psychology to Cognitive Science: The Case Against Belief* (Cambridge, Mass., 1983) 10, 246. (Hereafter *FFPTCS*.)

2. A. A. Milne, "Lines Written by a Bear of Very Little Brain," in "Kanga and Baby Roo," in Milne, *The World of Pooh* (New York, 1957), 95.

3. Those who balk at my generalizations about what is important to "us" may read 'I' and 'me' for 'we' and 'us' in the relevant contexts. I have neither the wherewithal nor the desire to defend the generalizations. If pressed on this, I would affirm the singular form, speculate that I am not altogether idiosyncratic in my assessment, and invite you to consider whether or not your assessment is relevantly like mine. None of the substance of my argument depends on generalizations about what is important to "us" or even on my own assessments of importance, though if, for instance, you do not care much about what you think, you are apt to have less interest in my claims than I would hope for.

4. Investigation of neurobiological elements in the etiology of behavior is in this sense a part of behavioral science. I do not know whether this usage is standard or not, but it is best for my purposes to have a term that covers both functionalistically conceived cognitive psychology and the relevant areas of neuroscience.

5. See especially Stich, *FFPTCS*, and Paul Churchland, "Eliminative Materialism and the Propositional Attitudes," *Journal of Philosophy* 78 (1981): 67–90. See also Stich, "Autonomous Psychology and the Belief-Desire Thesis," *Monist* 61 (1978): 573–91, and "On the Ascription of Content," in *Thought and Object*, edited by Andrew Woodfield (Oxford, 1982), 153–206; and Churchland, *Scientific Realism and the Plasticity of Mind* (Cambridge, 1979).

6. Or some other appropriate phrase in English (e.g., "I think that") or some other language (e.g., "Ich glaube dass").

7. It is clear that Stich and Churchland accept this last claim. It is less clear that they would accept my semantical formulation of its basis. Of what follows, nothing depends on the semantical claim that is not also a consequence of this essentialist corollary.

8. It should be noted that in both cases the suspicion is presented as just that. Neither Stich nor Churchland attempts to argue that behavioral science must evolve in the ways they describe, but only that present indications suggest that it might well so evolve.

9. My brief descriptions amount to little more than cartoons of the subtle and intricate positions of Churchland and, especially, Stich. I have not even sketched the arguments with which they support their prognoses. But since I propose to assume that the prognoses are correct in the one respect at issue (i.e., that behavioral science will eventually dispense with such notions as those of belief and desire), the lack of detailed exposition of their positions and arguments should not matter in what follows.

10. Stich calls this the Principle of Psychological Autonomy, and notes its incompatibility with our normal practices of content attribution. See "Autonomous Psychology and the Belief-Desire Thesis" and *FFPTCS* 164–70. See also Jerry Fodor, "Methodological Solipsism Considered as a Research Strategy in Cognitive Psychology," *The Behavioral and Brain Sciences* 3 (1980): 63–73.

11. See "The Meaning of 'Meaning'," reprinted in *Mind, Language and Reality* (Cambridge, 1975), 215–71.

12. See especially Tyler Burge, "Individualism and the Mental," *Midwest Studies in Philosophy*, 4 (1979): 73–121, and "Other Bodies," in Woodfield, *Thought and Object*, 97–120; and Stich, *FFPTCS*, Chap. 5, and "On the Ascription of Content."

13. An attitude's content depends on one of its referents in the sense I have in mind just in case necessarily any attitude that does not refer to the thing in question differs in content from the first attitude.

14. This characteristic is most commonly attributed to sentences containing proper names or terms for natural kinds. Regarding such sentences, see especially Saul Kripke, *Naming and Necessity* (Cambridge, Mass., 1980), and Putnam "The Meaning of 'Meaning'."

15. This is the approach of the functionalists whom Churchland ridicules in "Eliminative Materialism and the Propositional Attitudes," 77–82.

16. This is an instance of the general fact that the point of a body of discourse need not depend on the literal truth of the statements that it comprises. Many other examples may be found in H. P. Grice's work on conversational implicature and in the work of Peter Unger. See especially Grice's "Logic and Conversation," in *The Logic of Grammar*; edited by Donald Davidson and Gilbert Harman (Encino, Calif., 1975) 64–75, and Unger's *Philosophical Relativity* (Minneapolis, 1984).

17. The case is in this respect very different from that of the relativistic challenge to ordinary notions of the relation of space to time.

18. Apropos to this point, Hartry Field has argued at length that the actual uses of mathematics in scientific theorizing are consistent with the fact (as he takes it) that the mathematics in question is all false because of what he takes to be its false Platonistic commitments (Field, *Science without Numbers* (Princeton, N.J., 1980)). Regardless of the merits or faults of his detailed view of how this goes, the availability of a position like his illustrates the danger of taking the falsehood of a body of discourse to entail the falsehood of the understanding embodied in the discourse.

19. This group includes both Stich and Paul Churchland. Perhaps its most prominent member is Churchland's mentor, Wilfrid Sellars.

20. Presumably it will sometimes be possible to elicit an explicit statement of the speaker's genuine commitments regarding the phenomena in question, but sometimes that will not be possible. In the latter cases, speculation about such matters as whether the speaker would be shocked by certain scientific discoveries may give us our only access to "genuine views."

21. What is to count as an analysis and what a replacement in this context is not a simple matter. Presumably Dennett's instrumentalistic ascriptions of beliefs and desires would remain ascriptions of those states, and would thus remain committed to their existence. The instrumentalism comes in the attitude we take toward those commitments. If we, in fact, take our ascriptions to be true, going Dennett's route will involve at least a change in our attitudes toward our discourse. What Dennett wants to claim is that the attitudes in question are not centrally important parts of the self-image that is embodied in our ascriptions of belief and desire. See especially "Intentional Systems," in *Brainstroms* (Cambridge, Mass., 1978); "Three Kinds of Intentional Psychology," in *Reduction, Time, and Reality*, edited by Richard Healey (Cambridge, 1981); and "True Believers: the Intentional Strategy and Why it Works," in *Scientific Explanation*, edited by A. F. Heath (Oxford, 1981).

22. See especially David Armstrong, *Belief, Truth and Knowledge* (Cambridge, 1973).

23. See especially David Lewis, "An Argument for the Identity Theory," *Journal of Philosophy* 63 (1966): 17–25.

24. The word 'orectic' was recently coined by David O'Connor from a Greek root meaning desire. Orectic: desire :: doxic : belief.

25. In making this role the focus of my approach, I am following the example of Patrick Maher, who takes a similar line with respect to simple belief, though not to degrees of confidence as they appear in Bayesian decision theory. See Maher, "The Irrelevance of Belief to Rational Action," *Erkenntnis* 24 (May 1986): 363–86.

26. See especially Peter Geach, *Mental Acts* (London, 1957).

27. "How to Change Your Mind," in *Brainstroms*, 300–309.

28. There are also familiar problems about filling in the details of the qualifications. For the time being, though, I think it will be safe to neglect these matters. The fundamental ontological element in my account of opinion is the act of opining, and the existence and nature of that act is not affected by problems attending the specification of interesting dispositions to its performance.

29. This can sometimes happen even if I have previously reconsidered my earlier opinion and opined that $-\varphi$. I can forget that I have done so; my new opinion may fail to sink in. (This is no mere conceptual possibility; it has happened to me more than once.) This suggests that it may be useful to attribute to ourselves yet another sort of tacit worldview, consisting of claims that we are disposed to use as premises in reasoning, even if we are not disposed to accept them on explicit consideration.

30. It should be noted that having a somewhat ragged notion of tacit opinion is not as serious a problem as it would be if the central element in the general account were supposed to constitute a single genus

with explicit and tacit (or occurrent and dispositional) species. In the set of doxic notions that I am propos-ing, the central element is the act of (consciously, explicitly) opining. The notion of tacit opinion merely provides a way of accounting in terms of this element for claims that seem in some sense to be part of our views, even though we have not (yet) explicitly accepted them. Even total failure to come up with an adequate notion of tacit opinion would merely make it more difficult to account for these cases in terms of opinion, and cast no doubt on the existense or nature of opinion itself. On the other hand, it should be recalled that the notion of genuine affirmation as I explained it earlier does itself involve a dispositional element.

31. "On the Hypothesis that Animals are Automata," in *Methods and Results* (New York, 1896).

32. We may in fact use this as the basis for a fairly plausible story about how the full-blown notions of belief and desire evolved from those of opinion and wish.

33. It may be that the chief difference between my approach to the salvation of our self-image and Dennett's is one of emphasis. I take opinion and wish to do most of the work, and turn to an instrumentalist version of folk psychology to tie up some loose ends. Dennett takes instrumentalist, intentional psychol-ogy to do most of the work, and turns to opinion and wish to tie up loose ends.

34. An account of ordinary reason-giving explanations as teleological in a way that involves no appeal to antecedent events or conditions is persuasively defended by Arthur Collins in "Action, Causality, and Teleological Explanation," *Midwest Studies in Philosophy* 4 (1984): 345–69.

35. The issue here concerning action is parallel to the controversy about the need for causal elements in the account of what it is for one belief to be based on another. If such a noncausal account of an agent's operative reasons for belief can be devised, it could probably be applied *mutatis mutandis* to operative reasons for action. It should be noted that those who favor a noncausal account of belief-basing prefer not to invoke the counterfactuals available to accounts of purposive action of the second type. The success of such accounts of belief-basing would strongly confirm the possibility of a noncausal account of purpo-sive action, but their failure would not comparably disconfirm that possibility. For a bit of the controversy about belief-basing from the point of view of a noncausalist, see Keith Lehrer, *Knowledge* (Oxford, 1974), 122–26.

36. This view of rationality is defended by both Dennett and Alvin Plantinga. For Plantinga's version see his "Epistemic Justification," *Nous* 20 (1986): 3–18.

37. That role might be taken over by the beliefs and desires attributed in a Dennetty instrumentalist, intentional system theory. It may be that on such a theory, cognitive derangement would inevitably pre-vent the stable ascription of beliefs and desires to the deranged agent.

38. This should probably be modified in the direction of speaking of opinions about likelihoods and of wishes of various strengths. The need to move away from ungraded notions of belief and desire in this context is argued at length by Patrick Maher in "The Irrelevance of Belief to Rational Action." Ma-her's "belief" is roughly my "opinion"; his graded replacement is what he calls "degree of confidence." Maher argues that the proper role of belief is the satisfaction of curiosity, and degree of confidence is appropriate for determining the rationality of actions. But degrees of confidence might be understood ei-ther as themselves beliefs (about likelihoods) or as characteristics of beliefs (roughly, the degrees of strength with which the beliefs are held). Either way, any role played by degrees of confidence in deter-mining the rationality of actions would automatically bring with it a role for belief in that determination. In fact, everyday assessments of rationality often do invoke graded rather than ungraded belief and desire ("She wanted the money, but valued her honor more.") This would not detract from the primacy of curiosity-satisfaction to the notion of belief (as Maher understands it: roughly, opinion). In fact, it is Ma-her who convinced me that such a notion should be taken seriously as an alternative to the notion of belief that Stich and Churchland both presuppose and attack.

39. The availability of instrumentalist explanations in terms of unconscious beliefs and desires would, of course, remain.

40. A case can be made for the claim that the role most plausibly connected to the essence of belief and desire is that of constituting the agent's view of things as they are and as she would like them to be. The most natural description of how beliefs and desires function in the other two roles proceeds by iden-

tifying the actions that, given the agent's view of how things are, are best suited to getting them to be as she would like them. This approach seems to grant priority to the first role.

41. This conclusion is independent of whether or not the semantics are taken to involve verification-transcendent truth conditions. This may be seen clearly in the case of belief ascriptions. Surely there is nothing objectionably unverifiable about ascriptions that entail a theory of the etiology of behavior. One could hold that belief ascriptions entail such a theory whether or not one's semantics are verificationistic. All a verificationist need specify is that the theory itself is to be analyzed in terms of verification-conditions. And it should be clear that commitment to opinions and wishes (in the sense described earlier) does not entail commitment to the satisfaction of even the verification-conditions of a theory of the etiology of behavior.

How to Be an Ethical Antirealist

SIMON BLACKBURN

Some philosophers like to call themselves realists, and some like to call themselves antirealists. An increasing number, I suspect, wish to turn their backs on the whole issue.[1] Their strengths include those of naturalism, here counseling us that there is none except a natural science of human beings. From this it follows that there is no "first philosophy" lying behind (for instance) physics, or anthropology, enabling the philosopher to know how much of the world is "our construction" (antirealism) or, on the contrary, "independent of us" (realism).

This naturalism bestows small bouquets and small admonishments to each of the previous parties. The antirealists were right to deny that there exists a proper philosophical (a priori) explanation of things like the success of physics, which some people were acute enough to discern, from their armchairs, while others did not. A scientist can say that there was a certain result because a neutrino or electron did this and that, but a philosopher has nothing to *add* to this. If she tries to say, "Not only did the result occur because of the neutrino, but also because neutrino theory depicts (corresponds with, matches, carves at the joints) the world," she adds nothing but only voices a vain, and vainglorious, attempt to underwrite the science. This attempt may have made sense in a Cartesian tradition, when the mind's contact with the world seemed so problematical, but its time has passed. On the other hand, antirealists, sensing the futility of this road, stress instead the dependence of the ordinary world on us, our minds and categories, and again the additions they offer are unacceptable.[2] Characteristically, if realism fails because it is vacuous, antirealism fails because it strays into mistakes — making things dependent on us when they obviously are not, for example.[3] Again, and perhaps even more clearly, it is plausible to see antirealism as attempting to theorize where no theory should be — in this case, making the unnatural, Cartesian mind into a source of worlds. These theories are naturally described as "transcendental," and the word reminds us that for all his hostility to rational psychology, Kant himself failed to escape this trap.

The transcendental aspect can be seen if we put the matter in terms of what I call "correspondence conditionals." We like to believe that if we exercise our sensory and cognitive faculties properly and end up believing that p, then p. What kind of theory might explain our right to any such confidence? If p is a thesis from basic physical theory, only the theory itself. To understand why, when we believe that neutrinos exist, having used such-and-such information in such-and-such a way, then they probably do, is just to understand whatever credentials neutrino theory has. That is physics. Any attempt at a background, an underwriting of the conditional from outside the theory, is certain to be bogus.

When considering such global matters as the success of our science, the nature of our world, it seems that naturalism ought to win. But in local areas, it seems instead that battle can be joined. In this paper I would like to say in a little more detail why I think this is so. The main problem to which I turn is that of seepage, or the way in which antirealism, once comfortably in command of some particular area of our thought, is apt to cast imperialistic eyes on neighboring territory. The local antirealist faces the problem of drawing a line, which may prove difficult, or that of reneging on naturalism, and allowing that global antirealism must after all make sense. The second part of my paper is thus an exploration of this specific problem.

Why can battle be joined in local areas? What I said about physics might be retorted upon any area. To understand how, when we believe that twice two is four, we are probably right requires arithmetical understanding. To understand why, when we believe that wanton cruelty is wrong, we are also right requires ethical understanding. Where is the asymmetry?

Let us stay with the example of ethics. Here a "projective" theory can be developed to give a perfectly satisfying way of placing our propensities for values. According to me the surface phenomena of moral thought do not offer any obstacle to it. They can be explained as being just what we should expect, if the projective metaphysics is correct. (I call the doctrine that this is so "quasi-realism"—a topic I return to later.) I have also argued that this package contains various explanatory advantages over other rivals and alleged rivals. The projectivism is not, of course, new—the package is intended indeed to be a modern version of Hume's theory of the nature of ethics, but without any commitment to particular operations of passions such as sympathy. Emotivism and Hare's prescriptivism are also immediate ancestors. Anything new comes in the quasi-realism, whose point is to show that, since projectivism is consistent with, and indeed explains, the important surface phenomena of ethics, many of the arguments standardly used against it miss their mark. These arguments allege that projectivism is inadequate to one or another feature of the way we think ethically; the quasi-realism retorts that it is not, and goes on to explain the existence of the features. Such features include the propositional as opposed to emotive or prescriptive form, the interaction of ethical commitments with ordinary propositional attitude verbs, talk of truth, proof, knowledge, and so forth. I must urge the reader to look elsewhere for the details of the program; here, it is its relationship with naturalism that is to be determined.

I

The first link is this. I think that naturalism demands this view of ethics, but in any case it motivates it. It does so because in this package the fundamental state of mind of one who has an ethical commitment makes natural sense. This state of mind is not located as a belief (the belief in a duty, right, value). We may *end up* calling it a belief, but that is after the work has been done. In fact, we may end up saying that there really are values (such as the value of honesty) and facts (such as the fact that you have a duty to your children). For in this branch of philosophy, it is not what you finish by saying, but how you manage to say it that matters. How many people think they can just *announce* themselves to be realists or antirealists, as if all you have to do is put your hand on your heart and say, "I really believe it!" (or, "I really don't")? The way I treat the issue of realism denies that this kind of avowal helps the matter at all. The question is one of the best theory of this state of commitment, and reiterating it, even with a panoply of dignities—truth, fact, perception, and the rest—is not to the point.

The point is that the state of mind starts theoretical life as something else—a stance, or conative state or pressure on choice and action. Such pressures need to exist if human beings are to meet their competing needs in a social, cooperative setting. The stance may be called an attitude, although it would not matter if the word fitted only inexactly: its function is to mediate the move from features of a situation to a reaction, which in the appropriate circumstances will mean choice. Someone with a standing stance is set to react in some way when an occasion arises, just as someone with a standing belief is set to react to new information cognitively in one way or another. It matters to us that people have some attitudes and not others, and we educate them and put pressure on them in the hope that they will.

So far, two elements in this story are worth keeping in mind, for it will be important to see whether a projective plus quasi-realist story can do without them. These are: (1) the fundamental identification of the commitment in question as something other than a belief; (2) the existence of a neat natural account of why the state that it is should exist.

Obviously, the emergence of cooperative and altruistic stances is not a mere armchair speculation. It can be supplemented by both theoretical and empirical studies.[4] It is noteworthy that the account will insist upon the nonrepresentative, conative function for the stance. The evolutionary success that attends some stances and not others is a matter of the behavior to which they lead. In other words, it is the direct consequences of the pressure on action that matter. Evolutionary success may attend the animal that helps those that have helped it, but it would not attend an allegedly possible animal that thinks it ought to help but does not. In the competition for survival, it is what the animal *does* that matters. This is important, for it shows that only if values are intrinsically motivating, is a natural story of their emergence possible. Notice, too, the way the evolutionary success arises. Animals with standing dispositions to cooperate (say) do better in terms of other needs like freedom from fleas or ability to survive failed hunting expeditions by begging meals from others. No right, duty, or value plays any explanatory role in this history. It is not as if the creature with a standing disposition to help those who have helped it does well *because* that is a virtue. Its being a virtue is irrelevant to evolutionary biology. There is no such naturalistically respectable explanation.

The commitment may have psychological accretions consistently with this being its core or essence. The precise "feel" of an ethical stance may be a function of local culture, in its scope, or some of its interactions with other pressures and other beliefs. A pressure toward action can be associated variously with pride, shame, self-respect, and there is no reason to expect a simple phenomenology to emerge. The essence lies in the practical import, but the feelings that surround that can vary considerably. There is no reason for a stance to feel much like a desire, for example. Consider as a parallel the way in which a biological or evolutionary story would place attraction between the sexes, and the culturally specific and surprising ways in which that attraction can emerge – the varieties of lust and love (whose imperatives often do not feel much like desire either, and may equally be expressed by thinking that there are things one simply *must* do. I say more about this later.) So, if a theorist is attracted to the rich textures of ethical life, he need not, therefore, oppose projectivism. No "reduction" of an ethical stance to one of any other type is needed.

Now contrast the kind of evolution already sketched with any that might be offered for, say, our capacity to perceive spatial distance. Again, what matters here is action. But what we must be good at is acting according to the very feature perceived. A visual-motor mechanism enabling the frog's tongue to hit the fly needs to adapt the trajectory of the tongue to the place of the fly relative to the frog, and an animal using perceived distance to guide behavior will be successful only if it perceives distances as they are. It is because our visual mechanisms show us far-off things as far off and near things as near that we work well using them. That is what they are *for*. We can sum up this contrast by saying that although the teleology of spatial perception is spatial, the teleology of ethical commitment is not ethical. The good of spatial perception is to be representative, but the good of ethical stances is not.

The possibility of this kind of theory, then, provides the needed contrast between the general case of science, where an attempt to provide a further, background "theory" is transcendental, and the local particular case of ethics, where there are natural materials for such a story ready at hand. It also means that philosophers wanting a general realism versus antirealism issue cannot take comfort from the local case; the materials to generate theory there exist, as it were, by contrast with anything that can be provided in the general case.

These simple naturalistic points are not always respected. Consider, for example, the position associated with John McDowell and David Wiggins. This goes some way in the same direction as projectivism, at least in admitting that a person's ethical outlook is dependent on affective or conative aspects of his make-up. But it takes those aspects as things that enable the subject to do something else — to perceive value properties. It is only if one is moved or prone to be moved in a certain way that one sees the value of things, just as it is only if one is prone to be moved in some way that one perceives the sadness in a face.[5] This is supposed to do justice to the obvious point that sentiments have something to do with our capacity to make ethical judgment, yet to retain a "perceptual" and cognitive place for moral opinion.

Let us suppose that this is a substantial theory and different from projectivism (in the light of what is to come, neither supposition is beyond doubt). The view is substantial if it holds that changes in one's sensibilities enable one to do something else: *literally* to perceive ethical properties in things. Or if the "something else" is not literal perception, then at least its kinship with perception must be very close — so close that it cannot be explained as projection of a stance. For the view is no different from projectivism if this "something else" is nothing else at all, but merely a different label for reaching an ethical verdict because of one's sentiments. In other words, it is only different from projectivism if this literal talk of perceiving plays a theoretical role, and not just a relabeling of the phenomena. This is not at all obvious. Theoretically low-grade talk of perception is always available. Everyone can say that one can "see" what one must do or what needs to be done, just as one can see that 17 is prime. When I said that it is not what one finishes by saying, but the theory that gets one there, this is one of the crucial examples I had in mind.

Literal talk of perception runs into many problems. One is that the ethical very commonly, and given its function in guiding choice, even typically, concerns imagined or described situations, not perceived ones.[6] We reach ethical verdicts about the behavior of described agents or actions in the light of general standards. And it is stretching things to see these general standards as perceptually formed or maintained. Do I see that ingratitude is base only on occasions when I see an example of ingratitude? How can I be sure of the generalization to examples that I did not see (I could not do that for color, for instance. Absent pillar-boxes may be a different color from present ones; only an inductive step allows us to guess at whether they are). Or, do I see the timeless connection — but how? Do I have an antenna for detecting timeless property-to-value connections? Is such a thing that much like color vision? Perhaps these questions can be brushed aside. But in connection with naturalism, the question to ask of the view is why nature should have bothered. Having, as it were, forced us into good conative shape, why not sit back? Why should this be merely the curtain raiser for a perceptual system? It seems only to engender dangerous possibilities. It ought to make us slower to act, for we must process the new information perceived. Worse, it might be that someone moved, say, by gratitude comes to see the goodness of gratitude and then has, quite generally, some other (negative) reaction to what is seen. Perhaps typically, the conative pressure opens our eyes to these properties, about which we then have a different, conflicting feeling. Or is it somehow given that what comes back is what went in — that the property perceived impinges on us with the same emotional impact required for perceiving it? How convenient! But how clumsy of nature to go in for such a loop! And why did we not evolve to short-circuit it, as projectivism claims? In other words, we have here the typical symptoms of realism, which not only has to take us *to* the new properties but also has to take us back *from* them, showing how perception of them contrives to have exactly the effects it does.

This extravagance came from taking literally the talk of perception made possible by changes of sensibility. But the theory seems to be meant literally. Wiggins, for example, thinks that although projectivism can be dismissed (values "put into [or onto like varnish] the factual world"), the right view is that there are value properties and sensibilities for perceiving them "made for each other" as "equal and reciprocal partners."[7]

Can this be understood? Projectivism, from which the theory is supposed to be so different, can easily embrace one half of the doctrine—that the properties are made for the sensibility. The embrace ought to be a bit tepid, because we shall see better ways of putting the view that value predicates figure in thought and talk as reflections or projections of the attitudes that matter. But it is the other half, that the sensibilities are "made for" the properties, that really startles. Who or what makes them like that? (God? As we have seen, no natural story explains how the ethical sensibilities of human beings were made for the ethical properties of things, so perhaps it is a supernatural story.)

Wiggins, I think, would reply that nothing extraordinary or unfamiliar is called for here. Refinement or civilization makes both sensibility and property. It is the process of education or moral refinement that makes sensibilities end up in good harmony with values. "When this point is reached, a system of anthropocentric properties and human responses has surely taken on a life of its own. Civilization has begun." The implicit plea that we get our responses to life into civilized shape is admirable, but is it enough to locate a view of the nature of ethics, or is there a danger of confusing uplift with theory? Certainly, it is true that when we have gone through some process of ethical improvement, we can turn back and say that now we have got something *right*—now we appreciate the value of things as they are, whereas before we did not. This Whiggish judgment is often in place, but it is, of course, a moral judgment. It is not pertinent to explaining *how* sensibilities are "made for" values. Is it a good theoretical description or explanation of the fact that we value friendship that, first, it is good and, second, civilization has "made" our sensibilities "for" the property of goodness? It seems overripe, since it goes with no apparent theory of error (what if our sensibilities are unluckily not made for the properties?), no teleology, and no evolutionary background. Its loss of control becomes clear if we think how easy it is to generate parallels. Perhaps something similar made our arithmetical powers for the numbers, or our tastes for the niceness of things. Or, perhaps, on the contrary, the talk of our sensibilities being made for the properties is theoretically useless and the more economical remainder is all that is really wanted.

Might there still be room for a view that the properties are "made for" the sensibility, which avoids projectivism? The analogy with colors, for all its many defects, might be held to open such a possibility. But color at this point is a dangerous example. If we ask seriously what color vision is made for, an answer can be found—but it will not cite colors. Color vision is probably made for enhancing our capacities for quickly identifying and keeping track of objects and surfaces, and this asymmetry with, for instance, spatial perception remains the most important point of the primary-secondary property distinction.

Any analogy with color vision is bound to run into the problem of dependency. If we had a theory whereby ethical properties are literally made by or for sensibilities, ethical truth would be constituted by and dependent on the way we think. This might not repel Wiggins. It agrees with the analogy with colors, and in the course of discussing Russell's worry ("I find myself incapable of believing that all that is wrong with wanton cruelty is that I don't like it"), Wiggins freely asserts that "what is wrong with cruelty is not, even for Bertrand Russell, just that Bertrand Russell does not like it, but that it is not such as to call forth liking given our *actual* responses."[8] But is it? I should have said not. It is because of our responses that we *say* that cruelty is wrong, but it is not because of them that it is so. It is true that insertion of the "actual" into the sentence makes it wrong to test the alleged dependence by the usual device of imagining our responses otherwise and asking if that makes cruelty any better.[9] But our actual responses are inappropriate for the wrongness of cruelty to depend upon. What makes cruelty abhorrent is not that it offends us, but all those hideous things that make it do so.

The projectivist can say this vital thing: that it is not because of our responses, scrutinized and collective or otherwise, that cruelty is wrong. The explanation flows from the way in which quasi-realism has us deal with oblique contexts. It issues an "internal" reading of the statement of dependence, according to which it amounts to an offensive ethical view, about (of course) what it is that makes cruelty wrong. Critics of this explanation allow the internal reading, but complain that the quasi-realist is being wilfully deaf to an intended "external" reading, according to which the dependency is a philosophical thesis, and one to which the projectivist, it is said, must assent.[10] The crucial question, therefore, is whether the projectivist wilfully refuses to hear the external reading. According to me, there is only one proper way to take the question "On what does the wrongness of wanton cruelty depend?": as a moral question, with an answer in which no mention of our actual responses properly figures. There *would* be an external reading if realism were true. For in that case there would be a fact, a state of affairs (the wrongness of cruelty) whose rise and fall and dependency on others could be charted. But antirealism acknowledges no such state of affairs, and no such issue of dependency. Its freedom from any such ontological headache is not the least of its pleasures. A realist might take this opportunity for dissent. He might say, "I can just *see* that the wrongness of cruelty is a fact (perhaps an eternal one) that needs an ontological theory to support it—no theory that avoids providing such support is credible." In that case I gladly part company, and he is welcome to his quest—for what kind of ontology is going to help? The Euthyphro dilemma bars all roads there.[11]

It is tempting to think: on this metaphysics the world contains nothing but us and our responses, so that fact that cruelty is bad *must* be created by our responses. What else is there for it to be dependent upon? The prejudice is to treat the moral fact as a natural one, capable of being constituted, made or unmade, by sensibilities. The wrongness of wanton cruelty does indeed depend on things—features of it which remind us how awful it is. But locating these is giving moral verdicts. Talk of dependency is moral talk or nothing. This is not, of course, to deny that "external" questions make sense—the projectivist plus quasi-realist package is an external philosophical theory about the nature of morality. But external questions must be conducted in a different key once this package is brought in. We may notice, too, how this undermines a common way of drawing up the realist versus antirealist issue, according to which antirealism asserts that truth in some or all areas is "mind dependent" and realism denies this. For here is the projection, as antirealist a theory of morality as could be wished, denying that moral truth is mind dependent in the only sense possible.

The point can be made as follows. As soon as one *uses* a sentence whose simple assertion expresses an attitude, one is in the business of discussing or voicing ethical opinion. Such sentences include "The fact that *cruelty is wrong* depends on. . . . " or "Our refined consensus makes it true that *cruelty is wrong*," and so on. If one generalizes and says things like "moral facts depend on us," the generalization will be true only if instances are true or, in other words, if one can find examples of truths like those. Since these ethical opinions are unattractive, they must be judged incorrect, as must generalizations of them. If one attempts to discuss external questions, one must use a different approach—in my case, a naturalism that places the activities of ethics in the realm of adjusting, improving, weighing, and rejecting different sentiments or attitudes. The projectivist, then, has a perfect right to confine external questions of dependency to domains where real estates of affairs, with their causal relations, are in questions. The only things in this world are the attitudes of people, and those, of course, are trivially and harmlessly mind-dependent. But the projectivist can hear no literal sense in saying that moral properties are made for or by sensibilities. They are not in a world where things are made or unmade—not in this world at all, and it is only because of this that naturalism remains true.

The charge that projectivism refuses to hear an explanatory demand as it is intended can be returned with, I suggest, much more effect. I was severe earlier with Wiggins's theoretical description of us as indulging in a kind of coordination of responses and properties as we become civilized. But it is telling that the Whiggish appeal to a value ("civilization") is introduced at that point. For the introduction of values into explanatory investigations is echoed in other writings in this tradition, notably in those of John McDowell.[12] The strategy is that in a context purportedly comparing explanations of a practice—the practice of ethical judgment—we allow ourselves to invoke the very commitments of that practice. Why are we afraid of the dark? Because it is fearful. Why do we value friendship? Because it is good and we are civilized. Why do I dislike sentimentality? Because it merits it. And so on.

The refusal to stand outside ethics in order to place it is supposed to tie in with one strand in Wittgenstein. This is the thought that there is characteristically neither a reduction nor an explanation of the members of any major family of concepts in terms of those of another. Ethical notions require ethical sensibilities to comprehend them. Similarly, why should it not require an ethical sensibility to comprehend an explanation of the views we hold? Only those who perceive friendship as good will understand why we do so, and to them it can be explained why we do so by reminding them that it is good, or making them feel that it is so. The rest—aliens, outsiders, Martians—cannot be given the explanation, but this is as it must be. What I said about the explanation of our spatial capacities will make it apparent that the circularity exists there in exactly the same way. Only those who appreciate distance can understand the distance-centered explanation of visual perception.

This returns us to a theme that has been touched at many points in this essay. The insistence on hearing explanatory demands only in a way in which one can invoke values in answering them had a respectable origin. We agreed earlier that the parallel would be true of thinking about the correspondence conditionals in the case of physics. But I hope I have said enough to show that nature and our theory of nature surround our ethical commitments in a way that gives us a *place* from which to theorize about them. Nothing and no theory surround our physics. In other words, the difference in the ethical case comes in the theses I labeled (1) and (2)—the brute fact that an external explanatory story is possible. We already know that in even more local cases, where what is at question is not "the ethical" in a lump, but particular attitudes and their etiologies. Social anthropology is not confined to explaining the rise of puritanism to puritans or the evolution of polygamy to polygamists. Similarly, nothing in Wittgenstein offers any principled obstacle to explaining the general shape and nature of ethical attitudes and their expressions in projective terms.

Indeed much in Wittgenstein is sympathetic to doing so. Not only is Wittgenstein himself an antirealist about ethics. He is in general quite free in admitting propositions or quasi-propositions whose function is not to describe anything—the rules of logic and arithmetic, for instance. It is clear that what he wants to do is to place mathematical practice, not as a representation of the mathematical realm, but as "a different kind of instrument," commitment to which is not like central cases of belief, but much more like other kinds of stance. It is also interesting that some of the apparently irritating or evasive answers he gives when faced with the charge of anthropocentricity are exactly those which a projectivist can give if quasi-realism has done its work, and that according to me, no other philosophy of these matters can give. For example, when Wittgenstein approaches the question whether on his anthropocentric view of mathematical activity, mathematical truth is yet independent of human beings, he says exactly what I would have him say:

"But mathematical truth is independent of whether human beings know it or not!"—Certainly, the propositions 'Human beings believe that twice two is four' and 'twice two is four' do not mean the same. The latter is a mathematical proposition; the other, if it makes sense at all, may perhaps mean: human beings have *arrived* at the mathematical proposition. The two propositions have entirely different *uses*.[13]

The proposition expresses a norm that arises in the course of human activities, but it does not describe those activities, and it has no use in which the correctness of the norm (the truth of the proposition) depends upon the existence or form of those activities. *That* question simply cannot be posed; it treats what is not a dependent state of affairs belonging to the natural world at all, as if it were.

I have tried to show that naturalism, which turns away from realism and antirealism alike in the global case turns toward projective theories in the ethical case. This theory is visibly antirealist, for the explanations offered make no irreducible or essential appeal to the existence of moral "properties" or "facts"; they demand no "ontology" of morals. They explain the activity from the inside out—from the naturally explicable attitudes to the forms of speech that communicate them, challenge them, refine them, and abandon them, and which so mislead the unwary.

So far I have talked of the issue of mind dependency in fairly abstract terms, and relied upon a relatively subtle move in the philosophy of language to defend my view. I now want to discuss these points in practical terms. It is evident that a more fundamental mistake underlies some discomfort with projectivism. The mistake is visible in Wiggins's critique of "non-cognitive theories" in his British Academy Lecture.[14] It results in the charge that projectivism cannot be true to the "inside of lived experience." Other writers (I would cite Nagel, Williams, and Foot) seem to illustrate similar unease. The thought is something like this: it is important that there should be some kind of accord in our thinking about ethical stances from the perspective of the theorist, and from that of the participant. Our story about ethical commitment is to explain it, not to explain it away. But projectivism threatens to do the latter (many people who should know better think of Hume as a skeptic about ethics, and, of course, John Mackie saw himself as one). It threatens to do so because it shows us that our commitments are not external demands, claiming us regardless of our wills or in direct opposition to our passions. It makes our commitments facets of our own sentimental natures; this softens them, destroying the hardness of the moral must.

From the inside, the objects of our passions are their *immediate* objects: it is the death, the loved one, the sunset, that matters to us. It is not our own state of satisfaction or pleasure. Must projectivism struggle with this fact, or disown it? Is it that we projectivists, at the crucial moment when we are about to save the child, throw ourselves on the grenade, walk out into the snow, will think, "Oh, it's only me and my desires or other conative pressures—forget it"?

It ought to be sufficient refutation of this doubt to mention other cases. Does the lover escape his passion by thinking, "Oh it's only my passion, forget it"? When the world affords occasion for grief, does it brighten when we realize that it is we who grieve? (The worst thing to think is that if we are "rational," it should, as if rationality had anything to tell us about it.)

There is an important mistake in the philosophy of action that, I think, must explain the temptation to share Wiggins's doubt. The mistake is that of supposing that when we deliberate in the light of various features of a situation we are *at the same time* or "really" deliberating—or that our reasoning can be "modeled" by representing us as deliberating—about our own conative functioning. Representing practical reasoning as if it consisted of contemplating a syllogism, one of whose premises describes what we want, encourages this mistake. But just as the eye is not part of the visual scene it presents, the sensibility responsible for the emotional impact of things is not part of the scene it takes for material. Nor is our sense of humor the main thing we find funny. This does not mean that our sensibility is hidden from us, and when we reflect on ourselves we can recognize aspects of it, just as we can know when we are in love or grieving. But it does mean that its own shape is no part of the input, when we react to the perceived features of things. Furthermore, even when we reflect on our sensibility, we will be using it if we issue a verdict: when we find our own sense of humor funny, we are not escaping use of it as we do so.

This misconstruction leads people to suppose that on a projective theory all obligations must be "hypothetical," because properly represented as dependent upon the existence of desires. But the lover who hears that she is there and feels he has to go, or the person who receiving bad news feels he must grieve, has no thoughts of the form "if I desire her / feel sad then I must go / grieve." Nothing corresponds to this. The news comes in and the emotion comes out; nothing in human life could be or feel more categorical. In ordinary emotional cases, of course, a third party may judge that it is only *if* he desires her that he must go; this is not so in ethical cases. One ought to look after one's young children, whether one wants to or not. But that is because we insist on some responses from others, and it is sometimes part of good moralizing to do so.

Once these mistakes are averted, is there any substance left to the worry about failure of harmony of the theoretical and deliberative points of view? I think not. Sometimes theory can help to change attitudes. One might become less attached to some virtue, or less eager in pursuing some vice, after thinking about its etiology or its functioning. One might qualify it a little (we see an example in what follows). But sometimes one might become more attached to the virtue, and sometimes everything stays the same. Does the story threaten to undermine the promise that the stances cited in this theory of ethics make good natural sense (does it take something divine to make the claims of obligation so pregnant with authority)? Not at all—I have already mentioned the "musts" of love and grief, and those of habit and obsession are just as common.

There is one last charge of the would-be realist. This claims that projectivism must lead to relativism. "Truth" must be relative to whatever set of attitudes is grounding our ethical stances; since these may vary from place to place and time to time, truth must be relative. The very analogies with other conative states press this result: what to one person is an occasion for love or grief or humor is not to another. Consider a young person gripped by the imperatives of fashion. The judgment that people must wear some style, that another is impossible, has its (naturally explicable and perfectly intelligible) function; it appears quite categorical, for the subject will think that it is not just for him or her that the style is mandatory or impossible (it was so in the parents' time as well, only they did not realize it). Yet, surely this is a mistake. The verdict is "relative," having no truth outside the local system of preferences that causes it. The image is plain: a projectivist may inhabit a particular ethical boat, but he must know of the actual or potential existence of others; where, then, is the absolute truth?

The answer is that it is not anywhere that can be visible from this sideways, theoretical perspective. It is not that this perspective is illegitimate, but that it is not the one adapted for finding ethical truth. It would be if such truth were natural truth, or consisted of the existence of states of affairs in the real world. That is the world seen from the viewpoint that sees different and conflicting moral systems—but inevitably sees no truth in just one of them. To "see" the truth that wanton cruelty is wrong demands moralizing, stepping back into the boat, or putting back the lens of a sensibility. But once that is done, there is nothing relativistic left to say. The existence of the verdict, of course, depends on the existence of those capable of making it; the existence of the truth depends on nothing (externally), and on those features that make it wrong (internally). For the same reasons that operated when I discussed mind dependency, there is no doctrine to express relating the truth of the verdict to the existence of us, of our sentiments, or of rival sentiments.

What, then, of the parallel with the other emotions, or with the fashion example? The emotions of grief and love are naturally personal; if the subject feels they make a claim on others, so that those unstricken somehow *ought* to be, then, she is nonrelativistically, absolutely wrong. Similarly with fashion: the underlying story includes the need to a self-presentation that is admirable to the peer group, and if what is admirable changes rapidly as generations need to distance themselves from their immediate predecessors, then the teenager who thinks that her parents were wrong to like whatever clothes they did is mistaken in the same way as the subject of an emotion who imputes a mistake to those who cannot feel the same. But the strongest ethical judgments do not issue from stances that are properly variable. They may sometimes be absent, from natural causes, as if a hard life destroys a capacity for pity. But this is a cause for regret; it would be better if it were not so. In the variations of emotion, and still more of fashion, there is no cause for regret. In saying these things I am, of course, voicing some elements of my own ethical stances, but as I promised, it is only by doing this that ethical truth is found.

II

If projective theories have everything going for them in ethics, how much can they jettison and still have *something* going for them? The two ingredients I highlighted are: the possibility of identifying the commitment in a way that contrasts it usefully with belief, and a "neat, natural account" of why the state that it is should exist. In the case of ethics we have conative stances, and a visible place for them in our functioning. But what in other cases?

Color commitments might attract attention, because not everybody will be happy that the agreed story about what color vision is and why we have it leaves realism as a natural doctrine about colors. Here the second ingredient is present. There is a neat, natural story of our capacity for color discrimination, and in its explanatory side, both physically and evolutionarily, it makes no explanatory use of the *existence* of colors. But there is no way that I can see usefully to contrast color commitments with *beliefs*. Their functional roles do not differ. So, there will be no theory of a parallel kind to develop, explaining why we have propositional attitudes of various kinds toward color talk, or why we speak of knowledge, doubt, proof, and so forth in connection with them. If anything can be drawn from a realism versus antirealism debate over color (which I rather doubt), it would have to be found by different means.

Modal commitments are much more promising. Our penchant for necessities and possibilities, either in concepts or in nature, is not easy to square with a view that we are representing anything, be it a distribution of possible worlds, or (in the case of natural necessity) a timeless nomic connection between universals.[15]

First, consider the case of logical necessity. A theory insisting on a non-representative function for modal commitment is clearly attractive. Here, however, although I think the first desideratum is met—we can do something to place the stance as something other than belief in the first instance—the second is not so easy. The kind of stance involved in insistence upon a norm, an embargo on a trespass. Saying that $2 + 2$ is anything other than 4 offends against the embargo, and the embargo in turn makes shared practices, shared communication possible. So far so good, but what of a "neat, natural theory" of the emergence of the embargo? That shared practices should exist is good—but do they so clearly depend upon such policing? If they do, it appears to be because of something else: because we can make no sense of a way of thinking that flouts the embargo. It introduces apparent possibilities of which we can make nothing. This imaginative limitation is, in turn, something of which no natural theory appears possible, even in outline. For when we *can* make sense of the imaginative limitation, we do find it apt to explain away or undermine the original commitment to a necessity. If it seems only because of (say) confinement to a world in which relative velocities are always slow compared to that of light, that we find a relativistic view of simultaneity hard to comprehend, then that already shows how we would be wrong to deem the theory impossible. If it is only because of the range of our color vision that we cannot imagine a new primary color, then we would be unwise to rule out the possibility that some natural operation might result in our admitting one. Natural explanation is here the enemy of the hard logical must.

It is not obviously so in the case of natural necessity. Once more the paradigm is Hume—not the Hume of commentators, but the real Hume, who knew that talk of necessity was irreducible, but gave a projective theory of it. The explanation here has us responsive to natural regularity, and forming dispositions of expectation (we might add, of observing boundaries in our counterfactual reasoning), which in turn stand us in good stead as the regularities prove reliable. Here, once we accept the Humean metaphysics, the naturalism seems quite in place. The upshot—talk of causation—is not undermined but is explained by this interpretation. This accords exactly with the case of ethics. There is a difference, however. I do not think metaphysical obstacles stand in the way of the conception of nature that does the explanatory work in the example of ethics. But many writers have difficulty with the conception of nature that is supposed to do it in Hume's metaphysics of causation. Regularities—but between what? Events—but how are these to be conceived, stripped of the causal "bit" (to use the computer metaphor)? Events thought of as changes in ordinary objects will scarcely do, for as many writers have insisted, ordinary objects are permeated with causal powers. Nothing corresponds to the easy, sideways, naturalistic perspective that strips the world of values.

What is the option? All sides carry on talk of causation in whichever mode they find best. The new realists like to produce apparent ontologies—universals, timeless connections, and the rest. The Humean does not mind, so long as the explanatory pretensions of these retranslations are kept firmly in their place (outside understanding). Is there scope for a debate here? It is a place where the ghosts are hard to lay, and I for one do not like being there alone in the gloom.

Notes

1. For example, see Arthur Fine, "Unnatural Attitudes: Realist and Instrumentalist Attachments to Science," in *Mind*, 1986.

2. On Putnam in this connection, see Ruth Garrett Millikan, "Metaphysical Anti-Realism," in *Mind*, 1986.

3. My favorite example is Putnam, *Reason, Truth and History*, 52.

4. R. Axelrod, *The Evolution of Cooperation* (New York, 1984).

5. John McDowell, "Non-Cognitivism and Rule Following," in *Wittgenstein: To Follow a Rule*, edited by S. Holtzman and C. Leich (London, 1981). Also, Sabina Lovibond, *Realism and Imagination in Ethics* (Oxford, 1984). Other writers influenced by the analogy include Mark Platts, *The Ways of Meaning*, and Anthony Price, "Doubts about Projectivism," in *Philosophy*, 1986.

6. John Locke, *An Essay Concerning Human Understanding*, IV, chap. IV, 6-7.

7. D. Wiggins, *Truth, Invention and the Meaning of Life* (British Academy Lecture, 1976), 348.

8. "A Sensible Subjectivism," *Needs, Values, Truth* (Oxford, 1987), 210.

9. The use of 'actual' to make rigid the reference to our present attitudes, and thereby fend off some natural objections to dispositional subjective analyses, is exploited in this connection by Michael Smith.

10. Cassim Quassam, "Necessity and Externality," in *Mind*, 1986.

11. I enlarge upon this in "Morals and Modals," in *Truth, Fact and Value*, edited by Graham MacDonald and Crispin Wright (Oxford, 1986).

12. For instance in his "Values and Secondary Properties," in *Value and Objectivity: Essays in Honour of J.L. Mackie*, edited by T. Honderich (Oxford, 1985).

13. Ludwig Wittgenstein, *Philosophical Investigations* (Oxford, 1953), 226.

14. Ibid., (note 6) section 4.

15. David Armstrong, *What Is a Law of Nature* (Cambridge, 1983), Chapter 6.

MIDWEST STUDIES IN PHILOSOPHY, XII

Moral Realism and the Amoralist

WM. DAVID SOLOMON

I

The contemporary debate surrounding the issue of moral realism is complex and frequently confusing. The diverse set of issues from areas of philosophy other than ethics intersecting in the debate is surely partly responsible for this situation. Difficult issues from semantics, philosophy of mind, epistemology, and metaphysics are raised in the discussion of moral realism, and since the relevant issues from these other areas of philosophy are themselves often difficult and controverted, it should not be surprising that the discussion of moral realism often presents the student of the subject with an untidy bundle of difficulties. But this entanglement with other areas of philosophy is not the only reason the area presents special difficulties. Deep methodological issues arise in discussions of moral realism concerning how one may use features of ordinary moral practice as evidence for one or another of the standard realist or antirealist views.

In this regard a complicated dialectic has emerged. Some moral realists attack antirealism on the ground that it is a threat to moral practices that are at the heart of ordinary moral thought and talk. They suggest that if antirealism is adopted, then it will be impossible, conceptually or logically, to go on doing or saying some of the things that it is essential to do or say within the practice of morality. It is put forward, that is, as one of the virtues of moral realism that it allows us to save the appearances of moral thought and talk. Opposition to moral realism is regarded as tantamount to opposition to central features of the moral life; indeed, it is sometimes regarded as opposition to morality itself.

Opponents of moral realism take different approaches in responding to this line of criticism. Some, like John Mackie, admit at least part of the charge, but attempt to turn the point to their advantage.[1] Mackie has argued that his version of moral antirealism is an "error-view," that is, a view that, if true, will be in conflict with certain features of ordinary moral thought and talk. Mackie, indeed, is committed to the view that built into the ordinary practices of morality are certain errors which it is the task of moral theory to correct.[2]

Some other opponents of moral realism have reacted quite differently to this charge. Rather than admit, as Mackie does, that important features of moral practice are threatened by the rejection of moral realism, they claim that moral realism can be rejected relatively cheaply. Simon Blackburn, in particular, has argued that the opponent of moral realism need not concede to its defenders that moral realism is more in line with the ordinary practice of morality than is antirealism.[3] Blackburn has defended his irenic version of antirealism, which he calls quasi-realism, from charges that it cannot account for central features of ordinary moral practice, by attempting to show how those features of ordinary moral practice thought by the moral realist to be threatened by the rejection of realism can live comfortably within an antirealist setting.

The dialectic is further complicated by the fact that some moral realists seem to agree with Mackie that moral theory must have a significant revisionary role. The form of moral realism defended by broadly Kantian moral theorists like Thomas Nagel, for example, requires, as does Mackie's view, that certain features of ordinary moral thought and talk be sacrificed.[4] Nagel does not defend his version of moral realism as a purely descriptive theory, but rather as a theoretical account of the moral point of view that, while sacrificing some appearances, is true to the deep practical structure of the moral point of view.

The recent literature on moral realism, then, can usefully be seen as involving deep disagreements about two issues:

(1) The truth of moral realism; and
(2) The methodological question of the extent to which any developed view on the truth of moral realism must be true to the central features of moral practice.

The current discussion of moral realism would be much more manageable if contributors to it who agree in their response to the first question also agreed in their response to the second. But this agreement in response is not universally found. Moral realists, as well as antirealists, may hold their views in more or less revisionary forms. Mackie and Nagel, though certainly disagreeing with regard to the first question, are broadly in agreement with regard to the second. Blackburn and Mackie agree with regard to (1), but disagree concerning (2).

Perhaps the most difficult issues in trying to penetrate this dialectic further arise because insufficient attention has been paid to the question of how to identify the main features of ordinary moral practice to be preserved. What features should be preserved if a theory is to be broadly nonrevisionist? Surely not every feature, more or less idiosyncratic, of every person's participation in the practice of morality must be captured in an adequate moral theory. Moral theory must have some critical thrust. More generally, it seems necessary to sort out in some systematic fashion those features of human life essentially associated with the practice of morality. Moral practice involves, at minimum, various modes of talking and thinking, certain feelings, and particular tendencies to be moved in characteristic ways by experiences. It also may be regarded as encompassing substantive practical beliefs – beliefs, for example, that some features of experience necessarily give agents reasons, and perhaps overriding reasons, for acting in a particular fashion. Moral practice is, in short, complicated.

This otherwise obvious point is worth noting in that it may make one hesitate before responding too quickly to questions about the revisionary role of ethical theory. It is difficult to take a firm position on this revisionary role until one has sorted out all the potential candidates for revision. And it would not seem an unreasonable first view to suppose that some things might be better candidates than others. That is, rather than taking one of the extreme views (moral theory must leave moral practice exactly as it is, not disturbing a single linguistic convention or a single mode of feeling; or the view that nothing in moral practice is sacred, everything may be revised or rejected), it would seem most plausible to suppose that there are certain basic features of moral practice that will not be subject to revision, though other, less central, features may be revised. Ethical theory will be, according to this view, both conservative and critical. And surely this is what ought to be desired. It is difficult to see how one can reject the conservatism of ethical theory; after all, moral practice is the primary subject matter of ethical theory. If everything can be rejected or revised, one wonders what the resulting theory would be a theory of. But the critical pull is equally strong. The ultimate point of ethical theory must be practical. Moral practice is frequently beset with uncertainty, perplexity, and disagreement. Ethical theory is, at least in part, a response to these commonplace features of moral experience. But if the response is to be effective, the possibility must be allowed of revising certain features of moral practice – ideally, precisely those features that prevent moral practice from accomplishing the task it is suited to perform.

To say this, of course, is not yet to take a position on the dispute between the revisionist and the descriptivist. It may, indeed, appear to be merely the pusillanimous response to the dispute that says no more than, "There is something to what both of you say." There are two approaches that promise real progress, however, one much more ambitious than the other. The ambitious approach, alluded to above, would involve making some kind of inventory of the features of moral practice, and then attempting to sort these features into those subject to revision and those to be held immune from revision. A more modest approach would proceed in a piecemeal fashion. It would examine the points at which the realist claims that the antirealist cannot do justice to particular features of moral practice. The point of the examination would be to determine if the realist is right or if, perhaps, a more careful formulation of antirealism, or a more nuanced view of the particular feature of moral practice in question, might allow the antirealist to save this *part* of the moral appearances. Much labor has been expended on this more modest task, and not without success. Simon Blackburn, in particular, has developed ingenious strategies to show how antirealism with regard to value can sit relatively comfortably with features of moral practice that may appear initially incompatible with it.

This more modest strategy is, however, by its very nature inconclusive. Its task can never be completed in that it is always open to the realist to bring up some further feature of moral practice not yet considered, and to argue that *this* feature defies domestication by the antirealist. The prospect here is one of prolonged "trench warfare." In what follows, I would like to explore one of the issues that is presently being fought out "in the trenches." Some realists have argued that one aspect of moral practice that cannot be accounted for by the antirealist is the possibility that someone might hold a set of views associated with the "amoralist." These moral realists have argued that "amoralism" is to be regarded as a possible first-order set of moral views which, though possibly false, must be regarded as coherent and, in particular, not to be ruled out by any a priori features attributed to moral thought and talk by the antirealist. Further, they claim that standard versions of antirealism do render the views of the amoralist incoherent. If it is true that amoralism is not incoherent and that standard versions of antirealism would render it incoherent, then antirealism is in some difficulty. In order to escape these particular charges, the antirealist must be prepared to argue either (1) that amoralism is, indeed, incoherent (at least in the forms relevant to these particular arguments) or (2) that antirealism, properly understood, does not render it incoherent. I would like to explore these possible avenues of escape for the antirealist. In the following section, this particular argument against antirealism will be set out more fully and certain ambiguities in it explored. In the final two sections, I will argue that a more nuanced look at the phenomenon of amoralism tends to undermine this argument.

II

In recent moral philosophy, questions about the ontological status of moral facts or moral properties have been entangled in complicated ways with questions about the motivational force of moral judgments. The dispute between realists and antirealists in moral philosophy concerns the first set of issues. Although there is a bewildering variety of ways in which recent moral philosophers have characterized moral realism, all would agree that the moral realist is committed to the view that moral judgments can be true or false and that their truth or falsity is determined, in some way, by how they fit the facts about the world. There is also broad agreement, however, that moral realism requires certain restrictions on the range of facts that can serve as the truth-conditions for moral judgments. These facts must be independent, in some sense, of human powers of recognizing them, and, in particular, they must not be constituted by our beliefs about what is right or wrong. There are a variety of ways of stating this "independence" condition. Nicholas Sturgeon attempts to capture it in the following way:

We ought not to count a view as realist unless it holds that these moral truths are in some interesting sense *independent* of the subjective indicators—our moral beliefs and moral feelings, as well as moral conventions constituted by coordinated individual intentions—that we take as guides to them.[5]

David Brink characterizes the condition as one requiring that "there are moral facts and true moral propositions whose existence and nature are independent of our belief about what is right or wrong."[6] Mark Platts construes the independence condition much more strongly when he says that "the realist treats evaluative judgments as descriptions of the world whose literal significance (viz. truth conditions) make no reference, or generally make no reference, to human desires, needs, wants or interests."[7] The disagreements that underlie these different formulations of the independence condition are important ones, but for the purposes of our discussion of moral realism, we need not attempt to settle them. It is important to note, however, that any view that identifies the truth conditions for moral judgments as a function of human attitudes or cognitive states will fall short of realist requirements.

Antirealists deny either that moral judgments fit the facts or, if they admit "moral facts," that the facts satisfy the independence condition. Although antirealists may countenance our assessing of moral claims as true or false, they understand the use of 'true' in such contexts in such a way that the"truth" of a moral claim is not determined by how the judgment in question fits "independent" facts. Frequently, antirealists disparage the pretensions of moral judgments to express "genuine" truths by claiming that the function of moral judgment lies elsewhere: perhaps in causally influencing the attitudes of the speaker and audience (emotivism) or in prescribing behavior to the speaker and audience (prescriptivism).[8] In whatever way the details of the antirealist view are spelled out, however, it is essential that no commitment be made to truth conditions for moral judgments that involve "independent" facts.

The dispute between moral realists and their opponents concerns how moral judgments relate to the "world"; the dispute concerning moral motivation concerns how an agent's moral judgments relate to the motivational states of that person. The opposing views here are usually labeled "internalism" and "externalism." The internalist with regard to moral motivation holds that an agent's assent to a moral judgment is tied necessarily to some motivation to act in an appropriate way. The connection between assent to a moral judgment and appropriate motivation is unmediated by other desires or motivations that the agent might have. Thus, the internalist holds that if an agent genuinely assents to the judgment "I morally ought to A," that agent is necessarily, simply in virtue of his or her assent, motivated to A. Externalism denies this a priori connection. For the externalist, motivation to act in accord with moral judgments need only be contingently connected to assent to moral judgments. It is possible, according to the externalist, that someone assent genuinely to some particular moral judgment and be completely unmoved by that judgment. One might believe, for example, that one is morally required to perform some particular action but be completely unmotivated to perform that action.[9]

Both the dispute between the realist and the antirealist and the dispute between the externalist and the internalist are complicated enough in their own right; but additional complications arise because these two disputes cannot be neatly kept separate. For many philosophers, the central issue that determines the plausibility of moral realism is the question of whether internalism is true. They are driven to this view because they hold that the most powerful argument against realism presupposes the truth of internalism. They believe that realism requires an externalist account of moral motivation because they believe that a moral view that embraces both a realist ontology and an internalist motivational scheme must countenance moral facts or moral properties that are at once independent of an agent's evidence for assenting to a moral judgment and also necessarily motivating. John Mackie has argued that such properties are sufficiently "queer" that there should be no place for such properties in a plausible ontology.[10]

This general line of argument, which makes the truth of moral realism dependent on the falsity of internalism, might be criticized in a number of different ways. A number of philosophers, including John McDowell and David Wiggins, have been prepared to allow such queer properties into their world.[11] But there is no doubt that many moral philosophers, both realists and antirealists, have believed that an internalist account of moral motivation is fatal to moral realism. Antirealists have attacked moral realism by appealing to internalism; realists have defended themselves by attacking internalism and defending externalism.

One particular argument used by realists in this exchange involves the appeal to the possibility of amoralism as a device to undermine internalism. The amoralist, in the context of this argument, is someone who assents to moral judgments but is unmoved by them. The claim is made that amoralism is surely possible, and proponents of this view point to historical or fictional characters (for example, Thrasymachus, Uriah Heep, Hobbes's fool, and Bernard Williams) who appear to exemplify amoralism.[12] The significance of the amoralist in this context is that he appears to constitute a clear counterexample to internalism. Internalism holds that there is an a priori connection between assent to moral judgments and appropriate motivation. But the amoralist is someone for whom assent to moral judgments leads only to indifference. Thrasymachus, for example, assents to many of the same moral judgments as does Socrates. He agrees that it is unjust to steal, kill, and plunder. But although he assents to these judgments, he is unmoved by them. He appears happily to live a life that contains the moral belief that killing is unjust, but no particular motivation to avoid killing.

I will call the general argument that uses the possible existence of the amoralist to undermine internalism, and, in turn, to strengthen moral realism the *Amoralist Argument for Realism* (AAR). The general form of the AAR fits the pattern of "trench warfare" between the realist and the antirealist discussed in the previous section. The realist claims that ordinary moral practice allows the possible existence of the amoralist, while antirealism, because of its internalist presuppositions, must deny this possible existence. The general charge made by the realist in this argument is that the antirealist cannot do justice to ordinary moral practice in that antirealism is forced to render the views of the amoralist incoherent or conceptually confused.

David Brink has recently presented the AAR in a particularly sophisticated and compelling way.[13] He has argued directly that the possible existence of the amoralist both undermines internalism and, in doing so, strengthens the case for moral realism. Indeed he seems to regard the establishment of the possibility of amoralism as a particularly powerful argument to be used in defense of moral realism. One finds, however, a curious lack of argument on his part for the claim that the amoralist is conceivable.[14] He alludes to putative examples of amoralists (Thrasymachus and Uriah Heep), and then seems content merely to assert that amoralism is conceivable. Thus he says, "We can imagine someone who regards certain demands as moral demands — and not simply as conventional moral demands — and yet remains unmoved."[15] In another place, he says, "But we do think that such a person [the amoralist] is possible, and, if we are to take the amoralist challenge seriously, we must attempt to explain why the amoralist should care about morality."[16] Brink's position seems to be that we can establish the possible existence of the amoralist by mere ostention. We can point to historical or imaginative examples of amoralism, and this pointing is sufficient to establish their possibility.

He seems to suppose that there is a straightforward argument against internalism at his disposal that has the following form:

(1) Internalism entails the impossibility of the amoralist.
(2) Amoralists have existed or at least might have.
(3) Amoralism is possible. (from (2))
(4) Therefore, internalism is false. (from (1) and (3))

But a little reflection shows that this argument alone will not suffice to undermine internalism. An example of an amoralist, stripped of the historical associations of, say, Thrasymachus or Uriah Heep, may make this clear. This agent assents to moral judgments that we might call "the standard set." He recognizes the moral wrongness of theft, deception, exploitation, the gratuitous causing of pain in other humans, discrimination, and so on. His moral views are in most respects like those of a well-brought-up, morally sensitive person. Unlike such persons, however, he is unmoved by actions or states of affairs that possess these properties. He agrees with the "moralist" in his description of the world in moral terms, but regards such a description as irrelevant to action. That an action is morally wrong is, in itself, of no more moment to him than the fact that an action occurs at 12:45 a.m. or that an action is performed by the right hand rather than the left.

This description may appear to describe a possible agent. There may appear to be nothing incoherent or inconceivable in either what the amoralist says or what he feels. But it is not clear that even such a plausible description is sufficient to settle the question of the coherence of the amoralist. What is described above is a particular package of utterances and motivations found together in an agent. It is presumably the same package that Brink takes to characterize Thrasymachus and Uriah Heep.

But the possibility of describing such a package cannot demonstrate the conceivability of the amoralist. The internalist need not deny that such combinations of putative moral assent and moral motivation exist. His quarrel with the externalist is not over the existence of such packages, but over their interpretation. Just as one might attribute to someone a string of utterances that express incoherent views, one might attribute packages of utterances and motivations like those above to someone while recognizing that, on certain plausible interpretations of them, they constitute an incoherent position.

Although the description of the case above may seem relatively straightforward, there are at least three different points at which questions of interpretation may arise. First, it must be determined if the assent to the judgments in question is genuine and sincere. Perhaps the agent in question uttered certain words without really meaning them. He may have been deliberately attempting to mislead his audience, or perhaps he uttered the words in order to try to convince himself of their truth – and failed. Of course, one cannot determine whether assent was genuine by asking the agent. That only pushes the problem of genuine assent back one stage.

The internalist may choose, however, not to raise questions about whether assent was genuine, but rather about whether the judgment assented to, genuinely or not, is really a moral judgment. Here, very large questions may be raised about the "domain" of the moral. The person who uses examples like the above to refute the internalist must be prepared to argue that the judgments in question are moral judgments in a sense of moral that the internalist is willing to accept. Notoriously, as Brink points out, internalists have invoked interpretations of the meaning of certain putative moral judgments that render them nonmoral. Hare, for example, has interpreted certain judgments that appear to be moral judgments as judgments merely reporting what conventional morality requires. His claim is that these judgments involve "inverted commas," uses of terms that would in other usages be moral terms. Whether Hare's view on this matter is ultimately defensible need not be settled here. Brink clearly thinks it is not.[17] The more general point is that Brink must provide some plausible account of how genuinely *moral* judgments are to be identified if he is to argue persuasively that amoralism is possible.

There is a third tactic, however, which the internalist may use to question the interpretation of the example above. Rather than challenge the genuineness of assent, or the moral character of the judgment assented to, the internalist may choose to query the notion of "appropriate" motivation. Consider the case of someone who genuinely assents to the moral judgment that one ought not to vote for Republicans. What would be the appropriate motivation associated with this assent if internalism is true? At one extreme, there is the mere thought that, for example, it would be a good thing not to vote for Republicans. On the other extreme, there are full-blooded actions of not voting for Republicans. But surely neither of these is sufficient to establish appropriate motivation. The mere thought clearly won't do since it is a thought, and, as a thought, presumably it will have a certain propositional content. But the same question could be raised about the appropriate motivational upshot of having this thought as could be raised about assenting to the original judgment. Neither will, however, the full-blooded action do. The action of not voting for Republicans need not have been motivated by a belief that voting for them would be morally wrong. The agent might have been bribed by the opposition. But if neither the mere thought nor the full-blooded action provides conclusive evidence that the agent in question was appropriately motivated, what would? Here there seems to be a genuine problem. At least for someone in a third-person situation, it seems necessary to rely on what someone says or what someone does as evidence in this matter. But with regard to what someone says, one can raise questions about the motivational force of the thing said; with regard to what someone does, it is always possible that motivation arises from some other source.

This argument is not intended to generate a general skepticism about determining the motivations of others. Rather it is intended to emphasize that, in attributing motivational states (or their absence) to agents, difficult questions of interpretation arise. Any argument against internalism that claims that some particular agent lacks appropriate motivation must be prepared to defend this claim by appealing to some account of how motivational states are to be identified and their character determined.

The considerations above are intended to show that it is not as easy as it may first appear to demonstrate the conceivability of the amoralist. What we can conceive without difficulty are certain packages of utterance and action in particular agents that may be subject to interpretation as instances of amoralism. But the internalist has a number of resources that make the interpretation problematic for the defender of the conceivability of amoralism. The opponent of the conceivability of amoralism may argue that the assent attributed to the putative amoralist is not genuine, or that what is assented to is not genuinely a moral judgment, or that it has yet to be shown that there is a complete absence of motivation. The questions raised here are such large ones that it is difficult to see how the defender of the conceivability of amoralism will be able to respond without invoking a large-scale account of moral thought and action that goes far beyond the mere question of the conceivability of the amoralist.

One might put this same point another way by noting that the notion of an amoralist is theory-laden. It invokes accounts of genuine assent, moral judgment, and motivation that can be sustained adequately only by developing a more comprehensive theory of moral thought and action than proponents of the AAR typically give. The conceivability of the amoralist cannot be used as a fixed point prior to ethical theory that can be used to justify moves within ethical theory. It is too heavily laden with theory itself to play such a role. That is why the device of pointing to the conceivability of the amoralist has about it a question-begging air. From the standpoint of ethical theory the conceivability of the amoralist is the problem; it cannot be part of the solution.

The results of this line of argument are almost entirely negative, however. At most, the argument shows that proponents of the AAR who rely, as Brink does, on mere imaginative ostention of the amoralist cannot overturn internalism as easily as they suppose. Mere ostention of amoralists will not do. The picture of the *pure* amoralist has a kind of power, however, which, in spite of the arguments in this section, may appear to count against internalism. Someone might admit that Brink needs to do more than he does, but still be convinced that the task can be carried out. In the next section, I would like to consider the amoralist in more detail. In particular, I would like to argue that the picture of the amoralist we have been working with in this section may be in various respects oversimplified and one-dimensional. A deeper appreciation for the complexity of amoralism may go further than we have been able to in this section to render him harmless from the point of view of antirealism.

III

The amoralist is a familiar figure in the arguments of contemporary moral philosophers. He is usually taken seriously, however, for what he is not, rather than for what he is. Indeed, his standard role is to be the target of arguments designed to convert him from his amoralist ways. This is surely as it should be, but the fact that he is typically not taken seriously in his own right makes it likely that the variety and complexity of amoralist positions are seldom understood. Although moral philosophers recognize that the views of those who are moved by morality exhibit a remarkably wide diversity, it is all too easy to believe that amoralists (if there are any) share views that are (morally) indistinguishable. Even a little thought, however, would suggest that this view is surely false. There is every reason to believe that there are at least as many ways to distance oneself from the motivational pull of morality as there are ways of coming under the sway of morality. I would like to identify at least three ways in which amoralists may differ. Noting these differences is surely useful in itself, but it also provides a different perspective on the claims made by proponents of the AAR about the relations among internalism, moral realism, and the amoralist.

A first obvious way in which amoralists may vary is with regard to the *range* of moral judgments from which they are motivationally distanced. Amoralists are characterized by the fact that they assent to some range of moral judgments, but fail to be motivated appropriately by these judgments. But moral judgments form a large and multifarious class. One may presumably be an amoralist with regard to some members of this class while failing to be so with other members. One might distinguish *local* amoralists from *global* amoralists in this regard. At one local extreme will be the agent, for example, who is appropriately motivated by all moral judgments except those having to do with attributions of chastity. He is willing to assent to "standard" judgments about which actions are chaste, but he is completely unmoved by the fact that an action is chaste. Indeed, he may take the fact that an action is chaste as giving him a reason to avoid it. He is an amoralist concerning chastity, but a "moralist" regarding all other types of moral judgment. At the other extreme will be the *global* amoralist—the agent who is unmotivated by every moral consideration to which he assents.

This first point raises questions about the *extent* of the motivational disengagement of the amoralist. Is he unmoved by all moral claims, or only by some proper subset of moral claims? A second difference among amoralists concerns the *intensity* of motivational disengagement. With regard to any human practice, there are two quite different ways in which one might become distanced from it. One way is simply not to care about it. One may, for example, simply not care about gourmet cooking. It may be, of course, that one knows quite a lot about it, can participate in discussions of it, and, even, perhaps, render expert judgments. (Consider a jaded gourmet cook, someone who once cared very much, became expert in the area, but then lost interest.) One might call this kind of distance from a practice *disengagement*. For someone who is disengaged, the facts that would typically move persons within the practice to act a certain way would not move him.

There is more radical distancing of oneself from a practice, however, that one might call *disenchantment*. Imagine the gourmet cook who doesn't simply lose interest in gourmet cooking, but who comes to loathe gourmet cooking. He may, for example, think that it offends against health or justice or nature. He now becomes not only unmoved by the claims of the expert gourmet cook, but perhaps offended by them. That a certain fact about cooking would motivate a gourmet to act in certain ways, he regards as unfortunate. He believes that that very fact should motivate one to act in a quite different way. The disenchanted are not only unmoved, they are opposed. The form of their opposition, of course, will depend on the nature of their opposition to the practice in question. They may think it is only silly, in which case they may oppose it by writing the occasional ironic essay; on the other hand, they may think it is dangerous, in which case they may take to the streets—or go underground for guerrilla warfare.

The distinction between disenchantment with a practice and disengagement from it provides another dimension within which amoralists can be distinguished. The amoralist may either not care about morality or be, in some sense, opposed to it.[18] Brink's examples of amoralists, Thrasymachus and Uriah Heep, would seem clearly to fall into the latter class. Their motivational distance from morality is not a matter of lack of interest, but rather a matter of opposition. Amoralists generally could be divided along the lines of this distinction, although most of the examples that philosophers discuss, like those of Brink's, will surely be cases of disenchantment.

These first two differences among amoralists allow one to distinguish amoralists either with regard to the extent of motivational disengagement or with regard to its degree. Amoralists may be either partial or global, and they may be merely disengaged or disenchanted. A third difference concerns not the varieties of amoralism, but a particular feature that typical putative amoralists seem to exemplify. The standard examples of the amoralist in the history of moral philosophy— Thrasymachus, Nietzsche, and Marx, for example[19]—all provide, in more or less complete form, an account of morality. Thrasymachus, for example, is *not* merely disengaged from morality; he is disenchanted. And his disenchantment arises from a theory he holds concerning the origins and maintenance techniques of morality. According to his theory, the practice of morality has been promoted by powerful members of society as a device to forward their particular interests. It is necessary, if they are to achieve their goals, that the real origins of morality be obscured. According to Thrasymachus, morality's presentation is at odds with its origins. It is presented as being in the interest of everyone, but in fact it is only in the interest of the few. Nietzsche's account of the origins of morality is structurally similar to Thrasymachus's, but materially quite different. The same basic "conspiracy theory" is operative, but the conspirators for Nietzsche are not the strong, but the weak. One might call theories of the sort that Thrasymachus and Nietzsche put forward *deprecating theories of morality*, since they deprecate the status of morality. Deprecating theories typically indict either the standard story of the origin of morality or its maintenance techniques.

The notion of a deprecating theory introduces yet a third way to differentiate among types of amoralism. First, it suggests that we may distinguish types of amoralism that are based on deprecating theories from those that have no such basis. But, secondly, the variety of types of deprecating theories provides a further range of differences among those amoralists who base their amoralism on such a theory. The variety of possible deprecating theories of morality is much too great to discuss in detail here, but the following possibilities may be noted. Deprecating theories may be broadly *empirical* (as the theories of Marx and Nietzsche appear to be) or broadly *nonempirical* (as certain aspects of Bernard Williams's deprecating account of morality appears to be);[20] they may be *complete*, in that they indict all of morality, or they may be *partial*, in that they indict only some part or aspect of morality; they may indict either some *substantive* part of morality (for example, its treatment of future generations) or some *conceptual* part of morality (for example, the centrality of categorical imperatives); they may be *internal* theories, which rest on a more or less clearly defined moral base, or *external* theories, which depart from premises that are recognizably nonmoral in character.

It is a sign of how little attention contemporary moral philosophers have paid to the possible varieties of amoralism that these distinctions among possible deprecating theories of morality have been so little investigated. There can be no doubt, however, that there will be significant differences among forms of amoralism associated with deprecating theories that differ in these ways. One need only imagine an amoralist who holds an internal, substantive, and partial deprecating theory, and compare the possible form his amoralism will take with that of an amoralist who holds an external, conceptual, and complete deprecating theory. The differences would surely be substantial.

IV

It may seem that the claims made in the previous section about the variety of views apparently open to the amoralist are largely irrelevant to the AAR considered in section II. In fact, it may seem that, by considering the possible variations of the amoralist position, one gives proponents of the AAR the concession they need in order to make out their larger claim. Their central claim, as we have seen, is that the amoralist is possible, and that the possibility of the amoralist demonstrates the inadequacy of internalism as an account of moral motivation. By discussing the variety of amoralist positions, I may seem to be admitting the central point at issue: the possibility of the amoralist. If there are varieties of amoralism, then surely amoralism is possible.

This interpretation of the upshot of the analysis in the previous section is, however, too hasty. Given the larger context of argument in which proponents of the AAR imbed their defense of the possibility of the amoralist, it is clear that the possibility of just *any* amoralist will not serve the purposes required by the larger goals of their argument. The ultimate goal of the AAR is a defense of moral realism. The argument presupposes that the most serious threat to the truth of moral realism is an internalist account of moral motivation. If internalism gives the best account of moral motivation, then moral realism must be given up. The possibility of the amoralist is introduced as a difficulty for any internalist account of moral motivation. If the amoralist is possible, then internalism is inadequate; but if internalism is shown to be inadequate, then the most serious obstacle to moral realism will have been removed.

What is important to notice about this overall line of argument is that it makes the possibility of amoralism a *necessary* condition of the truth of moral realism. Without the possibility of amoralism, the moral realist will find it necessary to defend mind-independent but motivationally active properties: the kind of "queer" properties that Mackie believes the moral realist will be unable to defend. It does not follow, however, from the fact that the possibility of amoralism is necessary for moral realism that it is also sufficient for the truth of moral realism. Or, to put the same point in another way, it does not follow that moral realism is necessary for the possibility of the amoralist. Amoralism may be possible and moral realism still be false.

This point opens up the possibility that, though some forms of amoralism may be possible, they may, instead of supporting moral realism, be incompatible with it. If, for example, it could be shown that, though amoralism is possible, its possibility depends on the falsity of moral realism, then the overall goal of the AAR would hardly be satisfied. This point suggests that the defense of the possibility of the amoralist on the part of the proponents of the AAR must be more complicated than it first appears. Some proponents, like Brink, as we have seen in section II, seem content merely to point to the possibility of the amoralist. There are difficulties even in this procedure, as I have tried to show. Any argument for the possibility of the amoralist must be imbedded in a richer theoretical background than that which Brink employs. But even if these problems could be overcome, the point above suggests a further difficulty. Proponents of the AAR must not only provide convincing arguments for the possibility of the amoralist, but also must demonstrate that the amoralist is possible in a world in which moral realism is true. If the price they must pay to establish the possibility of the amoralist is to give up the truth of moral realism, then their overall argument will have failed.

The distinctions in the previous section provide grounds for questioning whether they can succeed in this task. The main point of these distinctions was to suggest that amoralism should not be conceived in an oversimplified and one-dimensional way. Amoralists appear to vary in a number of ways and along a number of different dimensions. Once the variety of amoralism is appreciated, however, one can raise questions about whether constraints might be imposed on the possible range of forms of amoralism. For example, it is clear that some varieties of amoralism could not possibly obtain. Consider, for example, a global form of amoralism that is based on an internal deprecating theory. Clearly, such a form of amoralism is impossible. If the deprecating theory is internal, then it must motivationally draw on some moral beliefs; but if the amoralism is global, there would be no motivationally active moral beliefs on which it could draw. This relatively simple kind of incoherence demonstrates how the possible range of amoralisms might be narrowed.

It also seems clear that some varieties of amoralism are not going to be useful in supporting moral realism. Suppose, for example, that local amoralism is the only possible form of amoralism. This form of amoralism will surely not serve the broadly realist purposes of the AAR. If only local amoralism is possible, then, necessarily, at least *some* of the moral beliefs of any agent who has moral beliefs will be motivating. But if the goal of the AAR is to show that *no* moral properties need have, in themselves, any motivating force, then mere local amoralism will not support this conclusion. The moral realist who makes use of the AAR wishes to avoid *all* mind-independent but motivationally active properties; reducing their number is of no help.

Consider, on the other hand, the form of amoralism associated with the kind of deprecating theory held by Thrasymachus. This theory holds that what is true in morality is constituted by the beliefs and actions of the most powerful members of society. Thrasymachus's deprecating theory is clearly antirealist, since, as we noted in section II, moral realism requires not only that moral judgments report facts, but that these facts not be constituted by the beliefs of moral agents. Thrasymachus agrees with the moral realist that moral judgments report facts, but he does not agree that these facts are independent of the beliefs of moral agents. A theorist who wants to make use, as proponents of the AAR do, of Thrasymachus's amoralism to defend moral realism must face an unpalatable choice. He must either agree with Thrasymachus's antirealist deprecating theory or disagree with it. But either alternative causes problems for the overall defense of moral realism. If the theorist agrees with this antirealist account, he is in conflict with the realist conclusion that he wants to draw. If he disagrees with Thrasymachus's antirealist account, however, he encounters a quite different problem. He must regard Thrasymachus as holding an account of the meaning and truth conditions of his moral judgments that is at variance with the truth about the meaning of moral judgments. But then it is unclear that he can regard Thrasymachus as assenting to *genuine* moral judgments. After all, on the realist's view, genuine moral judgments will be those that report agent-independent facts about the world. On Thrasymachus's view, however, the "moral" judgments he is assenting to report only what actions are regarded as being to the advantage of the stronger members of his society. It is at least not obvious that the realist can regard Thrasymachus in this case as assenting to genuine moral judgments.[21] But, if the judgments assented to are not genuine moral judgments, then Thrasymachus does not constitute a genuine instance of the amoralist. Either the proponent of the AAR must then agree with Thrasymachus's deprecating theory, in which case he must renounce realism, or he must disagree with the theory, in which case it is not clear he can continue to regard Thrasymachus as a genuine amoralist. Neither alternative will be of use in the AAR's larger project of defending realism.

These two examples of putative amoralists are intended to establish that not every possible instance of amoralism will serve the purposes of the AAR. Proponents of this argument must not only show that amoralism is possible, but that the right kind of amoralism is possible, where the right kind is a form of amoralism that is consistent with moral realism. It should also be noted, however, that these two cases constitute the most plausible forms of possible amoralism. When one thinks of possible examples of the amoralist, one typically thinks of cases like the two above: cases where the amoralism in question extends only to certain areas of morality; or cases where amoralism is sustained by a deprecating theory of morality that is broadly antirealist in form. And it seems only natural that amoralism should take one or another of these two forms. Resistance to the motivating force of (some) moral judgments is likely to have its source either within (a part of) morality itself or outside of morality. If it comes from within morality, the amoralism in question can at most be local; if it comes from without, it will typically be accompanied by a deprecating—and antirealist—account of morality. The only other alternative would seem to be a kind of global amoralism without any source in the agent's own commitments or beliefs. And it is surely far from clear that this is possible.

V

The arguments in this paper are intended to demonstrate that the rather quick movement the AAR makes from the possibility of the amoralist to the inadequacy of internalism, and then to the truth of moral realism, will not do. Two specific objections have been raised to his project:

    (1) The question of the possibility of the amoralist cannot be settled by merely

imaginatively pointing to a certain package of utterances and actions in an agent. In defending the possibility of the amoralist it is necessary to deploy a richer account of the necessary conditions for genuine assent to a moral judgment, and also to render more perspicuous than Brink does, how lack of motivation is to be detected.

(2) Even if it is admitted that the amoralist is possible, the variety of positions open to the amoralist makes it problematic whether the mere possibility of the amoralist will support moral realism. Indeed, a close look at the most plausible possible varieties of amoralism suggests that the defender of moral realism will not find them available for use in a general defense of moral realism.

The remarks in the opening section of this paper made it clear that the issues under consideration here are involved in one of the many instances of "trench warfare" now being conducted around the topic of moral realism. My purpose has been to attempt to close one gap that may have appeared to open in one part of the defensive perimeter of the antirealist. The particular challenge put to the moral realist who wishes to use the AAR is that he develop an account of the amoralist that is sufficiently rich and detailed for more substantive argument to get a grip.

Notes

1. John Mackie, *Ethics: Inventing Right and Wrong* (New York, 1977), chap. 1.

2. But Mackie's view is not as radical as it may first appear. For although he defends an error view in the opening chapter of his influential book on ethics, he goes on in the remaining chapters, which make up the bulk of the book, to practice normative ethics in a way that is quite similar to the traditional practice of normative ethics. One cannot resist the view that if Mackie thinks that there are errors built into the practice of morality, he does not believe that they are errors that importantly affect practical moral deliberation.

3. Blackburn has developed his views in a number of places. The most important are *Spreading the Word* (Oxford, 1984), chaps. 5 and 6, and "Errors and the Phenomenology of Value," in *Morality and Objectivity*, edited by Ted Honderich (London, 1985), 1–22.

4. Compare the discussion of Kantian views of this sort in Bernard Williams, "Ethics and the Fabric of the World," in *Morality and Objectivity*, edited by Honderich, 206–7.

5. Nicholas Sturgeon, "What Difference Does It Make Whether Moral Realism Is True?" in *Spindel Conference 1986: Moral Realism*, vol. 24, Supplement, edited by Norman Gillespie, *The Southern Journal of Philosophy* (1986): 117.

6. David Brink, "Externalist Moral Realism," in *Spindel Conference 1986: Moral Realism*, vol. 24, Supplement, edited by Norman Gillespie, *The Southern Journal of Philosophy* (1986): 24.

7. Mark Platts, "Moral Reality and the End of Desire," in *Reference, Truth and Reality*, edited by Mark Platts (London, 1980), 73.

8. Of course, these oversimplified ways of capturing the point of emotivism and prescriptivism are mere parodies of the sophisticated views that their proponents have developed. The point here, however, is merely to capture the sense in which each of these views treats moral language as having some point other than reporting moral facts.

9. My treatment of internalism as the view that assent to a moral judgment is conceptually tied to motivation is but one way of characterizing internalism. One might characterize it as the view that there is a necessary connection between the truth of a moral judgment and motivation; or the view that there

is a necessary connection between assent to a moral judgment and having reasons for action. Other obvious permutations are also available. These distinctions are important in any full treatment of moral motivation, and a number of them are explored in a useful way in David Brink's "Externalist Moral Realism." The characterization I give, however, is the one presupposed by the argument I wish to explore.

10. Mackie's "argument from queerness" is discussed in his *Ethics*, 38–42. He explains the metaphysical "queerness" in question as follows: "An objective good would be sought by anyone who was acquainted with it, not because of any contingent fact that this person, or every person, is so constituted that he desires this end, but just because the end has to-be-pursuedness somehow built into it. Similarly, if there were objective principles of right and wrong, any wrong (possible) course of action would have not-to-be-doneness somehow built into it"(40).

11. For McDowell's views, see John McDowell, "Virtue and Reason," *The Monist* 62: (1979). For Wiggins's views, see David Wiggins, "Truth, Invention and the Meaning of Life," *Proceedings of the British Academy* (Oxford, 1976), 331–78.

12. Thrasymachus and Uriah Heep are examples used by David Brink in "Externalist Moral Realism," 30; Nicholas Sturgeon uses Hobbes's fool and Bernard Williams as examples of amoralists in Nicholas Sturgeon, "What Difference Does It Make whether Moral Realism Is True?" in *Spindel Conference 1986: Moral Realism*, vol. 24, Supplement, edited by Norman Gillespie, *The Southern Journal of Philosophy* (1986): 121.

13. In David Brink, "Externalist Moral Realism."

14. There is some difficulty in knowing exactly how to characterize Brink's view concerning the amoralist. He says of the amoralist that he is "conceivable," "conceptually possible," that his position is "coherent," and that he "must be taken seriously." I take it that these various characterizations are supposed to be roughly equivalent. For the most part, I will talk about his view as the view that the amoralist is conceivable.

15. Brink, "Externalist Moral Realism," 30.

16. Brink, "Externalist Moral Realism," 30.

17. Thus he says, "The amoralist challenge need not depend upon a failure to recognize inverted commas usage of terms." In "Externalist Moral Realism," 30.

18. It is important to note that this is *not* the same distinction as one commonly drawn (and drawn by Brink) between motivational skepticism with regard to morality and cognitive skepticism with regard to morality. Both the morally disengaged and the morally disenchanted may stop short of cognitive skepticism. Thrasymachus, for example, is surely disenchanted with morality, but he is not a cognitive moral skeptic.

19. There may be some question, of course, about whether Nietzsche and Marx are amoralists in Brink's sense. Whether they are or not does not seem to me important for what I have to say about deprecating theories.

20. Although I do not agree with Sturgeon that Williams's views are genuinely amoralist, he does have a deprecating theory of morality. His views on this topic are found in a number of places, but perhaps most usefully in chap. 10, "Morality, the Peculiar Institution," in Bernard Williams, *Ethics and the Limits of Philosophy* (Cambridge, 1986), 174–96.

21. Of course, neither is it obvious that the realist cannot treat the Thrasymachean antirealist as assenting to genuine moral judgments. The issues here are complex, and I am not sure what I want to say. This much, however, seems clear: If someone treats putative moral judgments as having truth conditions that radically diverge from the truth conditions *I* attach to moral judgments, I will be justified in concluding that the judgments in questions are not genuine moral judgments. How radical the divergence must be to justify this conclusion, of course, is the difficult question. However this issue is ultimately to be settled, the point here is that the realist at least has to say more than he typically does to convince the antirealist that Thrasymachus can be used for his realist purposes.

Realism in Ethics

PANAYOT BUTCHVAROV

I

The general topic of realism is, once again, trendy. It dominated philosophy in the late nineteenth and early twentieth centuries. That realism was contrasted then with idealism and is contrasted now with just irrealism or antirealism is of less significance than it may seem, since what the idealists meant by "mind" or "spirit" included what is meant today by "our conceptual scheme." And, like the idealsm of the earlier period, contemporary irrealism rests on one or both of two assumptions that are not necessarily related (both are evident, for example, in Hilary Putnam's recent writings). The first is representationalism, the view that we are encircled by our ideas and sensations (whether these are understood as mental, or neural, or linguistic states or events), which at most *represent* an independent reality. If so, then it becomes plausible to suggest that we have no reason to believe they represent anything at all, and that even if they do, they could be taken to represent any one of a great variety of possible realities. G. E. Moore (and, later, Sartre) denied this assumption by arguing that to have an idea or sensation (understood as a mental state or event) is already to be outside the circle, to be in direct epistemic contact with something other than an idea or a sensation. (Putnam rejects such a view as magical.)[1] The second assumption is that we can have no epistemic access to an unconceptualized reality. H. H. Price, in his chapter on the given in *Perception*, in effect argued (I take some liberties with the text) that the very idea of our conceptualizing something presupposes that there is a thing that is (to be) conceptualized and that this presupposition is intelligible only if we allow for an independent, unmediated by concepts, epistemic access to the thing. That this is so is especially plausible if we think, as most philosophers do today, that conceptualization involves the employment of language. It takes years to learn to talk.

As with many trendy topics, the first rule a discussion of realism must enforce is: distinguish! For example, as Michael Devitt has recently argued,[2] realism must not be confused with a theory of truth, or a theory of meaning, or a theory of knowledge, though it may be dialectically connected with such theories. It is a metaphysical theory.

Very roughly, I shall mean by unqualified realism with respect to x the view that (1) x exists and has certain properties, a nature, and that its existence and nature are independent of (2) our awareness of it, of (3) the manner in which we think of (conceptualize) it, and of (4) the manner in which we speak of it. Obviously, a great variety of views can be called realist or irrealist. One principle of classification would be the meanings that are attached to the terms "exists" ("real"), "awareness," "independent," "conceptualize," and how conditions 3 and 4 are distinguished (as they should be by any phenomenologically sensitive philosophy of mind), crucial questions to which recent discussions of the topic accord very little attention. Another principle of classification would be which (if not all) of the four conditions are accepted. This question becomes even more complicated if we distinguish between the two parts of (1) and thus between realism with respect to the existence of x and realism with respect to the nature (properties) of x. It should be noted that the conditions are largely independent of each other. Perhaps (3) entails (4), but not vice versa; a Meinongian would hold that the second part of (1), as well as (2), (3), and (4) may be satisfied even if the first part of (1) is not; Moore held that almost nothing fails to satisfy (2), Berkeley held that almost everything does. A third principle of classification would be the subject matter of the view, the value of the variable x with respect to which one or more of the four conditions are accepted or rejected. In addition to what may be called unqualified global realism (more plausibly stated as "Whatever exists satisfies conditions 2, 3, and 4," rather than as "Everything satisfies conditions 1, 2, 3, and 4") and unqualified global irrealism (more plausibly stated as "Whatever exists satisfies none of conditions 2, 3, and 4," rather than "Nothing satisfies any of conditions 1, 2, 3, and 4"), and the many possible qualified but still global realisms and irrealisms between those extremes (qualified by excluding only one or two of conditions 2, 3, and 4), there are theories distinguished according to specific subject matter, for example realism or irrealism with respect to numbers, realism or irrealism with respect to the theoretical entities of physics, realism or irrealism with respect to the properties ethics is concerned with. Just as there are important differences among the varieties of realism (irrealism) distinguished according to the first two principles of classification, there are important differences among the varieties distinguished according to this third principle, differences that result from the differences in subject matter.[3]

In this paper I shall be concerned with realism in ethics. I begin by suggesting that, because of its subject matter, genuine realism in ethics should satisfy at least three metaphysical requirements. (1) The alleged reality of ethical properties must be understood in a straightforward, familiar, unsurprising fashion. What it is for something to be real or to exist is the deepest philosophical problem, but one does realism in ethics no service by resting it on highly dubious or unclear solutions of that problem. In such a case philosophical interest is to be found almost entirely in the latter, not the former. For example, arguing for realism with respect to ethical judgments, as Sabina Lovibond has recently done,[4] by appealing to the view that *all* judgments are founded in shared language games and "the world text is at least partly written by ourselves," is like defending the existence of theistic knowledge by claiming that there is no difference between knowledge and belief. (2) The argument for realism in ethics must not rest on definitions of all ethical terms in purely nonethical terms. Of course, if it is obvious that the definitions capture the senses of the ethical terms, this requirement would be unjustified. But it should be commonplace by now that this is not obvious in the case of any definitions so far proposed or that can even be conceived. For example, Gilbert Harman's remark that "there are relative facts about what is right or wrong with respect to one or another set of [social] conventions"[5] cannot be regarded as an argument for genuine realism. (3) The argument for realism in ethics must concern the realist interpretation of an ethical *theory*, not of isolated, haphazardly selected reports of alleged moral "intuitions." To take an often-used example,[6] whether Hitler's moral depravity is an irreducible moral fact, which might explain our belief that Hitler was morally depraved, cannot be judged in abstraction from a theory of moral depravity, which itself must be a part of a whole ethical theory. The reason is that outside such a theory, we can have no genuine understanding of moral depravity. A vapor trail in a cloud chamber (another much-used example!) is not a reason for concluding that a free proton has passed through the chamber except in the context of a physical theory; we need such a theory even to understand what a proton is. I suggest that in this respect, the case with ethics is quite similar.

There is also at least one epistemological requirement that genuine *cognitivism* (by which I mean one that entails realism) in ethics should satisfy: that our alleged knowledge of, or justified belief in, ethical facts be understood in a straightforward, familiar, unsurprising fashion. One does no service to realism by resting it on highly dubious epistemologies. For example, even if someday someone will work out an adequate purely coherentist theory of justification (one that is not wedded to a coherence theory of truth, yet preserves and elucidates the connection between justification as coherence and truth),[7] to rest cognitivism, now, on such a theory can only be described as misguided. So also can be described reliance on the view that the test of reality is explanatory necessity, which usually itself rests on a commitment to "the scientific picture of the world," a commitment that, philosophically, belongs in the century of the French *philosophes*, when science was still a wonderful novelty, not in the century of Husserl and Wittgenstein, when, despite its enormous advances, the limits of its relevance to philosophy should be evident.

The above requirements, when combined, call for a highly conservative approach to the topic of realism in ethics. We must defend realism by showing that a standard, traditional ethical theory describes ethical realities as these would be understood in a standard, traditional manner, and that (at least in part) it can be known to be true in ways that can be understood in a standard, traditional way. The rationale for this approach has to do with philosophical strategy. A solution to a philosophical problem is far more valuable if it does not depend on a change in the conditions in terms of which the problem arose and was originally understood. This is especially true in ethics. Unlike most other branches of philosophy, it is firmly rooted in everyday thought, in which its subject matter is often understood better than by academic philosophers, and from which it derives its identity, interest, indeed life. This is why the topic of realism in ethics differs importantly from that of realism with respect to some other subject matters. Realism in mathematics may allow severely reductive definitions. Realism with respect to some of the "theoretical entities" of science can be defended, perhaps, only by substantive modifications in our ordinary conception of knowledge. Not so with ethics. Only utter despair over finding a defense of realism that satisfies the requirements I have stated could justify tampering with them. The time for such despair, I suggest, is not yet upon us.

I shall now sketch the core of a standard, traditional realist theory that I believe satisfies those requirements, and suggest the manner in which it should be defended against what I believe is the most common objection to it. But I shall conclude that even this theory, which is as *realist* as a theory could be, whether in ethics or in any other discipline, must ultimately rest on an *irrealist* foundation if it is to be defensible. Needless to say, I can attempt here neither a full exposition nor a full defense of that theory.

II

I shall assume that realism in ethics is, fundamentally, unqualified realism with respect to the *properties* of goodness, rightness, and morality, and their contraries, in the ethically relevant senses of "goodness," "rightness," and "morality." I begin by taking the ethically relevant *notions* of goodness, evil (or badness), degree of goodness or of evil, and quantity of goodness or of evil as primitive, but will restrict my discussion here to the first. The notion of rightness (of right action) can be given a utilitarian definition in terms of goodness, though what I shall say about goodness will make clear that the resulting theory would be quite different from run-of-the-mill utilitarianism. The notion of morality can be defined as applicable primarily to certain dispositions and motives for performing what the agent believes would be right actions, and to the persons who exhibit them and the actions that follow from them. But I shall not attempt to defend these definitions. It is a sufficient task for this paper to offer a (partial) defense of realism with respect to the property goodness.

I shall assume that the metaphysical distinction between concrete entities and properties ("abstract entities," "universals") is legitimate and that goodness is a property, if it is anything at all. This assumption is a necessary part of the realist core of the view I am outlining and, I believe, of any defensible genuinely realist ethical theory. If to say of a certain thing that it is good is to describe it, to say something true or false about it, then it is to attribute to it a certain property. It follows that we must distinguish sharply between goodness itself and the things that are good, just as we must distinguish sharply between the geometrical figure triangularity and the concrete entities (if there are any) that are triangular.

For our purposes, we can regard as concrete entities not only what would ordinarily be called individual things, but also actions, as well as such things as a person's life, on grounds similar to those that would allow us to call a flash of lightning or yesterday's weather concrete entities. It may, of course, be asked whether events, for example, a flash of lightning, or a certain action, are not states of affairs and therefore not concrete. A detailed answer to this question cannot be attempted here. It is worth noting, however, that although an action, or a flash of lightning, can be said to have spatial and temporal properties, this cannot be intelligibly said of a state of affairs. And I am deeply skeptical about the very category of states of affairs.[8]

Goodness is usually attributed to concrete entities. But sometimes it is attributed to certain properties, to abstract entities. We may say that a certain person's life is good, but we may also say that happiness as such (that is, the property a life or a person may have of being happy) is good. Now, I suggest, a person's life can be said to be good on the grounds that it is happy only if happiness itself can be said to be good, and in general, that a concrete entity can be said to be good only on the grounds that it has some other property or properties that themselves have the property of being good. (A number of distinctions are needed here, which I shall make shortly.) This is the point, and I suggest, only clear and useful sense of describing the goodness of concrete things as a consequential or supervenient property, not an intrinsic property. I shall return to this point.

In addition to happiness, a number of other properties, or abstract entities, may be, and ordinarily would be, called good—for example, life, health, pleasure, desire-satisfaction, knowledge, strong will, justice, friendship, certain *kinds* of action such as promise-keeping, irreducibly societal properties such as the flourishing of the arts and sciences.[9] There is nothing mysterious, or queer, or nonnatural about these properties, though each requires detailed examination. Nor is there any ordinary reason for denying that there are such properties, that they are real, or that their existence and nature are independent of our awareness, thought, and talk of them. Nor is the description of them as good a matter of widespread disagreement, except in cases of ignorance or easily eliminable misunderstandings. The history of ethics, especially in modern times, has consisted largely in attempts (in my view, unsuccessful) to reduce the goodness of some of them to that of others, not in disagreements about their being good. I cannot here discuss further the constitution and order of the system of the properties that are good. But whatever they are, what is *philosophically* questionable about them is primarily that they are described as having a common property, namely, goodness. This is questionable because of the initial, crude but natural, assumption that this common property must be distinguishable from them in the way, say, the shape of an object is distinguishable from its color, and because of the then inevitable conclusion that they have no such common property. I shall postpone the consideration of this assumption. Continuing with the point with which we have been concerned so far, we may now say that goodness is, strictly speaking, a property of properties, and that good concrete entities, which we may call concrete goods, exemplify it only, so to speak, indirectly, by exemplifying some other property or properties that themselves exemplify goodness directly, and which we may call abstract goods. It follows that the sense in which a concrete entity may be said to be good is not the same as, but is derivable from and explainable through, the sense in which an abstract entity may be said to be good. The term "good" is not used univocally with respect to concrete entities and abstract entities. Indeed, it has also a third, also derivative sense, namely, that in which dispositions and motives to do what is right, the sort of person who generally has such dispositions and motives, and the actions issuing from them, may be said to be good—the sense of "good" roughly expressed by our term "moral." But the *kinds* of such dispositions, motives, persons, and actions may also be abstract goods when considered in themselves; they may be good also in the primary sense. I shall be concerned here only with the first two senses.

Indeed, the difference between these two senses is even greater than it appears to be at first glance. A concrete entity that has a good monadic property is to that extent good, "intrinsically good," "good in itself," just in the sense that it has a property that is itself good in the primary sense. Usually it is on the basis of such facts about concrete entities that we make our ethical decisions, however unjustifiably, and it is in relation to such facts, which of course are of great variety and richness, that moral life emerges. But a concrete entity may have any number of relevant properties, some good, some bad—somewhat as the waters in the Bahamas are, though mostly turquoise, at some places blue, at others brown, and at still others white. Also, a concrete entity may contribute to certain other things' being good; it can be "good as a means," in virtue of its relational properties, causally or by being an element of what Moore called an "organic unity." (Whether we should count such relational properties as being themselves abstract goods, perhaps species of the genus the Useful, as Max Scheler and Nicolai Hartmann did, is a question I shall not discuss here.) To describe it as good without qualification, that is, without adding after the adjective "good" some term F or a phrase such as "*qua* an F" or "insofar as it F's" or "to the extent it is F," can only be, I now suggest, to make a claim about the balance of goodness over badness in the sum total of all its own relevant monadic and relational properties, and of the relevant properties of what it is a means to. It would be analogous to saying that the waters in the Bahamas are turquoise.

This is why, ordinarily (but by no means always), the unqualified application of the term "good" to a concrete entity seems to have no determinate sense, a fact emphasized by P. T. Geach in his claim that "good" is an attributive rather than a predicative adjective, that a statement of the form "x is good" requires completion into a statement of the form "x is a good F."[10] (Yet millions have thought they understood Genesis 1:31: "And God saw every thing he had made, and behold, it was very good.") But a determinate sense *can* be specified in the way I have suggested, namely, by saying that a concrete entity is unqualifiedly good if and only if it contributes, through its intrinsic (monadic) properties or through its causal or noncausal relations to other things, more goodness or less badness than there would have been if the thing had not existed. In the special case of human actions, where the unqualified use of "good" is common, this would mean that the action contributes at least as much goodness (as little badness) as any of its alternatives open to the agent would contribute, in the wide sense of the term "contribute" just specified. We may express all this more succinctly by saying that a concrete entity is unqualifiedly good in the sense that it is optimizing. (But it can be optimizing even if not optimific.[11] It may contribute most goodness not in virtue of its consequences but in virtue of its monadic properties.) My point is not that the term "good" in fact has such a sense, though I believe it does, but that it can be given such a sense and that this sense is logically impeccable, though admittedly vague, as long as the concepts of goodness, badness, and degree and quantity of goodness or badness are left vague.

Geach seems aware that his view is less plausible regarding statements such as "Pleasure is good" and "Preferring inclination to duty is bad," in which "good" and "bad" are predicated of abstract, not concrete, entities, but dismisses them on the grounds that they involve peculiarly philosophical uses of words that require explanation. But, of course, nothing is peculiarly philosophical about these statements. And even if an explanation of them cannot be given, if this means providing definitions of "good" and "bad," an explanation in the sense of a theory of good and bad may still be available. Another author, Paul Ziff, avows that "Pleasure is good" sounds to him remarkably odd.[12] It does not sound so to me. One reason for skepticism about great concern with the ordinary uses of words is that discussions of them consist chiefly in exchanges of avowals about what sounds "odd" to one and what does not.

If such statements strike some of us as odd, the obvious reason is that they are seldom made in ordinary discourse, since we seldom have a reason for making them. "If something is blue then it is colored" also may strike us as odd, since we seldom need to contrast colored entities with colorless ones. In English it may be better to say "Pleasure is a good," and there would be philosophical reasons for preferring this if the relation of pleasure to goodness is that of a species to its genus. Then the statement would be analogous to "Blue is a color," again a statement we seldom have reason for making in ordinary discourse, yet one that is logically impeccable. Or, we may express ourselves informally with sentences such as "Pleasure is a good thing," "thing" being, of course, not a sortal word at all in such a context.

Except to human actions, we would seldom apply the word "good" to concrete entities in the sense of optimizing. The reasons are several and closely related. First, the existence of the concrete entity is ordinarily already a fact, not something we must decide whether to bring about or not (and when it is the latter, the action of bringing it about is what we may judge to be unqualifiedly good). Whether it is on the whole better that it exists or not is often of no clear practical importance. But what often *is* important is some property or relation of the entity, and so we qualify the description of it as good by saying that it is good for such-and-such purpose, or a good so-and-so, or good in such-and-such a respect. The second reason is that the totality of respects in which a concrete entity may be described as good is intellectually and epistemologically overwhelming; we can hardly comprehend it, and can know, at most, a very small part of it. Indeed, this is true also of actions. But there, overwhelmed or not, we must make a judgment, for we must make a decision whether or not to act. And the intrinsic nature (the monadic properties) of the action (for example, its being the keeping of a promise) or its immediate consequences (for example, another person's being harmed) are ordinarily quite easy to comprehend, and therefore form a convenient basis for judgment. The third reason is that, with respect to most concrete entities, we have no clear idea, perhaps no idea at all, of what would, or even could, have existed in their place if they did not exist. Is Germany good in the sense of optimizing? We have no clear idea of what the specific long-range alternatives to the existence of Germany might have been, even though we have some idea of what is meant by the existence of Germany and of what would be relevant to the judgment that it has contributed more goodness or less badness than there would have been if it had not existed. The case with actions is obviously and dramatically different. The idea of the alternatives *open to an agent* is reasonably clear, especially when we stipulate, as we should, that only actions the agent contemplates, of the possibility of which he or she is aware, are genuinely open to the agent.[13] It is not surprising, therefore, that the question Is Germany good? strikes us as nonsensical, though the question Was appeasing Germany in 1938 good? does not.

The richness of the dimension of appraisal of concrete goods, including actions, explains some of the phenomena of moral conflict, much discussed recently, and generates the illusion of pervasive and intellectually unresolvable ethical disagreements, which motivates so many, wholly or partly irrealist, views, such as that of Bernard Williams.[14] If I must choose between *a* and *b*, I may choose *a*, even though continuing to recognize the merits of *b*, which just happen to be lesser than those of *a*; and my recognition of the merits of *b* may lead to a feeling of regret, remorse, perhaps even guilt. If *a* and *b* are of equal merit, then the conflict would be intellectually unresolvable, but tautologically so. (Choice, of course, would remain possible, for example, by flipping a coin.) Nothing follows from this regarding the truth or falsehood of moral realism.

The richness of the dimension of appraisal of concrete goods, including actions, also explains the plausibility of what Sidgwick called perceptional intuitionism,[15] which has been revived in recent years, under the influence of Wittgenstein's later philosophy.[16] By perceptional intuitionism, Sidgwick meant the view that one can make an "immediate judgment as to what ought to be done or aimed at," without inference from past experience or general rules. Renford Bambrough gives as an example one's judgment that a child about to undergo an operation ought to be given an anaesthetic. The truth in this view is that often the goodness (badness) of one or more good (bad) qualities of a concrete entity, especially of an action, is striking and can be acknowledged without inference. But, of course, it would be a mistake to conclude that the concrete entity can be judged also to be unqualifiedly good (bad) in such an immediate way. A physician, I hope, would consider carefully the possible harmful effects of anaesthesia on the child before deciding to use it.

Our sharp distinction between abstract and concrete goods allows us also to see our way clear through some familiar puzzles. For example, Philippa Foot asks whether, granted that courage is a virtue, an inveterate criminal may be said to possess it and exemplify it in his bad actions.[17] What Foot calls the virtues are prime examples of abstract goods, but it does not follow that all their concrete exemplifications are unqualifiedly good.

III

So far I have attempted to elucidate what it is for a concrete entity to be good or, in the case of actions (if we define a right action as one that is optimizing), right. But what is it for an abstract entity, for a property, to be good? It is important, I believe, to answer this question by appealing to a clear sense in which several properties may be said to share a property, and not to rely on purely formal notions such as that of supervenience. That sense, I suggest, is the sense in which the different colors share the property of being a color, and the three species of triangle share the property of being a triangle. The relationship is familiar. It is the species-genus relationship, as holding between properties, not classes. W. E. Johnson referred to something very much like it as the relationship between determinate and determinable qualities. For a property to be good, I suggest, is for it to be a species (perhaps a subgenus) of the generic property goodness. If we understood goodness in this way, we would find the existence of such a property far less questionable. The property would be no more mysterious, queer, or nonnatural than its species.[18] And we would achieve clear understanding of what might be meant by "good-making" properties. Instead of being puzzled by the nature of such a mysterious relation of "making" (or its converse, "being consequential upon" or "supervening upon"), we would be guided by the paradigm of the relationship of the specific (phenomenal) colors to the genus color. We would then see as grotesque, arguments against the reality of goodness such as that of Ralph Barton Perry: "One who upholds this view of good must be prepared to point to a distinct *quale* which appears in that region which our value terms roughly indicate, and which is different from the object's shape and size, from the inter-relations of its parts, from it relations to other objects, or to a subject; and from all the other factors which belong to the same context, but are designated by words other than 'good.' "[19] W. D. Ross's timid reply that goodness is "discerned by intelligence" and that this is why it is "not as easily discerned as what is discerned by sense-perception" would hardly convince anyone.[20] More convincing might be Ross's further remark that, unlike yellow, goodness is a consequential property. But this remark does not help at all if we have no idea of what relation the word "consequential" expresses. (A purely formal definition does not provide us with such an idea.) The genus-species relation, I suggest, is exactly what should be expressed.

Then we can answer Perry's objection by agreeing that there is no *specific* quale that "good" indicates, but pointing out that goodness can be found in "the region which our value terms roughly indicate" as the *genus* of some specific quale present in that region. If we find in a person the property of being compassionate, we should not expect to find *in the same way also* the property of being good. But we can find the property of being good *in* the property of being compassionate, as we can find triangularity in an isosceles triangle and color in a shade of yellow.[21]

The view of the nature of goodness that I am suggesting was well expressed by Brand Blanshard, in the context of a criticism of Moore: "Can one draw a line within a given experience of pleasure between the pleasure and the goodness? Moore apparently thinks that one can, that the pleasure and the goodness are sharply distinct, though connected synthetically by a relation of entailment, as colour and extension are in 'what is coloured is extended.' I cannot think that this has caught the true relation between them. The relation is more intimate. The goodness of being happy is not some isolable quality supervening upon the happiness; the happiness is itself a kind of goodness; we call it *a* good, as we call love an emotion, meaning, I think, that it is one of the forms in which goodness presents itself."[22] But Blanshard did not use this conception of goodness in his own theory, probably because he believed that a generic property, so understood, "lies not in the reality thought about, but in our thought about that reality," that "the universal triangle or man or colour is not as such real," that one could not discern a self-identical nucleus in the species of a generic property.[23] Indeed, we cannot discern such a self-identical nucleus, for there is not one. If there were, the property would be specific, not generic. Following Aquinas, we must be clear that "the unity of the genus comes from its indetermination or indifference; but not in such a way that what is signified by genus is a nature numerically the same in different species, to which would be added something else (the difference) determining it."[24]

The nature of the genus-species relationship is a topic of extraordinary difficulty. The reason, I suggest, is that it makes especially evident, as I shall explain later, the unique character of the concept of identity. We do distinguish the property of being crimson and the property of being red, or the property of being an isosceles triangle and the property of being a triangle, as even Berkeley was forced to admit.[25] But to be aware of both in a particular instance, say in a particular crimson surface or a particular triangular surface, is not at all to be aware of two properties that are distinct but coexemplified, in the way in which, say, the color and the shape of the surface are distinct but coexemplified. Indeed, there is a clear sense in which the crimson color and the red color of the surface are one and the same property, since its being red consists entirely in its being crimson. But there is also a clear sense in which they are not one and the same property, since a scarlet surface is also red but is not crimson.

The fact is that the notion of a generic property and, therefore, the notion of an awareness of a generic property must be understood analogically, as extensions of the notion of a specific property and of the notion of awareness of a specific property. And the notion of awareness of a specific property understood as a universal is itself an analogical extension of the primary notion of awareness of an individual thing, or of an instance of a property. The analogical nature of these notions is evident when we consider their origin.

The notion of a universal property is based on the notion of the (numerical) identity of a property of one individual thing and a property of another individual thing. Indeed, the clearest and least questionable explanation of the technical term "universal" is that to say that a certain property of an individual thing is a universal is to say that it *can* be (numerically) identical with a property of another individual thing. If the identity is specific, such as (perhaps) that of the color (or shape) of this page and the color (or shape) of the next page, then we have a paradigm of identity, questionable only by philosophers. But the notion of a generic universal is grounded in the notion of *generic identity*, in the notion that allows us to say, for example, that a scarlet thing and a crimson thing are the same general color though not exactly the same color, or that an equilateral triangle and a scalene triangle are the same general figure, though not exactly the same figure. Clearly, this notion is no longer a notion of a paradigm of identity, since the qualifications just made ("though not exactly the same color," "though not exactly the same figure") are needed. But generic identity is more like indentity than like anything else. And the *generic property* is more like a single entity than like anything else (for example, it is much less like a mere collection of entities, or even like a structure composed of entities in relation to each other, as the so-called resemblance theories hold).[26]

It follows that the *awareness* of a generic property is awareness also only analogically, though now we have a case twice removed from the primary, paradigmatic case, that of awareness of an individual thing or of an instance of a property. The intermediate case is that of awareness of the specific property as such, which is more like awareness of an individual thing than is the awareness of a generic property, yet still not awareness in the same sense. The difference is evident from the fact that to be aware of a specific property as such is to be aware of it as it would be wherever and whenever it is instantiated, indeed to be aware of it as it would be even if it were nowhere and never instantiated; nothing like this is true of our awareness of an individual thing. But both awareness of a specific property and awareness of a generic property are more like awareness of a single individual thing than like awareness of a collection or structure of individual things, for the same reason that their objects are more like single individual things than like collections or structures of individual things. If we wish, we can call them intellectual awareness or *intuition*. Both kinds of awareness are present in the most fundamental kind of conceptual cognition, namely, in recognition,[27] the first, say, in the recognition of the color of a given individual thing as a certain familiar, even if nameless, specific shade of yellow, and the second in the recognition of that shade as a shade of *yellow*. For, in general, to *recognize* x as y, one must be conscious of both x and y, though in very different ways. It is not to *recall* some z such that one knows that x is identical with z. For example, I may recall seeing someone last year whose identity with the person before me now, whom I do *not* recognize, I infer from their similarities. And I may recognize the person before me now without recalling any past occasion on which I saw that person.

It is the analogical nature of the notions of generic identity, of generic property, and of our awareness of generic properties that explains and excuses the opinion that we are simply not aware of and, therefore, have no reason to believe that there is a property such as goodness. A generic property such as goodness is an entity in an analogical sense of "entity," and we are aware of it in an analogical sense of "aware."

We may find disturbing the need to rely on analogies for understanding our subject matter. But this would be a symptom of a rather narrow view of what it is to understand something. Indeed, in the simple, paradigmatic cases of the application of a concept, to understand something is to see it as unquestionably falling under the concept. But the intellectually challenging cases, whether in philosophical or legal or scientific or mathematical reasoning, are precisely those that are not paradigmatic. With respect to such cases, we must be willing to ask not so much What *is* it?, but rather, What is it *like*?[28] To understand something is to see it in the light of other things, sometimes easily, sometimes not. I hope the reader recognizes, therefore, that the important qualifications made in the previous paragraphs are needed not just because they are required for a defense of our notion of goodness as a generic property, but would need to be made in order to account for any notions likely to be of fundamental intellectual interest. And, if the reader takes my assertion that since goodness is a generic property it is, in a sense, not an entity and, in a sense, we cannot be aware of it, as constituting an admission that the irrealist has won, he or she would be reminded that exactly the same can be asserted also of triangularity and the color red, and of our awareness of them. Goodness and our awareness of it would be beyond the irrealist's reach if their reality could be questioned only by questioning the reality also of such properties as triangularity and the color red and of our awareness of them.

In fact, generic identity is perhaps the most striking application of the Hegelian dictum that all genuine identity is identity in difference, a dictum certainly applicable, though less obviously, also to the specific identities in which the existence of specific properties is grounded. Even if the color of this page is exactly the same as the color of the next page, there is a sense in which the colors are distinguishable, and this is why the judgment of their identity is informative. For example, when you see the one, there is a clear sense in which it is false that you see the other, though also there is a no less clear sense in which it is true that you see the other. Indeed, the Hegelian dictum applies also to individual identity, and this, I suggest, is the lesson to be learned from Frege's account of informative identity statements in terms of the different modes in which the referred-to entity is presented. (*This* is his fundamental account, not that in terms of difference of senses, since he defined his notion of a sense in terms of the notion of a mode of presentation; and by a mode of presentation Frege did not mean a sense-datum, or idea, but, arguably, the entity itself *as it presents itself*, and he denied that one could have access to the entity except via a mode of presentation. But there is no self-identical nucleus *in* the modes of presentation. If there were, the statement would not be informative.) When Blanshard rejected the reality of generic properties on the grounds that he could not discern a self-identical nucleus in the species of a generic property, he ignored the fact that no discernible nucleus of self-identity can be found in the subject matter of any genuine, informative identity statement, that such a nucleus exists only in the subject matter of empty statements of the form "x is x." As Wittgenstein suggested (see quoted material in the next section), philosophers' thinking about identity seems to be dominated by an obsessive picture that requires the genuine cases of identity to be cases of—nothing at all!

IV

Any ethical theory that reflects at all adequately everyday ethical thought would allow for a variety of species or subgenera of goodness, for example, those I mentioned earlier: life, health, pleasure, desire-satisfaction, knowledge, strong will, justice, friendship, *kinds* of actions such as promise-keeping, the flourishing of the arts and sciences. But how could all of these be species or subgenera of the same genus? Are they not evidently heterogeneous? Aristotle thought so, and so did Aquinas and Scotus, who regarded goodness as one of the transcendentals, not as a genus. The complete answer to this question cannot be given without a detailed account of each abstract good, but it should suffice for our purposes to point out that, as I have argued, even uncontroversial generic identity is not paradigmatic identity, but only analogous to paradigmatic identity, and, therefore, that generic properties are not paradigmatic single entities but are only analogous to single entities. (Indeed, even theories much simpler than ours, for example, those that regard only pleasure as good, presuppose the notion of generic identity. There is great variety in pleasures.) If so, then there is no exact point at which we may not attribute generic identity and must acknowledge heterogeneity. This is why, I suggest, the question whether goodness is a genus or a transcendental is not genuine. Of course, from this it does not follow that the classification of the abstract goods is a matter of caprice. That a certain property is a species or a subgenus of goodness is subject to justification. This justification involves an examination of the particular case, of the similarities and differences between it and the paradigmatic cases, the extent to which the resulting classification is illuminated by, and itself illuminates, the classification of other, nonethical properties, such as those constitutive of "human nature." In this paper I have tried to show how it would be possible for goodness to be a real property, albeit a generic one, the species and subgenera of which are of great variety. To show that *in fact* it is such a property would be the task of a detailed ethical theory, which, of course, cannot be attempted here. But I must now introduce a necessary qualification of the thesis that goodness is a real property, necessary even if that thesis were made evident by a detailed ethical theory, though it is a qualification also of the thesis that, for example, triangularity is a real property.

In defending the extension of the notions of identity, of entity, and of awareness of an entity beyond their paradigms, I have appealed to the fact that extensions of the application of our concepts are common, indeed indispensable, in any serious attempt to understand a given subject matter. The justification of such extensions in the case of a concept other than that of identity consists chiefly in our finding significant similarities between the cases in which they are made and the paradigmatic cases of the application of the concept. But these similarities are themselves nothing but generic identities! (I assume that resemblance theories of universals, which appeal to an irreducible resemblance relation, are unacceptable, for reasons familiar in the literature on the problem of universals.) As long as the attribution of the generic identity is defensible, so is the extension of the concept. But the notion of generic identity itself involves an extension of the application of a concept, though this time of the concept of identity itself. What justifies *this* extension? We may point out the inadequacy of the alternative accounts, those offered by the resemblance and strict nominalist theories. But in order to have a positive account, we must also appeal to the second-order identity ("likeness," "analogousness") of what we wish to describe as generic identity and paradigmatic identity. This appeal itself involves a further extension of the application of the concept of identity. What justification can we have of *this* extension? Clearly, none. We cannot find a genuine justification of the extensions of the concept of identity by engaging in yet further extensions. But neither can we have a genuine justification even of the application of the concept of identity to what I have called the paradigmatic, that is, standard and ordinarily uncontroversial, cases. (That they are paradigmatic does not by itself provide such justification; the paradigms of a concept can be justifiably changed.) Indeed, if we could, the ultimate nonjustifiability of judgments of generic identity might render these judgments suspect.

Wittgenstein wrote:

> 215. But isn't *the same* at least the same?
> We seem to have an infallible paradigm of identity of a thing with itself. I feel like saying: "Here at any rate there can't be a variety of interpretations. If you are seeing a thing you are seeing identity too."
> Then are two things the same when they are what *one* thing is? And how am I to apply what the *one* thing shews me to the case of two things?
> 216. "A thing is identical with itself." — There is no finer example of a useless proposition, which yet is connected with a certain play of the imagination. It is as if in imagination we put a thing into its own shape and saw that it fitted.[29]

How do we apply the concept of identity in the case of "two things," in the genuine cases of its application, those in which the application is informative, for example, to the color of this page and the color of the next page? By detecting between "them" a relation called identity? But, then, is the "nominalist," who denies their identity, just blind? And even if we detected *something*, how do we recognize it, how do we know that it is an *identity*? By finding that it is itself identical, whether specifically or generically, with some other relations of identity? But which are these? Surely such an appeal to a second (and third, fourth, and so on) order relation of identity would be mere fantasy. Surely the truth is that there is no relevant "something" that we can detect in a case of identity, no relation in the world that is called identity, even in the paradigmatic cases. Indeed, how could such a relation hold between "two" things and yet render them "one" thing? (Could the identity be, or be inferred from, the complete coincidence of the properties of the identicals? But does the color of this page have the property of being the color of the next page, which property the color of the next page does have? Only if first we decide that they are identical. In the basic cases identity is the criterion of complete coincidence of properties, not vice versa.) Ultimately, that is, in the basic, noninferential cases, we apply the concept of identity not because we find in them something called identity, but because of the manner in which we conceive of them. The concept of identity may be called transcendental in the sense that though it has application, it stands for nothing in the cases to which it applies. This is why there is ultimately no genuine justification of its applications, whether paradigmatic or nonparadigmatic. A few lines after the passage I quoted earlier, Wittgenstein says, about the justification for supposing that one is following the *same* rule, "If I have exhausted the justifications I have reached bedrock, and my spade is turned. Then I am inclined to say: 'This is simply what I do.' "[30]

It is thus that even a straightforward realism in ethics rests on a sort of *global irrealism* — irrealism with respect to the foundation of any conceptualization of the world, that is, the application of the concept of identity. But this sort of irrealism must not be confused with the sort of global irrealism that claims that there can be no appraisal of the adequacy of a conceptual scheme to reality, that we cannot justifiably criticize a conceptual scheme or the language in which it is embodied by comparing it with the facts. (Indeed, it is better to say that it is such criticizability that defines realism with respect to conditions 3 and 4, stated at the beginning of this paper.) We can do all this on the basis of the extent to which the conceptual scheme or the language reflects the identities and nonidentities ("similarities" and "differences") involved in the facts. But these identities and nonidentities are not themselves elements in the facts. Given our concept of identity, whether a certain conceptual scheme or linguistic practice is adequate to its subject matter has, at least in principle, a determinate answer; the concept of identity provides the basis for such an answer. But whether our concept of identity itself is adequate to the nature of reality (in its paradigmatic as well as nonparadigmatic applications) is a question that can have no answer since the concept of identity stands for nothing in reality. It (and concepts, such as the concept of existence, which I believe may be understood in terms of it),[31] is the basis of all criticism of the adequacy of any conceptual scheme or language as a representation of reality. This is why it is not itself subject to such criticism.

It must not be confused with any word or use of a word or linguistic practice, since it is presupposed even by our recognition of words, without which language would itself be impossible. Any essentially anthropological understanding of it, whether of the Wittgensteinian or Kantian variety, would be woefully superficial. Of course, this does not mean that its application is a matter of caprice, of whimsy, of purely "subjective" decision. We do have the concept of identity and thus are constrained by it in our applications of it. What we cannot do is to go beyond these constraints and discover an independent rationale for them. Yet the absence of such a rationale makes itself felt in the relative freedom we enjoy in extending the applications of the concept and in the possibility of different but equally adequate classifications and cross-classifications (the equilateral triangle is generically identical with the scalene triangle but also with the square, and pleasure is a good but also a psychological state). Should the reader feel that our conclusions may justify the adoption instead of a resemblance theory of universals, an alternative I have ignored here but discussed at great length elsewhere, he or she is invited to show that such a theory could be defended without acknowledging irrealism with respect to the alleged relation of resemblance.

So, there is a kernel of truth in irrealism with respect to ethics. I have, in effect, argued that a defensible realism in ethics must rest on the acceptance of irrealism with respect to identity. The reality of the property goodness can be shown only by acknowledging the unreality of the "relation" of identity. But this is in no way peculiar to ethics. It holds with respect to any conceptual activity, for example, the geometry of the triangle.

Would ordinary ethical thought find what I have said in defense of realism in ethics highly dubious and unclear, as it would find defenses that appeal to shared language games or to causal explanations of ethical beliefs? It is already part of that thought that a variety of things are regarded as good, and my defense of realism, namely, that such things have something in common, goodness, in the way the three species of triangles have something in common, would hardly appear dubious or unclear. Of course, my *account* of this fact in terms of identity is highly technical, and ordinary ethical thought would form no opinions about it. The nature of identity is not one of its objects of concern.

Notes

1. Hilary Putnam, *Reason, Truth and History* (Cambridge, 1981). Robert Nozick bases his "externalist" epistemology on the assumption that "we know mediately, not directly." *Philosophical Explanations* (Cambridge, Mass., 1981), 203).

2. Compare Michael Devitt, *Realism and Truth* (Oxford, 1984).

3. Compare Michael Dummett, "Realism," in *Truth and Other Enigmas* (Cambridge, Mass., 1978).

4. Sabina Lovibond, *Realism and Imagination in Ethics* (Minneapolis, 1983), 113 *passim*. See also S. L. Hurley, "Objectivity and Disagreement," in *Morality and Objectivity*, edited by Ted Honderich (London, 1985).

5. Gilbert Harman, *The Nature of Morality* (New York, 1977), 132.

6. Compare Nicholas L. Sturgeon, "Moral Explanations," in *Morality, Reason, and Truth*, edited by David Copp and David Zimmerman (Totowa, N.J., 1984).

7. The best attempt so far to accomplish this is Laurence BonJour's in *The Structure of Empirical Knowledge* (Cambridge, Mass., 1985). But it is not purely coherentist (see pp. 148–49 *passim*); it also employs the difficult and unexplicated notion of a priori probability to connect justification with truth, a notion not obviously other than a species of the notion of justification (see chap. 8).

8. Compare Panayot Butchvarov, *Being Qua Being: A Theory of Identity, Existence and Predication* (Bloomington, Ind., and London, 1979), appendix A, and "States of Affairs," in *Roderick M. Chisholm*, edited by Radu Bogdan (Dordrecht, 1986). For the most familiar defense of the view that events, including actions, are particulars (however complex in structure), see Donald Davidson, *Essays on Actions and Events* (Oxford, 1980), especially Essay 6. But Davidson's reasons for this view are different from, though not incompatible with, mine.

9. Compare Roderick M. Chisholm's lists of "intrinsically good things" and "intrinsically bad things," in his "Self-Profile," in *Roderick M. Chisholm*, 49.

10. P. T. Geach, "Good and Evil," *Analysis* 17, no. 2 (1956): 33–42.

11. Compare C. D. Broad, "Certain Features in Moore's Ethical Doctrines," in *The Philosophy of G. E. Moore*, vol. 1, edited by P. A. Schilpp (LaSalle, Ill., 1968), 48–49.

12. Paul Ziff, *Semantic Analysis* (Ithaca, N.Y., 1960), 216.

13. With this stipulation we may also avoid some of the difficulties for utilitarianism to which Lars Bergström drew attention in *The Alternatives and Consequences of Actions* (Stockholm, 1966).

14. See Bernard Williams, "Ethical Consistency" and "Consistency and Realism," in *Problems of the Self* (Cambridge, 1973), and *Ethics and the Limits of Philosophy* (Cambridge, Mass., 1985).

15. Henry Sidgwick, *The Methods of Ethics* (Chicago, 1962), xxv, 97–98.

16. Compare Sabina Lovibond, *Realism and Imagination in Ethics*; Renford Bambrough, *Moral Scepticism and Moral Knowledge* (Atlantic Highlands, N.J., 1979); David Wiggins, "Truth, Invention, and the Meaning of Life," *Proceedings of the British Academy* 62 (1976); John McDowell, "Virtue and Reason," *The Monist* 62 (1979), and "Non-Cognitivism and Rule-Following," in *Wittgenstein: To Follow a Rule*, edited by Steven H. Holtzman and Christoper M. Leich (London, 1981.)

17. Philippa Foot, *Virtues and Vices* (Berkeley and Los Angeles, 1981). 15–19.

18. In "That Simple, Indefinable, Nonnatural Property *Good*" (*The Review of Metaphysics*, September 1982), I argue that Moore's otherwise most puzzling view of the property goodness becomes intelligible and defensible if understood in this way.

19. Ralph Barton Perry, *General Theory of Value* (Cambridge, Mass. 1926), 30.

20. W. D. Ross, *The Right and the Good* (Oxford, 1930), 87–88.

21. This is how, I suggest, we should answer S. W. Blackburn's argument against moral realism in "Moral Realism," included in *Morality and Moral Reasoning*, edited by John Casey (London, 1971). See also *Spreading the Word* (Oxford, 1984), 182–89. The argument rests on the assumption that moral properties would have to be supervenient on nonmoral properties, yet that their exemplification is not entailed by the exemplification of the latter. Yet if "supervenience" is understood in the manner I have suggested, the entailment would hold, even though it would not be a formal entailment.

22. Brand Blanshard, *Reason and Goodness* (London, 1961), 269.

23. Brand Blanshard, *The Nature of Thought*, vol. 1 (London, 1939), 652; *Reason and Analysis* (La Salle, Ill., 1962), 402–3, 420–21.

24. *On Being and Essence*, 2d rev. ed., translated by Armand Maurer (Toronto, 1968), 42.

25. *Principles of Human Knowledge*, Introduction, #16.

26. See Panayot Butchvarov, *Being Qua Being*, 195–206, and *Resemblance and Identity: An Examination of the Problem of Universals* (Bloomington, Ind. and London, 1966), chap. 2 and 3.

27. The classic work on the topic is still H. H. Price's *Thinking and Experience* (London, 1953).

28. Compare Mary B. Hesse, *Models and Analogies in Science* (London, 1963); Nelson Goodman, *Ways of Worldmaking* (Indianapolis, 1978), especially chap. 6. Iris Murdoch writes: "The development of consciousness in human beings is inseparably connected with the use of metaphor. Metaphors are not

merely peripheral decorations or even useful models, they are fundamental forms of our awareness of our condition" (*The Sovereignty of Good* [New York, 1971], 77). Edward O. Wilson suggests that both art and science "rely on similar forms of metaphor and analogy, because they share the brain's strict and peculiar limitations on the processing of information" (*Biophilia* [Cambridge, 1984] 63–64).

29. *Philosophical Investigations*, 3d. ed., translated by G. E. M. Anscombe (Oxford, 1958).

30. *Philosophical Investigations*, #217. If we take #215 and #216 as central to Wittgenstein's argument, as I have in effect done, then we can see that the much discussed passages on following a rule and on private languages are essentially applications and explications of the far deeper thesis of those two passages.

31. Compare Panayot Butchvarov, *Being Qua Being*, and "Our Robust Sense of Reality," *Grazer Philosophische Studien* 25/26 (1985–86). The metaphysical thesis of the present article is developed further in the context of a detailed ethical theory in the author's *Skepticism in Ethics* (Bloomington, Ind., and London, forthcoming).

Realistic Interpretations of
Moral Questions

H.E. MASON

M oral questions deserve more attention than they have received. There are peculiarities of their use and treatment which cast a rather different light on many of the standing controversies in moral philosophy. That is particularly true of those controversies which focus on the semantic interpretation of the language used to express moral judgments. Non-cognitivist theories, for example, tend for the most part to have been developed with an eye to the assertion of moral judgments, and to controversies over those assertions. Their application to moral questions commonly results in paradox, and sometimes even in incoherence. But realistic interpretations of moral questions are almost equally problematic. There are some peculiarities of the use and treatment of moral questions which seem to presuppose a form of moral realism, but there are others which make it hard to understand how any form of moral realism could be sound. In this paper I consider the question whether moral questions can be given a realistic interpretation that is in keeping with their place in our discourse and our lives.

I

Realistic interpretations of moral questions and the judgments offered in answer to those questions take different forms and serve a variety of philosophical purposes, but they share the idea that well-formed moral questions are susceptible of true or false answers, the truth or falsity in question susceptible of recognition upon occasion, but not necessarily dependent upon our capacity to recognize or determine it. In moral philosophy as elsewhere, realists tend to focus their attention on the failings of alternative accounts, assuming, perhaps, that in the absence of a persuasive alternative account of moral judgment, the presumption favors realism. Evidence from our moral practices makes that assumption questionable. Focusing my attention on those modest forms of moral realism which hold that moral judgments are suscepti-

ble of truth or falsity and that their truth or falsity can under normal circumstances
be recognized, I will offer some reasons for thinking that those views offer a somewhat distorted picture of common moral practices.

Conscientious moral questions are seldom phrased in terms of truth or falsity.
It is unlikely that a person asking whether the maintenance of a first-strike capacity
is morally justified would phrase the question in terms of truth, asking 'Is it true that
a first-strike capacity is justified?' or 'Is it in fact the case that a first-strike capacity
is justified?' But, although moral questions are seldom explicitly phrased in terms
of truth or falsity, answers to the questions can be marked in that way without apparent distortion, and, as philosophers have often pointed out, must in many clearly appropriate forms of argument be treated as susceptible of truth or falsity. It is also
true that the conscientious consideration of a moral question is treated as a virtue
and often given high praise, and a thoughtless or careless consideration of a moral
question is often condemned. It clearly seems a presumption of both the question itself and of the fact that its careful consideration should be praised as a virtue that
the question has a true or a false answer, and that given sufficient care it is more
likely to receive a truthful answer. Not all of the indications point in that direction,
however. There are features of the treatment of moral questions which are quite out
of accord with that presumption.

Moral questions tend to be phrased in direct and straightforward ways. 'Must
I?' 'Can we?' 'Would there be any justification for it?' 'Does she have a right to know?'
But some responses normally appropriate to direct and straightforward questions
seem inappropriate in response to a moral question. In almost any area of inquiry
the result of a line of investigation can be unexpected, and the answers to questions
asked surprising and even astonishing. But it is difficult to think of circumstances
in which a person seriously considering a moral question could be said to be surprised at its answer. He might be surprised that he should have come to accept a certain answer, but he could hardly be surprised at the answer to the question. It would
be more than strange to hear a person say that she was surprised that the death penalty is sometimes justifiable, or that she was astonished to learn that it is never
justifiable. Such remarks would almost certainly be taken as ironic references to the
moral opinions of others. A person might ask another's opinion on a moral issue and
be astonished to learn her views. I might, for example, learn to my great astonishment that you and your party favor the reinstatement of the death penalty. But that
would be very different from learning to my astonishment that the death penalty is
sometimes justifiable. Even if I had given the matter long and careful thought and
had come to an opinion contrary to my earlier views, my report that I was astonished
to learn that the death penalty is sometimes justifiable would almost certainly be
received with perplexity and treated as betraying a misconception.

There are other responses which would seem equally inappropriate. There are
many circumstances in which a person might be relieved to learn the answer to a
troubling question. Concerned about the cause of his continuing indigestion, one
might be relieved to learn that it was an allergic response to a dispensable food. Dis-

tressed over reports of a potentially disastrous political development, one might be relieved to learn that the evidence had been exaggerated. In appropriate circumstances similar responses could be imagined for almost any question which might be of some concern. But that does not appear to be true of moral questions. Imagine a person deeply troubled over a moral question, uncertain what to think. It would be bizarre to suppose that such a person could learn the answer to the question in a way that would relieve her distress. Imagine, for example, a teacher distressed over the question of what counsel she could responsibly offer students reluctant to serve in an absurd and inhumane war, but uneasy over the heavy penalties of refusal they might face. It would be bizarre to imagine her saying that she had learned to her great relief that a teacher could with good conscience counsel her students to refuse service even where the legal penalties would be severe. Why would such a response seem bizarre? Presumably because the implication of the response that a person could somehow learn that the question had been settled would betray a misunderstanding at odds with the understanding of the question giving rise to her concern and distress over it.

Is it ever reasonable to say of a person that he or she has learned the answer to a moral question? Could a person be said to learn, for example, that the death penalty is sometimes justifiable, or that it never is? One might have been taught at home or in school that it is never justifiable, and if he continued to believe that, I would guess that he might say that he had learned that as a child. But saying it under those circumstances would not imply that the matter had been settled. It would not have the force of saying that it had been generally known and he had now learned of that, or that it had recently been established and he had learned of that, or that it had been discovered and as a result he now knew it to be so. None of these ways of marking the standing of an answer to a question has common application to answers to moral questions. If someone claimed to have discovered that the death penalty is never justifiable, people would almost certainly wonder what he could possibly have in mind. I believe that people would respond in a similar way if someone claimed that it had been established that the death penalty is never justified, or that it was generally known that it is never justified. If these expressions did have application to moral questions, there would surely be cases in which a person considering a moral question in appropriate circumstances might be informed that the answer had been discovered or established, and his concern relieved accordingly. But attempts to construct such a case result in the bizarre sort of incongruity outlined above.

It is interesting that guessing also appears to have no application to moral questions. Almost any question in any area of inquiry is under some circumstances fair game for guessing. I can guess about the details of human affairs, but I can also guess about matters of physical theory or biological fact and even about remote etymological histories. Mathematicians frequently offer guesses and conjectures. But it seems strangely incongruous to speak of guessing whether any wars are morally defensible, guessing whether it is wrong to eat meat, guessing what degree of energy conservation our obligations to future generations require, or guessing what disclosure of correspondence among public officials people have a right to expect. Facing any of these questions, one might be counseled to be thoughtfully tentative, but hardly to guess. One can take a guess at another's views on some moral issue, but not at the issue itself. In many moral situations the necessity of taking some action makes it impossible to avoid taking a position on a moral question, no matter how difficult the question may be. In like circumstances with other sorts of questions it is sometimes said, 'We'll have to guess; we have no other choice'. But that would be strangely out of place in the face of a difficult but forced moral decision. Imagine a young person unable to decide whether he should register for the draft but unable to defer his decision. Even if he professed no notion of what he should do, 'You'll have to guess' or 'Make the best guess you can' would seem a perplexing and inappropriate bit of counsel.

Why should guessing seem a misplaced response to a moral question? There may be a tendency to think that it is merely a matter of its being less than serious, a somewhat irresponsible way of addressing an important matter. But there are deadly serious matters which are quite open to guessing. A patient may hope that his surgeon does not have to proceed by guesswork, but if the surgeon does have to make guesses, that will ordinarily be quite understandable. Where there is no other choice, guessing can be as serious as any other approach. More to the point, there are several ways in which guessing can be out of place regardless of the seriousness of the question. A person cannot make a guess if she already knows what she is supposed to guess, and she cannot make a guess if there is nothing to guess, if, that is to say, there is no fact of the matter in question. I cannot guess my own name unless I have forgotten it or for some reason never learned it, and I cannot guess it if I have no name. Applied to the case of moral questions, one could not make a guess if one knew the answer to the questions, and one could not make a guess if there were no answer at all. But neither explanation seems in accord with the way moral questions are treated. A person seriously considering a moral question can be presumed not to know how to answer it, and would presumably say if asked that she did not know what to say or think about it. If she could not try to guess the answer, that could hardly be because she already knew what she was to guess. The explanation that there is nothing to guess seems equally out of accord with the way moral questions are treated. A person seriously considering a moral question can hardly be said to believe that it has no answer, nor can those who praise her for her careful and conscientious consideration of the question; and a person seriously considering a moral question, like those who praise her for that, is the very person most likely to find bizarre the suggestion that a guess might be in order. If we grant the seriousness and apparent point of moral consideration and deliberation, we thus seem unable to account for the fact that guessing has no apparent place within that undertaking.

I have mentioned a number of ways in which moral questions appear to be set apart. The question whether a person can lie in response to a moral question provides still another marker. Asked a moral question, a person can, of course, misrepresent his views. Asked his views on abortion, a proponent of legalized abortion might say that he was opposed or had not yet made up his mind, and in saying that he would be lying. But it is difficult to think of circumstances in which a person's flat and un-qualified answer to a conscientious moral question would occasion the charge that it was an outright lie. It is difficult, that is to say, to think of circumstances in which the flat answers 'It's justified' or 'It's clearly wrong' would occasion that charge. It is unlikely that a person who said that universal conscription worked fewer injustices than a volunteer army would be accused of lying, even by those who profoundly dis-agreed. While 'That's not so' or 'That's not true' would be possible responses, 'You're lying' seem most unlikely. To the extent that that is true, the expectation with which a person asks a moral question can apparently not be satisfied in a way allowing him to misinform others of the answer to the question. What success there may be ap-pears not to carry with it a commonly recognized authority which might be misused.

Like all observations of what might or might not be said in response to a ques-tion, what would seem strange and what bizarre, these observations depend upon the contexts assumed and the particular questions considered. There may be an incli-nation to think that the observations are plausible only to the extent that the examples considered are deliberative questions, questions like 'What should we do?' or 'What is the right thing to do in these circumstances?' The questions I have mentioned are difficult moral questions, but they are not necessarily deliberative questions, and the observations seem in any case to be equally true of deliberative questions and those somewhat more abstract questions which formulate moral considerations with a fairly direct bearing on deliberation. It is worthy of note, however, that none of the observations would hold true of deliberative questions asked in, not a moral, but a technical context. Suppose I am stripping down an engine and ask a knowledgeable friend, 'What do I do next?' His answer might come as a surprise or a relief; what he tells me to do I might have learned or discovered, or I might have guessed. What restrictions on the range of practical authority these observations suggest are thus almost certainly a matter of the subject matter, and not the degree of abstraction of the questions considered.

If these observations are an accurate reflection of the way in which moral ques-tions are understood and treated within the practices in which they have their place, they cast considerable doubt on a realistic interpretation of those questions. Al-though moral questions are asked in direct and straightforward ways, and their care-ful consideration is praised in a way that suggests that truth is an end in view, they are not treated as though truth could be achieved in a way justifying well-qualified assertion, and in the face of uncertainty, even guessing seems out of place. We thus seem faced with the apparent anomaly that questions to whose answers questions of truth have apparent application are not treated in the way that would seem to require: there appear to be no commonly acknowledged conditions of well-qualified asser-tion, and the very notion of an independent truth that would give guessing an occa-sional appropriateness seems not to be recognized.

II

How are these perplexing features of the treatment of moral questions to be explained? Any explanation must begin with some consideration of the grounds on which moral questions tend to be answered. The most striking fact is that general principles play a much less prominent role in deliberation and reflection over moral questions than the discussions of philosophers would suggest. Conscientious moral questions tend to be local and specific, focused on particular judgments and practices. We question the justice of a particular form of taxation or a particular institutional practice, and we question particular rights that are claimed or particular obligations proposed. Questions that are more global tend to arise out of and be supported by reference to particular doubts. Where particular doubts are raised they tend to be argued by reference to other judgments not questioned. Thus, for example, by contrast with an acknowledged form of taxation or an accepted way of dividing a burden, the justice of a proposed form of taxation is said to be doubtful. Where it is acknowledged that a person has a right to the disclosure of one sort of information, it seems doubtful that he should be denied access to information of a somewhat similar kind. Moral questions tend to be answered systematically, that is to say, their answers argued on a systematic basis, but the elements in the system are much more likely to be particular judgments and practices than general moral principles.

In considering the way in which moral questions arise and the grounds on which they are answered, it is instructive to recall some of Wittgenstein's suggestive observations in *On Certainty* about the conditions under which doubts arise. While the view suggested does not provide any account of the differences between moral questions and other sorts of questions, it does remind us of the extent to which moral questions may be dependent upon other moral beliefs not in fact questioned. "(The) questions that we raise and our *doubts* depend on the fact that some propositions are exempt from doubt, are as it were like hinges on which those turn."[1] In the examples offered above, those judgments which are cited in justifying a question or supporting a particular answer are like hinges on which the questions turn. Wittgenstein's remarks about those propositions he thinks serve in that way are both suggestive and puzzling. The propositions on which our doubts turn are said to be propositions we accept or acknowledge. They are not doubted, and could not all be doubted. We accept them in acting as we do, and they are said to provide the basis for our actions and our lives. "My *life* consists in my being content to accept many things."[2] The nest of propositions we accept in raising any doubt forms, moreover, a system or a structure. We have been taught the elements of this structure and share it with a community bound together by education and practice. "The child learns to believe a host of things. I.e., it learns to act according to these beliefs. Bit by bit there forms a system of what is believed, and in that system some things stand fast and some are more or less liable to shift. What stands fast does so, not because it is intrinsically obvious or convincing; it is rather held fast by what lies around it."[3] Wittgenstein's examples make clear that what stands fast may be related to a particular doubt in a variety of ways, but he disclaims the capacity to describe those relationships. Speaking of a particular unlikely doubt he says, "But this would not fit into the rest of my convictions at all. Not that I could describe the system of these convictions. Yet my convictions do form a system, a structure."[4]

Wittgenstein was apparently led to this way of looking at the conditions of reasonable doubt by the difficulty of specifying conditions under which one could reasonably doubt propositions like 'The earth has existed for a good many years' and 'This is a human hand' offered in its celebrated context. "I believe that I have forebears and that every human being has them. I believe that there are various cities, and, quite generally, in the main facts of geography and history. I believe that the earth is a body on whose surface we move and that it no more suddenly disappears . . . than any other solid body. If I wanted to doubt the existence of the earth long before my birth I should have to doubt all sorts of things that stand fast for me."[5] With such examples it appears that it is not the special standing of any particular proposition that makes it stand fast for a particular doubt, but its relationship in turn to other propositions not in fact doubted. I believe that it is the sheer number of such propositions and the complexity of their interrelationships that give Wittgenstein's view its plausibility. Considered in abstraction, none of the propositions on which Wittgenstein thinks our doubts and questions turn can be reasonably regarded as exempt from doubt. Considered in a context in which particular doubts are actually raised, most of those pivotal propositions will stand related to other propositions not actually doubted in ways that will make the pivotal propositions difficult if not impossible to doubt.

Whatever its merits as a general doctrine, this view of the conditions of doubt and uncertainty does provide a fairly accurate account of the conditions under which moral questions and doubts arise. General moral principles may play a predominant role in the philosophical discussion of moral questions, but relatively specific moral judgments play a much more important role in the daily consideration of moral questions; and those judgments tend to be lodged in a complex web of interrelated considerations. A person who doubts some particular right or responsibility will commonly be expected to make her doubt plausible by contrasting the case in question with cases in which an apparently similar right or responsibility is commonly acknowledged, and by taking into account all the variety of considerations that bear on the right or responsibility in question, each of the considerations likely to be a matter of judgment itself. Think, for example, of the variety of circumstances in which a person is said to have a right to be informed or to be consulted or even to have some say in what is done. Discussion in a particular case will focus on similarities and differences among cases, and it will proceed by consideration of a myriad of factors: the importance of the undertaking and any difficulties of consultation regarding it, the mutual relations and positions of the parties, any general expectations of consultation as well as particular understandings that there be consultation, the mutual respect of the parties, and even the feelings of those who might not be consulted. These considerations will enter into the discussion in different ways and they will be weighted differently, but they all contribute to the underlying complexity of the issue.

Even the simplest of moral questions will share this complexity to some degree. Suppose you wonder whether you can ask a friend or neighbor to care for your dog while you are away on vacation. You have no right to expect her to do it, you may be told. You know that, but you wonder whether it would be an imposition to ask her to do it as a favor. Told that it would, you wonder why it would be an imposition to ask her to take the dog, but not an imposition to ask her to feed the cat or water the plants. That is a matter of relative inconvenience and likely bother, you may be told. Granting that, you may wonder whether the friend might not welcome the opportunity to be of some help and even feel somewhat offended if she knew that in the belief that it would be an imposition, you had refrained from asking her to care for the dog. If you were in serious difficulty she would surely be offended if you did not turn to her for help. True enough, it may be said, but this is only a matter of your own convenience and surely not a matter of serious difficulty. The ensuing judgment that you could not ask her to take the dog is one that might be questioned, but not without some recognition of the force of all these diverse considerations. Even in a case so little fraught with telling consequences, the relevant considerations are both diverse and diversely related to the question at stake.

Moral instruction tends to bear out the view that relatively specific judgments determined by a variety of interrelated considerations play a critical role in the daily consideration of moral questions. We may be taught some absolute prescriptions and some general percepts, but we soon learn that it is relatively specific judgments that we are supposed to take seriously: 'A person in your position has no right to speak to her like that', 'You have to give them an opportunity to object: that's the least people in those circumstances can expect', 'It would be an imposition to ask anyone else to do that for you', 'You're not being fair to them in making that judgment without hearing their side of the story'. How many such judgments have we heard, in a tone of voice that exhibits an assumed and sometimes acknowledged authority? Wittgenstein's observation about empirical judgments is at least equally true of moral judgments: "We do not learn the practice of making empirical judgments by learning rules: we are taught *judgements* and their connection with other judgements. A *totality* of judgements is made plausible to us."[6] It is of course true that not all judgments offered in the course of moral instruction are accepted, and not all that are initially accepted continue to be. But it would be a mistake to focus on the instances of rejection. It is surely true that we come to accept a body of interconnected judgments, and that in moral instruction, as in moral argument, cases loom large, with attention focused on similarities and differences supposed to make a difference.

I have been arguing that relatively specific judgments play a critical role in deliberations over moral questions, and that it is a mistake to think that conscientious deliberations must be regarded as a matter of applying general moral principles or regulative concepts of one sort or another. That is not to say that it is never true that a person facing a difficult moral decision will simply appeal to a general principle and apply it to the case at hand. My contention is rather that in a great many cases in which a person is thought to address a moral question conscientiously, the question does not lend itself to the direct application of general principles, and that in the place of that there will be an appeal to judgments of relatively specific cases, and to a variety of moral considerations bearing in one way or another on cases of the sort in question. Moral questions must be understood, that is to say, as framed by reference to accepted judgments fixed in a web of moral considerations. Moral questions asked out of the blue are often incoherent. One could only wonder what a doctor had in mind, for example, if he dubiously questioned the right of a patient to crucial information but was unwilling to acknowledge or deny the rights of anyone to information of any sort. That apparent incoherence is to be explained by noting the formative role of relatively specific judgments accepted by those participating in the practices in question.

III

Suppose that moral questions are regarded in this way, with antecedently accepted judgments giving sense to the terms of the questions and providing what basis we have for answering the questions. Whether an action at hand would be inconsiderate, an imposition, or even unkind we will be said to learn in learning how to go on from case to case, and we will be said to learn in a similar way what ancillary questions to ask, whether the dog is unfriendly, for example, or the neighbor unlikely to be candid in responding to a plea for help. Anyone who supposes that moral questions are formed in this way is bound to face the question how moral questions differ from those empirical judgments Wittgenstein had his eye on. With some adjustment for the practical role of moral questions, it might in fact be thought that the application of Wittgenstein's suggestions to moral questions provides some support for a realistic interpretation of those questions. In "Non-cognitivism and Rule-following,"[7] John McDowell develops that line of thought. Exploiting some of Wittgenstein's conjectures about the supposed role of explicitly formulated rules, McDowell offers a realistic way of conceiving of value predications and, accordingly, of the answers to moral questions. The chinks in his line of thought provide a clear indication how Wittgenstein's remarks must be taken if they are to be cited in partial explanation of the anomalies with which I began.

  McDowell argues that value judgments are on occasion true, and that we are capable of perceiving that they are. A kind person, for example, is capable of perceiving what he or she should do in a particular situation, what would be, that is to say, the kind thing to do in that situation. Against typical non-cognitivist views that in such a case a person may respond positively to those independently recognizable features of the situation toward which he has pro-attitudes, but could not coherently be said to recognize values themselves in the situation, McDowell argues that there is no good reason to believe that a person applying a value concept must be responding to features of the world specifiable independently of the value concept itself.

Even if value classifications are supervenient on non-evaluative classifications, he argues, it does not follow that the set of items to which supervening terms are correctly applied must constitute a kind recognizable as such at the level supervened upon. There may be no way, expressible at the level supervened upon, of grouping just those items together, and no way of mastering at that level a term supposed to group together exactly the items to which competent users would apply the supervening term. "Understanding why just those things belong together may essentially require understanding the supervening term."[8] Knowing why a particular action in a particular circumstance was kind or courageous would thus require an understanding of the use of those expressions within the moral practices of the community in question, and that knowledge could not be otherwise expressed. Because the knowledge could not be otherwise expressed, recognizing an action as kind or courageous would be simply recognizing it as that, and could not be a matter of the reasonable application of independently specifiable criteria of kindness or courage. A person participating in the moral practices of the community would be able to go on from one case to another, and the way he went on would make perfectly good sense within the context of those practices. But he would be unable to explain in a way that an observer might have expected why he went on as he did.

Why should we be unready to accept our moral practices in these terms, trusting our moral sensitivities and confident in our capacity to go on in the same way, even to ostensibly new and different cases? Why should we expect an account specifying in independent terms the grounds of our judgments and explaining the responses they exhibit? McDowell speculates that the inclination to think that there must be some independently specifiable foundation of our moral practices arises out of a kind of vertigo, "induced by the thought that there is nothing that keeps our practices in line except the reactions and responses we learn in learning them."[9] If our practices are not to be groundless, the tracks we follow must be objectively there to be followed, there in a way transcending the reactions and responses of participants in the practices. Dread of proceeding in a groundless way thus leads to the thought that there must be some more secure foundation assuring us that our way of going on from case to case is justified. In McDowell's view this thought is misconceived. It requires a foundation satisfactory to a point of view external to our practices and transcending our normal ways of learning how things are. Rejecting those expectations leaves a place, he argues, for a form of realism which can allow that the apparent predications expressed with evaluative language are genuine instances of the application of a concept: in applying an evaluative concept correctly, we single out a kind which is there to be singled out. It is, in a way, a philosophically austere form of realism, permitting itself no independent explanations of the judgments or the practices in question. Taking our practices at face value, it allows judgments of value to be what they sometimes appear to be, judgments susceptible of truth or falsity, their truth or falsity perceptible upon occasion.

It is a striking feature of McDowell's defense of a realistic view of values that he takes as the primary motivation to its rejection the expectation of foundations inappropriate to value judgments, but equally inappropriate to a wide range of empiri-cal judgments. His appropriation of Wittgenstein's idea that we are able to go on from case to case without benefit of explicitly formulated rules does not envisage the possibility that there might be sufficiently great differences between our mastery of empirical concepts and our mastery of value concepts to cast doubt on a realistic treatment of the latter. The observations with which I began this paper suggest that doubts about a realistic treatment of moral questions can arise from within moral practices themselves, and are not necessarily caused by the adoption of a point of view external to those practices. I believe that there are peculiarities of the relation-ship between those judgments in place in a practice and the questions we ask as we go on which cast doubt on McDowell's idea that considered from within moral prac-tices, moral questions must be interpreted realistically.

Consider McDowell's idea that within a reasonably cohesive moral community there will be current specific conceptions of moral virtue classifying actions and dis-positions in ways those sharing the community's special concerns will be able to mas-ter. Those specific conceptions are supposed to come into play in the deliberations of members of the community deciding what to do in appropriate particular situa-tions. A person trying to decide what to do is to be regarded as asking of particular alternatives, 'Is this action of a sort to be done?' 'Is it of a sort to be avoided?' Granted the moral vocabulary of the community and the allied sensitivities, a participant will commonly be able to place the alternatives in question in a way facilitating a truthful answer to the deliberative question. Because a deliberative question is a matter of placing the alternatives in morally relevant classifications of actions and disposi-tions, the capacity of a person with a mastery of the relevant specific conceptions of virtue to answer such a question truly will in normal circumstances be un-problematic. It is a critical feature of this picture of moral deliberation that the moral force of a judgment applying a specific conception of moral virtue is entailed by the judgment's classification of an alternative under the specific conception. There can be no independent question of the bearing or the moral force of the peculiarity of the alternative singled out with the judgment.

If we think of specific examples of such virtues, even within relatively cohe-sive moral communities, it is difficult to do justice to the peculiar use of particular conceptions of virtue without leaving a place for independent questions of their moral force. Consider, for example, the various attitudes taken toward shoddy work within an academic community. It is easy to imagine both fiercely honest responses and extremely kind responses, and fairly easy to imagine how people taking each of those attitudes would explain their taking the attitudes they did. It would be reasonable to expect, moreover, that a person trying to decide for herself how to re-spond to the work, what to say, how much and how little to say, would give some thought to each of those quite different attitudes toward the work. In considering the question how she should respond, she might regard each possible response as an ex-pression of a kind of virtue, but where she had some doubt she would have to be regarded as trying to decide which virtue to allow to rule her own response. That question is not well conceived as simply a matter of placing possible responses in relation to others granted some standing in the community. It may be true that it is only as a member of a relatively cohesive moral community that a person is able to recognize fiercely honest or extremely kind responses as instances of kinds, and true, moreover, that people who share the peculiar concerns of the community recognize honesty and kindness as things to be admired or emulated. But the question which virtue to allow to rule arises within the context of the recognition, and is itself not merely a question of the kind of action in question. In such a case a person is commonly held responsible for the judgment he comes to and the way he responds. His response is taken as an expression of character, and judged accordingly. In asking which form of response to take, which virtue to allow to rule, he is asking, in a way, which he is willing to stand by. That question and the deliberations it occasions can hardly be regarded as no more than a matter of placing the possible responses among a class of responses forming a morally significant kind recognized within the moral practices of his community.

It may be helpful to put this point in the terms of another idiom. It is commonly said that moral considerations provide a prima facie reason for performing or refraining from a particular action. In a useful discussion Davidson[10] has suggested that 'prima facie' should be regarded as an operator on pairs of sentences relating evaluative judgments and grounds. The evaluative judgments are conditional on the grounds, and in a case in which there is at least a pair of prima facie reasons, the conditionalization of the evaluative judgments stands in the way of the supposition that there might be a line of practical reasoning from the grounds to a deliberative conclusion. In the cases I have been discussing, the grounds would be judgments of particular virtue made in accord with the usage of a particular moral community, the evaluative judgment a judgment of what should be done in light of the judgment of particular virtue.[11] The judgment that kindness would require one action, honest criticism another, can be regarded as prima facie judgments offering deliberative conclusions as conditional upon judgments of particular virtue. Those prima facie judgments are taken into account by a person deciding what he should do, and that judgment can be said to be made in light of the prima facie judgments. But the judgment of what should be done is independent of those prima facie judgments, and is not determined by them. Any particular prima facie judgment is silent about its relative weight in a deliberation in which it competes with other prima facie judgments. In a typical case a person will cite the judgment of particular virtue in favor of a deliberative judgment, thus invoking the prima facie judgment, but the deliberative judgment is, in a way, a further act. That act is, I have argued, an expression of character for which a person is responsible, and on the basis of which his character is assessed.

It is difficult to know how this feature common to a great many moral questions could be given a realistic interpretation. Couched in the rhetoric of philosophical realism, a question interpreted realistically must, in one way or another, be a matter of the accurate representation of a feature of the world. Thus, summing up his view,

McDowell speaks of moral values as "there in the world," and as making demands "on our reason."[12] But how could the question whether fierce honesty would be an admirable response to shoddy work be a matter of the recognition of values, somehow there in the world to be recognized, and why should the conscientious consideration of that question be regarded as a response of reason? There are, of course, extremely kind and fiercely honest people, and a person with a reasonably firm grasp of those predicates can commonly recognize those characteristics in conduct exhibiting them and project their appearance in conduct under consideration. But that recognition is not tantamount to the judgment that those forms of conduct are to be admired and emulated, or that particular actions exhibiting them are to be chosen. A person with a very clear view of just what forms of conduct were commonly described as kind or honest might still have the question whether those forms of conduct, or particular instances of them, deserved the place commonly given them within the moral practices of his community. He might, that is to say, know how to go on in his use of those concepts and still be uncertain of the virtue of the forms of conduct in question. In a particular case he might, as I have suggested, be uncertain which form of conduct to follow, a question which could give rise to the more general question of the relative virtue of the forms of conduct correctly described as kind or honest. Neither question is well conceived as a matter of the accurate representation of the forms of conduct in question.

The distinction between the question whether a particular action would be kind or generous and the question whether it would for that reason be virtuous is obscured by the fact that in many communities it is sufficient to object to an action in prospect by saying, 'That would be mean', or 'It would be unkind'. It is understood that an action that is mean or unkind or dishonest is objectionable, and, analogously, that the fact that an action would be kind or generous or honest is a consideration in favor of performing it. But the fact that even within those communities the relative virtue of actions so described can come into question in conscientious deliberations is sufficient to show that the common currency of those attributions does not necessarily give them moral standing.

Whether those attributions are correctly said to be an exercise of reason is also problematic. Suppose that an academic responding to a piece of shoddy work is thought to be excessively kind, indulgently excusing its carelessness. The distinction between the question whether her response would be less than honest and the question whether she should let that consideration rule shows that her failure is not well conceived as a failure to recognize features of the world which make demands on her reason. She recognizes the relevant features, but does not let them rule either her judgment or her action. Where she is held responsible for her response and faulted, she is not likely to be faulted for a failure of reason, but for a failure of character. She will be said to be less than honest, indulgent of careless work, or not a serious critic. In many instances there will, of course, be telling objections to such judgments, providing justification for the questionable response. But the issue at stake will be the academic's character, the particular virtue of her response, and not merely the accuracy of her representation of the morally significant features of the alternatives confronting her. By the same token, where a person has conscientious doubts and is uncertain how to respond despite a grasp of the relevant detail, her uncertainty can be and often is taken as a sign, not of misconception but of moral seriousness.

I believe that these considerations show that Wittgenstein's ideas about our way of going on with the application of concepts cannot be used in the way McDowell suggests to support a form of moral realism. In his remarks in the *Investigations* about following a rule, Wittgenstein attended for the most part to utterly unproblematic cases, cases in which there would have been no question how to go on or what to say. That there would have been no question how to go on is at the very heart of the perplexity. It is just the unproblematic character of our way of going on, its obvious correctness, that comes to seem impossible to conceive. In normal circumstances it is utterly unproblematic how an arrow pointing down the path should be taken, but approached with certain natural philosophical expectations, we may find that impossible to understand. By assembling an array of telling cases, Wittgenstein sought to exhibit the misconceptions underlying those expectations. McDowell takes the philosophical inclination to mark off value judgments as semantically and epistemologically irregular to exhibit the same misconceived expectation of inappropriate grounds. But the fact that in circumstances that are not abnormal a conscientious person with a command of moral language can be at a loss to know what to think or say about a moral question where others have no doubts shows that there are differences not invented out of misconception. If, as I have argued, a person's conscientious question how to respond to a piece of shoddy work can stand unanswered despite his knowledge of the case and command of the relevant vocabulary, that question and others like it resist realistic interpretation.

IV

The picture of moral deliberation and moral judgment as a matter of going on from accepted judgments in accord with the practices current within a community is misleading in its suggestion that a conscientious response to a moral question necessarily requires conformity to established expectations and patterns of response. If the moral vocabulary with which a conscientious person frames the considerations bearing on a moral question is rich and complex, and if general principles play a less prominent role than commonly supposed, the practices within which that vocabulary has come to be established and judgments exhibiting its use are bound to figure in conscientious deliberations. But focussing on that feature of conscientious deliberation gives a somewhat skewed picture. As a corrective it is important to note the extent to which deliberation requires decision. A person must decide which considerations to allow to determine his response, which analogous cases to take seriously, which to reject. I have stressed the extent to which a deliberative decision must be regarded as a decision to allow a consideration to rule, but that is also true in any case in which judgment is said to play a role. Saying of moral judgments that they are expressions of character is a way of marking that fact. But that, too, can be misleading if it is taken to mean only that a judgment may exhibit a person's character, his concerns and his sensitivities. If the place of appeals to accepted judgments and established expectations and patterns of response is to be well understood, the responsibility a conscientious person accepts for the judgments he makes must also be acknowledged.

How does the responsibility a conscientious person accepts for his judgments affect the role of antecedently accepted judgments in deliberation over a moral question? Where a person is responsible for the positions he takes and the things he does, he will in questionable or controversial cases consider what explanation he could offer to those people affected, and, in a more general way, to those whose admiration and respect he cherishes. But explanations which justify must appeal to something independent. They must appeal to considerations, that is to say, which it is reasonable to expect those people affected to accept. In the absence of commonly accepted and explicitly formulated principles, antecedently accepted judgments of relevantly similar cases serve as the touchstones of acceptable justification. Where people affected are likely to find a position or a policy objectionable, the responsibility a conscientious person accepts in saying of a position or a policy that it is fair or just or reasonable requires him to give consideration to those objections and the judgments from which they proceed. Responsibility thus imposes some constraints on the appeal to accepted judgments and practices in place, and stands in the way of the apparently conservative bias of that procedure. Consider again the person inclined out of kindness to blunt the force of possibly humiliating criticism of another's shoddy work. That inclination will doubtless find some support in judgments antecedently accepted within his community. But so will the contrary inclination to judge the work on its merits. Construed in this way the issue seems no more than a matter of choosing among virtues, each with some standing in the moral practices of the community. Recognizing the responsibility a reluctant critic would bear turns the question in another direction. Whose work depends on a continuing practice of full and honest criticism, and whose welfare otherwise considered? Are the standards in question no more than mannered styles whose celebration serves the pride of some practitioners, or are they standards facilitating work of some importance? Similar questions could be raised about the proffered kindness. Is the concern in question no more than a somewhat precious concern for a fellow academic? How serious would his humiliation seem to people forced by the institutions and practices of the society to suffer cruel and continuing humiliation? These questions are not supposed to be decisive, but they do suggest the constraints a responsible concern to hear the objections of people affected can impose on deliberations over a moral question.

There are moral questions which provide little or no occasion for serious moral consideration. 'Was it unfair to exclude those candidates who sent their applications by airmail?' 'Was it an imposition on her part to ask an advisee to clean out her office for her?' 'Did she have a right to read the correspondence, having been retained to represent the family in court?' Turning quite directly as they do on practices and accepted understandings well in place, such questions would in most circumstances offer no difficulty to anyone who understood them and accepted the terms in which they were framed. If a person did proceed to press such a question, that would almost certainly be greeted with perplexity. There are other questions, less dependent on practices and common understandings, which would normally provide as little occasion for serious consideration. I have in mind questions of the appropriate moral response to instances of striking generosity or courage, or, on the other hand, of inhumane and even brutal treatment. It seems likely that a person who affected not to know how to make up his mind about such cases would also be greeted with perplexity, the incongruity of his apparently serious question at odds with the moral sensitivity it affected. There are undoubtedly a great many other cases of a less extreme and even ordinary sort which would commonly raise as little question. They serve, moreover, to form the basis of consideration for more problematic cases.

The situation is very different in those cases in which moral questions are underdetermined by the relevant moral considerations.[13] In those cases the answer to the question asked may be, as we say, a matter of judgment, or it may be that there is no answer at all. 'Is a fetus a person with a person's right to live?' 'Is it inhumane to keep a dog in a high-rise?' 'Do animals have rights?' 'Can pensioners be justly taxed to support public education for the young?' 'Does a doctor have a right to withhold information from a patient in the interests of his health?' 'Is it fair to other taxpayers to grant agricultural subsidies to farmers for holding land out of production?' It may be that when these questions are adequately formulated and the relevant analogies considered, it will have to be said that the questions have no answer, or at least no answer in the terms in which they are posed. The applicability of the operative concepts or their moral force is problematic, the ruling analogies are too slight, or the case in all its complexity is too far from any ruling anaology to allow a settled judgment. The questions have a simple and direct ring, but we may not have the conceptual resources to handle them. In a way, then, they are like the philosophical questions about which Wittgenstein said, "Say what you please," but with a difference: the practical importance of the question makes us press for an answer even where none is forthcoming. In such a case the judgment a person comes to is tantamount to a decision to let certain considerations rule. He can be held responsible for his judgment, and, if he acts on it, the particular virtue of his action may come to be praised. But it cannot be said that the relevant considerations are determining.

There is another sort of case which is more difficult, but more to the point of the issues I have been discussing. If moral questions are ruled in a way that brings into play diverse and sometimes incommensurable considerations serving a variety of quite independent interests and concerns, it is reasonable to expect that there will be questions which are morally overdetermined. The considerations in question provide what would normally be decisive support to incompatible judgments. In such a case the question cannot be answered in a way that serves equally well all of the interests and concerns represented, and because the question does not serve a merely theoretical purpose, the agent is in no position to restructure the issue or dismiss recalcitrant considerations. Some cases of conflicting obligations are like that. The obligations may have been incurred in such a way that they are quite independent of one another and give an agent no right to dismiss them. A person may find her way through such a conflict, but not in a way that allows her to suppose that the question has been settled. There are a great many moral questions that are similarly overdetermined, but sometimes in a less well-defined way. Consider again the person who asks whether there might be extreme cases in which capital punishment is justified. One need not flag in thinking capital punishment a barbarous institution to acknowledge that the question whether it might be justified for a heinous crime arises in light of a requirement deeply embedded in the practice of criminal punishment: the requirement that a particular punishment be appropriate to the crime. As a requirement of justice it is, moreover, quite independent of the requirement of justice invoked when the discriminatory practices of existing courts and the patterns of the punishments they impose are cited against any use of capital punishment. Regarded in the simplest terms, the question is thus framed by a number of independent moral notions, each shaped by its particular history and each used to formulate considerations that could be decisive in other contexts. It might be sufficient, for example, to argue against a relatively light penalty imposed upon a drug firm distributing adulterated products that what the firm had done was terrible, or against some cruel and harsh restriction tending to separate refugee families that it was barbarous. But if someone asked whether there are crimes so terrible that only punishments that would otherwise be termed barbarous would be appropriate, the very language would be misleading, suggesting that the notions in question could allow the question to become a matter of careful judgment. Other apparently relevant considerations are subject to comparable qualifications. Noting how the question of capital punishment is framed, it is thus not at all surprising that it should seem bizarre to suppose that a person concerned over the question might learn to his astonishment that capital punishment was sometimes justifiable, or that it never was. So long as the use of capital punishment is regarded as a genuine possiblity, it may be the responsibility of serious and conscientious people to come to some conviction on the question of its justification. But anyone with a reasonably firm grasp of the question would surely recognize that it could not turn out that the question had been settled in a way allowing well-informed people to inform others of that fact, and if anyone did propose to take a guess one could only wonder what there was to guess.

There are a great many moral questions which are overdetermined in a similar way, requiring the weighing of apparently incommensurable considerations, each of which might have been decisive in other contexts. The considerations may be formulated in terms indicating their weight in normal deliberations, but the patterns of accepted judgments which will have established the sense of the expressions in question, and the relative weight of considerations couched in those terms, will not have precluded the possibility of deep and irresolvable questions over the priority of particular considerations in particular circumstances. The framing of particular considerations appears not to be subject to a regulative principle requiring or even allowing the rejection or assimilation of recalcitrant considerations. Any such principle would almost certainly run afoul of the independence of distinct considerations and the plurality of interests and concerns represented and acknowledged in any difficult moral deliberation. In this respect there is a marked difference between moral questions and those historical and geographical questions Wittgenstein was considering in *On Certainty*. In a geographical survey or a historical investigation, the overriding interest in a consistent account requires that an apparently recalcitrant consideration be rejected, or in one way or another, assimilated. In moral deliberation the responsibility a person bears to those affected by the actions in question may require instead that recalcitrant considerations be allowed to stand, their recognition a kind of acknowledgment of the legitimate interests and concerns of those people.

It is difficult to know on what grounds one could impose a realistic interpretation on either those moral questions underdetermined by framing judgments or overdetermined in the way I have described. In either case the peculiarities of the considerations framing the questions asked make it unreasonable to suppose that if they are well formed, the questions must be susceptible of true answers, their truth not dependent upon our particular capacities of reasoned judgment. The fact that there are some moral questions about which reasonable and conscientious people can have little or no doubt may seem to stand against this conclusion. But the treatment of failures of judgment and conviction within a moral context shows that inclination to be misconceived. Those failures are not taken as failures of insight or ingenuity. They are taken as failures of character and judged accordingly. Moral insensitivity is not treated as an accidental failing. It is treated instead as a failing for which a person can be held responsible. I have tried to offer a way of understanding that feature of moral practices. Noting the fact that in the face of a difficult moral question there is a distinction between recognizing a consideration and granting it moral force, I have argued that in weighing the considerations bearing on a moral question a conscientious person is, in effect, deciding which considerations to allow to rule. Those decisions are not incorrigible, but the corrigibility to which they are subject is internal to moral practices. They are judged, that is to say, as moral failures and not as failures of rationality or cognition. To mark that difference I have described moral judgments as expressions of character.

At the outset of this paper I characterized moral realism as the view that moral questions are susceptible of true or false answers, the truth or falsity in question susceptible of recognition upon occasion, but not necessarily dependent upon our capacity to recognize it. It is hard to know what role this view could play in the actual practice of moral reflection and moral deliberation, and there are several respects in which it is bound to distort those practices. Within the practice of moral deliberation there is no independent mark of successful recognition, and, correlatively, no uniform explanation of failure. The phenomenological observations with which I began suggest that there is no place for either within moral criticism and moral deliberation as they are practiced, and the features of moral argument I have noted, its particularity, its complexity, and its systematic character, make the very idea of an independent mark of successful recognition misplaced. But if that is true, a realistic interpretation could apparently be borne out only in the serious and conscientious way in which moral questions are deliberated, the effort and its praise showing a belief in an end to be achieved. The fact that failures are marked in moral terms, and judged as failures of character, counts against that view as well. What is said to be reasonable in moral deliberation is not a matter of the likely outcome, but of the willingness to take into account and give serious consideration to the full range of considerations, from whatever points of view might be relevant.

This last point should, perhaps, be emphasized. If a realistic interpretation of moral questions is rejected, it may seem puzzling that conscientious uncertainty and the careful consideration of moral questions should sometimes be praised. If, in the very circumstances in which they are likely to be most prominent, there may be no answer forthcoming, it may seem strange that the earnest worrying of moral questions should be regarded as a virtue. There is at least one feature of conscientious consideration that is worthy of praise even where what might have seemed the ostensible purpose of consideration may be frustrated. That is the recognition of the weight of all the variety of considerations bearing on the case in question. If it is true that our moral sensitivities are mostly formed by a congeries of relatively specific judgments concerning cases of many sorts with varying degrees of similarity, it should be no surprise if in the face of moral questions we are drawn in different directions and can sometimes find no answer. It would be surprising if that were not true. In those circumstances the conscientious consideration of a moral question may be praised, not for the concern for truth it exhibits, but rather for the apparent concern to do justice to all the various claims at stake, and thereby to the persons whose lives and interests may be at stake. A conscientious person may be praised, that is to say, for his recognition of responsibility to those people affected by the actions or practices under consideration. The hesitation and uncertainty which conscientiousness sometimes requires may not be the most desirable outcomes of a line of moral thought, but there are times when they are the most responsible.[14]

Notes

1. L. Wittgenstein, *On Certainty*, edited by G. E. M. Anscombe and G. H. von Wright, translated by D. Paul and G. E. M. Anscombe (Blackwell, Oxford, 1969), 44.

2. Ibid.

3. Ibid., 21.

4. Ibid., 16.

5. Ibid., 21.

6. Ibid., 21.

7. J. McDowell, "Non-cognitivism and Rule-following," in *Wittgenstein: To Follow a Rule*, edited by S. H. Holtzman and C. M. Leich (London, 1981), 141–62.

8. Ibid., 145.

9. Ibid., 149.

10. D. Davidson, "How is Weakness of the Will Possible?" in Davidson, *Intention and Action* (Oxford, 1980), 36–41.

11. Following McDowell we may think of the judgment of particular virtue as a ground for the judgment of what should be done, taking it that within a moral community people would be capable of making judgments of particular virtue without use of explicitly formulable criteria. Such a judgment, made by members of the community provides in turn prima facie reason for a judgment of what should be done.

12. J. McDowell, "Non-cognitivism," 156.

13. Compare D. Wiggins, *Truth, Invention, and the Meaning of Life* (Oxford, 1976), 366–75. Wiggins speaks of moral questions as underdetermined by relevant considerations. He does not draw the distinction I draw between those which are underdetermined and those which are overdetermined. I believe the need for the distinction is made clear in the text.

14. Earlier versions of this paper were read to the Department of Philosophy of the University of Hong Kong and to the Department of Moral Sciences at St. Andrews University. Some of the ideas in the paper were originally formulated in "On Moral Certainty," read at the Fifth International Wittgenstein Symposium in Kirchberg am Wechesel, Lower Austria, in August 1980, and subsequently published in the proceedings for that symposium, *Ethik-Grundlagen, Probleme und Anwendungen*, edited by E. Morscher and R. Stranzinger (Wien, 1981). I am grateful to Michael Root, John Wallace, and Joseph Owens for their helpful comments on earlier versions of this paper.

Moral Theory and Explanatory Impotence

GEOFFREY SAYRE-McCORD

1. INTRODUCTION

Among the most enduring and compelling worries about moral theory is that it is disastrously isolated from confirmation. The exact nature of this isolation has been subject to two interpretations. According to one, moral theory is totally insulated from observational consequences and is, therefore, in principle untestable. According to the other, moral theory enjoys the privilege of testability but suffers the embarrassment of failing all the tests. According to both, moral theory is in serious trouble.

After briefly defending moral theory against the charge of in-principle untestability, I defend it against the charge of contingent but unmitigated failure. The worries about untestability are, I suggest, easily met. Yet the very ease with which they are met belies the significance of meeting them; all manner of unacceptable theories are testable. The interesting question is not whether moral theory is testable, but whether moral theory *passes* the relevant tests. Recently, it has become popular to hold that a moral theory passes only if it is explanatorily potent; that is, only if it contributes to our best explanations of our experiences. The problem with moral theory is that it apparently contributes not at all to such explanations.[1] Working out a plausible version of the demand for explanatory potency is surprisingly hard. Even so, once a plausible version is found, I argue, (some) moral theories will in fact satisfy it. Unfortunately, this too is less significant than it might seem, for any argument establishing the *explanatory* potency of moral theory still falls short of establishing its *justificatory* force. (My arguments are no exception.) And, as I will try to make clear, the pressing worries concerning moral theory center on its claim to justificatory force; its explanatory force is largely beside the point. So much the worse for moral theory, one might be inclined to say. If moral theory goes beyond explanation, it goes where the epistemically cautious should fear to tread. Those who

433

demand explanatory potency, however, cannot afford the luxury of dismissing justificatory theory. Indeed, the demand for explanatory potency itself presupposes the legitimacy of justificatory theory, and this presupposition can be turned to the defense of moral theory's justificatory force. Or so I shall argue.

2. OBSERVATIONAL INSULATION

Keeping in mind that observation is theory-laden, one way to put the charge of untestability is to say that moral theory appears not to be appropriately observation-laden; unlike scientific theories, moral theories seem forever insulated from observational implications.

This objection to moral theory emerges naturally from a variation on the empiricist verification principle. Of course, as a criterion of meaning, the verification principle has for good reason been all but abandoned. Still, taken as a criterion of justifiability, rather than as a criterion of meaning, the principle seems to impose a reasonable requirement: If there is no way to verify observationally the claims of a proposed theory, then there is no way to justify the theory (unless all its claims are analytic).[2] Even if moral claims are meaningful, then, they might nonetheless be impossible to justify.

In favor of thinking moral theory untestable is the apparently unbridgeable chasm dividing what is from what ought to be.[3] After all, claims concerning moral obligations cannot be deduced from nonmoral claims ('ought', it is often said, cannot be derived from 'is'), which suggests (to some) that 'ought-claims' are not 'is-claims'. Since observation is always of what is, we may have reason to suspect that observation is irrelevant to what ought to be.

This argument for the is/ought distinction is too strong, though. It mistakenly assumes that definitional reducibility is a prerequisite for putting what ought to be on an ontologically equivalent footing with what is. No matter what we know about the nonmoral facts of the case, the argument emphasizes, we cannot uncontroversially infer the moral facts. Moral assertions are not definitionally reducible to nonmoral assertions. Since nonmoral assertions report what is, and since moral claims are not reducible to these others, then moral claims must not report what is. So the argument goes.

Remarkably, by similar lines of reasoning we would be constrained to admit that the claims made in psychology are not claims about facts; for psychology, no less than morality, resists definitional reduction. No matter what we know of the nonpsychological facts of the case, we cannot uncontroversially infer the psychological facts. Psychological assertions are not definitionally reducible to nonpsychological assertions. Since nonpsychological assertions report what is, and since psychological claims are not definitionally reducible to these others, then (the argument would have it) psychological claims must not report what is. Consequently, if the argument offered in support of the is/ought distinction worked, we would find ourselves stuck with an *is/thought* distinction as well. Psychology, we would have to say, reports not what is but merely what is thought—which is silly.[4]

Yet even if we put aside the is/ought distinction, the claim that moral theory is not properly observation-laden still extracts admirable support from common sense. For if people, or actions, or states of affairs have a worth, or a dignity, or a rightness about them, this is something we seemingly cannot sense directly. And most moral theories recognize this by construing moral properties as not directly observable. This cannot pose a special problem for moral theory's testability, however, since in *this* respect, moral theory is no different from those (obviously testable) scientific theories that postulate unobservable entities.

Moreover, on at least one standard construal of what counts as an observation, some moral claims will actually count as observation reports. Specifically, if one takes an observation to be any belief reached noninferentially as a direct result of perceptual experience, there is no reason to deny that there are moral observations. After all, just as we learn to report noninferentially the presence of chairs in response to sensory stimulation, we also learn to report noninferentially the presence of moral properties in response to sensory stimulation.

On this liberal view of observation, what counts as an observation depends solely on what opinions a person is trained to form immediately in response to sensory stimulation, and not on the content of the opinions.[5] Since such opinions are often heavily theory-laden and are often about the external world rather than about our experiences, the account avoids tying the notion of observation to the impossible ideal of theory neutrality or to the solipsistic reporting of the contents of sensory experience.

Of course, we may be too liberal here in allowing *any* opinion to count as an observation simply because it is reached directly as a result of perception. Surely, one is tempted to argue, we cannot observe what is not there, so that some opinions—no matter that they are directly reached as a result of perception—may fail to be observations because they report what does not exist. As a direct result of perception, I may believe I felt a friend's touch; but in the absence of her touch, my report seems most properly treated as an illusion, not an observation. Taking this into account, it is tempting to distinguish what are merely perceptually stimulated judgments from actual observations, thus reserving 'observation' for those perceptually stimulated judgments that are accurate.

If there were some observation-independent way to determine which judgments are accurate, we might legitimately dismiss a given class of purported observations (say, moral observations) on the grounds that they fail to report the facts accurately. Yet once the prospect of divining some set of basic (and indubitable) empirical statements is abandoned, so too must be the hope of establishing what things exist without appeal (at least indirectly) to observations. If some observations are needed to support the theories we then use to discredit other observations, we need some account of observation that allows us to isolate observations as such without assuming their accuracy has already been shown. Observations (in some ontologically noncommital sense) will be needed to legitimize the theories we use to separate veridical from nonveridical observations. It is this ontologically noncommittal sense of 'observation' that may be characterized simply as any opinion reached as a direct result of perception; and it is in this sense of 'observation' that we must allow that there are moral observations. Once moral observations are allowed, the admission that moral theories can be tested against these moral observations will quickly follow. Just as we test our physical principles against observation, adjusting one or the other in search of a proper fit, so we can test our moral principles against (moral) observation, adjusting one or the other in search of a proper fit. (Many have exploited the availability of this sort of observational testing and—unsatisfyingly—treated it as the sole criterion we have for the acceptability of theories.[6])

So neither the is/ought distinction nor the unobservability of moral properties seems to support the charge of untestability. In fact, there is reason to think moral theory passes the testability requirement in the same way any respectable scientific theory does—even if moral properties count as unobservable. Of course, how scientific theories manage to pass the testability requirement is a notoriously complicated matter. As Duhem and Quine have emphasized, scientific theories do not pass the testability requirement by having each of their principles pass independently; many of the theoretical principles of science have no observational implications when considered in isolation. Observationally testable predictions may be derived from these scientific principles only when they are combined with appropriate background assumptions.[7]

In the same way, certain moral principles may not be testable in isolation. Nevertheless, when such principles are combined with appropriate background assumptions, they too will allow the derivation of observationally testable predictions. To test the view that an action is wrong if and only if there is some alternative action available that will bring about more happiness, we might combine it with the (plausible) assumption that punishing the innocent is wrong. From these two principles taken together, we get the testable prediction that there will never be a time when punishing the innocent brings more happiness than any other action that is available. Alternatively, consider Plato's contention that 'virtue pays'. If combined with some account of what virtue is and with the (non-Platonic) view that 'payment' is a matter of satisfying preferences, we get as a testable consequence the prediction that those who are virtuous (in whatever sense we settle on) will have more of their preferences satisfied than if they had not been virtuous. Or again, if a moral theory holds that a just state does not allow capital punishment, and if we assume some particular state is just, we get as a testable consequence the claim that this country does not allow capital punishment.

In each case our moral principles have observationally testable consequences when combined with appropriate background assumptions. Experience may show that punishing the innocent does sometimes increase happiness, or that misery often accompanies virtue, or that the state in question does allow capital punishment. Upon making such discoveries we must abandon (or amend) our moral principles, or our background assumptions, or the confidence we place in our discoveries. Something has to give way.[8] Of course, we can often make adjustments in our overall theory in order to save particular moral principles, just as we can adjust scientific theories in order to salvage particular scientific principles. In science and ethics, background assumptions serve as protective buffers between particular principles and observation. Yet those same assumptions also provide the crucial link that allows both moral and scientific theories to pass any reasonable testability requirement. If the testability requirement ruled out relying on background assumptions, it would condemn science as untestable. If it allows such assumptions, and so makes room for the testability of science, it will likewise certify moral theory as testable. Once — but only once — background hypotheses are allowed, both scientific and moral principles will prove testable. Hence, if moral theories are unjustified, it must be for reasons other than that moral theories have no testable consequences.[9]

3. EXPLANATORY IMPOTENCE

Disturbingly, just as moral theory survives any reasonable standard for testability, so too do phlogiston theory, astrology, and even occult theories positing the existence of witches. Like moral theories, each of these theories (when combined with appropriate background assumptions) generates testable consequences, and each makes cognitively packed claims about the world. Still, given what we now know about the world, none of these theories has a claim on our allegiance. Although testable, they fail the test.

Quite reasonably, then, we might wonder whether moral theories likewise fail the empirical tests to which they may admittedly be subjected. Perhaps we ought to think of moral theories as failed theories — as theories betrayed by experience. Perhaps we ought to give up thinking there are moral facts for a moral theory to be about, just as we have abandoned thinking there is such a thing as phlogiston, just as we have abandoned the belief that the heavens control our destiny, and just as we have abandoned the idea that bound women who float are witches.

In our search for an understanding of the world, each of these theories seems to have been left in the dust; every phenomenon we might wish to explain by appeal to these theories can be explained better if they are put aside. Like phlogiston theory, astrology, and theories positing witches, moral theories appear explanatorily impotent.

The problem is that we need suppose neither that our particular moral judgments are accurate nor that our moral principles are true in order to explain why we make the judgments or accept the principles that we do. It seems we make the moral judgments we do because of the theories we happen to embrace, because of the society we live in, because of our individual temperaments, because of our feelings for others, but not because we have some special ability to detect moral facts, not because our moral judgments are accurate, and not because the moral theories we embrace are true. Given our training, temperament, and environment, we would make the moral judgments we do and advance the moral theories we do, regardless of the moral facts (and regardless of whether there are any).

To clarify the challenge facing moral theory, consider two situations (I take these from Gilbert Harman, who has done the most to advance the charge of explanatory impotence.[10]) In one, a person goes around a corner, sees a gang of hoodlums setting a live cat on fire, and exclaims, "There's a bad action!" In the other, a person peers into a cloud chamber, sees a trail, and exclaims, "There's a proton!" In both cases, part of the explanation of why the report was made will appeal to the movements of physical objects, and the effects these movements have initially on light and eventually on the observers' retinas. A more complete explanation would also have to make reference to the observers' psychological states as well as the background theories each accepted. Certainly the scientist would not make the report she did if she were asleep, nor even if awake and attentive, if she did not accept a theory according to which vapor trails in cloud chambers evidence the presence of protons. Had she thought witches left such trails, she might have reported a witch in the chamber instead of a proton. Similarly, the moral judge would not have made the report he did if he were asleep, nor even if awake and attentive, if he did not accept a view according to which burning live animals is wrong.[11] Had he thought cats the embodiments of evil, he might have reported the action as right instead of wrong.

Whatever explanations we give of the reports, one thing is striking: protons will form part of our best explanation of why the proton report was made; in contrast, moral properties seem not to form part of our best explanation of why the moral report was made. We will often explain the scientist's belief that a proton was present by appeal to the fact that one was. But, the argument goes, we will not explain the moral judge's belief that burning the cat is wrong by appeal to the wrongness of the act.

Harman elaborates on the problem with ethics by noting that

> facts about protons can affect what you observe, since a proton passing through a cloud chamber can cause a vapor trail that reflects light to your eye in a way that, given your scientific training and psychological set, leads you to judge that what you see is a proton. But there does not seem to be any way in which the actual rightness or wrongness of a given situation can have any effect on your perceptual apparatus.[12]

This emphasis on affecting (or failing to affect) an observer's perceptual apparatus suggests (mistakenly, I will argue) that the following *Causal Criterion* underlies the explanatory impotence attack on moral theory:

> The only entities and properties we are justified in believing in are those which we are justified in believing have a causal impact on our perceptual apparatus.

Unless moral properties are causally efficacious, and so figure as causes in the explanation of our making the observations that we do, moral theory will fail to meet this criterion's test.

Even though the argument from explanatory impotence turns on a different (and more plausible) principle, the Causal Criterion deserves attention because of its intimate ties to the causal theories of knowledge and reference.

4. THE CAUSAL CRITERION, KNOWLEDGE, AND REFERENCE

Any reasonable view of moral theory, and of the language(s) we use to formulate the theory, must (if moral theory is legitimate) be compatible with some account of how we come to *know* about moral properties and how the terms of the language come to *refer* to these properties. Assuming that the causal theories of knowledge and reference are substantially correct, the Causal Criterion is attractive simply because we could neither know about, nor even refer to, any class of properties that failed the Causal Criterion's test.[13] Thus, by requiring that we believe in only those entities and properties with which we believe we can causally interact, the Causal Criterion encapsulates the demands of the causal theories of knowledge and reference.

According to the causal theory of knowledge, we can get evidence only about that to which we bear some appropriate causal connection.[14] All our knowledge arises from the causal interaction of the objects of this knowledge with our bodies; anything outside all causal chains will be epistemically inaccessible.[15] So, if moral properties are causally isolated—if they fail to meet the Causal Criterion—they will be unknowable. More important, if moral properties make absolutely no difference to what we experience, we can never even form reasonable beliefs about what they are like.

The causal theory of reference makes moral theory look all the more hopeless because it suggests that we cannot even successfully refer to, let alone know about, moral properties (if they fail the Causal Criterion). As the causal theory of reference would have it, words in our language refer thanks to their standing at the end of a causal chain linking the speaker's use of the word to the thing to which the word refers. No appropriate chain can be established between speakers of a language (in this case a language containing moral terms) and causally isolated properties. Such properties will lie outside all causal chains, and so outside these causal chains which establish reference.[16]

Moral theory's trouble seems to be that the properties it ascribes to actions, people, and states of affairs, reflect no light, have no texture, give off no odor, have no taste, and make no sound. In fact, they do not causally affect our experience in any way. Were they absent, our experiences would be unchanged. Since we cannot interact with moral properties, there is no way for us to establish a causal chain between ourselves, our use of moral language, and moral properties. Consequently, our moral terms fail to refer.

So put, this criticism of moral theory is much too quick. Even the causal theory of reference allows success in establishing a referential tie between word and world by description as well as by ostension.[17] It is true that ostension works in establishing reference only if the properties (or entities) referred to are causally present (since we can succeed in our ostensions only by locating something in space and time).[18] However, we may still use descriptions to establish a referential link even to that from which we are causally isolated — as long as the appropriate terms of the description succeed in referring. If moral properties fail the Causal Criterion, we will not be able to refer to them by ostension; but we will nonetheless be able to refer to them as long as we can describe the moral properties in nonmoral terms. (Of course, if the description's terms were moral, they would be no help in grounding the requisite referential link.[19]) As a result, the causal theory of reference will serve to undermine ethics only if we cannot refer to moral properties by using nonmoral descriptions, and then only if moral properties are in fact causally isolated.[20] Any argument against moral facts using the causal theory of reference, then, must rely on some independent argument that shows that moral facts (if such there be) are both indescribable in nonmoral terms and causally isolated.

Plainly, our ability to refer to moral properties will be small consolation unless we can also secure evidence about the properties to which we refer. Successful reference may prove epistemically useless. So, even if we can succeed in referring to moral properties, the problems raised by the causal theory of knowledge remain.

Not surprisingly, these problems too are less straightforward than suggested so far. To tell against moral theory, the causal theory of knowledge (like the causal theory of reference) must be supplemented by an argument showing that moral properties are causally isolated (or that they do not exist).

Against theories concerned with abstract entities (like mathematics and Plato's Theory of Forms), the Causal Criterion, and the causal theories of knowledge and reference, apparently meet no resistance. The theories under attack grant right off that the entities in question are causally isolated (because outside space and time). That abstract entities fail the Causal Criterion appears to be a forgone conclusion.[21]

Against moral theories, in contrast, the charge of causal isolation meets with resistance. Unlike abstract entities, moral properties are traditionally thought of as firmly ensconced in the causal nexus: a bad character has notorious effects (at least when backed by power), and fair social institutions evidently affect the happiness of those in society. The ontology of moral theory will not be an unwitting accomplice in the causalist critique of ethics. Of course, moral theory's resistance does not establish that moral properties actually do satisfy the Causal Criterion (and so the causal theories of knowledge and reference); rather, the resistance imposes a barrier over which the causal critique of moral theory must climb. Some argument must be given for thinking moral properties fail to meet the Causal Criterion.

5. THE EXPLANATORY CRITERION

Regardless of whether moral properties satisfy the Causal Criterion, there are good reasons for thinking the criterion itself too strong. To hold tight to the Causal Criterion (and the causal theories of knowledge and reference that support it) is to let go of some of our most impressive epistemological accomplishments; the claims of mathematics, as well as both the empirical generalizations and the laws of the physical sciences, all fail the criterion's test.

We never causally interact with numbers, for instance.[22] So, if causal contact were really a prerequisite to knowledge (and reference), mathematical knowledge and discourse would be an impossibility. For similar reasons, empirical generalizations (like "all emeralds are green"), as well as natural laws (like the first law of thermodynamics), would fall victim to the Causal Criterion. Although these generalizations and laws may help *explain* why we experience what we do as we do, they *cause* none of our experiences. That all emeralds are green does not cause a particular emerald to be green, nor does it cause us to see emeralds as green.[23] These casualties of the Causal Criterion make it clear that we need to replace the Causal Criterion even if we wish to salvage its emphasis on the link between knowledge (or at least justified belief) and experience.[24]

In forging a new criterion, we should concentrate on the reasons that might be given for thinking it reasonable to believe (as I assume it is) in the truth of many mathematical claims, empirical generalizations, and laws of physics. According to one standard line in the philosophy of science (one embraced by Harman, J. L. Mackie, Simon Blackburn, and many other critics of moral theory), the key to the legitimacy of these scientific and mathematical claims is the role they play in the explanations of our experiences. "An observation," Harman argues, "is evidence for what best *explains* it, and since mathematics often figures in the explanations of scientific observations, there is indirect observational evidence for mathematics."[25] Empirical generalizations and physical laws will likewise find their justification by appeal to their role in the best explanations of our experience—"scientific principles can be justified ultimately by their role in explaining observations."[26] The legitimacy of a theory seems to ride on its explanatory role, and not on the causal impact of its ontology. From these points we can extract the *Explanatory Criterion* according to which

> the only hypotheses we are justified in believing are those that figure in the best explanations we have of our making the observations that we do.

Significantly, the Explanatory Criterion retains, even reinforces, the empiricist's demand that epistemology be tied to experience; not only does justification turn on experiential testability, it now requires an *explanatory* link between the truth of our beliefs and our experiences as well. Accordingly, an acceptable theory must do more than have observational consequences; it must also contribute to our explanations of why we make the observations we do.

Two versions of the Explanatory Criterion should be distinguished; the first sets necessary and sufficient conditions for reasonable belief; the second sets only necessary conditions. In its stronger version, the criterion would say:

A hypothesis should be believed *if and only if* the hypothesis plays a role in the best explanation we have of our making the observations that we do.

In its weaker version the criterion would say instead:

A hypothesis should be believed *only if* the hypothesis plays a role in the best explanation we have of our making the observations that we do.

Or, in its contrapositive (and more intuitively attractive) form:

A hypothesis should not be believed if the hypothesis plays no role in the best explanation we have of our making the observations that we do.

Accepting the stronger version of the criterion involves endorsing what has come to be called 'inference to the best explanation'. In this guise, the criterion licenses inferring the truth of a hypothesis from its playing a role in our best explanations of our experiences. To be even remotely plausible, of course, some bottom limit must be set on the quality of the explanations that would be allowed to countenance inferences to the truth of the hypotheses invoked. Despite their being the best we have, our explanations can be so bad that we may be quite sure they are wrong. It would be a mistake to infer the truth of a hypothesis from its being part of our best – but obviously flawed – explanation. Even with a quality constraint, the strong version of the Explanatory Criterion is hopelessly liberal because we have such good grounds for thinking that the best explanations we can come up with, at any given time, are not right.[27] In light of these difficulties, I shall concentrate on the weaker version of the criterion. The weaker version raises all the same difficulties for moral theory without endorsing inferences to the best explanation.

The problem with moral theory is that moral principles and moral properties appear not to play a role in explaining our making the observations we do. All the explanatory work seems to be done by psychology, physiology, and physics.[28] A scientist's observing a proton in a cloud chamber is evidence for her theory because the theory explains the proton's presence and the scientist's observation better than competing theories can. The observation of a proton provides observational evidence for a theory because the truth of that observation is part of the best explanation we have of why the observation was made. A moral 'observation' does not appear to be, in the same sense, observational evidence for or against any moral theory, since (as Harman puts it) the truth or falsity of the "moral observation seems to be completely irrelevant to any reasonable explanation of why that observation was made."[29]

Underlying the Explanatory Criterion is the conviction that confirmation mirrors explanation: theories are confirmed by what they explain. Added to this view of confirmation is the stipulation, motivated by an empiricist epistemology, that we should assume to exist only what we need to explain *our experiences*.

Put generally, some fact confirms whatever principles and hypotheses are part of the best explanation of the fact. So, the fact that some observation was made will confirm whatever is part of the best explanation of its having been made. But the making of the observation will not provide *observational* evidence for a theory unless the observation itself is accurate. And we will have grounds for thinking an observation accurate, on this view, only when its being accurate forms a part of our best explanation of the observation having been made. Thus, embedded within this overarching view of confirmation is a more specific account of observational confirmation. An observation will provide confirming observational evidence for a theory, according to this account, only to the extent that it is reasonable to explain the making of the observation by invoking the theory while also treating the observation as true.[30]

For this reason, moral facts, and moral theory, will be vindicated (in the eyes of the Explanatory Criterion) only if they figure in our best explanations of at least some of the accurate observations we make. Unfortunately, as Harman argues, "you need to make assumptions about certain physical facts to explain the occurrence of observations that support a scientific theory, but you do not seem to need to make assumptions about any moral facts to explain the occurrence of the so-called moral observations."[31] Of course, moral facts would be acceptable, according to the Explanatory Criterion, as long as they were needed to explain the making of some observation or other (regardless of whether it is a moral observation). Just as mathematics is justified by its role in explaining physical (and not mathematical) observations, moral theory might similarly be justified by its role in explaining some nonmoral observations. But the problem with moral theory is that moral facts seem not to help explain the making of *any of our observations*.

Importantly, the problem is not that moral facts explain nothing at all (they may explain other moral facts); the problem is that regardless of whether they explain something, they do not hook up properly with our abilities to detect facts. Even if there are moral facts, and even if some of these facts would help to explain others, none will be epistemically accessible unless some help to explain our making some of the observations we do. No matter how perfect the fit between the content of our moral judgments and a moral theory, no matter how stable and satisfying a reflective equilibrium can be established between them, the theory will not gain observational confirmation unless it enters into the best explanation of why some of our observations are made. We will be justified in accepting a moral theory on the basis of our observations only if we have reason to believe our observations are responsive to the moral facts. And we will have reason to believe this only if moral facts enter into the best explanations of why we make the observations we do. To be legitimized, then, moral facts must explain certain nonmoral facts; specifically, moral facts must explain our making observations.[32]

In order to highlight the problem faced by moral theory, it is a good idea to go back to the (dis)analogy between the scientist's making the observation "there's a proton" and the moral judge's making the observation "there's a bad action." Our best explanation of why the scientist made the observation she did will make reference to her psychology, her scientific theory, the fact that vapor trail appeared in the cloud chamber, and *the fact that a proton left the trail*. Our best explanation of why the moral judge made the observation he did will likewise make reference to his psychology, his moral theory, the fact that a cat was set on fire, and even (when the explanation is more fully elaborated) to the fact that the cat and the kids were composed of protons. Yet our explanation will not make reference to the (purported) fact that burning the cat was wrong: "It seems to be completely irrelevant to our explanation whether [the judge's moral] judgment is true or false."[33] That burning the cat was wrong, if it was wrong, appears completely irrelevant to our explanation of the judge thinking it wrong.[34]

6. EXPLANATORY RELEVANCE AND EXPLANATORY POTENCY

The explanatory critique of moral theory seems to rest on the claim that moral facts are *irrelevant* to explanations of our observations. So, to flesh out the problem, we need some test for explanatory irrelevance. Nicholas Sturgeon proposes the following:

> If a particular assumption is completely irrelevant to the explanation of a certain fact, then the fact would have obtained, and we could have explained it just as well, even if the assumption had been false.[35]

With this in mind, Sturgeon argues that, for those who are not already moral skeptics, moral facts will prove to be explanatorily relevant.

Sturgeon's argument runs as follows. To decide whether the truth of some moral belief is explanatorily relevant to the making of an observation, we must consider a situation in which the belief is false, but which is otherwise as much like the actual situation as possible. Then we must determine whether the observation would still have been made under the new conditions. If so, if the observation would have been made in any case, then the truth of the moral belief is explanatorily irrelevant (the observation would have been made even if it had been false); otherwise its truth is relevant. If a supervenience account of moral properties is right (so that what makes a moral judgment true or false is some combination of physical facts), then for some true judgment to have been false, or some false judgment true, the situation would have had to have been different in some physical respect.[36] Consider the hoodlums' cat-burning. According to Sturgeon,

> If what they are actually doing is wrong, and if moral properties are, as many writers have held, supervenient on natural ones, then in order to imagine them not doing something wrong we are going to have to suppose their action different from the actual one in some of its natural features as well.[37]

Whether we would still judge the action wrong given these changes is a contingent matter that turns on how closely tied our moral judgments are to the morally relevant physical features of the situation. In the case of a curmudgeon, who thinks badly of kids as a matter of principle (averring that "kids are always up to no good"), changing the moral (and so the nonmoral) features of the situation will probably not change his moral judgment. For him, the truth of the judgment is irrelevant to the explanation of his making it. Fortunately, though, many people do not share this bias and are therefore more attuned to the evidence. Such people would have different opinions had the hoodlums found their entertainment in more acceptable ways (say, by petting rather than incinerating the cat). For those to whom the difference would make a difference, part of the explanation of their judgment would be that burning the cat is wrong.[38]

Notice that the same contingency attaches to the scientist's sighting of a proton. Had the proton not been there, whether the scientist would have thought it was depends on how closely tied her scientific judgments are to the relevant features of the situation. If she is a poor researcher, she might well have reported the proton's presence had there really been only a passing reflection. Again fortunately, many scientists are well attuned to the difference between proton trails and passing reflections. At least these scientists would have made different reports concerning the presence of a proton had the proton been absent. For those to whom the difference would make a difference, part of the explanation of their judgment will be that a proton passed.[39]

Sturgeon holds that what separates his own position from Harman's is a differential willingness to rely on a background moral theory in evaluating the question: Would the moral observation have been made even if the observation had been false? Sturgeon assumes the observation to be true (relying as he does on his background moral theory), and believes that for it to be false, some nonmoral features of the situation must be assumed different (because the moral properties supervene upon natural properties). When these nonmoral features are changed, he points out, the moral judgments (along with the explanations of why they were made) will often change as well. Harman, though, does without the background moral theory, so he has no reason to think that if the observation were false, anything else about the situation (including the observer's beliefs) would have been different. Consequently, he holds that the observation would have been made regardless of its truth.

As a result, Sturgeon concludes that Harman's argument is not an independent defense of skepticism concerning moral facts, for its conclusion apparently rests on the assumption that our moral judgments are false (or, more accurately, on the assumption that moral theory cannot be relied on in estimating how the world would have been if it had been morally different).[40]

Unfortunately for moral theory, Sturgeon's argument fails to meet the real challenge. The force of the explanatory attack on moral theory may be reinstated by shifting attention from explanatory *irrelevance* to explanatory *impotence*, where

a particular assumption is explanatorily impotent with respect to a certain fact, if the fact would have obtained and we could have explained it just as well, *even if the assumption had not been invoked in the explanation* (as opposed to: 'even if the assumption had been false').

By charging explanatory impotence, rather than explanatory irrelevance, the explanatory challenge to moral theory survives the admission that we hold our moral theories dear. It also survives the supervenience account's provision of a necessary link between moral and nonmoral properties. For the question becomes: Do we honestly think appealing to moral facts in our explanations of moral judgments strengthens our explanations one bit? Behind this question is the worry that we have been profligate with our theory building (or, perhaps, that we've been unnecessarily and unwholesomely nostalgic about old, and now outdated, theories). The concern is that acknowledging moral facts adds nothing to our ability to explain our experiences. Everything we might reasonably want to explain can, it seems, be explained equally well without appeal to moral facts.[41]

If these worries are well-founded, if moral facts are explanatory 'fifth wheels', and if we accept the Explanatory Criterion for justified belief, then moral facts will become merely unjustified theoretical baggage weighing down our ontology without offering compensation. In the face of this threat, pointing out that we happen to rely on moral facts in explaining people's behavior is not sufficient to justify believing in (even supervenient) moral facts; actual reliance does not establish justified belief.

To see the force of the explanatory challenge, imagine that a belief in witches becomes popular among your friends. Imagine, too, that your friends teach each other, and you, how to give 'witch explanations'. You 'learn' that the reason some bound women float when tossed into ponds, and others do not, is that the floaters are witches, the others not; that the mysterious deaths of newborns should be attributed to the jealous intervention of witches; and so on. No doubt, with enough practice you could become skillful at generating your own witch explanations; so skillful, perhaps, that in your unreflective moments you would find yourself offering such explanations. In order to assuage your philosophical conscience, you might entertain a sort of supervenience account of being a witch. Then you might comfortably maintain that being a witch is explanatorily relevant (in Sturgeon's sense) to your observations. All this might come to pass, and still you would be justified in thinking there are not really any witches—as long as you could explain the floatings, the deaths, and whatever else, just as well without appealing to the existence of witches. Presumably, the availability of such alternative explanations is just the reason we should not now believe in witches.

Certainly, things could turn out otherwise; we might find that witch explanations are actually the best available. We might discover that postulating witches is the only reasonable way to account for all sorts of otherwise inexplicable phenomena. Should that happen, our conversion to a belief in witches would, of course, be quite justified.

The question is, to which witch scenario are our moral explanations more analogous? Are our appeals to moral properties just intellectually sloppy concessions to effective socialization, or do we really strengthen our explanatory abilities by supposing that there are moral properties? This is a substantial challenge, and one not adequately answered by the observation that we often rely on moral properties to explain behavior.

Two points about the explanatory challenge deserve emphasis. First, the challenge recognizes conditions under which a belief in moral facts, or witches, would be legitimate. Specifically, the Explanatory Criterion would take these beliefs to be justified if their truth figured in the best explanation of why we have the experiences we do. Second, the challenge will not be met simply by pointing out that witches, or moral facts, do figure in some of our best explanations of the world. For unless these explanations of the world can be properly linked to *our experiences* of the world, there will be no way for us to justify accepting some of the explanations rather than others. The truth of one or another will make no difference to our experience, and so will be epistemically inaccessible.

7. SUPERVENIENCE AND LENIENCE

The problem with concentrating on explanatory relevance, rather than on explanatory potency, is that it makes a defense of moral properties (and belief in witches) too easy. It permits as justified the introduction of any properties whatsoever, so long as they are construed as supervenient upon admittedly explanatory properties.

The Explanatory Criterion, when interpreted as demanding explanatory potency (rather than mere relevance), promises a stricter standard, which might separate those properties we are justified in believing instantiated from mere pretenders. Yet the criterion must be interpreted in a way that acknowledges as justified belief in two kinds of properties: those which can be reductively identified with explanatorily potent properties and those we have independent reason to think supervene upon, without being strictly reducible to, explanatorily potent properties. These properties demand special attention because, at least initially, they appear explanatorily expendable — despite our belief in them being justified.

For instance, though all the explanatory work of water may be better accomplished by H_2O; all the explanatory work of color, by the wave lengths of light; and all that of psychological states, by neurophysiological states of the brain; we are nonetheless justified in believing that the oceans are filled with water, that roses are red, and that people feel pain and have beliefs. Any criterion of justified belief that would rule these beliefs out as unjustified is simply too stringent. The difficulty (for those attacking moral theory) is to accommodate these legitimate beliefs without so weakening the Explanatory Criterion as to reintroduce excessive leniency.

Of course, some beliefs may plausibly find justification by relying on reductions: because water is H_2O, the justification of our belief in H_2O (by appeal to its explanatory potency) serves equally well as a justification of our belief in water. In cases where identification reductions are available, explanatory potency might well be transitive.[42]

Where identification reductions are not available, however, things become trickier; and it is here that the Explanatory Criterion runs into problems. It seems straightforwardly true that roses are red, for example, but our best explanations of red-rose-reports might well make reference to certain characteristics of roses, facts about light, and facts about the psychological and perceptual apparatus of perceivers—but not to the *redness* of the roses (and not to any particular feature of the roses that can be reductively identified with redness). Despite this, the availability of such explanations expands our understanding of colors; it does not show there are no colors. Similar points hold not just for those properties traditionally characterized as secondary qualities, but for *all* nonreducible properties.[43]

Recognizing this, Harman attempts to make room for nonreducible properties. In discussing colors, he maintains that they satisfy the demand for explanatory potency because

> we will sometimes refer to the actual colors of objects in explaining color perceptions if only for the sake of simplicity. . . . We will continue to believe that objects have colors because we will continue to refer to the actual colors of objects in the explanations that we will in practice give.[44]

Thus, pragmatic tenacity is supposed by Harman to be enough to establish explanatory potency; now the criterion will allow, as explanatorily potent, those properties and entities to which we appeal in our best explanations, plus those that are precisely reducible to properties or entities appealed to in our best explanations, plus those that are pragmatically tenacious.

Relying on such a lenient interpretation of the Explanatory Criterion, Harman is able to treat moral facts as threatened only by resorting to what is patently false: he is forced to argue that moral facts are not "useful even in practice in our explanations of observations."[45] If nothing else, however, moral facts are useful, at least in practice, when explaining our observations. Many very useful, and frequently offered, explanations of events in the world (and so our observations of those events) make reference to moral facts. Mother Teresa's goodness won her a Nobel Prize; Solidarity's popularity is caused by Poland's oppressive political institutions; millions died in Russia as a result of Stalin's inhumanity; people are starving unnecessarily because of the selfishness of others; unrest in Soweto is a response to the injustice of Apartheid. Even if such explanations could eventually be replaced by others that appeal only to psychological, social, and physical factors, without mention of moral facts, the moral explanations would still be useful in just the way talk of colors remains useful even in light of theories of light. If mere pragmatic tenacity is enough to legitimize color properties, it ought to be enough to legitimize moral properties.

If the Explanatory Criterion is to challenge the legitimacy of moral theory, it must require more than pragmatic tenacity for justification. Yet, almost certainly, any stronger requirement that remains plausible will countenance moral properties. For the Explanatory Criterion will be plausible only if it allows belief in those properties needed both to identify and to explain the natural regularities that are otherwise explicable only in a piecemeal fashion as singular events (and not as instances of regularities). Consider Hilary Putnam's example of the peg (square in cross-section) that will pass through the square hole in a board, but not through the round hole.[46] To explain a single instance of the peg's going through one hole, we might offer a microstructural description of the peg and the board in terms of the distribution of atoms, and then appeal to particle mechanics. But even if we could eventually work out such an explanation, it would suffer from a serious drawback; it would only explain why the particular peg went through a particular hole at a particular time. The explanation will be of no help when we are faced with another board and peg, or even with the same board and peg a moment later (when the distribution of atoms has changed). The explanation will not extend to new cases. And the properties appealed to in giving an explanation at the level of ultimate constituents will be useless in trying to identify and explain the general fact that pegs of a certain size and shape (whether made of wood, or plastic, or steel) will fail to go through holes of a certain size and shape (whether the holes are in a piece of wood, or plastic, or steel). This general fact will be identifiable and explicable only if we appeal to certain macrostructural features of pegs and holes.

In the same way, certain regularities—for instance, honesty's engendering trust, or justices's commanding allegiance, or kindness' encouraging friendship—are real regularities that are unidentifiable and inexplicable except by appeal to moral properties. Indeed, many moral virtues (such as honesty, justice, kindness) and vices (such as greed, lechery, sadism) figure in this way in our best explanations of many natural regularities. Moral explanations allow us to isolate what it is about a person, or an action, or an institution, that leads to its having the effects it does. And these explanations rely on moral concepts that identify characteristics common to people, actions, and institutions that are uncapturable with finer-grained or differently structured categories.

Of course, even if moral properties do have a role in our best explanations of natural regularities, we might still wonder whether these properties are anything more, anything over and above, psychological properties and dispositions of individuals; and we might wonder to what extent these 'vices' and 'virtues' have any normative authority. For all that has been said so far, we might have no good reason to think the 'virtues' worthy of cultivation and the 'vices' worthy of condemnation. So even if moral properties ultimately satisfy the demands of the Explanatory Criterion (once we get a reasonable interpretation of its requirements), we will at most have established that certain people, actions, and institutions have those properties we label 'moral'. We will not yet have shown that there is any reason to care about the properties, nor that some of the properties are better than others.[47]

As long as we concentrate on which properties satisfy the Explanatory Criterion, and which do not, the distinctive value of moral properties will remain elusive. The structure of a compelling defense of their value will emerge only after we turn our attention to the presuppositions of the Explanatory Criterion itself.

8. THE EVALUATION OF EXPLANATIONS

As the Explanatory Criterion would have it, which hypotheses are justified, and which are not, will depend crucially on our standards of explanation, since it is by figuring in the *best* available explanations that a hypothesis finds justification. No argument that depends on the Explanatory Criterion will get off the ground unless some explanations are better than others. This poses a dilemma for those who suppose that the Explanatory Criterion will support the wholesale rejection of evaluative facts. Either there is a fact of the matter about which explanations are best, or there is not. If there is, then there are at least some evaluative facts (as to which explanations are better than others); if not, then the criterion will never find an application, and so will support no argument against moral theory.

If we say that astronomers, and not astrologers, make the appropriate inferences from what is seen of the constellations, or that evolutionary theorists, and not creationists, have the best explanation of the origin of our species, we will be making value judgments. In trying to legitimize these judgments by appealing to our standards of explanation, a reliance on values becomes inescapable (even if the values appealed to are not themselves mentioned in our explanations).

The obvious response to this point is to embrace some account of explanatory quality in terms, say, of simplicity, generality, elegance, predictive power, and so on. One explanation is better than another, we could then maintain, in virtue of the way it combines these properties.[48]

When offering the list of properties that are taken to be the measures of explanatory quality, however, it is important to avoid the mistake of thinking the list wipes values out of the picture. It is important to avoid thinking of the list as eliminating explanatory quality in favor of some evaluatively neutral properties. If one explanation is better than another in virtue of being simpler, more general, more elegant, and so on, then simplicity, generality, and elegance cannot themselves be evaluatively neutral. Were these properties evaluatively neutral, they could not account for one explanation being better than another.

If we are to use the Explanatory Criterion, we must hold that some explanations really are better than others, and not just that they have some evaluatively neutral properties that others do not. Any attempt to wash evaluative claims out as psychological or sociological reports, for instance, will fail — we will not be saying what we want, that one explanation is *better* than another, but only (for example) that we happen to like one explanation more, or that our society approves of one more. What the Explanatory Criterion presupposes is that there are evaluative facts, at least concerning which explanations are better than others — regardless of whether these facts explain any of our observations.

Even assuming that the Explanatory Criterion presupposes the existence of some *evaluative* facts, the question remains whether we have any good reason for thinking there are moral facts as well. We might be convinced that some explanations really are better than others, but still deny that some actions, or characters, or institutions, are better than others. Significantly, though, once it has been granted that some explanations are better than others, many obstacles to a defense of moral values disappear. In fact, all general objections to the existence of value must be rejected as too strong. Moreover, whatever ontological niche and epistemological credentials we find for explanatory values will presumably serve equally well for moral values.[49]

Without actually making the argument, I shall briefly sketch one of the ways one might defend the view that there are moral values. The aim of such an argument would be to show that some actions, characters, or institutions are better than others—just as some explanations are better than others.

The defense of moral values rests on recognizing and stressing the similarities between the evaluation of actions, and so on, and the evaluation of explanations. The crucial similarity is that in defending our evaluations (whether of actions, institutions, or explanations) we must inevitably rely on a theory that purports to *justify* our standards of evaluation as over against other sets of (moral or explanatory) standards. In both cases, we will be engaged in the process of justifying our judgments, not of explaining our experiences. The analogy to keep in mind here is not that between moral theory and scientific theory, but that between moral theory and scientific epistemology.[50]

Since we must regard certain evaluative claims (those concerning which explanations are better than others) as true, we will be justified in believing those parts of value theory that support our standards of explanatory value. Just as we take the explanatory role of certain hypotheses as grounds for believing the hypotheses, we must, I suggest, take the justificatory role of certain evaluative principles as grounds for believing the principles. If the principles are themselves not reasonably believed, they cannot support our particular evaluations of explanations; and if we can have no grounds for thinking one explanation better than another, the Explanatory Criterion will be toothless.

Thus, if evaluative facts are indispensable (because they are presupposed by the Explanatory Criterion), we can invoke what might be called *inference to the best justification* to argue abstract value claims on the grounds that they justify our lower-level epistemic judgments. And these very same abstract evaluative principles might imply lower-level, distinctly moral principles and particular moral judgments. If so, then in defending moral values we might begin with evaluations of explanations, move up (in generality and abstraction) to principles justifying these evaluations, then move back down, along a different justificatory path, to evaluations of actions, characters, institutions, and so on. That is, to argue for a particular moral judgment (for example, that it is better to be honest than duplicitous), we might show that the judgment is justified by some abstract evaluative principle that is itself justified by its relation to our standards of explanatory quality (which are indispensable to our application of the Explanatory Criterion). In this way, particular moral judgments and more general moral principles might find their legitimacy through their connection with the indispensable part of value theory that serves to justify our judgments of explanatory quality.

To take one (optimisitic) example: Imagine that we justify believing in some property by appeal to its role in our best explanation of some observations, and we then justify our belief that some explanation is the best available by appeal to our standards of explanatory quality, and finally, we justify these standards (rather than some others) by appealing to their ultimate contributions to the maximization of expected utility. Imagine, also, that having justified our standards of explanatory value, we turn to the justification for cultivating some moral property (for example, honesty). The justification might plausibly appeal to its contribution to the cohesiveness of one's society, and we might in turn justify cultivating properties conducive to the cohesiveness of society by appeal to the benefits available only within society. Finally, we might justify these as benefits by appeal to their maximizing expected utility. Appeal to the maximization of expected utility would then serve both as the best justification for certain standards of explanatory value and as the best justification for cultivating particular moral properties. It would justify both our belief that some particular explanation is better than another and our belief that some moral properties (for example, honesty) are better than others (for example, duplicity). We could then deny the justifiability of moral judgments only by denying the justification of our evaluative judgments of explanations.

So, in pursuing justifications for our standards of evaluation, we might discover that the justificatory principles we embrace have as consequences not only evaluations of explanations but also recognizably moral evaluations of character, or behavior, or institutions. Justificatory principles might come most plausibly as a package deal carrying both explanatory and moral evaluations in tow.

No doubt this picture is overly optimistic. Most likely, the justificatory principles invoked in justifying particular standards of explanatory quality will not be so neatly tied with the justifications available for having or developing certain (recognizably moral) properties, nor with the justifications available for condemning other (recognizably immoral) properties. In following out the two lines of justification—that is, in justifying particular evaluations by appeal to principles, which we in turn justify by appeal to more general principles—we may never arrive at a single, overarching justificatory principle. Indeed, it is highly unlikely that we will ever get such a principle either in epistemology or in moral theory.[51] It is even less likely that we will ever find a single principle that serves for both.

Although inference to the best justification legitimizes both the lower-level standards of explanatory value (simplicity, generality, and so on) and—more important—the very process of justification, the substantive principles the process engenders will probably vary according to what is being justified. When we are justifying a belief that some property is instantiated, one set of justificatory principles will come into play; when we are justifying the having or cultivating of some property, a completely different set of justificatory principles may prove relevant. The two paths of justification might neither coincide nor converge.

Yet a failure of convergence would not undermine moral justifications. The legitimacy of moral theory does not require any special link between explanatory and moral justifications. What it does require is that moral properties figure both as properties we are justified in believing exemplifiable and as properties we are justified in cultivating.

In constructing explanatory and justificatory theories, we may discover any of four things: (1) that moral properties are neither possessable nor worth possessing, in which case (I assume) moral theory loses its point; (2) that moral properties (for example, honesty, kindness) are possessed by some but that there is no justification for thinking some better than others, in which case only an unexciting conclusion will have been established—like atomic weights, virtue and value would exist, and claims involving them would have a truth value, but they would be normatively inert; (3) that we have no reason to believe moral properties are exemplified, but we do have reason to cultivate them, in which case a unique version of the is/ought distinction will have been established—there are no instantiated moral properties, even though there ought to be; or finally, (4) that moral properties are actually possessed and (some) are worth possessing, in which case moral theory will have found its strongest defense. Which of these four positions is right can be settled only against the background of an accepted justificatory theory.

Of course, whether we are justified in believing moral properties are both possessable and worth possessing is an open question. Yet it is a legitimate question, a question that can be answered only by engaging in moral theorizing; that is, only by attempting the justifications and seeing where they lead.[52]

Notes

1. For example, see Gilbert Harman's *The Nature of Morality* (New York, 1977) and his "Moral Explanations of Natural Facts—Can Moral Claims be Tested Against Moral Reality?" in *Spindel Conference: Moral Realism, Southern Journal of Philosophy* 24 (1986), Supplement: 57–68; J. L. Mackie's *Ethics: Inventing Right and Wrong* (New York, 1977); Simon Blackburn's *Spreading the Word* (New York, 1984); Francis Snare's "The Empirical Bases of Moral Scepticism," *American Philosophical Quarterly* 21 (1984): 215–25; and David Zimmerman's "Moral Theory and Explanatory Necessity," in *Morality, Reason and Truth*, edited by David Copp and David Zimmerman (Totowa, 1985), 79–103.

2. Although this change in emphasis, from meaning to justification, represents a natural development of the verification principle, it constitutes a significant change. With it comes the rejection of the verifiability principle as grounds for noncognitivism.

3. As Reichenbach notes: "Science tells us what is, but not what should be." *The Rise of Scientific Philosophy* (Berkeley, 1951), 287.

4. Although it is true that what is thought to be is not always so (just as what ought to be is not always so), reports that something is thought to be (or that something ought to be), are still clearly assertions concerning what is the case. Moral theory is as concerned with what is as is psychology. In making claims about what ought to be, moral theory is claiming that what ought to be is such and such. Moral theory characteristically makes assertions such as "Killing humans for entertainment *is* wrong;" "An action *is* made worse if it results in excruciating pain for others"; "The Ku Klux Klan *is* a morally corrupt oganization."

5. Paul Churchland defends this account in *Scientific Realism and the Plasticity of Mind* (Cambridge,

1979). See also Norwood Russell Hanson's *Patterns of Discovery* (Cambridge, 1958) and Wilfrid Sellars's *Science, Perception, and Reality* (London, 1963).

6. See as examples John Rawls's *A Theory of Justice* (Cambridge, Mass., 1971), Ronald Dworkin's *Taking Rights Seriously* (Cambridge, Mass., 1977), and Philip Pettit's *Judging Justice* (London, 1980).

7. See Pierre Duhem's *The Aim and Structure of Physical Theory* (Princeton, N.J., 1954) and W. V. O. Quine's "Two Dogmas of Empiricism," in *From a Logical Point of View* (Cambridge, Mass., 1964), 20–46.

8. See Morton White's *What Is and What Ought to Be Done*, (Oxford, 1981), and Nicholas Sturgeon's "Moral Explanations," in *Morality, Reason, and Truth*.

9. The last few paragraphs reiterate points made in my "Logical Positivism and the Demise of 'Moral Science' " in *The Heritage of Logical Positivism*, edited by Nicholas Rescher (Lanham, 1985), 83–92.

10. Harman, *The Nature of Morality*, 6–7.

11. Of course, neither the scientist nor the moral judge need have had a well-worked-out theory in order to make observations. The ability to form opinions (about protons, witches, or morals) as a direct result of perceptual experience is more a matter of effective training than of the conscious application of theory to experience.

12. Harman, *The Nature of Morality*, 8.

13. Actually, the Causal Criterion will be attractive regardless of whether the causal theories are substantially correct, as long as we assume causal contact is a necessary condition for knowledge.

14. Goldman characterizes the appropriate connection in terms of there being a "reliable belief-forming operation." Alvin Goldman, "What Is Justified Belief?" in *Justification and Knowledge*, edited by George Pappas (Dordrecht, 1979), 1–23.

15. Mark Steiner defends mathematical entities from this objection in *Mathematical Knowledge* (Ithaca, N.Y., 1975), 10. See also Penelope Maddy, "Perception and Mathematical Intuition," *Philosophical Review* 89 (1980): 163–96; Paul Benacerraf, "Mathematical Truth," *Journal of Philosophy* 70 (1973): 661–79; Crispin Wright, *Frege's Conception of Numbers as Objects* (Aberdeen, Scot., 1983); and Philip Kitcher, *The Nature of Mathematical Knowledge* (Oxford, 1983).

16. All of this is compatible, of course, with there being a causal story of our use of moral language. Since we do live in a community of moral-language users, we are taught how to use moral words and we stand at the end of a causal (in this case, educational) chain that explains our use of moral terms. Despite there being such a causal story, if moral properties are causally isolated, our language will lack the grounding that would allow it to refer; the linguistic chain would lack an anchor.

17. See Saul Kripke's *Naming and Necessity* (Cambridge, Mass., 1980).

18. Incidentally, one may succeed in referring to an ordinary object, one located in space and time, even if the object does not actually have any causal impact on the referrer. Eyes closed, I may enter a room, point to my left, and declare, "I'll bet that chair is brown." I will have referred to the chair (assuming one is there), and made a bet about its color, despite my neither bumping into it, seeing it, nor in any other way being causally affected by it. At most, successful ostension requires causal *presence* and not causal *impact*.

19. In this paper I shall leave unchallenged the (eminently challengeable) assumption that there is some way to isolate moral from nonmoral language.

20. Note that we need not have naturalistic *definitions* in order to succeed in referring by *description*. Since the Causal Criterion rules out all causally inert properties, while the causal theory of reference allows reference to causally inert properties as long as they are describable, the strictures of the Causal Criterion actually go beyond those of the causal theory of reference.

21. Actually, even when applied to mathematical entities, the game is not quite so easily won. For instance, Kurt Godel maintained that we have a mathematical intuition akin to visual perception that establishes a causal link, of sorts, between numbers and knowers (in "What is Cantor's Continuum Problem?" *American Mathematical Monthly* 54 (1947): 515–25. Penelope Maddy (in "Perception and Mathematical Intuition") has defended this possibility by appeal to recent theories of perception. In the process, she

has argued that abstract mathematical entities (e.g., sets) will, contrary to initial appearances, satisfy the Causal Criterion.

22. As Harman notes, "We do not and cannot perceive numbers . . . since we cannot be in causal contact with them" (*The Nature of Morality*, 10).

23. As Harman argues in *Thought* (Princeton, N.J., 1973), 127. Adolf Grunbaum makes the same point in arguing that one scientific law may explain another, even though the first law does not *cause* the second. See "Science and Ideology," *The Scientific Monthly* (July 1954): 13–19.

24. Harman recognizes the shortcomings of the Causal Criterion, and it is in his pointing them out that it becomes clear that he does not accept the criterion. See *Thought*, especially 126–32.

25. Harman, *The Nature of Morality*, 10. My emphasis. There is room, of course, to agree that if the truth of mathematical claims contributes to our best explanations these claims should be believed, while also holding that their truth does not so contribute. This is Hartry Field's position in *Science Without Numbers* (Princeton, N.J., 1980).

26. Harman, *The Nature of Morality*, 9.

27. The one reasonable application of this strong version of the Explanatory Criterion would tie its use to the explanations reached at the ideal limit of inquiry—an explanation *we* will almost surely never get. At this Piercean limit, there is sense to saying we can infer the truth of the hypotheses invoked by the (very) best explanation; for only if there is some such link with epistemology will truth be accessible. So used, though, the principle will never actually countenance any of our inferences.

28. According to Harman, "Moral hypotheses never help explain why we observe anything. So we have no evidence for our moral opinions." *The Nature of Morality*, 13, see also 8.

29. Harman, *The Nature of Morality*, 7.

30. Theories find observational confirmation only from accurate observations, and some particular theory will find observational confirmation from an accurate observation only if the theory also plays a role in explaining the making of that observation. Nonetheless, the making of some observation O' will confirm a theory T' even if the observation is false, as long as T' explains why the false observation was made. Even supposing an observation inaccurate, then, the making of the observation will be confirming evidence (but not *observational* evidence) for whatever theories contribute to the best explanation of the making of that (false) observation. When the report is false, however, it will be the making of the observation, and not its content, that serves to confirm our explanatory theories; and it will be the accurate observation that the false observation was made (and not the false observation itself) that provides observational support for our explanatory theories.

31. Harman, *The Nature of Morality*, 6.

32. Implicit in the Explanatory Criterion, then, is the conviction that legitimate theories must be linked to an acceptable theory of observation. As Putnam argues, "it is an important and extremely useful constraint on our theory itself that our developing theory of the world taken as a whole should include an account of the very activity and process by which we are able to know that a theory is correct." *Reason, Truth and History* (Cambridge, 1981), 132.

33. Harman, *The Nature of Morality*, 7.

34. Of course, that the burning of the cat was wrong might be part of the moral judge's (as opposed to our) best explanation of why he made the observation he did, just as for some people the best explanations they had of their observations made reference to phlogiston.

35. Sturgeon, "Moral Explanations," 65. As Sturgeon recognizes, the test has its limits. It will not be a reliable indicator of explanatory relevance when dealing with two effects of the same cause; neither effect would have occurred without the other (because each would have occurred only if the cause of the other had), even though neither explains the other. And it will not be reliable when using 'that-would-have-had-to-be-because' counterfactuals; it may be that if Reagan had lost the Presidential election, that would have had to be because he failed to get enough votes, even though his being elected is not explanatorily relevant to his getting enough votes. Ibid., 75. For other limitations, see Warren Quinn's "Truth and Explanation in Ethics," *Ethics* 96 (1986): 524–44.

36. At this stage, the relevant feature of a supervenience account of moral properties is that if the

moral properties of something are changed, then so must be some nonmoral properties; there is no holding the nonmoral properties fixed while altering the moral properties, as there can be no moral difference without a nonmoral difference.

37. Sturgeon, "Moral Explanations," 66. Which nonmoral facts will have to be altered to change the moral facts is, obviously, open to dispute.

38. As Sturgeon emphasizes, "Hitler's moral depravity—the fact of his really having been morally depraved—forms part of a reasonable explanation of why we believe he was depraved" ("Moral Explanations," 54). Had he not been depraved we very likely would not have thought him depraved; for he would not have done all the despicable things he did, and it is his having done such things that leads us to our condemnation.

39. Our background theories will clearly play a central role in determining explanatory relevance. In the cat-burning case, we will rely on our moral theory in deciding what nonmoral features of the world would have been different had the hoodlums' activities been unobjectionable. Similarly, in the passing proton case, we will rely on our scientific theory in deciding what physical features of the world would have been different had a proton not passed. Such a reliance on background theories will certainly offend a thoroughgoing skeptic. But attacks on moral theory are interesting only if some of our views survive the skeptic's arguments, so I shall assume we may legitimately rely at least sometimes on our background theories

40. Sturgeon, "Moral Explanations," 71. Independently, John McDowell has made essentially the same point concerning skeptical attacks on moral explanations in his "Values and Secondary Qualities," in *Morality and Objectivity*, edited by Ted Honderich (London, 1985), 110–29.

41. Which, of course, is not to say that we can explain everything that we might reasonably want to explain.

42. Yet there is at least some question as to whether the reductive hypothesis itself satisfies the explanatory criterion. What, after all, do we explain with the help of the reductive hypothesis that we could not explain just as well by assuming the reduced claims fail to refer? See Quinn's "Truth and Explanation in Ethics" for more on the tension between the explanatory criterion and reductive hypotheses.

43. There are some significant differences between moral properties and secondary qualities, not least of which is that we can learn to ascribe secondary qualities without having any idea as to what properties they supervene upon, whereas learning to ascribe moral properties requires an awareness of the properties upon which they supervene. This difference will stand in the way of treating moral properties as strictly analogous to secondary properties. But I think it won't underwrite any plausible version of the explanatory criterion that is still strong enough to rule out moral properties. See Quinn's "Truth and Explanation in Ethics."

44. Harman, *The Nature of Morality*, 23.

45. Ibid.

46. Hilary Putnam, "Philosophy and Our Mental Life," in *Mind, Language, and Reality* (Cambridge, 1975), 291–303.

47. Just as reductions of the mental to the physical fail to capture intentionality, reductions of the moral to the mental fail to capture justifiability.

48. For discussions of the (often conflicting) criteria for explanatory value, see Paul Thagard's "The Best Explanation: Criteria for Theory Choice," *Journal of Philosophy* 75 (1978): 76–92, and William Lycan's "Epistemic Value," *Synthese* 64 (1985): 137–64.

49. Of course, this leaves open the possibility that more specific attacks may be leveled at moral values; the point is that once epistemic values are allowed, no general arguments against the existence of values can work.

50. Here I part company with other moral realists (for example, Boyd, Sturgeon, and Railton) who seem to hold that moral theory should be seen as being of a piece with scientific theory. See Richard Boyd's "How To Be A Moral Realist," in *Essays on Moral Realism*, edited by Geoffrey Sayre-McCord (Ithaca, N.Y., forthcoming); Nicholas Sturgeon's "Moral Explanations"; and Peter Railton's "Moral Realism," *Philosophical Review* 95 (1986): 163–207.

51. In "Coherence and Models for Moral Theorizing," *Pacific Philosophical Quarterly* 66 (1985): 170–90, I argue that we have good reason for rejecting any proposed unifying fundamental principle we might find. ,

52. Earlier versions of this paper were delivered at the 1985 Eastern Division meetings of the American Philosophical Association, at the Research Triangle Ethics Circle, and at University of Wisconsin-Madison, University of Notre Dame, Virginia Polytechnic Institute, University of California-Irvine, Duke University, and University of California-San Diego. This paper has benefited considerably from exposure to these audiences, and especially from comments made by Kurt Baier, Douglas Butler, Joseph Camp, Jr., David Gauthier, Joan McCord, Warren Quinn, Michael Resnik, Jay Rosenberg, Robert Shaver, and Gregory Trianosky.

A Putnam's Progress

ERNEST LEPORE AND BARRY LOEWER

In the medieval ages, before the arrival of scientific thinking as we
know it today, well, people could believe anything, anything could
be true. . . . But the wonderful thing that happened was that then
in the development of science in the western world was that certain
things came slowly to be known and understood. I mean, you know,
obviously all ideas in sciences are constantly being revised. . . . That's the whole point. But we do at least know that the
universe has some shape and order. And that trees do not turn into
people and goddesses and there are very good reasons why they
don't and you can't believe absolutely anything.

—*My Dinner with Andre*

Hilary Putnam tells us that metaphysical realism (MR) has been the dominant view
in philosophy of every historical period (at least until Kant) (1978, 1). One can find
it in Plato, Aristotle, Descartes, and Locke. In this century Russell and early Wittgenstein (on the usual interpretation) were explicit advocates, and currently Michael
Devitt (1981, 1984), Hartry Field (1972, 1982), Clark Glymour (1986) and David
Lewis (1986) confess to it. Putnam himself says he held it implicitly, if not explicitly
(1983, vii). Recently, however, Putnam announced that he has discovered MR is incoherent (1978, 124). And he wants to replace it with another kind of realism, internal realism (IR), a realism with a human face. Putnam argues that MR is committed
to a picture of the relation between thought (or language) and reality that is fundamentally implausible; it leads to an unacceptable view of the nature of truth and
to pernicious dichotomies. On the other hand, IR is claimed to maintain the scientific
aspects of realism while rejecting its metaphysical aspects. So, Putnam has given us
a characterization of MR, has produced a bill of indictment against it, and sketched
an alternative view, IR. We think it fair to say that Putnam has not succeeded in con-

vincing many metaphysical realists of the errors of their ways. The usual reaction to his arguments is puzzlement. It has seemed to many that Putnam has betrayed his previous realist contributions – he was even pronounced a renegade by a former student (Devitt 1984) – and adopted in its stead a soft, some would say, a quasi-mystical view. Our aim here is to relieve some of this puzzlement by constructing a "reading" of Putnam's progress from metaphysical to internal realism.

1. Scientific and Metaphysical Realism

Bas van Frassen characterizes scientific realism (SR) in this way:

> Science aims to give us, in its theories, a literally true story of what the world is like; and acceptance of a scientific theory involves the belief that it is true. (1980, 8)

Putnam would agree with this characterization and add that we sometimes have good reasons to believe that scientific theories, particularly those in the mature sciences, are true or approximately true and that the entities they posit exist. The truth of a theory is independent of our beliefs concerning it. Our present good reasons for believing a theory to be true do not guarantee that it is true or approximately true. Any theory we presently hold we may come to reject for good reasons. Furthermore, successive theories can often be viewed as better approximation to the truth. Thus, Bohr's 1934 theory of the electron is closer to the truth than his 1912 theory. Such comparisons require interpreting terms within successive theories as referring to the same entities, in this case, to electrons. One of Putnam's most important contributions to the defense of SR was to show how a causal account of reference can be used to support claims concerning intertheoretic reference. Bohr's 1912 term "electron" and his 1934 term "electron" were appropriately causally related to the same entity. Of course, this claim is made on the basis of present theory (and what we know of the history of the development of Bohr's views) and is itself defeasible. Putnam considers SR to be an overarching *empirical* hypothesis which best explains scientific practice and success (1978, 123).

We will not attempt to assess SR or Putnam's arguments for it.[1] Rather, we want to show how naturally it seems to fit into a more general philosophical view concerning the relationship between language and the world, namely, metaphysical realism. Putnam's official characterization is (1981, 49):

(1) The world consists of a *fixed* totality of mind-independent objects and properties

(2) Truth involves some sort of correspondence relation between words or thought-signs and external things and sets of things.

(3) There is exactly one true and complete description of the way the world is (though we may never have a language capable of expressing it or may never know it).

MR appears to lend philosophical support to SR by providing an account of truth and reference that applies to all theories. It allows for the possibility that terms in different theories refer to the same theory-independent entities. By characterizing truth nonepistemically (in terms of correspondence) it allows for the possibility that even our best theories might yet turn out to be false. And it seems to provide a way of making sense of the idea that successive theories converge on the one true description of reality.

But according to Putnam, there are important differences between MR and SR. He says that MR "is supposed to apply to all theories at once . . . and THE WORLD is supposed to be independent of any particular representation of it" (1978, 125). On the other hand, scientific-realist claims, for example, that Bohr's two uses of "electron" referred to the same phenomena, are made within a particular theory, present-day quantum theory. Putnam's alleged discovery is that MR, instead of supporting SR, actually undermines it. As we will see, the heart of his argument is that the reference and correspondence relations invoked by MR cannot be placed with a scientific account of the world.

2. THE ARGUMENTS AGAINST MR

In this section we discuss some of Putnam's arguments against MR. He observes that

the most important consequence of metaphysical realism is that *truth* is supposed to be *radically non-epistemic* — we might be "brains in a vat" and so the theory that is "ideal" from the point of view of operational utility, inner beauty and elegance, "plausibility", simplicitly, "conservativism", etc., *might be false*. "Verified" (in any operational sense) does not imply "true", on the metaphysical realist picture, even in the ideal limit. (1978, 125)

Putnam's claim is that the MR's (1), (2), and (3) entail:

    (4) Truth is radically nonepistemic.

    (5) It is possible that we are all brains in a vat even though we believe we are not.

    (6) Even an epistemically ideal theory may be false.

(5) and (6) are Putnam's glosses on (4), and he appears to take (5) to imply (6). The argument proceeds:

I assume THE WORLD has (or can be broken into) infinitely many pieces. I also assume T_1 *says* there are infinitely many things (so in *this* respect T_1 *is* "objectively right" about THE WORLD). Now T_1 is *consistent* (by hypothesis) and has (only) infinite models. So by the completeness theorem (in its model theoretic form), T_1 has a model of every infinite cardinality. Pick a model M of the same cardinality as THE WORLD. Map the individuals of M one-to-one into the pieces of THE WORLD, and use the mapping to define relations of

M directly in THE WORLD. The result is a satisfaction relation SAT – a "correspondence" between the terms of L and sets of pieces of THE WORLD – such that the theory T_1 comes out *true* – true of THE WORLD – provided we just interpret "true" as TRUE (SAT). So what becomes of the claim that even the ideal theory T_1 might *really* be false? (1978, 125–26)

The structure of the argument is this:

  (i) MR implies (6).
  (ii) But an epistemically ideal theory has an interpretation SAT which makes it true.
  (iii) So, the epistemically ideal theory is true.
  (iv) So, MR is false.

There are a number of places where one might take issue with the argument. It is not obvious that the concept of an ideal theory is clear.[2] And it may be objected that although "Even an ideal theory is false" is consistent with MR, it is not obvious that MR *entails* it is possible that an ideal theory is false.[3] But the place at which most will balk at Putnam's argument is the move from (ii) to (iii). If someone told us that a theory, for example, phlogiston theory, is true because it is consistent and so has a model in THE WORLD, we would think him crazy. We would point out the theory's defects – it makes false predictions. The case of an ideal theory is different since it has no epistemic defects, for example, fails to predict an observation (Putnam 1978, 126–27; 1981, 45–48, 55; 1983, 8–15). But the MR still may object that SAT is not the correct interpretation of the ideal theory; the correct interpretation SAT* is the one determined by the reference and correspondence relations between the terms of T_1 and THE WORLD. Interpreted by SAT* T_1 may turn out to be false. Now Putnam asks this question: What makes SAT* *the correct interpretation*? This is the key question. The force of the argument is to claim that the MR must answer it if he is to defend his view. We will consider answers he might give shortly. First, we want to consider a different response to the argument that seems to avoid the need for answering the question.

Suppose that an MR argues as follows: I cannot say what makes a particular reference relation the correct one, but I can show that whatever does allows for the possibility that even an ideal theory is false. Here is how (1978, 125):

  (i) It is possible that I am a brain in a vat experiencing the stimuli I experience even though I believe I am not a brain in a vat.
  (ii) The ideal theory that is epistemically ideal for a brain in a vat that experiences the same stimuli that I experience is identical to the epistemically ideal theory for me.
  (iii) Among the statements included in the ideal theory is that I am not a brain in a vat.
  (iv) But in that case the ideal theory constructed by the brain in the vat must be false.

This response to Putnam's argument, whatever its other features, depends on the assumption that a brain in a vat can entertain the thought that it is a brain in a vat. But Putnam has argued that, given the causal theory of reference, it is not possible for a brain in a vat to even entertain the thought that it is a brain in a vat (1981, chap. 1). Putnam's argument for this conclusion is usually taken to be a new (or not so new) argument against skepticism, but critics are quick to observe that as such it is not very convincing since the argument depends on a premise that the skeptic is unlikely to allow: the causal theory of reference (Brueckner 1986, Conee 1987, van Inwagen 1988). But the MR whom we imagine making this response to Putnam's original argument accepts the causal theory of reference. If we see the brain-in-a-vat argument as a reply to that MR's response, then Putnam's puzzling article seems to make sense.

In "A Problem about Reference," Putnam constructs an argument that is related to, but slightly different from, the argument based on Godel's completeness theorem. Putnam calls this the permutation argument:

> I shall argue that even if we have constraints of whatever nature that determine the truth value of every sentence in every possible world, still the reference of individual terms remains indeterminate. (1981, 33)

Suppose that there is a language L and an assignment to each sentence of L at world w a truth value. These assignments might be determined by whether or not the sentences satisfy certain constraints, for example, are part of an ideal theory at that world. Putnam shows that there are distinct interpretations of the predicates and constants of the language that agree on the assignment of truth values at possible worlds. He concludes that this shows no view about how content is determined, which works by assigning truth conditions to whole sentences, is capable of explaining the reference relation. We seem to have the following argument:

(i)   To defend MR one must specify the reference relation.
(ii) Specifying the reference relation by listing a collection of sentences even if we take those sentences to have truth conditions — functions from possible worlds to truth values — is not sufficient for specifying a unique reference relation.
(iii) So, MR cannot be defended.

A natural response to both of Putnam's "model-theoretic" arguments is to say that the interpretations of one's terms and thought-signs are fixed by their causal connections to items in the world. In fact, a number of commentators have expressed puzzlement as to why Putnam, who is one of the developers of the causal theory of reference, does not simply recognize that a causal theory of reference will succeed in specifying the "intended" interpretations (Blackburn 1984, 301; Brueckner 1984, 137; Devitt 1984, 86–87; Glymour 1982, 177; Harman 1982, 569, 573; Leeds 1978, 113; Lewis 1986):[4]

> The natural modern reply to the rhetorical question [What fixes reference?] is that all of the intended interpretations should be replaced by talk of causally

determined reference relations; roughly, our physical and social circumstances, and sometimes perhaps our beliefs as well, determine together a set
of links, connecting words and objects, and thus delimiting the admissible interpretations of our theories. (Glymour 1982, 177)

So Glymour's view is that the admissible interpretation of our language, the interpretation under which an ideal theory might turn out to be false, is determined not by
the sentences of the theory but by causal relations between bits of the world and
terms of the theory.

Putnam's response to the suggestion that a causal theory of reference will succeed in answering the key question has exasperated his critics. He says that the causal
theory of reference is just more theory and observes that the argument applies to it
as well; in particular, there are interpretations that assign "cause" some relation
cause*, which makes all the sentences in the causal theory of reference (and the rest
of the theory) come out true. Putnam thinks that the MR is begging the question by
appealing to the causal theory of reference (or any other account for that matter)
since the appeal works to single out a unique reference relation only if we assume
that "cause" refers to cause and not, say, to cause*. Glymour, Devitt et al. think that
at this point Putnam has moved from name-calling to game-playing. Their claim is
not that adding the causal theory of reference to their theory fixes reference, but
rather that causation itself fixes reference. The causal account of reference also is
supposed to apply to the terms appearing in it—so that the reference of "cause" is
causally determined to be cause instead of cause*. Devitt accuses *Putnam* of begging
the question:

> The question begging is most striking in Putnam's latest response to the idea
> of a causal theory of reference. He claims that "if reference is only determined
> by operational and theoretical constraints then the reference of terms in that
> theory of reference will themselves be indeterminate." . . . Maybe so but
> if reference is determined causally, as the theory says it is, then the reference
> of those terms will be determinate. He is not entitled to assume the theory is
> false in order to show it false. (1984, 190)

Devitt has missed the force of Putnam's argument that there are alternative reference
relations that result in identical assignments of truth values at every possible world.
If there is a causal characterization of reference, there also are alternative characterizations (in terms of cause*, cause**, and so on) that agree on the truth values of
statements at all possible worlds. The question Putnam asks the MR is why say that
the account of reference in terms of cause rather than in terms of cause* is the correct
one? On MR both accounts cannot be correct since presumably that x causes y is
a different (physical) fact than that x causes* y (even though the sentences are true
in the same worlds) and the MR says that x refers to y is a particular fact in the world.
So the challenge to the MR is to give some reason for holding one identification of
reference rather than another. The problem that confronts the naturalistically

minded MR (as those who put forward causal accounts claim to be) is that from the point of view of scientific explanation, the different identifications of reference are equally acceptable. That is, if the causal theory assigns truth conditions in such a way as to meet whatever standards placed on the theory, so will the causal* theory. Putnam is not, as Devitt says (1984, 189), like a small child delighting in discovering that there is no end to questions. Instead, he has asked a question – Why identify reference with cause rather than cause*? – that the naturalistic MR cannot answer.[5] Further, this question is not unanswerable because the MR lacks some added piece of information. It is in principle unanswerable as long as the MR keeps his empiricist (naturalist) credentials. If one were to give up naturalism, one could reply to Putnam that there simply is a brute metaphysical fact that reference is identified with causation and not causation*. Here name-calling – it is a magical, mysterious theory of reference – would be warranted (1981, 3). For this would be to suppose that an *intrinsic* property of an object can determine its relation to a particular object external to it.

We can now summarize our discussion of the model-theoretic arguments as follows: None proves that MR is false. Rather, they are vivid ways of putting to the MR the question what on his view determines the reference of representations? That Putnam also sees his arguments in this light is shown by the following remark:

> The only paper in this book which makes use of technical logic "Models and Reality" is not an attempt to solve the problem [how correspondence is fixed] but rather a verification that the problem really exists. (1983, ix)

3. PUTNAM AND KRIPKENSTEIN

The MR's picture of the relation between language and the world is this:

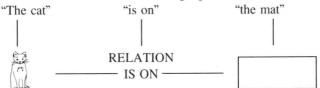

     "The cat"   "is on"   "the mat"

RELATION

——— IS ON ———

The vertical lines indicate reference relations between terms and parts of the world. The important feature is that the holding of these relations are themselves facts – facts that must obtain for "The cat is on the mat" itself to succeed in stating a fact. Putnam's question to the MR, then, is: What fixes these reference relations? Or, in what do these facts of reference consist? For an MR who is also a naturalist it is important that in answering this question he makes use only of naturalistic properties and facts. To complete Putnam's argument against MR, one would have to show that the MR cannot provide an answer to this question consistent with his naturalistic scruples. Although Putnam does not do this, it seems to us that the situation is exactly this: Reference and meaning are *not* naturalistically reducible. Kripke argues for this claim in his discussion of Wittgenstein on rule-following (1981).

The question he asks is similar to the one we have found in Putnam. What fact makes it the case that my use of "plus" refers to plus (or means that plus – in Kripke)? Kripke observes (as does Putnam) that citing images in my mind when I use "plus" or my intentions to use "plus" in a particular way cannot provide a satisfactory answer, since images and intentions are themselves open to interpretation. The heart of Kripke's objection is that if there were a fact that my use of "plus" means plus, then that fact would have to possess a certain normativity. It would have to make it the case that if I answer "5" to the question "What is 68 plus 57?" I would be *wrong*. Kripke argues that no "natural" fact possesses this normativity. For example, the fact that I have dispositions to answer various questions involving "plus" is not the appropriate kind of fact, since the dispositions do not themselves distinguish right answers from wrong ones. One might think that a causal theory of reference might be of use here.

A kind of causal theory suggested Fodor (1987) and Stalnaker (1984) is this: A predicate P (in the language of thought of person X) has as its extension, say, cats iff under optimal conditions X's tokenings of P are caused by cats and only by cats. There are many difficulties with this kind of account.[6] Here we will discuss two. One is that to make this account even slightly plausible, the specification of "optimal conditions" will make ample use of intentional notions, including specifications of X's other beliefs. Obviously, this is inadmissible in a naturalistic reduction of reference. Second, a Goodmanesque problem arises: If under optimal conditions tokenings of P are caused by all and only by cats, they will also be caused by all and only by cats*, where y is a cat* iff if conditions are optimal y is a cat and if conditions are not optimal y is a dog.[7] Although neither Kripke nor Putnam has produced a proof that a reduction of semantic facts to natural facts is impossible, given the preceding it seems an extremely poor bet. If we are right in our reading of Putnam, he has noticed the same problem that Kripke has for the MR. And the prospects for the MR answering the question seem extremely dim.

Must the MR solve the Kripke problem to defend his views? He might make a familiar move that cat* is a peculiar property and really is not, other things being equal, an eligible referent for a term. This amounts to there being a special class of "natural" properties that are better candidates than the gruesome properties to be the referents of our terms.[8] In the context of physicalistic MR, this is an odd view. What makes something a gruesome or natural property? That the natural properties just happen to be the ones we refer to might be taken to mean we simply *read* the structure of our language into nature.

A comparison with moral statements is useful. A naturalistically minded MR considers moral statements as non-fact-stating unless he can show how they are made true by natural facts. If he cannot do so he will consider them as performing some other function, say, expressing preferences or attitudes (for example, Ayer 1936; Mackie 1977). Is a similar move open to the MR? The following argument suggests that it is not (Wright 1984; Boghossian, unpublished manuscript). Suppose that S is true iff p. If "S is true" expresses an attitude, not a fact, then it seems to follow that "p" does not state a fact either. For the MR this is to throw the baby out with the bathwater. So, although an MR might be led to relegate ethics to a second-class status, he cannot do the same for semantics without undermining his own position.

We would like to consider briefly two other responses open to the MR. One is just to embrace semantical relations and facts as irreducible (or primitive). Putnam reserves his most creative name-calling for this position, accusing it of being "medieval" and "magical." It amounts, for Putnam, to saying that the mind somehow reaches out (perhaps by shooting noetic rays!) and touches objects. Beyond the name-calling, there is the irony that a position originally intended as a philosophical basis for scientific realism would end up appealing to nonnatural facts.[9] The second response is to try to mitigate the mysteriousness of nonnatural facts by claiming that they *supervene* on natural facts. But, as Simon Blackburn has argued in the case of the alleged supervenience of moral properties on natural properties, without a reduction of the former to the latter, "supervenience becomes, for the realist, an opaque, isolated logical fact, for which no explanation can be proffered" (1971). The problem is that if moral statements are realistically interpreted as stating facts, supervenience is itself a mystery unless there is a reduction of moral properties to natural ones. One can respond by abandoning moral realism while keeping supervenience as a constraint on the attribution of moral predicates. As we saw, this response is not available to the MR. So as long as he cannot produce a reduction of semantical properties to natural ones, the supervenience claim does little to dispel the mystery.

4. INTERNAL REALISM

Putnam tells us that it was Dummett who awakened him from his metaphysical slumbers, and it will be useful to describe briefly certain features of Dummett's account of meaning and truth as preparatory to discussing IR. Dummett, like Putnam, rejects the view that truth is radically nonepistemic. According to Dummett:

A statement is true only if we have established it as true; or only if we either have done so or shall do so at some future time; or only if we have some procedure which, were we to carry it out, would establish it as true; or, at least, only if there exists something of the sort that we normally take as a basis for the assertion of a statement of that class, such that, if we knew it, we should treat it as a ground for the truth of the statement. (1981, 443)

This idea is best illustrated in Dummett's philosophy of mathematics (1978, xxiv). Associated with a mathematical statement are conditions for proving it. *Understanding* the sentence is a practical ability to manifest a particular sort of behavior, namely, that behavior which brings us into the position in which, if the condition that conclusively justifies the assertion of S obtains, we *recognize* it as so doing. In case of a mathematical statement this requires that we recognize what would count as a proof of the statement. The recognizable conditions of a sentence's conclusively justified assertion are its verification conditions. Dummett denies that a sentence has truth conditions other than those associated with it recognitionally by the speaker's understanding. So, a sentence has only *verificationist* truth conditions. A mathematical sentence, thus, is "true" iff it has a proof (1973, 467–68; 1975, 115–23; 1976, 70–111).

All understanding for Dummett is verificationist. Although Dummett has not developed a well-worked-out account for nonmathematical sentences, he thinks the situation for these sentences is similar. To understand, for example, "There is a chair in the room," is to know what would count as a (conclusive) justification of it: perhaps seeing a chair in the room under good light conditions, not being intoxicated, and so on.[10] On this view, there may be sentences such that neither they nor their negations are true. (To justify the negation of S is to [conclusively] refute S.) We may know what counts as a (conclusive) justification (and refutation) of a sentence S, but none might exist. Finally, on this account, reality is mind-dependent (at least) in this sense: Whether the sentence "There is a chair in the room" is true depends on its justifiability conditions. Truth and rationality (justifiability) are conceptually bound—no truth without conclusive justifiability. For example, our finite abilities limit what we can justify.

Dummett's view contains numerous subtleties. Here we want to ignore most of them and pursue a line of thought that will be useful for our comparison with Putnam.[11] It is notorious that Dummett wavers between considering "justification" to mean "conclusively justified" and "sufficiently well justified" (1973, 146, 467, 514, 586; 1978, xxxviii). The problem is that on first reading, it may be that only mathematical and sense-perception statements, if even they, are ever justified. If truth is identified with conclusive justification, it would follow that only mathematical and sense-perception statements are capable of having truth value. Also, since for Dummett the justification conditions of a sentence are its meaning and since understanding a sentence is just knowing its meaning, it follows that anyone who understands a sentence knows its justification conditions, that is, the canonical conditions such that if they were satisfied the sentence would be true. An obvious difficulty with this view is that it makes it extremely unlikely that two different people, especially different people who live at different times or in different societies, speak languages that are translatable. For example, it is extremely unlikely that any sentence spoken by Tycho Brahe has the same justification conditions as our sentence "The sun revolves around the earth." The result is incommensurability. We would like to say that Tycho Brahe was wrong to believe that the sun revolves around the earth, but Dummett's theory together with the fact that our procedures for verifying or confirming sentences change seems to preclude us from doing so.

With this capsule summary of Dummett under our belts, we can describe IR by constrast. Putnam's own proposal, IR, is very sketchily presented. The heart of his view seems to be a rejection of the metaphysicalist realist picture. It is replaced with a view that truth is justification. He writes:

My own view . . . is that truth is to be identified with justification in the sense of *idealized* justification, as opposed to justification on the present evidence. (1983, xvii)

Consider the sentence "There is a chair in my office right now." Under sufficiently good epistemic conditions any normal person could verify this, where sufficiently good epistemic conditions might, for example, consist in one's having good vision, being in my office now with the light on, not having taken a hallucinogenic agent, etc. . . . There is no single general rule or universal method [contra Dummett] for knowing what conditions are better or worse for justifying an arbitrary empirical judgement. (1983, xvi)

Putnam is not trying to give a formal definition of truth but an informal elucidation of the notion. The two central ideas of his idealization theory of truth are:

(a) Truth, though independent of justification here and now, is not independent of all justification. To claim a statement is true is to claim that it could be justified under ideal conditions.

(b) Truth is expected to be stable or convergent; if both a statement and its negation could be "justified," even if conditions were as ideal as one could hope to make them, there would be no sense in thinking of the statement as having a truth value. (1981, 56).

His view seems to be this: Our practices of forming judgments, testing them, arguing about them, and so on, are sufficient to associate with statements what would count as reasons for believing the statements. For some statements we have a pretty clear idea of what it would take to justify them and the conditions under which they would be justified, for example, "There is a chair in my office right now." Putnam offers no account of knowledge, but presumably he has in mind that there is some account of better and worse reasons for my believing that there is a chair in my room right now. Somehow, community practices result in associating justification conditions with statements. These are conditions such that if we believed they obtained we would be justified in stating that X believes that p. Since truth is idealized justification, it is not the case that "The sun revolves around the earth" changed truth value and/or meaning between the time of Tycho Brahe and now. It is rather that views have changed about whether that statement is (ideally) justified. This is an improvement over Dummett's views, but it is committed to the position that it is impossible (by definition) for our ideally justified beliefs to be false. We saw before that despite the MR's protests, Putnam argues that the MR cannot maintain his intuition about the logical possibility of the ideal theory being false. IR does not rule out the possibility that we might be very well (ideally) justified in believing another to be a brain in a vat. But IR seems to rule out the possibility that for any individual he can think of himself that he is a brain in a vat and also be (ideally) justified in this thought.

It is important to clear up certain misconceptions, perhaps owing to Putnam's own rhetoric, about IR. In denying the MR's (1), in the first section of this paper,

Putnam is denying that the world consists of a fixed totality of mind-independent objects. This smells of "idealism," and Putnam's favorite metaphor that the mind and the world together make up the mind and the world encourages the charge that IR has idealist tendencies. One way of expressing these tendencies would be to say that under IR, ordinary commonsense counterfactuals fail to be true. But it is no consequence of IR that counterfactuals like "If we had not constructed the theory of electrons, then there would be no electrons" are true. In fact, on Putnam's, but perhaps not on Dummett's, account the counterfactual "Even if we had not constructed the theory of electrons there would be electrons" is justified. So we have reason to think it is true. In general, whenever S is justified, so is "Even if I had not thought of S it would be justified." (Of course, this counterfactual is not justified for every S.) This may not satisfy an MR since he wants to say not merely that one would be justified in asserting the counterfactual, but that it is a *fact* that even if I had never thought of electrons they would have existed. But the IR *is* justified in saying this as well. So whatever the alleged mind-dependence of the world consists in for the IR, it cannot be expressed by him counterfactually since he and the MR agree on (most) counterfactuals they assert.[12] The difference, rather, is in what they think the truth of these counterfactuals consists in. For the MR it is correspondence to facts. For the IR it is in being ideally justified.

As early as 1978 (50–51), Putnam made some rather strong statements about the relationship between realism and equivalent descriptions. He stated that we cannot ignore the existence of pairs of equivalent descriptions. Scientific realism is not committed, he contends, to there being one true theory (and only one). He says that "assuming there is a 'fact of the matter' as to 'which is true' if either whenever we have two intuitively 'different' theories is naieve." Putnam's intuition is well accommodated by his IR. Since idealized justification is theory relative, then, for example, relative to field theory "Fields are real" may be ideally justified, though relative to particle theory it may not be ideally justified. Therefore, it is consistent with IR that there be more than one "true" theory or description of the world (contra the MR's (3)). It is not surprising, therefore, that Putnam should be charged with relativism (Pears 1982). He is a relativist inasmuch as whether a statement is true is relative to a theory. But it is a very limited relativism (1978, 38–41; 1981, 117–19). Putnam claims that ordinary statements about ordinary objects, for example, "There is a chair in the room," are, if true, true relative to all acceptable theories (Putnam ms$_2$). Relativism applies only to statements on the periphery, for example, the one about fields above, statements in set theory. Whether Putnam's "relativism" is this confined or not, he argues that IR does not possess what he takes to be the two most pernicious features of relativism: (1) relativism cannot distinguish between "P is true" and "I (we) think that p is true" and (2) relativism leads to rampant incommensurability. We cannot go into why Putnam's views escape these charges here except to remark that (a) there is a distinction on IR between ideally justifying "I think that p" and ideally justifying "p" (1981, 124) and (b) as we have mentioned a number of times, Putnam thinks that translation-claims between theories can themselves be ideally justified and we frequently have good reason to believe these claims are satisfied (1981, 116–17).

The obvious question that one is itching to ask Putnam is this: Doesn't a problem analogous to the MR's problem of explaining how the reference relation is fixed arise for IR? What makes it the case that a particular sentence has the justification conditions it has as opposed to other justification conditions? Similar questions could be asked concerning the reference and meanings of terms. The MR may smugly suppose that the IR will have as much difficulty specifying the naturalistic facts that make these semantical relations hold as he had. This way of asking the question reveals an MR bias. The MR is asking what *fact* makes it the case that "There is a chair in the room" has whatever ideal justification conditions it has? But the IR has rejected the account by which facts make assertions true. This being so he need not satisfy the MR's demand in order to defend his theory. (In contrast, the MR did need to satisfy the IR's request since the MR held that there is a fact about what terms refer to.) What he needs to do instead is to show that the sentence "It is part of the ideal justification conditions of 'There is a chair in the room' that . . . " is itself justified — similarly, for sentences like " 'Cat' refers to cats" and "Bohr's term 'electron' in 1912 has the same reference as his term in 1934." Someone may ask what fact makes it the case that these semantical sentences have the justification conditions they have. The IR answer is that there is no such fact. Rather, certain assertions about their justification conditions are justified. As Putnam says (quoting Dummett), "Facts are soft all the way down" (1978, 128).

The IR can reply to the permutation argument as follows: He says that " 'Cat' refers to cats, not to cats*" is justified. He can support this by pointing out that "cat" is appropriately causally related to cats but not to cats*. Neither objection made against the MR applies here since the IR is *not searching for a naturalistic fact* with which to identify reference.

5. CONCLUSION

The IR's response to the Kripkenstein problem may appear to be a sleight of hand. Simply say that sentences have justification conditions, not realist truth conditions, and — Voilà! — the problem of intentionality vanishes. But does it? Isn't there, for example, still a problem of accounting for the causal efficacy of intentional (and other mental) states, if these are not naturalistically reducible? These are questions we address elsewhere.[13] Here we rest, content to have uncovered what we think to be a provocative "interpretation" of Putnam's text.[14]

Notes

1. For a detailed assessment of SR and Putnam's arguments for it see Devitt 1984.

2. Putnam has himself on several occasions remarked that the notion of an (epistemically) ideal theory is far from clear (1983; 12, 161).

3. MR does not mention "ideal" theory. So it is hard to see how it could imply "It is possible that

an ideal theory is false." But since MR is supposed to provide a nonepistemic characterization of truth, it does seem that the MR would embrace (6). See Glymour (1982, 176).

4. Carsten Hansen writes:

> That Putnam in "Models and Reality" does not discuss his previous work in "The Meaning of 'Meaning' " is quite puzzling. For in the latter, after having argued that 'meanings aren't in the head', he goes on to give a realistically acceptable account of the extensions in a nonsolipsistic, social setting. . . . It needs to be explained why Putnam no longer thinks this explanation is available to a realist" (1987, 91).

There are two reaons why the causal theory of reference, which Putnam *continues* to hold, does not provide a sufficient response to the challenge. The first is that the causal theory as developed by Putnam provides at most constraints on what counts as an acceptable interpretation and it itself uses intentional notions and so presupposes that the problem of specifying an interpretation has already been solved. For my use of "water" to refer to water on Putnam's theory requires that I have certain perceptions and intentions, for example, that I intend to refer to the same substance that whoever I acquired the term used it to refer to. The second response concerns a particular feature of reference. On some versions of the causal theory of reference certain terms in my language – names and natural kind terms – can refer only if there is a causal chain connecting my use of the term with its reference. This causal chain may go via other speakers. [It is not clear that Kripke holds the view that there must be such a causal chain.] This requirement seems much too weak to single out a unique interpretation or even to remove from consideration the interpretation SAT which makes the ideal theory true.

5. When I ask why is reference fixed by causation and not by causation*, the only answer a physicalist can give me is "because that is the nature of reference." To say that Nature itself singles out objects and put them into correspondence with words is a claim that has no meaning that I can make out at all (Putnam ms_1).

6. See Loewer 1987.

7. A slightly different theory is found in Dretske 1981: If the original tokens (those that occurred during what Dretske calls the "learning period") of the predicate P carried the information cats are present, then subsequent tokens (those that occur subsequent to the learning period) refer to cats even if they are not caused by cats. The trouble with this is that the appropriate notions of information and the learning period will likely include intentional concepts. See Loewer 1987.

8. David Lewis has recently (1986) taken up the suggestion that there are certain classes of things "out there" that are intrinsically distinguished and he suggests it is a "natural constraint" on reference, that is, a constraint that is built into nature, that as many of our terms as possible should refer to these classes. Lewis's natural constraint is not brought into existence by our interests. It has to be thought of as something that operates together with those interests to fix reference (Putnam ms_1).

9. In some places Putnam makes the stronger charge that this view of taking reference as primitive is unintelligible. In "Models and Reality," Putnam says that this move is unintelligible only if you resist making certain kinds of moves that some do not resist (1983, 14). For example, Chisholm, following Brentano, contends that the mind has a faculty of referring to external objects which he calls Intentionality. The MR Putnam is criticizing, though, is naturalistically minded and would find the postulation of an unexplained mental faculty unhelpful epistemologically and almost certainly bad science as well (1983, 5).

10. Dummett is well known for his subscription to the dictum "a theory of meaning *is* a theory of understanding" (1975, 99; 1976, 69–70).

11. See Dummett 1978, xxxviii, where he articulates various worries about the plausibility of his antirealism.

12. Peter van Inwagen (1988) for reasons unspecified seems to think otherwise.

13. See LePore and Loewer 1987.

14. We would like to thank for comments on earlier drafts of this paper Bruce Aune, Michael Hand, Peter van Inwagen, Tim Maudlin, Eva Piccardi, Michael Root, and especially Hilary Putnam.

References

Ayer, A. J. 1936. *Language, Truth and Logic*. London.

Blackburn, Simon. 1971. "Moral Realism." In *Morality and Moral Reasoning*, edited by J. Casey. London.

Blackburn, Simon. 1984. *Spreading the Word*. Oxford.

Boghossian, Paul. "A Survey of Recent Work on Rule Following." Unpublished manuscript.

Brueckner, A. 1984. "Putnam's Model-Theoretic Argument against Metaphysical Realism." *Analysis* 44: 134–40.

Brueckner, A. 1986. "Brains in a Vat." *Journal of Philosophy* 83: 148–67.

Conee, Earl. 1987. "Hilary Putnam, *Reason, Truth and History*." *Nous* 21: 81–95.

Devitt, M. 1981. *Designation*. New York.

Devitt, M. 1984. *Realism and Truth*. Princeton.

Dretske, Fred. 1981. *Knowledge and the Flow of Information*. Cambridge, Mass.

Dummett, M. 1973. *Frege: Philosophy of Language*. London.

Dummett, M. 1975. "What is a Theory of Meaning?" In *Mind and Language*, edited by S. Guttenplan. Oxford.

Dummett, M. 1976. "What is a Theory of Meaning? (II)." In *Truth and Meaning*, edited by G. Evans and J. McDowell. Oxford.

Dummett, M. 1978. *Truth and Other Enigmas*. Cambridge, Mass.

Dummett, M. 1981. *The Interpretation of Frege's Philosophy*. Cambridge.

Dummett, M. 1983. "Language and Truth." In *Approaches to Language*, edited by Harris and Roy. Oxford.

Field, Hartry. 1972. "Tarski's Theory of Truth." *Journal of Philosophy* 69: 347–75.

Field, Hartry. 1982. "Realism and Relativism." *Journal of Philosophy* 79: 553–67.

Fodor, J. 1987. *Psychosemantics*. Cambridge, Mass.

Glymour, C. 1982. "Conceptual Scheming or Confessions of a Metaphysicalist Realist." *Synthese* 51: 169–80.

Hansen, Carsten. 1987. "Putnam's Indeterminacy Argument: The Skolemization of Absolutely Every-thing." *Philosophical Studies* 51: 77–99.

Harman, G. 1982. "Metaphysical Realism and Moral Relativism." *Journal of Philosophy* 79: 568–74.

Kripke, Saul. 1981. *Wittgenstein on Rules and Private Language*. Oxford.

Leeds, Stephen. 1978. "Theories of Reference and Truth." *Erkenntnis* 13: 111–29.

LePore, E., and B. Loewer. 1987. "Mind Matters." *Journal of Philosophy* 84: 630–42.

Lewis, David. 1986. "Putnam's Paradox," unpublished manuscript.

Loewer, B. 1987. "From Information to Intentionality." *Synthese* 70: 287–317.

Mackie, J. L. 1977. *Ethica, Inventing Right and Wrong*. New York.

Pears, David. 1982. "Review of Putnam's *Reason, Truth and History*." *London Review of Books*.

Putnam, H. 1975. "The Meaning of 'Meaning'." In *Mind, Language and Reality*, Philosophical Papers. Vol. 2. Cambridge.

Putnam, H. 1978. *Meaning and the Moral Sciences*. London.

Putnam, H. 1981. *Reason, Truth and History*. Cambridge.

Putnam, H. 1983. *Realism and Reason*, Philosophical Papers. Vol. 3. Cambridge.

Putnam, H. "A Defense of Internal Realism." Unpublished manuscript[1].

Putnam, H. "A Note on Internal Realism," Unpublished manuscript[2].

Stalnaker, R. 1984. *Inquiry*. Cambridge, Mass.

van Fraassen, B. 1980. *The Scientific Image*. Oxford.

van Inwagen, P. 1988. "On Always Being Wrong." This volume, pp. 95–111.

Wright, C. 1984. "Kripke's Account of the Argument against Private Language." *Journal of Philosophy* 81: 759–77.

Contributors

Simon Blackburn, Pembroke College, Oxford University

Thomas S. Blackburn, Department of Philosophy, University of Notre Dame

Robert Brandom, Department of Philosophy, University of Pittsburgh

Curtis Brown, Department of Philosophy, Trinity University

Panayot Butchvarov, Department of Philosophy, University of Iowa

Hector Neri-Castañeda, Department of Philosophy, Indiana University

Arthur W. Collins, Department of Philosophy, City University of New York, Graduate Center

Michael Devitt, Department of Philosophy, University of Maryland

Aron Edidin, Department of Philosophy, University Notre Dame

Evan Fales, Department of Philosophy, University of Iowa

Mark Heller, Department of Philosophy, Northern Illinois University

Eli Hirsch, Department of Philosophy, Brandeis University

Paul Humphreys, Department of Philosophy, University of Virginia

Peter van Inwagen, Department of Philosophy, Syracuse University

Jaegwon Kim, Department of Philosophy, The University of Michigan

Ernest LePore, Department of Philosophy, Rutgers, The State University of New Jersey

Barry Loewer, Department of Philosophy, University of South Carolina

Penelope Maddy, Department of Philosophy, University of California at Irvine

H. E. Mason, Department of Philosophy, University of Minnesota

Alan McMichael, Department of Philosophy, Virginia Polytechnic Institute and State University

Geoffrey Sayre-McCord, Department of Philosophy, University of North Carolina at Chapel Hill

Wm. David Solomon, Department of Philosophy, University of Notre Dame

Peter Unger, Department of Philosophy, New York University

Crispin Wright, Department of Logic and Metaphysics, University of St. Andrews, and Department of Philosophy, The University of Michigan

Peter A. French is Lennox Distinguished Professor of Philosophy and chairman of the philosophy department at Trinity University in San Antonio, Texas. He has taught at the University of Minnesota, Morris, and has served as Distinguished Research Professor in the Center for the Study of Values at the University of Delaware. His books include *The Scope of Morality* (Minnesota, 1980), *Ethics in Government* (1982), and *Collective and Corporate Responsibility* (1984). **Theodore E. Uehling, Jr.,** is professor of philosophy at the University of Minnesota, Morris. He is the author of *The Notion of Form in Kant's Critique of Aesthetic Judgment* and articles on the philosophy of Kant. **Howard K. Wettstein** is associate professor of philosophy at the University of Notre Dame. He has taught at the University of Minnesota, Morris, and has served as a visiting associate professor of philosophy at the University of Iowa and Stanford University. Wettstein has published papers in the philosophy of language and the philosophy of mind.